"*A Contextual Approach to Human Development* is a vital resource for students and researchers in psychology, education, human development, and related fields. With a comprehensive focus on diverse aspects of human development, this book uniquely integrates theories, concepts, and research, from India and other Asian and African countries, offering culturally relevant perspectives with meaningful applications often overlooked in books originating from Euro-American tradition. Its interdisciplinary approach, lifespan perspective, and emphasis on sociocultural context make it an invaluable and refreshing guide for understanding human development."

Professor Janak Pandey, *Former Vice-Chancellor of Central University of South Bihar, Gaya, and Ex-President, International Association of Cross-Cultural Psychology (IACCP)*

"Understanding of development must necessarily be rooted in the cultural context. Professors Srivastava and Misra present in this book a comprehensive and integrated view of human development which adds a clear cultural perspective to the accumulated global understanding of the processes of growth and development over the lifespan. Their meticulous attempt in this remarkable work sets it apart from other purportedly "universal" accounts of human development. It stands out due to its thorough and insightful treatment of facets of human development from an Indian perspective along with the extant views from the Global North. This book will be seen as a milestone work in the years to come and will provide a much-needed sourcebook for students and researchers of human development in India and abroad."

Professor Ajit K. Mohanty, *Former Professor of Psychology and ICSSR National Fellow, Jawaharlal Nehru University, New Delhi*

"*A Contextual Approach to Human Development* is a refreshing and invaluable resource for teachers and students of human development. The multidisciplinary approach and a focus on the multifaceted aspects of context augur a holistic treatment of human development hitherto missing in books available on the subject. The book presents exemplary insights from ancient Indian texts and approaches and the latest research inputs from the majority world. The dialogic style of writing in several places makes the book very appealing. The book covers various topics with a focus on new theoretical and methodological approaches to development. The contextualist perspective runs as a thread throughout the book. The book orients students and teachers, informing them, appealing to them, exciting them, and helping them to connect to their reality, allowing for a deep and meaningful understanding of the subject."

Purnima Singh, *PhD, Professor of Psychology, Indian Institute of Technology Delhi*

"Students, researchers, and teachers of developmental psychology have been experiencing the void of connections between aspects of human development (physical, cognitive, moral, etc.) and cultural ethos and structural context shaped by the social and economic policies of the nation. By highlighting the need to situate human development within the context of culture and sustainable development goals of nations and providing examples of such development from the Western and Indian contexts, this book comes up as a highly meaningful and refreshing resource for the learners of developmental psychology. To this end, besides the contributions of eminent thinkers such as Sigmund Freud and Jean Piaget, the seminal work of Indian contributors such as S. Anandalakshmy, T.S. Saraswathi, and Malavika Kapur marks the uniqueness of this volume.

The questions for reflection at the end of chapters have the potential to foster critical research in human development towards meaningful integration with cultural and structural contexts as well as significant contemporary societal issues of poverty, healthcare, environment, and social justice."

Kumar Ravi Priya, *PhD, Professor of Psychology, Indian Institute of Technology Kanpur*

"The book provides a fresh and integrative perspective towards understanding human development. Describing the entire spectrum of human development from an Indian perspective, the book highlights a cultural and contextual approach. Focus on human strengths, sustainable development, lifelong learning, and inclusive development adds interesting and valuable insights. An interdisciplinary approach is reflected in the various chapters of the book, which is in tune with the National Education Policy 2020. Scientific as well as cultural rootedness makes the book stand out as an invaluable contribution to the field of human development."

Swati Patra, *PhD, Professor of Psychology, Indira Gandhi National Open University, New Delhi*

A Contextual Approach to Human Development

This textbook offers a unique insight into the theoretical and applied aspects of human development in relation to the cultural traditions of non-Western countries.

Presented in a modular form, this comprehensive and thematic approach to lifespan development will help students develop an understanding of human development in varied Indian social contexts. Covering all stages of development, including the development of self and personality, social understanding, human strengths, sustainable development, lifelong learning, and many more, the book highlights current research in these areas as well as provides learning objectives, points for reflection, web links, and a glossary.

This book is an essential reading for undergraduate students of psychology, human development, and allied fields, as well as for postgraduates with an interest in studying human development in a non-Western context.

Ashok K. Srivastava, PhD, was at the National Council of Educational Research and Training (NCERT), New Delhi, for more than three decades. During this period, he served as Professor of Educational Psychology and Dean (Research).

Girishwar Misra, PhD, served as Professor of Psychology at the University of Delhi for two decades. He also served as Vice-Chancellor of Mahatma Gandhi Antarrashtriya Hindi Vishwavidyalaya, Wardha.

A Contextual Approach to Human Development
Integrating an Indian Perspective

Ashok K. Srivastava and Girishwar Misra

LONDON AND NEW YORK

Cover image: Yana Iskayeva via Getty Images

First published 2025
by Routledge
4 Park Square, Milton Park, Abingdon, Oxon OX14 4RN

and by Routledge
605 Third Avenue, New York, NY 10158

Routledge is an imprint of the Taylor & Francis Group, an informa business

© 2025 Ashok K. Srivastava and Girishwar Misra

The right of Ashok K. Srivastava and Girishwar Misra to be identified as authors of this work has been asserted in accordance with sections 77 and 78 of the Copyright, Designs and Patents Act 1988.

All rights reserved. No part of this book may be reprinted or reproduced or utilised in any form or by any electronic, mechanical, or other means, now known or hereafter invented, including photocopying and recording, or in any information storage or retrieval system, without permission in writing from the publishers.

Trademark notice: Product or corporate names may be trademarks or registered trademarks, and are used only for identification and explanation without intent to infringe.

British Library Cataloguing-in-Publication Data
A catalogue record for this book is available from the British Library

ISBN: 978-1-032-57820-0 (hbk)
ISBN: 978-1-032-54752-7 (pbk)
ISBN: 978-1-003-44116-8 (ebk)

DOI: 10.4324/9781003441168

Typeset in Times New Roman
by Apex CoVantage, LLC

Dedicated to the memory of Professors Durganand Sinha, S. Anandlakshmy, and Rajalakshmi Muralidharan, pioneers in the field of human development in India

Contents

Foreword	*xi*
Preface	*xvi*
Acknowledgements	*xx*

PART I
Human Development from a Contextualist Perspective   1

1 Introduction to the Study of Human Development   3
2 Understanding the Human Life Course   23
3 Theoretical and Methodological Approaches to Development   41

PART II
Foundational Processes of Human Development   63

4 Physical and Motor Development   65
5 Socialization and Development   85

PART III
Perspectives on Cognitive and Language Development   107

6 Cognitive Development   109
7 Language Development   139

PART IV
Perspectives on Self and Affective Development   161

8 Development of Self and Personality   163
9 Affective Development   184
10 Moral Development   203

PART V
Social Understanding and Prosocial Development   223

11 Development of Social Understanding   225

12 Human Strengths and Their Development   243

PART VI
Towards Inclusive Development: Emerging Issues   261

13 Development under Vulnerable Circumstances   263

14 Sustainable Development and Lifelong Learning   281

Glossary of Sanskrit Terms   *296*
References   *301*
Index   *337*

Foreword

It is not an exaggeration if I declare this as an "aurora borealis", the best book on Indian psychology to appear on the Indian horizon! I had despaired over the past decades about the quality of psychological research and applications across India along the applied-practitioner spectrum, characterized by an absence of interest in what is indigenously produced in the distant past and the present. The miracle that Professor M.N. Srinivas's seminal work, *The Remembered Village* (1976), did 45 years ago to Indian sociology did not happen in the field of psychology in India. Now we have arrived at this book *A Contextual Approach to Human Development: Integrating an Indian Perspective* by Professors Ashok K. Srivastava and Girishwar Misra. A holistic and multi-disciplinary approach is the hallmark of this volume. "Contextual" refers to the bio-psycho-social and cultural contexts. Looking back at the ancient approaches and viewing the current endeavours, both are paid equal attention, turning the mined gold into exquisite, handcrafted jewellery.

Indian psychology has finally arrived. Transplanting Euro-American theories and practices on Indian soil was adopted, and it was an elitist approach. It failed to recognize the grassroot-level realities. It is reflected in the view of a renowned psychiatrist trained abroad that can be paraphrased as "Most Indian patients are unsuited for psychotherapy". I counter the argument that most psychiatrists or psychologists, who cannot do psychotherapy with most of the patients across class, caste, gender, ethnicity, and religion, are themselves unfit to be counsellors in their own country. This volume is eminently designed to break this barrier of "othering" our own people.

I am delighted that such a book has arrived, though 45 years late. It has avoided the natural bane of edited books by multiple authors lacking connectivity among themes and stylistic differences with a lack of focus and purpose. These two authors' efforts are very simple and precise, providing an easy and interesting read instead of being an academic tome. It provides a broad canvas of Western work, focusing sharply on Indian work with even passing references to pan-Asian and African work, which makes it so fascinating.

The book is organized into six interconnected sections that provide a comprehensive exploration of human development. These sections cover the contextual perspective, foundational processes, perspectives on cognitive and language development, insights into self and affective development, social understanding and prosocial development, as well as inclusive development. These interesting clusters make the linkages meaningful, dynamic, and interactive, though these aspects are conventionally known as the domains. This makes a dialogue with the reader possible. This format itself, going beyond the domains, allows a nuanced and multidisciplinary context, adopting a holistic approach. Kudos to Professors Srivastava and Misra for coming up with this ideal format for conveying profound thoughts most briefly and lucidly. The chapters end with an excellent overview and a few questions that are open-ended and thankfully not multiple-choice.

The book begins by introducing the indigenous concepts of development and milestones. The term "context" in the title encompasses the past, present, and future contexts as well as the bio-psycho-social and cultural contexts. At the core lies the "developmental or lifespan approach" as against a static cross-sectional one. This is an icing on the cake! My grouse has always been that child psychology is the most neglected field among all the branches of psychology except as a subject at the graduate or master's level or in the home science departments. The developmental approach brings the child to the centre stage where he rightfully belongs in the scheme of things. After all, "child is the father of man".

The holistic nature of human development across life stages is presented in a subsequent chapter. Childhood is anchored into the developmental or lifespan approach. It is important to note that development starts at the embryonic stage and not at birth, as it is generally believed to be. The Indian view negates that the child's mind is a "clean slate" as held by John Locke and several other early thinkers like William James. The point of interest is that there is evidence for rapid total development and amazing receptiveness and plasticity in learning very early in the life cycle. Early language development too is very rapid and extensive. Indian babies have a special affinity for multilingualism, where multiple languages are naturally spoken. This is found to be linked to social development due to their ability to communicate and be empathic with those around them. In the Western context, adolescence is considered a distinct phase of stress and storm while Indian studies have not observed such clear boundaries. Scholars like Saraswathi consider it a myth – the term employed instead is "emerging adulthood". Early adulthood consists of transition and transformations. Middle adulthood is the "blossoming" stage and is followed by old age. Indian scholars offer a fine distinction to describe old age. It is speculated that the belief in the afterlife represents pan-Asian regions; perpetual bonding exists with the living and the dead.

Excellent summaries of theoretical and methodological approaches to evaluate applications and integrate them with real-world applications are given. Beyond the typical Western approaches, indigenous approaches are incorporated. The importance of longitudinal as against static cross-sectional approach is rightly emphasized in "developmental inquiry" and in clinical consideration as well. It highlights the need for interdisciplinary and collaborative research in promoting the mining of knowledge in depth and width.

The chapter on physical and motor development presents various indicators of the physical growth of Indian children. It also describes the importance of adequate nutrition through free mid-day meals provided in schools to children, a serendipitous boon, that has led to multiple physical, social, and psychological benefits to children. The ancient approach to physical development is holistic, highlighting the interconnectedness of the body, mind, and spirit. The implications of handedness and eye–hand coordination are given. Traditional physical activities such as martial arts, dance forms like Bharatanatyam, and sports like Kabaddi as well as the importance of games and toys are delved into. The history of traditional folk healing and traditional health systems such as Ayurveda is given in detail. Nursery books and contemporary classic literature for children promote psychosocial development. The chapter ends with a special section on yoga and recommendations for a sustainable and environmentally healthy lifestyle.

A shift in socialization practices is seen from descriptive accounts to child-centred child-rearing. A wonderful description of how socialization practices are nested in the Indian context is presented. The roles of physical and psychological learning in the integration of the individual into one's society are highlighted. Several new approaches are described. Transgender issues are covered from historical and current perspectives. Socialization and its link to competence are examined at cognitive, affective, and motivation levels. The revelation that child and parent bonding are mutually beneficial and not one-sided is a high point of the chapter, as revealed by contemporary Indian work.

The chapter on cognitive development describes Piagetian studies that provide anchoring points. Common conceptions of intelligence across different cultures are covered extensively. In addition, Sri Aurobindo's contribution to the understanding of compliances, cognitive, social, intellectual, and emotional realms are provided. Cultural variations are brilliantly portrayed. The high point of the chapter is that Western approaches are analytical while Indian approaches are holistic. An interesting comparison of the "theory of minds" is included together with the fostering of creativity in the Indian context. Finally, the contribution of schooling, even the alternative system of schooling, is examined. The *Guru–Shishya Parampara* is yet another facet brought to our attention.

Language development is an exquisitely detailed chapter focusing on the complex issues surrounding language. For example, it starts with simple literacy rates across the country. It highlights the benefits of bilingualism and multilingualism. Language has a major cognitive connotation. Indian thought from the *Nyaya Sutra* is given in detail. Just to discover the delights of understanding language, this chapter is exceptional and needs to be studied in depth. It is too exquisite to be summarized.

The chapter on the development of self and personality provides an excellent description of the self. It contains various Western theories of self and personality. Self is associated with social and cultural influences and the development of self across life stages is described. Indian selfhood is brought under *ashrama dharma*. In Indian thought the variants used are *Atman, moksha, brahman*, cosmic entity, self-knowledge, and intimate relationship with God. The Indian view of personality is reflected in *purusharthas*, exemplified by *Triguna* consisting of *Sattvik, Rajasik*, and *Tamasik* characteristics in varying proportions. The tools for measuring personality are described aptly. Culture-specific innovative tools need to be yet developed. Perhaps, emic models need to be adopted to study cross-cultural differences, and the etic model needs to be discarded as emic provides the "insider" view while etic provides an "outsider" view of a specific culture.

The relationship between affect and emotions offers multiple descriptions. Affect resides in the prefrontal cortex and is an overall mood status. Emotion is subcritical, resides in the amygdala, and is intense and short-lived. Major theories are described in brief. However, the complexity of emotion in the Indian context is a riveting part of the chapter on affective development. These occur in varied contexts such as aesthetics as *rasa* and devotion as *bhakti*. Tantric, mystical, spiritual, and philosophical aspects are illuminated to reveal their complex nature. Patanjali's understanding and description are extensive, such as *klesha, raga, dvesha, avidya, dukkha, abhinivesha*, and egoism. According to Ayurveda, emotions are linked to *tridosha* (*vata, pitta*, and *kapha*). *Natyashastra* describes emotions in terms of *rasas*. All religions agree on control of senses and self-control and provide sets of instructions about controlling emotions.

Morality has been studied by philosophers, theologians, and social scientists. It is a deep-rooted concern in India. *Dharma* is righteousness, a related construct being *karma*. Ahimsa is promoted in Hinduism, Jainism, Buddhism, and Sikhism. Moral development as described by Piaget, Kohlberg, and Turiel are described. Turiel believed that different cultures have distinct domains of morality. The chapter also covers current ethical concerns such as euthanasia, capital punishment, abortion, and so on. Carol Gilligan described moral reasoning in women. Shweder proposed moral relativism between genders. Gandhi's "Satyagraha" was an influential idea. However, morality is easy to preach but hard to practice. Possibly, Mahatma Gandhi was the only one who did it!

The development of social understanding encompasses individualism and collectivism that vary according to horizontal and vertical dimensions. Asian and African countries are high on collectivism. In contrast, Western cultures are high on individualism. In India, rapid urbanization has led to the emergence of individualistic values. Indians however behave according to *desha*, *kala*, and *patra*. The theory of cognitive dissonance and concepts of money and greed are aptly discussed. In collective societies, extravagant weddings or funerals to promote one's social status are common though many poor and middle-class people go bankrupt to repay.

The development of human strengths is an interesting basket consisting of positive emotional states, happiness and well-being, wisdom, optimism, hope, courage, and self-efficacy. The mystery of consciousness is explored along with mindfulness and spiritualism. Life skills find an important place which forms the building blocks of communication, cooperation, teamwork, resilience, and digital literacy. Prosocial behaviours, altruism, gratitude, and forgiveness, descriptions are abundant. The *Swastika* is a symbol of the Indian goal of life.

Developmental challenges are caused by vulnerabilities in a large population and the impact of adverse circumstances faced by families and the community, such as war, violence, terrorism, migration of refugees, abandoned and neglected children, child labour, and so on. Mental health crisis also forms a part. The chapter highlights that the policy and legal endeavours to effectively deal with them are in place, but they hardly reach the needy sufferers at the grassroots level as these get lost in translation. Natural disasters are on the rise due to climate change. Solutions need to be local but controlled by the Centre.

The chapter on sustainable development has a Box with 17 global goals. Psychosocial aspects of sustainable development are covered. Major Indian efforts are highlighted. There is a need to bring in change in our attitude, values, and skills to promote sustainability.

The psychology in India has steadfastly ignored the elephant in the room. Jerome Kagan (2012) in his *Psychology's Ghosts* pointed to drug dependence being promoted by the pharmaceutical industry, highlighting the use of stimulants in children or attention deficit hyperactivity disorder (ADHD) and suggesting that the diagnosis itself is an artefact. I concur with this as I discovered no case of ADHD in 800 tribal residential school children. In his book *Science and Politics of IQ* in 1974, Leon Kamin demolished the heritability of IQ and how it was used to promote racism, bringing about the downfall of Sir Cyril Burt for misuse of science to promote political agenda.

In India, in the last decade, corporate greed has submerged the psychological needs of psychologists. A decade back we had a thriving group of test manufacturers and distributors selling at affordable prices, such as the Test Bureau of Allahabad, Manasayan, Purohit and Purohit of Pune and others. The entry of multinationals swallowed them up. Now, with a very low budget for education, government colleges and provincial colleges across the nation no longer can maintain well-equipped psychological labs. Today's master's in psychology may even not be exposed to tests! Once again corporate greed comes in. The only solution is to start a test collective drive and revive the indigenous group of test manufacturers.

The bane of Indian education at all levels is tuition and guidebooks. Children spend as much time in their tuition classes as their regular classes resulting in a loss of play time. This is due to the collision of teachers and parents. At the college level, they have the alternate "KOTA" syndrome in the name of coaching causing enormous stress to children and financial burden to the family. If our children are provided quality education in government schools, this entire menace would end.

Presently, IoT and AI are paraded as the new panacea for all problems of the world while their disastrous impacts are overlooked. Once again corporate greed!

Finally, research should also be used for the benefit of the masses in a poor country. Be it policy or intervention, it should have "outcome evaluation". To give an example, if Pratham and ASER are doing a laudable job, the assessment of achievement should not be an end in itself. The same groups of data gatherers in the field can be trained to give simple instructions to be communicated to the teachers as to how to simplify maths and demonstrate interesting picture books to read for children. Epidemiology needs to be interventional. Research that leaves the stakeholders high and dry is not worth pursuing if it benefits only the researchers.

These are significant concerns that Indian psychologists need to address. This book, I would say, is not a Scandinavian Smorgasbord but a healthy Indian Thali Meal that leaves one satisfied. It is hoped that this volume will herald the beginning of Indian research, theories, and applications in that order so that we can stop transplanting theories and applications from the West.

Malavika Kapur, PhD
Honorary Visiting Professor
National Institute of Advanced Studies
Indian Institute of Science Campus
Bangalore 560 012

References

Kagan, J. (2012). *Psychology's ghosts: The crisis in the profession and the way back.* Yale University Press.
Kamin, L. (1974). *The science and politics of IQ.* Lawrence Erlbaum Associates.
Srinivas, M. N. (1976). *The remembered village.* Oxford University Press.

Preface

The concept of "development" has captured the imagination of common people as well as policymakers globally. Indeed, it has earned substantial currency in everyday vocabulary as a societal and personal goal, as well as the processes involved in pursuing and accomplishing those goals. As such, it entails a positive and desirable state having implications for health and mental well-being. Within the field of developmental psychology, however, development characterizes the processes of change in living organisms often reflected in behaviour. Its study is meant to monitor and regulate the pattern of developmental changes to ensure that it is proceeding according to the norms and to make necessary interventions to bring it on track. Moving according to the normal development plan requires consistent and regular environmental support and stimulation. The welfare departments in governments are highly concerned with making suitable provisions to facilitate development. The Human Development Index has become a key tool to assess the level of overall attainment by any country. In this context, the study of human development becomes a theoretical as well as an applied enterprise. Also, it is intimately connected to almost all areas of human lifeways.

For long, the study of development has fascinated scholars from diverse traditions and approaches, and there has been a spate of research on various aspects of development. Information from studies emerging from evolutionary, cultural, gender, and neuroscience perspectives is constantly surprising us with discoveries. Also, the ecological and social contexts of development have been drastically changing. Furthermore, scientific and technological changes are becoming increasingly profound and complex. They have been constantly changing the nature of developmental tasks and setting the agenda across life stages. This has, however, not been occurring at the same pace across the globe. There are significant differences between developed and developing countries, and any analysis of human development will fall short if we do not take into account variations and diversity across regions. However, the production and dissemination of knowledge have been primarily centred in the Euro-American region. Therefore, it is imperative to continue updating our learning and integrating the emerging knowledge from other regions.

Our goal in preparing this book has been to make available a current overview of the field of human development from a contextualized perspective that reflects major theories, research, interventions, and applications that developmental researchers have to offer. Throughout many years of teaching and research, we had longed for a compact and substantive text that was interesting, accurate, up to date, and presented in clear, concise language that students could easily understand. We consider students as active participants having questions and interests in developmental processes. We aspired to emphasize the processes and contexts of development to allow the students to understand the patterns, causes, and complexities of human development. We also tried to keep the concern for relevance at the centre stage in this journey so that the students may prepare themselves to apply their learning in real-life settings. The treatment of human development in textbooks often opts for a chronological (ages/stages) approach or thematic approach. We have chosen to present developmental processes thematically or topically. This allowed the uninterrupted treatment of developmental sequence in a specific domain.

The process of development deals with changes in behaviour that unfold with time. These changes are correlated with the processes of growth or maturation. Thus, transformations as well as continuities are taken into account. While attending to develop, we have tried to keep the holistic spirit of development intact. The dynamic interplay among biological, social, and cultural influences is also taken into account. It may be noted that the study of development has evolved based on contributions from evolutionary, social, cognitive, biological, clinical, cultural, and individual difference perspectives.

The study of human development encompasses growth and development that occurs throughout the entire lifespan. Indeed, the ideas about human development have changed over the years. Most contemporary conceptualizations of development expand the exploration of age-related changes from childhood and adolescence to encompass the entire lifespan. Young adults, their younger siblings, their middle-aged parents, and their elderly grandparents differ from each other in important ways. The human brain develops throughout life, and a person can form new connections in old age. New research has shown that human infants are not as dependent on experience as earlier thinkers believed them to be. They are born with many capabilities. Also, the different aspects of development, that is, social, cognitive, and physical, constantly interact with each other.

Human development takes place in the physical, social, and cultural contexts. This necessitates that the context must receive its due attention in all phases of human development research and teaching. Unfortunately, the available textbooks in this area have been drawn from the Euro-American context, and the same are being used as major academic resources at the centres of higher learning. There is enough research available in the non-Western context which needs to be used in teaching the students so that they can develop the necessary sensitivity and relate to their context. As of now, there is a scarcity of good books on human development focusing on Indian as well as other non-Western contexts. India possesses a rich array of traditions and practices for stimulating all-round development, including developing values and social capacities in young children. The textual sources, demographic variations, and subcultural differences observed in India provide a rich and variegated opportunity to understand the myriad facets of human development.

The present volume attempts to address some of these concerns. It integrates pertinent research carried out in the Indian context with a focus on contextual features and influences. We have made efforts to make the text rigorous and applied. It challenges students to think about the fascinating process of human development, to share the excitement, and to acquire knowledge of principles that will serve them in their varied roles as parents, teachers, psychologists, consultants, or in any other capacity by which they may influence the lives of developing persons.

It is a common realization that diverse theories are used to understand the complexity of human development. Also, different theoretical perspectives have diverse emphases and therefore, they appear complementary. Indeed, theories and systematic research contribute immensely to our understanding. Developmental processes are shaped by the interplay of biological and environmental factors. We believe that historical eras and sociocultural contexts shape every aspect of development. The similarities and differences in processes and outcomes of development are very crucial. Families, neighbourhoods, media, and peer groups need to be understood. These form the immediate sociocultural context. Also, we believe that human development is holistic. The different facets such as physical, social, cognitive, and emotional are part of a whole and therefore are influenced by other areas rather than being treated in isolation. The researchers are becoming over-specialized and forget the reality of holistic perspective. The growth of research is fast, and findings are becoming quickly obsolete. This requires adopting a balanced approach so that classic studies as well as new research are included. The book is divided into six parts as given below.

Part I: Human Development from a Contextualist Perspective. Three chapters of this introductory part of the book offer an orientation to the meaning and process of human development and the methodology adopted in its study. The salient features of human development are presented in Chapter 1. The scope and changes taking place during various stages in the life course are described in Chapter 2. Finally, Chapter 3 introduces the major theoretical perspectives and methodological approaches adopted in human development research.

Part II: Foundational Processes of Human Development. This part presents the details of two basic aspects of development focusing on the development of the body and the transformation of human beings into social beings. To this end, the physical and motor development is presented in Chapter 4. It includes patterns of physical growth and motor development, their assessment and relationship between motor and other aspects of development, the use of toys, and a discussion on healthy living. The processes of socialization and related issues of parenting are detailed in Chapter 5.

Part III: Perspectives on Cognitive and Language Development. The two chapters constituting this part offer developmental perspectives on cognition and language. The unfolding of cognitive development is presented in Chapter 6. It includes a discussion of intelligence, creativity, and emotional intelligence. The role of culture and schooling in cognitive development is also described. Chapter 7 describes the processes involved in language development and the relationship between language and thought and addresses the problem related to the medium of instruction and cognitive development.

Part IV: Perspectives on Self and Affective Development. This part contains three chapters. The developmental changes in self and personality are described in Chapter 8. The chapter especially focuses on self-esteem and social identity. Chapter 9 discusses the process of affective development. It also includes a discussion of emotions, aesthetic development, resilience, and meeting the diverse challenges. Chapter 10 focuses on moral development. It also includes the development of the concepts of justice, human rights and duties, democracy, and citizenship.

Part V: Social Understanding and Prosocial Development. Chapter 11 deals with the development of social understanding. It includes understanding the notions of family, group, and nation false beliefs, understanding other people, social dynamics, and relationships, and the development of religious identity and prejudice and discrimination. Chapter 12 is dedicated to the development of human strengths and virtues. Positive emotional states and processes (e.g., happiness, self-efficacy, courage, flow, spirituality, and mindfulness), life skills, and development of prosocial behaviours (e.g., altruism, gratitude, forgiveness, attachment, love, and forgiveness) are discussed.

Part VI: Towards Inclusive Development: Emerging Issues. The final section of the book attempts to delineate the developmental problems at different levels of our existence. Chapter 13 focuses on vulnerable circumstances of various kinds emerging in the context of development, community, and family violence. Also, problems related to terrorism, natural disasters, violence, and war are discussed. The problem of destitute children is also discussed. Finally, the chapter attempts to discuss the potential of conflict resolution and the promotion of values. Chapter 14 examines the implications of the emerging conceptualization and policies of sustainable development and lifelong learning. To illustrate the possible efforts, interventions developed in India are described. The competencies, skills, and good practices related to sustainability are mentioned. The issues of sustainability are also examined in the cultural context.

We have, thus, endeavoured to create the engagement of students in the processes of development as embedded in a cultural context, especially from the majority world setting of India. The approach has been integrative. We have tried to relate human development with other aspects of psychology as well as with other disciplines. The readers will find frequent connections to the material in other chapters. We encourage readers to experience the developmental phenomena, think scientifically, and connect to research. We hope that this book will promote interest in developmental enquiry, critical thinking, and integration of principles and applications.

Acknowledgements

The genesis of this book stems from the collective wisdom of several individuals, including students, teachers, teacher educators, researchers, and colleagues. Over the years, our engagement in teaching, research, development of learning resources, and grassroots-level training across various institutions and universities has shaped our professional journey. The Educational Research and Innovations Committee (ERIC) of NCERT played a catalytic role in this process. Our sincere gratitude goes to all those who have contributed their insights, making the creation of this book possible.

A pivotal call to indigenize psychology in the Indian cultural context was given by the late Professor Durganand Sinha in the 1970s. His advocacy inspired researchers nationwide to examine cultural processes and develop measures sensitive to the Indian context. The book integrates the analyses and findings of Indian studies, striving for cultural relevance.

In the course of our research endeavours spanning more than the last three decades, we have been exploring various facets of the cognitive, social, developmental, and health domains of human development in the Indian context. Previous works, including *Researches in Child and Adolescent Psychology* (1993), *Child Development: The Indian Perspective* (1997), *Rethinking Intelligence: Conceptualizing Human Competence in Cultural Context* (2007), and *Basics in Education: Textbook for B.Ed. Course* (2014), along with contributions to journals and edited volumes, reflect our engagement. We express our gratitude to the editors and publishers of these volumes for recognizing our efforts and motivating our exploration of contextual factors in human development. Our experience in editing journals, namely the *Indian Educational Review* (AKS) and *Psychological Studies* (GM), further reinforced our commitment to the study of sociocultural influences.

We shall remain indebted to Professors B.B. Chatterjee, E.G. Parameswaran, B.N. Puhan, R. Muralidharan, Ajit K. Dalal, T.S. Saraswathi, A.K. Mohanty, Adesh Agarwal, and M.K. Raina in sharpening our academic acumen.

Our heartfelt appreciation goes to our families for their unwavering support, understanding, and encouragement throughout the highs and lows of this creative journey. Saurabh and Vibhor Srivastava's inquisitiveness and technical support were invaluable.

Special thanks are extended to Molly Selby, Editor at Routledge, and Shivranjani Singh, Editorial Assistant for their invaluable support while developing and finalizing the manuscript. Thanks are also due to Pallavi Ramanathan for help in finalising the manuscript.

Finally, we extend our appreciation to everyone, whether in a significant or small role, who contributed to bringing this book to fruition. Their support has been the cornerstone of this journey, and we are genuinely thankful for the privilege of sharing this volume with the world.

AKS
GM

Part I
Human Development from a Contextualist Perspective

1 Introduction to the Study of Human Development

Contents

Introduction	4
What is Development?	4
Concepts of Growth, Development, and Evolution	5
Key Issues in Understanding Human Development	6
Culture and Human Development	9
Human Development in Societal Context: The Case of India	10
Box 1.1: Population Pyramid	11
Box 1.2: Empty Nest Syndrome	12
Indigenous Developmental Concepts	12
Box 1.3: What is Your Age?	13
Box 1.4: The Indian Conception of Body (*Sharira*)	13
Box 1.5: The Concept of *Atman*	14
Box 1.6: *Ashrama Dharma* in Hindu Tradition	14
Box 1.7: *Samskaras* (Rituals)	15
Societal Goal of Human Development: An Indigenous Approach	16
Milestones in the Study of Human Development: A Historical Overview	17
Scope of Human Development Research	20
Overview	21
Key Terms	21
Questions for Reflection	22

Learning Objectives

After studying this chapter, the learner will be able to:

Describe the concepts of growth, development, and evolution;
Describe the concepts of development, change, and evolution;
Explain major debates in the field of human development;
Discuss the issues involved in understanding development in the Indian context;
Appreciate concepts related to development in the Indian tradition; and
Describe the contributions of prominent Western and Indian developmental psychologists.

Introduction

The study of human development is a multifaceted journey that explores the intricate interplay of biological, psychological, cultural, and ecological factors shaping changes in individuals and communities. This chapter seeks to orient the readers to change-related processes. In doing so, the concepts of growth, development, and evolution are examined. It further dissects the influence of culture on the developmental trajectory, offering insights into how societal contexts, exemplified by the case of India, shape the unfolding narrative. Within this discourse, concepts unique to Indian indigenous perspectives are introduced, exploring the ideas encapsulated in age, body, self, rituals, and tradition. The indigenous perspective on human development is discussed. To further enrich our understanding, a historical overview of the contributions of prominent international and Indian thinkers and scholars who have shaped this field is presented. The chapter finally delves into the scope of developmental psychological study and research that illuminates the processes of becoming and being. In this intellectual journey, we unravel the aspects of human development, guided by a curiosity to comprehend the complexities that define the essence of human existence.

What is Development?

The concept of development relates to diverse changes occurring in human life over time and across the developmental stages. From birth to death, human beings undergo a series of transformations in all aspects of life, including physical, psychological, social, and behavioural. Interestingly, development in its various manifestations in the different domains of social life has become a prime mover as well as a goal for societies. Accordingly, countries are often categorized as developed, developing, and underdeveloped. In societal discourse, "development" is adopted as a keyword indicating movement from one stage to another and often denotes a process leading to positive changes. Though the study of development within developmental psychology shares some features with societal development, it is more focused on the processes and outcomes of change located in the individual's bio-psycho-social characteristics. Also, the study of developmental changes helps in planning and regulating developmentally relevant activities in various life stages and taking steps to redress the problems encountered. This chapter introduces the key concepts involved in the study of individual or person-focused understanding of development.

Human growth and development are self-regulated phenomena taking place in the ecological context. Therefore, the pace of development relates to a variety of physiological, psychological, and environmental processes. Traditionally, these processes were considered to be continuous and orderly. In recent years, however, developmental processes are thought to be probabilistic outcomes of somewhat indeterminate combinations of genetic and environmental factors. Genetic factors do substantially guide developmental changes in specific directions. At the same time, the course of development is shaped by the life events of every individual, which makes it variable and probabilistic. These life events are emergent and therefore can neither be predicted nor explained by general laws. It is often remarked that "human beings are neither made of glass that breaks in the slightest adverse situation nor of steel that will remain unaffected by devastating hurricanes". Human beings are like plastic that may bend with environmental pressures and may resume their shape when the pressure is relieved (Baltes & Reese, 1984). Thus, human beings are unlikely to be permanently distorted by adverse circumstances.

Mery and Burns (2010) noted that plasticity is the result of a complex interaction between innate behavioural responses and cumulated lifetime experiences. The plasticity in behaviour makes human beings adaptive to varied life situations. That is, human beings learn to become socially and practically competent to meet the demands of everyday living. To meet the demands of their environments, each person must acquire a set of skills. As environments change, people must continuously learn new skills to meet the demands. Making a phone call is an example of adaptive behaviour that has changed over time. The skills needed to make a call today are very different from the skills that were required two or three decades ago. The adaptive skills change from one life stage to another and also with time.

Concepts of Growth, Development, and Evolution

To understand the concept of development, it is necessary to distinguish it from other related concepts such as "growth", "evolution", and "maturity". Growth refers to an increase in physical size and is quantitative (e.g., height, weight, vocabulary etc.). It is concerned with getting bigger or larger. The growth rate is not uniform across the various life stages. Growth is fast during childhood, reaches its peak during adolescence, and slows down during later years.

Development, on the other hand, refers to functional or non-organic changes and is mainly qualitative. It covers the qualitative changes during the entire spectrum of life. It is concerned with the psychological (e.g., cognitive, affective, social, and behavioural) changes with advancing age. In simple terms, the skills learnt such as reading and arithmetic are indicative of development. In some sense, growth seems to be an external phenomenon while development appears as an internal one. Thus, development can be inferred from the sophistication evinced in a child's performance on tasks of reasoning, imagination, creativity, and so on. It is also to be noted that though development usually refers to a positive change, it may also result in performance deterioration. For example, researchers have noted that some areas of psychometric intelligence, such as fluid intelligence (e.g., reasoning, problem-solving, and adapting to the environment) begin to decline during early adulthood. In the case of crystallized intelligence (which is the result of experience, education, and cultural background), development proceeds in an incremental fashion over the lifespan up to late adulthood (Horn & Cattell, 1967). Similarly, in the field of social development, relationships with the opposite-sex peers may show a discontinuous pattern with a decline in the elementary school years, followed by an increase during adolescence and young adulthood (Arnett, 2000). Development may, thus, be viewed more appropriately as a process characterizing a gain–loss relationship. Developmental changes need not always be of growth or progression but may also involve some loss in functional efficacy.

The term "evolution" is used for the species-specific patterns of change. It is concerned with any gradual directional change in the characteristics of a species over generations. It is a natural process involving irresistible changes in the genetic composition of a species from one generation to another. Such changes may affect the physical characteristics of the organism. The evolution of Homo sapiens from apes over about six million years ago is an example of the process of evolution (Lewin & Foley, 2004). When guided by natural selection, evolutionary changes tend to produce populations that are better adapted to the environments in which they live. In this way, evolution may be considered species-specific (phylogenetic) while development is individual-specific (ontogenetic).

Related to development is another term called "maturity". Maturity refers to the optimal development of a person. In some sense, it is a normative specification of the state of mental and emotional patterns of development. In common parlance, a mature person, therefore, becomes responsible as per one's age. It is reflected in how one chooses to respond and react to life situations. Viewed in this sense, development refers to the process through which an individual grows up while maturity refers to the end product.

Key Issues in Understanding Human Development

Understanding human development has engaged scholars to attend to several issues, such as the relative role of heredity and environment, the nature of development and change, organismic and contextual factors in development, the multidirectional and multidimensional nature of development, holistic nature, the role of culture in development, and so forth (see Srivastava, 1998). This section briefly introduces some of these issues.

Heredity and Environment

There has been a perennial debate regarding the contributions of biological and environmental factors to the processes and outcomes of development. The problem has been traditionally discussed as the heredity–environment issue, the nature–nurture controversy, and by many other names. The main question has been what roles heredity and environment play in human development. Heredity refers to the genetic transmission of certain biological and psychological characteristics from parents to children. On the other hand, the environment comprises the complete surroundings in which an individual lives and develops. It can be of two types – natural and social. The natural environment consists of all physical things and forces on and around the earth that have the potential to influence the development of a person. The social environment refers to the man-made environment that the person sees around himself/herself based on his/her awareness (i.e., language, religion, customs, traditions, means of communication, family, school, social groups, etc.). It is structured in the context of cultural and civilizational history. Both environments influence each other. The recent advances in information and communication technology are refashioning both kinds of environments and their influences.

Arnold Gesell (1933), a maturation theorist, has been the principal spokesperson of the position favouring nature (heredity) as a more potent or critical factor. He believed that the development plan was contained almost totally within the organism itself, and the environment was of little significance in terms of its contribution to that plan. The environment works merely as a background against which development occurs. This view was supported by researchers and thinkers like Francis Galton, Karl Pearson, William McDougall, and others. In his book *Hereditary Genius* (Galton, 1869), Galton attempted to show that the probability of the occurrence of gifted children is vastly higher when the fathers are of superior intelligence. Pearson (Pearson & Lee, 1903) also believed that heredity is more potent than the environment. McDougall (1908) emphasized the role of inherited instincts in shaping human behaviour and social interactions. He proposed a list of innate instincts, including instincts for self-preservation, reproduction, gregariousness, and other fundamental aspects of human functioning.

The behaviourists, most notably John B. Watson (1919), were opposed to the maturation or nativist view. Watson argued that human behaviour and development were controlled by external factors and rejected the significance of heredity and other inborn tendencies. The behaviourists treated the human organism as reactive and passive, as being receiving and being moulded in a sculptor's hand. Watson claimed that the principles of learning hold the key. They are key factors regulating the acquisition of human behaviour.

The recent theorization does not take a polarized view in favour of either heredity or environment. It appreciates the importance of both and favours an interactionist position: human behaviour is a product of the interaction of heredity and environment. It is assumed that the interaction of the two explains the variability in human attributes (refer to Monroe & Simons, 1991; Plomin et al., 1977). In simple terms, it is held that heredity sets the upper limit of what an individual can attain while the environment affects the degree to which the potentialities can be realized. Therefore, the debate is not framed as either heredity or the environment. Rather, it is more plausible that both sets of factors shape human development and how various factors interact at any point in time.

Development and Change

As stated earlier, development leads to some kind of change, but the reverse may not be true. To develop means to grow and evolve. In the literal sense, to develop means to unwrap or open up. It is a change that enhances or corrects existing qualities (e.g., brain functions, cognitive abilities, communication skills etc.). In human development, successive stages (or patterns) do not merely follow one another but emerge directly from the one that precedes it. Non-developmental change, in contrast, is a transition requiring no evolution or no unfolding. The non-developmental change is discrete, and therefore, one instance may occur without necessarily having any relationship with the other.

Lifespan Perspective on Development

Two main perspectives have been adopted in studying human development: *child development* and *lifespan*. The field of child development focuses on understanding the basis of individual development during the early years. In doing so, it emphasizes the first decade of life. It places greater stress on early experience and/or maturation for later development. Such a focus has led to a concern with examining general developmental trajectories and the more proximal contexts of human life, such as the family, the peer group, and the school. In contrast, the lifespan perspective studies all phases of life, beginning from prenatal and childhood to adulthood and ageing. It even studies the effect of changes in one partner's life on the life of another partner. For instance, when a partner dies, another partner's life changes drastically in social, physical, and intellectual aspects (Berger, 2011).

In recent studies, researchers are increasingly preferring the lifespan approach. In these efforts, five characteristics of human development are taken into account: multidirectional, multidisciplinary, multi-contextual, multicultural, and plasticity.

Multidirectional

Multidirectionality refers to all the possible directions of development, including gains and losses, growth and decline throughout life. For example, when infants learn to walk they also fall. Sometimes, we may have several friends, but we also feel lonely on other occasions. However, during the loss human beings consolidate the skills learnt and restart with new zeal.

Multidisciplinary

The multidisciplinary nature of human development suggests that understanding and explaining human development requires the integration of knowledge from various disciplines, including biology, psychology, sociology, culture, education, environment, economics, and so on. For example, we cannot understand the physical changes of puberty without discussing its psychological effects. Similarly, it is not possible to examine the outcomes of socialization without examining the nature of one of our major social institutions, the family. It is therefore essential to consider the perspectives from various disciplines in a complementary and integrated manner.

Multi-Contextual

The multi-contextual nature of human development recognizes that individuals do not exist in isolation but are shaped by several interconnected factors and settings throughout their lives.

8 Human Development from a Contextualist Perspective

These contexts relate to different levels, including microsystem (the immediate environment in which an individual lives, such as family, peers, and school), mesosystem (or the connections and interactions between various microsystems such as family and school or between family and peer groups), exosystem (or environments or settings that the individual may not be directly involved in but that still influence their development such as parent's workplace or community resources), macrosystem (or the broader cultural, social, economic, and political systems that shape the individual's development (Bronfenbrenner, 1979; Sinha, 1977). Cultural norms, societal values, and historical events are part of the macrosystem and chronosystem (e.g., life events, transitions, and historical changes that occur throughout a person's life).

Multicultural

The multicultural nature of human development refers to the idea that individuals grow, learn, and develop within the context of multiple cultural influences. For example, they are exposed to a variety of influences from their family, community, society, and the broader societal context. People develop a sense of cultural identity, acquire cultural competence or the ability to interact effectively with people from different cultural backgrounds, and so on.

Plasticity

Plasticity emphasizes the fact that the individual is malleable and prone to change proving that they, along with their characteristics, can undergo alterations at any point in the lifespan. However, when circumstances change, they come back to their normal position.

Organismic and Contextual Factors

Human development has been conceptualized as a function of the interaction between an active individual and an active, organized environment or context. The individual manipulates different aspects of the environment, evoking behaviour from others, selecting settings, and discriminating among stimuli. The context includes variables such as the individual's experiential environment, the family, the peer group, the community, and the entire ecology.

The lifespan perspective acknowledges that there are several social contexts in which the process of development unfolds. According to Baltes (1987), the influence of context can be of three types: normative age-graded, normative history-graded, and non-normative.

Normative Age-Graded Influences

A specific age group such as childhood, adolescence, or adulthood may be prone to specific influences. Humans of a particular age group have similar social experiences (such as going to school, joining the workforce, and retiring) and biological changes (e.g., puberty) and so on. These influences are common to a particular age group and are considered normal within a given culture.

Normative History-Graded Influences

The period when one is born or the generation to which one belongs (cohort) influences his/her experiences. Some commonly recognized generations are Silent, Baby Boomers, Generation X, Millennials, Generation Z, and Generation Alpha.

> *Silent Generation* or Traditionalists (born roughly 1928–1945) grew up during the Great Depression and experienced World War II. They value loyalty, hard work, and respect for authority.

Baby Boomers (born roughly 1946–1964) experienced a significant increase in birth rates post-World War II. They witnessed cultural shifts and hold a strong work ethic, loyalty to organizations, and a desire for social change.

Generation X (born roughly 1965–1980) witnessed increased divorce rates and both parents working. They experienced the advent of personal computers, the rise of MTV, and economic uncertainty. Generation X emphasizes independence, adaptability, and scepticism towards institutions.

Millennials, also known as Generation Y (born roughly 1981–1996) grew up with rapid technological advancements, including the internet and mobile devices, embrace diversity, value work–life balance, and hold a strong sense of community and social awareness.

Generation Z (born roughly 1997–2012) grew up in a digital era, with smartphones and social media as integral parts of their lives, embrace diversity, and tend to be socially and environmentally conscious. They value individual expression and entrepreneurial pursuits.

Generation Alpha, people born roughly after 2010 are tentatively given this name, and the defining characteristics of the generation may evolve as individuals within the generation grow. They are likely to be true digital natives, tech-savvy, globally aware, environmentally conscious, and have an entrepreneurial spirit.

Non-Normative Influences

Non-normative influences are irregular or atypical. These influences do not follow a predictable or common developmental trajectory and, as a result, can have a significant impact on an individual's life. These are unique and unpredictable life events, such as immigration, accidents, and unfortunate deaths in the family.

Holistic Nature of Human Development

This view is based on the assumption that the whole is greater than the sum of its parts (Haynes, 2009). The holistic nature of human development draws attention to the interconnectedness and complementarity of the functioning of mind, body, and spirit. It is, therefore, essential to pay attention to the physical, intellectual, social, emotional, and spiritual well-being of the individual. Changes in body size, brain development, perceptual and motor capacities, and physical health are covered under physical development. Cognitive development includes changes in an individual's thinking, intelligence, and language. Changes in an individual's relationships with other people, changes in emotions, and personality changes are covered in socio-emotional processes. Spiritual development brings changes in one's awareness of and relationship with God and the cosmos. The existential questions (such as Who am I? Why am I here? What is the meaning of life? What happens after death?) are the subject matter of spiritual development. The development of all these abilities is required to make humans competent to face the challenges of the world.

Thus, understanding human development involves grappling with several complex issues. The issues discussed above represent a fraction of the multifaceted landscape of human development research. Exploring these issues provides valuable insights into the factors that shape human development, informs research and intervention strategies, and contributes to the overall well-being of individuals across the lifespan.

Culture and Human Development

In simple terms, culture is a way of life. It represents a set of beliefs, behaviours, ideas, values, and practices shared by a group of people. It is a way of expressing oneself as an individual and as a group. Comprising meanings and practices, culture gives you a distinct identity – Indian,

English, American, Mexican, Japanese, Asian, and so on. Cultures vary from one another in practices (e.g., sleeping, eating, and dressing) and behaviour patterns and affect the development of cognitive, affective, and social competencies (refer to Cole, 1996; Markus & Kitayama, 1991; Rogoff, 2003; Valsiner, 1987).

The influence of culture on development is seen from the moment the child is born and continues to regulate developmental processes and outcomes throughout life. For instance, culture operates with shades of socialization processes, values, language, artefacts, belief systems, and an understanding of individuals and as members of society. Also, the organization of the home environment, parent's education, occupation, economic status, peer group, community, school, and workplace environment occurs in a cultural context. They do exert influence on the development of the child as located in the cultural context.

In summary, it can be said that exploring the key issues in understanding human development unveils a rich tapestry of interconnected factors that shape the journey of life. Understanding these key issues not only deepens our comprehension of individuals but also fosters a broader appreciation for the intricate dance between nature and nurture that defines the human experience.

Human Development in Societal Context: The Case of India

Since India gained independence in 1947, it has witnessed significant strides in various indicators of human and social development, such as education, healthcare, gender equality, and poverty alleviation. A brief description of the progress is given here. The details are given at appropriate places in subsequent chapters.

Education

One of the most noteworthy achievements is the expansion and improvement of the education system. Significant progress has been made in increasing literacy rates and enhancing access to education. Various schemes of the government and Acts (such as the *Samgra Shiksha* and Right to Education Act) have played pivotal roles in ensuring primary education for all, irrespective of gender, socio-economic status, and disability. However, there persist regional and socio-economic disparities in access to quality education. Rural areas often face infrastructure challenges and a shortage of qualified teachers, hindering the educational experience for many children. Additionally, the quality of education needs improvement to meet the demands of a rapidly evolving global economy. Practices like child marriage and child labour, though reduced, continue even in recent times.

Healthcare

Advancements in the healthcare sector have resulted in improved life expectancy and a decline in infant mortality rates. The successful implementation of vaccination programmes, maternal health initiatives, and disease control measures have contributed to these positive outcomes. The disparities in healthcare facilities between rural and urban areas demand our attention. Also, improvements in healthcare have increased the population of the elderly. The elderly population faces different kinds of challenges that demand our attention (Boxes 1.1 and 1.2).

Gender Equality

There has been a gradual but significant shift towards gender equality. The government has implemented policies and programmes to empower women socially, economically, and politically. Additionally, the increased participation of women in various fields, including education, science, and technology, reflects a changing societal mindset. However, the country continues to grapple with issues of gender-based violence, including domestic violence, sexual assault, and harassment.

Poverty Alleviation

Various anti-poverty programmes and schemes have played a crucial role in providing employment opportunities and improving the livelihoods of rural communities. While challenges persist, such as underemployment and unemployment, regional disparities, and urban poverty, the progress made is commendable.

Environmental Sustainability

The rapid pace of industrialization and urbanization has led to environmental challenges, including air and water pollution, deforestation, and climate change impacts. Balancing economic development with environmental sustainability is a complex task that demands strategic policies, technological innovations, and public awareness campaigns to foster responsible and sustainable practices.

To address these challenges one would need to adopt a holistic and integrated approach. A singular focus on one aspect of development is insufficient, and a comprehensive strategy involving multiple dimensions and coordinated efforts is essential for sustained progress in improving the well-being of the people. The democratic system in India provides a framework and opportunities for interventions aimed at improving the social conditions and well-being of its citizens.

Box 1.1   Population Pyramid

A population pyramid is a graphical representation of the age and gender structure of a population. In India, population pyramids have undergone significant changes over the years, reflecting changes in fertility rates, mortality rates, and migration patterns.

In the early 20th century, India had a pyramid-shaped population structure, with a large proportion of young people at the base and a smaller proportion of older people at the top. However, with improvements in healthcare, sanitation, and education, the mortality rate declined, leading to an increase in the proportion of older people. In addition, with increasing urbanization and education, the fertility rate declined, leading to a decrease in the proportion of young people.

According to the 2011 census, the population pyramid in India is no longer pyramid-shaped but rather an "inverted pyramid" with a large proportion of older people and a smaller proportion of younger people. This trend is expected to continue with the proportion of older individuals projected to reach 19% by 2050 (United Nations, 2019).

The changing population structure in India has important implications for social and economic development. An ageing population can put pressure on health and social care systems, as well as lead to a decline in economic productivity. However, it also presents opportunities for innovation and growth in sectors such as healthcare and technology.

Box 1.2 Empty Nest Syndrome

The term empty nest is used to describe a phase in a parent's life when their children have grown up and moved out of the family home to pursue education or work opportunities. In India, the concept of the empty nest has become increasingly relevant to changing social and economic factors.

Traditionally, in India, the family system was based on joint family structures, where multiple generations lived together under one roof. However, with urbanization and increased mobility, the nuclear family system has become more common (Sinha, 1988), and an empty nest has become a growing concern for parents. Females are likely to experience empty nest syndrome more than males (Budhia et al., 2022). The transition from a full house to an empty nest can be emotionally challenging for parents, particularly for mothers, who may have dedicated their lives to raising their children. Jhangiani et al. (2022) have developed a scale for the measurement of empty nest syndrome among Indians.

Studies (e.g., Agrawal, 2023; Nayak et al., 2022) have shown that parents in India experience a range of emotions during the empty nest phase, including loneliness, sadness, and a sense of purposelessness. However, there are also positive aspects of this phase, such as increased freedom, opportunities for self-care and personal growth, and the ability to strengthen relationships with their spouse or other family members. Social support from family and friends, as well as participation in community activities, helps parents navigate the empty nest phase and maintain a sense of well-being. Interventions such as family therapy and support groups can also be beneficial in helping parents adjust to this phase of life.

Overall, the concept of an empty nest in India highlights the changing family dynamics and the need for support and resources to help parents navigate this phase. As India continues to experience rapid social and economic changes, it is essential to recognize the emotional and psychological impact of the empty nest on parents and provide appropriate support and interventions.

Indigenous Developmental Concepts

India is one of the oldest continuing civilizations. It has a rich heritage of concepts and practices about human life. The textual knowledge and lifeways were connected. However, the learning of related concepts was marginalized during the British colonial rule of about two centuries, and alien concepts and practices were imposed. Today, the country is involved in self-introspection and recovery of these concepts and practices. Ayurveda (the Indian science of life and medicine) and yoga are being received internationally. The need to understand, critically examine, and use indigenous concepts is being seriously felt. Keeping this in view, this section describes some developmentally pertinent indigenous concepts in Boxes. These are the conceptions of age (or *ayu*) (Box 1.3), body (*Sharira*) (Box 1.4), *Atman* (Box 1.5), *ashrama dharmas* (Box 1.6), and *samskaras* (Box 1.7).

Box 1.3 What is Your Age?

There are variations in the conceptions of age. Four primary conceptions include chronological age, biological age, psychological age, and social age. The interplay of chronological, biological, psychological, and social dimensions provides a more holistic perspective on the ageing process, acknowledging the diversity and uniqueness of each individual's journey through the different stages of life.

Chronological age indicates the number of years a person has lived since birth. You ask someone "What is your age?", and the answer, for example, is that I am 20 years old. This shows the number of years since birth.

Biological age refers to the physiological condition and functional capabilities of an individual's body, often measured by assessing factors like organ function, cellular health, and genetic markers. It shows the health and susceptibility to age-related diseases. Biological age depends upon several factors including nutrition, level of physical activity, sleeping habits, smoking, use of alcohol, handling of stress mentally, and genetic history.

Psychological age reflects an individual's mental and cognitive abilities, emotional well-being, and overall psychological development. Individuals may age differently psychologically, with some maintaining a youthful mindset and cognitive agility while others may experience cognitive decline or emotional changes. A 65-year-old might be emotionally strong and travels all around the world while some 45-year-olds might be reluctant to travel even short distances.

Social age considers the roles, relationships, and societal expectations associated with a particular age. It encompasses cultural norms, societal roles, and the impact of one's interactions and relationships on the ageing process. Social age recognizes that the expectations and responsibilities assigned to individuals at different life stages influence their overall well-being and sense of purpose.

The Indian concept of age (or *ayu*) incorporates all four types of age as mentioned earlier. The elderly wish the children and others with the blessing "Ayushman Bhava", which means a long life. At the same, it also implies that you should also possess low biological age (remain fit) and have high cognitive, emotional, and behavioural competencies which may enable you to conquer the world. The Vedas aspire for 100 years long and active life: *Pashyem sharadah shatam, adiinah syam sharadah shatam.*

Box 1.4 The Indian Conception of Body (*Sharira*)

The Indian view recognizes the existence of three bodies in a human being (Das, 2022):

The Gross, Physical Body or "*Sthula Sharira*": It is the material and mortal body that performs acts like eating, drinking, and breathing. It is composed of five elements: ether, air, water, fire, and earth. The three main features of the *Sthula Sharira* are *Sambhava* (birth), *Jara* (old age), and *Maranam* (death). Of the three states of existence (i.e., waking, dream, and deep sleep), it is characterized by the state of waking.

The Subtle Body or "Sukshma Sharira": This form of the body is composed of *Pranamaya Kosha* (vital breath or energy), *Manomaya Kosha* (mind), and *Vijnanamaya Kosha* (intellect). It keeps the physical body alive. It continues to exist after death and serves as a vehicle of reincarnation. It is characterized by the state of the dream.

The Causal Body or "Karana Sharira": This form of the body is a combination of the gross and subtle bodies as it compels the soul to take another birth. It is characterized by emptiness, ignorance and darkness. However, it contains the expression of experience. It is characterized by the state of deep sleep.

Box 1.5   The Concept of *Atman*

Atman is a Sanskrit word, defined in terms of an individual's inner self, spirit, or soul. *Atman* is regarded as eternal and imperishable, distinct from the physical body, mind, and consciousness. It is believed to be found within every living being, though some individuals do not recognize this true self due to ignorance or illusion, known as *Maya*. It is generally accepted that the union of *Atman* and *Brahman* (or universe) through cultivating self-knowledge is a means of achieving liberation from suffering. Practices such as yoga and meditation can help to increase *Atma Jnana*, a form of self-awareness or self-knowledge that lifts the veil of ignorance and relieves practitioners from suffering.

Box 1.6   *Ashrama Dharma* in Hindu Tradition

The Hindu tradition visualizes life as consisting of four stages and has specified duties for each stage. These stages regulate life from beginning to end and take one's life to perfection. There are duties specified for the four stages of life. Of the four stages, the first two pertain to *Pravritti Marg* or the path of work and the last two to *Nivritti Marg* or the path of renunciation. The four *Ashramas* are:

1) *Brahmacharyashrama* (or the period of studentship)

Starting from the age of around 8–9 years, the person strives to maintain celibacy to conserve physical, moral, and mental energy and to devote him to the studies for a period of about 12–15 years. During this period, importance is given to the acquisition of knowledge and securing physical and moral fitness, that is, strengthening of body, mind, and intellect.

2) *Grhasthashrama* (or the stage of the householder)

The person gets married and settles down. The emphasis during this stage is on leading an honest and purposeful married life and family life, earning legitimate income and through it serving the family and society.

3) *Vanaprasthashrama* (or the stage of the forest dweller or hermit)

Around the age of 60, the person becomes a forest recluse and, without much attachment to worldly life, engages himself in *Vedic karma*. The individual is required to entrust the family responsibility to his grown-up sons/daughters and to devote himself mainly to the *seva* (selfless service) of the society.

4) *Sannyasashrama* (or the life of renunciation or asceticism)

In this stage, the individual renounces the world completely (even Vedic activities) and becomes a hermit (*Sanyasi*). He devotes himself completely to God.

The ashramas were organized with the principles of *Rinas* (debts). An individual is considered to be born with debts to parents, teachers, human beings, and other living beings. One is required to perform *Yajnas* or sacrifices (actions, performances) to repay the debts. Four life goals were also articulated: *Dharma* (righteousness), *Artha*, (wealth), *Kama* (desire and action), and *Moksha* (liberation). Life has to be pursued with the principle of enjoyment with renunciation (*Bhoga* with *Tyaga*). An important characteristic of *ashrama dharma*, together with the *samskaras*, as Chakkarath (2013) noted, is that they provide a framework for transmitting culture-specific information from generation to generation.

Box 1.7 *Samskaras* (Rituals)

Traditionally, in the Indian/Hindu view of life, 16 *samskaras* (or rituals) are performed from conception till death at different stages of life. These *samskaras* are performed to initiate the child into the world, purify the soul, clean sins from the body and soul, build character, and bring stability, calmness, and inner peace (refer to Sarangi, 2021). Eight major *samskaras* are described here.

Namakarna or ceremony for naming the child is performed on the eleventh or twelfth day in the presence of family and friends.

Annaprasana or first-time feeding the baby with solid food during around six months for good health and physical strength of the baby.

Chudakarna or haircut (*mundan samskara*) is generally done when the child is around one year of age. The child's hair is cut, and nails are trimmed, which symbolizes cleaning, renewal, and new growth.

Karnavedha or piercing the earlobes. Research has shown links between earlobes and hemispheres, the *samskara* is performed to develop intelligence and immunity against respiratory diseases.

Vidyarambha or beginning of learning numbers and alphabets. This is usually performed around five years of age.

Upanayana or Holy thread ceremony is performed when the child begins going to the guru for learning.

Vivaha or marriage ceremony marks the entry into *grihasthaashrama*.

Antyesti or last rites of funeral is performed after the death of the person by close relatives.

Societal Goal of Human Development: An Indigenous Approach

The Indian approach to human development adopts a cosmogenic perspective with an emphasis on time, place, and person. It relates to the socio-economic and cultural trajectory of the society. In contrast to mainstream development paradigms that often prioritize economic growth with an anthropocentric view, the Indian model takes a more holistic stance, considering well-being comprehensively and inclusively. Classical concepts such as "Dharma" and "Karma" (moral and ethical duty) and action orientation and the recent one of "Sarvodaya" (the welfare of all) have played a pivotal role in shaping the perspective on development. The Indian model stresses holistic development (social, cultural, economic, and environmental), inclusivity and social justice, promotion of cultural values and identity, sustainable development, and participatory governance. The work of scholars like Amartya Sen and Jean Dreze contributes towards understanding human development in India. In their book, *An Uncertain Glory: India and its Contradictions*, Dreze and Sen (2013) argue that India's problem lies in the lack of attention paid to the essential needs of people, particularly of the poor and women, which cannot be solved by the rapid economic growth alone. It requires adopting a participatory approach and utilizing social and economic resources. Jean Dreze was instrumental in advocating for a rural guarantee scheme, which took the shape of the Mahatma Gandhi National Rural Employment Guarantee Act (MGNREGA) (see Chapter 14).

The two terms *Dharma* and *Sarvodaya* need to be discussed in some detail. The concept of "dharma" is deeply rooted in the philosophical and religious traditions of the country. It encompasses a broader understanding of the moral and ethical order that encompasses the universe, including human lives. The concept is shared by almost all faiths of Indian origin including Hinduism, Buddhism, Jainism, and Sikhism. Certain common elements define the concept of *dharma* across these traditions. It involves fulfilling one's duty and adhering to righteous conduct in all domains of life, promoting social harmony by prescribing ethical behaviour in relationships and societal roles, emphasizing a balance between individual aspirations and societal well-being, as well as a balance between material pursuits and spiritual growth and adapting to changing circumstances while maintaining its core ethical principles. *Dharma* is defined in the following words: *Yatobhyuday nihshreyas siddhih sa dharmh*. *Dharma* is thus not a static concept; rather it is contextual and connects with *desh* or place, *kala* or time, and *patra* or person. In essence, the concept of *dharma* provides a moral and ethical framework for individuals to lead a virtuous life and contribute positively to the well-being of the self, society, and environment. It reflects a deep understanding of the interconnectedness of all life and the importance of living in harmony with the cosmic order.

The *Sarvodaya* movement, which gained prominence during the 20th century, was concerned with the social and economic development of the people. It aimed to achieve social upliftment and well-being for the entire community. The *Sarvodaya* movement emerged as part of Mahatma Gandhi's vision for a just and equitable society. It was rooted in Gandhian principles of non-violence (ahimsa), truth (*satya*), self-reliance (*swaraj*), and the pursuit of social justice. *Sarvodaya* emphasizes decentralized and self-governing communities, fostering a sense of self-sufficiency and autonomy among them. The movement promoted the idea that development should not be pursued at the expense of certain segments of society and should uplift the marginalized and underprivileged. The Sarvodaya movement emphasizes rural development and the well-being of villages, having access to basic amenities, education, and healthcare, thereby reducing the migration from rural to urban areas.

One of the practical manifestations of the Sarvodaya movement is the concept of "Shramadana", which translates to "the contribution of one's labour". Sarvodaya Shramadana is a community-driven voluntary work initiative where individuals contribute their time and effort for the betterment of the community. This grassroots approach helps in building a sense of community and shared responsibility. *Sarvodaya* also draws inspiration from India's spiritual and cultural heritage, emphasizing the values of compassion, self-discipline, and the interconnectedness of all living beings. Notable figures like Vinoba Bhave, Jaya Prakash Narayan, Nirmala Deshpande, and Dhanraj Bhati prominently led the Sarvodaya movement. The movement emphasized the welfare and uplift of all, especially the marginalized and economically disadvantaged sections of society. It also laid stress on the importance of self-reliance, community empowerment, and non-violent social change. Although the impact of the movement has evolved over time, the essence of *Sarvodaya* continues to resonate with those advocating for a more equitable and humane world.

The Indian model of human development, thus, represents a distinctive approach that transcends narrow economic perspectives. It seeks to carve out a path that aligns with its historical and cultural ethos. While challenges persist, the Indian model offers valuable insights about how to prioritize the well-being of all citizens. This book focuses on delineating the social and cultural aspects while discussing different aspects of human development.

Milestones in the Study of Human Development: A Historical Overview

The scientific study of human development (or developmental psychology) began in the 20th century. This section briefly introduces the researchers and their contributions from a historical perspective who have shaped the modern enquiry concerning the processes of human development.

The origin of modern developmental psychology can be traced in the writings of John Locke (a 17th-century English philosopher), Jean-Jacques Rousseau (an 18th-century Franco-Swiss philosopher and nativist), and Charles Darwin (a 19th-century British biologist). John Locke considered a newborn's mind as *tabula rasa* (blank slate), which can be moulded through learning and experience. Rousseau gave importance to innate processes. Darwin, who had proposed the theory of evolution, postulated that human behaviours have their origins in successful adaptations in the past as "ontogeny recapitulates phylogeny".

G. Stanley Hall (1844–1924) is regarded as the father of developmental psychology. Hall and his students devised several tools for the study of child development. In his book *Adolescence* (1904), Hall postulated that mental growth proceeds by evolutionary stages.

James M. Baldwin (1861–1934) proposed the first stepwise theory of cognitive development. He is also known for his idea of infant imitation. He proposed that through imitation, individuals come to understand and internalize the mental states and processes of others (Baldwin, 1895).

John B. Watson (1878–1958) popularized the scientific theory of behaviourism. He (Watson, 1913) believed that human behaviour is the result of learning and experience. Emphasizing the notion of objectivity, he considered only observable and measurable behaviour as the subject matter of scientific psychology.

Sigmund Freud (1856–1939) postulated the role of psychoanalysis in understanding human behaviour and psychopathology. Freud (1905) gave a stage model of development which he believed to be biologically determined. Freud gave importance to early years of experience (particularly those before five years of age).

Arnold Gesell (1880–1961), a student of G. Stanley Hall, proposed the maturation theory. Gesell (1928) believed that human behaviour is the outcome of biological maturation and that environment plays a minimal role. His research led to the development of norms for a variety of children's early behaviour including cognitive, motor, language, and social development. For this, he adopted the method of one-way observation to identify the typical age at which skills are acquired. These milestones are still used as a way to assess a child's development today.

Another landmark development at the beginning of the 20th century was Alfred Binet's engagement in experimental methods to develop tests of intelligence. In 1905, Binet developed a test of intelligence which underwent several revisions later on and revolutionized the field of intelligence testing.

Over the 20th century, one would observe a paradigmatic shift from behaviourism to cognitivism. Noam Chomsky took the lead in this direction. His theory of transformational grammar (Chomsky, 1957) earned wide recognition.

Jean Piaget (1896–1980) is one of the most influential developmental psychologists. His theory of genetic epistemology though gave primacy to genetic factors and also valued the importance of experience in determining behaviour. Piaget (1954) proposed a stage theory of cognitive development. He believed that the way children think is qualitatively different from that of adults. The constructivist theory of Piaget suggests that people actively construct their knowledge of the world based on the interaction between their ideas and experiences.

Lev Vygotsky (1978) advocated the importance to sociocultural factors. He proposed that human development is primarily a socially mediated process. Children learn cultural values, beliefs, and problem-solving strategies through active dialogues with more knowledgeable members of society. Vygotsky's theory comprises concepts such as culture-specific tools, private speech, and the zone of proximal development (ZPD).

Paul Baltes is known to have put forth a lifespan perspective of development (Baltes & Baltes, 1990). In addition, he worked substantially on historical cohort effects, cognitive development, a dual-process conception of lifespan intelligence, and the study of wisdom. He successfully brought changes in the study of human development from child psychology to developmental psychology to developmental science (Lerner, 2008).

Contributions of Modern Indian Thinkers and Scholars

In India, the philosophical thoughts of several thinkers influenced the course of child/human development. Prominent among them are Mahatma Gandhi, Rabindranath Tagore, and Sri Aurobindo. Mahatma Gandhi (1869–1948) believed in the all-round development of children: morally sound, individually independent, socially constructive, economically productive, and responsible citizens. He gave primacy to the values of ahimsa (non-violence) and *Satya* (truthfulness). His concept of basic education (*Buniyadi Talim*) focused on developing the three Hs – Head, Heart, and Hand – in addition to the learning three R's – Reading, Writing, and Arithmetic.

Rabindranath Tagore (1861–1941) believed in the development of innate faculties of children that lead to their all-round development through natural processes. Children should be provided opportunities to explore and play, and learning should be joyful. Education should develop creativity and aesthetics in children. The medium of instruction should be the mother tongue.

According to Sri Aurobindo (1872–1950), education should begin at birth and continue throughout life. It should begin before birth. The education should be child-centred and should be according to the mental aptitudes and psychological needs of the child. It should train the senses of the child. He believed in the development of five aspects of the individuals: physical, vital, mental, psychic, and spiritual. His ideas about the evolution of consciousness and integral yoga offer a new approach to development as the manifestation of the divine.

Several modern scholars have contributed to the field of human development. Prominent among them are Sudhir Kakar, S. Anandalakshmy, Amita Verma, T.S. Saraswathi, Rajalakshmi Muralidharan, Durganand Sinha, Girishwar Misra, Ajit K. Mohanty, and Malavika Kapur.

Sudhir Kakar was trained in psychoanalysis at Sigmund Freud's Institute in Frankfurt. He highlighted the relationships between culture and the unconscious. In his book, *The Inner World: A Psychoanalytic Study of Childhood and Society in India*, Kakar (1978) discussed the development of Indian identity. In doing so, he uses anthropological evidence, clinical data, mythology, and folklore to open the door to the daily lives of the Hindu family. His other book *Indian Childhood* (Kakar, 1979) provides a rich and vivid portrait of a pivotal moment in Indian history and a personal reflection on the complexities of growing up in a rapidly changing world. His books have been translated into 21 languages around the world.

S. Anandalakshmy is credited to have started a master's course on child development at Lady Irwin College in New Delhi in the 1970s. She was involved in developing and implementing programmes to promote child development and well-being, particularly in underprivileged communities in India. Her work focused on understanding the cultural and contextual factors that influence child development, and she advocated for a more culturally sensitive approach to studying and promoting child development (Anandalakshmy et al., 2008).

Amita Verma was instrumental in launching full-fledged master's and postgraduate programmes in early childhood education in the Department of Human Development and Family Studies at MS University of Baroda. She documented social change in traditional child-rearing practices in rural Gujarat (Verma & Poffenberger, 1970). Her work has explored how parenting practices, family dynamics, and cultural beliefs shape children's development. She worked closely with communities and policymakers to create interventions that address the specific needs of children in diverse cultural contexts.

T.S. Saraswathi worked in the Department of Human Development and Family Studies at MS University of Baroda. She has contributed to the field of cross-cultural development psychology. Her research explored how cultural beliefs and practices shape children and adolescents' development. Saraswathi has also been involved in developing and implementing programmes to promote the well-being of children and adolescents in India. She worked closely with policymakers and educators to create interventions that address the specific needs of young people in diverse cultural contexts. She proposed developmental theories grounded in Hindu world views and provided new directions in family studies and human development (Scott, 2013). She brought out a book *Childhoods in India: Traditions, Trends and Transformations* (Saraswathi et al., 2018).

Rajalakshmi Muralidharan contributed significantly towards enriching preschool education in the country. She has been involved in devising developmental norms for Indian children between the ages of 2 years and 5 years (Muralidharan, 1986). Her research primarily focused on the area of cognitive stimulation of children. She established a play laboratory for preschool children at the National Council of Educational Research and Training, New Delhi.

Durganand Sinha proposed an ecological model for understanding the development of children in the Indian context. He emphasized the role of sociocultural factors in understanding cognitive development. An ardent promoter of culturally rooted psychology, Sinha focused on socialization (Sinha, 1981), development in the context of poverty and disadvantage (Sinha et al., 1982), and intergenerational transformation of values (Sinha, 1974).

Girishwar Misra is a leading cultural development psychologist. His work has focused on exploring perceptual, cognitive, and motivational patterns among children and young adults, culturally rooted empirical explorations of various psychological processes, including cognition, morality, reasoning, and well-being. Misra's (Misra et al., 2021) recent book *Psychology in Modern India: Historical, Methodological, and Future Perspectives* provides an insight into the current state of psychology in India.

Ajit K. Mohanty is an educational psycholinguist working on Multilingual Education (MLE), Language Policy in Education and Education of Indigenous, Tribal, Minority and Minoritized Communities. His current research focuses on multilingual education for indigenous minorities. He edited a book *The Multilingual Reality: Living with Languages* (Mohanty, 2019). He drafted the 2014 Policy for Mother Tongue-Based Multilingual Education of tribal children in Odisha (India).

Malavika Kapur worked at the National Institute of Mental Health and Neurosciences, Bengaluru. She has been interested in developmental psychology and community mental health programmes for children and adolescents. She has developed integrated models of mental health service delivery for children and adolescents. Her book *Mental Health of Indian Children* (Kapur, 1995) sensitizes practitioners to issues related to the mental health of children. She has explored the indigenous roots of childcare practices in India (Kapur, 2016) and examined the challenges of digital technology in a developmental context (Kapur, 2021, 2024).

Scope of Human Development Research

In the contemporary period, the scope of human development research has expanded significantly. It covers dimensions that reflect the complexities and diversities of human existence. The interplay of globalization, technological advancements, socio-economic shifts, and evolving cultural norms has moved human development research to new heights. This expanded scope not only addresses existing challenges but also paves the way for innovative approaches and solutions.

The scope of human development research has expanded in diverse ways. First, it draws insights from an array of disciplines, such as psychology, sociology, economics, anthropology, public health, and more. This multidisciplinary approach allows researchers to examine human development from various angles, fostering a holistic understanding of the factors that influence growth and well-being. Second, globalization has interconnected societies like never before. Researchers are now analysing how global trends impact local communities and individuals. This includes the study of migration, cultural exchange, and the diffusion of ideas, which significantly shape developmental trajectories. Third, the digital revolution has transformed the way people interact, learn, work, and communicate. Human development research investigates the impacts of technology on cognitive development, social relationships, and skill acquisition, as well as addresses concerns related to digital divides and online well-being. Fourth, with growing concerns about climate change and ecological degradation, the scope of human development research now extends to sustainable development. It examines the intricate relationship between human progress, economic activities, and environmental preservation, seeking solutions for a balanced and resilient future.

Fifth, contemporary human development research adopts a lifespan perspective, examining how individuals develop and adapt across different stages of life. Sixth, the study of human development places a strong emphasis on addressing inequality, social justice, and marginalized populations. Researchers analyse how structural inequalities impact access to resources, opportunities, and overall life outcomes, seeking ways to create more inclusive societies. Lastly, the insights gained from human development research are now directly influencing policymaking and intervention strategies. Governments, organizations, and communities use research findings to design programmes that promote education, health, social equity, and economic development.

In essence, the scope of human development research in the contemporary period is dynamic, broad, and responsive to the intricate challenges and opportunities of the modern world. As our understanding of human development continues to evolve, this research plays a pivotal role in shaping policies, fostering positive change, and ensuring a brighter and more equitable future for all.

Overview

In conclusion, this introductory chapter provided an overview of the multifaceted field of human development. We delved into the fundamental question of "What is Development?" and explored the nuanced concepts of growth, development, and evolution. The key issues in understanding human development were examined, emphasizing the intricate interplay of biological, psychological, and sociocultural factors. Culture emerged as a pivotal influence on human development, prompting an exploration of human development in the Indian cultural context. Our journey through indigenous developmental concepts shed light on the rich tapestry of beliefs and practices that shape the developmental trajectories of individuals within specific cultural frameworks.

Furthermore, we took a closer look at demographic structures using the population pyramid and delved into the emotional dimensions of family life through the lens of the empty nest syndrome. We also discussed that addressing human development in India needs to go beyond the economic model and incorporate the social and cultural ethos of India. The chapter also provided insights into significant milestones in the study of human development, offering a historical perspective on the evolution of this interdisciplinary field. Finally, we explored the vast scope of human development research, emphasizing its relevance across diverse domains. As we embark on this exploration of human development in subsequent chapters, we will continue to unravel the intricacies of this dynamic field, bridging theory and practice to gain a deeper understanding of the complex processes that characterize the human journey from conception to old age.

Key Terms

Age	Home Environment
Ashrama	Maturation
Atman	Mortality
Body	Normative Influence
Childbirth	Non-Normative Influence
Development	Plasticity
Empty Nest Syndrome	Population Pyramid
Evolution	*Samskara*
Environment	*Shramadaan*
Growth	*Sarvodaya*
Heredity	Satyagraha

Questions for Reflection

1) How would you define the term development, and what aspects do you think are crucial for a comprehensive understanding of development in a societal context?
2) How do concepts like growth, development, and evolution differ, and why is it essential to grasp these differences when studying human development?
3) What do you believe are the key issues that shape our understanding of human development?
4) How does culture influence individual and societal perspectives on development, and how might cultural diversity impact the trajectory of human development in different regions?
5) How do demographic patterns and family structures influence human development within a societal framework?

Suggested Further Readings

Books

Arnett, J. J., & Jensen, L. J. (2019). *Human development: A cultural approach* (3rd ed.). Pearson.
Boyd, D. R., & Bee, H. L. (2019). *Lifespan development*. Pearson.
Lally, M., & Valentine-French, S. (2022). *Lifespan development: A psychological perspective* (4th ed.). Open Textbook. https://open.umn.edu/opentextbooks/textbooks/540.
Santrock, J. (2021). *Life-span development*. McGraw Hill.

Website/Online Resources

Psychology Today (*psychologytoday.com*)

2 Understanding the Human Life Course

Contents

Introduction	24
Embryonic Beginning: Exploring the Prenatal Stage	24
Infancy Stage: A Journey of Growth and Exploration	25
Early Childhood Stage: The Wonder Years	27
Box 2.1: Early Childhood Care and Education (ECCE)	28
Box 2.2: Nurturing the Foundation Through ECCE: The Case of India	28
Late Childhood Stage: Expanding Horizons	29
Adolescent Development: A Transformative Phase	30
Box 2.3: Adolescence in the Indian Context	31
Box 2.4: The Notion of "Emerging Adulthood"	32
Early Adulthood: Transitions and Transformations	33
Middle Adulthood: A Blossoming Stage	34
Old Age: Embracing Change and Ageing Gracefully	35
Box 2.5: Cognitive Development in Old Age	36
Death as a Life Stage: Embracing the Final Passage	37
Overview	39
Key Terms	40
Questions for Reflection	40

Learning Objectives

After studying this chapter, the learner will be able to:

Describe the key stages of human development and their distinctive characteristics;
Analyse the sociocultural, environmental, and biological influences on development;
Examine the nuances of early childhood care and education;
Examine the transformations associated with early and middle adulthood;
Identify challenges faced during old age; and
Explore the cultural diversity in ideas about death.

DOI: 10.4324/9781003441168-3

Introduction

The stages of human development encompass the remarkable journey of growth and change across the lifespan, from conception to death. From the very first moments of existence, through pre-natal, infancy, childhood, adolescence, adulthood, and into old age and death, individuals transform, physically, cognitively, emotionally, and socially. Each stage brings with it unique challenges, opportunities, and milestones that contribute to shaping one's identity, abilities, and understanding of the world. This chapter focuses on providing a sketch of these developmental stages. The details of developmental changes are provided in subsequent chapters.

Embryonic Beginning: Exploring the Prenatal Stage

Human life begins at conception and undergoes fascinating phases of development in the womb of the mother for nine months. This period, called the prenatal or embryonic stage, lays the foundation for a person's life. The prenatal period can be divided into three sub-phases: germinal, embryonic, and foetal. The following description is an account of the developmental changes in normal pregnancy (e.g., Carlson, 2019; Moore et al., 2019).

Germinal Stage

The germinal stage takes place during the first two weeks after conception. It begins with fertilization, where a sperm cell penetrates the ovum, forming a zygote. The zygote consists of 23 pairs of chromosomes; half of them are received from the father and the other half from the mother. The mother provides 23 X chromosomes. The father provides 22 X chromosomes. The twenty-third chromosome of the father may be X or Y, which determines the sex of the baby. In the case of the daughter, the twenty-third chromosome of the father is X, and it is Y in the case of the son. Thus, the zygote in the case of females consists of 23 pairs of X chromosomes, and in the case of males, the zygote consists of 22 pairs of X chromosomes and the last pair comprises XY chromosomes. The zygote undergoes numerous cell divisions, each cell consisting of 23 pairs of chromosomes, as it travels through the fallopian tube towards the uterus. By the time it reaches the uterus, the zygote has become a blastocyst, a hollow ball of cells. Once in the uterus, the blastocyst attaches to the uterine wall in a process known as implantation, marking the end of the germinal stage. In recent times, in vitro fertilization (IVF), a medical procedure, is used to help individuals or couples with fertility issues in conceiving a child.

Embryonic Stage

The embryonic stage spans from the third week to the eighth week after conception. During this period, the embryo undergoes differentiation and organogenesis. At the start, rapid cell differentiation occurs, and the blastocyst begins to differentiate into three primary germ layers: *ectoderm*, *mesoderm*, and *endoderm*. Each germ layer gives rise to specific tissues and organs in the body. The key patterns are as follows:

1) The *ectoderm* is the outermost germ layer, giving rise to various structures, including the nervous system and the skin.
2) The *mesoderm* is the middle germ layer and is responsible for forming a wide range of tissues and organs, such as the musculoskeletal system, cardiovascular system, reproductive system, kidney and urogenital system, and so on.

3) The *endoderm*, the innermost germ layer, contributes to the development of the gastrointestinal and respiratory systems.

Thus, organogenesis, the process of forming major organs, occurs during the embryonic stage. By the end of the embryonic stage, all major organs are present, although they are not fully functional yet. During this stage, limb buds appear, fingers and toes become distinct, and the embryo starts to exhibit human-like characteristics. Sensory organs, such as the eyes and ears, start to form. By the end of the embryonic stage, the basic body plan is established, and the embryo's shape becomes more recognizable as a human. Also, sexual differentiation begins, and the embryo's sex becomes distinguishable.

The embryonic stage, however, is a highly vulnerable period for the developing embryo, and exposure to teratogens (negative environmental factors such as tobacco, wine, cigarette smoke, and so on) can cause birth defects, having long-lasting effects on the baby's health and development.

Foetal Stage

The foetal stage spans from the ninth week until birth. During this phase, the foetus grows from being just a few centimetres long to a size capable of surviving outside the womb by the time of birth. The heart, brain, lungs, liver, kidneys, and other vital organs become fully functional to support independent life after birth. The foetus becomes increasingly active, with movements that can be felt by the mother. These movements are essential for muscle development and the maturation of the nervous system. The sensory abilities start to develop. The foetus can hear sounds from the external environment and may respond to touch and light, showing early signs of sensory perception. The lungs undergo crucial maturation during the third trimester. They produce surfactant, a substance necessary to keep the air sacs open and facilitate breathing after birth.

Towards the end of the foetal stage, usually around the twenty-fourth week of gestation, the foetus reaches a stage of development where it can survive outside the womb with intensive medical care. As the foetal stage nears its end, the foetus moves into a position suitable for birth. In the weeks leading up to delivery, the foetus usually assumes a head-down position, readying itself for the journey through the birth canal.

Infancy Stage: A Journey of Growth and Exploration

The infancy stage spans from birth to two years of life. This stage is characterized by exponential growth and boundless exploration. This phase lays the foundation for an entire range of future development, shaping their physical, cognitive, emotional, and social competencies.

During the first four weeks, the baby is medically referred to as a neonate. Traditionally, a neonate was considered a passive and dependent being. However, growing research evidence (e.g., Aydlett, 2011; Grusec & Hastings, 2015) challenges the traditional view and considers them "competent neonates" because they are equipped with the necessary tools to communicate, learn, and adapt to their surroundings. Neonates are born with a set of primitive *reflexes*, such as sucking, rooting (turning their head in the direction of touch on the cheek), and grasping. Although they cannot speak, they do communicate through crying, facial expressions, and body movements to express their needs and emotions. They are born with sensory capabilities, such as the ability to see light and shadows, hear sounds, and feel touch. While their social interactions are limited, neonates can respond to social stimuli, such as eye contact and the sound of familiar voices. The Indian tradition also does not believe in what John Locke (1689, cited in Uzgais, 2022) advocated for newborn babies, to be a "white paper" or blank slate.

Infants achieve various physical and motor developmental milestones, such as fine and gross motor skills, brain growth, sensory refinement, and overall growth (O'Connor & Daly, 2016). The brain reaches approximately 80% of its adult size by the age of two years. Infants rapidly gain the ability to perceive and process information from their environment. The senses of sight, hearing, touch, taste, and smell gradually refine and become more acute. Infants achieve various cognitive milestones related to perception, memory, language, problem-solving, and social cognition. They progress from being reflexive beings to curious explorers of the world.

Infants develop the ability to understand and respond to the world around them. They develop attachment or emotional bonds with parents or caregivers (Bowlby, 1969). Ainsworth and her colleagues (1978) identified three primary attachment styles: *secure attachment, insecure-avoidant attachment*, and *insecure-resistant attachment*. Later, Main and Solomon (1986) added the fourth attachment style called *disorganized attachment*. Securely attached infants feel secure in their caregiver's presence, readily explore their environment, and are easily comforted when distressed. Unresponsive or rejecting parenting styles often lead to insecure-avoidant attachment where infants remain independent and indifferent. They may avoid seeking comfort from their caregivers and show little distress during separations. Insecure-resistant kind of attachment is the result of inconsistency in the caregiver's behaviour. Such infants remain anxious and may become clingy and distressed. Disorganized attachment refers to a pattern of behaviour where infants display contradictory and disoriented behaviours in the presence of their caregivers, such as freezing, repetitive movements, or a lack of a coherent strategy for dealing with stress. Disorganized attachment is often associated with caregivers who are frightening, abusive, or neglectful. Babies also engage in a process called social referencing, where they look to their caregivers' emotional expressions to gauge how they should respond to a new situation.

Infants are born with a limited range of emotions, such as joy, sadness, fear, and anger. As they grow and interact with their environment, they gradually learn to recognize and express a broader spectrum of emotions (Ekman, 1992). Thompson (2014) found that warm and nurturing relationships between children and adults promote social competence among children, and their ability to succeed in school and life.

Assessment tools have been developed and are used to evaluate various aspects of an infant's development. Bayley Scales of Infant and Toddler Development in 1969, which were revised in 1993 and 2006 (Bayley, 2006), are the popular ones. They evaluate cognitive, language, motor, social–emotional, and adaptive behaviour skills. The age range for the assessment is from one month to 42 months. Based on an earlier version of the Bayley scale, Phatak and Khurana (1991) devised the Baroda Screening Test for Infants for use with children up to 30 months. Also, Madaan et al. (2021) have recently developed "The Developmental Assessment Scale for Indian Infants (DASII)", which is an Indian adaptation of Bayley Scales of Infant Development. Additionally, some other tests like Denver Developmental Screening Test (Frankenburg & Dodds, 1967), Peabody Developmental Motor Scales (Folio & Fewell, 2000), Ages and Stages Questionnaires (Squires & Bricker, 2009), and so on are available for assessment.

Early Childhood Stage: The Wonder Years

Spanning from infancy to around six years of age, the early childhood stage is marked by rapid growth in various domains. Children transform into more active and coordinated individuals and from complete dependency to increased autonomy and mobility. Growth in height and weight is observed. Gross motor skills progress to more complex movements, such as crawling, walking, and running. Fine motor skills, like grasping and using utensils, also develop during this stage (Berk, 2017). Several factors such as a balanced diet, regular physical activity, and playtime contribute to the development of gross and fine motor skills, as well as overall physical health and well-being.

The brain undergoes significant growth, and neural connections are formed at an astounding rate, making early childhood a time of incredible plasticity and receptiveness to learning (Kolb, 2019). In terms of Piaget's theory, this developmental stage is characterized by pre-operational thinking (refer to Chapter 6). The executive functions, such as working memory (responsible for holding information in mind and mentally working with it), inhibitory control (such as self-control, selective attention, and cognitive inhibition), and cognitive or mental flexibility required for creative activities, undergo significant development, allowing children to plan, organize, and regulate their behaviours effectively (Diamond, 2002, 2013). They also develop a theory of mind or meta-understanding that people have their own beliefs, desires, and intentions that may differ from one's own (Flavell & Miller, 1998).

This is the time when children enter the preschool years which results in significant expansion in their specific languages. Vocabulary develops exponentially and, by the age of two to three years, children start combining words to form short phrases or sentences, expressing more complex thoughts. As they reach three to five years of age, children begin to grasp grammar rules (e.g., use of plural words, past tense, and pronouns) and sentence structure, leading to grammatically correct speech (Hoff, 2013). Also, early childhood is an opportune time for learning multiple languages. Children develop the abilities for bilingualism/multilingualism by engaging with several languages which offer various advantages to them (Mohanty et al., 1994). Interestingly, the Indian scenario is such that people are exposed to different linguistic settings in life (e.g., home, office, market), and therefore they are generally multilingual.

During early childhood, children learn to recognize basic emotions such as happiness, sadness, fear, and anger. With the development of language skills, they can communicate their feelings effectively. Also, they begin to develop the ability to manage and regulate their feelings appropriately. They learn how to cope with frustration, disappointment, and other challenging emotions. Empathy or the capacity to understand and share the feelings of others develops in the course of socialization. Children undergo a transition from being primarily reliant on parents or caregivers to actively engaging with the world around them. Parenting style significantly influences children's social development (see Chapter 5).

During this stage, proper stimulation, supportive environments, and high-quality early childhood education programmes are essential for maximizing their potential. By providing children with nurturing and enriching experiences, we can help shape the trajectory of their lives, ensuring that they reach their full potential and become confident, curious, and well-adjusted individuals as they progress through subsequent stages of development. Realizing this fact, efforts are being made the world over to offer quality early childhood education (Boxes 2.1 and 2.2).

Box 2.1 Early Childhood Care and Education (ECCE)

Early childhood education programmes, offered the world over, have been found effective in shaping a child's physical, cognitive, emotional, and social development. Historically, it was the German educator Friedrich Frobel who, in 1838, opened "Play and Activity School", which was soon named "Kindergarten". This was followed by the introduction of a method of education by Maria Montessori in 1907. It is based on self-directed activity, hands-on learning, and collaborative play.

In the 1960s, the Head Start Program was introduced in the United States, which aimed to provide comprehensive early education, health, and nutrition services to children from low-income families, to improve school readiness and long-term outcomes. Encouraged by the positive effects of these programmes, there has been a mushroom expansion of ECCE programmes, with a focus on quality standards and evidence-based practices.

Early childhood, often referred to as the "critical period", is a time of rapid brain development and learning. There is growing evidence that high-quality ECCE programmes contribute to improved cognitive skills, enhanced socio-emotional development, and greater school readiness. Research (e.g., Heckman et al., 2013) has shown that investments in ECCE yield significant returns, leading to higher educational achievements, improved social competence, planning and organization, and reduced social inequalities later in life.

Box 2.2 Nurturing the Foundation Through ECCE: The Case of India

Traditionally, early childhood education was deeply embedded in the sociocultural fabric of India. These practices emphasized the holistic development of children. For example, there existed family centric education in which children were taught essential life skills, cultural values, and traditions. In the Gurukul system, a young child would live with a Guru (teacher) in an ashram and receive a holistic education, which addressed the needs of physical, moral, and intellectual development.

The focus on formal education after gaining independence often ignored early childhood education in India. However, some pioneering efforts, like *Balwadi* movement, emerged, which aimed to provide basic education and nutrition to young children, particularly in rural and underprivileged areas. It was a community-based approach which focused on holistic development and providing preschool education. Some *Balwadis* also provided nutritious meals and basic healthcare services to improve children's overall well-being.

The introduction of the Integrated Child Development Services (ICDS) scheme by the Government of India in 1975 was the most significant development. This scheme includes the delivery of an integrated package of services including supplementary nutrition, immunization, health check-ups, preschool education, referral services and nutrition and health education to children through *Anganwadis*. Currently, the ICDS is operative throughout the country and has helped children in improving their nutritional status and immunization (Behera & Acharya, 2020; Dixit et al., 2018; Gupta et al., 2013). It has led to the decline in infant and child mortality and has spread awareness about immunization and health and nutrition education (NIPCCD, 2009).

The preschool component of ICDS has, however, been found weak and children are not being readied for primary education (Ramachandran, 2004). In another study (Rao et al., 2021), variations in access to early childhood education among children of Bangladesh, China, India, and Myanmar were reported. Kaul and Sankar (2009) suggested ensuring basic learning conditions (such as availability of trained teachers, developing curriculum in ECCE, increasing coverage, and decentralized and holistic planning). In a longitudinal study covering four years from age 4 to age 8, Kaul and associates (2017) found that regular participation in a preschool between the ages of 4 and 5 improved children's school readiness, although at age 5+ average readiness levels were still well below what is expected at this age. The Samgra Shiksha does have an ECCE component for children aged 6 and below.

At the policy level, several initiatives have been taken to promote ECCE in India. The National Policy on Education (NPE) of 1986 recognized the importance of early childhood care and education, emphasizing the need for a strong foundation. National Early Childhood Care and Education (ECCE) Policy, introduced in 2013, emphasizes the importance of providing comprehensive ECCE services by integrating ECCE into the formal education system and promotes holistic development and strengthening partnerships between government, civil society, and communities. The Protection of Children from Sexual Offences (POCSO) Act of 2012 highlighted the importance of safe and child-friendly environments, impacting ECCE programmes' implementation.

The National Education Policy–2020 recognized ECCE as the foundation of learning and resolved to strengthen the ECCE. The National Curriculum Framework for Foundational Stage (2022) recognizes three distinct phases of early childhood education: ages 0–3 years, 3–6 years, and 6–8 years. During the first phase, children are at home and parents need to be made aware about children's developmental needs. Children in the age group 3–6 years need to participate in ECCE centres/preschools. The third group of children from ages 6–8 are in regular schools studying in classes I and II. The education of children aged 3–8 years is now known as the Foundational Stage.

Late Childhood Stage: Expanding Horizons

Late childhood, also known as middle childhood, spans from approximately 6 to 11/12 years of age. This period, according to Piaget, is characterized by the concrete-operational stage. Children develop the ability to engage in logical reasoning and problem-solving about concrete, observable, or tangible objects; events; and situations (see Chapter 6). Further, children's working memory capacity reaches adult-like levels by the age of 14 (Gathercole et al., 2004). With improved attention, they can sustain focus for more extended periods, which enhances their ability to process and understand complex information.

The peer group grows in size and verbal and relational aggression (insults, derogation, threats, gossip) gradually replaces direct physical aggression (Rubin et al., 2006). Children engage in bullying and victimization. However, within the friend circle, they cooperate, negotiate, and resolve conflicts, laying the foundation for future interpersonal relationships. Late childhood may also involve experiences of peer rejection and social challenges.

As regards emotional development, children become more adept at recognizing and identifying their own emotions. Masten and Narayan (2012) have noted that this stage is crucial for developing emotional strength and adaptive responses to adversity and making them resilient. Cultural factors and gender differences also shape emotional expression. For example, in individualistic societies (such as the West), the emotions of happiness, anger, and frustration are openly expressed. In contrast, people shy away from expressing these emotions openly in collectivistic (such as Asian and African societies) (Markus & Kitayama, 1991). Further, in some cases, boys are socialized to suppress certain emotions, whereas girls are encouraged to express emotions more openly (Chaplin & Aldao, 2013). In India, girls are socialized to express the emotion of *Lajja*, which signifies modesty and self-sacrifice (refer to Chapter 9).

Understanding the concepts of right and wrong (values) and forming their sense of morality constitute other key features of social development during this stage. Kohlberg's (1981) theory of moral development suggests that during late childhood, children enter the conventional level of moral reasoning. They become more aware of societal norms and adopt a rule-based approach to moral decision-making. They engage in moral reasoning, weighing the pros and cons of different choices, and considering the potential impact on others (Turiel, 2006).

Thus, children during late childhood undergo major changes that shape their personalities, relationships, and world views. Understanding the characteristics of late childhood is crucial for parents, teachers, and society to provide appropriate support and opportunities for children to grow and thrive.

Adolescent Development: A Transformative Phase

Adolescence is a transformative stage, marked by experiencing a journey of self-discovery, identity formation, and preparation for adult responsibilities. This period, roughly spanning between ages 10 and 18, is also considered the transition from childhood to adulthood.

One of the hallmark features of adolescence is the onset of puberty, typically occurring between ages 10 and 14 in girls and 12 and 16 in boys. During puberty, hormonal changes occur that lead to the secretion of sex hormones such as testosterone in males and oestrogen in females. The ovaries start to release mature eggs (ova). There is onset of menstruation (menarche) between the ages of 11 and 15 in females. In males, the testes begin to produce sperm, and boys experience their first ejaculation during sleep, known as nocturnal emission or wet dreams. The hormonal surge also results in a growth spurt, characterized by a rapid increase in height and weight that typically occurs around the age of 10–11 years in girls and 12–13 years in boys. Changes in body composition in terms of muscle mass, bone density, and body fat distribution are also observed (Wang & Lobstein, 2006; WHO, 2021a). Secondary sexual characteristics develop during adolescence. These include breast development, growth of pubic hair, and the widening of hips in girls and growth of facial hair, the deepening of the voice, and the enlargement of the Adam's apple (or the protrusion on the front of throats) in boys.

Cognitive development in adolescence is characterized by the refinement of cognitive skills, abstract thinking, and the ability to consider multiple perspectives. Adolescence is also a crucial period for brain development. It has been reported (Blakemore & Choudhury, 2006) that the prefrontal cortex undergoes significant change allowing adolescents to process complex information more rapidly. According to Piaget, cognitive development is characterized by the formal operational stage (approximately ages 11–19), where individuals become capable of abstract thought, hypothetical reasoning, and deductive logic (Bjorklund, 2023; Inhelder & Piaget, 1958). Adolescents often experience egocentrism, perceiving themselves as the centre of attention and believing that others are intensely focused on their behaviour and appearance. This sense of an "imaginary audience" can lead to heightened self-consciousness and the belief that their every action is under public scrutiny.

G. Stanley Hall (1904) characterized adolescence as a period of storm and stress. However, Hall's view is considered an extreme characterization in recent times. Arnett (1999) argued that there are three domains in which adolescents exhibit the storm and stress characterization of behaviour. These include risk behaviour, mood disruption, and conflict with parents. According to Buchanan et al. (2023), the characterization of storm and stress speaks that adolescents show more negative behaviours (such as dangerous risk behaviour, mood disruptions, anxiety, sadness, and conflict with their parents) than younger and older individuals. However, the level of negative behaviours during adolescence has not yet been established in absolute terms. It needs to be established that the level of negative behaviour is higher than the positive or desirable behaviours (e.g., kindness, empathy, responsibility). Buchanan et al. (2023) propose that adolescence can best be characterized as a time of "promise and possibility", "openness and opportunity", or "exploration and discovery".

Adolescents bother about who they are, what they believe in, and their place in society. This search for identity sometimes leads to conflicts with parents and authority figures (Erikson, 1968). Adolescents experiment with different identities and roles, ultimately forming a coherent self-concept. Friendships become more meaningful and important, providing a sense of belonging and acceptance. Adolescents report greater levels of intimacy in their friendships than younger children (Rubin et al., 2006). Peer pressure and the desire to fit in may lead to both positive and negative outcomes, including risky behaviours if not guided by positive role models and supportive environments.

As regards moral development, adolescents typically move from the conventional to the post-conventional stages as they mature and gain exposure to diverse perspectives and ethical dilemmas (see Chapter 10). Adolescents begin to form a moral identity, which is a sense of themselves as individuals with moral principles and values. Parenting styles that emphasize warmth, open communication, and setting clear expectations contribute to moral development in adolescents (Smetana, 2013). Cultural diversity exposes adolescents to varied moral perspectives. Exposure to diverse cultures promotes tolerance, respect, and open-mindedness, fostering a more comprehensive and inclusive moral compass. Box 2.3 describes the status of adolescence in the Indian context.

Box 2.3 Adolescence in the Indian Context

The existence of adolescence as a distinct stage of life worldwide is a debated notion. Many researchers (e.g., Cobb, 1995) believe that it probably did not exist in traditional societies in the same way as it is understood today. The concept of adolescence gained prominence in the late 19th and early 20th centuries, influenced by factors such as increased urbanization, industrialization, and changes in education systems. After studying ethnographic data from more than 170 pre-industrial societies, Schlegel and Barry (1991) reported its existence in almost all societies with adult-like responsibilities (e.g., productivity or fertility) (Chen & Farruggia, 2002).

In the context of India, Saraswathi (1999) also considered adolescence a myth. She found the transition from childhood to adolescence almost invisible, particularly in the case of rural adolescent girls who assumed the roles of wives, mothers, and home managers even in their early teens. Saraswathi (1999) asserted that the modern notion of adolescence as a conception was not indigenous to India, and it is an import. She documented that adolescence is a middle-class phenomenon; more pronounced in boys than girls, who experience greater continuity with adulthood. Kapadia and Bhangaokar (2013) found variations in adolescence across class, caste, race, geographic location, and time in the Indian context. In the urban population pursuing modern ways of living, tasks like fulfilling demands of education, entering into employment and getting married (Saraswathi, 1999; Verma & Saraswathi, 2002) are being extended into the late twenties. In this context, a distinct phase of "emerging adulthood" is observed between the adolescence and adulthood stages.

As per UNICEF (2023), the adolescent population in India is highest in the world, and about 21% people are in the age group of 10–19 years. They have limited opportunity to develop their competencies. The adolescent girls are affected the most as there is limited scope for them to move freely and make decisions related to work, education, marriage, and social relationships. More than 40% of the girls drop out before completing secondary education for various reasons, including child labour, household responsibilities, early marriage, and so on. Thirty per cent of girls are married before age 18. However, in recent years, there has been an increase in awareness about the importance of education of girls in the country (Saraswathi & Oke, 2013). Also, social awareness campaigns and participation in the education process has made an impact on the age of marriage and fertility. Parents are also willing to invest in the welfare of their daughters.

The lifestyle of adolescents is also a matter of concern in India as they are affected by deficiency disease. In a study (Singh & Misra, 2012), it was reported that a large section of Indian adolescents engage in unhealthy dietary habits, unfavourable food consumption (i.e., bakery items, fast food, cold drink), irregular sleep habit, inactive leisure time engagement (mobile, videogame, TV, internet), and some of the risk behaviours pertaining to victimization of violence, physical fights, and suicidal attempts. Verma and Sharma (2003) also noted change in the leisure time activities of urban Indian adolescents under the pervasive impact of technology and market economy. The studies thus suggest the need for taking remedial actions for promoting healthy behaviours among adolescents.

Box 2.4 The Notion of "Emerging Adulthood"

The concept of emerging adulthood was coined by Jeffrey Arnett (2000, 2004, 2007, 2015), which is particularly relevant in today's rapidly changing world. The complexities of modern society, increased emphasis on personal growth, and the evolving nature of work and relationships have created a need for a flexible and adaptive transition to adulthood. Emerging adults often report feeling "in-between" adolescence and full adulthood. They may not fully identify with either stage and often grapple with uncertainty and ambivalence. Factors like prolonged education, economic pressures, changing norms regarding career, education, and marriage, and technological advancements have given rise to this life stage.

There are several characteristics of emerging adulthood. First, individuals engage in self-discovery and exploration of personal values, interests, and goals. They often experiment with different life paths, career choices, and relationships to solidify their sense of identity. Second, emerging adulthood is characterized by instability or frequent changes in living situations, educational pursuits, and career trajectories. Third, emerging adulthood is marked by a period of heightened self-focus, where individuals prioritize personal growth, experiences, and autonomy. Fourth, they have a sense of optimism and belief in multiple possibilities for their future. This stage provides individuals with the time and space to build a foundation for a fulfilling adult life while navigating the challenges of an uncertain and dynamic environment.

Cultural variations in the concept of emerging adulthood are observed. In the context of India, Seiter (2009) found this stage to be non-existent. A large majority of the participants (17–26 years of age) felt that they have already achieved adulthood; with males reporting in greater numbers than females. They believed that they were carrying out adult responsibilities, such as keeping the family physically safe, becoming capable of caring for ageing parents, fulfilling their duties, and so on. Seiter posited that Indian culture makes the transition into adulthood different from other cultures. Kapadia and Bhangaokar (2013) noted that in India emerging adulthood is observed in rich and urban societies where individuals have the opportunity for self-development. In rural and poor societal contexts, it is almost non-existent, as children begin adult-like work at an early age.

Early Adulthood Development: Transitions and Transformations

Spanning from approximately 18 to 30 years of age, early adulthood is a time of significant growth, exploration, and transition. During this period, individuals navigate through major responsibilities with long-term implications concerning education, career, building relationships and marriage, and personal identity. The period represents a time of peak physical growth including strength, endurance, and agility (Malina, 2001). Many people engage in sports, fitness activities, and recreational pursuits that may become more challenging with age. This period is also marked by sexual maturation and reproductive health changes.

Scholars (e.g., Commons & Richards, 2003) argue that early adulthood introduces a new cognitive phase known as *post-formal thought*. The stage of post-formal thought acknowledges the limitations of purely abstract and logical thinking by incorporating emotional and subjective elements into decision-making processes. This integration of emotion and rationality allows individuals to approach complex real-life situations with flexibility, leading to more adaptive and context-sensitive problem-solving (Labouvie-Vief, 2015). During this period, cognitive functions, such as working memory, attention, and processing speed, typically reach their peak. However, it is essential to note that while certain cognitive functions reach their peak (e.g., memory and reasoning), others (speed and spatial visualization) may gradually decline with age (Salthouse, 2009).

Individuals seek to establish their identities and understand their values, beliefs, and aspirations. This process is influenced by personal experiences, societal expectations, and cultural norms (Arnett, 2000). Compared to adolescence, the period is also characterized by increased emotional stability. As they gain life experiences and face challenges, they develop adaptive strategies to cope with emotional ups and downs, enhancing their overall emotional well-being.

Early adulthood is characterized by striving for increased autonomy and independence. Arnett (2015) reported that the drive for independence can sometimes lead to conflicts with parents but is essential for fostering personal growth and emotional maturation. Developing emotional resilience is crucial during this period (Ong et al., 2006). Also, individuals often engage in civic and community activities, such as volunteering (Finkelstein, 2009).

Understanding developments during early adulthood can assist individuals, parents, educators, and policymakers in providing appropriate support and guidance during this critical phase of life. This would also help societies foster a generation of well-rounded, capable, and resilient individuals.

Middle Adulthood Development: A Blossoming Stage

Middle adulthood, spanning from approximately 40 to 65 years of age, stands as a turning point in the human lifespan. During this period, individuals confront various new challenges and opportunities for personal growth, self-realization, and concern for fulfilling obligations.

This is the time when physical decline and changes in bodily functions gradually begin. Some of the primary physical changes include experiencing menopause in women and andropause in men, which have physiological and emotional effects, impacting overall well-being. There is a gradual decline in sensory functions, such as vision, hearing, and taste. While some middle-aged individuals maintain their physical prowess, many may notice a decline in muscle strength and endurance. The period is also associated with a reduced risk of certain health issues, such as infectious diseases, as immune systems tend to be more robust during this stage.

Middle adulthood is also characterized by changes in cognitive abilities. While some cognitive functions (e.g., fluid intelligence involving reasoning and problem-solving abilities) may decline with age, there may be improvements in other areas (e.g., crystallized intelligence) due to accumulated knowledge and experience (Salthouse, 1996). Life experiences enable people to display greater wisdom and a more nuanced understanding of the world (Baltes, 1987). They may become more adept at balancing emotions and rational thinking.

Erikson's theory of psychosocial development proposes that middle adulthood is a period when individuals experience a conflict between generativity, a desire to contribute positively to society and future generations, and stagnation, a feeling of unfulfilment and lack of purpose (see Chapter 11). Establishing a legacy through work, family, or community involvement becomes essential for many individuals. This period involves a shift in parent–child relationships. Thus, in joint families particularly, many adults become caregivers for their ageing parents while also nurturing their children. This "sandwich generation" may face challenges in balancing their responsibilities. Some people experience a midlife crisis during middle adulthood, which is characterized by questioning one's accomplishments, values, and goals. It can lead to significant life changes, such as career shifts or the pursuit of new passions. Many adults face crises and need counselling to figure out the different issues.

While there may be a decline to some extent in certain domains, middle-aged individuals have an edge as they also possess accumulated knowledge, wisdom, and experience. This advantage positively influences their lives and the lives of others. Embracing these changes and challenges with resilience and adaptability can lead to personal growth and fulfilment during this stage of life.

Old Age: Embracing Change and Ageing Gracefully

The Indian thought conceptualizes life of hundred years and aspires to be active throughout these years (कुर्वन्नेवेह कर्माणि जिजीविषेत् शतं समाः). The United Nations regards all persons above the age of 60 as older people. These people, for the sake of convenience, are further subdivided into the young-old (60 to 75), the old-old (75–90), the oldest (90 and above), and the centenarians (those above 100 years of age) (cited in Ramamurti & Jamuna, 2010). According to the United Nations (2015a), 12% of the world population is aged 60-plus, and this segment is growing at a rate of 3.26% annually (cited in Cheng, 2020). Indian population contained 8% aged people in 1999, which is expected to increase to 21% by 2050.

During old age, individuals experience unique challenges and opportunities for growth. Physical decline is a normal and natural part of the ageing process. In general, there are changes in appearance, mobility, and overall health. Included among the other physical changes are the emergence of sarcopenia, osteoporosis, problems in the cardiovascular system, and reduced visual and hearing acuity (for details, see Cheng, 2020). Sarcopenia refers to a decrease in the number and size of muscle fibres, leading to reduced muscle function and strength (Cruz-Jentoft et al., 2019). Osteoporosis is a condition characterized by reduced bone density making bones weak and brittle (Raisz, 2005). As a result, older people become more prone to fractures, especially in the spine, hips, and wrists. The reduction in bone density is largely attributed to hormonal changes and decreased calcium absorption in the body. A decline is noted in the cardiovascular system with age, including reduced elasticity of blood vessels and increased stiffness of the heart muscle (Lakatta & Levy, 2003). This leads to an increased risk of hypertension, heart disease, and stroke in older individuals. Old age also brings changes in vision and hearing. The lenses of the eyes become less flexible, resulting in presbyopia and difficulty focusing on nearby objects. Additionally, the ageing process can lead to presbycusis causing decreased hearing acuity, particularly in higher frequencies (Gates & Mills, 2005).

Among all challenges, cognitive changes are significant during old age. Though there is a decline in short-term or working memory, long-term memory (or the ability to retain procedural and distant events) often remains relatively stable or even improves with age (Cabeza et al., 2018). This enables older people to remember past events, but they easily forget immediate events showing a decline in prospective memory. Further, the speed of processing information is reduced, which interferes with decision-making and increases reaction time (Salthouse, 2010). Executive functions, including cognitive flexibility, problem-solving, and inhibitory control, are also on the decline during old age. The decline of these functions affects an individual's ability to manage complex tasks effectively (Fjell et al., 2014). Neurodegenerative diseases, such as Alzheimer's disease and dementia, are more prevalent in elderly individuals and can cause severe cognitive impairment. The prevalence of dementia for those aged 60 years and older in India is 8.44% (Jin et al., 2023). It may, however, be noted that some elderly people display extraordinary resilience and adaptability. They maintain cognitive functioning despite encountering difficult challenges.

There is a change in social networks due to factors like retirement from a job, relocation, or the loss of friends and family members forcing older people to adapt to new social circumstances. During old age, individuals often engage in life review processes, reflecting on their life experiences and accomplishments. As Erikson (1968), those who feel proud of their accomplishments may feel a sense of integrity. Evaluation of being unsuccessful may bring the feeling of despair implying that their life has been wasted.

In general, social connections and active participation in social activities are essential for the elderly to experience a sense of belonging and combat feelings of loneliness and isolation.

Likewise, continued cognitive engagement, such as participating in mentally stimulating activities (e.g., reading, learning new skills, or engaging in puzzles and games) can help older adults maintain cognitive function and enhance mental well-being. In the MacArthur Studies of Successful Aging (Rowe, 2023) it was reported that intellectual stimulation and active learning are associated with better cognitive health and successful ageing. Maintaining a sense of purpose and engaging in meaningful activities contribute to a fulfilling life for the elderly. Volunteering opportunities, pursuing hobbies, mentoring, or participating in community initiatives empower older adults to utilize their skills, knowledge, and life experiences, fostering a sense of contribution and personal growth. Cheng (2020) argues for adopting a humanistic approach towards older adults and considering them as "Elegant Seniors" to eradicate their marginalization and promote manageability.

In India, Ramamurti and associates have extensively examined the psychosocial aspects of ageing. In their review of studies (Ramamurti & Jamuna, 2010), it was noted that people, in general, show a positive attitude towards the elderly. Physical and psychological activity levels, flexibility in behaviour, and significant social support were observed to be associated with longer living of older people. Women, people living in rural areas, and belonging to middle-income families had a history of long lives. Such persons also lived in joint families, had spiritual orientation, and were temperamentally calm. Adlakha and associates (2020) found that access to neighbourhood amenities such as transportation, parks and green spaces, and opportunities for leisure and social interaction play a key role in determining older adults' health and quality of life in urban localities.

Thus, while old age is characterized by challenges, there are also unique opportunities for growth and development. Understanding these characteristics of development during old age can help society provide better support and care for older adults, fostering a more inclusive and age-friendly environment.

Box 2.5 Cognitive Development in Old Age

Ageing or old age is associated with several physiological, anatomical, biochemical, and hormonal changes. The changes during old age, which are deteriorative, sometimes give rise to the development of one or another kind of disability or disease. This may lead to the false belief that ageing has many incurable diseases. Though the risk of developing some debilitating illness with advancement in age is relatively high, it does not mean that in old age impairment or decline happens across all domains including cognitive abilities. A few abilities get strengthened with age. The lifestyle, internal strength, and one's ability to cope with situations help in maintaining our cognitive reserve. Pandey et al. (2018) argue that a peaceful, calm, composed, and conflict-free environment with an active lifestyle does wonders in developing a cognitive reserve for the elderly. Many people set goals at every stage of life including old age and believe that every stage brings with it meaning in life as well as associated challenges. They prefer to work productively till their last breath and remain cognitively healthy. Such people generally have a resilient mindset with principles and discipline.

Cognitive abilities are the key to performing daily chores independently including taking care of one's health (Tucker-Drob, 2011). Though a decline in some abilities, such as fluid intelligence, speed of processing information, working memory, and executive cognitive functions (Murman, 2015) is observed, age-related gains in crystallized intelligence until the seventh decade of life are observed (Tucker-Drob et al., 2022). Wisdom comes with age and experience. Cumulative knowledge and experiential skills are well maintained. With age and experience our understanding of the self and surroundings becomes better. People start working proactively and engage themselves in meaningful activities, which decreases the chances of pathological decay.

In the *Ashrama dharma* (see Chapter 1), a goal was set for every stage of life. *Manusmriti* (6.08) recommends the following for old age.

Svadhyaye nityayuktah syad danto maitrah samahitah;
Datta nityam-anadata sarvabhutanukampakah.

The verse states that after performing the duties of a householder one should get engaged in his/her regular study to improve the sense of well-being, regulate wishes, remain observant to motivate self for regulating senses, be a responsive and social being by maintaining friendly behaviour with everyone having a calm and peaceful mind. At this stage of life, one must indulge in sharing (charity), should not accept gifts from others, and have mercy on all living beings.

Some people perform exceptionally well during old age. For example, Dr C. Radhakrishna Rao, who received a Padma Bhushan award in 1968 and a Padma Vibhushan award in 2001, after his retirement at the age of 60, went to live with his daughter in the United States. There he became Professor of Statistics at the University of Pittsburgh at the age of 62 and Head of the Department at the University of Pennsylvania at the age of 70. He became a US citizen at the age of 75, received the National Medal at the age of 82 (a White House honour for Science), and recently, at the age of 102, received the Nobel Prize equivalent in statistics. There are other examples as well.

When one gets actively involved in strengthening his/her ability without claiming anything and without doubting oneself, s/he enables the self to explore the right pathway to drive self. Such individuals think thoroughly and try to function in every situation. Though they face challenges, they are not defeated and always remain ready to encounter challenges. As a result, the level of motivation to achieve goals remains intact and clarity of thought allows one to lead life positively. Both positivity and strength of mind help a person in moulding the situation.

Nisha Mani Pande
King George Medical University, Lucknow

Death as a Life Stage: Embracing the Final Passage

Throughout history, humans have grappled with the enigma of death, the final frontier of existence. As the last stage of human life, death has sparked countless philosophical, religious, and scientific enquiries. The perception of death and dying has shifted over the centuries, from a more integrated and accepted part of daily life in medieval times to a more private and taboo topic in modern Western societies. As Kastenbaum and Costa (1977) have noted, the present-day technological society is characterized as a "death-denying" society.

From a scientific perspective, death is often regarded as the irreversible cessation of all biological functions that sustain life. Modern medical advancements have enabled physicians to understand and classify different types of death, such as clinical death (cessation of heartbeat and breathing) and brain death (irreversible loss of brain function). Gire (2014) noted eight criteria, all of which must be met before a person is declared medically dead: absence of spontaneous response to any stimuli; completely unresponsive to even the most painful stimuli; lack of spontaneous respiration for at least one hour; absence of postural activity, swallowing, yawning, or vocalizing; no eye movements, blinking, or pupil responses; a flat electroencephalogram (EEG) for at least ten minutes; a total absence of motor reflexes; and that there ought not to be any change in these criteria if tested again after 24 hours.

The cultural interpretations of death differ markedly across the globe, with rituals, beliefs, and practices reflecting the unique perspectives of each society. In Indian tradition, death is seen as a natural part of the life cycle and an opportunity for spiritual growth. Indian beliefs about death are deeply rooted in the concepts of reincarnation, *karma*, and the ultimate goal of liberation (*moksha*) (Ganguli, 2008). The text of *Bhagavad Gita* states that the *Atman* is without beginning and end and that is the true nature of a person. The body is like the clothes of *Atman*, and *Atman* appears and disappears. The text states:

न जायते म्रियते वा कदाचि न्नायं भूत्वा भविता वा न भूयः ।
अजो नित्यः शाश्वतोऽयं पुराणो न हन्यते हन्यमाने शरीरे ॥2.20॥

(For the *Atman* (soul!), there is neither birth nor death at any time. It has not come into being, does not come into being, and will not come into being. It is unborn, eternal, and timeless and is never destroyed when the body is destroyed.)

One would, however, observe variations in practices and beliefs concerning death and dying in different parts of India, particularly among the ethnic communities (Sen & Chakraborty, 2024). The Hindus include elaborate rites or *Antyeshti* as one of the *samskaras* of life.

Christianity often views death as a passage to an afterlife. It teaches that death is a transition to either heaven or hell, depending on one's actions and beliefs in life. Consequently, funeral ceremonies in Western societies often involve prayers, hymns, and rituals to guide the soul to its eternal destination. Many African cultures exhibit a deep reverence for ancestors and the spiritual realm. Death is seen as a continuation of existence within the ancestral realm, where the deceased maintains a powerful influence on living beings. Funerals in African cultures often involve elaborate ceremonies that honour the deceased and strengthen community ties. Many indigenous societies maintain a close connection with nature and believe in the interconnectedness of all living beings. Death is often seen as a return to the earth and a continuation of the life cycle. Rituals and ceremonies are performed to honour the deceased, maintain harmony with the natural world, and seek guidance from ancestral spirits. Indigenous cultures prioritize communal mourning, with extended grieving periods and collective support for the bereaved.

As death remains an inevitable part of life, humans have developed diverse coping mechanisms to deal with the emotional, psychological, and spiritual impacts of mortality. Religion and spirituality often play a vital role in providing solace and offering explanations for what lies beyond death. For instance, exploring the role of religious coping in dealing with grief and loss, Pargament (1997) observed that individuals often turn to their religious beliefs as a source of comfort and guidance during difficult times.

Kubler-Ross (1969), a prominent figure in thanatology (the study of death and dying), outlined the five stages of grief. These are (1) denial (i.e., the initial shock and disbelief), (2) anger (i.e., frustration and resentment, often directed outward), (3) bargaining (i.e., seeking compromise or negotiation to avoid the inevitable), (4) depression (i.e., a sense of loss and deep sadness), and (5) acceptance (i.e., coming to terms with one's fate and finding a sense of peace). These stages are not necessarily experienced in a linear or predictable sequence. Individuals may move back and forth between stages, skip stages, or experience them in a different order. Therapists, such as Yalom (2008), emphasize the importance of confronting mortality and embracing the finitude of life as a means to live more fully.

Recent years have increasingly witnessed debates on issues like euthanasia. Euthanasia refers to a good, dignified, and easy death. It is particularly important in the case of terminally ill patients. There are ethical, philosophical, religious, medical, and legal aspects of euthanasia. It has been accepted in a few countries, but in the majority of the countries, it has not been allowed so far (for details, Kumar et al., 2021).

Thus, the perspectives on death have evolved. The cultural interpretations of death vary widely, shaping rituals and beliefs that reflect unique societal perspectives. Humans employ diverse coping mechanisms to navigate the emotional, psychological, and spiritual impacts of mortality.

Overview

The exploration of the human life course provides a comprehensive understanding of the diverse and dynamic stages that individuals traverse from embryonic beginnings to the final passage of death. Each stage, from the prenatal stage to old age, offers insights into the unique challenges, developments, and experiences characteristic of that particular life phase. Also, each stage is preparation for the next stage of life. People in different cultures endorse diverse views of life and accept the challenges differently.

Embarking on the exploration of human life, we delved into the miraculous journey of embryonic development, witnessing the intricate processes that shape the foundation of human existence. The infancy stage unfolded as a period of rapid growth and exploration, laying the groundwork for cognitive, emotional, and physical development. The early childhood years emerged as the wonder years, a time of curiosity and foundational learning while late childhood marked the expansion of horizons, paving the way for increased autonomy and social awareness. Historical developments in early childhood care and education showcased the evolution of practices that shape the early experiences of children.

Transitioning into adolescence, we witnessed the transformative phase characterized by identity exploration and self-discovery. The sections on early and middle adulthood provided insights into the challenges, transitions, and blossoming developments that accompany these life stages. Variations in the conception of adulthood across time underscored the evolving nature of societal expectations. Old age emerged as a stage of embracing change and ageing gracefully. The specific challenges faced by the elderly in the Indian context were discussed. Finally, we explored death as a life stage, recognizing it as the final passage that completes the human life course. Throughout this journey, we encountered the cultural, historical, and contextual nuances that shape human experiences at each stage. The inclusion of boxes highlighting specific developments in the Indian context added a valuable layer of cultural sensitivity and relevance.

This chapter provided a rich tapestry of the human life course, weaving together biological, psychological, social, and cultural threads. Through a multidimensional lens, readers gain a profound understanding of the complexities and nuances embedded in each stage of human development, fostering a holistic perspective on the journey from birth to death.

Key Terms

Adolescence	Implantation
Adulthood	Infancy
Ageing Gracefully	Endoderm
Blastocyst	Invitro Fertilization (Ivf)
Childhood	Integrated Child Development Services
Chromosomes	(ICDS)
Cell Divisions	Mesoderm
Death	Old Age
Early Childhood Care and Education	Post Formal Thought
(ECCE)	Pre-Natal
Ectoderm	Primitive Reflexes
Embryonic Stage	Teratogens
Emerging Adulthood	Zygote

Questions for Reflection

1) How does understanding the embryonic beginning contribute to our appreciation of the complexity and uniqueness of the human life course?
2) How does Early Childhood Care and Education (ECCE) shape the foundation of an individual's life? Illustrate the importance of nurturing this early stage.
3) Explore the challenges and opportunities presented during the adolescent phase. How does the Indian context influence the transformative experiences of adolescence?
4) How do the stages of adulthood contribute to the overall narrative of the human life course, and how might cultural and historical factors influence the conception of adulthood?
5) How can society create environments that facilitate positive experiences and contributions from older individuals?

Suggested Further Readings

Books

Kaur, R. (2022). *Constructions of childhood In India: Exploring the personal and sociocultural contours*. Routledge.

Paris, J., Ricardo, A., Raymond, D., & Johnson, A. (2019). *Child growth and development* (Open Textbook). College of the Canyons.

Patra, S. (2022). *Adolescence in India: Issues, challenges and possibilities*. Springer.

Rubin, K. H., Bukowski, W. M., & Parker, J. G. (2006). Peer Interactions, Relationships, and Groups. In N. Eisenberg, W. Damon, & R. M. Lerner (Eds.), *Handbook of child psychology: Social, emotional, and personality development* (pp. 571–645). John Wiley & Sons.

Smith, J. P., & Majumdar, M. (Eds.). (2012). *Aging in Asia: Findings from new and emerging data initiatives*. The National Academic Press.

3 Theoretical and Methodological Approaches to Development

Contents

Introduction	42
Theoretical Approaches to Development	42
Methodological Considerations in Developmental Research	49
Research Designs for Developmental Studies	50
Approaches for Conducting Developmental Research	51
Box 3.1: Example of Quantitative Research	52
Box 3.2: Examples of Qualitative Research	53
Box 3.3: Example of a Mixed-Methods Research	54
Key Techniques of Research	54
Box 3.4: Examples of Ethnographic Studies	59
Ethical Considerations	59
Overview	60
Key Terms	61
Questions for Reflection	61

Learning Objectives

After studying this chapter, the learner will be able to:

Describe the key tenets of different theoretical approaches to human development;
Differentiate between various research designs and critically assess their strengths and limitations;
Distinguish between quantitative, qualitative, and mixed-methods research approaches and evaluate their applications;
Explain the uses of data collection techniques, such as self-report measures, interviews, observations, and case studies; and
Integrate theoretical frameworks and methodological approaches to interpret real-world developmental scenarios.

DOI: 10.4324/9781003441168-4

Introduction

Understanding the diverse pathways of growth and change in human development requires appreciating both theoretical frameworks and methodological approaches. This chapter introduces various theoretical perspectives such as psychoanalytical, biological, learning, cognitive, humanistic, ecological, and indigenous approaches. Further, it examines various methodological approaches that underpin developmental research. From research designs like cross-sectional, longitudinal, and cross-sequential studies to the nuanced exploration of quantitative, qualitative, and mixed-methods approaches, this chapter unravels the intricate tapestry of developmental enquiry. Alongside the exploration of key techniques such as self-report measures, interviews, observation, focused group discussions, case studies, and ethnography, the chapter also addresses ethical considerations in conducting human development research. Thus, the chapter provides an intellectual voyage as it unravels the complexities of theoretical frameworks and methodological nuances that shape the study of human development.

Theoretical Approaches to Development

Theoretical approaches serve as lenses through which the complex processes of growth and development are interpreted and understood. Diverse frameworks, ranging from psychoanalytic and biological perspectives to learning, cognitive, ecological, and cultural, provide diverse vantage points. These varied approaches, however, need to be treated more as tools to illuminate different facets of development than as alternative approaches. Though their foci and proposed policies are different, in many ways they complement the exploration of development. This section briefly introduces the basic tenets of these theories. Details are given at appropriate places in subsequent chapters.

Psychoanalytic Approach

The psychoanalytic approach emphasizes the role of unconscious processes and early childhood experiences in shaping personality and behaviour. While the approach has grown in many directions, the seminal work by Sigmund Freud and Erik Erikson figures prominently in our endeavour to understand human development in distinctive ways.

Freud and Psychosexual Development

Sigmund Freud (1856–1939), an Austrian neurologist and the founder of psychoanalysis, gave importance to the unconscious mind and childhood experiences that drive our behaviour. He proposed three layers of consciousness: unconscious, subconscious, and conscious. Freud (1905) further proposed that human development occurs in stages, known as psychosexual stages: *oral, anal, phallic, latent,* and *genital*. Each stage is characterized by a different erogenous zone and a conflict that must be resolved for healthy development. Freud (1920) introduced the concepts of life and death instincts. Freud (1923) also proposed a structural model of the mind consisting of three components: *the id, ego,* and *superego*. He further proposed several defence mechanisms that individuals use to cope with anxiety and protect the ego (see Chapter 8).

Erikson's Psychosocial Theory

Erik Erikson (1902–1994), a German-American psychoanalyst, was greatly influenced by Freud. Erikson (1950) expanded on Freud's ideas by introducing eight psychosocial stages that span the entire lifespan. Each stage represents a conflict or crisis that individuals must navigate successfully to achieve healthy development. These stages include trust versus mistrust, autonomy versus shame and doubt, initiative versus guilt, industry versus inferiority, identity versus role confusion, intimacy versus isolation, generativity versus stagnation, and ego integrity versus despair (see Chapter 11).

Freud laid the groundwork for the development of various psychological schools of thought. However, his ideas have been criticized and modified over time. Erikson's psychosocial stages have had a significant impact on developmental psychology, and his focus on the influence of social and cultural factors has resonated with later theorists. The differences in the approach of Freud and Erikson reflect evolving perspectives within the broader psychoanalytic tradition.

Biological Approach

The biological approach focuses on the role of biological factors, such as genetics and physiology, in shaping an individual's growth and behaviour. Prominent among the advocates of the biological approach are Charles Darwin, Jean-Baptiste Lamarck, Arnold Gesell, and John Bowlby.

Darwin's Theory of Evolution

Charles Darwin (1809–1882) was an English naturalist and biologist. He (Darwin, 1859) proposed the theory of evolution through natural selection, suggesting that species evolve in response to environmental pressures. That is, within a population, individuals exhibit variations in traits. Some of these variations are heritable and can be passed on to offspring. Populations tend to produce more offspring than the environment can support. There is a competition for limited resources, leading to a struggle for survival. Individuals with advantageous variations are more likely to survive and reproduce, passing on these favourable traits to the next generation. Over time, the frequency of advantageous traits increases in the population, leading to adaptation to the environment. Darwin's theory, thus, revolutionized our understanding of the diversity of life on earth, highlighting the role of natural processes in shaping the complexity and adaptability of species over time.

Lamarck's Theory of Inheritance

Jean-Baptiste Lamarck (1744–1829), a pioneering French biologist, proposed the idea of the inheritance of acquired characteristics, suggesting that traits acquired through an individual's experiences or environmental interactions could be passed on to future generations (Lamarck, 1809).

Gesell's Maturation Theory

Arnold Gesell (1880–1961), an American psychologist and paediatrician, emphasized the role of maturation in human development. He (Gesell, 1928) believed that there is a genetically predetermined sequence of development, and children progress through stages at their own pace. He termed it as readiness (the internally timed unfolding of the individual's characteristics) of children when they are biologically ready to learn behaviours, concepts, or skills. Gesell's work contributed to the understanding of typical developmental milestones and the importance of biological factors in shaping these milestones.

Bowlby's Attachment Theory

A British developmental psychologist and psychiatrist, John Bowlby (1907–1990) proposed attachment theory. Bowlby (1969) focused on the biological basis of emotional bonds between caregivers and infants. He argued that a strong emotional connection, or attachment, is crucial for the child's social and emotional development. Bowlby's work highlights the role of attachment in promoting survival and well-being.

In summary, the biological approach integrates concepts from evolution, genetics, and physiological maturation to understand how individuals grow and develop over time. However, this approach is criticized for oversimplifying complex human behaviour, neglecting the impact of environmental and experiential factors.

Learning Approach

The learning approach is grounded in the idea that much of human behaviour and development can be understood through the process of learning. This perspective emphasizes the role of experiences and interactions with the environment in shaping an individual's thoughts, emotions, and behaviours. Three influential figures in the learning approach are John B. Watson, B.F. Skinner, and Albert Bandura.

Watson's Behaviourism

John B. Watson (1878–1958), an American psychologist, is considered the founder of behaviourism, which is a school of thought that emphasizes observable behaviours as the primary focus of study. Watson (1913) stressed the role of environmental factors and learning experiences in shaping behaviour. He argued that behaviour could be explained through the establishment of associations between stimuli and responses. Watson's work laid the foundation for the behaviourist approach.

Skinner's Operant Conditioning

B.F. Skinner (1904–1990), an American psychologist, expanded upon Watson's behaviourism, introducing the concept of operant conditioning to explain how voluntary behaviours are learned. Skinner (1938) proposed that behaviours are strengthened or weakened through reinforcement or punishment. Positive reinforcement increases the likelihood of behaviour while punishment decreases it. Skinner's work laid the foundation for understanding how voluntary behaviours are influenced by their consequences, shaping subsequent research in behaviourism and psychology.

Bandura's Social Learning Theory

Albert Bandura (1925–2021) was a Canadian-born American psychologist. He (Bandura, 1977) integrated cognitive and social elements and introduced the social learning theory. He emphasized the role of observational learning, where individuals learn by observing the behaviours of others. This process involves modelling and imitating the behaviours of role models. Bandura introduced the concept of reciprocal determinism, suggesting that personal, behavioural, and environmental factors interact and influence each other bidirectionally.

In sum, the learning approach contributes to our understanding of how individuals acquire and modify their behaviours based on their experiences with the environment. However, the excessive emphasis on the environment as well as on the study of observable behaviour has not been well taken in recent years. The approach overlooks internal cognitive processes and individual differences and, thus, may not fully capture the complexity of human cognition and emotion.

Cognitive Approach

The cognitive approach focuses on understanding how individuals acquire, process, and use information. This perspective emphasizes mental processes, such as perception, memory, language, problem-solving, and decision-making, as central to human development. Three prominent figures, Jean Piaget, Lev Vygotsky, and Jerome Bruner, have made significant contributions to our understanding of cognitive development.

Piaget's Theory of Cognitive Development

Jean Piaget (1896–1980), a Swiss zoologist and psychologist, is considered the most influential developmental psychologist. Piaget visualized that children's thinking is qualitatively different from adults, and children play an active role in the learning process. By interacting with the world, children develop new knowledge (assimilation), build upon existing knowledge (accommodation), and adapt to earlier knowledge to accommodate new information (adaptation). Piaget (1954) proposed a stage theory of cognitive development, suggesting that children progress through distinct stages of thinking. The stages are sensorimotor (0–2 years), preoperational (2–7 years), concrete operational (7–11 years), and formal operational (11+ years) (see Chapter 6). Piaget argued that cognitive development occurs through the interaction of biological maturation and environmental experiences.

Vygotsky's Sociocultural Theory

Lev Vygotsky (1896–1934), a Soviet psychologist, asserted the role of social and cultural factors in development. He argued that learning is an active process and not a natural or passive process. Vygotsky (1978) highlighted the importance of social interactions, language, and cultural tools (such as symbols and signs) in cognitive development. He proposed the notion of a zone of proximal development (ZPD) (see Chapter 6).

Bruner's Constructivist Theory

Jerome Bruner (1915–2016), an American psychologist and educator, advanced constructivist theory, which viewed the learner as an active agent of learning (Bruner, 1961). Based on the existing schema and the available information, children discern links between different facts, concepts, and theories. He postulated three stages of intellectual development: enactive, iconic, and symbolic. Bruner further proposed the concept of discovery learning, which states that children should be provided opportunities to discover relationships between different facts and concepts (see Chapter 6).

Thus, the cognitive approach underscores the importance of internal mental processes, social interactions, and active engagement in learning. Critics argue that this approach does not adequately address the emotional and social aspects of development, and it might oversimplify complex cognitive processes.

Humanistic Approach

The humanistic approach highlights the subjective experience, self-actualization, and the inherent goodness of individuals. It focuses on understanding people's unique experiences, personal growth, and the realization of their full potential. Central to the humanistic approach is the concept of self-actualization, a process through which individuals strive to fulfil their inherent potential. Major contributors to the humanistic approach are Abraham Maslow, Carl Rogers, Rollo May, and Eric Fromm.

Maslow's Hierarchy of Needs

Abraham Maslow (1908–1970), an American psychologist, is perhaps best known for his hierarchy of needs. Maslow (1943) proposed that human motivation is organized in a hierarchical structure. Basic needs such as physiological needs and safety must be satisfied before individuals can progress to higher-level needs like love and belonging, esteem, and self-actualization. Maslow's concept of self-actualization is foundational to the humanistic approach (see Chapter 8).

Rogers's Person-Centred Therapy

An American psychologist, Carl Rogers (1902–1987) developed person-centred therapy, which emphasizes the importance of the therapeutic relationship, empathy, and unconditional positive regard (Rogers, 1946). Rogers introduced the concept of the self-concept, which refers to an individual's perception of themselves.

May's Existential Psychology

Rollo May (1909–1994), an American psychologist, contributed to the humanistic approach through his work in existential psychology. May (1958) explored themes of human existence, freedom, responsibility, and the search for meaning. May highlighted the importance of individuals confronting existential challenges for personal growth.

Fromm's Social Psychology

Eric Fromm (1900–1980), a German-American psychologist, integrated social and psychological perspectives into his work. He (Fromm, 1941) explored the impact of societal structures on individual development and emphasized the need for individuals to transcend societal constraints to achieve authentic self-expression.

The humanistic approach to human development has influenced fields such as psychology, counselling, and education. Some critics argue that humanistic theories may be overly optimistic and lack scientific rigour. The emphasis on subjective experience can make it challenging to study and measure.

Ecological Approach

The ecological approach emphasizes the importance of understanding the complex interplay between individuals and their environments in the process of development. Several theorists have made significant contributions to the ecological approach, including Urie Bronfenbrenner, Charles Super and Sara Harkness, and Durganand Sinha.

Bronfenbrenner's Ecological Systems Theory

Urie Bronfenbrenner (1917–2005), a Russian-born American psychologist, proposed the ecological systems theory. According to him, the development of a child does not occur in a vacuum; rather, it takes place in a context. Bronfenbrenner (1979) advanced five nested-level contexts. These levels are categorized from the most immediate level to the farthest: (1) microsystem or the immediate environment in which children live and interact like parents and siblings, (2) mesosystem or the larger institutional structures such as family, school, religion, and so on, (3) exosystem or the larger contexts such as extended family, parent's workplaces, and the community in which family lives, (4) macrosystems or the social and cultural values, perceptions and beliefs, as well as the political and economic systems, and (5) chronosystem or the historical context (such as migration from one place to another, generation gap, and so on) in which these changes occur. Bronfenbrenner model is quite comprehensive and helps us to understand different environments that influence a child's development. However, the theory is not easy to use. It is difficult to research to determine the impact of different environments.

Super and Harkness's Concept of Developmental Niche

Charles Super and Sara Harkness are known for their work on cultural and ecological influences on human development. Based on their research in Africa, they (Super & Harkness, 1986) proposed a model known as the developmental niche, consisting of three interacting subsystems: (1) physical and social settings in which the child is raised, such as the home, neighbourhood, and the people, (2) customs of childcare involving the cultural beliefs, values, and practices related to child-rearing, and (3) psychological niche involving the cultural goals and expectations that parents have for their children. The model underscores the idea that cultural variations in child-rearing practices contribute to the diversity of developmental outcomes observed across different societies.

Sinha's Ecological Model

To understand the development of children in the Indian context, Durganand Sinha (1922–1998), an Indian psychologist, presented an ecological model. Sinha (1977, 1982) viewed the ecology of the child in terms of two concentric layers: (a) the upper and most visible layers and (b) the surrounding layers. The upper and visible layers consist of factors like (1) home (overcrowding, space available for each member, toys, technological devices used, etc.), (2) nature and quality of schooling, and (3) nature of interactions and activities undertaken with a peer group from childhood onward. These factors do not operate independently but constantly interact with each other. The surrounding layers constantly influence the upper layer, but the influence is not visible. The following factors constitute the surrounding layer: (a) general geographical environment – space and facilities for play and other activities available outside the home, general congestion of the locality, and the density of population, (b) institutional setting provided by caste, class, and other factors, and (c) general amenities available – drinking water, electricity, means of entertainment etc.

The ecological approach, thus, highlights the importance of considering multiple environmental influences on development. It promotes a holistic understanding of individuals within their contexts. Critics, however, suggest that the ecological approach does not provide sufficient guidance on how to intervene or promote positive development. It could be seen as descriptive rather than explanatory.

Indigenous Approach

The indigenous approach to human development is deeply rooted in the cultural ethos of a specific community or region. It originates from the traditional knowledge, beliefs, and practices of various indigenous cultures around the world. The indigenous theories present a holistic view of the self and consider the interconnectedness of physical, mental, emotional, and spiritual dimensions. The individual is seen as part of a larger whole, and personal well-being is linked to the well-being of the community and the environment. Nature is not seen merely as a resource but as a living entity with which humans share a reciprocal relationship. Many indigenous theories incorporate spiritual dimensions, recognizing the importance of a connection to the sacred or the transcendent.

The indigenous approach in India stands as a distinctive paradigm shaped by centuries-old traditions, philosophies, and wisdom. At the heart of this approach lies a profound connection to the land, traditions, and spirituality. Indigenous communities draw upon ancestral knowledge, oral traditions, and symbiotic relationships with nature to inform their understanding of human development. A unique approach to human development through cultural practices and rituals, such as *ashrama dharma, samskaras, deeksha* (or initiation), and so on, is followed. *Purushartha* or the fourfold objective of human life forms the foundation of the indigenous approach. Rites of passage, ceremonies, and communal festivities play pivotal roles in shaping an individual's identity and sense of belonging. Nature is seen as an integral part of human existence and is viewed as a teacher, healer, and provider. Practices such as eco-spirituality and sustainable living underscore the interconnectedness between humans and the environment, promoting a harmonious relationship that fosters both personal and collective well-being. There is an emphasis on holistic integration of physical, mental, and spiritual dimensions, emphasizing the interconnectedness of individuals with their environment and community. For example, Sri Aurobindo's notion of integral philosophy aims to harmonize the spiritual, mental, vital, and physical aspects of an individual, leading to a transformative and integrated development (Sundararajan et al., 2013).

In summary, the indigenous perspectives challenge the dominant Western paradigms and offer a world view that prioritizes interconnectedness, community well-being, and a harmonious relationship with the environment. Indigenous approaches are, however, diverse, and generalizations can be challenging.

Recent Developments and Theoretical Underpinnings

A scrutiny of the theories of human development discussed earlier would reveal several points. First, the theories were influenced by the disciplinary background of the theorists. Accordingly, stress was laid on biological factors, environmental influences, or the interaction between heredity and the environment. None of the theories alone are sufficient to fully explain the dynamic process of development taking place among humans. Second, some of the theories are based upon the experiments conducted in laboratories on non-humans, and some are derived from the observations of individual children devoid of the context in which they lived. The validity of such theories has been questioned. Third, Western theories conceptualize development in terms of hierarchical and discrete stages. At the core of each stage is a developmental task that a child is expected to achieve to move to the next stage. However, these theories overlook culturally specific themes that can be observed across these stages. These theories attempt to understand human development in terms of universal laws in an acontextual, culture-free manner.

In recent years, studies in cross-cultural and cultural psychology have established the universals as well as cultural variations in human development. The studies indicate that development is a constructive and continuous process of co-construction made possible by several participants in the context of historical–cultural and physical, phylogenetic time. The anthropological studies of Margaret Mead, Ruth Benedict, John Whiting, and others have shown that the linear model of the cause–effect relationship for understanding development is inadequate.

The research conducted in Africa, Japan, and India (e.g., Anandalakshmy, 1994; Holloway, 2006; Saraswathi, 1999, 2011; Super & Harkness, 1986) has shown that there are central themes around which the development takes place in non-Western societies. For example, the development is centred around obedience and responsibility in African countries, social harmony in the Indian continent, and insistence on otherness in Japan. Culture mediates the development, and children develop different competencies in different cultures depending on what values or cognitive abilities are emphasized in the particular society. This brings us to the importance of understanding practices and conceptions prevalent in a particular society. Thus, there is a need to integrate multiple perspectives that can provide a more nuanced understanding of the complexities of human development, acknowledging the interplay between biological, psychological, social, and cultural factors.

Methodological Considerations in Developmental Research

Methodological considerations are crucial for designing studies that yield valid and reliable results. As human development research involves individuals of different age groups, the studies need to be planned and executed carefully. Some key considerations include deciding about the response category, research design, research approach, key techniques of data gathering, ethical considerations, and interdisciplinary collaboration. By addressing these methodological considerations, the quality, validity, and ethical integrity of studies can be enhanced.

Response Categories

People engage in three kinds of behaviours that are primarily studied in human development research: involuntary, voluntary, and psycho-physical. As infants have limited motor control, they have difficulty sitting, keeping their heads erect for a longer time, and so on. They, however, show involuntary responses like an increase or decrease in heart rate, movement of the eye, and so on. One such research method that uses involuntary response is the procedure of habituation. For example, if a 4-year-old child is shown a photograph, she looks at it until she gets bored with the picture and turns away her attention. When shown a different picture, she shows interest and looks at the new picture. This is known as the method of habituation, taking advantage of the involuntary responses of the infants. The infants continuously look around and observe their environments; they do not have to be taught to engage with the world in this way.

Behaviours that a person completes by choice fall under voluntary responses. For example, a person chooses a dress to wear, games to play, persons with whom she wants to study or play, and so forth. These behaviours indicate diverse aspects of development and are used by researchers to study. Psycho-physiological data refers to measurements that capture the relationship between psychological processes (such as thoughts, emotions, and mental states) and physiological responses (bodily functions and activities). The study of how the brain develops or how biological changes (e.g., heart rate, hormone levels) influence behaviour requires collecting psycho-physiological data (e.g., blood pressure, electroencephalograph (EEG), electrocardiograph (ECG), electromyography (EMG), galvanic skin response (GSR), etc.). All three types of responses are studied in human developmental research.

Research Designs for Developmental Studies

Research in human development aims to find out how development takes place and the factors influencing development across different life stages. In doing so, three types of research designs are employed: cross-sectional, longitudinal, and cross-sequential.

Cross-Sectional Research Design

A cross-sectional research design is used to examine the development of individuals of different ages at any given time (Table 3.1). If the researcher wants to study, for example, cognitive development of children, she may select samples of children of different age groups (i.e., children aged 6 years, 7 years, 8 years, 9 years, and so on) and study these groups together. This approach provides a snapshot of a population's characteristics and allows researchers to examine age-related differences.

The strengths of cross-sectional design are that it, (1) is quick, inexpensive, and allows the researcher to collect data from children of different age groups at a time, (2) helps in identifying differences due to age, (3) allows researchers to collect data from a diverse and large sample, providing a broader perspective on human development within a population, and (4) provides normative developmental milestones and patterns across different age groups. The value of this kind of research for establishing challenging educational curricula, creating appropriate television or reading materials, designing interesting toys and games, and provoking further studies of continuous individual development has been unparalleled.

The limitations are the following: (1) since people of different age groups are studied at a time it tells us about the age differences and not the development *per se* or individual developmental trajectory, (2) differences observed between age groups may be attributed to generational or cohort effects rather than true developmental changes, making it challenging to disentangle age-related changes from cultural or historical influences, and (3) it cannot establish causation or determine the direction of developmental changes, as they capture only correlations at a single point in time.

Longitudinal Research Design

A Longitudinal research design, unlike cross-sectional research, studies individuals or groups over an extended period at different intervals (Table 3.1). For example, the cognitive development of the same group of children is studied when they are six years old and re-examined when they become 7 years old, and so on. By tracking individuals over time, researchers can observe how developmental processes unfold, identifying patterns, milestones, and critical

Table 3.1 Examples of Cross-Sectional and Longitudinal Research Design

Cross-sectional	Child A 6 years old	Child B 7 years old	Child C 8 years old	Child D 9 years old
Longitudinal	Child A 6 years old	Child A 7 years old	Child A 8 years old	Child A 9 years old

periods. Also, it enables researchers to infer the cause-and-effect relationships between various factors. Longitudinal designs allow for the exploration of developmental trajectories, offering insights into the stability or change of individual characteristics, behaviours, and experiences. Longitudinal studies are well-suited to identify sensitive and critical periods in development. Longitudinal studies are widely employed in investigating various aspects of human development, educational interventions, physical and mental health trajectories, career development, and social and cultural influences.

The limitations of longitudinal studies are the following: (a) they demand significant time, financial resources, and commitment from both researchers and participants, (b) attrition rates may also pose challenges as participants may drop out or become difficult to track over time, (c) changes in measurement tools or methods for the study may introduce inconsistencies in data collection, and (d) since the same group of subjects take the test more than once, familiarity with the measuring instrument may affect the results of the study.

Cross-Sequential Research Design

This design combines the elements of both cross-sectional and longitudinal research designs (Table 3.2). Similar to longitudinal research, the participants are examined at different periods. Further, similar to cross-sectional designs, participants of different age groups are included in the study. In this design, children of different ages are enrolled into a study at various points in time to examine age-related changes and development within the same individuals as they age and account for the possibility of cohort effects. As it combines the elements of both cross-sectional and longitudinal design, it is considered more powerful. When considering the best research design to use in the research, the researcher looks into the main research question and the best way to come up with an answer.

Approaches for Conducting Developmental Research

Three primary approaches – quantitative, qualitative, and mixed-methods – are generally employed in human development research. The choice of a research approach depends on the research question, the available resources, and the nature of the phenomena being studied.

Quantitative Approach

The quantitative approach is concerned with the process of collecting and analysing numerical data. It is based on the assumption that only factual knowledge gained through observation or "senses", which is measurable is trustworthy. The role of the researcher is limited to data collection and analysis objectively and systematically. Objectivity refers to the fact that if two or more persons independently study a phenomenon or event, both of them to a large extent should arrive at similar conclusions. The second characteristic is that it follows a systematic procedure:

Table 3.2 Example of Cross-Sequential Research Design

	2018	*2020*	*2022*	*2024*
Cohort A	Age 5	Age 7	Age 9	Age 11
Cohort B	–	Age 5	Age 7	Age 9
Cohort C	–	–	Age 5	Age 7
Cohort D	–	–	–	Age 5

conceptualizing the research problem, collecting data with the help of samples and tools, subjecting data to statistical analysis, drawing conclusions, and revising research conclusions and theory. The goal is often to generalize findings from a sample to a larger population.

In the quantitative approach, the researcher remains independent of the research being conducted. Her role is limited to the collection and analysis of data without any bias for description, explanation, and prediction of behaviour. This approach relies purely on facts and considers the world to be external and objective. Data is collected using standardized and structured methods, often employing surveys, experiments, or structured observations. Data is analysed using statistical techniques to identify patterns, correlations, or cause-and-effect relationships. Results are often presented in tables, charts, and graphs. Box 3.1 contains an example of quantitative research.

Box 3.1   Example of Quantitative Research

T.S. Saraswathi (1976) examined changes in the immediate memory span of preschool children who were 3–5 years old. The study employed a longitudinal design for 15 children who were tested individually at an interval of six months. The cross-sectional data was collected on 36 children. They were tested on a digital number series with a score of one for a correct answer and zero for a wrong answer. A significant increase in memory span (from 3 to 4 digits) between 3½ and 4 years was noted (the average for adults being 7 plus/minus 2). The study concluded that information storage capacity increases with advancement in age.

Quantitative research, though a powerful tool, has its limitations. First, it simplifies complex human behaviours and experiences into measurable variables. Second, a particular behaviour is studied in isolation, devoid of the context. Third, though it provides a wide range of data from large samples, an in-depth exploration of individual experiences or reasons for certain behaviours is not feasible. Fourth, it is also challenging to study people's interpretation of certain phenomena (e.g., emotions concerning the loss of a dear one, suffering due to major setbacks in life, etc.) using quantitative research.

Qualitative Approach

Qualitative research is exploratory and seeks to understand human experiences, behaviours, and social phenomena through non-numerical data. It involves in-depth, context-rich data collection and analysis. Qualitative research focuses on understanding the subjective meanings individuals attribute to their experiences. It involves using methods such as interviews (semi-structured or unstructured), focus group discussions, participant observation, case studies, ethnography, and so on. Data is often textual (e.g., sentences, statements, critical incidences etc.) and pictorial with researchers providing detailed, contextually rich descriptions of the phenomena under study. It helps in collecting detailed in-depth information about a few people, groups, cultures, and so on.

The qualitative research paradigm assumes that the reality or the world is socially constructed through interaction with others. The researcher aims to understand the meaning of reality by immersing himself/herself in the situation. Further, it follows inductive reasoning, and ideas are developed based on induction from data. It employs not one but several methods to understand different aspects of an event or phenomenon. Qualitative research often employs an emergent design, allowing the research questions and methods to evolve as the study progresses. The emphasis is on understanding how the social and cultural contexts influence behaviour. It is labelled as a subjective interpretation of facts, events, or phenomena. Coding and thematic analysis are common techniques for analysing data. Qualitative research is frequently used in anthropology, education, sociology, and psychology to explore complex social processes, cultural phenomena, and individual experiences (see Box 3.2 for an example of qualitative research).

To address the issue of subjectivity in qualitative research, the methodology of triangulation is followed. Triangulation refers to using multiple sources, methods, theories, or researchers to study a phenomenon to enhance the validity of the findings. The idea is to cross-verify information from different perspectives. There are several types of triangulation, such as method triangulation (e.g., using different types of methods such as interviews, observations, and document analysis), researcher triangulation (e.g., using multiple researchers or observers), data source triangulation (e.g., collecting information from diverse groups of respondents including students, peers, teachers, parents), theory triangulation (e.g., using multiple theoretical perspectives to interpret the data), and time triangulation (e.g., studying the same phenomenon at different points in time).

Box 3.2 Example of Qualitative Research

To understand the world view of impoverished rural children and adolescent girls, R. Dutta (1983) lived in the setting, talked to adolescent girls, played with children, and learnt their language. She observed their activities, interviewed the mothers, and informally interacted with other community members. She cooked *chapatis* with adolescent girls, accompanied them to the marketplace, and fetched water from the well. Slowly, she began to understand their way of life, the complex culture that gave meaning and shape to their lives. She recorded and described the information so gathered.

Though qualitative research is a valuable and insightful approach, it has certain limitations. First, qualitative research relies heavily on the interpretation of researchers, which introduces the potential for subjectivity and bias in data collection and analysis. Second, the generalization of findings is challenging because of the involvement of small, non-random samples. Third, as qualitative research is context-dependent, replicating studies exactly can be challenging due to the uniqueness of each setting and group of participants. Fourth, data analysis is time-consuming due to the need for detailed coding and interpretation. Fifth, the essence of qualitative research is highly dependent on the skills of the researcher in data collection, analysis, and interpretation.

Mixed-Methods Research

Mixed-methods research combines the elements of both quantitative and qualitative research within a single study. Researchers collect and analyse both quantitative and qualitative data, using a sequential or concurrent design. For example, data may be collected using unstructured interviews, participant observation, and administering questionnaires/tests. It is to be noted that the mixing of methods is purposeful and is guided by the research questions that the researcher attempts to answer. Mixed-methods research often involves an iterative process, with the findings from one phase informing the design and analysis of subsequent phases. Mixed-methods research is particularly useful when researchers seek a comprehensive understanding of a phenomenon by combining the breadth of quantitative data with the depth of qualitative insights. It is employed in various disciplines, including education, health sciences, and social sciences. Box 3.3 presents an example of mixed-methods research.

In summary, the choice between quantitative, qualitative, or mixed-methods depends on the nature of the research question, the level of understanding required, and the strengths and limitations of each approach. Researchers often select the approach or combination that best aligns with their study objectives and the characteristics of the phenomena they are investigating.

> **Box 3.3   Example of a Mixed-Methods Research**
>
> Access to health and education for street children from 6 to 18 years of age in Mumbai and Kolkata was studied (Dutta, 2018) using a combination of quantitative and qualitative methodologies. The study was conducted on 100 children selected through the convenience sampling method. Data were collected on a one-to-one basis through semi-structured interview schedules and by non-participant observation. Extreme poverty, a lack of awareness among illiterate parents about educational facilities, and a lack of educational ambience at home were the primary reasons that kept street children away from school attendance. Children living with their parents had better access to healthcare facilities than children living on their own.

Key Techniques of Research

Research tools and techniques are integral components of the research process. They play distinct roles in gathering, analysing, and interpreting data. Research tools are instruments or resources used to collect, organize, or analyse data. These can be physical devices, software applications, or even conceptual frameworks. Examples of research tools include questionnaires, interview guides, laboratory equipment and measuring devices, observation forms, statistical software, and so on. Research techniques refer to the specific methods or procedures employed by researchers to gather, analyse, and interpret data. Techniques are the practical applications of research methodologies. Self-report methods, case studies, content analysis, experimental design, observational research, focus group discussion, ethnography, and meta-analysis are some examples of research techniques. The use of these tools/techniques in research depends upon the objectives of the research, the characteristics of the respondents (e.g., infants, young children, adolescents, parents, literate/illiterate), as well the research approach (e.g., quantitative, qualitative, or mixed-methods) proposed to be employed. Some of the tools and techniques are described in this section.

Self-Report Methods

In self-report methods, individuals provide information about their thoughts, feelings, behaviours, or experiences. These methods are commonly used to gather data directly from the individuals being studied. Here are some key aspects and examples of self-report methods.

Surveys

Surveys are a widely used research method that involves collecting data from a sample of individuals by administering a set of structured questions. Surveys use a predetermined set of questions, which are either closed-ended (multiple-choice, Likert scales) or open-ended, depending on the research objectives. To generalize survey findings to a larger population, researchers aim for a representative sample, using sampling methods, such as random sampling or stratified sampling. Surveys can take different forms, including online, paper-and-pencil surveys, telephone interviews, and face-to-face interviews. Surveys primarily generate quantitative data, allowing for statistical analysis. This enables researchers to identify patterns, trends, and relationships among variables. Surveys are suitable for collecting data from large samples and diverse populations, which enhances the generalizability of findings.

Surveys are a cost-effective way to collect data from a large number of participants. Online surveys, in particular, eliminate the need for printing and manual data entry. Advances in technology have made survey administration more accessible. Online survey platforms (such as Google Survey and others) and mobile applications simplify the process of data collection and analysis. Surveys can be used to investigate a wide range of topics, including social attitudes, consumer preferences, health behaviours, and educational outcomes. The versatility of surveys makes them applicable in various fields of study.

Though surveys yield useful information, some precautions need to be taken while using this method. First, greater attention should be given to question wording, response options, and the order of questions while preparing the survey questionnaire as they can influence participants' answers. Second, surveys provide information with limited depth when compared to qualitative methods. Follow-up interviews or additional qualitative research may be necessary to explore participants' perspectives more thoroughly. Proper design and implementation, along with attention to potential biases, contribute to the reliability and validity of survey findings.

Questionnaires

You must have come across a questionnaire or psychological test (e.g., intelligence test, personality test etc.) in which you were asked to express your views, opinions, or attitudes on a certain issue or problem. It is the most common, simple, versatile, and low-cost method of collecting data. Questionnaires often consist of structured and closed-ended questions (e.g., yes/no type, true/false, multiple-choice, rating scales, or pictorial), where participants select responses from predetermined options. This format simplifies data analysis and ensures uniformity in participant responses. Some questionnaires allow for flexibility by using open-ended questions that allow participants to provide detailed responses. This can add qualitative depth to the data collected.

Questionnaires are well-suited for collecting data from large samples of participants. They can be distributed widely, either in person or through online platforms, reaching a diverse and extensive audience. Further, respondents may have the choice to reveal their identity or answer the questions remaining anonymous. One of the primary strengths of questionnaires is their ability to generate quantitative data. Researchers can assign numerical values to responses, allowing for statistical analysis and the identification of patterns or trends. Ensuring the validity (accuracy) and reliability (consistency) of questionnaire items is crucial. Pilot testing or trying out of the questionnaire is done to ensure that the research tool is valid, reliable, and effectively measures what it is intended to measure.

The use of questionnaires should be done with caution. First, it cannot be used with infants, young children, or illiterates who are not proficient in understanding the language of the questionnaire. Second, the words or phrases used in the questionnaire should be easy to understand. If the questions are unclear, the respondent may give an irrelevant response. Third, two similar questions should not be combined. Rather, they should be asked separately. Fourth, the questionnaire should not be too lengthy. A lengthy questionnaire takes longer time to answer, and the respondents may also feel fatigued, losing their interest in answering the questions. Fifth, it is essential to frame questions carefully to avoid socially desirable responses from the participants. That is, participants may provide answers they perceive as socially acceptable rather than their true opinions or behaviours. For example, when you ask questions like "Do you show respect to elders", there is a possibility that all participants will reply in affirmation. A researcher needs to take care of these issues while designing a questionnaire.

Experimental Method

The experimental method is a systematic and controlled approach to scientific enquiry, aiming to investigate the effects of independent variables (IV) on dependent variables (DV). In the context of human development research, IVs might include interventions, treatments, or specific experiences while dependent variables are the measurable outcomes or changes observed in individuals. Examples of IVs might include responsiveness of parents during infancy, different teaching methods in KG, duration of exposure to screen times during adolescence, and so on, with corresponding DVs attachment of children to parents, cognitive abilities, and development of social skills, respectively. Random assignment, control groups, and manipulation of variables are fundamental elements of the experimental method.

Random assignment of participants to different experimental conditions is a crucial aspect of experimental research. In experimental studies, participants are typically divided into two groups: the experimental group, which receives the treatment or intervention, and the control group, which does not. By comparing the outcomes of these groups, researchers can discern whether the changes observed in the experimental group are a result of the intervention or an external factor. The experimental method allows researchers to manipulate variables intentionally to investigate their impact on human development. For instance, in studies examining the effect of teaching methods, one group may be taught by the traditional method and the other by the play-way method, and the learning levels of the two groups are compared.

The experimental method plays a pivotal role in understanding the intricate tapestry of growth across the lifespan. It allows the researchers to establish cause-and-effect relationships, control extraneous variables, and generate replicable results. However, it also has limitations. Ethical concerns may arise when manipulating variables that could have lasting effects on participants. Additionally, the artificial laboratory setting may not fully capture the complexity of real-world developmental processes. Despite its limitations, the experimental method remains a powerful tool, contributing significantly to our understanding of how individuals change and develop over time. As technology and research methodologies evolve, the experimental approach will continue to be a cornerstone in advancing our knowledge of human development.

Interview Method

Interviews are a powerful and flexible research tool widely employed to explore the intricacies of individuals' experiences, thoughts, and behaviours. As interviews are a face-to-face relationship between interviewer(s) and interviewee(s), they help establish a personal connection or rapport between the two. This leads to a more open and honest exchange of information, fostering trust and enhancing the quality of data. By conducting interviews in natural settings, researchers can gain insights into the contextual factors that shape human development. Understanding the influence of environment, culture, and relationships is crucial for a holistic perspective. In this method, the interviewer asks questions and the interviewee or the respondent gives answers to the questions, which are recorded by the interviewer in written form or electronically.

The flexibility of interview formats allows researchers to adapt to the unique needs of each study. Interview formats can be structured, semi-structured, and unstructured. In *structured interviews*, the questions, the wording, and the order of questions are pre-decided. The interviewer asks the same questions to all the respondents. The questions are generally closed-ended. Asking predetermined questions helps in comparing the responses of different people. *Semi-structured interviews* involve a mix of predetermined questions and the flexibility for the interviewer to explore topics in more detail based on the respondent's answers. There is a core set of questions, but the interviewer has the freedom to ask follow-up questions and probe for deeper insights. The questions are open-ended. This type of interview is best suited for experienced researchers because asking spontaneous questions is not easy. In *unstructured interviews*, there is no predetermined set of questions, and the conversation is more like a free-flowing discussion. The interviewer may have a general topic in mind but allows the conversation to evolve naturally. The questions in unstructured interviews are open-ended, allowing the researcher to gather in-depth descriptive data. The research questions are exploratory trying to understand the meaning of the responses. Unstructured interviews are characteristic of qualitative interviewing. The responses have meaning in a particular context which cannot be generalized. This type of research requires forming a deeper connection with the respondent to encourage him/her to reveal the true picture of his/her emotions, motives, and personality.

Interviews offer valuable insights, as they allow the researcher to gather rich information from the respondents. Also, it takes into consideration non-verbal cues including postures and gestures, and emotional responses. However, the interview is a time-consuming technique and requires skill and expertise to conduct interviews. It also suffers from an inherent risk of interviewer bias or systematic errors introduced into the data due to the interviewer's influence, perceptions, or personal preferences.

Observation Method

The observation method involves watching and recording behaviours as they occur in a natural setting, without direct intervention or manipulation by the researcher. In our daily life, we do observe people, objects, events, and phenomena. The scientific observation is, however, characterized by several salient features. The researcher selects behaviour for observation. For example, if the researcher wants to study aggressiveness among adolescents, she identifies behaviours that indicate aggressiveness (e.g., physical violence, shouting, teasing, bullying, use of harsh language, etc.). At certain times, the researcher provokes or creates a situation in which the desired behaviour is most likely to occur. The observed behaviour is recorded through different means (e.g., taking field notes, video recording) and subsequently classified into categories, these categories are interrelated, and meaning is provided to these categories (called encoding). Finally, the behaviour is observed as it occurs in diverse natural settings. For example, aggressiveness is observed when the person is at home interacting with children and other family members, at the workplace, at play, with friends, and so on.

An important feature of observation is *participant observation*. This refers to the extent to which the observer participates in the setting being studied. The extent of participation of the observer can vary from complete separation from the setting as a spectator to complete immersion in the setting as a full participant. Complete participation helps in understanding the respondent's (or insider's) perspective and provides exact meaning to the behaviour observed.

Though participant observation is an effective tool, it needs to be conducted with caution. When the researcher becomes a part of the setting to which she does not belong naturally, the problem of acceptance by group members arises. Group members may not accept the researcher, and this may result in a reflection of distorted behaviour by the group. Another problem is the social class difference between the observer and the observed or the participants. The social class difference refers to distinctions in social and economic status (such as income, education, occupation, and wealth), which can influence the dynamics of the research process. The third problem is the recording of the observed behaviour. When the participants see that their behaviour is being recorded, the participants become conscious of it and may not display their natural behaviour. Efforts need to be made to minimize the effects of these factors. Technology can be used for recording the behaviour, but analysis of recorded behaviour is a time-consuming task.

Focus Group Discussion

Focus group is another variation of qualitative interviewing in which a group of participants (generally 6 to 10 persons) are brought together to answer questions related to the topic of study. A question is asked and each member of the group has an opportunity to express his/her views. In addition to their answers, the focus group also helps in the study of group dynamics and body language. Focus groups can provide more nuanced and unfiltered feedback than individual interviews and are easier to organize. Group discussion is more useful during the early phase of the study when the researcher wants to explore the nuances of a research topic. This helps in finding out new questions or future research ideas.

Case Studies

A case study involves an in-depth and detailed examination of a specific individual, group, event, or situation. It provides a rich understanding of the nuances of human experiences, behaviours, and development over time. Case studies are conducted for unique, extreme, or unconventional cases, which are different from the normal. The intricacies of a particular case are explored in depth adopting a holistic perspective. This comprehensive view helps researchers capture the interconnectedness of different aspects of human development.

Case studies often rely on qualitative research methods, such as interviews, observations, and document analysis, to gather detailed and context-rich data. This qualitative approach allows researchers to capture the subjective experiences and meanings attributed to different aspects of human development. Case studies are sensitive to the context in which development occurs. Researchers can examine how cultural, familial, educational, and environmental factors influence human development within a specific case.

While case studies offer a deep understanding of specific cases, it is important to note that findings from individual cases may not be generalizable to larger populations. Researchers often use case studies in conjunction with other research methods to provide a more comprehensive and nuanced understanding of human development phenomena.

Ethnography

Ethnography (ethno refers to culture and graphic refers to description) refers to presenting a detailed and thick description of a culture, group, institution, society, village, etc. Ethnography requires immersion in the culture by becoming a member of the group, a functionary in the school, a resident of a village and participating in all their activities as the natives do. While doing so, the researcher does not shift his/her attention from the central theme of research; interacts with the members of the group, takes part in their daily rituals, and records the conversation/observation. It is a long and time-consuming process. It requires constant interviewing supported by observation. This enables the researcher to collect and elicit natives' views of reality and ascription of meaning to events, intentions, and consequences. Examples of ethnographic studies conducted in India are given in Box 3.4.

> **Box 3.4 Examples of Ethnographic Studies**
>
> Margaret Trawick (1992), an American researcher, was interested in understanding the concept of love in India. For this she chose to live with an Indian family in a small village in Tamil Nadu state for about a year. To understand the meaning of the concept of *anpu* (love in English), she took part in the daily activities, customs, and rituals of the village, talked to different persons, and observed their activities. This allowed her to discern the meaning of love in that particular context.
>
> Anjum Sibia (2006) carried out an ethnographic study to explicate the pedagogic processes taking place in the classroom at Mirambika School to examine the school organization, teaching–learning process, and students' development. An understanding of the school was built mainly through personal observations, informal interactions, and by examining the perceptions of the participants, namely the teachers, students, and parents. It attempted to provide an interpretation of the various school processes by giving a feel of what they mean to the participants. While highlighting the significant issues, an attempt was made to reconstruct the ambience of the school and to examine the influence of ideology on it.

In conclusion, the key techniques discussed here represent a diverse toolkit for understanding and exploring human behaviour and experiences. These methodologies offer unique advantages and limitations, highlighting the importance of selecting the most suitable approach based on the research objectives and context.

Ethical Considerations

Human development research raises complex ethical considerations that must be carefully addressed to ensure the well-being and rights of research participants. The ethical considerations are briefly described here.

Informed Consent

One of the fundamental ethical principles is obtaining informed consent from participants. Researchers must provide comprehensive and understandable information about the study. This information typically includes the purpose of the research, the procedures involved, potential risks and benefits, the voluntary nature of participation, and any alternatives. Participants must voluntarily agree to participate without coercion or undue influence.

Privacy and Confidentiality

Respecting the privacy and confidentiality of participants is another critical consideration. Participants' sensitive information should be kept confidential and securely stored. This is particularly relevant in longitudinal studies that involve collecting data over an extended period.

Minimizing Harm and Risks

Human development research may involve interventions, assessments, or observations that could pose risks to participants. Researchers must take proactive measures to reduce any potential negative effects that participants may experience as a result of their involvement in a study. This principle is rooted in the broader ethical framework of beneficence, which emphasizes the researcher's responsibility to promote the well-being of participants and minimize any potential harm that might arise during the research process.

Respect for Diversity and Cultural Sensitivity

Research participants may come from diverse backgrounds, which should be considered in the design and implementation of studies. This involves respecting cultural norms, values, and practices, as well as adapting research methods to suit diverse populations. Collaborating with local communities and involving them in the research process helps ensure that studies are culturally relevant and ethically sound.

Equitable Participation and Access

Ethically sound research requires a commitment to equitable participation and access to diverse groups of people in the studies to avoid any kind of bias. This is essential for a more comprehensive understanding of human development across different demographic groups.

In sum, ethical considerations are paramount to safeguarding the rights, well-being, and dignity of research participants. By upholding these principles, the research community can contribute to the betterment of society while respecting the individuals who contribute to our understanding of human development.

Overview

This chapter provided a comprehensive exploration of theoretical and methodological approaches to development. It delved into various lenses through which scholars examine human growth and behaviour. Theoretical frameworks such as psychoanalytical, biological, learning, cognitive, humanistic, ecological, and indigenous perspectives offer diverse paradigms for understanding the complexities of development.

Methodological considerations have been scrutinized, shedding light on the crucial decisions researchers make when designing studies. The exploration of research designs, including cross-sectional, longitudinal, and cross-sequential approaches, has emphasized the nuanced choices researchers must navigate. The delineation of research approaches, encompassing quantitative, qualitative, and mixed-methods research, highlighted the breadth of tools available to researchers. Boxes have provided concrete examples, offering a glimpse into the real-world application of these approaches and illustrating the dynamic nature of developmental enquiry. The discussion on key techniques has showcased the diversity of tools researchers can leverage to capture the multifaceted aspects of human development. These techniques serve as invaluable instruments for researchers seeking a deeper understanding of individual and collective developmental processes. Finally, ethical considerations have been woven into the fabric of this chapter, emphasizing the paramount importance of upholding ethical standards in developmental research. The ethical compass guides researchers in their interactions with participants, ensuring that the pursuit of knowledge is ethically sound and respects the rights and well-being of those involved.

In essence, this chapter serves as a comprehensive guide for researchers, educators, and practitioners, offering a road map through the theoretical and methodological landscape of developmental studies. The integration of diverse approaches, techniques, and ethical considerations underscores the richness and complexity of the field, inviting scholars to engage in thoughtful and impactful research that contributes to the broader knowledge base of human development.

Key Terms

Attachment	Longitudinal Research
Behaviourism	Mesosystem
Biological	Microsystem
Cognitive	Mixed-Methods Research
Cross-Sectional Research	Observation
Cross-Sequential Research	Psychoanalytic Approach
Developmental Niche	Psycho-Physiological Data
Ecological	Qualitative Research
Ethical Considerations in Research	Quantitative Research
Exosystem	Response Categories
Humanistic	Self-Report Measures
Indigenous	Social Learning Theory
Interview	

Questions for Reflection

1) How do diverse theoretical perspectives enhance our understanding of human development?
2) How does the choice of research design impact studying different aspects of developmental changes over time?
3) In what ways can combining quantitative and qualitative methods contribute to a more comprehensive understanding of developmental processes?
4) How can researchers ensure the well-being and rights of participants, especially when using different methods?
5) How might working with experts from diverse fields enhance the depth and breadth of our understanding of human development?

Suggested Further Readings

Books

Denzin, N. K., & Lincoln, Y. S. (2005). *The SAGE handbook of qualitative research*. Sage.
Miller, P. H. (2016). *Theories of developmental psychology* (6th ed.). Worth Publisher.
Slater, A. M., & Quinn, P. C. (2021). *Developmental psychology: Revisiting the classic studies*. Sage.
Swamy, S. (1965). *Methods of knowledge: Perceptual, non-perceptual and transcendental*. George Allen & Unwin Ltd.

Websites/Online Resources

American Psychological Association (APA) – Research Methods Resources.
Methods in Behavioral Research – Online Learning Center: Hosted by Gregory J. Privitera.

Part II
Foundational Processes of Human Development

4 Physical and Motor Development

Contents

Introduction	66
Concepts of Physical Growth and Motor Development	66
Pattern of Physical Growth	67
Box 4.1: Birth and Mortality Rates in Indian Population	69
Box 4.2: Prevalence of Obesity in Indian Population	70
Box 4.3: Health Norms	70
Box 4.4: Immunization Schedule for Babies and Mothers in India	71
Box 4.5: Mid-Day Meal Scheme in India	72
Physical Development: An Indian Approach	74
Pattern of Motor Development	75
Box 4.6: Developmental Milestones for Indian Children	76
Relationship of Motor Development With Other Aspects of Development	77
Role of Toys in Child Development	79
Box 4.7: Nursery Books: Nurturing Young Minds Through Literature	80
Healthy Living: A Lifelong Commitment	81
Overview	83
Key Terms	84
Questions for Reflection	84

Learning Objectives

After studying this chapter, the learner will be able to:

Describe the concepts of physical growth and motor development;
Explore the patterns of physical growth and identify key milestones across different developmental stages;
Recognize the interplay between physical development and broader societal concerns;

DOI: 10.4324/9781003441168-6

> Differentiate between gross and fine motor development and examine the factors influencing the progression of these skills; and
> Understand the relationship between motor development and other aspects of growth, including handedness and hand–eye coordination.

Introduction

This chapter delves into the nuanced patterns of physical growth and motor development, with a specific focus on the Indian context. It contains diverse facets, from birth and mortality rates to the prevalence of obesity and the immunization schedule for babies and mothers in India as the essential components of ensuring a healthy start to life. The mid-day meal scheme in India stands as a testament to the nation's commitment to nourishing its young population. The chapter further explores the unique perspective on physical development in the Indian context, emphasizing the cultural and societal influences on growth. The intricate dance between gross and fine motor development, the assessment of motor skills, and the factors affecting motor development form the crux of the chapter. Delving into developmental milestones, it unravels the intricate threads of motor development and its interconnectedness with broader aspects of a child's growth. The role of nursery books is highlighted. The significance of handedness, hand–eye coordination, and the influential role of toys in child development are carefully examined. The narrative expands to the holistic view of healthy living as a lifelong commitment, encompassing organic living, yoga, and the interplay with overall well-being. The intellectual odyssey thus, deciphers the intricacies of physical and motor development, laying the foundation for a comprehensive understanding of the fascinating tapestry that is human growth.

Concepts of Physical Growth and Motor Development

Physical growth refers to the changes observed in the size, shape, and proportions of the body as an individual progresses from infancy to adulthood. These changes occur in various aspects of the body, including height, weight, skeletal structure, muscles, internal organs, hormones, and brain structures. There is a noticeable increase in height and weight during the first year of life, which continues at a slower pace throughout childhood and adolescence until adulthood. There are significant changes in the skeleton system. Bones increase in length, width, and density. As children grow, the number of bones also decreases as separate bones fuse through a process called *ossification*. For example, the skull bones fuse, and the number of ossification centres in long bones decreases. The muscle mass increases, and muscles become stronger and more developed. The development of muscle strength and coordination contributes to improvements in gross motor skills and physical abilities.

Physical growth is also characterized by the development and maturation of internal organs. For example, the heart increases in size and pumping capacity, the lungs grow and become more efficient in exchanging oxygen and carbon dioxide, and the digestive system matures to support increased nutritional requirements. Hormones play a vital role in physical growth and development. Physical growth is also closely linked to brain development. The brain undergoes structural changes, including the formation of new neural connections, synaptic pruning, and myelination, which enhance cognitive abilities and motor skills.

Motor development refers to the progression of motor skills and abilities as children grow and mature. It involves the acquisition and refinement of both gross motor skills, which involve large muscle movements (such as rolling over, sitting up, crawling and creeping, walking, and so on), and fine motor skills, which involve precise movements of the hands and fingers (such as grasping, writing and drawing, and so on).

Motor development involves changes in both the structure and function of the neuromuscular system in many ways. The central nervous system (brain and spinal cord) undergoes significant maturation and refinement during motor development. Muscles become stronger and more coordinated over time. Muscle fibres increase in size and number, leading to increased muscle strength and endurance. Motor development also involves the development of coordination and balance skills. As motor development progresses, there is an improvement in postural control (i.e., the ability to maintain a stable and balanced body position).

Likewise, fine motor skills, involving precise movements of the hands and fingers, develop and become more refined. This includes improvements in hand–eye coordination, manual dexterity, and the ability to manipulate objects with increased precision. Motor development also involves the development of spatial awareness and is closely linked to perceptual development. The ability to perceive and interpret sensory information (e.g., visual, auditory, proprioceptive) and integrate it with motor responses improves over time. This integration allows for more accurate and efficient motor planning and execution.

Various factors, such as genetic factors, environmental experiences, overall health, and opportunities for practice and exploration, contribute to the physical and motor development. It is important to provide children with a supportive and stimulating environment to facilitate their physical and motor development. Medical professionals often refer to growth charts and milestones to monitor and assess a child's physical growth and some aspects of motor development.

Pattern of Physical Growth

Assessment of Physical Growth

The assessment of physical growth provides valuable insights about children's health and overall development, including their nutritional status and well-being. The key aspects of the assessment of physical growth in children are given here.

Anthropometric Measurements

These are essential tools used to assess physical growth in children, such as their height/length, weight, head circumference, and body mass index (BMI). Height is measured using a stadiometer, weight by a weighing scale, head circumference by using a measuring tape, and BMI by dividing weight (in kilograms) by height (in metres squared).

Growth Charts

Growth charts are standardized tools that compare a child's measurements to those of a reference population. World Health Organization (WHO) Growth Charts are widely adopted globally and are based on a diverse, multi-ethnic population. They provide percentile curves for height, weight, and head circumference from birth to 5 years and 5 years to 19 years of age. The Office of the Registrar General and Census Commissioner (India) also provides data related to the physical growth of Indian children.

Interpretation of Growth Measurements

Interpreting growth measurements involves comparing a child's measurements to the growth charts and assessing the trends over time. Key considerations include the following.

1) Percentiles: Growth percentiles indicate how a child's measurements compare to those of a reference population. The fiftieth percentile represents the median while higher or lower percentiles indicate above-average or below-average growth, respectively.
2) Growth Velocity: Monitoring the rate of growth over time is crucial. Growth velocity is typically assessed by calculating the change in height or weight over a specific period, such as a year.

Factors Influencing Physical Growth

Several factors influence a child's physical growth, including genetic factors, nutritional status (such as the availability of a balanced diet), hormones, and environmental factors (such as socio-economic status, access to healthcare, and exposure to toxins).

Milestones in Physical Growth

In humans, physical growth is characterized by different stages and milestones. During the first year of life, infants experience rapid growth. Table 4.1 contains the child's height and weight median growth standards as per data collected by the WHO.

The average weight of a newborn baby in India is reported to be low (2.8–3.2 kg for males, and 2.7–3.1 kg for females) (Bulletin of Registrar General of India, 2022). Growth during the first year is more pronounced, and it slows down during childhood. Height and weight increase steadily. Permanent teeth start to emerge, replacing primary teeth. Fine motor skills develop further, allowing children to perform activities like writing, drawing, and tying shoelaces.

Adolescence marks a period of rapid growth and development. Puberty begins, triggered by hormonal changes, leading to secondary sexual characteristics such as breast development in females and facial hair growth in males. Growth spurts occur, resulting in a significant increase in height and weight. Sexual organs mature, and reproductive capabilities develop. Muscles, bones, and organs continue to grow and develop.

By early adulthood (early to mid-twenties), physical growth typically slows down and reaches its peak. Most individuals have achieved their full adult height by this stage. Muscle and bone density continue to increase, reaching maximum levels in the late twenties or early

Table 4.1 WHO (1997–2003) Child Growth Standards

Months	Median Height (cm)		Median Weight (kg)	
	Girls	*Boys*	*Girls*	*Boys*
Birth	49.1	49.9	3.2	3.3
6	65.7	67.6	7.3	7.9
12	74.0	75.7	8.9	9.6
18	80.7	82.3	10.6	10.9
24	85.7	87.1	11.5	12.2
36	95.1	96.1	13.9	14.3
48	102.7	103.3	16.1	16.3
60	109.4	110.0	18.2	18.3

(*Source*: www.who.int/tools/child-growth-standards/who-multicentre-growth-reference-study)

thirties. After reaching adulthood, physical growth generally stabilizes, and changes primarily occur due to ageing rather than growth. Ageing processes, including a gradual loss of muscle mass and changes in skin elasticity, become more prominent later in adulthood.

Issues Related to the Physical Growth of Children

Related to physical development are some important issues concerning the survival of children and the nutrition of children who survive. Box 4.1 contains birth and mortality rates, and the prevalence of obesity is described in Box 4.2. Health norms are included in Box 4.3. The Government of India has launched programmes for the immunization of children against killing diseases (Box 4.4) and providing adequate nutrition through a mid-day meal scheme (Box 4.5).

Box 4.1 Birth and Mortality Rates in Indian Population

The birth rate, also known as the crude birth rate (CBR), represents the number of live births per 1,000 people in a specific population over a given period. Likewise, the mortality rate, specifically the crude death rate (CDR), represents the number of deaths per 1,000 population in a given year. Table 4.2 contains birth and death rates in India.

India has traditionally experienced high birth rates due to factors, such as cultural norms, fertility preferences, and limited access to family planning services. However, in recent decades, there has been a declining trend in the country's birth rate due to increased education and awareness, improvements in healthcare infrastructure, urbanization, and rising female empowerment. Similarly, there has been a gradual decline in the mortality rate over the years, indicating improvements in healthcare, sanitation, and overall living conditions.

The National Family Health Survey (NFHS) reported the infant mortality rate to be 40.7% during 2015–16 (NFHS 4) and 35.2% during 2019–21 (NFHS 5).

The percentage of stunted children (i.e., height for age) under five years of age has declined from 38.4 during NFHS 4 to 35.5 during NFHS 5. A similar decline from 21.0% to 19.3% (NFHS 5) is observed in the percentage of children under five years of age who are wasted (weight for height) in the surveys.

Table 4.2 Birth and Death Rates in India

Year	Birth Rate	Death Rate
1950	44.175	28.161
1960	42.066	22.481
1970	39.231	17.454
1980	36.216	13.498
1990	31.817	11.007
2000	26.635	8.804
2010	21.508	7.589
2020	17.592	7.273
2023 (provisional)	16.949	7.416

Source: www.macrotrends.net/countries/IND/india/birth-rate

Box 4.2   Prevalence of Obesity in Indian Population

Obesity is a global health concern with significant implications for public health. The WHO (WHO, 2021b) defined overweight and obesity as excessive accumulation of fat in the body. It is calculated by body mass index (BMI), which refers to the weight for height in adults. BMI is the ratio of a person's weight in kilograms divided by the square of his height in metres (kg/m^2). The WHO defines overweight and obesity for adults as having a BMI greater than or equal to 25, and greater than or equal to 30, respectively. For children, age needs to be considered when defining overweight and obese. Obesity poses significant health risks and is associated with various chronic diseases, including diabetes, cardiovascular diseases, and certain types of cancer.

Obesity in India has increased from 20.6% (NFHS 4) to 24% (NFHS 5) among women and 18.9% (NFHS 4) to 22.9% (NFHS 5) among men (both in the age group 15–49 years). Variations in the prevalence of obesity were observed between rural (women 19.7%, men 19.3%) and urban (women 33.2%, men 29.8%) populations during NFHS 5. The prevalence of overweight children under five years of age has increased from 2.1% (NFHS 4) to 3.4% (NFHS 5). A recent study (Singh et al., 2023) estimated childhood obesity to be 8.4% while the prevalence of childhood overweight was estimated to be 12.4%. Also, children studying in private schools, children of working women, and those with a family history were at a higher risk of developing obesity.

Thus, the incidence of obesity in the Indian population has been steadily increasing. Factors such as urbanization, sedentary lifestyles, and dietary changes are the major contributors to this increase. In a study (Awasthi et al., 2018), it was found that Indian women believed that obesity cannot be controlled by internal factors; rather, it can be cured by doctors or supernatural powers.

Box 4.3   Health Norms

Health norms are established criteria, or recommendations that serve as benchmarks for promoting and maintaining optimal health and well-being. The National Institute of Nutrition (Indian Council of Medical Research), Hyderabad, has developed a manual concerning dietary guidelines for Indians of different ages, sexes, activity levels, and specific health conditions (National Institute of Nutrition, 2011). It suggests healthy eating patterns and is designed to promote overall well-being and prevent chronic diseases.

The manual recommends consuming a balanced diet that includes a variety of foods from different food groups in appropriate proportions. The basic food groups are (a) cereals and millets, pulses, and legumes; (b) fruits and vegetables; (c) milk and dairy products; and (d) fats and oils. The manual recommends consuming the following foods.

Cereals and Millets: About 400 grams/day of whole grains like rice, wheat, maize, and millet, and their products are recommended.

Pulses and Legumes: A variety of pulses (lentils, beans, chickpeas) and legumes need to be included in the diet (about 80 grams/day) at least twice a week, as they are rich in protein, fibre, and other essential nutrients.

Fruits and Vegetables: The manual recommends consuming a wide variety of fruits and vegetables (about 300 grams) daily. Both raw and cooked vegetables should be included in meals.

Milk and Dairy Products: Consumption of milk and milk products like yoghurt, paneer (cottage cheese), and buttermilk should be a regular feature (about 300 grams/day). They provide essential nutrients like calcium, protein, and vitamins.

Fats and Oils: Cooking oils should be used sparingly, and one should choose healthier options like vegetable oils (sunflower, safflower, mustard, or groundnut oil) over solid fats (ghee, butter). The recommended dietary allowance is about 30 grams/day. The intake of trans fats and saturated fats should be restricted as they can increase the risk of cardiovascular diseases.

Sugars and Salt: The intake of foods and beverages high in added sugars, such as sweets, desserts, sugary drinks, and processed foods should be limited. The consumption of high-sodium foods like pickles, papads, and processed snacks needs to be restricted to reduce the risk of hypertension.

Hydration: Drinking an adequate amount of water (around 8–10 glasses) throughout the day is essential. Intake of sugary beverages should be limited and healthier options like infused water, herbal teas, or freshly squeezed juices without added sugar need to be taken.

Moderate Alcohol Consumption: If one chooses to drink alcohol, do so in moderation. It is recommended that men limit their alcohol consumption to two standard drinks per day, and women should limit it to one standard drink per day.

Physical Activity: Engaging in regular physical activity for at least 150 minutes per week, spread over 5–6 days is essential. Include a combination of aerobic activities (such as brisk walking, jogging, or cycling) and strength-training exercises.

Note: These guidelines are general recommendations and are available at www.nin.res.in/downloads/DietaryGuidelinesforNINwebsite.pdf

Box 4.4 Immunization Schedule for Babies and Mothers in India

Immunization plays a vital role in safeguarding the health of both babies and mothers by preventing the occurrence and spread of various diseases. In India, the government has implemented a comprehensive immunization programme for babies and mothers to protect against a range of infectious diseases. An overview of the recommended immunization schedule is given in Table 4.3.

Table 4.3 Immunization Schedule for Babies

Age	Vaccines Given
Birth	Bacillus Calmette Guerin (BCG), Oral Polio Vaccine (OPV)-0 dose, Hepatitis B birth dose
6 Weeks	OPV-1, Pentavalent-1, Rotavirus Vaccine (RVV)-1, Fractional dose of Inactivated Polio Vaccine (fIPV)-1, Pneumococcal Conjugate Vaccine (PCV) - 1*
10 weeks	OPV-2, Pentavalent-2, RVV-2
14 weeks	OPV-3, Pentavalent-3, fIPV-2, RVV-3, PCV-2*
9–12 months	Measles and Rubella (MR)-1, JE-1**, PCV-Booster*
16–24 months	MR-2, JE-2**, Diphtheria, Pertussis and Tetanus (DPT)-Booster-1, OPV –Booster
5–6 years	DPT-Booster-2
10 years	Tetanus and adult Diphtheria (Td)
16 years	Td
Pregnant Mother	Td-1, Td-2 or Td-Booster***

Source: https://nhm.gov.in/New_Updates_2018/NHM_Components/Immunization/report/National_%20Immunization_Schedule.pdf
* PCV in selected states/districts: Bihar, Himachal Pradesh, Madhya Pradesh, Uttar Pradesh (selected districts) and Rajasthan; in Haryana as a state initiative
** JE in endemic districts only
*** One dose if previously vaccinated within three years

Box 4.5 Mid-Day Meal Scheme in India

There is a provision for providing food to school-going children in several countries. This measure not only provides nutritional supplements to children but has also been found effective in improving enrolment and attendance and reducing dropouts among school-age children (Jayaraman, & Simroth, 2015), particularly in children of low-income groups.

In India, though isolated efforts to provide food to school students were made by states like Tamil Nadu, Gujarat, Kerala, and the Union Territory of Pondicherry, a nationwide programme was launched in 1995 under the National Programme of Nutritional Support to Primary Education (NP-NSPE). It aimed at providing nutritious meals to school children to address malnutrition, encourage regular attendance in schools, improve health, and social equity, and enhance learning outcomes. It is now one of the largest school meals programmes, benefitting 11.80 crore children studying in grades 1 to 5 (since 1995) and also grades 6 to 8 (since 2008) in 11.20 lakhs government, government-aided, local bodies schools, as well as the EGS/AIE centres including *Madrasas* and *Maqtabs* supported under SSA/*Samgra Shiksha* across the country. The scheme is proposed to be extended to students studying in pre-primary or *Balvatikas* in government and government-aided primary schools.

Since its introduction at the national level, the Mid-Day Meal Scheme has undergone various changes to enhance its reach, efficiency, and impact. The scheme was initially introduced in 2,408 revenue blocks for students in grades 1 to 5. By the year 1997–98, it was introduced in all blocks of the country. The students studying in EGS/AIE centres were covered in 2002. In 2003, the government introduced the provision of cooked meals in addition to the existing option of providing dry rations. The Supreme Court of India issued a directive in 2004, making the provision of cooked mid-day meals in all government and government-aided primary schools mandatory. This directive added legal weight to the scheme and ensured its implementation across the country.

In 2006, the government introduced nutritional guidelines, specifying the minimum nutritional content and quality standards for the meals. From 2008–09, the scheme was extended to students studying in grades 6 to 8. The scheme was integrated with the Integrated Child Development Services (ICDS) programme, which focuses on early childhood care and development. The National Food Security Act was enacted in 2013, which included the provision of mid-day meals as a legal entitlement for children aged 6–14 years. The government introduced the use of technology in 2015 to monitor the scheme effectively. Initiatives like the Mid-Day Meal Monitoring System (MDMMS) and mobile applications were implemented to track the scheme's progress, enhance transparency, and address issues promptly. In recent years, the government has placed a greater emphasis on improving the quality of meals, including diversification of food items, hygiene standards, and kitchen infrastructure. Efforts have been made to leverage public-private partnerships, community participation, and local sourcing of food grains to ensure efficiency and sustainability. Since 2021, the scheme is known as the Pradhan Mantri POSHAN ((*POshan SHAkti Nirman*) Scheme.

The scheme places emphasis on providing wholesome and balanced meals to children. The meals typically consist of items like rice, dal (pulses), vegetables, fruits, and milk. The calorific value of a mid-day meal has been fixed at a minimum of 450–700 calories and 12–20 grams of protein by providing 100–150 grams of food grains (rice/wheat) per child/school day, at the primary and upper primary stages respectively. The quality of the meals is monitored through regular inspections and adherence to prescribed standards.

Studies endorse the fact that MDMS has made a positive impact on the enrolment of children in the schools, particularly, socially disadvantaged groups and girls (Kaur, 2021). An increase in the retention rate of students has also been reported (e.g., Bonds, 2012; Dreze & Goyal, 2003; Paltasingh, & Bhue, 2022). Studies also show that the nutritional status of students has increased (Paltasingh, & Bhue, 2022). It serves as a safety net for children (Singh et al., 2014).

Continuous feeding of mid-day meals to students in schools has a positive effect on learning achievement (Afridi et al., 2014; Chakraborty & Jayaraman (2019). The results of studies examining the effect of MDMS on social equity are inconclusive. For example, studies (Dreze & Goyal, 2003; Khera, 2006; Thorat & Lee, 2005) reported some forms of discrimination in various parts of the country on account of caste. However, there are another set of studies (e.g., Angom, 2008; Chauhan, 2011; Wizarat, 2009) which report that MDMS has been successful in breaking the caste, class, and gender barriers, and all students take the meals together.

In sum, it can be said that the mid-day meal has been successful in achieving its goal. It has led to improved attendance and retention of students in the school and enhanced their nutritional status. It has also been able to address the issue of social equity to some extent. However, some more efforts are required to tackle the social equity issue throughout the country.

Physical Development: An Indian Approach

The Indian conception of physical development encompasses a holistic approach that recognizes the interconnectedness of the body, mind, and spirit. Physical development is considered an integral part of overall well-being and is closely linked to spiritual and mental growth. Consider the following verse from Bhagavad Gita (18.78):

Yatra yogeshwaraḥ Kṛṣhṇo yatra pārtho dhanurdharaḥ ।
Tatra śrīr vijayo bhūtir dhruvā nītiḥ matir mama ॥.

(Wherever there is Shri Krishna, the Lord of all Yoga, and wherever there is Arjun, the supreme archer, there will also certainly be unending opulence, victory, prosperity, and righteousness. Of this, I am certain.)

The verse highlights that when the mind (represented by Krishna) and the body (represented by Arjuna) are in harmony and aligned with higher principles, there will be prosperity, success, strength, and righteousness in life. It acknowledges the interplay between the physical, mental, and spiritual dimensions and the importance of their integration for overall well-being. Some key aspects of the Indian conception of physical development are enumerated here.

Yoga and Ayurveda

Yoga emphasizes the integration of physical postures (*asanas*), breathing exercises (*pranayama*), and meditation for achieving physical and mental harmony. Ayurveda promotes a balanced lifestyle, including proper diet, exercise, and daily routines to maintain physical health.

Mind–Body Connection

The Indian view recognizes the significance of mental and emotional well-being for optimal physical health. Practices such as meditation and mindfulness are often incorporated to cultivate mental clarity and inner peace, which are believed to positively impact physical health.

Traditional Physical Activities

Traditional Indian physical activities, such as martial arts (e.g., Kalaripayattu), classical dance forms (e.g., Bharatanatyam), and traditional sports (e.g., Kabaddi), are not only seen as physical exercises but also as artistic expressions and means of self-discipline. These activities promote physical strength, agility, endurance, and a sense of cultural identity.

Dietary Considerations

The importance of a balanced and nutritious diet for overall health has been recognized. Traditional Indian cuisine, with its emphasis on whole grains, legumes, vegetables, and spices, provides a rich source of essential nutrients. Recently, the importance of millets has been recognized and the United Nations celebrated 2023 as the International Year of Millets.

Social and Environmental Factors

The Indian view acknowledges the influence of social and environmental factors on physical health. It recognizes the importance of supportive social relationships, community engagement, and a harmonious relationship with nature for overall well-being.

Healing Practices

India has a long history of traditional healing practices, such as Ayurvedic medicine, naturopathy, and traditional massages (e.g., Ayurvedic *Panchakarma*). These practices focus on restoring balance and vitality in the body and are often used in conjunction with physical exercises and lifestyle modifications.

The Indian conception of physical development is diverse and varies across different regions and cultural practices within India. While traditional perspectives continue to be valued, modern approaches to physical development, including Western scientific knowledge, are also incorporated into contemporary Indian lifestyles.

Pattern of Motor Development

Motor development typically follows a consistent sequence. For example, a baby who learns to sit early also walks early. Motor development occurs in stages and follows two developmental laws. Gross motor development follows the cephalocaudal law and fine motor development follows the proximodistal law. According to cephalocaudal law, development proceeds in a head-to-tail or top-to-bottom direction. The law suggests that during prenatal and early postnatal stages, the head and upper body develop before the lower body and extremities. For example, during embryonic development, the brain and sensory organs begin to form and develop earlier than the legs and feet. Similarly, infants typically gain control over their head and neck muscles before they develop the ability to sit up, crawl, and eventually walk.

The proximodistal law proposes that development tends to progress from the centre or core of the body outward to the extremities. In other words, children typically gain control over muscles and motor skills in the central parts of their bodies before they gain control over the muscles in their arms, legs, and fingers. For example, infants start by being able to control their torso and trunk, followed by gaining control over their arms and hands, and finally developing fine motor skills in their fingers. This principle can be observed in various aspects of motor development. For instance, infants learn to sit up before they can crawl, and they develop the ability to reach and grasp objects before they can perform more intricate tasks such as writing.

Gross Motor Development

Locomotion is a good example of gross motor development. As per cephalocaudal law, the first stage in the locomotion sequence is head movement. Studies indicate that average or normal children usually lift their heads for a short period when on their stomachs by about the second month, and their head is held steady in a sitting position by about the fourth month (WHO-ICMR Study, 1991). Both these skills are critical for later development because they allow the child an increased visual field and offer more opportunities for learning new skills. Urban–rural differences were also observed in some of the gross motor skills such as lifting the head while on the stomach, standing alone, walking backwards, and hopping. Urban children attained these skills at a slightly younger age. Other gross motor skills such as standing on one foot with support, carrying a wooden block on the head, and getting up from a squatting position are attained at a younger age by rural tribal children as compared to urban children (WHO-ICMR Study, 1991).

Fine Motor Development

Vision plays an important role in the acquisition of fine motor skills. Seeing not only stimulates a child to learn and do more, but eye–hand coordination is important for fine motor activity such as grasping an object. Children begin to develop voluntary control over their hand movements and can grasp objects between four and seven months of age. Initially, they use a palmar grasp (grasping with the whole hand), which later evolves into a pincer grasp (using the thumb and index finger) around 9–12 months of age. Around 8–10 months, babies learn to release objects intentionally rather than involuntarily dropping them. Preschool-aged children typically develop the ability to hold and control a pencil or crayon, and they start to draw recognizable shapes and letters. This milestone varies but is often observed between three and five years of age. Box 4.6 contains developmental milestones for Indian children.

Box 4.6 Developmental Milestones for Indian Children

The Indian Academy of Pediatrics (2021) has provided a short list of activities that we can expect Indian children to do at different ages.

2 months:
- Smiles on social contact; listens to voice; and coos. Follows objects with eyes.

3–6 months:
- Holds head steady; turns over; sits with support.
- Reaches out; grasps large objects; enjoys mirrors.
- Laughs aloud; makes sounds; shows joy, interest, fear, and surprise.

6–9 months:
- Sits unsupported; crawls
- Observes, picks, transfers from hand to hand; bangs and drops large objects.
- Notices small objects → raking movement → immature grasp → mature pincer grasp with thumb and index finger (9 months)
- Waves bye-bye; separation anxiety

9–12 months:
- Stands without support.
- Plays with objects; enjoys inserting and dumping out.
- Retrieves hidden toy; enjoys "peek-a-boo".
- Points to body parts.
- Responds to his name and to "No".
- Two to three words with meaning.
- Non-verbal gestures.

15 months:
- Walks alone
- Follows simple commands; names familiar object

18 months:
- Runs stiffly
- Explores
- Scribbles
- 10 words; names pictures

24 months:
- Runs well; climbs stairs; jumps
- Tower of seven cubes; imitates horizontal stroke
- Three-words sentences
- Handles spoon; helps to undress.

36 months:
- Rides tricycle; throws ball.
- Copies circle; imitates cross.
- Knows age and sex; counts three objects; speaks fluently. Listens to stories.
- Plays simple games; pretends.
- Helps in dressing; washes hands.

It may, however, be noted that children vary greatly in the attainment of specific skills. Some children achieve at a faster pace and others may be slow. The traditional explanation of motor development is based on the process of maturation. That is, children acquire the abilities for gross and fine motor skills biologically (Gesell, 1940/1993). Genetic predispositions, such as inherited muscle strength and body composition, can influence the rate and quality of motor skill acquisition. Other factors, such as opportunities available for the development of skills, also influence skill acquisition (Adolph, 2008).

Assessment of Motor Skills

The psychological assessment of motor development during infancy is made through observation using a schedule or checklist. The child's attainment of skills is compared to a reference standard in terms of the age of the child. This method is used because the baby is mostly lying down or held in the mother's lap. Schedules and checklists used for assessing the psychomotor and psychosocial development of infants and preschool children include a series of developmental skills in broad areas of gross and fine motor development, adaptive behaviour, and psychosocial development. For older children, tests of cognitive functions are also used. The most well-known scales for the assessment of motor development are the Gesell Developmental Schedule and Bayley Scales of Infant Development. Muralidharan (1971) modified the Gesell scale for the Indian condition. The Indian adaptation of Bayley scales is also available (Balasundaram & Avulakunta, 2022; Pathak, 1990). The National Institute for the Mentally Handicapped (Peshawaria & Venkatesan, 1992) has developed Behavioral Assessment Scales for Indian Children With Mental Retardation (BASIC-MR). Other scales developed in the West can also be used after developing norms for the Indian context.

Factors Affecting Motor Development

Motor development is influenced by several factors including stimulation at home, opportunities to practice, nutrition, and health conditions (Murthy & Dharmayat, 2020). Intellectual and social–emotional development are related to the emergence of motor skills and the age of attaining them. Intellectually brighter children attain complex motor skills earlier than backward children. Certain emotional states like fear and anxiety may have a negative influence on motor development. Accidents and parental anxiety may prevent a child from practising new skills. Overenthusiasm on the part of parents may develop a fear of failure among the children against parental expectations.

Studies in India (e.g., WHO-ICMR Study, 1991) indicate age differences in rural–urban children in the attainment of motor skills. Urban children are found better in the development of fine motor skills (Muralidharan, 1971; Murthy & Dharmayat, 2020); rural tribal children perform better at tasks such as sustained attention to objects, reaching for and grasping objects, and picking up a pebble (WHO-ICMR Study, 1991). Other factors like debilitating diseases, chronic and repeated infections, and a lack of nourishing diet negatively influence motor development. They can impair the immune system and thereby not only cause growth retardation but also affect physical strength and motor function in children.

In sum, physical growth and motor development are interrelated and mutually interdependent. Progress in physical development facilitates the acquisition of more complex motor skills, which in turn stimulates further development. Acquisition of gross and fine motor skills may vary across children of different ecological backgrounds. This may be due to opportunities available to children to master different skills.

Relationship of Motor Development With Other Aspects of Development

Motor skills not only develop and mature in themselves but also influence the development of skills in other areas. For example, the development of manipulatory skills during infancy facilitates the development and functioning of basic mental processes. Malfunctions in motor coordination are the earliest signs of possible brain damage. Dyspraxia (difficulty with movement and coordination) is one of several such diseases.

While developing motor skills, the child learns to make finer movements by using her hands. The development of fine motor skills involves maturity in hand movements, which progresses initially from the use of both hands to finally a preference for either the right or the left hand. The preference for the use of either hand is referred to as handedness. Also, the development of fine prehension (i.e., the act of grasping) involves the integration of visual and neuromuscular components (hand–eye coordination).

Handedness: Exploring Manual Preference

Handedness refers to the preference for using one hand over the other in performing manual tasks. The majority of individuals (about 90%) are right-handed, meaning they prefer using their right hand for tasks such as writing, throwing, and grasping objects. However, a significant minority (about the remaining 10%) comprises left-handers, ambidextrous individuals (those who lack a strong hand preference), and mixed-handers (who prefer different hands for different tasks). A recent meta-analysis of 262 studies estimated the prevalence of left-handedness at 10.60% (Papadatou-Pastou et al., 2020). Mandal et al. (1992) reported a 6.8% incidence of left-handedness in India. In a tribal Mizo student population in India, Srivastava (1987) found an overall incidence of 7.24% (boys 8.19%, girls 6.21%; rural 6.93%, urban 7.51%). The number of male left-handers is usually higher than females. Further, the incidence of left-handedness is higher (15%) in young people (below 20 years of age) than in the elderly above 50 years of age (5%) (Coren & Halpern, 1991).

Theories of Handedness Development

Several theories have been proposed to explain the development of handedness. Twin studies have shown that identical twins are more likely to have concordant hand preferences than non-identical twins, indicating a hereditary influence (Medland et al., 2006; Procopio, 2001). However, the specific genetic mechanisms underlying handedness remain unclear.

According to another theory, the brain's division of labour between the left and right hemispheres, known as brain lateralization, plays a role in handedness. Annett (2002) suggests that the left hemisphere of the brain, which controls the right hand in the majority of individuals, is dominant in most right-handers, and it is responsible for language and fine motor control. In contrast, left-handers may exhibit either right-hemisphere dominance or a more distributed pattern of brain activation. The right hemisphere is suggested to be more involved in visuospatial processing. The prenatal environment (such as exposure to differing levels of hormones including testosterone) may also influence handedness development (Tan & Tan, 2001).

Cultural attitudes and practices do influence the expression and perception of handedness (Coren, 1993). Some cultures (e.g., agrarian societies) favour right-handedness, considering left-handedness as unusual or even taboo. This may result in left-handed individuals being encouraged or forced to use their right hands for various activities. Indeed, a low prevalence of left-handedness has been repeatedly found in societies with high levels of conformity (MacManus, 2009; Suar et al., 2013). In contrast, hunting and fishing societies are more permissive and do not force their children to conform to a right-hand norm for daily activities (Dawson, 1977).

Implications for Development

Handedness has implications in various aspects of life. Right-handers have higher longevity, less prone to allergies, accidents, and schizophrenic disorders (for details, Mandal & Dutta, 2001). In a study (Misra et al., 2008), left tapping of the foot was found faster than right tapping in left-handers, and right tapping was faster than left tapping in right-handers. There was no difference between the left and right tapping performance in the mixed-handers. Research also reports differences in language processing, spatial abilities, and mathematical skills between right-handed and left-handed individuals. Left-handers exhibit a higher incidence of cognitive advantages such as divergent thinking, including mathematical thinking, arts, aesthetics, and creativity. As language processing occurs in the left hemisphere, right-handers seem to have an advantage in language competence. Handedness can influence performance in sports and the choice of professions. Certain sports, such as tennis or boxing, may favour right-handers due to the prevalence of right-handed opponents. Additionally, left-handers are often overrepresented in professions such as art, music, and mathematics.

In India, all auspicious works are done by the right hand. The left hand is considered unclean. Therefore, the use of the left hand is not promoted. In recent years, left-handedness has been accepted in urban centres. In rural areas, left-handers are forced to switch over to the use of the right hand.

Hand–Eye Coordination: A Skill for Motor Control and Performance

Hand–eye coordination is a skill that allows individuals to synchronize visual perception with motor movements. It refers to the ability to coordinate visual information processing with manual dexterity, enabling precise control and manipulation of objects. The visual system processes information about the object's location, speed, and trajectory while the motor system translates this information into appropriate motor commands. Indian mythology is replete with tales of great people and deities who possessed exceptional hand–eye coordination. Arjuna's skills to shoot the eye of a fish, which was positioned on top of a rotating wheel, by merely looking at its reflection in the water; Lord Shiva's cosmic dance (i.e., *Tandava*) representing his rhythmic coordination between his hands, feet, and eyes; and Goddess Durga's flawlessly handling multiple weapons simultaneously are some examples.

Hand–eye coordination is essential for both children and adults as it underpins numerous activities across various domains, including sports, fine motor skills (such as writing, drawing, painting, sewing, playing musical instruments, and performing surgical procedures), and occupations (such as surgeons, dentists, artists, craftsmen, and pilots). Athletes with superior hand–eye coordination exhibit enhanced accuracy, reaction time, and overall performance. Hand–eye coordination facilitates various everyday tasks, including driving, cooking, typing, using electronic devices, and playing video games. Several factors contribute to the development and refinement of hand–eye coordination skills including sensory integration (i.e., the ability to integrate and process sensory information from multiple sources, particularly visual and proprioceptive inputs), practice and experience, neurological development, clear vision, knowledge of the results (Thomas et al., 1982), and so on.

Role of Toys in Child Development

Toys are powerful tools that foster cognitive, social, emotional, and physical growth. The act of playing with toys engages children's senses, stimulates their imagination, enhances their problem-solving abilities, and promotes crucial skills necessary for their overall development (Tarapore, 1998). Using toys in childhood influences the development of key skills (Tom & Gisli, 2017). It must be remembered that it is not necessary to go out and play with toys; rather, play is everywhere. For example, exploring nature is also a kind of play. Anything which stimulates the child's creativity and imagination is a play.

Toys contribute to the development of fine and gross motor skills. According to a study by Logan and colleagues (2017), active play with toys improves motor skills and physical fitness in children. Toys are instrumental in nurturing cognitive development in children. Simple toys like building blocks, puzzles, and shape sorters encourage imagination, logical thinking, spatial awareness, and problem-solving skills. They play an important role in developing social skills, such as negotiation, solving conflicts, perspective-taking, and prosocial behaviours. Toys also serve as companions to children facilitating emotional exploration and understanding. Research (e.g., Havighurst et al., 2011) has shown that doll play improves children's emotional regulation and empathy skills. The colour of the toy plays a role in the development of emotions and, if implemented in the design, can motivate children to learn Saikia et al. (2023).

Diversity in Indigenous Toys and Play in India

The rich cultural heritage of India is deeply intertwined with traditional toys and play. These indigenous toys reflect the diversity, creativity, and cultural ethos of various regions across the country. Passed down through generations, research (e.g., Dhanakar, 2020; Yadav, 2020) has shown that these indigenous toys not only entertain children but also serve as educational tools, fostering creativity, imagination, and motor skills. Variations in the use of toys are observed across culture, age, gender, and economic status. There has been a shift, in recent years, in gender-specific use of toys with girls preferring to play with toys traditionally considered male-oriented (Guha & Murthy, 2017). Some of the most popular indigenous toys are *Guddi Bazi* (Kite Flying), *Latto* (Spinning Tops), *Pachisi* (*Ludo*), *Chaupar (Pallanguzhi)*, *Moksha Patamu* (Snakes and Ladders), *Gulel* (slingshot), etc. Dolls and puppets are also very popular, each representing a specific region's cultural and artistic traditions. *Kathputli* from Rajasthan, *Gombeyata* from Karnataka, and *Bommalattam* from Tamil Nadu are some examples. Several traditional sports played in India (e.g., Kabaddi, Kho-Kho, *Gilli-Danda*, and *Lagori*) have a strong connection to indigenous culture.

Indigenous toys and play in India not only entertain children but also offer a glimpse into the rich heritage and creativity of the country. Preserving and promoting these traditional toys and play forms are essential for nurturing cultural identity, creativity, and playfulness among future generations in India. Recognizing the significance of toys, NCERT (2022a) developed a handbook for toy-based pedagogy for the development of skills like critical thinking, problem-solving, and holistic development of children. In this context, nursery books also play important roles in fostering the motor, cognitive, and socio-emotional development of young children (see Box 4.7).

Box 4.7 Nursery Books: Nurturing Young Minds Through Literature

Nursery books introduce young children to the joys of reading and plant the seeds of a lifelong love for literature and learning. These books, with their engaging visuals, interactive elements, and captivating stories, open doors to new worlds, foster creativity, and nurture young minds as they embark on their literary journey.

Nursery books have many salient features. First, the books are known for vibrant, colourful, and eye-catching illustrations. These visuals not only attract young readers but also aid in comprehension, as children can associate images with the text and develop visual literacy skills. Second, nursery books often feature simple and repetitive text patterns, which help young readers grasp basic vocabulary, sentence structure, and language patterns. Third, many nursery books incorporate interactive elements like lift-the-flap, touch-and-feel, or pop-up features. These interactive elements stimulate sensory exploration, promote fine motor skills, and make reading a hands-on and multisensory experience. Lastly, these books typically feature engaging and age-appropriate storylines that capture children's attention and spark their imagination. These stories often revolve around themes such as friendship, family, emotions, animals, nature, and everyday experiences that children can relate to. The use of these books depends on home literacy environment (Pandith et al., 2022).

There are several benefits of nursery books. They facilitate language acquisition and expand vocabulary as the books introduce young children to new words, sentence structures, comprehension abilities, and language patterns. The books stimulate cognitive development by encouraging critical thinking, problem-solving, and memory recall. Through stories and characters, children learn about cause and effect, sequencing, and logical reasoning. These books also foster emotional and social development by exploring different emotions, relationships, and social situations and thus, help children develop empathy, emotional intelligence, and social skills. Their role in igniting children's imagination and creativity is immense as they transport children to new worlds, introduce fantastical characters, and inspire imaginative play. They encourage children to think beyond the literal and explore their ideas and storytelling abilities.

In India, several popular nursery books are loved by children. Some of the popular nursery books are *Panchatantra* by Vishnu Sharma, *Chhota Bheem* series by Rajiv Chilaka, *The Jungle Book* by Rudyard Kipling, *Tenali Raman Stories*, *Akbar and Birbal Stories*, *Malgudi Days* by R.K. Narayan, *Jataka Tales* depicting the previous lives of Gautama Buddha before he attained enlightenment, and *Geronimo Stilton* series.

As a follow-up of National Education Policy 2020, the Ministry of Education (Government of India) has brought out *Jadui Pitara* (as per the release by the Press Information Bureau on 20 February 2023) in 13 Indian languages. *Jadui Pitara* comprises playbooks, toys, puzzles, posters, flashcards, storybooks, and worksheets and reflects the local culture, social context, and languages to pique curiosity and accommodate the diverse needs of learners in the foundational stage (3–8 years of age).

Healthy Living: A Lifelong Commitment

Healthy living is a lifelong commitment. It is about making small, sustainable changes and adopting healthy habits that promote overall well-being. In this section, two aspects of healthy living, that is, organic living and yoga and holistic development, are discussed.

Organic Living

The theme of organic living emphasizes adopting a sustainable and environment-friendly lifestyle. The Indian tradition for long has emphasized the importance of living in harmony with nature, maintaining a balanced lifestyle, and consuming foods that promote well-being. They convey the principles of Ayurveda and the holistic approach to living a healthy and sustainable life.

The concept of organic living encompasses various aspects of our lives, including food, agriculture, personal care products, and overall well-being. It involves the adoption of strategies, such as (a) organic farming which prioritizes the use of natural fertilizers, crop rotation, and biological pest control; (b) eco-friendly practices by reducing waste, conserving energy, adopting renewable energy sources, minimizing the use of plastics, and practising responsible consumption; (c) organic living practices by avoiding synthetic pesticides and fertilizers; and (d) being mindful of the products we use and the impact they have on our health and the environment.

The organic farming movement in India has witnessed a surge in recent years, with farmers adopting organic practices to protect soil health, conserve water resources, and safeguard biodiversity (also see Chapter 14). The demand for organic food has also increased as people have become more conscious of the benefits of consuming chemical-free, nutritious produce. India has witnessed the rise of organic food markets and stores, offering a wide range of organic products, including fruits, vegetables, grains, dairy products, and spices. The Indian government has taken several initiatives to promote organic living. The National Program for Organic Production (NPOP) and the Pramparagat Krishi Vikas Yojana (PKVY) support the adoption of organic farming practices and provide financial assistance to farmers. Additionally, the Swachh Bharat Abhiyan and campaigns like "Say No to Plastics" promote sustainable practices and environmental conservation.

Yoga and Holistic Development

Yoga is a holistic discipline that encompasses physical postures and exercises (*asanas*), breathing exercises (*pranayama*), deep relaxation, and meditation. Beyond being a mere exercise routine, yoga offers a comprehensive approach to personal growth and development, fostering a harmonious balance between the body, mind, and spirit. B.K.S. Iyengar (cited in Carr, 2022) observed that yoga is like music. The rhythm of the body, the melody of the mind, and the harmony of the soul create the symphony of life. By integrating various practices, yoga facilitates the enhancement of physical health, mental well-being, emotional stability, and spiritual awakening. However, research (e.g., Pandit & Satish, 2014) shows that the positive effects of yoga on a cluster of factors termed as "positive health" emerge only in the long term.

Physical Development

Regular practice of yoga *asanas* helps in developing strength, flexibility, and balance. *Asanas* stimulate the muscular and skeletal systems, improving overall physical fitness. Research has shown that yoga can alleviate chronic pain, enhance cardiovascular health, and reduce the risk of conditions such as hypertension, diabetes, and obesity (Field, 2016). The positive effect of yoga on physical health among visually impaired children has also been reported (Mohanty, 2017).

Mental and Emotional Well-Being

The mind–body connection in yoga plays a vital role in promoting mental and emotional well-being. Through mindful movement and breath awareness, yoga cultivates a state of present-moment awareness, reducing stress, anxiety, and depression (Nanthakumar, 2018; Ranjani et al., 2023; Woodyard, 2011). Telles et al. (2013) found a positive effect of yoga on improving self-esteem. Regular practice of meditation and mindfulness helps individuals develop emotional resilience, self-awareness, and the ability to manage negative thoughts and emotions

(Cramer et al., 2018). Nagaratti (2020) found significant improvement in quality of life (including physical, psychological, social relationships, and environmental domains) among adults. Further, yoga positively influences cognitive function, memory, attention, and concentration (Gothe et al., 2016).

Spiritual Growth

Yoga delves into the realm of spirituality, providing a pathway to self-realization and inner growth. Yoga philosophy embraces concepts such as unity, interconnectedness, and finding one's true nature. This spiritual exploration contributes to a sense of purpose, meaning, and a greater understanding of the interplay between mind, body, and spirit.

Social Harmony

Yoga's impact extends beyond the individual to the social realm. The practice of yoga promotes ethical principles such as non-violence, truthfulness, and compassion. These principles form the foundation for harmonious relationships and the development of empathy towards others. By cultivating qualities of kindness and understanding, yoga practitioners contribute to creating a more compassionate and interconnected society.

Yoga, thus, serves as a powerful catalyst for holistic development, improving physical health, mental well-being, and a deeper sense of spirituality. Moreover, yoga fosters a greater sense of connection with oneself, others, and the world, leading to the development of empathy and ethical values.

Overview

The study of physical and motor development reveals the intricate journey that unfolds as individuals grow and interact with their environment. This chapter has delved into the concepts of physical growth and motor development, recognizing that these processes are biological and deeply influenced by cultural, social, and environmental factors. The pattern of physical growth, from infancy through childhood and into adolescence, is marked by milestones that reflect the unique trajectory of each individual. However, these milestones are not isolated from broader societal concerns, as evident in discussions surrounding birth and mortality rates, obesity, and health norms. The importance of comprehensive care, as seen through immunization schedules and nutrition initiatives, underscores the imperative of ensuring a healthy start for every child.

Motor development, both gross and fine, adds another layer of complexity to this journey. As children master their physical abilities, they engage with the world in increasingly sophisticated ways. The significance of developmental milestones is particularly highlighted within the Indian context, where cultural norms and expectations shape the progression of motor skills. Moreover, the relationship between motor skills and other facets of development, such as handedness and hand–eye coordination, emphasizes the interconnectedness of different developmental domains. It is also crucial to recognize the role of play and education in fostering physical and motor development. As evident from the discussions, toys and literature serve as powerful tools that facilitate growth and learning. Moreover, adopting a holistic approach to healthy living, encompassing organic practices and practices like yoga emphasize the lifelong commitment required for optimal development.

In summary, physical and motor development are not isolated processes; they are threads intricately woven into the fabric of human growth. By understanding the nuances of these processes, acknowledging their cultural and contextual variations, and fostering environments that encourage healthy living and learning, we pave the way for individuals to embark on a journey of holistic development – one that encompasses the body, mind, and soul.

Key Terms

Birth Rate
Cultural, Social, and Environmental Influences on Physical Development
Fine Motor Development
Gross Motor Development
Health Norms
Handedness
Hand–Eye Coordination
Healthy Living Practices
Hormone
Immunization Schedules
Milestones Across Stages
Motor Development
Motor Development and Other Areas of Growth
Mortality Rates
Myelination
Nutrition Initiatives
Organic Living
Obesity
Ossification
Play
Physical Growth
Puberty
Patterns of Physical Growth
Yoga and Holistic Development

Questions for Reflection

1) How do cultural factors influence physical growth and motor development? Give examples from your context.
2) In what ways does the Indian approach to physical development differ from or align with global perspectives on child growth and motor skills?
3) Explore the significance of developmental milestones. How do these milestones contribute to understanding and assessing motor development?
4) Reflect on the interconnection between motor development and other aspects of child development, specifically focusing on handedness, hand–eye coordination, and the role of toys.
5) How do the practices like organic living and yoga contribute to a lifelong commitment to healthy living?

Suggested Further Readings

Book

Adolph, K. E., & Robinson, S. R. (2015). Motor development. In L. S. Liben, U. Müller, & R. M. Lerner (Eds.), *Handbook of child psychology and developmental science: Cognitive processes* (7th ed., pp. 113–157). John Wiley & Sons, Inc.

Websites/Online Resources

Indian Academy of Pediatrics (*iapindia.org*)
National Institute of Child Health and Human Development (NICHD) (*www.nichd.nih.gov/*)

5 Socialization and Development

Contents

Introduction	85
Nature of Socialization	86
Dynamics of Socialization	87
Variations in Parenting Styles	93
Patterns of Socialization in India	94
Box 5.1: Socialization: An Interplay of Continuity and Change	99
Building an Inclusive Society	101
Socialization and Development of Competencies	103
Overview	105
Key Terms	105
Questions for Reflection	106

Learning Objectives

After studying this chapter, the learner will be able to:

Explain the nature and contribution of socialization;
Identify and analyse the key agents of socialization;
Understand the different parenting styles and their impact on socialization outcomes;
Understand the nuances of socialization studies;
Explain the relationship between culture and changes in socialization patterns; and
Analyse contributions of socialization to cognitive, emotional, and social development.

Introduction

The chapter embarks on an exploration into the intricacies of socialization and development, where the profound influence of societal interactions on individual growth comes to the forefront. It begins with an examination of the nature of socialization, unravelling the fundamental dynamics that shape human behaviour and identity. The multifaceted agents of socialization

DOI: 10.4324/9781003441168-7

86 *Foundational Processes of Human Development*

(e.g., family, peer groups, schooling, mass media, religion, and culture) and their role in shaping perspectives are elucidated. Further, it focuses on the process of socialization as embedded in the Indian context. Delving into the rich tapestry of parenting, variations in parenting styles are discussed, offering insights into the diverse approaches that contribute to the development of young minds. Socialization practices in India are illustrated with the help of some exemplary studies and a nuanced comparison of traditional and modern views. One of the goals of socialization is building an inclusive society. Towards this end, the chapter addresses the unique challenges and experiences of children with disabilities and transgender persons. The intricate connection between socialization and the development of competencies is unveiled, highlighting the crucial role of this interplay in shaping well-rounded individuals. The chapter, thus, takes you on a thought-provoking journey, laying the groundwork for a comprehensive understanding of the process of socialization and its impact on human development and societal harmony.

Nature of Socialization

Human babies are born in families where a social environment awaits and welcomes their arrival. The newborn depends on others in the family/society to meet its needs. In this way, diverse social influences start operating from early life, helping the child to develop as a member of society as well as build their identity. Socialization stands for the set of processes through which children learn and acquire norms, values, beliefs, and customs of their family/community/society. It is a two-way process that begins during childhood and continues throughout life, helping individuals to become socialized members of society in diverse contexts. Socialization is crucial for developing an individual's identity, self-concept, social skills, and abilities to function effectively within a given social and cultural context.

Family, peers, and institutions such as schools, religious organizations, and the media play important roles in the socialization process. These are often called the agents of socialization. The family, especially the quality of the parent–child relationship reflecting positive and nurturing interactions, open and effective communication, mutual respect, trust, and emotional responsiveness play the most crucial role. Peer groups, particularly during adolescence, contribute to social, emotional, cognitive, and identity development, shaping individuals' understanding of themselves and others. Schools afford opportunities for children to interact with peers and learn from significant others such as teachers and parents of peers. They develop social skills and learn about teamwork and cooperation in school. Religious institutions provide a framework for understanding morality, spirituality, and the meaning of life. The media, including television, video games, and social media, influence children's attitudes, behaviours, and beliefs about gender, race, and other social issues. It may be noted that the socialization of children is also regulated by broader influences such as culture, gender, and socio-economic status. The study of socialization has been and continues to be a subject of multidisciplinary interest.

While conceptualizing socialization, sociologist G.H. Mead (1934) identified its two major types: primary and secondary. Primary socialization helps young children to learn the basic skills, values, and beliefs of their culture. The family is particularly important in this process, as children socialize through interactions with their parents and siblings. They learn basic social skills, such as how to interact with others, how to express and share emotions, and how to follow rules. In this context, family structure becomes a crucial factor. Primary socialization is crucial for the development of a stable sense of self. The process of secondary socialization occurs throughout life and involves learning more complex skills and behaviours that are necessary for functioning in specific social contexts. For example, individuals learn new skills and behaviours when they start a new job, join a new social group, or move to a new place. Secondary socialization refers to the deliberate efforts of individuals to actively seek out opportunities to master new skills and behaviours. It helps people to navigate more complex social situations.

Dynamics of Socialization

Socialization is a dynamic process that is shaped by the complex interplay of familial, educational, religious, cultural, and other influences. Additionally, in the Indian context, socialization refers to a complex interplay of celestial influences, symbiotic relationships, and deeply entrenched gender roles. The interweaving of spiritual beliefs, mythology, and societal norms creates a unique tapestry that shapes individual identities and societal structures. This section examines these and other aspects of the social fabric that contribute to socialization.

Agents of Socialization

Various agents of socialization are involved in shaping individuals during their developmental journey. Included among these agents are family, peers, school, media, religious institutions, and culture.

Family and Socialization

The role of the family is critical in the socialization process. There are primarily two types of family structures: nuclear and joint or extended. A nuclear family, popular in Western countries, consists of a married couple and their children living together in the same household. The extended families, prevalent in many African and Asian cultures, often include grandparents, aunts, uncles, and cousins living together in the same household or nearby. In the Indian context, joint families are more common in traditional and rural areas while nuclear families are more prevalent in urban areas. The ideology of the joint family influences resource distribution within a family even when most of its members spend some or the greater part of their lives in nuclear households (Uberoi, 2003). In addition to the two types, in recent years, same-sex families (families consisting of lesbian, gay, bisexual, and transgender), single-parent families (one parent with one or more children), blended families (two families merging into one with their children), grandparent families (grandparents and grandchildren), and so on are also on the rise.

Diverse family structures uniquely influence socialization practices by offering different demands and opportunities shaping how children perceive themselves and their place in society. The close relationships and daily interactions within a family unit contribute to the formation of a child's personality and behavioural style. The extended families provide additional support and resources, including emotional, financial, and social support, and often play a significant role in child-rearing. In single-parent households, children may experience an intense bond with one parent, necessitating increased self-reliance and adaptability (see Chaudhary & Shukla, 2019). Blended families introduce the challenge of navigating relationships with step-siblings and adapting to new parental figures, fostering resilience and interpersonal skills. Same-sex parent families challenge heteronormative expectations, encouraging children to embrace diversity and question traditional gender roles. In families with grandparents, there is an interplay between the wisdom of older generations and the needs of younger ones, leading to a reduction in the generation gap. Dual-career families in which both wife and husband work provide a new context for parenting, requiring the restructuring of responsibilities and participation in the socialization process.

Indian families are characterized by the transmission of cultural values between generations. Elders within the family hold a revered position as bearers of cultural wisdom. Respected for their experience and knowledge, grandparents and elder family members actively contribute to the socialization of young members. They play a crucial role in imparting cultural traditions, rituals, and moral values (Srinivas, 1996). Through daily practices, festivals, and religious ceremonies, joint families provide a rich cultural backdrop for socialization. Oral traditions of cultural transmission are still valuable. Indian families contribute to the socialization of gender roles, reinforcing traditional expectations. While changing social dynamics have influenced gender roles (Sinha, 1988), familial expectations continue to play a crucial role in shaping individual identities (Jeffery & Jeffery, 1996). With increasing degrees of social and spatial mobility, families are becoming nuclear.

Peers and Peer Groups

As children grow, peer groups become increasingly influential in the socialization process. Peer interactions provide opportunities to develop social skills, learn about conformity, and develop identity outside the family context. Cooley's (1902) concept of the "looking-glass self" suggests that individuals shape their self-concept based on how they believe others perceive them, emphasizing the role of peers in identity formation. During adolescence, peers play a pivotal role in identity formation. Adolescents observe and imitate the behaviours of their peers, acquiring new skills, attitudes, and social norms. Peer groups establish standards of acceptable behaviour and reasonableness. Thus, they shape the moral compass of individuals. The quality of peer relationships has been linked to emotional well-being and resilience in the face of stressors (Rubin et al., 2006).

In India, the peer group consists of individuals from various linguistic, religious, and regional backgrounds. The interactions within these groups expose individuals to a multitude of perspectives, influencing an individual's sense of self and fostering cultural awareness and inclusivity (Bhatia & Ram, 2001). Peer interactions in informal and academic settings contribute to the development of cognitive and social skills. As urbanization accelerates in India, peer groups in urban settings often reflect modern influences and global trends, influencing the fashion, language, and attitudes of the individuals (Appadurai, 1996).

Educational Institutions

Formal education institutions, such as schools, colleges, and universities, act as dynamic environments where individuals not only acquire academic knowledge but also internalize cultural norms, societal expectations, and interpersonal skills. According to sociologist Durkheim (1897), education fosters social integration by instilling shared values and promoting a collective conscience. Through curricula, classroom discussions, and extracurricular activities, students are exposed to moral and ethical standards and principles. Students also learn practical skills that prepare them for their roles as citizens, workers, and community members. Education also cultivates active and informed citizens capable of engaging in democratic processes and questioning societal norms.

In India, the curriculum often includes lessons on historical events, religious teachings, and cultural practices that are integral to the Indian way of life. It allows students to connect with their cultural heritage, promotes social cohesion and unity in diversity, and fosters a sense of pride and belonging (Kumar & Oesterheld, 2007). Education provides opportunities to marginalized communities for social mobility and challenge caste-based prejudices (Thorat &

Attewell, 2007). In the Indian context, efforts to encourage female school enrolment, scholarship programmes, and the introduction of gender-sensitive curricula aim to challenge traditional gender roles and empower women through education, thereby contributing to broader social change (Govinda & Sedwal, 2017). However, there is a gap in the educational opportunities available to different sections of the society. Thus, education in India serves as a potent agent of socialization, influencing individuals' identities, values, and perspectives.

Religious Institutions

Religious institutions impart moral values, ethical principles, and a sense of community. Religious institutions and practices are repositories of cultural values and beliefs passed down through generations. The rituals, ceremonies, and teachings within religious settings contribute to the preservation of cultural identity and shared values. Participation in religious activities provides individuals with a network of like-minded individuals, creating a support system and a sense of belongingness. Research suggests that religious individuals may experience greater psychological well-being and a sense of purpose, attributing their coping abilities to their faith (Pargament, 1997). In India, religious ceremonies, festivals, religious institutions, and rituals provide individuals with a sense of identity and belonging within the larger societal framework (Bhatia & Pathak-Shelat, 2019; Srinivas, 1966). The coexistence of various religions (i.e., Hinduism, Islam, Christianity, Sikhism, Jainism, and Buddhism) contributes to the cultural richness of Indian society, emphasizing pluralism, sharing, and mutual tolerance. Indeed, it resonates with Vedic wisdom that reality is one but perceived in different ways (*ekam sad viprah bahudhaa vadanti*).

In the contemporary period, mass media has emerged as a powerful agent of socialization. Television, the internet, and other media platforms shape cultural trends, influence public opinion, and inform people about societal norms and expectations. With globalization, social media is increasingly providing opportunities for individuals to connect with people from different backgrounds and cultures, learn new things, and share their own experiences and perspectives. Social media, being interactive, also provides platforms for social activism and advocacy. As Arnett (2007) has observed, digital media allows adolescents opportunities for identity formation, along with entertainment, coping, and identifying with a larger youth culture.

Social media have also been found to have negative effects on the aspects of social development. For example, it exposes individuals to harmful or inappropriate content, such as cyberbullying, pornography, hate speech, and fake news. Moreover, social media promote a culture of comparison and competition, leading to feelings of anxiety, depression, and low self-esteem. The overuse of technology and social media interferes with the development of social skills, such as face-to-face communication, conflict resolution, and empathy. The social life of teenagers is always susceptible to such influences (Singh, 2019). Excessive screen time interferes with sleep and physical activity, which are important for overall health and well-being. It is thus important to be aware of these effects and to use technology and social media in a responsible and balanced manner.

CULTURE AND CHANGES IN SOCIALIZATION PATTERNS

Culture stands as a dynamic agent of socialization. According to Rogoff (2003), human development is not simply a biological or psychological process but a cultural process. Family, education, media, and religion collectively contribute to the transmission of cultural values. Cultural variations are prominent in socialization practices. Thus, the parents in collectivistic cultures emphasize obedience, respect for elders, and family loyalty (Markus & Kitayama, 1991). In contrast, individualistic cultures emphasize characteristics such as independence, self-expression, and personal achievement (Triandis, 1995). Socialization practices in India have a strong emphasis on obedience and conformity to social norms and traditions (see Bhangaokar & Kapadia, 2021). However, as more young people are exposed to Western culture and values, they are increasingly questioning traditional norms and seeking greater autonomy in their lives. Cultural interactions lead to new patterns in socialization. John and Montgomery (2012) noted that Indian immigrants to the United States showed both blended (combination of autonomy and family centred) and traditional (ethnic behaviours and family centred) goals of socialization.

There are cultural variations in the practices the societies adopt to meet the requirements of their people and ecologies. In Western cultures, particularly in the United States and Europe, there is a prevailing trend of infants sleeping in separate cribs or bassinets. This practice aligns with the emphasis on independence and individualism within these societies (Brazelton, 1992). In contrast, many Asian cultures, such as Japan and China, encourage co-sleeping, where infants share the bed with their parents. This is often viewed as fostering a strong parent–child bond and promoting a sense of security (Teti et al., 2016). Indian parents consider children fragile, vulnerable, and needy and therefore do not leave them alone and unprotected during the night (Shweder et al., 1995). Research suggests that co-sleeping fosters a sense of security and attachment (Feldman, 2015).

Studies show that mothers' responses to their baby's crying vary across cultures. Japanese mothers tend to respond more promptly to crying, viewing it as a natural and expected behaviour. Japanese mothers instil a strong sense of dependence in their young children by being available at all times (Grossman et al., 1985). The American mothers employ strategies that encourage self-soothing, emphasizing the development of independence. German mothers remain quite unresponsive to their children's crying since they believe that infants should become independent at an early age and learn that they cannot rely on the mother's comfort at all times. Barry and Paxson (1971) found that the Kipsigis people of Kenya adopt a communal approach to caregiving. Infants are cared for by multiple individuals, leading to less immediate responses to crying. The Indian child-rearing practices are characterized by carrying the child by the mother or family members frequently, sleeping with it, nursing on demand, making little effort to control urination or defecation, and soiling accidents. As a result, the child develops a strong emotional attachment to the mother. This situation is, however, slowly changing, and there is an increase in direct maternal control over children's discipline and more training for responsibility and assertiveness.

As another example, force-feeding is a routine practice in Nigeria. In Europe and the United States, these techniques include feeding games, rewards for finishing a meal, punishment for not finishing a meal, and passive restraint. Indian mothers try to distract their children and offer them food again after some time. Kakar (1978) noted that Indian caregivers emphasize pleasure between the adult and the child and exercise little pressure to mould the child in a given direction.

Cultural variations are common in gender socialization. Girls are often socialized to be nurturing, emotional, and passive while boys are encouraged to be competitive, assertive, and independent (Eagly & Wood, 2013). In some societies, gender roles may be very rigidly defined while in others they may be more fluid and subject to change over time. These gender expectations are communicated through various social institutions, such as families, schools, and media, and significantly impact children's development and sense of identity (Ruble & Martin, 2018). The roles of boys and girls across cultures vary widely depending on geography, religion, history, and socio-economic status. In India, an increasing emphasis on gender equality and women's empowerment is being witnessed.

The transition from childhood to adolescence is marked by some sort of public recognition or rituals in many cultures. These rituals are used as a way of helping adolescents arrive at an understanding of their identities. For example, the beginning of adolescence is marked by *upanayana samaskara* in India. In North America, though there are no marked rituals, adolescence is characterized by graduation from high school to college, successful passing of a driver's test, marriage, or the first job. During adulthood, cultural variations are observed in the expected roles to be performed by the adult members. The European American cultures expect adults to accept responsibility for one's self, make independent decisions, and become financially independent. The Asian cultures, on the other hand, expect their adults to become capable of taking care of one's parents. Asian cultures tend to place greater value on the elderly than American or Western cultures do. Indian adolescents show respect for their parents and believe that parents want the welfare of their children (Kapadia, 2008).

The agents of socialization play an integral role in shaping individuals throughout their lives. From the foundational influence of the family to the pervasive impact of media and culture, each agent contributes to the development of an individual's identity and social integration.

Embeddedness in the Indian Context

Socialization in the Indian context is rooted in a rich tapestry of traditions, beliefs, and practices that have evolved over centuries. This section explores the embeddedness of socialization in India, focusing on symbiotic relationships, beliefs about celestial events, and gender dynamics.

Symbiotic Relationships and Interconnectedness

Symbiotic relationships, both in the natural world and within human societies, are integral to Indian socialization. The "self" in India is described as ensembled and relational (Misra & Gergen, 1993). That is, the identity of the person is situated in the group and collectivity. The Indian social reality, despite urbanization, industrialization, and liberalization, has maintained certain traditional features which inform the social arrangements and functioning of the cultural system. The core themes of *dharma, karma* (action), *neeti* (ethics), *gunas* (qualities), desire for children particularly the male child, observing various codes of conduct and rituals, symbiotic relationship between the child and parents, role of social hierarchy, and adherence to norms regulating affairs in everyday life emphasize the interconnectedness of individuals within a societal framework (Kakar, 1979; Kapadia & Sayajirao, 2009; Misra, 1995; Saraswathi & Pai, 1997; Sinha, 1977; Seymour, 1974, 1976). From family structures to community bonds, the symbiotic nature of relationships shapes socialization by instilling a sense of responsibility and interdependence.

According to Roland (1988), Indian society subscribes to an embedded notion of "we-self" – a kind of group ego in which a given individual is embedded. The physical closeness denotes the early symbiotic union between the Indian mother and her child which is carefully prolonged rather than gradually subdued. The young child is treated as godlike, which develops narcissistic well-being in the child (Roland, 1988). Kurtz (1992) noted that motherhood in India involves multiple mothering, in types and forms. The mother occasionally frustrates but regularly gratifies the child. In the joint family system, the task of gratifying or satisfying is shared by other family members. Outside the home, the task is shared by other male members of the family. The child belongs more to the family as a whole than to any one particular individual. Children are brought up in the context of "Many by Many" (many children by many adults) (Chaudhary, 2013). In rural households, the care of children is not the responsibility of parents alone. Rather, it is a shared activity, which is taken care of by older adult members of the family as well as siblings, cousins, visiting kin, and often even selected neighbours (Chaudhary et al., 2021). Social conventions and moral obligations keep this tradition alive (Sharma, 2003).

There is a strong belief shared in the traditional communities that parents transfer merits and demerits to their children. A son tends to follow in his father's footsteps and adopts his father's values, attitudes, and behaviours. The son is considered the father's seed, the daughter the mother's vine. Children reap the fruits of their parents, the same soul with the same habits and similar behaviour patterns. Thus, the parent–child relationship goes beyond biological inheritance and involves emotional bonds and shared experiences. Children are the reflection of their parents, carrying their parents' legacy and values forward into the future. They are viewed as extensions of their parents (*santati*) (Misra & Gergen, 1993). Within this orientation, socialization happens to be an occasion of self-articulation for many parents. The locus of this articulation is often perceived as lying within the parents themselves. Indian parents usually find it difficult to separate and distance themselves from their children. This situation characterizes the social life in rural India and less urbanized regions, which is changing in urban areas (Misra et al., 1999).

Misri (1986) conceptualized the Indian child in three dimensions: *human-divine, individualism-collectivism*, and *alterable-transformative*. The human-divine axis sees the child simultaneously as a creation of parents and a gift from God. The individualism-collectivism axis assumes that a child is both a collective being and a unique individual. The concept of *karma* emphasizes individuality while the relationship with family and others emphasizes collectivity. Lastly, the child is born being transformed by *samskaras* and rituals, the alterable-transformative axes. Within this paradigm, which rests on contradictions, society attempts to simultaneously integrate and separate the newborn. Being an agrarian society, a continuity between the worlds of an adult and that of a child is maintained through the constant sharing of life spaces (Kumar, 1996).

Beliefs About Celestial Events

The context of childhood in traditional Indian families involves a complex structure in which the role of diverse factors is visualized. Anandalakshmy (2013) has drawn attention to the pervasive role of "sacred" in the life of Indians. These are sacred places (temple, gurudwara, mosque, and place of pilgrimage), sacred time (*muhurta* for weddings and inaugurations based on planetary positions), and sacred persons (Gurus, Swamis, religious leaders, and learned elders). This cosmocentric view of life considers the alignment of stars and planets a significant source of influence. It is believed to influence destinies and life paths and plays a pivotal role in guiding major life decisions, such as marriage, career choices, and even child-rearing practices. The horoscope (or *janampatri*) is often made and consulted on such critical occasions. Zodiac predictions (or *Rashiphal*) constitute a popular column in newspapers, magazines, and on television. The fortune-telling industry thrives in India and fortune-tellers forecast the future of people based on the placement of stars at the time of one's birth. This kind of belief informs the scope for parental socialization. At the same time, it helps reduce uncertainties and overcome ambiguities in life (Misra et al., 1998). It gives a sense of connectedness to human beings to a larger reality (Anandalakshmy, 2013). Sundararajan et al. (2013) propose a concentric system framework for self for collectivistic or relational cultures which is multi-layered and inhabits a ritual space, a space marked by inner and outer self. The person is located within a series of interdependent and interactive forces that extend from family to nature and the gods and spirits.

Additionally, the socialization of children in India is influenced by factors like rituals (refer to Chapter 1 for *samskaras* or rituals) and norms; social structures like caste, region, and religion; and urban and rural environments (Bhogle, 1981, 1983; Chakkarath, 2013). Thus, the context or ecology of childhood in Indian society presents a world of multiple influences, though the texture of these influences is changing. This context has operated in India for many centuries.

Gender Roles and Socialization

Socialization for gender roles refers to the process by which individuals learn and internalize societal expectations, norms, and behaviour patterns associated with masculinity and femininity. It plays a crucial role in shaping gender identities and their understanding of gender roles within the respective cultures. This process occurs within the cultural context and is shaped by various social institutions, such as family, peers, media, and education.

Traditionally, in India, there are different expectations for boys and girls. Thus, male children are supposed to extend the family lineage, and girl children are considered *paraya dhan* (another's wealth) as they are to be given to someone in marriage (for details, Anandalakshmy, 2013). Accordingly, male and female children are expected to develop different traits in which parents and family members play a significant role. Girls are often taught to be obedient, submissive, and nurturing, whereas boys are encouraged to be strong, assertive, and competitive. From an early age, Indian girls are told that their proper place is in the home, fulfilling domestic duties and attending to the needs of men, whereas males learn that they are superior to women and must exercise authority over them (Das gupta, 1996). Gender-discriminatory practices are more common in rural areas and urban poor (Basu et al., 2017). Gender inequality is also manifested in certain harmful practices, such as higher rates of child marriage in the case of girls and female genital mutilation/cutting (Lashkar, 2021). These gendered expectations are reinforced through various social institutions, including schools, religious institutions, and media.

As India undergoes rapid modernization and urbanization, the dynamics of gender socialization are experiencing a shift. Educational institutions emerge as key agents challenging traditional gender roles by providing opportunities for both boys and girls to pursue academic and professional aspirations (Kapadia, 2019). Efforts are being made to develop gender-sensitive curricula to dismantle stereotypes and empower women through education, fostering a more egalitarian society. While traditional media may have reinforced stereotypes, the rise of digital platforms has enabled a more diverse representation of gender identities. The workplace, a modern societal institution, has become a major site for changing gender dynamics. As women increasingly participate in the workforce, notions of traditional gender roles are being challenged. However, the workplace itself can become an arena where gender-based stereotypes persist, highlighting the ongoing complexities in the socialization of gender roles in modern India.

In India, gender norms and expectations are deeply entrenched and have significant implications for individuals' lives and opportunities. Research (e.g., Ram et al., 2014) reports that gender discriminatory practices negatively influence mental health. To promote gender equality and reduce gender-based violence and discrimination, it is crucial to challenge traditional gender norms and promote inclusive gender socialization practices.

It may be noted that the agents of socialization operate in an intricate pattern of relationships. The unique form of embeddedness in Indian culture, characterized by symbiotic relationships, interconnectedness, the cosmocentric view of life, and the shaping of gender roles, underscores the multifaceted nature of socialization. Understanding these complex interactions is essential for appreciating the arena of influences that guide individual development and societal norms within the diverse cultural landscape of India.

Variations in Parenting Styles

Parenting styles are patterns of behaviour and attitudes that parents use in interactions with their children. Researchers have identified several kinds of parenting styles, each with its characteristics and effects on children's development. In a classic work, Baumrind (1991) has identified the following four parenting styles.

1) *Authoritative*

Authoritative parents are warm and supportive while also setting clear boundaries and expectations for their children. They are responsive to children's needs and emotions but also firm in enforcing rules and discipline. Children raised by authoritative parents tend to be independent and confident and have better social and emotional development and academic performance.

2) *Authoritarian*

Authoritarian parents are strict and controlling, often relying on punishment and harsh discipline to enforce rules. They are less responsive to their children's needs and emotions and may be less warm and affectionate. Children raised by authoritarian parents may tend to be obedient and have lower self-esteem, poorer social skills, and higher levels of anxiety and depression (Chao & Tseng, 2002).

3) *Permissive*

Permissive parents are warm and supportive but tend to have few rules or expectations for their children. They may avoid disciplining their children or setting limits, leading to a lack of structure and consistency in the child's life. Children raised by permissive parents may have lower academic performance and higher levels of impulsivity and risk-taking. Also, they struggle with issues of discipline and self-regulation (Baumrind, 1991).

4) *Neglectful/uninvolved parenting*:

This parenting style is characterized by low levels of warmth, responsiveness, and control. Neglectful/uninvolved parents are disengaged and uninvolved in their children's lives, often neglecting their basic needs. Children raised by neglectful/uninvolved parents tend to have poor social and emotional outcomes, such as low self-esteem, poor academic performance, and behavioural problems.

It has been found that in collectivist cultures, parenting is often more authoritarian and emphasizes obedience and conformity to group norms (Kim & Rohner, 2002). This is in contrast to individualistic cultures, where parenting tends to be more permissive and focuses on promoting independence and self-expression (Darling & Steinberg, 1993). In a review of studies conducted in India during 2000–2018 on parenting styles, Sahithya et al. (2019) reported that parental constructs such as warmth, acceptance, and encouragement are positively associated with child well-being and low levels of aggressive behaviour and substance abuse. Overprotection and control as well as rejection from parents were associated with behaviour problems, expression of indirect aggression, stress, anxiety, low self-esteem, feelings of loneliness, depression, and substance abuse in children.

Patterns of Socialization in India

This section is divided into two subsections. The first subsection describes a few exemplary studies on child-rearing practices in India. The second subsection compares the traditional and contemporary views on child-rearing practices.

Some Exemplary Studies

Some landmark studies on socialization practices in India have been conducted, which set the tone for future research. The number of such studies is large. For want of space, five studies have been identified which have been widely acclaimed. A summary of these studies is given in this section.

Six Cultures Study: Findings from India

The Six Cultures Study of Socialization, conducted by John Whiting and his colleagues, was a cross-cultural study that aimed to investigate the relationship between cultural factors and child-rearing practices (Whiting, 1963; Whiting & Whiting, 1975). The study was conducted in six different societies, including the United States, Mexico, Kenya, India, Japan, and the Philippines. The study in India was conducted by Leigh Minturn at Khalapur town in Uttar Pradesh (predominantly occupied by the Rajput community) during 1954–56. The researchers examined a wide range of factors, including child-rearing practices, cultural values, beliefs, and socialization practices.

One of the key findings of the study was the significant cross-cultural variation in child-rearing practices. For example, mothers in the United States were more likely to use verbal communication to control their children's behaviour while mothers in Kenya and the Philippines used more physical punishment. Additionally, American parents placed a higher value on independence and autonomy than parents in other cultures. It was also observed that religion and social class influenced child-rearing practices. Religious beliefs played a significant role in India and the Philippines while social class influenced child-rearing practices in the United States and Mexico. Twelve categories of social behaviour were found to occur in the children of all six cultures. These included nurturance, dependence, sociability, dominance, and aggression. The relative frequency with which children express any one of these kinds of behaviour was shown to depend to varying degrees upon their sex and age, what culture they were brought up in, and the situation or setting in which they were observed.

Indian parents emphasized the importance of early weaning of infants and introducing solid food. This practice was believed to help babies develop faster and become more independent. Indian parents also tended to be more protective of their infants and young children than parents in other cultures, and they typically kept their children closer to them. Indian parents placed a high value on obedience and respect for authority. Physical punishment was not commonly used as a disciplinary tool, and parents tended to rely more on verbal reprimands and scolding. Another significant finding was that education was highly valued in Indian culture, and parents placed a lot of emphasis on academic achievement. Children were expected to perform well in school, and parents often made significant sacrifices to ensure their children had access to education (Minturn, 1966).

Susan Seymour's Case Study of Child-Rearing

Seymour (1974) studied child-rearing practices in the old and new townships of Bhubaneswar. Seymour noted that traditionally children were raised in an extended family setting and had access to multiple caregivers, including grandparents, aunts, and uncles, which provided them with a strong support system. Children were taught to be obedient and respectful to their elders and were often discouraged from expressing their own opinions. However, with the process of modernization, Seymour noted that child-rearing practices in India have started to shift. For example, families became nuclear in the new township, and there are fewer caregivers available to look after children. Additionally, as women became more educated and entered the workforce, they were no longer able to devote as much time to child-rearing as they once did. Despite these changes, Seymour noted that many traditional child-rearing practices remain in India. For example, parents still place a strong emphasis on obedience and respect for elders.

Seymour (1976) also examined variations in child-rearing practices in relation to SES. She found that while nurturance was limited up to three years of age in low socio-economic status (SES) families, a much larger proportion of nurturant acts was directed to non-infants in the middle and upper SES families. The kind of nurturance act primarily consisted of comforting and nursing children in low SES families. The proportions of nurturant acts such as hand feeding, bathing, dressing, and offering instrumental help were relatively higher in middle- and upper-SES families for infants as well as for older age groups of children. This practice followed in low-SES families though developed self-reliance, interdependence, and responsible behaviours in children, they were more prone to adopting attention-seeking behaviour (such as teasing, hitting others, and destroying property). Seymour's research stresses the importance of recognizing the heterogeneity of behaviour which occurs in any society and which can be particularly striking in a society as complex as India.

After about three decades, Seymour (1999) reported the results of a follow-up in-depth study of families, who lived in a newly urbanized part of Bhubaneswar. She captured the voices and changing perspectives of women in a series of intergenerational interviews. It was noted that, in urban centres, parents have to rely on paid childcare providers who have different cultural backgrounds and may not share the same values and beliefs about child-rearing as the parents themselves. This created tension in terms of providing appropriate care to children.

Sudhir Kakar's "The Inner World"

Kakar (1978) provided an in-depth psychoanalytic study of childhood and society in India, drawing on both Western and Indian perspectives. He explores how traditional Indian family structures and cultural values shape the psychological development of children. He argues that Indian children experience a unique form of "psychic nurturance", which emphasizes emotional attachment and interdependence with the family rather than individual autonomy and independence. This psychic nurturance is reflected in the mother–child relationship, with mothers showing indulgence and overprotection.

Kakar also examines the role of religion and spirituality in Indian society and their impact on child development. He suggests that traditional Indian beliefs about *karma* and reincarnation may lead to a greater emphasis on conformity and obedience, which can be both beneficial and problematic for child development. He also explored how Indian culture and mythology shape children's imagination and contribute to the development of their inner worlds. Kakar offers a unique and nuanced perspective on childhood and society in India, highlighting how cultural values and family structures shape the psychological development of children.

S. Anandalakshmy's Study on Weaver's Community in Varanasi

Anandalakshmy and Bajaj (1982) explored the socialization practices in the weaver community of Varanasi. The research is based on observations and interviews with families in the weaver community. The weaver community is a close-knit, traditional community, where socialization practices are deeply embedded in everyday life. It was found that socialization in the weaver's community is based on an apprenticeship model, where children learn the craft of weaving from a young age by observing and assisting their parents and other adult weavers. Children learn by observing and participating in household tasks, and as they grow older, they are given more responsibilities. The research also highlighted the role of gender in socialization practices. Girls are expected to learn household tasks such as cooking and cleaning while boys are taught weaving skills. Anandalakshmy and Bajaj also noted that many children drop out of school early to help with the weaving business, which limits their opportunities for formal education. Overall, the research provides a detailed account of the socialization process of children in a weaver's community in Varanasi and highlights the importance of family, religion, and education in shaping the attitudes and behaviours of children in this context.

T.S. Saraswathi's Study of Socialization Practices in Gujarat

Saraswathi and Dutta (1988) conducted extensive fieldwork in the rural and urban slums of Baroda. They used a qualitative approach and employed methods such as participant observation, interviews, and case studies. They spent considerable time in the field, living with families, and observing their daily lives. They observed and analysed the everyday experiences of children, adolescents, and adults in these settings using content analysis and thematic analysis techniques.

It was observed that socialization practices were influenced by cultural beliefs, values, and practices. In the rural setting, socialization was centred on family and kinship relationships, and children were expected to conform to traditional gender roles and expectations. In contrast, in the urban slum setting, socialization was influenced by the economic and social conditions of the families, with children often taking on adult responsibilities to help support the family. It was also found that poverty had a significant impact on socialization practices in both settings. Children from poor families had fewer opportunities for education and were often expected to work from a young age. Poverty and socialization were intertwined, with poverty perpetuating certain cultural beliefs and practices that limited opportunities for social mobility. In the urban slum setting education provided a way for children to escape poverty and to challenge traditional gender roles and expectations. Overall, the study provides valuable insights into the complex interactions between poverty, culture, and socialization. The researchers highlighted the need for policies that address poverty and promote education as a means of breaking the cycle of poverty and improving social and cultural values.

Child-Rearing: Traditional and Contemporary Views

The traditional view of child-rearing is rich and varied. It prescribes practices based on *dharma* and *neeti* as reflected in *dharma shastras* (*Manusmriti*), epics such as *Ramayana* and *Mahabharata*, and others (see Kane, 1968; Prabhu, 1954). It is more prescriptive and stresses the interdependence between the individual and the larger social settings in which he/she is embedded (Saraswathi & Pai, 1997). Also, it considers the present life as stationary in an ongoing journey. Thus, it is related to the past and future lives. Indian people, therefore, believe that one's actions (*karmas*) continue to accumulate and contribute to (mis)fortune. Analysing the traditional and contemporary views, Krishnan (1998) noted the following salient features in child-rearing practices in India.

1) The traditional view considered a child as a pure, innocent, amoral, asocial being, born in the image of the divine, which represents inherited dispositions presumably carried over from previous births. The child needs love and protection but also needs to be moulded through discipline, which is more in the form of punishment than love-oriented. The contemporary view gives importance to affection and warmth, in place of punishment, generating a sense of acceptance rather than rejection in the child.
2) The parent–child bond, though considered special in the traditional view, parents are warned not to get too involved in this bond, which can be a source of *asakti* (attachment) and *moha* (illusion). The contemporary view, however, considers the parent–child relationship as symbiotic, one of mutual benefits.
3) The traditional view acknowledges mother and father as equally important, but in some situations, one may be glorified more than the other. It has been stated in the *Mahabharata* that wise men know that the father is an assemblage of all gods but, because of her affection, within the mother dwells the whole community of humans and gods. In contemporary

studies, the parental role is mother-centred, as the majority of the studies deal with maternal practices and attitudes.

4) The traditional view assigns parents a near-divine role: पितृ देवो भव, मातृ देवो भव, आचार्य देवो भव (Treat the father as God, treat the mother as God, treat the mentor as God). Some practices indicating parental authority, such as children touching their parents' feet and receiving their blessings, reinforce the superiority of parents. To a large extent, the contemporary view also portrays a similar picture. In place of love withdrawal or induction, mothers use power assertion as a disciplinary technique (Saraswathi, 1999; Saraswathi & Sundaresan, 1979). While the parenting style was more of an authoritative type in ancient times, it is more authoritarian in the contemporary period.

5) The traditional view prescribes a stage-wise differentiation in parental attitudes. The following verse emphasizes the different approaches that parents and educators should take in raising and guiding children through different stages of their development.

लालयेत् पञ्चवर्षाणि दशवर्षाणि ताड्येत् ।
प्राप्ते तु षोडशे वर्षे पुत्रं मित्रवदाचरेत् ॥

This verse states that for the first five years, a child should be treated with love and affection; for the next ten years, he should be treated with strict discipline; and upon attaining the age of 16 years, he should be treated like a friend and companion while always maintaining the role of a guide and teacher. Indian tradition also prescribes carrying out various *samskaras* to ensure that the physical–nurturant, social–moral, and intellectual needs of the child are fulfilled (refer to Chapter 1).

6) The Indian tradition prescribed practices keeping in view the gender of the child. The child-rearing practices were shaped diversely in the cases of boys and girls (Bhogle, 1991; Saraswathi & Dutta, 1990). There is a general preference for male children to ensure the continuation of the family tree. Though the girl child was treated as *Lakshmi* (the goddess of prosperity), she needed to be constantly protected. A son was to be brought up to be independent, courageous, educated, and equipped with skills required by the occupation followed by the family. The daughter was expected to be submissive, quiet, chaste, nurturant, and with the ability to maintain harmonious relationships within the family. These traditional gender roles and expectations are, however, gradually changing, especially among younger generations. Many families are now prioritizing education and career opportunities for daughters and encouraging them to pursue their interests and passions.

Role of Fathers in Child-Rearing

The study of parental role in child-rearing has been largely mother-centric, and very few studies have examined the father's role. A study by Roopnarine et al. (2013) shows that despite economic and social changes within the Indian family context, the ideological beliefs about men's and women's roles and responsibilities within the family have not changed appreciably. Fathers are more responsive to the needs of young children, but mothers still assume major responsibility for child-rearing. However, there has been a cultural shift in recent years, and the active involvement of fathers in parenting is increasing (Bhattacharyya & Pradhan, 2015). Contrary to the belief that fathers are strict disciplinarians, children viewed their fathers as loving, caring, and sharing individuals (Subramanyam & Chadha, 2002). In a recent study, Sriram (2023) examined children's accounts of how fathers connect and contribute to their lives. Most children reported experiencing a deep connection and communication with their fathers and appreciating their care and nurture. The socialization practices of fathers are influenced by the ideals of their parents followed by close relatives and other sources such as the media, mythology, friends, and their respective spiritual gurus (Sriram & Navalkar, 2012). Fathers in urban middle-class families are fully committed to their children. The involvement of fathers leads to the success of children, brings happiness to the fathers, and positively impacts the father's self-esteem (Sriram, 2011).

In summary, child-rearing in India reveals a shift from a more prescriptive and discipline-oriented approach to one emphasizing affection, warmth, and mutual benefits in the parent–child relationship. While traditional practices emphasize the divine role of parents and gender-specific expectations, contemporary perspectives are witnessing a gradual evolution towards gender equality and a more flexible parenting style (Box 5.1 for details). The stage-wise differentiation in parental attitudes reflects a nuanced understanding of child development. However, the persistence of mother-centric research and the limited exploration of the father's role highlight a need for a more comprehensive understanding of evolving family dynamics in the Indian context. As societal changes unfold, the delicate balance between tradition and adaptation becomes evident in shaping the narratives of child-rearing practices in India.

Box 5.1   Socialization: An Interplay of Continuity and Change

Socialization is a process that unfolds along the culture-context interface. Core socialization goals evolve from deep-rooted cultural mentalities and practices and hence are likely to continue in the long term. At the same time, changes in the context necessitate adjustment in goals and related practices. The interplay of cultural continuity and change is thus an integral part of socialization.

Contextual changes modify the relative importance and influence of the role of core socialization agents – family, school, peers, educational and religious institutions, and media. Whereas family and parents continue to be the primary agents for the growing child, the rising penetration of globalization is strengthening the role and influence of "external" agencies. The influx of information and ideas on myriad topics including child development and parenting is presenting opportunities as well as challenges to socialization (Kapadia, 2017). Consequently, adaptations in socialization are required to adjust to the continual changes (Keller, 2007). The context is persuading parents to question and revisit their socialization beliefs and practices in the best interest of preparing their child to do as well as possible in this rapidly transforming global context. At the same time, they are keen on ensuring the continuity of core cultural values, especially the interconnectedness and primacy of family.

Children have always been the fulcrum of Indian families. In the present times, however, the "child-centric" orientation is markedly evident. A key change that one observes, mostly in urban middle-class families, is the shift towards greater consciousness about parenting, laced with concern about one's performance as a parent and how this will translate to the child. This is a departure from the traditional model of "enculturation" of children into adult and family life.

The increasing discussions and write-ups in popular magazines and social media sites on topics such as, "how to parent" and "steps to effective parenting", as well as planned social interventions on parenting by international agencies (e.g., UNICEF) for instance, are indicative of the increasing consciousness and concern about the "right" way to socialize children. Phrases such as "I need to spend quality time with my child" or "Weekends are reserved for children", commonly expressed by parents, are also suggestive of conscious parenting.

Adaptations to the changing context involve reinterpretation and reappropriation of traditional parenting beliefs and practices (Kapadia, 2017, 2019). For instance, the persistence of the traditional cultural notion that family care is the ideal care model for the child is observed in dual-earner couples' inclination to invite either set of parents to live with them to ensure the constant presence of a family member with the child. Yet another example is the formation of family groups on WhatsApp to facilitate sustained contact and interaction among extended family members. Technology is thus used to support and advance the cultural goal of connection.

One aspect that poses a challenge to parents and children is the growing ethos of comparison and competition. It permeates every aspect of children's (and even adults') lives, including education, extracurricular activities, and social domains. Educational achievement is a cherished goal among Indian families and much socialization revolves around this domain. The Indian education system demands high performance that puts pressure on children as well as parents. Given the "enmeshed" nature of the parent–child relationship and strong parental concern and identification with the child's achievement, parents typically exert tacit and/or direct pressure on the child to perform well. The child's achievement is the family's achievement. Children, on their part, consider it their duty and responsibility to meet parents' expectations, which intensifies academic stress and potentially creates mental health problems for the child (Sarma, 2014).

Social media is perceived as a hindrance to children's focus on studies. Increasing popularity, access and appeal of social media platforms prompt children, especially adolescents, to constantly scroll through platforms such as Instagram, Facebook, WhatsApp, YouTube, Telegram, and so on. Children and adolescents spend considerable time on such platforms to post pictures or reels and keep track of the likes or dislikes that they receive, often in comparison with their friends. The downside of this is the double burden that it creates – one is the pressure for academic achievement from parents, and the other is the pressure to be liked and admired by peers.

A factor that further complicates the socialization process is children's greater familiarity and adeptness with technology use. Today's children are "digital natives", whereas parents are on a continuum about digital know-how. Overall, technology is playing a crucial role in inculcating a more agentic orientation to childhood rather than viewing children as passive recipients of an adult culture. Under such circumstances, the child often becomes the expert and is seen to provide help and support to parents in navigating digital devices, especially in low-resource contexts. This leads to a kind of "reverse socialization", which poses new challenges to the parental role. The influx of technology is also creating a sense of mistrust in the socialization process. On the one hand, parents want their children to become competent in the use of digital media, and at the same time, they are keen on monitoring and even restraining its use.

Such changes have implications for disciplining. Parents realize that allowing some independence and freedom to the child is necessary in the present context. Hence, they are adapting their disciplinary practices to incorporate a more flexible approach. Authority is balanced with support for the child's autonomy by taking the child's perspective and offering space for mutual exchange of views. The traditional hierarchical authority orientation is gradually giving way to a more accommodating outlook, especially during adolescence (Kapadia, 2017).

Gender socialization is also changing. Girls are being encouraged to pursue their interests, education, and careers. At the same time, the essential cultural norms are slow to change. Certain restrictions continue to prevail as girls are considered to be vulnerable, and hence boundaries or "Lakshman Rekhas" are drawn around their activities and behaviours.

In general, we observe an active interaction and intersection between tradition and modernity in the socialization process. Parents ensure that core cultural values continue (such as value for family and relationships); and at the same time, they are trying to tune their beliefs and practices to meet present-day requirements and devise practices that will enable the child to thrive in the changing world.

Shagufa Kapadia
The MS University of Baroda

Building an Inclusive Society

Building an inclusive society is essential for promoting equality, diversity, and social cohesion. An inclusive society acknowledges and values individual differences and tries to ensure equal opportunities, access to resources, and participation for all members. The United Nations Sustainable Development Goals 4 (United Nations, 2015) and the Universal Declaration of Human Rights (1948) are steps in this direction. The efforts made towards the inclusion of children/persons with disabilities and transgender persons in India have been discussed here.

Children With Disabilities

Children with disabilities are individuals under the age of 18 years who have one or more physical, intellectual, or sensory impairments that significantly limit their ability to function in daily life activities, such as communication, mobility, self-care, and learning. Disabilities can be congenital or acquired, and they can range from mild to severe. As per UNICEF, one in ten of all children worldwide have disabilities (UNICEF, 2021) and one in 11 in South Asia. In India, as per the Census 2011, about 2.21% of the total population (rural=2.17%, urban=2.24%, male=2.41%, female=0.01%) was disabled. Of all disabilities, the incidence of persons having disabilities such as movement (20.3%), hearing (18.9%), seeing, (18.8%), and speech (7.5%) are more prominent. Further, of the total population of Persons with Disability, nearly a quarter is in the school-going age group of 5–19 years, but only 7% are enrolled in regular schools. Earlier, only seven disabilities were identified. However, the recent Rights of Persons with Disabilities (RPWD) Act 2016 has increased the list of disabilities from 7 to 21.

In recent years, disability has been looked at more from a social perspective rather than a medical perspective. That is, they are viewed as being disabled by the society rather than their bodies. It has been argued that people with physical disabilities suffer more due to societal prejudices than due to the physical conditions in which they live (Dalal, 2006; Ghai, 2019). However, there is a need to view medical and social models as dichotomous, and an appropriate weightage to both aspects would be necessary. It is important to provide support and accommodations that meet the unique needs of each child.

Many barriers prevent people with disabilities from fully participating in society. These barriers include physical barriers (e.g., buildings, transportation, toilets, and playgrounds that cannot be accessed by wheelchair users), communication and information barriers (such as textbooks unavailable in Braille or public health announcements delivered without sign language interpretation), and attitudinal barriers (like stereotyping, low expectations, pity, condescension, harassment, and bullying). Gowramma et al. (2018) have extensively reviewed the challenges, opportunities and developments concerning children with disabilities. They note that people with physical disabilities tend to have low levels of self-esteem and high levels of depression, inferiority, fear of social ridicule, lack of self-confidence, limited social participation, and stress and anxiety in comparison to those without disabilities.

In India, inclusive education for children with disabilities has been one of the major interventions of the *Samagra Shiksha*. Various measures have been taken to improve the quality of education for children with disabilities. In this context, the development of tools for identifying disabilities and suitable material development are essential. NCERT (2022b) has developed the Pre-Assessment Holistic Screening Checklist for Schools (PRASHAST), a statistically standardized screening instrument, in Hindi and English, that facilitates screening of all 21 disability conditions, recognized in the RPWD Act 2016 and applies to all stages of school education. Adapted textbooks for the primary and upper primary levels (NCERT, 2015) have been developed. A reading series for all to give equal access to reading with inbuilt features that facilitate every child to read is available (NCERT, 2018). Awareness packages (Julka, 2003) and manuals (Julka, 2007) have been designed and tried out for professionals dealing with the education of children with disabilities. Cornelius and Balakrishna (2012) have suggested a model curriculum emphasizing the removal of grade placement. Home-based education (or the education that is provided to the child in their home) is an alternative to traditional classroom-based education for children with disabilities. Subashini (2017) has developed technology to support independent living and learning such as a smart walking device and GPS-based university navigation system that enables persons with visual impairment to move independently, Talk 'N' Learn-based English phonic software, digital talking book (DTB), Fixture App, and talking book application (TBA).

Transgender Persons

According to India's Transgender Persons (Protection of Rights) Bill, 2019, a transgender person is

> one whose gender does not match the gender assigned at birth. It includes trans-men and trans-women, persons with intersex variations, gender queers, and persons with socio-cultural identities, such as *kinnar* and *hijra*. Intersex variations are defined to mean a person who at birth shows variation in his or her primary sexual characteristics, external genitalia, chromosomes, or hormones from the normative standard of the male or female body.

The Bill prohibits discrimination against such persons and provides rights of residence, education, employment, and healthcare.

Historically, a reference to third-gender persons can be found in ancient texts such as the *Ramayana* and *Mahabharata* and also during the Mughal rule in India. Recently, the Supreme Court of India, in the landmark National Legal Services Authority (NALSA) vs. Union of India case (2014), recognized transgender people as a "third gender" and upheld their fundamental rights, including the right to self-identified gender, equality, and protection against discrimination. In 2014, it was estimated that around three million third-gender people live in India alone. A study conducted by the National Human Rights Commission in 2014 found that transgender persons are often denied basic rights, such as access to education, healthcare, and public spaces, and are subjected to violence and abuse by police and other authorities (National Human Rights Commission, 2014). However, in recent years the doors of education and job opportunities have been opened to *hijras*. While progress has been slow, in 2015 the first *hijra* mayor in India was elected in the city of Raigarh, and the city of Kochi hired 23 *hijras* to work for their public transit system in 2017. According to a newspaper report, a transgender person has been appointed to the Senate of Patna University in December 2023. The Government of Odisha, through the scheme *Sweekruti* 2017, seeks to provide transgenders with equal opportunity, protection of rights, and full participation in society. Still, progress is slow, and most third-gender people remain in poverty, even as they continue to bless Hindu families with prosperity.

Transgender individuals face several challenges, such as social stigma (societal rejection, limited educational and sustainable employment opportunities, denial of housing, healthcare, and violence) and healthcare disparities. Efforts are underway to sensitize society, schools, and workplaces about transgender issues, aiming to reduce discrimination and promote inclusivity. NCERT (2023) has developed a module for school staff (e.g., principals and teachers, including academic, non-academic, and ancillary staff) to facilitate the acceptance and seamless integration of transgender children within schools and in the larger society.

Indeed, fostering an inclusive society for children with disabilities and transgender persons is not just a moral imperative but a societal commitment. It requires a collective effort. By doing so, we pave the way for a future where every individual can thrive, regardless of their abilities or gender identity.

Socialization and Development of Competencies

The influence of socialization on the development of cognitive, affective, and motivational competencies is discussed in this section.

Cognitive Competencies

Socialization facilitates the development of cognitive competencies in several ways. First, it provides the context and environment in which cognitive competencies develop. The stimulating and supportive environment provided by parents to their children facilitates the development of language, memory, and problem-solving skills. Examples of stimulating environments include providing a rich language environment (e.g., frequent verbal interactions, storytelling, and exposure to diverse vocabulary), play-based learning activities that foster problem-solving, creativity, and imagination, providing hands-on experiences and opportunities for exploration, stimulating materials such as books, puzzles, toys, and so on, and encouraging social interaction with peers and adults (Levine et al., 2012). Second, positive and supportive social environments nurture a child's self-esteem, confidence, and belief in their capabilities, whereas negative or unsupportive environments can hinder their cognitive and emotional development (Dweck, 2017). Third, socialization experiences that emphasize participation in real-world activities and interaction with others enhance cognitive development. For example, Rogoff (2003) found that children in Mayan communities in Guatemala, who participated in everyday activities with adults and older children, developed better problem-solving abilities and attention spans compared to children in more individualistic cultures.

In traditional Indian families, parents and elders transmit cultural values and beliefs to their children and provide them with intellectual stimulation and educational opportunities. Language development is an important cognitive competency. Children in India are exposed to multiple languages, including regional languages, national languages, and English. The ability to speak and understand multiple languages is seen as a sign of intelligence and cultural competence (Sinha, 2014).

Affective Competencies

Through interactions with parents, caregivers, peers, and others, children learn to recognize, express, and regulate their emotions in socially appropriate ways. Thus, expressing positive emotions, warmth, and sensitivity by parents have been linked to the development of positive affective competencies. In contrast, harsh discipline, emotional neglect, and abuse can develop negative affective patterns in children (Eisenberg et al., 1998). Parents help children develop a positive sense of self, empathy, and emotional awareness by responding appropriately to their emotional needs.

Research shows that mothers in India do not respond to their children's negative emotions with encouragement; rather, by "making the child understand" (Raval & Martini, 2011) the consequences of emotional displays. Children are taught to control expressions of negative emotions within the broader context of familial interdependence (McCord & Raval, 2016). To Indian mothers, negative emotions are inevitable and they wish their children to "move on" without disrupting their daily activities and relationships (Fishman et al., 2014). However, given the existing diversity in the Indian context (caste, SES, rural–urban, multiple caregivers), it is difficult to discern a uniform pattern, and variations in emotional socialization are obvious (Kathuria et al., 2023). Recent studies in the tradition of positive psychology suggest that human strengths are built with positive parenting. The experience of well-being in life requires emotional regulation and resilience which are acquired in the course of socialization.

Motivational Competencies

Motivational competencies refer to the skills and abilities that allow individuals to set goals, regulate their emotions and behaviours, and achieve desired personal and social outcomes. Children develop motivational competencies through their interactions with parents, peers, and other adults in their social environment (Ryan & Deci, 2000). Parenting styles influence children's motivational competencies. Authoritative parenting is associated with higher levels of motivational competencies in children (Grolnick et al., 1997; Wentzel & Wigfield, 2018). Also, children with supportive, achievement-oriented friends who share similar goals are likely to develop stronger motivational competencies (Wentzel & Wigfield, 2018). In the context of India, studies show that factors such as parental involvement, particularly in the educational activities of children, social support from parents and peers, and collectivist values together with religious and spiritual practices (Singh, 2019), promote the development of motivation and academic achievement among children and adolescents.

In conclusion, through interactions with peers, family, and societal structures, children navigate a dynamic social environment that fosters not only cognitive growth but also emotional intelligence and the drive to achieve. Recognizing the interconnectedness of these developmental facets underscores the importance of nurturing a holistic approach to education and social engagement, which are essential for success in an ever-evolving world.

Overview

This chapter examined the intricate processes that shape individuals within society. By exploring and understanding the contribution of the agents of socialization, such as family, peers, education, and media, this chapter provided a comprehensive but selective overview of the forces that contribute to our identity and behaviour. It also discussed the unique context that India provides for socialization. The exploration of variations in parenting styles, with a focus on positive parenting, underscores the critical role caregivers play in the socialization journey. The examination of socialization practices in modern India highlighted the dynamic interplay of cultural contexts and individual competencies.

Moreover, the chapter critically addressed the inclusive aspects of socialization, exploring how it shapes the lives of children with disabilities and transgender persons. By recognizing the need for an inclusive society, we pave the way for a more compassionate and understanding future. Finally, the analysis of competencies developed through socialization, including insights into the schooling system in India, shed light on the broader societal impact of these processes. As we navigate the complexities of socialization, it becomes evident that fostering positive experiences and inclusive practices is crucial for shaping individuals who contribute positively to society. This chapter serves as a gateway to understanding the nuanced interconnections between socialization and development, inviting readers to reflect on their own experiences and the broader societal implications of these processes.

Key Terms

Affective Competency
Agents of Socialization
Authoritative
Authoritarian
Children With Disabilities
Context Embeddedness
Cognitive Competence
Culture
Development of Competencies
Dynamics of Socialization
Family
Inclusive Society
Media
Nature of Socialization
Neglectful/Uninvolved Parenting
Parenting Styles
Peers and Peer Groups
Permissive
Positive Parenting
Religious Institutions
Socialization for Gender Roles
Socialization Practices in India
Symbiotic Relationships and Interconnectedness
Traditional and Modern Views
Transgender Persons

Questions for Reflection

1) How does the nature of socialization impact an individual's identity formation and sense of self in different cultural contexts?
2) In what ways do various agents of socialization contribute to the dynamics of shaping an individual's beliefs, values, and behaviour?
3) How does embeddedness in a particular context influence the development of an individual? Give examples.
4) Explore the variations in parenting styles and their effects on a child's socialization and development. How do cultural factors play a role in shaping these parenting styles?
5) What efforts are required to build an inclusive society?

Suggested Further Readings

Books

Cohen, D., & Kitayama, S. (2019). *Handbook of cultural psychology* (2nd ed.). The Guilford Publications.

Grusec, J. H., & Hastings, P. D. (2014). *Handbook of socialization: Theory and research* (2nd ed.). The Guilford Publications.

Roopnarine, J., & Yildirim, E. D. (2019). *Fathering in cultural context: Developmental and clinical issues.* Routledge.

Research Paper

Harkness, S., & Super, C. M. (2020). Culture and human development: Where did it go? And where is it going? *New Directions for Child and Adolescent Development*, 101–119.

Part III
Perspectives on Cognitive and Language Development

6 Cognitive Development

Contents

Introduction	110
Theories of Cognitive Development	110
An Indian Perspective on Cognition	119
Box 6.1: Indigenous Concepts: *Antahkarana, Jnana, Pragya, Smriti,* and *Panch Kosha*	119
Box 6.2: Yoga and Cognitive Development	122
Exploring the Multifaceted Nature of Intelligence	122
The Interface Between Cognition and Emotion	126
Box 6.3: Indian View of Emotional Intelligence	127
Culture and Intelligence	128
Box 6.4: Common Conception of Intelligence in India	129
Box 6.5: Development of Theory of Mind in the Indian Context	131
Creativity	132
Schooling and Cognitive Development	133
Box 6.6: The *Guru–Shishya* Relationship: A Timeless Bond of Learning and Transformation	135
Overview	136
Key Terms	137
Questions for Reflection	137

Learning Objectives

After studying this chapter, the learner will be able to:

Explain key theoretical perspectives on cognitive development;
Analyse the Indian perspective on cognition;
Explore the role of culture on cognitive development;
Trace the historical overview and changing conceptions of intelligence;
Explore the interface between cognition and emotion, including the Indian perspective; and
Investigate the role of schooling in cognitive development.

DOI: 10.4324/9781003441168-9

Introduction

The term cognition refers to a wide spectrum of intellective or mental processes such as perception, learning, memory, thinking, intelligence, problem-solving, and decision-making. It is primarily through these processes that we acquire abilities for understanding, representing, imagining, and communicating about ourselves and the world. They allow functioning at concrete and abstract levels and enable us to solve our problems along a flexible time horizon. The cognitive capacity, therefore, becomes an important tool for adaptation to diverse situations and the attainment of goals. Human cognitive functioning, however, undergoes several noticeable quantitative and qualitative changes indicating the existence of a series of interrelated phases or stages. In the course of development, each preceding phase is preparatory for the next phase. Further, while cognitive processes are available to everyone, the use of these processes does partly vary across cultures and the contexts available to the growing child. The same event or phenomenon may be interpreted differently by people living in different cultures. The question of how cognitive changes occur and which processes transform the mind of a newborn baby into the mind of a mature adult has been approached from many theoretical vantage points. This chapter discusses some of the key issues related to cognitive development and introduces major theories advanced to explain the pattern of changes in the cognitive domain.

Theories of Cognitive Development

Various theories have been put forward, each offering unique insights into the cognitive milestones and mechanisms that shape the unfolding of human intellect. This section examines the theories proposed by Jean Piaget, Lev Vygotsky, Neo-Piagetian, Barbara Rogoff, Jerome Bruner, and the information processing perspective.

Jean Piaget's Theory of Cognitive Development

Piaget employed the methods of observation and clinical interview to study various aspects of human development. Piaget believed that the development of children is the result of interaction between hereditary and environmental factors. The hereditary factors set the limit of development and, within that limit, the development is facilitated by exposure to environmental factors. Also, he believed that children are not passive but are active learners and constructors of knowledge. Through interactions with the environment, they actively construct their knowledge by doing things and not just by listening or reading things.

Piaget (1936, 1957, 1964, 1977) described children's cognitive development based on three components: schemas, adaptation, and stages of development as detailed in the following.

Schemas

Schemas are mental structures in which information is stored into interrelated categories (e.g., parents, peers, teachers etc.) and webbed with each other. They describe the pattern of thinking and behaviour about the world. For example, when a child visits a doctor for immunization, the doctor inserts the medicine through injection which is painful. This entire set of information is stored in the form of a "schema". If the child experiences pain or discomfort on subsequent visits, the related schema gets associated with the visit to the doctor or hospital and the experience of pain. The schema gets modified with subsequent experiences and exposure, and, therefore, schema changes with age.

Cognitive Development

The Process of Adaptation

According to Piaget, cognitive development takes place through the process of adaptation or adjustment to new information and experiences. This takes place through the processes of assimilation, accommodation, and equilibration. Assimilation refers to grasping or taking in any new information from the outside world and relating it to the existing schema. For example, a child has learnt that an apple is a fruit. Later on, when she sees an orange she relates it to the existing schema of fruit as both are similar in size and are consumed raw by the child.

However, assimilation is not so easy. For example, a child sees a watermelon which is big but wants to eat. Similarly, the surface of a pineapple is rough and needs to be peeled before eating. The child has to make changes in the pre-existing schema related to fruit in the sense that the size and surface of fruits can vary. This is called accommodation. However, during the process of accommodation, the child may experience difficulty. When successful in accommodating new information into existing schemas, the child takes recourse to equilibration. The state of disequilibrating brings unpleasantness and discomfort to the child, and she gets motivated to achieve equilibration by assimilating further information. Thus, equilibration is essentially an act of balancing between assimilation and accommodation.

Stages of Cognitive Development

Based on his minute observations of growing children, Piaget posited that cognitive development takes place through four stages. The stages involve qualitative changes in the behaviour of children as they progress from one stage to another. Also, the stages follow a specific order. That is, each subsequent stage occurs after the previous one is accomplished. It may also be noted that ages corresponding to the stages are approximations, and each child develops at his/her rate. The stages are as follows: sensorimotor stage (0–2 years old), preoperational stage (2–7 years old), concrete operational stage (7–11 years old), and formal operational stage (11 years through adulthood).

1) *Sensorimotor Stage*

This stage spans from birth to two years of age. During this period, children learn through their senses and motor functions. A variety of cognitive abilities, such as object permanence, representational play (or symbolic play or pretend play; for example, using a block as a phone and engaging in conversation), imitation, and self-recognition, develop during this stage. The stage is divided into six sub-stages.

  a) *Use of reflexes* (0–2 months): This sub-stage is characterized by the use of reflexes. They are unable to consolidate the information obtained through the senses into any category or schema.
  b) *Primary circular reactions* (1–4 months): This sub-stage shows the beginning of combining information received through different sense organs. They begin to engage in behaviours as per the needs of their bodies (e.g., repeating pleasurable behaviours). Also, they turn their heads to sounds and sights in the environment.
  c) *Secondary circular reactions* (4–8 months): During this sub-stage, children's behaviour becomes more deliberate, and they start taking more interest in their environment. They begin to perform behaviours that attract the attention of others. For example, the child places whatever comes to her hand into her mouth.

d) *Coordinating secondary schemes* (8–12 months): In this sub-stage, children begin to perform more intentional behaviours and combine different behaviours to achieve the goal. They show signs of the ability to combine knowledge to reach a goal.
e) *Tertiary circular reactions* (12–18 months): In this sub-stage, children do not perform the same actions but attempt new behaviours and actions to achieve different goals. Instead of performing spontaneous actions, their behaviours become more purposeful. They perform different types of behaviours to achieve the desired goals.
f) *Symbolic thought* (18–24 months): This sub-stage is characterized by the beginning of symbolic thought. They can now form a mental representation of objects. They start performing deliberate and careful actions. Mental representation is the development of the ability to visualize things that are not physically present before the child. This is crucial for attaining object permanence.

Object permanence refers to the child's understanding that objects continue to exist even if they cannot be heard or seen. For example, if you show a toy to a young infant and then remove it from her vision, the child will believe that toy does not exist. However, older infants who have achieved object permanence do not believe this and continue to seek the object here and there in the environment.

2) *Preoperational Stage*

This stage begins at the age of two years and lasts approximately till seven years of age. Here, it is important to understand the meaning of the term *operation*. The word "operation" is used by Piaget to refer to the ability to manipulate information logically. The stage is called pre-operational as the child has not developed this ability by the end of this stage. The main characteristics of development during this period include egocentrism, centration, conservation, animism, parallel play, symbolic representation, artificialism, and irreversibility. Let us examine these processes in some detail.

Egocentrism: It refers to the quality of the child to remain self-focused and be concerned about her welfare only. The child refuses to acknowledge others' point of view. If the child wants a toffee or a sweet, she will insist on getting the same despite your arguments against having it. An egocentric child is unable to differentiate between self and others and believes that everyone sees things as she sees. By the time the child becomes four years old they begin to understand other's perspectives.
Centration: This refers to the tendency to focus on one aspect of a task or situation at a time. For example, if you ask a child to differentiate between two objects based on their height and width, they have difficulty in doing so. They can do so based on either their height or their width.
Conservation: Similar to centration, conservation refers to the development of understanding that quantity remains the same even if other features such as shape, size, or container are changed. For example, take two glasses of identical shapes and sizes and fill the same amount of water in both glasses in front of the child. Now ask the child whether the amount of water in both the glasses is same. The child will reply in the affirmative. Now take a third glass which is longer in shape than the other two glasses and transfer the water from one glass to the longer one in front of the child. Naturally, the level of water in the long glass will go up. Ask the child whether the amount of water in the small and long glasses is the same. The child will say no following the logic that the long glass contains more water than the small one. This ability develops in children around five years of age.

Animism: It is a belief that objects are capable of performing actions and have life-like qualities. For example, a child believes that when she stumbles with a chair and hurts herself, it is the fault of the chair which needs to be punished. Similarly, a doll can eat and sleep like her. Around age 3, children begin to realize that physical objects are not alive.

Parallel Play: Play is essential for the development of children. During the pre-operational stage, two or more children remain in each other's company but play independently. They imitate what the other child is doing but do not interact with each other directly. If one child is running, the other child may also decide to run but a lack of coordination between them may be observed. This reflects a transition from solitary play to the development of cooperative behaviour among children.

Symbolic Representation: During the early pre-operational period (2–3 years), children increasingly use symbols (e.g., gestures and postures), in addition to the use of words and sentences, for communication. Also, they may use the same symbol for two or more things.

Artificialism: It refers to the belief of children that the natural events in the environment (e.g., clouds) are man-made.

Concrete Operational Stage

During this period (7–11 years of age), children develop the ability of logical thinking, particularly inductive thinking (i.e., drawing inferences from specific experiences to general principles). An example of inductive reasoning could be that the child finds that whenever it rains she gets a runny nose and swollen throat. The child draws the inference that she should take precautions whenever it rains. The stage is called concrete operational as their thinking is tied to concrete objects/events only (whatever is physically present before them). However, children find it difficult to use deductive reasoning.

Children's cognitive abilities (e.g., categorization, numerical, and spatial) are more developed during this stage. They can solve conservation problems, understand reversibility (i.e., items can be returned to their original states), can decentre (i.e., concentrate on multiple dimensions of items rather than just one), and better understand the concept of identity (i.e., an item remains the same even if it looks different).

Formal Operational Stage

This stage begins around 11–12 years of age and lasts up to adulthood. This stage is characterized by the emergence of the ability to use abstract thought. The thinking of children is not limited to the current time, person, or situation. They can do imagination about hypothetical persons, objects, and events, do deductive reasoning (e.g., application of general rules to specific instances), problem-solving and future planning, and ponder about "what–if" type of situations.

Evaluation of Piaget's Theory

Piaget's theory has inspired a tremendous amount of research throughout the globe. Reviewing available evidence, Dasen (2022) has noted a few strengths and weaknesses of Piaget's theory. First, the development of children mostly follows the same pathways in most cultures, but the age at which various sub-stages appear varies across cultures (for details, see Harkness & Super, 2020). Second, in several societies, older children and adults do not seem to display the concrete operational stage. Third, the emergence of abstract reasoning during the formal operational stage has been questioned by several researchers. Some children do not develop the requisite thinking skills to fully approach this stage. Here it may be worthwhile to note that Piaget (1972) had revised his earlier position that formal operational reasoning is evident only under favourable circumstances (Dasen, 2022). Finally, Piaget did not take into cognizance the role of training in advancing cognitive development. The rate of cognitive development is often influenced by providing appropriate training to children.

Piaget's theory did attract a considerable degree of research attention in India (refer to Bevli et al., 1989; Mishra, 2014; Misra & Tripathi, 1998). Attempts have been made to examine the effect of contextual factors (e.g., socio-economic status, age, schooling, rural/urban, tribal/non-tribal, etc.) on Piagetian tasks. Based on the review of studies, Mishra (2014) concluded that the cognitive development of children in India passes through stages as suggested by Piaget. However, sociocultural factors sometimes facilitate and sometimes create hindrances in the rate of cognitive development. The implications of Piaget's theory in education have also been examined, but the results are mixed.

Lev Vygotsky's Sociocultural Theory

Vygotsky's (1978) sociocultural theory emphasizes the role of social interactions, language, and cultural factors in shaping the mind. At the core of Vygotsky's theory is the belief that cognitive development is intrinsically a socially mediated process, which occurs within a sociocultural context (see Wertsch, 1985). The main features of his theory are described as follows.

Zone of Proximal Development

One of the key concepts in Vygotsky's theory is the zone of proximal development (ZPD). This refers to the range of tasks that a learner can perform independently or without any assistance and the level of development which the child can achieve under the guidance of an adult or teacher or more able peers. For example, suppose there are two learners of the same chronological age (e.g., 8 years), and their mental age is also the same (e.g., 8 years). Now, both children get coaching on the type of material used in a problem-solving task and how the task can be solved. After coaching, one child may still be able to solve problems meant for 8-year-old children while another child can solve problems meant for 11-year-old children. It is this difference (11 minus 8) that indicates ZPD.

Scaffolding

Scaffolding stands for the support provided by a knowledgeable person to help a learner accomplish a task within their ZPD. As the learner gains proficiency, the support is gradually withdrawn, allowing for independent performance. Scaffolding facilitates the internalization of knowledge and skills. It is more useful when the child attempts to learn new skills, offering more support early and gradually withdrawing as the child learns.

Language and Thought

Vygotsky believed that language not only represents or reflects but also shapes thought. Through language, individuals internalize cultural knowledge and engage in self-regulation. The use of private speech, or talking to oneself, is a manifestation of this internalization process, serving as a tool for planning, problem-solving, and self-reflection.

Cultural Tools and Symbols

Vygotsky emphasized the importance of cultural tools and symbols in cognitive development. These include not only language but also writing, counting systems, and other forms of symbolic representations. Cultural tools, acquired through social interactions, serve as mediators for thought and problem-solving. The cultural context, therefore, provides the foundation for the development of higher mental functions. Subsequent work by Michael Cole (1996) on cultural psychology established that the mind emerges in the joint activity of people in a cultural context and, in an important sense, co-constructed. It assumes that individuals are active agents in their development.

The use of scaffolding in an educational setting is effective in promoting learning and cognitive development. Additionally, ZPD has been used to inform teaching practices and curriculum design (Verenikina, 2010). The limitations of Vygotsky's theory are as follows: (1) it is not clear whether ZPD refers to the needs of children, their capability, or their motivations. The ZPD also does not explain how the development occurs; (2) it disregards the role of the individual and gives emphasis on the group; and (3) the social groups may not extend equal support to all learners, hence unequal opportunities for learning to each learner.

Neo-Piagetian Theories

Neo-Piagetian theories build upon Piaget's work. While Piaget's theory emphasized qualitative changes, Neo-Piagetian theories focus on quantitative changes in cognitive development. These theories emphasize an increase in efficiency, speed, and capacity of cognitive processes rather than solely on qualitative shifts in thinking. Case (1992), a prominent Neo-Piagetian, argued that children develop general conceptual structures in domains that are applied across different domains, such as mathematics, language, and reasoning. Smith (1995) stressed the role of environmental and social factors in shaping cognitive development. She believes that cognitive processes are inherently dynamic and interconnected, which involves the continuous adaptation of cognitive processes to changing environmental demands. This process is shaped by factors such as experience, motivation, and social interaction. Ericsson (1996) focused on the role of deliberate practice and feedback in developing expertise in specific domains. The Neo-Piagetians recognize the role of individual differences and acknowledge the contributions of genetics, experience, and culture.

Barbara Rogoff's Theory of Apprenticeship

Rogoff (1990, 2003) emphasizes the importance of cultural and social contexts for understanding how individuals learn and develop cognitive skills. Her theory of "Cultural Apprenticeship", explores how learning is situated within cultural practices and is often a collaborative and socially mediated process. Here are some key elements of her theory.

Guided Participation

Rogoff emphasizes the concept of "guided participation", which refers to the idea that learning occurs through participation in culturally meaningful activities under the guidance of more knowledgeable significant others. This guidance can come from parents, peers, or other members of the community.

Apprenticeship in Everyday Activities

Rogoff argues that learning is not confined to formal educational settings but is embedded in everyday activities. Children learn through active engagement in practices such as cooking, storytelling, or problem-solving within the community. Rogoff and Mejía-Arauz (2022) have termed it "Learning by Observing and Pitching Into family and community endeavours (LOPI)". Rogoff (2003; Rogoff & Mejía-Arauz, 2014) conducted a study in a rural village in India, where children learnt by participating in household and community activities. For example, children might learn math by counting money or measuring ingredients while helping their mothers prepare meals. Another example is children's learning of crafts by observing and assisting parents and other adults (refer to Chapter 5).

Cultural Variation in Learning

The theory acknowledges the importance of cultural variation in learning processes. Rogoff contends that how individuals learn and the skills they develop are influenced by the specific cultural practices and social structures in which they are immersed. In a study conducted in a school in Bengaluru, Rogoff and Mejía-Arauz (2014) noted that children who come from cultures that value cooperation and collaboration may struggle in a school system that emphasizes individual achievement and competition.

Social Interaction and Collaboration

Social interaction and collaboration are central to Rogoff's theory. Learning is seen as a socially mediated process, with individuals actively participating in shared activities and receiving guidance from more experienced individuals.

Rogoff's theory has been subject to criticism on certain counts. First, it overlooks the role of individual differences and innate cognitive abilities in shaping development. Second, it places too much emphasis on informal learning contexts and does not adequately account for the role of formal instruction and motivation in learning (Deci & Ryan, 2000). Third, it does not provide a clear and detailed account of how learning takes place.

Jerome Bruner's Socio-Cognitive Theory

Bruner was a leading proponent of constructivism, emphasizing the active role of learners in constructing their knowledge. Bruner's (1961, 1990, 1996) theory posits that cognitive development is deeply intertwined with social and cultural factors. The theory proposes that individuals learn best when engaged in meaningful social interactions and when the learning context reflects real-world problem-solving.

Stages of Cognitive Representation

Bruner identified three stages of cognitive representation: enactive, iconic, and symbolic. Enactive representation (0–1 year) involves learning and representing knowledge through action and movement. In this stage, children acquire understanding by interacting with the environment and performing actions. For example, an infant learns about a doll by physically handling it, through direct bodily experiences. Iconic representation involves working with mental images or pictures that resemble the physical objects or events they represent. For example, if a child mentally visualizes a doll in their mind, forming a mental image that resembles the actual doll.

Finally, symbolic representation is the most advanced mode, involving the use of symbols such as words, mathematical symbols, or abstract concepts to represent ideas or objects. This mode allows for the manipulation of abstract symbols and the development of language and thought.

These three modes are not mutually exclusive, and individuals often use a combination of them to understand and represent information. Bruner's theory suggests that as cognitive development progresses, individuals shift from relying on enactive and iconic representation to increasingly using symbolic representation, which plays a crucial role in language development and higher-order thinking.

The Spiral Curriculum

Bruner introduced the idea of a "spiral curriculum", suggesting that learning should be organized in a way that revisits fundamental concepts at increasing levels of complexity. This approach aligns with the notion that individuals build on their existing knowledge through iterative exposure to related ideas. By revisiting topics in a spiral manner, learners gain a deeper and more nuanced understanding over time.

Cultural Tools and Symbols

According to Bruner, cultural tools and symbols (such as language, symbols, and other shared cognitive artefacts) mediate the learning process. Language, in particular, serves as a means for individuals to internalize and organize their thoughts, facilitating the construction of knowledge within a cultural context.

Social Interaction and Collaboration

Bruner emphasizes the significance of social interaction in organizing the learning process. Collaborative learning, in which individuals engage in dialogue and shared problem-solving, is seen as a catalyst for cognitive development. Through interactions with more knowledgeable peers or instructors, learners can scaffold their understanding, gradually taking on more complex cognitive tasks.

Discovery Learning

Bruner advocated for the value of discovery learning, wherein learners actively explore and uncover knowledge rather than passively receive information. He argued that this approach promotes a deeper understanding and encourages problem-solving skills. However, Bruner also recognized the need for guidance and support, as pure discovery learning may not be effective in all situations.

Bruner's socio-cognitive theory has significant implications for education and instructional design. Educators can apply these principles by creating learning environments that foster collaboration, provide meaningful contexts for learning, and encourage students to actively construct their knowledge. In India, the NCERT (2005) developed the National Curriculum Framework (2005) following the constructivist approach. However, the theory is not without its criticism. Some argue that the emphasis on social interaction may not adequately address individual differences in learning styles and preferences. Additionally, the application of discovery learning has been debated, with concerns about the need for structured guidance to ensure effective learning outcomes.

Information Processing Approach

Information processing theories seek to elucidate the mechanisms by which individuals acquire, store, retrieve, and utilize information. These theories have evolved, drawing inspiration from computer science and psychology. Researchers like Ulric Neisser and George Miller have contributed significantly to laying the foundation for information processing theories. The key concepts of information processing theories are described here.

Encoding and Input Processes

Information processing begins with the encoding of stimuli from the environment. This process involves transforming sensory input into a format that the brain can understand and process. Encoding, thus, refers to the process of taking in information from the environment and storing it in memory. This process involves attention, which is the ability to focus on relevant information while ignoring irrelevant information. According to Atkinson and Shiffrin (1968), when information is received, it goes through various stages. The sensory memory holds information that the mind receives through sense organs (e.g., eyes, ears etc.). From sensory memory, the information goes to short-term memory (STM), whose capacity is limited. From STM, the information goes to long-term memory (LTM), which has unlimited space.

Storage Processes

Miller (1956) proposed that STM can hold only 7 plus or minus 2 items or chunks at a time. The information stays in STM for about 30 seconds. He also advanced the concept of chunking, which says that information belonging to one domain is stored in one category or chunks.

Retrieval Processes

Retrieval involves the process of accessing information from LTM when needed. The retrieval cues play a crucial role in accessing memories. Tulving's encoding specificity principle (Tulving & Thomson, 1973) suggests that, as memory is context-dependent, retrieval from memory is influenced by the similarity or specificity of the cues present during encoding and retrieval. For example, if you study for an exam in a quiet room (encoding context) and then take the exam in a similar quiet environment (retrieval context), you are more likely to recall the information effectively. However, if there is a mismatch between the encoding and retrieval contexts (e.g., studying in a quiet room but taking the exam in a noisy one), memory retrieval may be less efficient.

Working Memory

Baddeley and Hitch (1974) proposed the concept of working memory, expanding the concept of STM. It is the working memory which is responsible for the temporary storage and manipulation of information for various cognitive tasks before the information is finally stored in long-term memory. Working memory is crucial for tasks requiring attention, problem-solving, and decision-making.

Parallel Distributed Processing (PDP)

Unlike traditional models that view cognitive processes as a series of sequential steps, the PDP model suggests that information is processed in parallel across a network of interconnected processing units. As a result, several pieces of information can be processed together. This parallelism is thought to mimic the simultaneous activation of neurons in the brain (Rumelhart & McClelland, 1986).

The information processing theories have, however, been criticized for oversimplifying the complexity of human cognition and neglecting emotional and social factors. Future research may address these limitations by integrating information processing theories with other perspectives, such as embodied cognition and sociocultural theories.

In summary, the array of cognitive development theories discussed underscores the multifaceted nature of the cognitive growth process. Each theory contributes a valuable facet to our comprehension of how individuals construct knowledge and adapt to the challenges presented by their environment.

An Indian Perspective on Cognition

The Indian tradition recognizes cognition to be closely linked to the concept of consciousness, which is seen as the fundamental basis of all mental processes. The *Samkhya* system advocated a dualistic view of consciousness and matter. According to this view, consciousness is a non-material entity that pervades all living beings and is distinct from matter. It also proposed that the mind, which is a part of the material world, is responsible for cognition and perception. Another school of Indian thought, the *Advaita Vedanta*, proposed a monistic view of consciousness, where all reality is seen as a manifestation of the same underlying consciousness. In this view, cognition is seen as a process of becoming aware of the fundamental unity of all things.

The Indian tradition of Ayurveda, a system of medicine that has been practised for thousands of years, emphasizes the importance of maintaining a balance between the body, mind, and spirit for optimal cognitive functioning. Ayurvedic remedies such as the use of certain herbs and spices (such as Sage, *Tejpatta*, *Brahmi*, Turmeric, *Ashwagandha*, and so on) are believed to enhance cognitive abilities. A few indigenous concepts related to cognition such as *Manas, Chitta, Panch Kosha, Jnana, Pragya,* and *Smriti* are briefly discussed in Box 6.1. In the Indian spiritual tradition, various practices such as yoga and meditation are believed to enhance cognitive abilities (see Box 6.2).

Box 6.1 Indigenous Concepts: *Antahkarana, Jnana, Pragya, Smriti,* **and** *Panch Kosha*

Antahkarana

The term *Antahkarana* refers to the inner instrument or the internal aspect of the mind. The word is derived from Sanskrit, where "Antah" means inner and "Karana" means instrument or tool. *Antahkarana* encompasses several components of the inner being, including *Manas, Buddhi, Chitta,* and *Ahamkara. Manas* (or mind) is considered the faculty of the mind that processes sensory input and generates thoughts and emotions. It is responsible for perception, cognition, and decision-making. The *Bhagavad Gita,* considers *Manas* as the "instrument of thought" and emphasizes the importance of controlling it through meditation and detachment. *buddhi* (intellect) is the higher intellect or discriminative faculty. It is responsible for decision-making, judgement, and discernment. *Buddhi* helps in understanding, analysing, and making choices based on wisdom. *Chitta* (or consciousness) refers to the "mind-stuff" or the totality of the psyche, including thoughts, emotions, memories, and experiences. *Chitta* is considered to be the repository of all our experiences, both conscious and unconscious. It is said to be like a mirror that reflects our thoughts and emotions and like a lake that can be disturbed by external factors, leading to turbulence in the mind. *Ahamkara* (or ego) is the sense of individuality or ego. It gives a person the sense of "I" and is responsible for the identification of one's body and personality. Thus, *Chitta* remembers, *Manas* forms representations of an object or event, *buddhi* selects one of the representations, and *Ahamkara* acts on the selected representation (Das, 2013).

The *Antahkarana*, when purified and harmonized through practices like meditation (*dhyan*), self-reflection (*adhyavasay*), and other yogic disciplines, is believed to lead to a state of inner clarity, balance, and spiritual evolution. In many spiritual traditions, the goal is to transcend the limitations of the mind and ego, allowing one to connect with higher levels of consciousness and realize their true nature.

Jnana

Jnana, a Sanskrit term, refers to knowledge or wisdom, particularly spiritual or philosophical knowledge that leads to liberation or enlightenment. The Upanishads emphasize the importance of realizing the true nature of the Self through knowledge and contemplation and describe the path of *jnana* as a means of achieving liberation from suffering and ignorance. The *Bhagavad Gita* emphasizes the importance of discerning between the eternal (*anitya*) and the temporary (*nitya*) and describes the path of *jnana* as a means of realizing the unity of all existence and achieving liberation from the cycle of birth and death. The *Yoga Sutras* of Patanjali describe *jnana* as a means of achieving liberation from the fluctuations of the mind and emphasize the importance of cultivating a clear and steady intellect through the practice of meditation.

The Vedanta school distinguishes between two types of knowledge: lower knowledge (*avidya*) and higher knowledge (*jnana*). Lower knowledge refers to knowledge of the external world, including the physical sciences and worldly affairs. Higher knowledge, on the other hand, refers to knowledge of the Self or *Brahman*, the ultimate reality that underlies all existence. Overall, the concept of *jnana* emphasizes the importance of spiritual knowledge and understanding as a means of attaining liberation from the cycle of birth and death and realizing one's true nature as a spiritual being.

Pragya

In Indian philosophy, *pragya* (or *prajna*) refers to a state of higher consciousness or wisdom that is attained through spiritual practice and meditation. It is often translated as "wisdom", "knowledge", or "intuition". It is considered an important aspect of the spiritual path, particularly in the *Advaita Vedanta* school of Hindu philosophy. According to this school, the ultimate reality is non-dual and can be directly realized through the state of *pragya*. This state is characterized by a deep understanding of the nature of reality and the true self, as well as a sense of inner peace and contentment. In Buddhist philosophy, *pragya* is considered to be one of the six *paramitas* or "perfections" that are cultivated on the path to enlightenment. *Pragya* is associated with the realization of the emptiness of all phenomena and the development of insight into the true nature of reality.

In both Hindu and Buddhist traditions, the cultivation of *pragya* is considered to be a gradual process that involves the development of mindfulness, concentration, and insight through the practice of meditation and other spiritual disciplines. It is seen as an essential component of spiritual growth and the attainment of liberation or enlightenment.

Smriti

Smriti (memory) refers to the capacity of the mind to remember past experiences, knowledge, and information. The term "Smriti" is derived from the Sanskrit word "Smṛ", which means "that which is remembered?" In the Indian tradition, there are two types of texts: *Smriti* and *Sruti*. *Smriti* refers to a category of texts that are considered to be derived from human memory. They are the result of human efforts and are believed to have been compiled by sages and scholars over time. The *shruti* texts (e.g., Vedas) are believed to have been directly revealed to sages and seers through divine inspiration and passed down through generations by sages and seers in deep states of meditation and spiritual realization.

The two primary categories of *smriti* literature are "dharma shastras" and "itihasas". *Dharma shastras* are texts that deal with the principles of *dharma*, such as righteousness, ethical duties, and societal norms. The *Manusmriti* (Laws of Manu) is one of the most well-known *dharma shastras*. *Itihasas*, on the other hand, are epic narratives that include the Ramayana and the *Mahabharata*. While the events in *itihasas* are traditionally believed to have happened, they also serve as vehicles for imparting moral and ethical teachings.

Panch Kosha

The concept of *Panch kosha* has been described in the *Taittiriya Upanishad*, part of *Yajurveda*, one of the four Vedas. It describes the five sheaths or layers that cover the true Self or *Atman*. These five sheaths are:

Annamaya kosha: The physical sheath, which is made up of the physical body and its organs.
Pranamaya kosha: The vital sheath, which is made up of the life force or energy that sustains the physical body.
Manomaya kosha: The mental sheath, which is made up of the mind and emotions.
Vijnanamaya kosha: The intellectual sheath, which is made up of the intellect or the power of discrimination.
Anandamaya kosha: The blissful sheath, which is made up of pure consciousness and represents the true Self or *Atman*.

According to *Panch kosha*, each of these sheaths must be transcended to realize the true nature of the Self, which is pure consciousness or bliss. By understanding and meditating on each of these sheaths, one can move closer to a state of spiritual realization and liberation.

> **Box 6.2 Yoga and Cognitive Development**
>
> Yoga, an ancient system of thought and practice originating in India, has garnered increasing attention in contemporary research for its potential impact on cognitive development. This holistic discipline, encompassing physical postures (*asanas*), breath control (*pranayama*), meditation (*dhyana*), and ethical principles (*Yama and Niyam*), has been associated with a range of cognitive benefits. Research has shown that regular practice of meditation can lead to improved attention, memory, and emotional regulation (Dwivedi, 2019; Shetty et al., 2022).
>
> The practice of yoga involves mindfulness and relaxation techniques, which can contribute to stress reduction and improved emotional regulation. This, in turn, positively influences cognitive performance and mental well-being (Pascoe & Bauer, 2015). Yoga has been associated with changes in brain wave patterns, including increased alpha and theta waves, indicative of relaxed and focused states. It increases blood flow and oxygenation to the brain, which can enhance neuronal function and communication (Gard et al., 2014). Thus, the integration of yoga into one's lifestyle appears to offer a holistic approach to cognitive development.

Exploring the Multifaceted Nature of Intelligence

Intelligence, a cornerstone of human cognition, has been a subject of intense scrutiny and exploration across various disciplines. From the early philosophical musings of ancient scholars to the cutting-edge research in contemporary neuroscience, the concept of intelligence has evolved significantly. It was during the 20th century that the scientific study of intelligence gained prominence with the development of standardized intelligence tests. The psychometric approach, exemplified by the work of Alfred Binet and Theodore Simon in the early 1900s, focused on measuring intelligence through standardized tests. The intelligence test, developed by Lewis Terman and others, became a widely used tool to quantify cognitive abilities. In 1912, Stern introduced the concept of the intelligence quotient (IQ), which is calculated by dividing the test taker's mental age (obtained based on his/her performance on an intelligence test) by his/her chronological age and multiplying this number by 100. For example, if the test taker's mental age is 14 and chronological age is 12, then IQ will be 116: $(14/12) \times 100 = 116$.

Several scholars, including Binet, Spearman, Thurstone, Guilford, Cattell, Vernon, Wechsler, Piaget, and Simonton, have defined intelligence. Their definitions emphasize that intelligence refers to learning from experience, thinking abstractly using concepts and symbols, or adapting to new situations. Different types of IQ tests (e.g., verbal, non-verbal, and performance; speed and power tests) have been developed and are in vogue. The performance on IQ tests is often used to predict personal attributes, school performance, years of education, social status and income, job performance, social behaviour, non-academic knowledge, etc.

While IQ tests have been widely used to assess cognitive abilities, they are not without limitations. Here are some key limitations associated with IQ tests. First, IQ tests imply a unitary (or single ability), relatively fixed and stable view of intelligence, suggesting that an individual's cognitive abilities remain constant over time. However, research has shown that intelligence is dynamic and can be influenced by various factors, including education, experiences, and environmental stimulation (Baltes et al., 1999). Second, IQ tests primarily focus on cognitive abilities such as problem-solving, logical reasoning, and memory. However, they often neglect other important aspects of intelligence, such as creativity, emotional intelligence, and practical problem-solving skills. Third, performance on IQ measures is influenced by socio-economic factors. The limited access to educational resources by persons belonging to lower socio-economic backgrounds negatively affects their performance on IQ tests (Neisser et al., 1996). Fourth, IQ tests do not effectively measure an individual's ability to navigate real-world challenges. Practical skills, adaptability, and creativity, which are essential for success in various professions, are not fully captured by traditional IQ measures (Sternberg, 2003). Fifth, IQ tests yield numerical scores to represent cognitive abilities, which oversimplify the multidimensional nature of intelligence (Sternberg, 2004a).

Sixth, there is an inherent cultural bias in IQ tests. Test items may include language, references, or experiences that are more familiar to individuals from certain cultural backgrounds, leading to an unfair advantage for those individuals. For example, in a study (Serpell, 1979), Zambian and English children were required to reproduce patterns in three different media: wire models, pencil and paper, and clay. The Zambian children excelled in the wire medium to which they were most familiar while the English children were best with paper and pencil. Both groups performed equally well with clay. In the context of Brazilian schoolchildren, it was reported that children who were able to do mathematics required to run their street business were unable to do school mathematics (Carraher et al., 1985). These studies suggest that the cultural context and exposure to certain types of information play a role in test performance, challenging the notion of a fixed and universally applicable intelligence.

Changing Conceptions of Intelligence

The prevailing notion of IQ views intelligence in a decontextualized manner. Studies have shown that performance on IQ measures varies due to variations in culture including linguistic differences, test motivation, and exposure to particular environmental stimuli. Further, intelligence is not simply an adaptation to an environmental context (or reacting to the demands of the situation). Rather, human beings shape or bring changes in their environment and, at times, select a new environment. Robert Sternberg (1997, p. 1030) has, thus, defined intelligence as follows:

> Intelligence comprises the mental abilities necessary for adaptation to, as well as shaping and selection of, any environmental context.

Let us take an example. When you go to stay at a relative's place during holidays, you try to behave according to their expectations (adaptation). Slowly, you begin to suggest changes according to your likings or dislikes (shaping). However, bringing out the change in the environmental context may not always be possible due to various reasons. In that case, an intelligent person tries to find another suitable environment (selection). It is to be remembered that intelligence does not simply mean mere possession of certain abilities as such; rather use of these abilities in real-life situations is important. Recently, Sternberg (2021) has proposed the concept of *adaptive intelligence* – intelligence that is used to adapt to current problems and anticipate future problems in the real world. It consists of a diverse set of skills, attitudes, and behaviours required to achieve the common good. Also, recent theories of intelligence conceptualize intelligence as having multiple dimensions.

Howard Gardner's Theory of Multiple Intelligences

Gardner (1983, 1993) initially proposed seven kinds of intelligences. Later on, he added two (naturalistic and existential) intelligences (Gardner, 1999). The intelligences do not subsist as independent, isolated entities; rather, they relate with each other and ultimately don't exist at all. They do, however, provide an important medium for describing and understanding individual and cultural differences in our approach to the world. These intelligences are:

1) *Linguistic–Verbal Intelligence*: Persons possessing this intelligence are "word smart". They are sensitive to the meaning and order of words and use words well both while writing and speaking. Poets and writers exhibit this kind of intelligence.
2) *Logical–Mathematical Intelligence*: This type of person is "number and reasoning smart". Exhibited in scientific work, such people can solve mathematical problems and complex logic systems and enjoy thinking about abstract ideas.
3) *Visual–Spatial Intelligence*: Also known as "picture smart", it refers to the ability to "think in pictures", perceive the visual world accurately, and recreate (or alter) it in mind or on paper. Sailors, engineers, surgeons, pilots, sculptors, and painters have highly developed spatial intelligence.
4) *Bodily Kinesthetic Intelligence*: Also referred to as "Body smart", people who are high on this intelligence can use their body in a skilled way for self-expression or towards a goal, such as those required for dancing, athletes, surgery, craft making, and the like. Such people have hand–eye coordination and dexterity.
5) *Musical Intelligence*: "Music smart" people are good at thinking about rhythms, patterns, and sounds. Such people enjoy singing and playing musical instruments and have an understanding of rhythms, notes, and musical patterns. Musicians, singers, composers, and dancers are high on musical intelligence.
6) *Interpersonal Intelligence*: Also known as "people smart", this type of intelligence refers to the ability to perceive, understand, and relate with other individuals. The persons high on this intelligence are capable of accurately judging the intentions, motives, and desires of other individuals. Salespersons, politicians, counsellors, clinicians, and religious leaders possess a high degree of interpersonal intelligence.
7) *Intrapersonal Intelligence*: Referred to as "self-smart", people high on this intelligence can understand one's self (emotional states, feelings, motivations) and develop a sense of identity. They analyse their strengths and weaknesses well and have well-developed self-awareness. Philosophers, writers, and scientists are high on this type of intelligence.
8) *Naturalistic Intelligence*: Such people are "nature smart" and can recognize flora and fauna and make distinctions in the natural world. They are more interested in exploring the environment and knowing about other species. Hunters, farmers, tourists, and biologists are high on this intelligence.
9) *Existential Intelligence*: This is more concerned about the questions of life, its meaning and existence. Gardner puts Plato and Buddha in this category. Saints, philosophers, and theologians possess a high degree of existential intelligence.

Gardner's theory assumes that, though born with all types of intelligences, one may tap individual and cultural differences in the range of competencies that individuals enjoy. For example, one person may be good at verbal intelligence, the other at musical intelligence. Similarly, cultures may stress the acquisition of some of the intelligences more than others.

The development of a particular kind of intelligence depends on the available opportunity to the individual, the importance of particular intelligence in that culture, and the individual's efforts.

The theory has several implications for children's learning and cognitive development. First, children possess an array of skills and can be highly talented in some areas. Second, children should be presented with the learning materials in such a way that engages most or all of the intelligences to facilitate a deeper understanding of the material. Schools should instead foster creativity, critical thinking, and a deep understanding of the subject matter by encouraging students to explore and experiment with different ways of learning (Gardner, 1991). Third, as children have different sets of developed intelligences, the set determines how easy or difficult it would be for a particular child to learn information. Fourth, adults who find themselves misfit in a job that does not allow the optimal use of their highly developed intelligence should look for an opportunity for maximum expression of the same.

The educational programmes have been designed and implemented that cater to different types of intelligences in countries like Brazil, the United States, Canada, New Zealand, and so on based on Gardner's theory. At the same time, the theory has faced criticism for the fact that his definition of intelligence is too broad and different intelligences simply represent talents, personality traits, and abilities. Also, Gardner's theory is primarily based on a Western cultural perspective, and some of the intelligences, such as musical and spatial, may be valued differently in different cultural contexts. Further, though a series of educational programmes were launched based on Gardner's theory, not much empirical evidence is available in support of his claim.

Robert Sternberg's Triarchic Theory

Sternberg (1985) proposed that intelligence is composed of three distinct components: *analytical, creative*, and *practical intelligence*. Analytical intelligence is the ability to analyse and solve problems using logical reasoning and critical thinking. Creative intelligence is the ability to generate novel and useful ideas and solutions. Tasks that require innovation and originality, such as scientific research, entrepreneurship, and the arts, require this component of intelligence. Practical intelligence is the ability to adapt to real-world situations and solve practical problems. It refers to the ability to evaluate and adapt to different situations and to identify the most effective strategies for solving problems. Tasks that involve social interaction, such as leadership, communication, and negotiation as well as tasks requiring adaption to new environments and situations, such as starting a new course or job, demand the use of practical intelligence. Though Sternberg's theory has important implications for education and training, it has been criticized that components are too broad and vague, and they overlap with other constructs such as personality and motivation. Additionally, it lacks empirical support, particularly in terms of the measurement of creative and practical intelligence.

PASS Model of Intelligence

J.P. Das and colleagues (Das et al., 1994; Das & Naglieri, 1997) suggested the PASS model of intelligence that describes the cognitive processes consisting of four key processes: planning, attention, simultaneous, and successive (PASS). Each process represents a unique aspect of cognitive functioning that contributes to overall intelligence. Planning involves the ability to formulate a plan or strategy to solve a problem or achieve a goal. Attention refers to the ability to focus and sustain attention on relevant information while filtering out distractions. Simultaneous processing involves the ability to process multiple pieces of information at the same time. Successive processing refers to the ability to process information in a step-by-step or sequential manner.

The PASS model has important implications for understanding how students learn and how to optimize their learning experiences. For example, the model suggests that students with difficulties in one or more of the PASS processes may require specialized instruction. The PASS model has been extensively researched in a variety of cultural and linguistic contexts such as the United States (Flanagan & Ortiz, 2011), China (Pan & Detterman, 2013), and India (Dash, 1991; Das & Dash, 1989; Dash & Mahapatra, 1989).

In response to the limitations of psychometric measures, emerging theories offer more comprehensive frameworks that acknowledge diverse cognitive abilities, including creativity, practical skills, and dynamic problem-solving, fostering a broader understanding of human intelligence. These alternative models advocate for a shift from a one-size-fits-all approach to a more nuanced and inclusive perspective on cognitive capabilities.

The Interface Between Cognition and Emotion

The concept of intelligence has traditionally been associated with cognitive abilities and intellectual prowess. However, in recent decades, there has been a growing recognition of the importance of a more comprehensive understanding of intelligence – one that encompasses emotional, social, and even spiritual dimensions. This section discusses concepts such as emotional intelligence, spiritual intelligence, and wisdom.

Emotional Intelligence

In the 1990s, the concept of emotional intelligence (EI) gained prominence, with the work of Peter Salovey and John Mayer (1990), and was popularized by Daniel Goleman (1995). EI refers to the ability to understand and manage one's own emotions, as well as the emotions of others. It is the capacity to perceive, understand, and regulate emotions in oneself and others effectively. According to Mayer and Salovey (1997, p. 10),

> Emotional intelligence involves the ability to perceive accurately, appraise, and express emotion; the ability to access and/or generate feelings when they facilitate thought; the ability to understand emotion and emotional knowledge; and the ability to regulate emotions to promote emotional and intellectual growth.

This theory emphasizes the role of emotional awareness and interpersonal skills as crucial components of overall intelligence. EI has become increasingly popular over the years.

Mayer et al. (2000, p. 400) have listed certain characteristics of emotionally intelligent persons. Such persons are more likely to (a) have grown up in bio-socially adoptive homes (i.e., have had emotionally sensitive parenting), (b) be non-defensive, (c) be able to reframe emotions effectively (i.e., be realistically optimistic and appreciative), (d) choose good emotional role models, (e) be able to communicate and discuss feelings, and (f) develop expert knowledge in a particular emotional area such as aesthetic, moral or ethical feeling, social problem-solving, leadership, or spiritual feeling. Also, such people develop quality social interaction with peers.

Various models of EI have been put forth. The cognitive model (Mayer & Salovey, 1997) argues for emotional reasoning in everyday life and argues that emotions convey knowledge about a person's relationship with the world. For example, fear indicates the threat the person is facing, happiness indicates one's harmonious relationship with others, and anger generally reflects injustice. Goleman's (1995) model of affective regulation viewed EI as the ability to know and manage one's own emotions, recognize them in others, and handle relationships. The emotional competence model (Saarni, 1997) identified emotional competence as the ability to understand, manage, and express the social and emotional aspects of one's life in ways that enable the successful management of life. The relational model (Bar-On, 1997) defined EI in terms and an array of emotional and social knowledge and abilities that influence our overall ability to effectively relate to environmental demands.

The models discussed earlier emphasize harnessing others' emotions for one's benefit and are thus applicable in individualistic societies. Studies (e.g., Leung, 2005; Shanwal, 2004; Sharma et al., 2009; Srivastava, 2013) suggest that the concept of EI in collectivist societies is different, which takes into account obligations and social responsibilities. Sibia et al. (2005) developed a model of EI suitable to the Indian context (Box 6.3).

EI has been linked to numerous positive outcomes in both personal and professional settings (Mayer & Salovey, 1997). Individuals with high levels of EI are more successful in their careers, are better able to handle stress, and have higher levels of job satisfaction. Also, they tend to have more satisfying personal relationships and are better equipped to handle conflicts and resolve disputes.

Box 6.3 Indian View of Emotional Intelligence

Keeping in view the differences in the perspectives of the West (which is more individualistic) and East (context-sensitive nature), attempts have been made to develop a model of EI suitable for the Indian context. In India, the well-being of others and fulfilling obligations and responsibilities are important social concerns. Social skills such as respecting elders, helping others, caring, kindness, benevolence, and non-violence are typical emotional expressions. The Indian self is constructed around "we", "our", and "us" in contrast to the Western "I" and "me". There is more emphasis on looking inward and discovering the true self by following practices like yoga and *vratas* (ordinances) and faith in concepts like *dharma* (duty), *karma* (deeds), and *jitendriya* (a person who can manage and regulate one's emotions).

Given the distinguishing features mentioned earlier, Sibia and colleagues (Sibia et al., 2005) developed a model of EI for the Indian context. The model includes five dimensions: (a) social sensitivity (e.g., showing respect for significant others, prosocial activities, expressing and experiencing affection, building social support for oneself, and control of negative emotions), (b) time orientation (preparedness to meet future contingencies and ability to monitor progress in one's life course), (c) prosocial values (values related to the welfare of the society such as patience, affect, tolerance, kindness, endurance, and so on), (d) action tendencies (competencies such as persistence, dedication, discipline, punctuality, and so on), and (e) affective states (quality of emotional life such as being happy, contended, creative, open to exposure, optimism, and so on). The model has also been empirically tested in the Indian context (Srivastava et al., 2008).

Spiritual Intelligence

Spiritual intelligence (SQ) refers to the ability to explore and understand existential questions, transcend the ego, and connect with a higher purpose or meaning in life. SQ involves the integration of spiritual values and principles into daily life, leading to a sense of purpose, inner peace, and a deeper understanding of oneself and others (Emmons, 2000; Zohar & Marshall, 2000). It is concerned with the inner life of mind and spirit and its relationships to being in the world (Vaughan, 2002).

Empathy, compassion, and altruism are essential for developing SQ. The ability to connect with others in a deep and meaningful way is an important component of SQ. It guides individuals in making ethical decisions that align with their spiritual values. Also, SQ contributes to emotional resilience by providing individuals with a sense of inner strength and peace in the face of adversity. Wadhwani (2014) argues that spiritual intelligence leads to transpersonal, integrating, transcendental, searching, persisting, and transforming thinking. Thus, the development of spiritual intelligence has far-reaching implications for personal growth, enhancing well-being, fostering meaningful connections with others, and contributing to a more harmonious society. Meditation and mindfulness practices are effective in developing SQ. Religious and spiritual practices help in developing SQ as they provide a sense of community and support and offer opportunities for reflection and self-exploration. Engaging in activities that promote social and environmental justice also helps individuals develop a sense of purpose and meaning and connect with others.

In the Indian cultural context, spirituality is integrated into daily life through religious practices, festivals, and rituals. Children are exposed to these practices from a young age, and they are often taught spiritual values and concepts as part of their upbringing. Concepts of *karma* (action) and *dharma* (duty/righteousness) contribute to the moral and ethical dimensions of spiritual intelligence (Radhakrishnan, 1923). India's cultural diversity and pluralism afford an environment that encourages tolerance, acceptance, and understanding of diverse perspectives. Research has demonstrated the potential benefits of developing SQ. A positive relationship between SQ and psychological well-being has been reported (Thakur et al., 2022).

Wisdom

Wisdom is an enduring virtue that transcends the boundaries of time and culture. It is a holistic integration of cognitive, emotional, and reflective dimensions, shaping individuals into discerning and compassionate beings. Wisdom offers timeless guidance in the pursuit of a meaningful and purposeful life. In a world marked by constant change, the quest for wisdom remains a noble endeavour, as it equips individuals with the tools to navigate the complexities of the human experience (see Chapter 12 for details).

Thus, as individuals navigate the complex web of life, the cultivation of emotional intelligence and spiritual intelligence becomes a transformative journey, fostering not only intellectual acuity but also emotional resilience and spiritual depth. It is at this intersection that the profound essence of wisdom unfolds, transcending mere knowledge to illuminate the path towards a more enlightened and compassionate existence.

Culture and Intelligence

The cultural view assumes that the intellectual processes are rooted in the sociocultural milieu of people during a specific socio-historical time. It assumes that culture influences behaviour that is considered intelligent, processes underlying intelligence behaviour and the course of its development. Greenfield (1998, p. 83) has argued that "cultures define intelligence by what is adaptive to their particular eco-cultural niche". This view endorses the fact the behaviours considered intelligent are culture-specific, and the processes and course of intellectual development are guided by culture. Sternberg (2020) has also argued that intelligence needs to be understood in the cultural context in which it is displayed.

The societies in the West are highly urbanized, having advanced technology and modern schooling facilities. As Goodnow (1976) remarked, such developed societies stress the development of characteristics, such as generalization (i.e., drawing broader inference based on observation of a few instances), speed (i.e., acting fast or faster performance is superior), minimal moves (i.e., finding solutions of the problems in the fewest steps), no hands (i.e., a preference for mental rather than physical manipulations), and something of one's own (something original or creative to one's credit). Thus, an intelligent person in the Western world places more emphasis on the material or physical world than the social world and its practices, thinks more in terms of personal welfare than the societal norms and compliance with the norms, and has a preference for speed rather than slowness. As a consequence, the intelligence tests which were developed in the West attempted to capture this uniqueness which Mundy-Castle (1974) termed "technological intelligence".

Intelligence in non-Western societies is viewed in terms of the social competence of the individual. A person who fulfils social obligations, behaves in a socially responsible manner, and conforms to the established social norms is considered intelligent (refer to Cocodia, 2014; Srivastava, 2013 for review of studies). Research shows that intelligent people are more conforming and slow in Africa (Wober, 1974). They emphasize capability in specific situations and social responsibility such as cooperativeness and obedience (Serpell, 1982). In Kenya, intelligence refers to the ability to do what is needed to be done around the home without someone asking for the same (Harkness et al., 1992). The Leo (in Kenya) conception of intelligence revolves around two aspects: socio-emotional competence and cognitive competence (Grigorenko et al., 2001). To Yoruba, an intelligent person (a) does more listening than talking, (b) responds to an issue by placing it in proper cultural context, and (c) offers constructive rather than destructive views or cunningness.

Azuma and Kashiwagi (1987) reported that the Japanese concept of intelligence consists of five factors. These are (a) positive social competence (sociable, humorous, effective speaker), (b) receptive social competence (ability to appreciate other's point of view, sympathy, modesty, admitting mistakes, knowing one's place), (c) task efficient (working efficiently, good insights, future planning, clear decisions), (d) originality, and (e) reading and writing. The Chinese conception stresses more on reflection and self-efficacy and sees a close connection between intelligence and morality (Chen, 1994). The Indian notion of intelligence integrates cognitive, social, entrepreneurial, and emotional competencies (see Box 6.4). Thus, the studies show that the unidimensional approach to intelligence cannot be applied universally. It is essential to understand the local definition of intelligence and develop suitable measures for assessing intelligence in a particular context.

Box 6.4 Common Conception of Intelligence in India

In the Indian context, the Sanskrit term *buddhi* is used for intelligence which incorporates cognitive, affective, and motivational functions. It refers to waking up, noticing, recognizing, understanding, and comprehending (Das, 1994). To Sri Aurobindo, *buddhi* can be translated as understanding and Krishnamurti conceptualizes it in terms of harmony of reason, emotion, and action. Intelligence is the inherent capacity to feel as well as to reason (Das, 2013). It is of two types: *dharma* (good) and *pap* (bad) *buddhi*. Srivastava and Misra (1999a, 1999b, 1999c, 2001, 2007) studied commonly understood characteristics of intelligent persons in India by analysing ancient scholarly tradition, folk literature, and the lay people's conception. Towards this end, the researchers first collected Sanskrit *suktis* (good words) from different *sukti koshas*. A total of 339 *suktis* having reference to intelligence were analysed. Likewise, in the second stage, the researchers identified 393 proverbs in Hindi related to intelligent behaviour and intelligent persons from four dictionaries of Hindi proverbs. In the third stage, 1,885 persons from five different localities were individually asked to describe the characteristics/attributes/behaviours of an intelligent person. The participants came from different age groups (12–14 years, 16–18 years, 20–25 years, 45–50 years, and 60+), gender (male/female), schooled versus unschooled, and rural versus urban background.

Results revealed that intelligence is conceptualized in terms of four facets: cognitive competence, social competence, entrepreneurial competence, and emotional competence. Included among the cognitive competence of an intelligent person were characteristics such as context sensitivity (e.g., behaving according to *desh* (context), *kala* (time), and *patra* (person)), felicitous speech (*Priyambada*), problem-solving ability, discrimination between good and bad, future planning, etc. Social competence encompasses characteristics such as following social norms, respecting elders, carrying out family responsibilities, and helping the needy. The characteristics such as hard work, commitment, practicality, goal orientation, and moderation in behaviour were included in the entrepreneurial competence. Emotional competence includes control over emotions, sensitivity to others, open-mindedness, and good conduct.

It is thus evident that the Indian conception of intelligence is process-oriented and tied to the context. It refers to the adaptive potentiality of a person in diverse domains of life. This adaptive potentiality consists of a range of skills that help one to overcome life problems, grow and become what one wants to be. Considering these dimensions, Misra and Srivastava (2002) termed the Indian view of intelligence as "Integral intelligence".

Cultural Variations in Thinking

Analytical and holistic reasoning are two distinct types of thinking. Analytical reasoning emphasizes breaking down complex problems into smaller parts and analysing each part separately (deductive reasoning). Holistic reasoning, on the other hand, involves viewing problems as interconnected and considering the larger context in which they exist (inductive reasoning). For example, you show a picture of a face to two persons. One person looks at it globally and says it looks good, bright, charming etc. The second person makes comments on different parts of the face, such as the nose, the eye, and so on. The first one is an example of holistic reasoning, and the second one is analytical reasoning.

Research has shown that individuals from Western cultures tend to have a more analytical thinking style while individuals from East Asian cultures (including India) tend to have a more holistic thinking style (Nisbett, 2003). For example, in a study (Ji et al., 2004), it was observed that East Asian participants were more likely to group objects based on their relationships with one another while Western participants were more likely to group objects based on their characteristics. In another study (Nisbett et al., 2001), participants from the United States and China were asked to identify which of two pictures was the odd one out, with one picture showing a large fish in a small fish tank and the other showing a small fish in a large fish tank. Americans were more likely to focus on the fish itself and chose the picture that showed the fish in the small tank. Chinese participants, on the other hand, were more likely to focus on the relationship between the fish and its environment and chose the picture that showed the small fish in the large tank. East Asian individuals tend to have better memory for contextual information compared to Western individuals, which may be related to their more holistic reasoning style (Masuda et al., 2019).

In conclusion, it can be said that the cultural perspective on intelligence goes beyond the practice of decontextualized understanding of the cognitive domain. It is more inclusive, places competencies in context, and gives importance to obligations and responsibilities towards self, society, and environment. Integration and adaptation, rather than change and innovation, are the hallmarks of this tradition.

Theory of Mind Across Cultures

Theory of mind (ToM) refers to the ability to understand and predict the mental states of oneself and others, including beliefs, desires, emotions, and intentions. ToM is considered a universal human trait and influences social processes (such as empathy, sympathy, and compassion) and facilitates social interactions including prosocial behaviour, moral judgements, and conflict resolution (Bruneau et al., 2012).

Cultural variations in ToM can be observed in both the content and the context of social interactions. For example, the interests of the group are prioritized over individual interests in collectivist cultures (e.g., Asian and African). Such cultures value personality traits and attributes like cohesion, harmony, responsibility, interdependence, group goals, context sensitivity, and so on. The ToM in collectivistic cultures focuses on understanding and predicting the thoughts and feelings of others to maintain group harmony. Western societies, characterized by individualism, focus on characteristics such as the uniqueness of the individual, personal goals, independence, self-sufficiency, self-reliance, and so on. The ToM may be more focused on understanding and predicting individual behaviour based on internal states in individualistic cultures (Sabbagh, 2017). Box 6.5 contains a note on ToM in the Indian context.

Box 6.5 Development of Theory of Mind in the Indian Context

The ability to represent and attribute mental states to self and others, called theory of mind development, constitutes an important milestone in social cognitive development. Closely associated with perspective-taking ability, research studies across the globe point towards the universality of its development during preschool years. However, the understanding follows a different timetable in terms of its occurrence across cultures (Liu et al., 2008).

In one of the studies (Joshi et al., 2019) in the Indian context, only 12% of 4-year-old could pass the false belief task, a standard test of the theory of mind development. They concluded that Indian children's understanding of first-order false belief is relatively late since the mastery in understanding false belief develops at around 6–7 years of age. This indicates a relative delay in the onset of the understanding compared to that of Western children who develop it around 4–5 years of age. In another study of Indian children (Wahi & Johri, 1994), the mental-real distinctions could not be performed by 3- and 4-year-old children whether they were from privileged or deprived homes. Several East-Asian communities report similar findings. Japanese children (Naito & Koyama, 2006) developed false belief understanding around 6–7 years of age. Children belonging to Hong Kong (Liu et al., 2008) were found to perform well on certain false belief tasks around the age of five years, whereas Canadian children passed these tasks at around three years of age. However, in a recent study with Indian children, the order and pattern of acquisition in the theory of mind were found to follow that of the children in the United States and Australia (Vishwanath et al., 2023).

These variations might have been related to the prevalent societal folk psychologies, socialization process, linguistic factors, and so on that might interact with the development process of the theory of mind. Development of mental state vocabulary is related to achievement in the theory of mind, and there is a mutual interdependence (Babu, 2009; Patnaik & Babu, 2001) as evident in studies in the Indian context. Parental literacy and mother–child interaction have been known to facilitate the use of meta-representational language and thereby the development of the theory of mind. That the development of metalinguistic abilities is influenced by socio-environmental factors as well as the language maturity of the child has been demonstrated (Raisa et al., 2019) in a study exploring the development of the higher-order theory of mind abilities in bilingual Indian children of 3–9 years of age. Rather than general intelligence, it is the social intelligence that this mind-reading ability was significantly related to in another study (Rajkumar et al., 2008) of 8- to 11-year-old Indian children.

Bhaswati Patnaik
Utkal University, Bhubaneswar
Fostering Creativity

Creativity

Creativity refers to the ability to generate something novel and useful, be it ideas, solutions, or products. Any creation is deemed creative to the extent it is different from earlier creations and useful to society. While creativity is related to intelligence, highly intelligent people are not necessarily highly creative. However, at least average intelligence is found in creative people. Formal schooling, which is considered to nurture knowledge, is also not very strongly related to creativity. Creativity is often considered an outcome of sudden insight, but most people tend to agree with the view that endurance too is important. Poets, artists, scientists, and other thinkers generally agree that seeing, thinking, and acting in novel ways require hard work, motivation, and concentration. It is to be noted that creativity is not a single or unitary ability; rather, it is a cluster of abilities. Some of the important abilities include flexibility in responding to a situation in a variety of ways, such as fluency, speed of responding, originality, understanding contradictions, elaboration, recognition of future possibilities, and divergent thinking.

Creativity is undoubtedly universally valued. However, as Misra, Srivastava, and Misra (2006) have argued, the expression of creativity takes place in a sociocultural milieu that may help or hinder its growth in an individual. Diverse cultures do appear to selectively nurture specific domains of creativity. Nisbett (2019) notes that creativity often involves the ability to think outside of established cultural norms and conventions and that individuals from different cultures may have different ideas about what constitutes creative or innovative thinking. For example, some cultures may value originality and risk-taking while others may place a greater emphasis on tradition and conformity. He further suggests that creativity may be more closely linked to practical problem-solving skills (e.g., weaving and pottery making) in some cultures while in others it may be seen as a more abstract and aesthetic pursuit (e.g., art and design). Thus, different forms and domains of creativity flourish in different cultures, which, in turn, shape the culture. Creativity can be fostered by encouraging curiosity and exploration, providing a supportive and collaborative environment, opportunities for play and experimentation, and recognizing and rewarding it (Csikszentmihalyi, 1996).

It may be mentioned that the need for creation is located in the demand for people's adjustment to their environment, as required by the struggle for survival. For example, in a study of *Jnanapith* awardees, the highest literary award in India, Raina et al. (2001) found that most of the awardees were born in remote villages where they went through a lot of frustration and suffering, including attending schools with an empty stomach. Failure and the pain associated with failure accelerate the process of creativity. The need for perfect adjustment or harmony involves transcendence on the part of artists' minds from the world of change of which they are a part. Keeping an open mind, remaining sensitive to the environment, and imaginatively viewing possibilities are the foundations for creativity (Misra et al., 2006). Creativity engages inspiration and imagination that help one to think beyond the given and bring in the elements of novelty in our world of experience.

In ancient Indian traditions, creativity was often seen as a divine gift, and individuals were encouraged to develop and express their creative potential for personal and societal well-being. The emphasis on innovation, adaptability, and holistic thinking can be found woven into the fabric of ancient texts, providing valuable insights for fostering creativity in various aspects of life. Patanjali's *Yoga Sutras* discuss the concepts of "dharana" (concentration) and "dhyana" (meditation). These practices are considered essential for fostering creativity by calming the mind, enhancing focus, and tapping into higher states of consciousness. The *Natyashastra* (or dramaturgy) emphasizes the role of creativity in performing arts and outlines the principles for artists to express their creativity through emotional and aesthetic experiences. The Bhakti movement emphasized the importance of devotion and emotional expression in spiritual practice. The movement inspired a rich tradition of poetry, music, and dance that expressed emotional devotion to the divine. Thus, the creative imagination is seen as a tool for exploring the depths of the mind and unlocking the secrets of the universe.

Schooling and Cognitive Development

Schooling is a social phenomenon reciprocally related to societal demands. The society, which embodies a value system and culture, determines what is expected of schools, and the institution of schooling shapes the social order by selectively nurturing certain skills and talents (Srivastava, 2009). Schooling involves the formal transmission of knowledge, skills, and values with a view to socializing and integrating individuals into society and preparing them for economic and civic participation (Dasen & Mishra, 2011). It brings sophistication to a person, changes his/her mentality, and opens new possibilities. Schooling brings changes in the world view of a person and the way he/she thinks.

Schooling affords opportunities for children to learn and develop cognitive abilities and skills; thereby, it is responsible for making minds and creating rational human beings. The physical (e.g., infrastructure, educational and ICT resources, safety and health) and social (e.g., peer interactions, teacher–student relationships, school culture, teamwork, and collaboration) environments of the school significantly influence cognitive development. The curriculum and pedagogical processes provide children with opportunities to think critically and creatively, analyse information, and make decisions. Further, schooling is seen as a dynamic and evolving system that is shaped by the cultural, political, and economic contexts in which it operates. Baveja (2019), therefore, proposed adopting a "person-in-context" approach to learning, which assumes culture and cognition as two enmeshed entities that inform pedagogic practices. This demands situating learning in everyday contexts where learners use concrete referents and tools extensively, giving authenticity to learning and promoting the transfer of learning within and between domains (Mishra & Baveja, 2014).

The Indian education system is faced with the challenge of bringing every child to school and ensuring their sustained participation and learning. Even though the dropout rate has reduced over the years, it is still a challenge for children belonging to socially disadvantaged groups (e.g., SCs, STs, Muslims, girls, etc.) (Nambissan, 2020), differently abled children, children in civil strife or calamity-affected areas, and those in urban slums. The quality of schooling also needs revisiting, as it has been reported that children in government schools in India learn little (ASER, 2024; NCERT, 2021).

Attempts have been made to promote the education of children through the formal system of schooling by adopting programmes like Sarva Shiksha Abhiyan (now Samagra Shiksha) and enacting the Right of Children to Free and Compulsory Education (RTE) Act, 2010. However, the situation demands adopting innovative approaches. There is a need to provide children with meaningful access to education in terms of high attendance rates, progression through grades without repetition, and learning outcomes which confirm that basic knowledge and skills are being mastered (Govinda, 2011). Keeping students in school through a provision of interesting, useful and child-friendly material, engaged teaching, and above all, a non-authoritarian and enriching atmosphere in the classroom continues to be a challenge (Thapan, 2020). It is in this context that alternative systems of schooling have flourished in the country for quite some time.

Alternative Schooling in India

Realizing the limitations of formal schooling, alternative schemes of education have been in place, which aim to provide an opportunity for the all-round development of the child by keeping her nature at the centre. Indian thinkers have visualized that education should develop inherent possibilities in a person, maintaining closeness with culture, and symbiosis with nature. Mahatma Gandhi emphasized the development of the heart, hand, and brain. Sri Aurobindo emphasized the integrated development of the individual's soul. One would find a yearning in the thinking and experiments of Swami Vivekananda, Swami Dayanand Saraswati, Rabindra Nath Tagore, Giju Bhai Badheka, and Jiddu Krishnamurthy who wanted to touch the dimensions of curiosity and creativity beyond the shackles of the normal school. They stressed the natural development of the person and the sense of joy in life.

Several schools are making efforts in this direction. Based on Gandhi's philosophy, a school named Anand Niketan in Wardha offers an opportunity to learn through artistic and productive work (such as agriculture and kitchen work). Sri Aurobindo's ideas of integrated development are used to organize education in Pondicherry. Chinmaya Mission, Sadhu Vaswani Trust, Dayalbagh Educational Institute etc. are also working in this direction. Hoshangabad Science

Education Project and Adharshila Shikshan Kendra in Madhya Pradesh, the Valley School in Bengaluru, Digantar in Rajasthan, Rishi Valley School in Andhra Pradesh, Siddha School in Uttarakhand, Vidyodaya School in Tamil Nadu, Shepherd School in Bihar are some such attempts. Schools of the Gurukul system are also running at many places in which students are being initiated based on Indian knowledge tradition. The alternative experiments tend to foster a sense of symbiosis with nature and community, where education loosens its mechanical constraints, where education within itself creates choices, provides opportunities for different paths for expression of individual differences in the true sense, where education bridges the gap between discovery and repetition (see Kumar, 1991; Sarangpani, 2003). It ends and prepares the student for the joy of learning.

The Government of India has also taken initiatives in the direction of alternative education. The National Institute of Open Schooling (NIOS) and Indira Gandhi National Open University (IGNOU) are two examples. The NIOS is making innovative efforts and gives the students the freedom to choose study subjects and take exams according to their preparation (for details, visit www.nios.ac.in/). The IGNOU is making such efforts in higher education (visit http://ignou.ac.in/).

There are two models of alternative education – one is a model where parents of affluent families manage the education of their children in small schools keeping the freedom of the individual at the centre, bearing the expenses. The second type of experiment is one in which children have no access to formal education, and if there is access then there is no connection with the culture. In the second type of situation, alternative education provides opportunities for children to read and write, keeping in mind the language, productive works, and science of the community. The Imli Mahua School in Chhattisgarh and the experiments of Adharshila in Madhya Pradesh are such examples. Research shows that alternative efforts for educating children have been successful (Konantambigi et al., 2008; Sibia, 2006; Thapan, 1991).

It may be noted that alternative schools emphasize project-based learning, experiential learning, and interdisciplinary learning and attempt to inculcate the responsibilities in life along with the spiritual, social, and moral values. They provide experiential learning. Alternative schools are continuously moving towards fostering the all-round development of children. Such elements must be adopted from alternative schools, which will help the mainstream of education to get rid of its captivity and focus more on learning skills and values than examination and marks. It is in the context of alternative schooling that *Guru–Shishya Parampara* assumes significance (Box 6.6).

Box 6.6 The *Guru–Shishya* Relationship: A Timeless Bond of Learning and Transformation

गुरुर्ब्रह्मा गुरुर्विष्णुर्गुरुर्देवो महेश्वरः । गुरुरेव परं ब्रह्म तस्मै श्रीगुरवे नमः ।

(The Guru is Brahma, the Guru is Vishnu, the Guru is Maheshwara. The Guru is the Supreme Absolute; I bow to that Guru).

The *Guru–Shishya* relationship, a sacred and profound connection between a teacher (*guru*) and a student (*shishya*), has held a significant place in the cultural, spiritual, and educational ethos of India for millennia. The earlier verse underscores the divine nature of the *Guru*. It suggests that the *Guru* is not just a teacher but embodies the qualities of the trinity (Brahma,

Vishnu, Maheshwara) and represents the ultimate reality (*Brahman*). *Guru* converts darkness into light and makes the invisible God visible (Raina, 2002). The 15th-century saint-poet Kabir asks that if *Guru* and *Govind* stand before me, whose feet should I touch? The answer is the *Guru* gets the offering. He shows the way to *Govind* (Gold, 1987). The Upanishads describe learning as a junction (*sandhi*) of the student which is the first part (*Poorva paksha*) and the teacher is the later part (*Uttar paksha*). The lesson or discourse is called *sandhan* or *exploration*.

Rooted in ancient scriptures, the importance of passing down knowledge from a wise *guru* to an eager *shishya* has been highlighted. The *guru* was not just an instructor; rather, they were a spiritual guide, a mentor, and a custodian of wisdom. The *shishya*, on the other hand, was not merely a student but a devoted disciple willing to embark on a journey of self-discovery under the guru's tutelage. The relationship is characterized by deep respect, unwavering loyalty, and a profound sense of duty.

There are examples showcasing the diversity of *Guru–Shishya* relationships spanning spiritual, philosophical, social, and artistic domains. There are also instances where the *shishya* overshadowed the *guru*. For example, Sant Kabir surpassed his guru Ramanand in spiritual insights, Adi Shankaracharya excelled his guru Govinda Bhagavatpada in spiritual prowess, and musician Tansen outshined his guru Swami Haridas in musical talent and innovation. The *Guru–Shishya* relationship is a cultural treasure that transcends time and continues to influence education, spirituality, and personal growth. It is a relationship built on mutual trust, respect, and an unbreakable bond of learning. Through this connection, knowledge becomes a living experience, and wisdom is passed down from one generation to the next.

Overview

This chapter has offered a multifaceted exploration of the intricate processes underlying the maturation of cognitive abilities. The journey through this chapter has traversed the seminal works of Piaget, Vygotsky, Neo-Piagetian, and Rogoff shedding light on diverse perspectives that have shaped our comprehension of cognitive growth. The socio-cognitive view of Bruner and the information processing approach have enriched our understanding, emphasizing the dynamic interplay between individual and societal influences. The cultural dimensions introduced in this chapter, particularly the Indian perspective on cognition and indigenous intellective concepts, contribute to a global understanding of cognitive development. As highlighted in the discussion on culture and cognition, the dichotomy between technological and social competence underscores the impact of cultural nuances on cognitive processes.

Intelligence and creativity explored through the historical lens and the contributions of Gardner, Sternberg, and J.P. Das showcase the evolving conceptions in these domains. The chapter has not only provided theoretical foundations but also delved into the practical aspects of fostering creativity, as well as positive schooling and learning skills.

The exploration of the intricate relationship between cognition and emotion, including emotional intelligence and spiritual intelligence, brings a nuanced dimension to our understanding. Incorporating an Indian perspective on emotional intelligence adds cultural richness to the discourse. The closing sections delving into educational strategies and alternative schooling provide a comprehensive view of the practical implications of cognitive development. The diverse topics covered, from the *Guru–Shishya* relationship to yoga's impact on cognitive development, illustrate the holistic approach this chapter adopts.

In essence, the chapter invites readers to appreciate the complexity and richness of cognitive development by intertwining diverse theories, cultural perspectives, emotional considerations, and practical applications. As we conclude this exploration, the chapter serves as a gateway to further enquiry, encouraging educators, researchers, and learners to continue unravelling the intricacies of the fascinating journey of cognitive development.

Key Terms

Antahkarana
Alternative Schooling in India
Apprenticeship in Thinking
Bruner's Theory of Cognitive Development
Concrete Operational Stage
Conservation
Culture and Cognition
Cultural Variations in Thinking
Emotional Intelligence
Equilibration
Fostering Creativity
Formal Operational Stage
Guru–Shishya Relationship
Indian View of Emotional Intelligence
Indian Perspective on Cognition
Indigenous Intellective Concepts
Jnana
Information Processing
The Interface Between Cognition and Emotion
Neo-Piagetian Theory
PASS Model
Panch Kosha
Piagetian Theory
Pragya
Positive Schooling
Scaffolding
Social Representation of Intelligence in India
Schooling and Cognitive Development
Sensory Motor Development
Smriti
Spiritual Intelligence
Theories of Cognitive Development
Theory of Mind (ToM) Across Cultures
Theory of Multiple Intelligences
Triarchic Theory of Intelligence
Vygotsky's Theory of Cognitive Development
Wisdom
Yoga and Cognitive Development
Zone of Proximal Development

Questions for Reflection

1) How do the indigenous concepts of cognition and the Indian view of emotional intelligence challenge or complement Western theories of cognitive development?
2) How might an understanding of the multifaceted nature of intelligence influence educational practices and assessments in different contexts?
3) How do cultural variations in thinking influence the development of emotional intelligence, and how can educators leverage this understanding to enhance learning experiences?
4) What implications does the traditional mentor–student relationship have for cognitive development in a modern, globalized world?
5) How does the development of the Theory of Mind in the Indian context differ from Western perspectives, and what insights does this offer into the cultural nuances shaping cognitive development?

Suggested Further Readings

Books

Eysenck, M. W., & Groome, D. (2023). *Cognitive psychology: Revisiting the classic studies.* SAGE.

Galinsky, H. (2010). *Mind in the making: The seven essential life skills every child needs.* Harper Collins.

Rogoff, B. (2003). *The cultural nature of human development.* Oxford University Press.

Shoda, Y., Cervone, D., & Downey, G. (Eds.). (2007). *Persons in context: Building a science of the individual.* The Guilford Press.

Website/Online Resources

Cognitive Development Society (*www.cogdevsoc.org/*)

National Institute of Child Health and Human Development (NICHD) – Child Development (*www.nichd.nih.gov/health/topics/child-development*)

7 Language Development

Contents

Introduction	140
What is Language?	140
Box 7.1: Significance of Language in the Indian Tradition	141
Stages of Language Development	141
Box 7.2: Manifestation of Language (*Vak*): An Indian View	142
Theories of Language Development	143
Subsystems of Language	144
Attending and Receiving Initial Sounds	146
Bilingualism and Multilingualism	147
Box 7.3: Literacy Rate in India	150
Box 7.4: Three-Language Formula in India	151
Language and Thought: An Inseparable Connection	152
Box 7.5: Relationship Between Language and Thought in the Indian Tradition	154
Development of Para-Speech Communication (PSC)	154
Box 7.6: *Mudras* and *Asanas* in the Indian Tradition	155
Factors Influencing Language Development	156
Overview	157
Key Terms	158
Questions for Reflection	158

Learning Objectives

After studying this chapter, the learner will be able to:

Describe the components of language and explain their role in communication;
Explore various theories of language development;
Analyse the interplay of different factors that shape language development;

DOI: 10.4324/9781003441168-10

140 *Perspectives on Cognitive and Language Development*

> Familiarize with the linguistic diversity in India and its implications for language development in the contemporary context; and
> Apply their knowledge to practical contexts, fostering language development.

Introduction

Sarvam shabden bhasate

—(Words make everything visible to us.)

– in Bhartrihari's *Vakyapadiya*

—(5th century BC)

Language is a remarkable phenomenon that sets humans apart from other species. It is a tool for communication, representation, and creative engagement. It is a vehicle for expressing ideas and emotions and a window to understanding the world around us. The statement "Sarvam Shabden Bhasate" is a profound realization by an Indian grammarian, Bhartihari. It implies that the world becomes visible or appreciable through words. In various streams of Indian thought including grammar, Vedanta and Tantra, there is a recognition of the power of language, sound, and vibration. The idea is that the entire universe, in its manifold forms, is an expression of a divine sound or vibration. In this context, "word" or "sound" is considered a fundamental aspect of creation, and everything in existence is a manifestation of this primal sound. This concept aligns with the broader notion of *Nada Brahman*, which translates to "the world is sound" or "sound is divine". It underscores the idea that the universe is not just a physical reality but is intricately connected to the vibrational or sound-related processes of existence.

In human life, the journey of language development is a fascinating one. It is shaped by a complex interplay of biological, cognitive, social, and environmental factors. In this chapter, we shall explore aspects of language development, delving into its various aspects, theories, and issues. It is estimated that there are 6,909 distinct languages (see Ethnologue). In India, there are 122 major languages and 1,599 other languages. They belong to several language families. About 78% speak Indo-Aryan, 19% speak Dravidian, and the remaining 3% speak Austroasiatic, Sino Tibetan, and other minor language families. Out of these, 22 languages are given the status of official languages. It may be noted that many languages do not have scripts. So they exist in oral form. Also, languages differ in numerous other ways, but they do have some common features. They have infinite generativity, and users of a language can generate an infinite number of sentences using a set of rules. This chapter introduces some of the fascinating aspects of language development.

What is Language?

Human language is a unique form of communication that involves the use of words, symbols, and rules to convey meaning. Language uses symbols, which can be spoken sounds (phonemes), written characters (letters or hieroglyphs), or gestures (sign language) to represent objects, actions, ideas, and concepts. These symbols are arbitrary and have meanings only because society has assigned them particular meanings. Languages have rules and structures governing how words and symbols are arranged to form meaningful sentences. Meaning is conveyed through the use of words and their relationships. Language serves as a means of communication, enabling the transmission of knowledge from one generation to the next. Language is highly creative, enabling speakers to combine words in novel ways to express new ideas or convey subtle nuances of meaning. It reflects the values, beliefs, and customs of the communities that speak them and thus shapes our identity and sense of belonging. Language is multimodal which uses spoken and written forms as well as non-verbal means such as body language, facial expressions, and gestures. It is not exclusive to humans; other animals have some forms of communication, but human language is distinguished by its complexity, adaptability, and ability to convey abstract concepts. Language holds a special place in the Indian thought tradition (Box 7.1).

Box 7.1 Significance of Language in the Indian Tradition

Language in the Indian tradition is conceptualized in terms of "Vak". *Vak* is a Sanskrit term that can be loosely translated as "speech" or "sound". However, its significance goes far beyond mere verbal communication. *Vak* is often personified and revered as a divine principle or goddess, known as "Vak Devi" or "Saraswati". The goddess represents the creative and transformative power of speech and is associated with wisdom, knowledge, and artistic expression.

Panini, an ancient Indian scholar, made significant contributions to the study of phonetics and grammar. Panini's work, the "Ashtadhyayi" provides a set of linguistic rules and notations known as "sutras" (aphorisms). *Sutras* are short, formulaic statements that capture essential aspects of Sanskrit grammar. Panini meticulously analysed the sounds and components of the Sanskrit language and formulated rules governing word formation, sentence structure, and linguistic transformations. He had a lasting impact on the study of linguistics worldwide. Contributions of sages like Katyayan, Patanjali, and Bhartihari have extended this tradition.

Language is considered one of the means of acquiring knowledge (*Pramana*). It is categorized as "Shabda" (word or testimony) along with perception (*Pratyaksha*) and inference (*Anumana*). Texts like the *Nyaya Sutras* discuss the epistemological role of language.

Speech can be a tool for spiritual growth and self-realization. The sound of "OM" (pronounced as *a u m*) has received great significance. Thus, the Indian tradition also recognizes the power of language in expressing devotion, acquiring knowledge, and facilitating spiritual growth. These concepts and practices have had a profound influence on Indian culture, philosophy, and spirituality.

Stages of Language Development

Language development begins in infancy and continues throughout a person's life. The development of language involves several stages and is influenced by various biological, cognitive, social, and environmental factors. Studies have shown that language development proceeds through several stages as discussed in the following.

1) *Pre-Linguistic Stage*

Between birth and six months, children do not show developed language skills. They communicate with sounds; they cry, make cooing sounds and utter nasal murmur as their vocal tract develops. Infants can also recognize voices and sounds in addition to facial expressions and voice tones.

2) Babbling

Infants begin by making various sounds, known as babbling, between six and nine months. Children begin to babble, making noises and syllables that are not yet words. This stage lays the groundwork for speech as they experiment with different vocalizations.

3) Holophrastic or One-Word Stage

Around their first birthday (between 9 and 18 months), children start to use single words to express entire ideas. For instance, a child in this stage might say "dada" as a way of getting their father's attention. These words may have a range of meanings depending on context and intonation.

4) Two-Word Stage

Around 18–24 months, children start combining two words to form basic phrases. For example, they say "more food", "doggy small" etc. These combinations often follow simple grammatical patterns.

5) Telegraphic Stage

In the next phase (between 24 and 30 months), children begin to use telegraphic speech, which consists of short, concise sentences with essential words. For instance, a child might say "Mommy go" instead of "Mommy is going".

6) Multi-Word Stage

Children beyond 30 months of age can generate complex sentences that allow them to better communicate their ideas. Around the ages of 4–5 years, children begin forming more complex sentences with conjunctions and clauses, expressing more nuanced thoughts. As children grow older, they develop the ability to think about and analyse language itself, including understanding puns, metaphors, and wordplay. Box 7.2 contains the Indian view on language development.

Box 7.2   Manifestation of Language (Vak): An Indian View

The early Indian tradition has been oral and ancient texts including the Vedas dating back to about 5,000 years were preserved through oral transmission from one generation to the other. Vedic scholars followed very rigorous practices of pronunciation.

According to Panini's *Ashtadhyayi* and Bhartrihari's *Vakyapadiya*, speech or sound undergoes four stages of manifestation, known as *Para, Pashyanti, Madhyama,* and *Vaikhari*.

- *Para* is the transcendental or supreme stage of sound. It is considered the unmanifested form of sound, existing in a potential or latent state.
- *Pashyanti* is the second stage where sound is conceptualized or visualized. In *Pashyanti*, the sound is still in a subtle form, not yet differentiated into individual words or distinct units. It is the stage where the speaker begins to form the sound within their mind.

- *Madhyama* is the intermediate stage where the sound takes a more concrete form. It is the stage where the mental concept of sound transforms into a more structured linguistic form, though it may not be fully articulated.
- *Vaikhari* is the final, overt, or articulated stage of sound. It is the stage where the sound is spoken or expressed in its fully manifested form, audible to others. *Vaikhari* is the stage of speech that we hear and understand in everyday communication.

In the Indian literary tradition, the power of words lies not only in their literal meaning (*Abhidha*) but also in their ability to convey nuanced, suggested meanings (*Lakshana*) and to evoke emotions and imagery (*Vyanjana*).

Theories of Language Development

Understanding how children acquire language has been a key concern of research in developmental psychology and linguistics. Various theories have emerged to explain the mechanisms and stages involved in this process. Some of the key theories of language development are discussed herewith.

Behavioural Perspective

The behaviourist theory proposes that language development is a product of environmental influences and conditioning (Skinner, 1957). According to this theory, children learn language through imitation and reinforcement. They mimic the speech of adults and receive positive feedback when they produce correct words and sentences. Skinner's theory emphasizes the role of external factors (e.g., reinforcement) in shaping language acquisition. However, this theory is criticized for its inability to explain the creative and generative nature of language. Children often produce novel sentences that they have never heard before, suggesting that language development involves more than mere imitation and reinforcement.

Biological Perspective

In contrast to the behaviourist view, the biological view argues that humans have an innate predisposition for language acquisition. Noam Chomsky (1957) posited that all human languages share a common underlying structure, and children are born with an innate knowledge of some kind of universal grammar. They are equipped with a language acquisition device (LAD). Children are genetically programmed to acquire language, and their exposure to language in the environment triggers the unfolding of this innate linguistic knowledge. Children all over the world display language milestones at about the same age and in about the same sequence.

Chomsky's Universal Grammar (UG) posits that certain principles and parameters are common to all natural languages. These principles form the foundation upon which individual languages build their specific grammatical structures. Languages differ from each other by setting these parameters in unique ways. For example, in some languages (e.g., English) the word order in a sentence is Subject–Verb–Object (e.g., she reads a book). In Hindi, the word order is Subject–Object–Verb (e.g., *Vah kitab padhati hai*). However, despite this difference, both languages adhere to the universal principle that sentences have subjects, verbs, and objects. Chomsky's theory addresses the "poverty of the stimulus" problem, which highlights the fact that children are exposed to limited and often incomplete linguistic input, yet they acquire complex grammatical structures. UG is seen as the source of knowledge that helps children fill in the gaps and deduce the grammatical rules of their language.

Chomsky's theory is supported by evidence that children, regardless of their linguistic environment, follow almost the same sequence of language development and display attainment of linguistic milestones. However, it has been critiqued for not fully accounting for the influence of environmental factors and the diversity of language acquisition experiences.

Interactionist Theory

Interactionist theories of language development propose that both biological and environmental factors interact to facilitate language acquisition. For example, Vygotsky's (1978) social interactionist theory posits that social interactions and cultural context influence language development (see Chapter 6).

Cognitive Theory

Cognitive theories, such as Piaget's theory, propose that language development is closely linked to other aspects of cognitive development (Piaget, 1952). According to his theory, language development is not solely about acquiring words and grammar but also about developing abstract thinking and problem-solving abilities. Piaget's theory underscores the idea that cognitive and linguistic development are intertwined and mutually supportive processes. However, it has been criticized for underestimating children's linguistic abilities and overlooking the influence of social interactions on language development.

Each theory of language development contributes to our understanding of how children acquire language. While each theory has its peculiarities, strengths and limitations, all of them highlight the complex interplay of genetic, environmental, social, and cognitive factors that shape the remarkable journey of language acquisition and growth in children. A holistic view of language development recognizes the multifaceted nature of this phenomenon, offering insights into how humans come to master the most powerful tool of communication and knowledge acquisition.

Subsystems of Language

Language is a multifaceted system that encompasses various interconnected subsystems. These subsystems work in harmony to enable us to convey thoughts, emotions, and ideas with precision. The key subsystems of language are discussed here.

Phonemes

Phonemics is the scientific study of speech sounds. It is concerned with investigating the physical properties of sounds and how they are produced by the vocal tract and attended to by the human ear (Lodefoged & Johnson, 2011). Phonetics is of three types: articulatory, acoustic, and auditory. Articulatory phonetics focuses on the production of speech sounds (e.g., movements of the lips, tongue, vocal cords, and palate). Acoustic phonetics delves into the acoustic properties of speech sounds, including their frequencies, durations, and amplitudes. Auditory phonetics examines how humans perceive and process speech sounds. This involves investigating the way the human auditory system discerns differences in pitch, loudness, and timbre, allowing for the recognition of speech sounds and linguistic patterns.

Morphemes

Morphemes are the smallest meaningful units of language, which can be words or parts of words (e.g., syllables). Morphology is the branch of linguistics concerned with the structure of words and the way they are formed and understood. It is the study of the rules for combining morphemes. Morphemes can be classified into two main categories: free morphemes, which can stand alone as words (e.g., "book", "run"), and bound morphemes, which must be attached to other morphemes to convey meaning (e.g., "-ed" to indicate past tense).

Syntax

Syntax is referred to as the "grammar" of a language and is concerned with how words are combined to form coherent and meaningful expressions. It establishes a systematic framework for communication. The principles governing syntax are universal across languages. Chomsky's (1965) transformational–generative grammar revolutionized the study of syntax by introducing the concept of innate linguistic knowledge and a universal grammar underlying all languages. Chomsky distinguished between deep structure and surface structure. The deep structure represents the underlying meaning of a sentence while the surface structure is the actual arrangement of words in a sentence. Transformational rules mediate the relationship between deep and surface structures. For example, in the sentence "The cat chased the mouse", the deep structure might abstractly represent the action of chasing, the agents involved (the cat and the mouse), and the direction of the action. Transformational rules then guide the conversion of this deep structure into various types of surface structure, such as passive voice ("The mouse was chased by the cat") or questions ("Did the cat chase the mouse?").

Semantics

Semantics is the study of meaning in language. It is concerned with the way words, phrases, sentences, and discourse convey information. It is responsible for linking linguistic signs (words and phrases) to the concepts they represent. Without semantics, language would be a mere collection of arbitrary sounds or symbols, devoid of any meaningful communication. At the most basic level, semantics deals with the meaning of individual words. Word meanings can be classified into two main categories: denotation (the core, dictionary definition) and connotation (the associated or implied meanings and emotions). For example, the word "dog" denotes a domesticated animal but can also communicate ideas like loyalty or affection. Semantics also involves the study of how words combine to form phrases and sentences, and how these combinations create new meanings.

Pragmatics

Pragmatics situates the meaning of a word or sentence in a context. It is the study of the way the users interpret meaning in a given social and situational context. It is concerned with questions like, "What does the speaker mean by this?" or "How is this sentence interpreted differently in various contexts?" It, thus, delves into the intricacies of communication beyond the mere words and phrases uttered, examining the role of context, speaker intentions, and the shared conventions that underlie successful interactions. The meaning of a sentence can change drastically depending on the context in which it is uttered. For example, in Hindi, the term "आप" is used to address elders or persons in authority and "Tum" to youngsters. But sometimes youngsters are addressed as "आप" in sarcasm. Thus, pragmatics is concerned with the "implications" of what is said and how it is said.

Discourse

Discourse is concerned with the larger units of language. Its study focuses on how sentences and utterances are connected and organized to convey meaning effectively within a given context. Discourse consists of several sentences that are interrelated on a given topic and purpose and work together to convey a communicative intent. Discourse encompasses cohesion, coherence, and structure to facilitate effective communication. Cohesion refers to the binding of sentences and utterances together by including pronouns (e.g., he, she, it), conjunctions (e.g., and, but, because), and lexical repetition. Coherence makes the discourse logically and semantically consistent. Information structure involves the arrangement of information within a discourse. This includes topics, themes, and how new information is introduced and developed. An effective information structure ensures that the most important or relevant information is presented in a way that captures the audience's attention and guides their understanding.

Indeed language comprises several interconnected subsystems, each with its unique role and significance. These subsystems collectively contribute to our ability to communicate effectively, conveying words and emotions, ideas, and cultural nuances.

Attending and Receiving Initial Sounds

Infants are born with a remarkable ability to attend to and receive sounds from the environment. Even in the womb, the auditory system is functioning, and the foetuses can hear and respond to external sounds. Studies indicate that newborn babies recognize their mothers' voices (DeCasper & Fifer, 1980). An important characteristic of a newborn's sensitivity to auditory stimuli is the Moro Reflex or Startle Reflex. It is an automatic and involuntary response that is typically exhibited by infants in response to a sudden or loud noise. The reflex begins with the infant suddenly extending her arms and legs outward while arching their back, resembling the shape of the letter "C". This is often accompanied by a brief, sharp inhalation of breath. Following the retraction, the infant may cry or make fussing noises. They may also seek comfort by reaching for or clinging to their caregiver. The Moro Reflex is a protective response that is most pronounced during the first few months of an infant's life and tends to diminish and eventually disappear as the baby grows and their nervous system matures.

Attending to Initial Sounds

Infants possess the ability to attend to and discriminate different speech sounds. In a landmark study (Kuhl et al., 2003), it was found that infants as young as two months old were capable of distinguishing between two languages based on phonetic cues and displayed a preference for the language they were exposed to. Infants pick up the frequency of specific speech sounds, which allows them to recognize patterns in their linguistic environment and differentiate between languages.

Social Interaction

Through social interaction, infants learn to attend to initial sounds, discriminate between different speech sounds, and eventually acquire language skills. One prominent example is the use of "motherese" or infant-directed speech by mothers and other caregivers. Mothers modify their speech when communicating with infants, often using a higher pitch, exaggerated intonation, and simplified language. For example, a mother might say, "Look at the biiiig doll!" while emphasizing the initial sound of "big" as "biiiig". Research has shown that infants as young as six months of age are highly responsive to motherese (Kuhl, 2007). They can distinguish between motherese and adult-directed speech and show a preference for the former.

Significance of Early Auditory Experiences

The ability of infants to attend to and receive initial sounds is a dynamic process. Early auditory experiences lay the groundwork for vocabulary acquisition, grammar development, and ultimately, the ability to communicate effectively. Also, it affects other cognitive skills, including problem-solving, memory, and spatial awareness. This underscores the importance of attending to and receiving initial sounds in infancy as a critical factor in overall cognitive development.

Cross-Cultural Variations

Cultural variations are observed in infant's initial sound preferences based on the phonetic characteristics of their native language (Singh et al., 2014). For example, the sound patterns of different languages vary significantly, with some languages having more complex consonant clusters or vowel systems than others. The language Hawaiian is known for its relatively simple phonological structure. Russian is a language that is known for its rich system of consonant clusters and complex consonant sounds. Xhosa, a Bantu language spoken in South Africa, is known for its extensive use of click consonants. Click sounds are made by creating a vacuum in the mouth and releasing it suddenly, producing distinct sounds. Among the Indian languages, Hindi has a relatively straightforward consonant–vowel syllable structure. Sanskrit also has a well-organized system of consonants and vowels. Tamil has a rich inventory of consonants and vowels. Bengali is known for its vowel-rich phonology and a distinctive sound system that includes nasalized vowels (e.g., *shubho sondhya*). Punjabi has a rich inventory of consonants.

Thus, it is clear that infants are born with a remarkable ability to perceive and distinguish speech sounds, setting the stage for their journey into language acquisition. Understanding this process holds implications for early intervention and support for children with language and communication disorders.

Bilingualism and Multilingualism

In a world characterized by diversity and interconnectedness, the ability to speak and understand more than one language is increasingly valuable. In the diverse Indian context, people often speak more than one language. Thus, bilingualism and multilingualism are in practice. This section examines the complexities and benefits of bilingualism and multilingualism.

Bilingualism

Bilingualism refers to the proficiency in speaking and understanding two or more languages. Bilinguals use two or more languages (or dialects) in their everyday lives (Grosjean, 2010). It may be noted that bilingualism is defined in terms of the use of more than one language, irrespective of the degree of proficiency in the use of languages (Bhatia, 2017). It is not a binary concept; individuals are not either monolingual or bilingual. Rather, there exists a continuum, ranging from individuals who have basic knowledge of a second language to those who are fully proficient in several languages. As noted by Chen and Padilla (2019), bilingualism can be of several types. Some of these types are described here.

1) *Limited, Partial, and Proficient Bilingual*

A limited bilingual has basic knowledge of a second language (e.g., knowing a few phrases, words, or sentences) but cannot engage in meaningful conversations in the second language. A partial bilingual has a moderate level of proficiency in a second language, allowing them to engage in basic conversations and understand straightforward written and spoken content. A proficient bilingual is highly skilled and fluent in both languages, capable of using them interchangeably in various contexts.

2) *Balanced and Non-Balanced Bilingual*

A balanced bilingual is someone who has roughly equal proficiency and fluency in two or more languages and can use them without any difficulty. On the other hand, non-balanced bilingualism refers to a situation where the individual is more proficient in one language and uses it frequently.

3) *Receptive and Productive Bilingual*

A receptive bilingual understands a language fluently but has less developed skills in using the language for speaking and writing. A productive bilingual is someone who possesses the ability to both understand and effectively use the language.

4) *Early or Late Bilingual*

Early bilingualism refers to the situation where an individual starts acquiring a second language during their early childhood, typically before the age of seven, through exposure at home, community, or school. Late bilingualism, on the other hand, occurs when an individual begins to learn a second language after childhood, typically during adolescence or adulthood.

5) *Simultaneous or Sequential Bilingual*

Simultaneous bilingualism occurs when a person is exposed to and learns two languages simultaneously from birth or early childhood with native-like proficiency in both. Sequential bilingualism, on the other hand, refers to the acquisition of a second language after the individual has already established proficiency in their first language.

6) *Coordinated, Compound, and Subordinated Bilingual*

Coordinated bilinguals have a balanced proficiency in two languages and can comfortably switch between them based on the situation or context. Compound bilinguals are individuals who use each language in specific domains or contexts and maintain clear distinctions between them. Subordinated bilinguals use one language as dominant or primary while the other language is relegated to a secondary or subordinate role. In this case, one language is typically more proficient, and the less dominant language may not be used as frequently or in as many contexts.

The Development of Bilingualism

The development of bilingualism is a gradual process involving several stages, including language acquisition, proficiency development, and language maintenance.

1) *Early Language Acquisition*

The foundation of bilingualism is often laid down in childhood. Individuals who learn two languages from birth (simultaneous bilinguals) progress through language development milestones in both languages similar to monolingual children (Genesee, 2015). Research has shown that infants as old as seven months and raised in a bilingual home environment develop sensitivity to learning multiple languages (Ferjan et al., 2017). They learn to differentiate between the two languages and develop a natural ability to switch between them.

2) *Language Proficiency Development*

As children grow, their proficiency in both languages continues to grow, depending on factors like exposure, usage, and the societal context. Cummins's (1979) theory of language proficiency suggests that cognitive development and language skills in one language can transfer to the other, enhancing overall language proficiency.

3) *Societal and Environmental Factors*

The development of bilingualism is also influenced by societal and environmental factors, such as opportunity for use, peer pressures, and educational environment. A bilingual placed in a monolingual setting is likely to activate only one language, whereas in a bilingual environment, the person can easily shift into a bilingual mode to a differential degree (Martin et al., 2009).

Two interesting language-mixing phenomena – code-mixing and code-switching – are observed in bilinguals. Code-mixing refers to the use of words or sentences from different languages (e.g., "ek aur chance milega?" meaning Will I get one more chance?). Code-switching is repeating the same message in two languages for socio-psychological reasons (e.g., "*ek aur mauka milega.* repeating it . . . Will I get one more chance"). Bhatia (2017) noted that language mixing is guided by factors like social roles and relationships of the participants, situational factors, language attitudes, and so on.

4) *Maintenance and Balance*

Achieving and maintaining a balance between two languages is a continuous process. Some bilingual individuals may experience language attrition, where one language becomes less proficient over time due to lack of use. Strategies for maintaining both languages, such as attending bilingual schools or engaging in regular practice, are essential for sustaining bilingual proficiency.

Thus, the linguistic composition of a region plays a significant role in bilingualism. Children in multilingual regions are more likely to develop bilingual skills naturally. Exposure to television, movies, and digital media in different languages, socio-economic factors, locality (urban/rural), and educated backgrounds of parents play important roles in the pattern of language use in Indian children.

150 *Perspectives on Cognitive and Language Development*

The Indian Context

Due to prevalent linguistic diversity, bilingualism is a grassroots phenomenon in India (Bhatia & Ritchie, 2004). The Hindi proverb commonly used in India "Kos-kos par badle paani, chaar kos par vaani" (The taste of water changes every few miles, and the language changes every four miles) highlights the linguistic and cultural diversity found within relatively short distances in India, emphasizing the richness of languages and dialects in the country. Despite these diversities, communication in India is not impaired (Khubchandani, 1978; Pattanayak & Illich, 1981); rather, a complementarity of relationships is observed in languages. Mohanty (2006) observed that, from early in life, Indians adapt to the presence of several languages and use some of them in their day-to-day communication. Box 7.3 contains details about the literacy rate in India.

Box 7.3   Literacy Rate in India

Literacy, a cornerstone of human development, empowers individuals and societies by enhancing access to information, knowledge, and economic opportunities. The literacy rate is defined as the percentage of literate persons aged seven years and above to the corresponding population. A person who can read and write a short simple statement on his/her everyday life in any language with understanding is considered literate.

India's literacy journey has evolved significantly over the years. During the colonial period, widespread illiteracy prevailed due to limited access to education. After gaining independence in 1947, the government implemented policies and initiatives to promote literacy, leading to notable progress over the decades (Table 7.1).

A large-scale disparity in the literacy rate across locality and socio-economic groups was observed in 2011. The literacy rate of the rural population was 67.8% (females 58.75%; males 78.57%), and it was 84.1% for the urban population (Females=79.92%; Males=89.67%). According to the National Family Health Survey (NFHS-5), the literacy rate currently is 77.70%, with literate males at 84.70% and literate females at 70.30%.

Table 7.1 Literacy Rates in India

Year	Female	Male	Total
1951	8.86	27.15	18.32
1961	15.35	40.4	28.31
1971	21.97	45.96	34.45
1981	29.76	56.38	43.57
1991	32.29	64.13	52.21
2001	53.67	75.26	64.83
2011	65.46	82.14	74.04

(*Source*: Census of India, Office of Registrar General, India)

India's educational system adopts a bilingual or multilingual approach. The Three-Language Formula (Box 7.4) adopted in Indian schools ensures that children develop functional proficiency in more than one language. Children are typically taught in their regional language or mother tongue alongside a regional language and also a widely spoken language, such as Hindi or English. It is now established that learners, during the initial stage of learning, learn more effectively if the language used in the classroom corresponds to the language they know best as compared to teaching in a foreign language. Pattanayak (1988) observed that it is against the pedagogical principle to use a language for instruction other than the home language.

Box 7.4 Three-Language Formula in India

The three-language formula was first stated in the National Policy of Education 1968. It recommended adopting a three-language formula for teaching in the schools, as per the following scheme. The three-language formula sought to serve three functions, namely accommodating group identity, affirming national unity, and increasing administrative efficiency.

1) Mother Tongue/Regional Language: The first language of instruction is often the student's mother tongue or a regional language.
2) Second Language: The second language typically includes another regional language or an official language of the state.
3) Third Language: The third language usually includes a widely spoken language like Hindi, English, or a classical language.

The exact languages taught can vary from state to state, depending on the linguistic diversity and preferences of the region. States with a majority of speakers of a particular language may emphasize that language in the curriculum. The National Education Policy 2020 also endorsed to continue the three-language formula.

Benefits of Bilingualism

Bilingualism offers numerous opportunities leading to cognitive, social, and economic benefits. Bilingual individuals exhibit enhanced cognitive abilities, such as improved problem-solving skills and multitasking capabilities as well as superior executive functions (e.g., attention, concept formation, problem-solving etc.) (Bialystok, 2017). On tasks involving conflicting situations, bilingual children perform better than monolingual children (Barac et al., 2014). Moreover, it promotes cultural diversity and fosters intercultural understanding. The active use of two or more languages in old age protects against cognitive decline, and in some cases reverses the effects of ageing (Kroll & Dussias, 2017). In the context of India, Mohanty and associates (Mohanty, 1982, 1990; Mohanty & Babu, 1983; Mohanty & Das, 1987; Mohanty & Perregaux, 1997; Mohanty & Saikia, 2004) have shown the superiority of bilingual children, irrespective of schooling, in cognitive and intellectual skills, metalinguistic and metacognitive task performance, and academic achievement. Proficiency in multiple languages can provide Indian children with a competitive edge in a multilingual job market, both within India and internationally.

While bilingualism offers numerous benefits, it also poses some challenges in the context of India. In bilingual environments, one language may dominate over the other. This can lead to unequal proficiency, where a child may be stronger in one language while lacking fluency in the other. In some cases, due to social, economic, or educational pressures, children may gradually shift towards speaking one language predominantly, leading to language attrition. This has been the case in some parts of the country. Further, ensuring that children receive quality education in both languages can be challenging, especially for less widely spoken languages due to the non-standardization of the particular language.

Multilingualism

Multilingualism refers to the ability of an individual to use two or more languages proficiently. As Crystal (2006) observed, multilingualism or speaking two or more languages is a way of life for three-quarters of humanity in the modern world. It often results from language contact, where two or more languages influence each other. This gives rise to *creole* languages, which develop in situations where different linguistic and cultural groups come into contact, such as during migration or trade. Creoles often have simplified grammatical structures compared to their parent languages. They frequently borrow vocabulary from the languages spoken by the different groups in contact. For example, in India, "Bazaar Hindustani" developed as a contact language between different linguistic and ethnic groups in Indian bazaars and trade centres during the colonial period. This pidgin language incorporates elements of languages like Hindi, Urdu, English, and various regional languages to facilitate communication among people from diverse linguistic backgrounds.

Globalization has facilitated the spread of certain languages as lingua fracas (global/common languages). In today's world, English, for instance, is widely used in international business, diplomacy, and academia (Crystal, 2003). This has led to the development of English proficiency in many non-English-speaking countries, further contributing to multilingualism. Also, in the digital age, technology has played a significant role in the development of multilingualism. Translation apps, language learning platforms, and social media have made it easier for individuals to engage with multiple languages, breaking down linguistic barriers.

Government policies and educational systems play a vital role in promoting or inhibiting multilingualism. Many countries have bilingual or multilingual education programmes to ensure that citizens are proficient in multiple languages, fostering a more inclusive and culturally rich society. It has been observed that though schooling plays a prominent role in promoting multilingualism, most minority and indigenous children are deprived of the opportunity (Mohanty et al., 2009). Box 7.5 contains information on the medium of instruction followed in Indian schools.

Thus, in today's world, bilingualism and multilingualism stand as vital assets that foster communication, understanding, and cultural enrichment. These linguistic abilities enhance cognitive flexibility and problem-solving skills, empowering individuals to adapt to an ever-changing, interconnected world. Moreover, they facilitate access to diverse perspectives, fostering empathy and tolerance.

Language and Thought: An Inseparable Connection

Language and thought are two intertwined phenomena that shape the way humans perceive and interact with the world. The relationship between language and thought raises the question of whether our thoughts are constrained by the limits of our language or does language merely serve as a tool to express pre-existing thoughts. This section explores the dynamic interplay between language and thought.

Language as a Cognitive Tool

Language is often described as a cognitive tool that enables us to organize, categorize, and communicate our thoughts. Chomsky's theory of universal grammar posits that humans are born with an innate ability to acquire language, suggesting that language is deeply embedded in our cognitive architecture (Chomsky, 1965). This view implies that language is more than just a means of communication; it plays a central role in shaping our thought processes.

One way in which language influences thought is through linguistic relativity, often referred to as the Sapir-Whorf hypothesis. This hypothesis suggests that the language we speak can shape our perception of the world and influence the way we think (Sapir, 1921; Whorf, 1956). For example, languages with a rich system of tenses, such as English, may lead speakers to be more attuned to the concept of time, whereas languages with less emphasis on tenses, like Mandarin (Chinese), may foster a different temporal perspective (Boroditsky, 2001). In the ancient Indian tradition, the concept of time is more context-sensitive. For example, the Vedas talk about "yugas" (*Satya Yuga, Treta Yuga, Dvapara Yuga,* and *Kali Yuga*). Empirical evidence shows that speakers of different languages may exhibit distinct cognitive patterns. For instance, when asked to arrange a series of pictures depicting temporal sequences, speakers of Aymara, a language spoken in the Andes, arrange them from right to left, reflecting their language's reverse temporal orientation (Nunez & Sweetser, 2006). Such findings suggest that language indeed influences the way we think about abstract concepts like time.

Thought as a Precursor to Language

In contrast to the Sapir-Whorf hypothesis, it is also important to recognize that thought precedes and influences language. People think and reason before they develop the linguistic skills necessary for full-fledged communication. Piaget's theory emphasizes that children progress through distinct stages of cognitive development before acquiring language. This implies that thought processes are not wholly dependent on language; rather, language emerges as a tool to externalize and refine pre-existing thoughts. Further, some cognitive processes, such as visual perception and basic emotions, are believed to operate independently of language. Ekman's (1973) studies on the universality of facial expressions for emotions suggest that certain aspects of human emotional experience are biologically hardwired rather than shaped by language.

Language and Thought: A Reciprocal Relationship

In reality, the relationship between language and thought is not unidirectional but rather reciprocal. While language influences thought by shaping the way we conceptualize the world, thought also affects language by generating new words, expressions, and metaphors to convey complex ideas (Gibbs, 2006). Language reflects and shapes cognitive structures, and thought drives the evolution of language. This interplay between language and thought is central to the human experience, allowing us to express our innermost ideas, emotions, and experiences and, in turn, shape the very fabric of our cultural and intellectual endeavours. The relationship between language and thought in the Indian tradition is discussed in Box 7.6.

Box 7.5 Relationship Between Language and Thought in the Indian Tradition

The relationship between language and thought has been examined across various Indian philosophical schools and texts. For example, in the *Nyaya Sutras*, language is considered not only as a means of communication but also as a tool for precise thought and understanding. The *Nyaya* tradition posits that language and thought are intimately connected, with language serving as a vehicle for the expression and refinement of thought. According to *Nyaya* philosophy, thought precedes language. This aligns with the Indian philosophical notion of "manas" or mind, which is seen as the inner faculty responsible for generating thoughts and cognitions. Through language, individuals can analyse, categorize, and convey their thoughts with precision. The *Nyaya Sutras* advocate the use of rigorous logical methods and language to arrive at valid knowledge (*Praman*). Thus, language is not merely a vehicle for communication but also a means for the systematic development of thought and the pursuit of truth.

The *Nyaya* tradition further categorizes language into different types based on its relationship with thought. These categories include "Shabda" (word), "Artha" (meaning), and "Prakriti" (object). *Shabda* refers to the spoken or written word, *Artha* is the meaning conveyed by words, and *Prakriti* represents the external object or referent to which words and thoughts correspond. This tripartite distinction underscores the idea that language, thought, and the external world are interconnected through a complex web of relationships. Thus, Indian tradition visualizes both as interdependent and essential for human understanding and communication. The detailed study of language by Sanskrit grammarians such as Panini, Patanjali, Bhartihari have deliberated in a nuanced manner on the nature of word, sentences, meaning, and related issues.

Development of Para-Speech Communication (PSC)

Human communication extends beyond spoken language and includes non-verbal or para-speech communication. PSC consists of a wide range of non-verbal cues and behaviours, including facial expressions, gestures, body language, posture, tone of voice, appearance, clothing, use of objects and symbols (e.g., emojis), and even the use of silence and pauses, such as hesitation, thoughtfulness, or discomfort. Also included are paralinguistic features, such as laughter, sighs, and vocal pitch variations that convey emotional nuances. These elements operate in tandem with spoken language, enhancing and sometimes even replacing verbal messages.

The development of PSC begins in infancy and continues to evolve throughout one's lifetime; from the subtle cues of an infant's smile to the complex non-verbal signals used by adults in various social contexts. From birth, infants display a range of facial expressions, such as smiling, crying, and eye contact, to convey their needs and emotions (Messinger & Fogel, 2007). As they grow, the use of gestures predicts the development of language (Iverson & Goldin-Meadow, 2005).

During childhood and adolescence, individuals develop a deeper understanding of body language and posture. They learn to interpret subtle cues like crossed arms (defensiveness) or open postures (openness) (Knapp et al., 2013). The modulation of tone of voice conveys the emotional states, intentions, and attitudes. Sarcasm, irony, or humour in the tone requires nuanced interpretation. In adulthood, individuals convey empathy through non-verbal listening behaviours or use non-verbal cues for persuasion and negotiation.

Cross-Cultural Variations in Para Communication

The patterns of PSC differ significantly from one culture to another. For example, the meaning of a nod or a handshake varies widely across cultures (Matsumoto, 2006). While a firm handshake is seen as a sign of confidence and trustworthiness in the Western world, a handshake should be gentle and not too firm in the Middle Eastern countries, as a strong grip may be perceived as aggressive. In some Asian cultures, a bow or a slight bow combined with a handshake is more common than a traditional Western handshake. In some Asian cultures, such as South Korea or China, physical contact like handshakes may be avoided, especially in formal situations. A nod or a slight bow is more appropriate. In traditional Indian culture, physical contact between the opposite genders may be avoided, so handshakes might be replaced with a polite nod or saying "Namaste" with folded hands.

In some Asian cultures, people may smile when they feel uncomfortable or anxious, which may create confusion among those from other cultures where smiling is primarily associated with happiness. Eye contact during conversations can vary widely. In many cultures, prolonged eye contact is a sign of showing confidence, respect, and attentiveness to the speaker. But when eye contact becomes too prolonged, it can be perceived as confrontational or disrespectful. High-pitched tones may indicate excitement or enthusiasm in some cultures while in others, it might be seen as childish or insincere. In some cultures (e.g., Asian and African), silence during a conversation can be seen as a sign of thoughtfulness and respect (see Chapter 6) while in others, it might be interpreted as discomfort.

PSC is essential in human interactions for several reasons. It complements verbal messages and allows individuals to convey emotions, such as joy, anger, sorrow, and empathy more effectively through non-verbal means. Further, it plays a significant role in building trust, forming relationships, and fostering social cohesion (Knapp et al., 2013). However, understanding and correctly interpreting non-verbal cues is crucial for effective communication. Box 7.6 describes a different form of PSC in the Indian context.

Box 7.6 *Mudras* **and** *Asanas* **in the Indian Tradition**

Indian tradition acknowledges the power of non-verbal cues, body language, and silence in conveying profound messages, emotions, and meanings. For example, ancient art forms, particularly classical dance and theatre, incorporate intricate hand gestures known as "mudras". *Mudras* convey emotions, stories, and messages without the need for spoken words. Each *mudra* has a specific meaning and conveys a wide range of emotions and ideas. The communication of *rasa* to the audience relies heavily on non-verbal elements, including facial expressions, body movements, and music. Similarly, in Yoga, the *asanas* (yoga poses) and *pranayama* (breathing exercises) are not just physical exercises but also tools for subtle communication with the body and mind. Ayurvedic practitioners pay attention to non-verbal cues, such as facial expressions, pulse diagnosis, and body language, to assess a person's overall health and well-being. In *Guru–Shishya Parampara*, spiritual knowledge is often transmitted not only through spoken words but also through the presence, aura, and energy of the guru. Disciples learn to attune themselves to the guru's non-verbal cues and the subtle vibrations of spiritual energy.

Factors Influencing Language Development

Though the ability to acquire and use language is an inherent human trait, its development is influenced by several factors. Some of the key factors that influence language development are described herewith.

Interaction of Nature and Nurture (Genes and Environment)

Language development is influenced by both biological factors (nature) and environmental experiences (nurture). Biological factors lay the foundation for language acquisition. As stated earlier, Chomsky (1965) advanced the view that the "language acquisition device" (LAD) allows children to generate and understand the rules of their native language. This inherent linguistic ability sets a universal blueprint that guides language development across cultures. It has also been found that genetics plays a role in determining certain speech and language disorders, such as verbal dyspraxia, which runs in the family. A person affected by this disorder has difficulty placing muscles in the correct position to produce speech. Research (Vargha-Khadem et al., 2005) has shown that mutations in the FOXP2 gene are linked to this particular language disorder.

The behaviourist perspective holds that children learn language through imitation, repetition, and reinforcement of correct language usage by caregivers and peers. Hart and Risley's (1995) famous "30 Million Words Study" demonstrated that the quantity and quality of language input children receive during their early years significantly impacts their language skills and future academic success. Additionally, cross-cultural studies have shown that linguistic exposure and cultural context can lead to variations in language development trajectories (Ochs & Schieffelin, 2011).

The contemporary perspective, however, acknowledges the interplay of nature and nurture in language development. The nativist and interactionist views are not mutually exclusive; instead, they complement each other. Steven Pinker's (1994) theory of the "language instinct" suggests that while humans possess a biological predisposition for language, inputs from the environment are necessary to trigger language development.

Critical Period

The concept of a critical period postulates that there exists a specific time frame during which language acquisition occurs most effectively, and thereafter it becomes more challenging. This notion was popularized by Lenneberg (1967), who proposed that the neurological plasticity, observed during early childhood, allows for efficient language acquisition. The critical period hypothesis aligns with observations that individuals who learn a second language during childhood tend to achieve higher levels of fluency and native-like pronunciation compared to those who start later in life. The duration of the critical period is subject to debate, and the exact age boundaries remain unclear. Generally, the critical period is believed to end around puberty, after which language acquisition becomes more challenging. However, the extent of this window may vary based on individual factors, such as cognitive aptitude, socioenvironmental factors, and the complexity of the language being acquired.

Role of Cultural Factors

Different cultures have unique linguistic norms, and children learn language by interacting within their cultural context. For instance, in individualist cultures, direct and explicit communication is valued. In contrast, indirect and nuanced communication is preferred in collectivist cultures. In India, the use of titles and honorifics, such as "Saheb" or "ji" is deeply ingrained depending on the level of formality in addressing someone. Code-switching is also quite common in India. A person might start a sentence in Hindi, switch to English for a technical term, and then end the sentence in their regional language. This fluidity in language use is a reflection of India's linguistic diversity and variations observed in cultural norms.

Cultural diversity can affect the timing of vocabulary development in children. In cultures with rich oral traditions and extensive storytelling, children may acquire a broader vocabulary earlier because they are exposed to a wider range of concepts and narratives. Conversely, in cultures where communication is more context-dependent, vocabulary development may progress differently (Slobin, 1996).

Role of Imitation

Children imitate the sounds they hear, refining their pronunciation over time (Ferguson & Menn, 1996). They also display a remarkable ability to imitate facial expressions, gestures, and vocalizations. Imitation is an adaptive strategy that allows individuals to rapidly acquire and adapt to culturally specific linguistic norms and nuances. In addition, imitation also plays a significant role in syntax and grammar acquisition (Tomasello, 2003). Bruner (1983) proposed the concept of a "Language Acquisition Support System" (LASS), suggesting that caregivers need to adapt their language to make it more understandable for the child. The use of simplified syntax, exaggerated intonation, and repetition by the parents helps children to imitate and ultimately fosters language development.

Indeed, language is a multifaceted communication system that develops through stages influenced by a combination of biological, cognitive, social, and environmental factors. The process is a testament to the complexity of human cognition and the interplay between nature and nurture. Language allows not only the representation and conservation of knowledge but also all creative endeavours including literary compositions which vary in form (e.g., prose, poetry, drama, story). The use of language to invoke and shape emotions is a significant aspect of our social and personal lives. Words used by us can make or break human relationships. That is why it is widely believed that one should speak in pleasant ways. Literary people often use various figures of speech to convey meanings that go beyond the literal meanings. Also, language helps us to reflect and organize our thoughts to perform different cognitive functions. Language itself becomes a special kind of performance or behaviour that shapes our lives and if suitably used enriches its users. Competence in spoken and written language, therefore, is given prime importance in formal education. Competence in the use of language is both a means and a goal to form our identities and realize our cherished goals.

Overview

This chapter dealt with the intricate world of human communication, from the earliest coos of infants to the rich tapestry of linguistic diversity found in India. It discussed the various components of language, analysed major theories that illuminate the pathways of language acquisition, and delved into the complex interplay of factors that influence language development.

Throughout this chapter, you must have gained a deeper appreciation for the multifaceted nature of language. We have learned that language is not merely a means of conveying information but a reflection of our cognitive processes, cultural identities, and social interactions. From the smallest phonemes to the most intricate discourse structures, language offers us a vast canvas for expressing our thoughts, emotions, and ideas. The chapter highlighted the significance of language development. Language is the bridge that connects us to our world and one another.

It is the foundation of education, the key to accessing knowledge, and a tool for empowerment. Language development is not a solitary endeavour but a shared journey, influenced by the dynamic interplay of nature and nurture, society, and culture. Through different boxes, an attempt has been made to deepen our understanding of language development with practical insights for promoting language skills in children, fostering emergent literacy, and appreciating the value of indigenous practices in language acquisition.

In a world where communication knows no bounds, where the tapestry of languages weaves a rich cultural mosaic, and where the ability to express and understand ideas is paramount, the study of language development remains as relevant and vital as ever. It is a journey that extends far beyond this chapter, as language continues to evolve, adapt, and shape our understanding of the human experience. In closing, language development is not merely an academic pursuit but a celebration of the human capacity to communicate, connect, and create. It is a reminder that in the intricate patterns of phonemes and syntax, in the nuances of semantics and pragmatics, and the richness of linguistic diversity, we find the essence of what it means to be human.

Key Terms

Attending and Receiving Initial Sounds
Bilingualism and Multilingualism
Critical Period
Discourse
Imitation and Language Development
Influences on Language Development
Language in the Indian Tradition
Language and Thought
Literacy Rate in India
Linguistic Diversity in India
Manifestation of Language
Medium of Instruction in Indian Schools
Moro Reflex
Morpheme

Mudras and *Asanas*
Nature of Language
Nature–Nurture
Para Speech Communication
Phonemes
Pragmatics
Semantics
Social Interaction
Stages of Language Development
Subsystems of Language
Syntax
Theories of Language Development
Three-Language Formula

Questions for Reflection

1) How do cultural perspectives shape the understanding of language?
2) What role does language play in preserving and transmitting cultural values?
3) Are there any cultural variations in the milestones of language acquisition? Give examples.
4) What are the challenges and benefits associated with promoting multiple languages in educational settings?
5) How can we provide equitable language development opportunities to all learners?

Suggested Further Readings

Books

Costa, A. (2020). *The bilingual brain: And what it tells us about the science of language*. Penguin Books.
Cunningham-Andersson, U., & Andersson, S. (2020). *Growing up with two languages: A practical guide*. Routledge.
Davis, M. (2021). *Becoming bilingual: A guide to language learning*. MIT Press.
Rosseel, L. (2021). *The multilingual mind: A modular processing perspective*. Oxford University Press.

Website/Online Resources

Bilingualism Matters (*www.bilingualism-matters.org/*)
Center for Applied Linguistics (*www.cal.org/*)
International Journal of Bilingual Education and Bilingualism (*www.tandfonline.com/journals/rbeb20*).

Part IV
Perspectives on Self and Affective Development

8 Development of Self and Personality

Contents

Introduction	164
Nature of Self and Personality	164
The Emergence of Self: An Evolutionary Journey of Consciousness	165
Theoretical Perspectives on Self	166
Concept of Self-Esteem	167
Development of the Self Across Life Stages	168
Culture and Development of the Self	170
Box 8.1: The Self in Indian Thought	170
Theories of Personality	170
Development of Personality	178
Cultural Variations in Personality	179
Box 8.2: The Indian View of Personality	180
Measurement of Personality Development	181
Overview	182
Key Terms	182
Questions for Reflection	182

Learning Objectives

After studying this chapter, the learner will be able to:

Differentiate between the concepts of self and personality;
Evaluate various theoretical perspectives on the self and personality;
Trace the development of self and personality across different life stages;
Examine the impact of culture on the development of self and personality; and
Evaluate and select appropriate methods for measuring personality development.

DOI: 10.4324/9781003441168-12

Introduction

The chapter focuses on the essence of individual identity and its development. It begins with an enquiry into the nature of self and personality, unravelling the complex interplay of intrinsic and extrinsic factors that shape the core of our being. The emergence of the self unfolds as an evolutionary journey of consciousness. Diverse theoretical perspectives on self provide insights into the kaleidoscope of frameworks that attempt to capture the essence of human identity. The interplay of culture and the development of the self emerges as a crucial facet. The evaluative aspect of the self, explored through self-esteem, adds another layer to our understanding of personal development. The chapter further examines theories of personality (such as psychoanalytic, biological, humanistic, social cognitive, and trait theories), uncovering the diverse pathways through which individual characteristics are forged. The Indian view of personality is examined in some detail. The discussion on the measurement of personality development enriches our understanding. The discourse on the multifaceted dimensions of self and personality lays the groundwork for a comprehensive understanding of the intricacies that define who we are.

Nature of Self and Personality

The concept of "self" refers to an individual's unique and enduring sense of identity, consciousness, and subjective experiences about herself/himself. It encompasses one's thoughts, emotions, memories, beliefs, desires, and perceptions, all of which contribute to a coherent and consistent understanding of oneself as a distinct entity. Human beings are unique in the sense that they are simultaneously subjects and objects. The view of self that is formed by a person provides a powerful lens to view the external world as well as personal qualities and attributes. It constitutes the centre of one's existence.

Scholars from different disciplines have pondered over the nature of the self for a long time. French philosopher Rene Descartes declared, "Cogito, ergo sum" (I think, therefore I am) (Burns, 2001), suggesting that self-awareness is the foundation of human existence. Existential philosopher Jean-Paul Sartre explored the notion of an "authentic self", emphasizing the individual's responsibility in shaping his or her own identity and purpose (Due, 2000). Psychologist William James (1890) drew attention to the distinction between the "I" (the observing self) and the "Me" (the object of self-awareness). The "Me" is further divided into the social self (how one is perceived by others) and the personal self (one's unique traits and experiences). Sigmund Freud (1923) viewed the self as composed of the id, the ego, and the superego. Carl Rogers (1961) emphasized the importance of congruence between the self-concept and the ideal self for psychological well-being. Sociologist George Herbert Mead (1934) introduced the concept of the "social self", emphasizing that the self emerges through interactions with others. Erik Erikson's (1968) theory of psychosocial development emphasized the development of a sense of self-identity. According to Erikson, the formation of a positive self-identity is a crucial task of adolescence.

The term personality is used to refer to the stable and enduring patterns of thought, feelings, and behaviours of an individual. It includes a unique set of traits and psychological features, such as temperament, attitudes, values, and motivations. It is assumed to be relatively consistent over time and across different situations and is thought to have a genetic and environmental basis. In contrast, the self is considered a dynamic and evolving construct that can change over time in response to different situations and experiences. Both self and personality often interact and influence each other. For example, an individual with traits of high self-esteem and extraversion may seek out social situations while an individual with low self-esteem and neuroticism may avoid social situations.

The Emergence of the Self: An Evolutionary Journey of Consciousness

The emergence of the self, or the awareness of one's individuality and existence, is rooted in biological, psychological, and sociocultural contexts. The role of these factors in the emergence of the self is discussed herewith.

Biological Foundations of Self

The emergence of the self can be traced back to the biological development of the human brain and the capacity for self-awareness that evolved over millions of years. The prefrontal cortex (PFC), a region responsible for higher cognitive functions, plays a crucial role in self-awareness. Mirror self-recognition or the mirror test is used to assess an individual's ability to recognize themselves in a mirror. This is a cognitive ability associated with higher-order thinking and consciousness. It suggests that the individual has a concept of self as a separate entity from the environment and can differentiate themselves from other objects.

Psychological Aspects of Self

The psychological aspect of the self encompasses a range of concepts as mentioned in the following.

Self-Concept

Self-concept refers to an individual's perception and understanding of themselves. It encompasses beliefs, ideas, and feelings about one's identity, abilities, values, and roles in society. Self-concept includes both cognitive aspects (what you think about yourself) and emotional aspects (how you feel about yourself) (Rosenberg, 1965).

Self-Esteem

Self-esteem is an individual's evaluation of his or her worth and the emotional response to that evaluation. It can be positive (or high) and negative (or low). More details are given later in this chapter.

Self-Identity

Self-identity or personal identity refers to the way people perceive themselves and how they are perceived by others. Self-identity includes various aspects such as biological identity (e.g., physical appearance and health conditions), psychological identity (e.g., personality traits, cognitive abilities, and emotional states), social identity (e.g., gender, ethnicity, religion, nationality or socio-economic status), cultural identity (e.g., belongingness to a cultural group), and so on.

Self-Regulation

This refers to an individual's ability to monitor, control, and manage their thoughts, emotions, behaviours, and impulses to achieve specific goals, adapt to changing circumstances, and maintain psychological well-being (for details, see Chapter 8).

The development of the theory of mind (ToM) (i.e., our ability to understand that others have thoughts, feelings, and beliefs distinct from our own) is another critical aspect of the emergence of the self. This capacity allows us to distinguish ourselves from others and form complex social relationships.

Social and Cultural Aspects of Self

The emergence of the self is also influenced by social and cultural factors. Socialization practices including parent–child relationships, peer groups, and other socializing agents contribute to the formation of self-concept. As children grow, they learn the norms and values of the particular culture that shape the emergence of the self. For example, collectivistic cultures emphasize the importance of group harmony and interdependence, which can lead to a more holistic and relational sense of the self (Markus & Kitayama, 1991). In contrast, individualistic cultures emphasize independence and self-expression, which can lead to a more independent and self-focused sense of the self (Triandis, 1989). According to Mead (1967), there are two parts of the self: the "I" which is the part of the self that is spontaneous, creative, innate, and is not concerned with how others view us and the "me" or the social definition of who we are. When we are born, we are all "I" and act without concern about how others view us. But the socialized self begins when we start considering how one important person views us. With advancing age, children become more aware of social comparisons and begin to evaluate themselves from the perspectives of others (Harter, 2012).

The emergence of the self is, thus, a multifaceted and intricate process that combines biological, psychological, social, and cultural factors. It is a testament to the complexity of human consciousness and identity.

Theoretical Perspectives on Self

In this section, an attempt is made to familiarize oneself with the basic tenets of some of the prominent theories of the self. These theories deal with different facets of self, such as self-efficacy, social identity, self-determination, and self-perception.

Self-Efficacy Theory

Albert Bandura's (1977, 1997) self-efficacy theory drew attention to an individual's belief that (s)he has the necessary skills, abilities, and resources to succeed in a particular situation. Self-efficacy beliefs can influence motivation, emotional states, and decision-making. Bandura discusses the four sources of interrelated self-efficacy beliefs: mastery experiences (e.g., successful completion of tasks), vicarious experiences (e.g., observing others completing a task), social persuasion (e.g., positive feedback received from others), and physiological and affective states (e.g., physical and emotional experiences while performing a task). Self-efficacy may be enhanced through adequate intervention addressed to these sources. The self-efficacy theory has been influential in several fields, including education, health psychology, and organizational psychology (Zimmerman & Bandura, 1994).

Social Identity Theory

Proposed by Tajfel and Turner (1979), the social identity theory refers to the part of an individual's self-concept that is derived from their membership in social groups, such as gender, ethnicity, region, or religion. Thus being an Indian or American citizen evokes certain attributes simply because of the membership of a particular country, irrespective of the fact whether those attributes belong to you. Individuals strive to maintain a positive self-image by identifying with social groups that have a positive reputation and distancing themselves from groups with a negative reputation.

Self-Determination Theory

Deci and Ryan's (1985) self-determination theory focuses on the psychological needs that motivate human behaviour. Individuals have three basic psychological needs: autonomy (the need to be in control of one's behaviour), competence (the need to feel capable and effective), and relatedness (the need to feel connected to others). When these needs are met, individuals are more likely to experience intrinsic motivation and a sense of well-being.

Self-Esteem Theory

Proposed by Morris Rosenberg (1965), the self-esteem theory suggests that self-esteem is a key aspect of the self-concept. Self-esteem refers to an individual's evaluation of his/her worth and competence. Self-esteem is developed through a process of social comparison, in which individuals evaluate themselves with others. This process can be influenced by factors such as culture, upbringing, and social norms. This theory has been very popular among researchers and practitioners.

Self-Perception Theory

The self-perception theory of Daryl Bem (1967) proposes that people infer their attitudes and beliefs by observing their behaviours and the contexts in which they occur and that this process is similar to how people perceive the attitudes and beliefs of others. According to Leary (1999), people use their behaviour to signal their self-esteem to others, and this process is influenced by social norms and expectations.

These theories illustrate that the self is treated in different ways. Also, the way individuals perceive themselves, interact with others, and navigate their social environments plays a significant role in pursuing goals and struggling with challenges in life. Together, they offer a comprehensive framework for understanding the multifaceted concept of the self and its role in shaping our thoughts, feelings, and actions.

Concept of Self-Esteem

Self-esteem refers to the subjective evaluation and perception that individuals have of their self-worth and value. It involves the thoughts, beliefs, feelings, and attitudes that a person holds about themselves. Baumeister et al. (2003) define self-esteem in terms of the value people place on themselves while evaluating themselves. Self-esteem is typically composed of two main components: global self-esteem (or overall assessment of one's self-worth) and specific self-esteem (or evaluation of oneself in specific domains, such as physical appearance, intelligence, social skills, or achievements). People may have varying levels of self-esteem in different areas of their life.

Self-esteem can vary in its strength and may change over time. Thus, people with high self-esteem generally have a strong sense of self-worth, believe in their abilities, and value themselves as individuals. They show confidence in their abilities, have a favourable perception of their physical appearance, intelligence, and overall competence, show resilience, and maintain

168 *Perspectives on Self and Affective Development*

healthy relationships with others (Orth & Robins, 2014). People with low self-esteem tend to doubt their abilities, feel unworthy, and may harbour self-critical thoughts. Also, they experience higher levels of stress and anxiety and struggle with establishing and maintaining healthy relationships (Sowislo & Orth, 2013). It is influenced by various factors, including childhood experiences, social and cultural factors, and personal achievements and failures. Efforts to improve self-esteem among individuals with low self-esteem often involve therapeutic approaches, such as cognitive-behavioural therapy (CBT), self-help strategies, and social support.

The concept of self-esteem in the Indian tradition encapsulates a holistic understanding of the self as interconnected with the cosmos and society. It emphasizes self-knowledge (*Atmanam viddhi*). The model of five *koshas* as developed in the text of Taittiriya Upanishad illustrates this idea. It states that there are five sheaths or *koshas* of one's being including body (*Annamaya*), vital function (*Pranamaya*), mental function (*Vigyanama*y), intellect (*Manomaya*), and bliss (*Anandamaya*) (see Sinha & Naidu, 1994). Drawing from philosophical wisdom, spiritual practices, and ethical principles, the Indian approach to self-esteem offers profound insights that resonate even in contemporary times. By cultivating self-awareness, self-compassion, and a sense of purpose, individuals can harness their inner potential and contribute positively to the world around them, thereby enriching their lives and the lives of others.

Development of the Self Across Life Stages

The concept of the self is not a static phenomenon. Rather, it changes and develops over the lifespan. Each stage of life brings with it unique challenges and opportunities that can shape an individual's sense of self. In a meta-analysis of 331 independent longitudinal studies conducted across the globe (Orth et al., 2018), it was found that people's self-esteem changes systematically across the lifespan. There is an increase in average levels of self-esteem from age 4 to 11 years, which remains stable from age 11 to 15 years, then increases strongly until 30 years of age and more slowly until the age of 60 years, peaks between age 60 and 70 years, and declines after 70 years of age. The development of self includes both cognitive and social processes which change with the advancing age. For example, cognitive processes including perception, attention, thinking and memory develop as a result of maturation and interaction with the environment. The interaction with parents, peers, teachers, and others helps consolidate their conception of self.

The Indian tradition emphasized changes in selfhood within the framework of four life stages called *Ashramas*, namely *Brahmacharya, Grihastha, Vanaprastha, and Sannyas*. These life stages covering a hundred years emphasized developing various competencies, performing household duties, gradual withdrawal from socially engaged life, and renunciation, respectively, as life tasks and framing an ideal scheme of selfhood which ultimately directed towards emancipation (*Moksha* or *Nirvana*). Of course, all the stages involved work or action. It is desired that one must live actively during the whole life (*Kurvanneveh karmani jijivishet shatam samaah* – Ishavasyopanishad) (see Box 8.1).

The Self During Early Childhood (Preschool Years)

Self-awareness emerges during the second year of life and becomes pronounced as children reach their third year (Lewis & Brooks-Gunn, 1979). Children become aware of their bodies, recognize themselves in the mirror, grasp body parts, and understand basic physical attributes. They begin to express preferences for certain activities, toys, or foods, indicating the beginnings of self-awareness and personal likes and dislikes. Positive reinforcement and encouragement from parents and significant others contribute to the development of positive self-esteem. Also, children start identifying and imitating gender-specific behaviours. The increasing use of pronouns like "I" and "me" indicates a growing awareness of their own identity.

Middle Childhood (Elementary School Years)

Children in this age group develop the capacity to engage in more sophisticated self-reflection and self-awareness. Children's self-concepts become more differentiated in various domains, including academic, social, and physical domains, where they start forming evaluations of their abilities and attributes (Harter, 2012). Research by Rubin et al. (2006) underscores the significance of peer relationships in shaping social identity and self-esteem. Positive peer relationships contribute to the development of social skills, emotional regulation, and a sense of belonging, all of which are integral to the formation of a positive self-concept.

The Self During Adolescence

As children progress from concrete to formal operational thinking, they develop the ability for introspection and self-reflection. The adolescents seek to gain acceptance and validation from their peers (Brown & Larson, 2009). They may experience identity confusion or exploration as they try to figure out who they are and what their values and beliefs are. For example, an adolescent may experiment with different styles of dress, music, or hobbies to explore their identity. As adolescents experience hormonal and neurological changes brought about by puberty, they may experience body dissatisfaction, which can distort their self-esteem and self-image.

In the Indian context, the family and the society determine the formation of identity among adolescents (Sharma, 1999). The Indian family is an extended one, which includes a larger network of grandparents, uncles, aunts, and cousins. Even if they do not live together, they relate emotionally. Further, the family belongs to a community (i.e., Brahmin, Jat etc.), a language group (e.g., Hindi speaking, Kannada speaking), and a caste group (e.g., Scheduled caste). A person may live in a rural or a small town, a large town, or a metro city. He/she may be engaged in different professions, such as teacher, medical or legal practitioner, or engaged in some business. All these provide an identity to the person.

The Self During Adulthood

In early adulthood, individuals continue to refine their view of self and make important life choices related to education, career, and relationships (Arnett, 2000). Middle adulthood is marked by increased stability and a focus on fulfilling the diverse responsibilities related to work, family, and community. Some may experience a midlife crisis or re-evaluation of their goals and values. In late adulthood, individuals reflect on their life experiences and accomplishments, which can either enhance or challenge their sense of self (Erikson, 1950).

The Self During Old age

During old age, individuals often engage in reflective processes that encompass their past achievements, regrets, and life's purpose (Baltes & Baltes, 1990). Erikson characterized this stage as ego integrity versus despair. Older adults may experience shifts in self-concept related to roles and identities. For instance, after retirement, individuals may no longer define themselves through their work roles and must adapt to a new self-concept based on different aspects of their lives, such as family roles, hobbies, or community involvement. Maintaining a strong social support system can positively impact an individual's self-esteem and well-being. On the other hand, social isolation can lead to feelings of loneliness, which negatively affect self-perception.

Thus, self-concept appears to change across the lifespan as individuals develop a greater understanding of themselves and their place in the world. These changes are influenced by both internal factors, such as cognitive and emotional development, and external factors, such as social and cultural experiences.

Culture and Development of the Self

The development of the self is a universal phenomenon. It is accomplished by people across the globe. There are, however, several aspects of the self that are specific to a particular cultural context. It has already been mentioned that in individualistic cultures self is viewed as an autonomous, independent entity that is separate from others. In contrast, collectivistic cultures place a greater emphasis on the interconnectedness of all things, including the self (Heine et al., 1999). The cultural differences in self-construal can influence a range of psychological processes, including self-esteem, motivation, and emotion (Kitayama & Markus, 1999). Indians' self-concept is more relational, which places a strong emphasis on social harmony and interdependence (Mascolo et al., 2004). Indian youth view parents' involvement in their lives as stemming from concern and interest, and not as interference, reflecting a collectivist orientation (Kapadia et al., 2005). Misra and Kashyap (2016) reported that Indian students were more likely to use interdependent coping strategies, such as seeking social support, while American students were more likely to use independent coping strategies, such as problem-solving. Box 8.1 contains the concept of self in the Indian context.

Box 8.1   The Self in Indian Thought

In Indian philosophy, the concept of self is deeply intertwined with the idea of *Atman*, the eternal and unchanging essence that resides within every individual (Radhakrishnan & Moore, 1957). The Upanishads declared that the true nature of self (*Atman*) is blissful (*Anand*). The Upanishads further emphasize that the realization of one's true nature is the ultimate path to liberation (*moksha*) and profound happiness. The Chandogya Upanishad famously proclaims, "Tat Tvam Asi" (You are That), highlighting the unity of the individual self with the cosmic reality (*Brahman*). The ultimate goal of human life is to realize the *Atman* through self-knowledge, which is attained through meditation, introspection, and contemplation. As Bhawuk (2011, p. 91) noted, the self in India emphasizes an inward journey and the potential discovery of an inward self. Tripathi and Ghildyal (2013) have argued that Hindus seek an intimate relationship with their God and, in the process, attempt to realize divinity in self.

Theories of Personality

Several theories have been proposed to explain the nature and development of personality. Some of the influential theories of personality are psychoanalytic, biological, humanistic, social cognitive, and trait theories. However, as Feist et al. (2018) argued, there is no one correct theory of personality. Different theories offer different perspectives, and each theory has its strengths and limitations.

Sigmund Freud's Psychoanalytic Theory

The psychoanalytic theory of Freud (1900) delves into the depths of the unconscious mind to elucidate the forces that drive human behaviour. At the core of this theory lies the belief that much of human behaviour is driven by unconscious processes, which are hidden from our conscious awareness. It emphasizes the role of early experiences and internal conflicts in shaping personality development. The basic tenets of the theory are given here.

The Id, Ego, and Superego

Freud (1923) introduced three distinct components of the human psyche that interact and influence behaviour: the id, ego, and superego. The id represents primal instincts and desires, the superego embodies societal norms and morality, and the ego mediates between the id and superego to achieve balance and harmony.

Defence Mechanisms

Defence mechanisms are psychological strategies that individuals unconsciously use to protect themselves from anxiety, discomfort, and emotional distress. These mechanisms operate on an unconscious level and serve to distort or manipulate reality to manage difficult emotions or thoughts. The defence mechanisms are described here.

1) *Repression* or pushing distressing or threatening thoughts, memories, or desires out of conscious awareness and into the unconscious.
2) *Denial* or refusing to accept the reality of a situation or a thought that causes discomfort. For example, a person diagnosed with a serious medical condition might deny the diagnosis itself.
3) *Projection* or attributing one's unwanted thoughts, feelings, or impulses to someone else. For instance, an individual who has repressed aggressive tendencies might accuse others of being aggressive.
4) *Displacement* or redirecting emotions from their source to a less threatening target. For instance, a person who is upset about a work-related issue might come home and take out frustration on a family member.
5) *Regression* or reverting to an earlier stage of development or behaviour in response to stress or discomfort. For example, an adult might exhibit childlike behaviours when feeling overwhelmed or anxious.
6) *Rationalization* or creating logical explanations for behaviours, thoughts, or decisions that are driven by emotional motives. For instance, someone who didn't get a desired job might rationalize that the company culture wouldn't have been suitable for him.
7) *Sublimation* or channelling unacceptable or socially inappropriate impulses into socially acceptable activities. An example of sublimation is channelling aggressive energy into competitive sports.
8) *Intellectualization* or distancing oneself emotionally from a situation by focusing excessively on abstract reasoning or logic. This defence mechanism can help individuals cope with distressing situations by approaching them from a detached, analytical perspective.

Defence mechanisms are thus crucial tools the human psyche employs to manage anxiety and distress. While they can be adaptive in moderation, excessive reliance on defence mechanisms can lead to psychological rigidity and hinder personal growth.

Stages of Psychosexual Development

Freud described five distinct psychosexual stages through which a child progresses from infancy to adolescence. Each stage is characterized by the focus on different erogenous zones and the potential conflicts that arise during each stage. According to Freud, the successful resolution of these conflicts is crucial for healthy personality development. The psychosexual stages as given in the classical psychoanalytical exposition are briefly presented.

1) *Oral Stage* (Birth to 18 months): During this stage, the infants seek pleasure and satisfaction from oral activities, such as sucking, biting, and exploring objects through the mouth. Freud believed that conflicts during this stage, such as weaning from breastfeeding, could lead to fixation. An individual who is fixated on the oral stage might exhibit behaviours like overeating, smoking, or excessive talking, reflecting an unresolved need for oral gratification.
2) *Anal Stage* (18 months to 3 years): The anal stage centres on the satisfaction the child drives by controlling bowel movements. Thus, toilet training becomes a pivotal experience during this stage. Conflicts can arise when there is an imbalance between the child's desire for autonomy and the parent's expectations for proper toilet training. If toilet training is overly strict or lax, it might lead to anal-retentive (obsessively neat and orderly) or anal-expulsive (disorganized and messy) behaviours in adulthood.
3) *Phallic Stage* (3 to 6 years): This stage is marked by the child's increasing awareness of their own gender identity and the focus on genital pleasure. This stage also introduces the Oedipus complex, where a boy develops feelings of affection towards his mother and rivalry with his father. Similarly, girls experience the Electra complex, where they develop feelings for their father and rivalry with their mother. Successful resolution of these complexes involves identification with the same-sex parent, which serves as a foundation for the development of gender roles and moral values.
4) *Latency Stage* (6 years to puberty): This is a relatively calm period during which sexual and aggressive desires are temporarily suppressed. Instead, children focus on developing social skills and relationships and acquiring knowledge.
5) *Genital Stage* (Puberty onwards): During this stage, the focus shifts back to sexual desires and relationships. Successful resolution of earlier stages contributes to a well-adjusted individual with a balanced and mature attitude towards sexuality and relationships. Those who have unresolved conflicts from earlier stages might face challenges in forming healthy relationships or might experience difficulty in managing sexual urges.

Psychodynamic thinking has undergone enormous expansion over the years (for details, Mitchell & Black, 1995). Critics argue that the theory lacks empirical evidence and is often criticized for its limited generalizability and overemphasis on the unconscious. Furthermore, the theory's gender bias and limited cultural applicability have been points of contention.

Biological Theory

This theory advocates the role of genetic factors, brain structure, and other biological factors in the development of personality. For example, Eysenck's (1967, 1990) theory of personality proposes three personality dimensions that are rooted in the individual's underlying physiological and genetic make-up. These dimensions are psychoticism, extraversion, and neuroticism ("PEN" model). The PEN model suggests that these traits exist on a continuum, and each individual falls somewhere along these dimensions.

Psychoticism

This dimension pertains to the degree to which an individual exhibits traits related to aggression, impulsivity, and antisocial behaviour. High levels of psychoticism are associated with a tendency towards aggression, interpersonal difficulties, and a disregard for social norms.

Extraversion

Extraversion refers to the level of outgoing and social behaviour in an individual. Extraverted individuals are sociable, assertive, and seek stimulation from the external environment while introverted individuals are more reserved and tend to prefer solitary activities.

Neuroticism

Neuroticism measures emotional stability and resilience. Individuals high in neuroticism are more prone to experience negative emotions, anxiety, and mood swings. On the other hand, individuals low in neuroticism are more emotionally stable and handle stress better.

Eysenck developed personality measures such as the Eysenck Personality Inventory (Eysenck & Eysenck, 1964) and the Eysenck Personality Questionnaire (Eysenck & Eysenck, 1975) to tap the three dimensions postulated in his theory. These instruments are widely used in personality research and have contributed to the validation of his model. Both the measures have been adapted for use in the Indian context (e.g., Thakur & Thakur, 1986; Tiwari et al., 2009).

Eysenck's theory has been questioned regarding the universality of his dimensions across cultures, suggesting that cultural factors might influence the expression and interpretation of personality traits. Additionally, the PEN model has been criticized for oversimplifying the complexity of human personality and omitting certain important dimensions that other theories include.

Humanistic Theory

The humanistic theory emphasizes the inherent value and potential of each individual, by focusing on their conscious experiences, self-awareness, and personal growth. The core tenets of the humanistic theory, pioneered by Abraham Maslow and Carl Rogers, revolve around self-actualization, personal agency, and the importance of subjective experiences.

Abraham Maslow's Self-Actualization

At the core of the humanistic theory is the concept of self-actualization. Abraham Maslow's (1943, 1954, 1968) hierarchy of needs theory posits that humans have a set of basic needs that must be met before they can focus on higher-level needs such as self-actualization. The hierarchy is typically depicted as a pyramid, with lower-level needs at the base and higher-level needs at the top. The five levels of hierarchy, from the bottom, are physiological needs (such as food, water, shelter, and sleep), safety needs (physical safety as well as the need for stability, order, and predictability in one's environment), love and belonging needs (seeking social connections and relationships), esteem needs (desire for self-respect and respect of others), and self-actualization needs (desire to reach one's full potential and achieve personal growth and fulfilment). He believed that self-actualization was the ultimate goal of human development and that individuals have an innate drive to reach their full potential. Subsequently, Maslow added self-transcendence to this model.

Figure 8.1 Maslow's Hierarchy of Needs

Self-Concept and Congruence

Carl Rogers (1951, 1961) introduced the idea of self-concept and the relationship between the individual and their environment. He posited that individuals strive to maintain a consistent self-concept and that discrepancies between the self-concept and one's experiences can lead to psychological distress.

Personal Agency

Humanistic theory emphasizes personal agency – the capacity of individuals to make intentional choices and take control of their lives. This contrasts with deterministic views that suggest that behaviour is shaped solely by external factors.

Subjective Experience

Unlike other theories that focus on objective measures, humanistic theory emphasizes an individual's subjective experiences and their unique interpretation of the world. This recognition of subjectivity allows for a more comprehensive understanding of human behaviour.

The humanistic theory has profound implications for counselling, therapy, education, and personal development. Humanistic therapies, like Rogerian therapy, create a non-judgemental and empathetic environment where individuals can explore their feelings and experiences freely. This approach is often used in fostering personal development, improving self-esteem, and addressing issues like anxiety and depression. However, the humanistic theory has not been without criticism. It has been argued that its concepts are difficult to quantify and measure.

Social Cognitive Theories

These theories are rooted in the belief that personality is not solely determined by genetics or environmental factors but is shaped by the interplay between cognitive processes, social interactions, and environmental influences. These theories emphasize the importance of observational learning, self-regulation, and the impact of social modelling on the development of personality traits.

Albert Bandura's Social Cognitive Theory

Bandura's (1977, 1997) theory, also known as social learning theory, emphasized the importance of cognitive processes, observational learning, and self-regulation in shaping human behaviour and personality. Central to Bandura's theory is the concept of observational learning, which posits that individuals learn by observing the actions, behaviours, and outcomes of others. Bandura (Bandura et al., 1961) did groundbreaking research on the Bobo doll experiment. In the experiment, children were exposed to a scenario where an adult model engaged in either aggressive or non-aggressive behaviour towards an inflatable doll named Bobo. The adult model interacted with the doll by hitting, punching, and verbally attacking it in the aggressive condition, while in the non-aggressive condition, the adult played quietly with other toys. The children were divided into different groups to observe different conditions: aggressive model, non-aggressive model, or no model. The results of the study showed that children who had observed the aggressive model were more likely to imitate the aggressive behaviours and physically attack the Bobo doll, hitting it with a mallet, kicking it, and even imitating the aggressive phrases they had heard. On the other hand, children who had observed the non-aggressive model or had not seen any model displayed fewer aggressive behaviours towards the doll.

Bandura's theory introduces the concept of "reciprocal determinism", which emphasizes the dynamic interaction between an individual's cognitive processes, behaviour, and environment (Bandura, 1986). According to this concept, individuals not only respond to their environment but also actively shape the environment through their actions and interpretations. This bidirectional influence underscores the complexity of human behaviour and personality development.

Bandura's theory has profound implications for various fields, including education, therapy, and media influence. In education, the theory highlights the importance of providing students with opportunities for successful experiences and role models to enhance their self-efficacy and motivation. In therapy, interventions that focus on improving self-efficacy can lead to more effective behaviour change and improved mental health outcomes.

Julian Rotter's Locus of Control

Rotter (1966) introduced the concept of locus of control – internal and external locus of control. This theory suggests that individuals have a belief about the degree of control they have over their lives. People with an internal locus of control believe that their actions and decisions influence their outcomes while those with an external locus of control attribute their successes or failures to external factors like luck or fate. Locus of control is closely related to how individuals approach challenges and perceive their ability to shape their own lives.

Social cognitive theories have contributed significantly to our understanding of personality by highlighting the intricate interplay between cognitive processes, social influences, and environmental factors. However, criticisms have arisen concerning the extent to which these theories account for the influence of biological factors and the relatively limited attention paid to the unconscious aspects of personality.

Trait Theories

One of the prominent frameworks for understanding personality is the trait theory. This theory posits that individuals possess relatively stable traits. Included among some prominent trait theories are the five-factor model, Cattell's 16 personality factors, and Allport's trait theory.

The Five-Factor Model (FFM)

Perhaps, the most well-known trait theory, the five-factor model (McCrae & Costa, 1987) proposes that personality can be understood in terms of five broad dimensions or traits: openness to experience, conscientiousness, extraversion, agreeableness, and neuroticism (OCEAN or CANOE).

1) *Openness to Experience*: This dimension describes the extent to which individuals are open to new experiences, ideas, and values. People who score high on openness tend to be curious, creative, imaginative, and intellectually curious. They enjoy novelty, appreciate beauty, and are open to new perspectives and ways of thinking. Those who score low on this dimension tend to be more conventional, conservative, and resistant to change.
2) *Conscientiousness*: This dimension refers to the degree of organization, responsibility, and self-discipline exhibited by individuals. People who score high on conscientiousness tend to be reliable, organized, hardworking, and goal-oriented. They are careful and thorough in their work and tend to be self-disciplined and responsible. Those who score low on this dimension tend to be more careless, impulsive, and disorganized.
3) *Extraversion*: This dimension describes the degree to which individuals are outgoing, sociable, and assertive. People who score high on extraversion tend to be talkative, energetic, and outgoing. They enjoy socializing and being around people and tend to be assertive and confident. Those who score low on this dimension tend to be more introverted, reserved, and quiet.
4) *Agreeableness*: This dimension refers to the degree of kindness, empathy, and cooperation exhibited by individuals. People who score high on agreeableness tend to be compassionate, cooperative, and considerate. They are generally easy to get along with and tend to be more concerned with the well-being of others than their interests. Those who score low on this dimension tend to be more competitive, argumentative, and critical.
5) *Neuroticism*: This dimension describes the degree to which individuals experience negative emotions such as anxiety, worry, and sadness. People who score high on neuroticism tend to be more emotionally reactive and prone to negative feelings. They may experience more stress and anxiety in response to life's challenges. Those who score low on this dimension tend to be more emotionally stable and resilient.

It has been observed (Rentfrow & Jakola, 2019) that the Big Five is a useful framework for conceptualizing and measuring individual personality differences. It is useful for predicting a wide range of behaviours, such as job performance, health behaviours, and relationship satisfaction (McAdams, 2018). As noted by McCrae and Costa (2013), the five-factor model guides not only personality psychologists but also developmentalists, cross-cultural psychologists, industrial/organizational psychologists, clinicians, and researchers interested in personality disorders.

Research supports the five-factor model in the Indian context (e.g., Lodhi et al., 2002). In an interesting study, Dutta et al. (2017) analysed the personality traits of Indian celebrities. Sportspersons were found to be low on openness and high on conscientiousness and agreeableness. Indian politicians were high on openness and low on extraversion and agreeableness. The study reported an overlap in the personality traits of actors and sportspersons. Like sportspersons, actors were low on openness and high on agreeableness. However, unlike sportspersons, Indian actors were high on extraversion. Age, gender, and socio-economic differences in the development of personality traits have been reported. For example, Magan et al. (2014) found an increase in conscientiousness with increasing age, neuroticism decreased with age in women aged 26–35 years, and extraversion increased with increasing age in men aged 35–46 years. Significant gaps along caste lines in India have been reported. Individuals belonging to Scheduled Castes, Scheduled Tribes and Other Backward Communities scored lower on conscientiousness, extraversion, agreeableness, and openness to experience (Dasgupta et al., 2023).

However, the five-factor model has some limitations. For example, it does not capture all aspects of personality, such as individual differences in motivation and self-concept. Additionally, the five-factor model may not be equally relevant for all individuals and situations (McAdams, 2018).

Raymond Cattell's 16 Personality Factors

Cattell's (1946) 16 personality factors (16PF) is a comprehensive trait theory that captures the complexity of human personality by breaking it down into 16 primary source traits. He used the statistical method of factor analysis to identify the 16 dimensions (Cattell et al., 1970; Cattell & Schuerger, 2003). According to Cattell, each person contains all of these 16 traits to a certain degree, but they might be low on some traits and high on others. Thus, 16 PF can be represented on a continuum from low to high. Here is a brief overview of the 16 personality factors.

1) *Warmth* or the degree of friendliness, kindness, and warmth.
2) *Reasoning* or the inclination to use rational thinking and logical problem-solving.
3) *Emotional Stability* or the extent to which one remains composed under stress and emotional pressure.
4) *Dominance* or the tendency to take control and lead in various situations.
5) *Liveliness* or the level of energy, enthusiasm, and spontaneity an individual exhibits.
6) *Rule-Consciousness* or the degree to which a person adheres to rules, norms, and societal expectations.
7) *Social Boldness* or the willingness to engage in new or unfamiliar social situations.
8) *Sensitivity* or the receptiveness to sensory stimuli and emotional cues from others.
9) *Vigilance* or the level of cautiousness and alertness in one's interactions and surroundings.
10) *Abstractedness* or the inclination towards abstract thinking and imagination.
11) *Privateness* or the tendency to keep personal thoughts and emotions private.
12) *Apprehension* or the extent to which one experiences anxiety or self-doubt.
13) *Openness to Change* or the willingness to embrace change and new experiences.
14) *Self-reliance* or the degree of independence and self-reliance exhibited by an individual.
15) *Perfectionism* or the pursuit of perfection and attention to detail.
16) *Tension* or the presence of nervousness or unease in various situations.

Each of these factors contributes to an individual's personality profile, and Cattell's 16PF assessment aims to provide a comprehensive understanding of how these traits interact and shape behaviour. For this, the 16PF questionnaire, a self-report instrument, published in 1949 was used. The questionnaire was revised in 1956, 1962, and 1969. Its recent and fifth edition, released in 1993 (Cattell et al., 1993), contains 185 multiple-choice items, which are written at a fifth-grade reading level. The 16 PF questionnaire has been adapted in India and is available in several Indian languages (such as Hindi, Tamil, Bengali, Marathi, Telugu, Kannada, Malayalam, Gujarati, and so on).

Gordon Allport's Trait Theory

Allport's (1937) theory paved the way for a more nuanced understanding of traits, emphasizing their dynamic interplay and impact on behaviour. His theory proposed three levels of traits: cardinal traits, central traits, and secondary traits, each contributing to the complexity of an individual's personality.

1) *Cardinal Traits*: These are the most dominant and pervasive traits that define an individual's overall personality. Cardinal traits are so influential that they shape a person's behaviour across a wide range of situations. For instance, a cardinal trait like "altruism" might drive an individual to consistently prioritize others' well-being in various contexts. Allport believed that cardinal traits are relatively rare, and not everyone possesses them. When present, they have a profound impact on an individual's behaviour. People with cardinal traits are known for these traits and are often recognized by them.
2) *Central Traits*: Central traits are general characteristics that describe an individual's personality but are not as all-encompassing as cardinal traits. They form the core of an individual's personality. For example, someone with a central trait of "extraversion" tends to be outgoing, sociable, and energized by social interactions. This central trait influences their behaviour in various contexts, whether at work, with friends, or in public settings.
3) *Secondary Traits*: These traits are more specific and context-dependent. They are not consistently present and may manifest only in certain circumstances. For example, a person possessing the central trait of introversion generally prefers solitary activities and finds social interactions draining. However, they might also have a secondary trait of gregariousness. This means that in certain situations or with specific people, they can exhibit sociable and outgoing behaviour, even though it is not their default mode of interaction.

Allport emphasized that traits are not solely responsible for behaviour; they interact with the unique experiences and situations individuals encounter. He believed that individuals are not reducible to a fixed set of traits but are characterized by their individuality and how their traits interact. Persons against trait theory argue that traits might not fully capture the complexity of human personality, as they don't account for situational influences and cultural variations. Critics suggest that traits may be less stable and more context-dependent than traditionally assumed.

Development of Personality

Like self, personality also undergoes the process of development throughout a person's lifespan. From infancy to old age, personality evolves in response to biological, psychological, and environmental factors. The salient features of the development of personality across life stages are given here.

Infancy and Early Childhood

The early stages of life lay the groundwork for personality development. Thomas and Chess (1977) introduced the concept of temperament. Temperament is the set of individual traits and characteristics that influence how people react and self-regulate while interacting with the world around them. The authors identified nine temperament traits that were grouped into three categories.

Easy: Infants with this temperament exhibited regular eating, sleeping, and elimination patterns, approached new situations with curiosity and adapted easily to changes in routine.

Difficult: Infants with a difficult temperament were characterized by irregularity in biological functions, intense emotional reactions, and resistance to change or new experiences.

Slow-to-Warm-Up: Infants in this category displayed a gradual approach to new situations, initially showing caution and withdrawal before gradually adapting.

The researchers found that infants with an "easy" temperament were more likely to develop secure attachments, whereas those with a "difficult" temperament faced challenges in forming positive relationships. According to Saucier and Simonds (2006, p. 118), temperament is the "early-in-life framework" out of which personality traits develop. Longitudinal studies (e.g., Caspi et al., 2003) have found an association between infants' temperament and personality traits in their young adulthood (mid-twenties).

Childhood and Adolescence

Adolescence is also characterized by the development of narcissistic tendencies (Hill & Edmonds, 2017). Narcissistic tendency refers to the presence of traits and behaviours characterized by a grandiose sense of self-importance. They believe they are exceptional, unique, or superior to others in various ways. Such adolescents also show a lack of empathy for others and a constant need for admiration and attention. While some levels of self-confidence and self-esteem are healthy, individuals with narcissistic tendencies take these traits to an extreme, often leading to interpersonal difficulties in maintaining healthy relationships.

Adulthood

Personality traits tend to stabilize during adulthood, with many foundational traits persisting over time. It has been noted (Mlacic & Milas, 2015) that after adolescence extraversion decreases, openness (intellect) increases, while agreeableness and conscientiousness follow a curvilinear trend, decreasing in adolescence and increasing in early adulthood. Also, adults develop the ability to change in response to life events (Roberts & Mroczek, 2008).

Old Age

Research (e.g., McAdams & Olson, 2010) shows some general patterns of change during old age, such as people becoming more socially dominant, more agreeable, more conscientious, and less neurotic. In this period, personality development often takes on a reflective and introspective quality. As individuals age, they may focus on existential questions and the legacy they leave behind. Wisdom, characterized by a deep understanding of human nature and a capacity for empathy, can emerge as a hallmark of personality in older adults.

Individuals encounter varying challenges and experiences from infancy through late adulthood that shape their personality traits, behaviours, and self-perception. While some aspects of personality tend to stabilize over time, others remain malleable, demonstrating the complexity and adaptability of human nature. Nature and nurture play pivotal roles in shaping personality development.

Cultural Variations in Personality

Cross-cultural studies have revealed that certain personality traits may be more valued or emphasized in specific cultures. As Triandis and Suh (2002) noted, there are cultural differences in the way people perceive themselves and the environment. In a collectivist culture, the environment is fixed (stable societal norms, duties, obligations etc.), and people tend to fit themselves. In individualist cultures, the reverse is true. That is, people see themselves as fixed and the environment is changeable.

Research on the five-factor model (FFM) of personality traits has also shown variability across cultures (McCrae & Terracciano, 2005). Openness to experience, for instance, may be valued differently in cultures that emphasize tradition and conformity. Neuroticism might manifest differently in cultures where emotional expression is discouraged. People in Central and South American cultures tend to score higher on openness to experience, whereas Europeans score higher on neuroticism (Benet-Martinez & Karakitapoglu-Aygun, 2003). Studies (Allik & McCrae, 2004; McCrae & Terracciano, 2005) reveal the geographical distribution of five factors: people in Asian cultures including India score high on agreeableness and low in extraversion; Central and South American cultures score high in openness; and Southern and Eastern Europe score high in neuroticism. East Asians have a higher tolerance for contradictions than Americans (Choi & Nisbett, 2000).

The concepts of "dharma", "gunas", and "karma" in Indian philosophy encourage individuals to fulfil their roles and duties within their social hierarchy. This results in the development of personalities that are more oriented towards duty, responsibility, and self-sacrifice for the greater good. The religious teachings in India emphasize values like humility, compassion, and detachment, influencing the development of personalities that are more oriented towards spiritual growth and inner harmony (Saraswathi, 1999). Qualities like adaptation and resilience are integral to the Sikh psyche (Kapur & Misra, 2003).

Cultural variations in personality are, thus, a fascinating testament to the intricate interplay between human nature and cultural contexts. Different societies emphasize and encourage specific traits, leading to diversity in the expression and manifestation of personality characteristics. Box 8.2 contains the Indian view of personality.

Box 8.2 The Indian View of Personality

Indian philosophy offers a unique lens through which personality is understood. In place of the term personality, the concept of *Swabhaava* has been used in scriptures, which cover all aspects of personality. *Swabhaava* is the essential quality. It is that speed of spirit which manifests itself as the essential quality in all becoming. The Indian conception revolves around the notion of "Purusharthas". Concepts like "Karma" and "Dharma" guide individuals in their behaviour and life choices (Paranjpe, 2013). Gunas like *Sattva*, *Rajas*, and *Tamas* (often called *Triguna*) influence an individual's personality and behaviour. A lexical analysis of the Hindi language confirmed the presence of *Sattvika*, *Rajasika*, and *Tamasika* personality traits (Singh et al., 2013). Bhangaokar et al. (2023) noted a positive correlation between *Sattavika* traits and *karma* yoga among young adults. Yogic practices such as "Dhyana" (meditation) and "Pranayama" (breath control) aim to cultivate inner peace, emotional balance, and self-awareness. These practices contribute to nurturing a harmonious and well-rounded personality. The Indian view underscores the interconnectedness of individuals with the universe and encourages self-realization and inner growth.

Measurement of Personality Development

Understanding the measurement of personality is crucial for appreciating how personality evolves across the lifespan. Longitudinal, cross-sectional, and sequential research designs are used in the study of personality. Different types of tools are used in personality studies, such as self-report measures, personality inventories, observers' ratings, narrative and identity analysis, projective tests, and others.

Self-report measures involve individuals responding to a series of questions or statements about themselves, reflecting their thoughts, feelings, and behaviours. Some of the widely used self-report measures include Costa and McCrae's (2008) NEO Personality Inventory instruments, Goldberg's (1992) Trait Descriptive Adjectives, and John et al.'s (1991) Big Five Inventory.

Personality inventories are standardized questionnaires designed to assess specific personality traits or dimensions. They provide a structured framework for assessing various aspects of an individual's personality. For example, the 16 personality factor questionnaire (16PF) (Cattell et al., 1970) measures 16 primary personality factors, including factors such as warmth, dominance, and emotional stability.

Observer-based assessments involve having others rate an individual's personality traits. This approach provides an external perspective and can mitigate biases inherent in self-report measures. The California Q-Sort is an observer-based method that requires sorting a set of personality descriptors based on their applicability to the individual.

The narrative and identity analysis method focuses on individuals' life stories, narratives, and sense of identity. McAdams (1996, 2011) emphasizes the importance of storytelling in understanding one's life and identity. This method recognizes that people construct their self-concepts and personalities through the stories they tell about themselves, the experiences they have had, and the way they perceive their identity over time.

Projective techniques are tools that present individuals with ambiguous stimuli, such as images, words, scenarios, inkblots, or incomplete sentences/stories and ask them to respond with their thoughts, feelings, or associations. The rationale behind these techniques is that, as the stimuli are unstructured and ambiguous, every individual sees them differently and projects her/his inner thoughts and emotions onto the stimuli, providing insights into their unconscious mind and personality traits. Rorschach Inkblot Test and Thematic Apperception Test (TAT) are the most widely used projective techniques.

There are other measures such as Behavioural Observations, Situational Judgement Tests (SJT), and Implicit Association Tests (IAT). In Behavioural Observations, an individual's behaviour is observed in natural or controlled settings, which can provide insights into their personality traits. Situational Judgment Tests present individuals with realistic work-related scenarios and ask them to choose the most appropriate response. Implicit Association Tests measure automatic associations between concepts and attributes, uncovering implicit biases and attitudes.

Thus, various methods are employed to measure personality, each with its strengths and limitations. Self-report measures provide direct insight into how individuals perceive themselves while personality inventories offer structured assessments of specific traits. Projective tests tap into deeper, unconscious aspects of personality, and other measures like behavioural observations, SJTs, and IATs provide additional dimensions of understanding. Researchers and practitioners choose these methods based on the context, goals, and intended applications, ultimately contributing to a more comprehensive understanding of personality.

Overview

In this chapter, an attempt was made to explore the human psyche through the study of self and personality. We began by pondering the nature of self and personality, recognizing them as cornerstones of our existence, shaping our thoughts, emotions, and behaviours. From there, we embarked on an enlightening voyage through various theoretical perspectives, each offering a unique lens through which we can comprehend different facets of our identity. Moreover, we discussed the emergence of the self throughout a lifetime, from the earliest moments of infancy to the wisdom of old age. We discovered that the self is not a static entity but a dynamic and evolving construct that adapts to the challenges and experiences of each life stage.

Our exploration also revealed the profound influence of culture on the development of self and personality. We had the privilege of exploring Indian thought, uncovering insights into the self and personality that expand our global perspective. Furthermore, we navigated the intricate realm of personality theories, each shedding light on the complexities of what makes us who we are.

Towards the end, we explored methods for measuring personality development, equipping ourselves with valuable tools to assess and understand the ever-evolving facets of our personalities. The journey of self and personality development is ongoing, and each individual's path is as unique as a fingerprint. By understanding the intricacies of ourselves and the diverse tapestry of human personalities, we not only gain insight into ourselves but also foster empathy and understanding for the rich mosaic of humanity that surrounds us.

Key Terms

Biological Approach to Personality
Concept of Self
Concept of Personality
Culture and Development of Self
Cultural Variations in Personality
Emergence of Self
Humanistic Approach
Measurement of Personality
Personality in the Indian Thought
Psychodynamic Perspective
Self-Efficacy

Self-Determination
Self-Esteem
Self-Perception
Self in Indian Thought
Self-Esteem
Self-Development Across Life Stages
Social Identity
Social Cognitive Theory
Trait Approach
Temperament
Triguna Theory

Questions for Reflection

1) After reading this chapter, how has your understanding of the nature and development of self and personality evolved?
2) Of the various theoretical perspectives discussed regarding the self, which perspective resonates with you the most, and why?

3) In what ways do cultural influences shape the understanding and expression of personality, and how it will enhance your interactions with individuals from diverse cultural backgrounds?
4) What are the specific instances in your life where self-esteem played a significant role?
5) Reflect on how your self-perception and personality have evolved from childhood to the present and identify any key milestones or challenges that have influenced this developmental journey.

Suggested Further Readings

Books

Leary, M. R., & Tangney, J. P. (Eds.). (2012). *Handbook of self and identity*. The Guilford Press.
Mroczek, D. K., & Little, T. D. (2006). *Handbook of personality development*. Psychology Press.

Website/Online Resource

Psychology Today – Self-Help (*www.psychologytoday.com/us/basics/self-help*)

9 Affective Development

Contents

Introduction	185
Conceptions of Affect and Emotions	185
Theories of Emotions	185
Indian Perspective on Emotions	188
Box 9.1: Indian Conception of *Doshas* – *Vata*, *Pitta*, and *Kapha*	189
Box 9.2: Theory of *Rasa* and *Bhava*	190
Box 9.3: The Concept of *Bhakti*	191
Positive and Negative Emotions	192
Box 9.4: The Concept of *Sthitapragya*	194
Understanding and Expressing Emotions: A Developmental View	195
Aesthetic Development	198
Stress and Coping: A Developmental View	199
Box 9.5: Stress of Schooling Among Indian Children	200
Overview	200
Key Terms	201
Questions for Reflection	201

Learning Objectives

After studying this chapter, the learner will be able to:

Define the fundamental concepts of affect and emotions;
Explore prominent theories of emotions, including the Indian perspective;
Examine cultural variations in the understanding and expression of emotions;
Explore positive and negative emotions, with a focus on the concept of *Sthitapragya*; and
Investigate the developmental aspects of positive and negative emotions.

DOI: 10.4324/9781003441168-13

Introduction

We all experience emotions such as joy, sorrow, hope, happiness, anger, shame, guilt, and fear in some form in our everyday life. People across cultures experience these emotions. In a study, students from 37 countries across the world reported experiencing the following emotions: joy, fear, anger, sadness, disgust, shame, and guilt (Scherer, 1997; Scherer & Wallbott, 1994). This chapter discusses the conceptions of affect and emotions, the related theories, the Indian perspective on emotions, salient features of a few positive and negative emotions, the development of emotions across the lifespan, the development of emotional competence and aesthetics, and stress with coping mechanisms adopted by individuals of different ages. In doing so, the Indian conceptions and research findings have been included in appropriate places.

Conceptions of Affect and Emotions

Though the concepts of affect and emotions are often used interchangeably and belong to the same family, they refer to distinct phenomena. Affect refers to the overall mood and emotional tone, more enduring or lasting, and reflects a person's general state of mind. In contrast, emotions are more specific and discrete experiences tied to events or stimuli that are often intense, significant, and short-lived. For example, if someone is generally happy and positive by nature, they have a positive affect. However, if they receive bad news, they may experience a negative emotion, such as sadness or anger, which is a temporary shift in their state of affect.

Researchers have shown that affect and emotions have different neural and physiological underpinnings. Affect is thought to be associated with the prefrontal cortex while emotions are associated with the amygdala and other subcortical structures (Davidson & Scherer, 2019). Affect is more closely linked to social behaviours and interpersonal relationships while emotions are more closely linked to individual experiences. For example, positive affect is associated with increased sociability, friendliness, and approach-oriented behaviours, and negative affect is linked to withdrawal, avoidance, and more cautious or defensive behaviours (Baumeister et al., 2003). Emotions, on the other hand, are subjective experiences characterized by specific psychological and physiological responses. They are more closely tied to individual experiences and can vary based on personal circumstances and interpretations. For instance, someone experiencing the emotion of fear may have specific subjective thoughts, bodily sensations, and behaviours associated with their unique interpretation of a threatening situation.

Theories of Emotions

Emotions are complex psychological phenomena that have been the subject of several theories, such as physiological, cognitive, social constructivist, and multi-componential theories. A brief description of these theories is given here.

Physiological Theories

The physiological theories argue that the origin of emotions lies in physiological responses to stimuli. Included among physiological theories are the James-Lange theory, Cannon-Bard theory, and Affect Script theory.

186 *Perspectives on Self and Affective Development*

The James-Lange Theory

Proposed by James (1884) and Lange (1885), this theory suggests that emotions are a result of physiological reactions to stimuli. In other words, our emotional experiences follow our physiological responses to a situation. According to the James-Lange theory, an event triggers a physiological response in the body, and the perception of these physiological changes is what we experience as an emotion. For example, if you encounter a lion in the forest, you may first experience a rapid heartbeat, then interpret that as fear.

The Cannon-Bard Theory

Walter Cannon (1927) and Philip Bard (1928) challenge the James-Lange theory by suggesting that physiological changes do not necessarily cause emotions. Instead, emotions and physiological responses occur simultaneously and independently of each other. For example, if an individual sees a lion in the forest, he/she will experience both physiological responses such as increased heart rate and sweating and emotions such as fear at the same time. According to the Cannon-Bard theory, the brain processes emotional information separately from physiological information.

Tomkins's Affect Script Theory

Tomkins (1962) argued for a biological basis for facial expressions associated with different emotions and that certain facial expressions are innate and universal across cultures. Tomkins identified a set of innate, universal emotional expressions that he called "primary affects". These are facial expressions associated with basic emotions such as joy, surprise, anger, fear, and distress. Tomkins proposed that emotions are modulated by the interaction of primary affect. He suggested that our emotional experiences are shaped by the patterns of emotional responses we develop over time, known as "scripts". Facial expressions, according to Tomkins, play a crucial role in the experience and communication of emotions.

Cognitive Theories

Cognitive theories, such as two-factor and appraisal theories, opine that cognition or thought has a primary role in generating and guiding emotions.

Schachter and Singer's Two-Factor Theory

Building upon the work by Cannon and Bard, this theory (Schachter & Singer, 1962) suggests that emotions are the result of a two-step process involving physiological arousal and cognitive interpretation. Emotions are triggered by physiological arousal. The cognitive component involves the interpretation or labelling of the physiological arousal based on the individual's cognitive appraisal of the situation. Emotion is a result of the interaction between physiological arousal and cognitive interpretation. The theory proposes that neither factor alone is sufficient to create emotional experiences; both are necessary. Different people may interpret the same physiological arousal differently, leading to distinct emotional experiences in response to similar stimuli.

Lazarus's Appraisal theory

According to Lazarus (1966, 1991), emotions are the results of our appraisal of a situation or event. Lazarus identified two types of appraisals: primary and secondary. Primary appraisals involve evaluating the situation in terms of its relevance to our goals, desires, and well-being.

If we perceive the situation as a threat to our well-being or goals, we are likely to experience a negative emotion and vice versa. Secondary appraisals involve evaluating our ability to cope with the situation. If we believe we have the resources and skills to cope with the situation, we are likely to experience a positive emotion, such as pride or confidence. If we believe that we cannot cope with the situation due to a lack of resources or skills, we are likely to experience a negative emotion, such as anxiety or helplessness.

Social Constructivist Theories

The social constructivist theories argue that emotions are not just individual experiences but are also shaped by social and cultural factors. These theories emphasize the importance of language, cultural norms, and social interactions in the development and expression of emotions. The salient features of these theories are described here.

Hochschild's Social Constructionist Theory

Hochschild's (1983) theory introduces the concept of "emotion work", which refers to the management of one's emotions to meet societal and organizational expectations. Hochschild argues that societies have implicit or explicit "feeling rules" that dictate how individuals should feel and express emotions in various situations. Hochschild distinguishes between "surface acting" (or faking emotions) and "deep acting" (or genuine emotions).

Lutz and White's Cultural Theory of Emotions

Lutz and White (1986) proposed that different cultures have different emotional regimes, which prescribe how people should feel and express their emotions in different situations.

Thomas Scheff's Interactionist Theory

Scheff's (1990) theory focuses on the symbols (e.g., words, gestures) people use to give meaning to their experiences. Scheff suggests that emotions are communicated and interpreted through symbols exchanged in social interactions. Scheff identifies shame and guilt as central emotions that often go unacknowledged in social interactions. These emotions may arise from perceived violations of societal norms or personal expectations. Unacknowledged shame and guilt may lead to emotional discomfort and affect subsequent interactions.

Multi-Componential Theories

These theories argue that emotions have both biological and cultural components. These components interact with each other in various socio-relational contexts, leading to the emergence of different emotional experiences. The following theories emphasize the multidimensional nature of emotions.

Scherer and Ekman's Component Process Model

Scherer and Ekman (1984) proposed that emotions consist of different components such as cognitive appraisal, physiological changes, expressive behaviour, and subjective experience. Appraisal refers to the individual's assessment of the significance of an event concerning their goals and well-being. Emotions are associated with physiological changes in the body, such as changes in heart rate, blood pressure, and hormonal levels. Emotions are expressed through facial expressions, body language, and other observable behaviours. Emotions are not only observable through external behaviours but also involve an internal, subjective experience unique to everyone. Emotion processes are of two kinds – automatic and effortful (controlled). Some aspects of emotion, such as immediate physiological responses, are automatic and rapid, while cognitive appraisal may involve more deliberate and effortful processes. The model also acknowledges the existence of universal emotional expressions and physiological responses across cultures.

Ellsworth and Smith's Component Process Model

Ellsworth and Smith (1988) advocated that emotions are composed of three components: cognitive appraisals, motivational states, and relational themes. Cognitive appraisals determine the motivational state of an individual, which in turn leads to the expression of a particular emotional response.

Gross's Emotion Regulation Theory

Gross (1998) provided a framework for understanding how individuals manage their emotions. Gross proposed a process model that distinguishes between different stages of emotion regulation. These stages include the selection of strategies, implementation of strategies, and the monitoring of the effectiveness of these strategies. Gross (2001) proposed that the effectiveness of emotion regulation depends on the fit between the chosen regulation strategy and the specific emotional situation. Different strategies may be effective depending on the context.

Thus, we find that the theories of emotions provide different perspectives on how emotions arise, are experienced, and are expressed. Some theories emphasize the biological basis of emotions while others focus on the cultural and social factors that shape them. Many contemporary theories take a multi-componential approach, suggesting that emotions are complex experiences that involve cognitive, physiological, and behavioural components.

Indian Perspective on Emotions

In the Indian tradition, emotions have been discussed in several contexts, such as aesthetics (e.g., *rasa*), Bhakti movement (devotion to deity), tantric (mysticism and spiritual) traditions, and philosophical contexts. There is no Sanskrit term equivalent to emotion. Terms like *vedana* (anguish) and *bhava* (feeling), as well as the names of individual emotions, such as *raga* (love), and *dvesh* (hatred) have been used (Tuske, 2021). The Indian view emphasizes freeing the mind from feelings and emotions because it considers them the cause of attachment resulting in obstacles to attaining *moksha* (liberation). According to the *Samkhya* philosophy, the human mind is composed of three fundamental elements: *sattva* (purity, harmony), *rajas* (activity, passion), and *tamas* (inertia, ignorance). Emotions are considered the products of the interplay of these three qualities. While *sattva* is associated with positive emotions such as joy, love, and compassion, *rajas* represents emotions like desire, anger, and attachment. *Tamas*, on the other hand, is linked to negative emotions such as fear, sadness, and delusion. The *Samkhya* philosophy aimed at achieving liberation (*moksha*) by transcending these emotional states and attaining a state of pure consciousness.

The *Yoga Sutras* of Patanjali provide a comprehensive framework for understanding and managing emotions. Patanjali described emotions as fluctuations of the mind and identified five types: afflictions (*kleshas*), ignorance (*avidya*), egoism (*asmita*), attachment (*raga*), aversion (*dvesha*), and fear of death (*abhinivesha*). According to Patanjali, suffering is due to ignorance about one's true "self" (*avidya*). Hence, suffering or *dukkha* arises from within and not from outside the world. Patanjali advocated the practice of meditation, self-discipline, and self-awareness to transcend these afflictions and attain a state of equanimity. According to Ayurveda, the traditional system of medicine, emotions are closely linked to the three *doshas* or bodily humour (*vata*, *pitta*, and *kapha*), and imbalances in these *doshas* can cause emotional disturbances (Box 9.1).

The *Yoga* philosophy recognizes the importance of emotional balance and self-awareness as a path to spiritual enlightenment (Feuerstein, 1998). *Yoga* practice also includes various techniques, such as *pranayama* (breathing exercises) and *asanas* (physical postures), that can help regulate emotions and promote mental well-being. The *Bhagavad Gita* also emphasizes the need to cultivate emotional balance and detachment to overcome the cycle of birth and death and attain liberation.

Box 9.1 Indian Conception of *Doshas* – *Vata, Pitta,* and *Kapha*

The conception of *doshas* is an important part of Ayurvedic medicine. According to Ayurveda, the three *doshas* – *vata, pitta,* and *kapha* – are the three fundamental energies or principles that govern all biological and psychological functions in the body (Tirtha, 1998).

Vata is responsible for movement and communication in the body, including breathing, circulation, and elimination. When *vata* is in balance, it promotes creativity, enthusiasm, and flexibility. However, when it is imbalanced, it can cause anxiety, restlessness, fear, insomnia, constipation, and joint pain.

Pitta is responsible for digestion and metabolism in the body. It governs all bodily functions related to transformation, including digestion, metabolism, and temperature regulation. When *pitta* is in balance, it promotes intelligence, courage, and leadership. However, when it is imbalanced, it can cause anger, jealousy, frustration, and inflammation. Some common symptoms of a *pitta* imbalance include heartburn, diarrhoea, and skin rashes.

Kapha governs all bodily functions related to growth and maintenance, including immunity, strength, and lubrication. When *kapha* is in balance, it promotes love, forgiveness, and stability. However, when it is imbalanced, it can cause lethargy, depression, lack of motivation, and weight gain. Some common symptoms of a *kapha* imbalance include congestion, sinusitis, and obesity.

Concepts of Rasa and Bhava

There are two key concepts related to emotions in the Indian tradition: *rasa* and *bhava*. *Rasa* refers to the aesthetic experience of emotions in art, literature, and drama. It is believed that different emotions evoke different *rasas* in the viewer or reader. The concept of *rasa* is believed to be a way of experiencing and understanding emotions in a more profound and meaningful way (Box 9.2). *Bhava* is close to emotion. (Box 9.3).

Box 9.2 Theory of *Rasa* and *Bhava*

The theory of *rasa* and *bhava* deals with poetic, dramaturgical, and aesthetic experiences having a direct bearing on the psychology of emotions (Misra, 2004, Paranjpe, 2009; Shweder, 1993). *Rasa* is a Sanskrit term that means "essence" or "flavour" and is used to describe the emotional experience that is evoked by a work of art, such as a poem, a play, or a piece of music. The concept of *rasa* can be traced back to the *Natyashastra*, an ancient treatise on the performing arts, written by sage Bharata in the 2nd century BCE. Bharata assigned specific emotional values to musical notes (*svaras*) and melodic patterns (*jatis* or *ragas*) when they are used in stage presentations. *Rasa* is a refined mental state to which the dancer/poet and spectator get transported. It is a meta-emotion – a sui generic form of consciousness. The core of this view is *bhava*, which means existence as well as mental state (*Bhavantiti bhavah; bhavayanti iti bhavah*). The theory suggests that it is through the *samyoga* (union) of *bhavas* that *rasa* becomes manifest (*vibha- vanubhavasanchari samyoad rasa nishpattih*). There are four kinds of *bhavas*, that is, *sthayi bhava* (enduring, common, frequent), *vibhava* (the determining/eliciting conditions), *anubhava* (the consequences, such as somatic responses, action tendencies, and expressive modes), and *vyabhichari* bhava (the accompanying mental states) (refer to Misra, 2005).

The *Natyashastra* talks about eight *rasas*. The *rasas* and the corresponding *bhavas* are given in Table 9.1.

Each *rasa* evokes a specific emotion that can resonate with the audience, and when combined together in a performance, they can create a rich and complex emotional experience for the viewers. The process of evoking a *rasa* begins with the creation of a work of art that is designed to elicit a particular emotion in the viewer or listener. This is achieved using various elements, such as language, rhythm, melody, and gesture, which are carefully crafted to create a specific mood or atmosphere. Once the work of art has been created, the audience must engage with it to experience the *rasa*. This requires a certain level of receptivity and openness on the part of the viewer or listener, as well as an ability to understand and appreciate the artistic elements that are being used. The experience of *rasa* is subjective, and different people may experience the same work of art in different ways, depending on their own emotional state and cultural background.

Table 9.1 Description of Rasas and Bhavas

	Rasa	Bhava
1	*Shringara* (erotic/romantic love)	*Rati* (passion)
2	*Hasya* (comedy)	*Hasa* (mirth)
3	*Karuna* (pathos or sorrow)	*Shoka* (sorrow)
4	*Raudra* (anger or rage)	*Krodha* (anger)
5	*Veera* (heroism)	*Utsaha* (enthusiasm)
6	*Bhayanaka* (fear)	*Bhaya* (fear)
7	*Bibhatsa* (disgust)	*Jugupsa* (disgust)
8	*Adbhuta* (wonder or amazement)	*Vismaya* (astonishment)
9*	*Shantha* (happiness or calmness)	*Sama* (freedom)

*The ninth *rasa* was introduced by Abhinavagupta, one of the greatest Kashmiri musicians and dramatists of his times, in the 17th century AD. Thus, the *rasas* are known as *Navarasas* (or the nine *rasas*).

Box 9.3 The Concept of *Bhakti*

Bhakti is a devotional practice that is central to Indian religious traditions. The term "bhakti" is derived from the Sanskrit root "bhaj", which means to worship or adore and emphasizes a personal relationship with a deity. It takes many forms, including singing, chanting, and dancing. Its central tenets include love, devotion, surrender, and service to the deity. It is seen as a path to spiritual liberation. Prominent among the followers of the *bhakti* practice are Chaitanya Mahaprabhu, Mirabai, Tulsidas, Kabir, Surdas, Saint Tukaram, Namdev, Ravidas, Guru Nanak, Ramkrishna Paramhans, to name a few. *Bhakti* is not limited to any caste, gender, or social class and can be practised by anyone regardless of their background. At its core, *bhakti* is a devotional practice that emphasizes love, devotion, surrender, and service to a divine being. For instance, Chaitanya Mahaprabhu devoted his life to Lord Krishna, and Mirabai took the idol of Lord Krishna as her husband incarnate. *Bhakti* has been a vital aspect of Indian culture and spirituality for centuries.

The Notion of **Jitendriya**

From a developmental angle, the optimal state of emotional functioning is conceived by the quality of being *jitendriya*. It refers to the mastery or control of the senses. The term "jita" means "conquered" or "subdued" while "indriya" refers to the sense organs. Thus, it refers to the ability to master and control one's senses and desires, leading to self-discipline, restraint, and ultimately spiritual growth. The practice of *jitendriya* involves learning to control the senses through various techniques, such as meditation, *pranayama* (breathing exercises), and *asanas* (physical postures). By learning to control the senses, one can achieve a state of inner calm and focus, which is seen as essential for spiritual growth and self-realization.

The Indian texts contain several examples of the importance of the concept of *jitendriya*. For example, in *Bhagavad Gita*, Lord Krishna advises Arjuna to conquer his senses to achieve inner peace and focus. The Patanjali's *Yoga Sutras* include detailed instructions for achieving mastery over the senses through the practice of *pratyahara* (withdrawal of the senses) and *dharana* (concentration), which lead to the state of *dhyana* (meditation) and ultimately *samadhi* (absorption). Buddhism emphasizes the cultivation of awareness and equanimity, allowing individuals to observe their sensory experiences without being consumed by them. Jainism believes in the importance of self-control and restraint in all aspects of life, including the senses. Thus, the concept of *jitendriya* is seen as a key step in the path to self-realization and inner peace. It helps to achieve the state of *sthitapragya* or steady wisdom. Gautam Buddha, Ramakrishna Paramahansa, Swami Sivananda are a few examples of *jitendriya* from India. The Indian view of emotion thus emphasizes the regulation of emotions. The *Bhagavad Gita* states that the agitated mind cannot achieve the state of happiness (*Ashantasya kuto sukham*).

Salient Features of Emotions in the Indian Context

There are some key aspects of the conception of emotions in the Indian context. First, emotions are seen as a natural and inevitable part of human experience, and they are not viewed as inherently good or bad. The goal is to understand and manage them rather than eliminate them. Second, emotions are seen as interconnected and interdependent, and they are viewed as part of a larger system of mental states (Nussbaum, 1994). For example, anger may be linked to desire or attachment, and compassion may be linked to empathy and love. Third, it is recognized that emotions are shaped by cultural and social contexts and that they are not solely determined by the individual. Fourth, emotions can be modified through various practices, such as meditation, mindfulness, and self-reflection.

Positive and Negative Emotions

Positive and negative emotions are two broad categories used to describe the wide range of human emotions. Positive emotions refer to feelings that are generally pleasant, such as happiness, joy, love, contentment, and gratitude. Negative emotions, such as fear, anger, shame, and sadness, refer to feelings that are generally unpleasant. It is important to understand the nature of positive and negative emotions, as well as strategies for coping with them for promoting well-being and helping individuals lead happier, more fulfilling lives.

Positive Emotions

Of all positive emotions, the nature and effects of three emotions, happiness, gratitude, and *lajja*, on human life are described herewith.

The Emotion of Happiness

Happiness is a positive emotion that is universally sought after and cherished. It is often described as a state of well-being, contentment, and joy and can manifest in a variety of forms, ranging from a subtle sense of satisfaction to an overwhelming feeling of euphoria. The experience of happiness is deeply interconnected with both our internal states and external circumstances. Internally, it is influenced by factors such as positive thoughts, gratitude, and a sense of purpose or fulfilment. Externally, it can be influenced by relationships, achievements, and the overall quality of life (see Chapter 12 for details).

The Emotion of Gratitude

Gratitude is a positive emotion that is characterized by feelings of thankfulness, appreciation, and recognition of the good things in life. It arises from acknowledging help, support, kindness, and blessings received from others or higher powers (such as God). Gratitude is a multifaceted construct that includes cognitive, affective, and behavioural components (Emmons & McCullough, 2003) (refer to Chapter 12). The youth in India acknowledges the relevance of gratitude in their lives and also that it helps enhance the overall quality of life (Kumar & Dixit, 2014) and personal growth (Nagar et al., 2021). Studies show that gratitude interventions have a positive impact on well-being in Indian populations (Iqbal & Dar, 2022; Sirois & Wood, 2017), including adolescents. Gratitude is significantly related to the subjective experience of feeling good or pleasantness, work–family enrichment (Garg, 2022), lower levels of depression and anxiety in women (Anand et al., 2021), and social dysfunction (Singh et al., 2014).

The Emotion of Lajja

Richard Shweder and his colleagues (Menon, 2013; Menon & Shweder, 1994, 1998; Shweder, 2004) have extensively studied the emotion of *lajja* in the temple town of Bhubaneswar (Odisha). Though the English equivalent of the term, that is, shame or embarrassment, is considered a negative emotion in the Western context, *lajja* is a positive emotion in the Indian cultural system which emphasizes modesty, obedience, and self-sacrifice (Sinha & Chauhan, 2013). It means possessing the virtue of behaving in a civilized manner, and it is closely tied to notions of honour, respect, and reputation. To experience *lajja* is to experience a sense of graceful submission and a virtuous, courteous, well-mannered self. It is equated with respectful restraint. "Bite your tongue" is an idiomatic expression for *lajja* and is also the facial expression used by women as an apology when they fail to follow social norms. It is exhibited in day-to-day behaviour by women, such as covering their faces and going out of the room to avoid direct contact with elder members, particularly males, of the family or society. Thus, *lajja* is experienced in response to a variety of different situations, including social interactions, moral transgressions, and personal failures and attachment.

Negative Emotions

Negative emotions are a normal and essential part of the human experience, as they alert individuals to potential threats and motivate them to act. However, when these emotions persist or become overwhelming, they can have adverse effects on individuals' well-being. Negative emotions are typically characterized by feelings of distress, discomfort, or pain. The nature and consequences of two negative emotions, anger and fear, are discussed herewith.

The Emotion of Anger

Anger refers to a strong feeling of displeasure or hostility that can be directed towards a person, object, or situation. Several factors give rise to anger, such as feelings of righteousness, unfulfilled desire, tiredness, and so on. While anger is a normal and healthy emotion in moderation, excessive or uncontrolled anger can have negative consequences for both individuals and society as a whole. In the Indian culture, there is a strong emphasis on maintaining social harmony and avoiding confrontation, which results in the suppression or inhibition of anger (Suchday, 2015). The *Bhagavad Gita* considers anger as the root cause of destruction:

क्रोधाद्भवति सम्मोहः सम्मोहात्स्मृतिविभ्रमः ।
स्मृतिभ्रंशाद्‌बुद्धिनाशो बुद्धिनाशात्प्रणश्यति ॥

(Anger leads to delusion; delusion confuses memory. When memory is confused, intelligence is lost, and when intelligence is lost, one is ruined.)

A survey conducted by NIMHANS (Sharma & Marimuthu, 2014) in six localities in India reported a rise in the anger level among youth, and eight out of ten youth in the age group of 15–26 years were found to be angry. The younger group (16–19 years), and males showed relatively higher levels of aggression. Several factors were identified for this behaviour, such as physical abuse in childhood, substance abuse, family violence, negative childhood experiences, and mass media. In another study (Singh & Misra, 1997), gender differences were observed in the targets of anger, with females displaying anger predominantly towards individuals, and males additionally included institutions, natural forces, and other things as targets. During anger, people are likely to engage in violent and aggressive behaviour. When anger is suppressed and not let out, it negatively influences psychological well-being (Dhasmana et al., 2018; Prabhu et al., 2016).

The Emotion of Fear

The experience of fear is a common human emotion that can be triggered by a variety of stimuli, such as a loud noise, a sudden movement, or an unexpected event. While fear can be a normal and healthy response to certain situations, it can also be debilitating and interfere with daily life (Ahuja et al., 2021). By seeking help and support, individuals can overcome their fears and improve their overall quality of life.

In India, studies have examined the emotion of fear in varied contexts: college students, workplace, fear of crime and social disorder, fear of terrorism, fear of sexual assault, and many other topics. For example, a study (Acharya et al., 2018) examined the prevalence of fear among urban adolescents and found that about 85% of adolescents suffered from fear, with girls reporting a greater number and level of fear. Based on their survey in Uttar Pradesh, Schutte et al. (2023) concluded that witnessing or experiencing violence leads to increased fear of violence. The fear of caste-based discrimination and the perpetuation of social inequalities contributes to a pervasive sense of fear within low-caste communities (Thorat & Newman, 2010). Incidents of sexual harassment, assault, and gender-based violence contribute to an environment of fear and restrict the freedom and mobility of women. The fear of public spaces, known as "eve-teasing", is a persistent concern for women across the country (Bhattacharyya, 2016; Chakraborty et al., 2021).

Coping With Negative Emotions

Effective strategies for coping with negative emotions include cognitive reappraisal, emotional regulation, and mindfulness-based techniques. Cognitive reappraisal involves reframing negative thoughts or interpretations of events in a more positive light while emotional regulation involves using strategies such as relaxation techniques, deep breathing, or physical exercise to manage intense emotions. Mindfulness-based techniques involve paying attention to the present moment and developing greater awareness and acceptance of one's emotions, thoughts, and sensations. Becoming *sthitipragya* is the Indian way of managing positive and negative emotions (Box 9.4).

In summary, it can be said that understanding the nature of positive and negative emotions is crucial for promoting mental and emotional health, building strong relationships, and achieving a sense of fulfilment in life. By embracing all emotions and learning to manage them effectively, individuals can lead healthier, happier, and more fulfilling lives.

Box 9.4   The Concept of *Sthitipragya*

Sthitipragya refers to a state of being in which an individual remains calm and composed in all situations. It is a Sanskrit term that means "one who has attained knowledge stability". In the *Bhagavad Gita*, *sthitipragya* is described as a person who has attained a state of mental equilibrium, where they are neither disturbed by pleasure or pain nor swayed by desire or anger. They are also free from ego and do not identify themselves with their body or mind. According to the Bhagavad Gita, *sthitipragya* is the highest state of consciousness that a human being can attain. Lord Krishna describes the qualities of a *sthitipragya* person in the *Bhagavad Gita*:

दुःखेष्वनुद्विग्नमनाः सुखेषु विगतस्पृहः ।
वीतरागभयक्रोधः स्थितधीर्मुनिरुच्यते ॥

(2: 56)

(He whose mind is untroubled amid sorrows and is free from eager desire amid pleasures, he from whom passion, fear, and rage have passed away, he is called a sage of settled intelligence.)

A *sthitipragya* person possesses certain traits. First, such a person is balanced and equanimous, regardless of external circumstances. They do not get elated by pleasure or disturbed by pain. Second, a *sthitipragya* person has complete control over their senses and emotions. They are not swayed by desire or anger. Third, the person is non-attached to material possessions or worldly pleasures. They are content with what they have and do not crave more. Fourth, a deep sense of compassion, kindness, and empathy is expressed towards all beings. Fifth, a *sthitipragya* person has a deep understanding of the nature of reality. They are aware of the impermanence of all things and have a broader perspective on life. Lord Krishna, Adi Shankaracharya, and Ramana Maharshi are a few examples of *sthitipragya*.

Research has shown that *sthitipragya* helps in the management of pain and the regulation of emotion (Nambi et al., 2011; Van Gordon et al., 2013). Thus, *sthitipragya* is a valuable concept for improving mental and physical well-being. Further research is needed to explore the full potential of *sthitipragya* in various contexts.

Understanding and Expressing Emotions: A Developmental View

It is accepted that emotions play an important role in our daily lives. They allow us to connect with others, respond to different situations, and make sense of our experiences. From infancy to adulthood, individuals develop a greater capacity to recognize, interpret, and communicate their own emotions as well as the emotions of others. In early infancy, babies are able to express only basic emotions, such as joy, sadness, and anger, through facial expressions and vocalizations (Denham, 1998). With age, they begin to develop more advanced cognitive skills, and their ability to identify and label emotions also improves. For instance, by the age of two, children can recognize and label the basic emotions of happiness, sadness, anger, and fear (Dolan, 2002). During childhood and adolescence, children develop the understanding that emotions are complex and can have multiple causes and consequences. They also become more skilled at regulating their own emotions and responding appropriately to the emotions of others. Several factors influence the development of emotional understanding and expression in children, including genetics, socialization, cultural factors, and environmental influences.

Genetic Factors

Studies have shown that some aspects of emotional competence, such as temperament and emotional sensitivity, have a genetic component (Rothbart & Bates, 1998), which accounts for a significant portion of individual differences in emotional competence (Knafo & Plomin, 2006). Genes influence the development of emotional competence by regulating brain function, personality traits, and temperament. The precise nature of these genetic influences is still the subject of ongoing research.

Neurological Factors

Neurological factors also play a role in emotional development. The brain regions involved in emotion regulation, such as the amygdala and prefrontal cortex, undergo significant changes during development. The prefrontal cortex, which is responsible for impulse control and decision-making, continues to develop well into adolescence. Adolescents show increased connectivity between the amygdala and prefrontal cortex than children (Tottenham et al., 2011). In a review of studies, Herba et al. (2006) observed differential patterns of activation in the amygdala and prefrontal regions during childhood and adolescence, suggesting ongoing development and maturation of emotion processing and regulation systems. Thus, the ability to regulate emotions and make appropriate decisions based on emotional cues improves with age.

Role of Socialization

Social learning theory suggests that children learn about emotions through observation and imitation of others' emotional expressions and behaviours. Parental responses to children's emotions can have a significant impact on their emotional development. For example, research (Denham, 1998; Eisenberg et al., 2010) has shown that by providing positive emotional support, validation, and understanding, parents help their children develop better emotion regulation skills, social competence, and academic achievement. According to attachment theory (Bowlby, 1969), the emotional bond formed between infants and caregivers sets the stage for the way individuals understand and express emotions throughout their lives.

In India, parents and caregivers are known to adopt an affectionate and nurturing style of parenting, where children are often co-slept and carried for prolonged periods (Crittenden, 1990). These practices foster a strong emotional bond between parents and children and provide a secure base for emotional exploration and development. Authoritative parenting (characterized by warmth, support, and consistent discipline) leads to the development of better emotion regulation skills (Das, 2022). However, Indian mothers are relatively low on emotional expressiveness compared to mothers in Western societies (Malhotra & Dutta, 2019), and this may limit children's exposure to different emotions and the way they learn to regulate and express their own emotions.

The interactions with peers and teachers also play a crucial role in shaping children's emotional development. Children who have positive experiences with peers and teachers are more likely to develop emotional competence and expressiveness (Denham et al., 2003). On the other hand, children who experience rejection, bullying, or other negative social experiences may have difficulty recognizing and expressing emotions in healthy ways.

Cultural Factors

Culture influences emotional development by shaping socialization practices, values, and beliefs surrounding emotions. Also, there are cultural differences in the way emotions are expressed and recognized. For example, some cultures encourage the expression of emotions while others discourage overt displays (Matsumoto & Hwang, 2012; Tsai & Clobert, 2019). Studies (Matsumoto et al., 2008; Mesquita et al., 2015) have reported that people from individualistic cultures tend to express their emotions more openly while people from collectivistic cultures tend to largely suppress their emotions. Markus and Kitayama (1991) have argued that people with independent selves (as is the case with individualistic societies) tend to express ego-focused emotions (e.g., anger, frustration, and pride) more while people with interdependent selves (as is the case with collectivistic societies) tend to express other-focused emotions (e.g., sympathy, feelings of interpersonal communion, and shame) and suppress the expression of ego-focused emotions.

The collectivist and family oriented nature of Indian culture plays a significant role in shaping the emotional development of children. In Indian families, emotions are often expressed in a restrained manner, with an emphasis on self-control and composure (Kathuria et al., 2023). Children are socialized to suppress negative emotions, such as anger, sadness, and fear, and to express positive emotions, such as happiness, gratitude, and respect, towards elders and authority figures. Indian children tend to use cognitive reappraisal as a coping mechanism to regulate their emotions. Cognitive reappraisal involves changing one's perception of a situation to regulate the associated emotions. This strategy is particularly effective in Indian children because it aligns with the cultural norm of emotional restraint.

Environmental Factors

Environmental factors such as poverty, stress, and trauma also influence emotional development in children. Exposure to chronic stressors such as poverty or family conflict impairs emotional regulation and increases the risk of emotional problems such as anxiety and depression (Evans & Kim, 2013). Traumatic experiences such as abuse or neglect also disrupt emotional development and increase the risk of emotional and behavioural problems (Perry, 2002).

The development of social media and technology has also provided new ways of understanding emotional expression. For example, facial recognition software can analyse facial expressions to identify specific emotions. This technology has been used in fields such as psychology and marketing to understand emotional responses to stimuli.

Emotional Development During Adolescence and Adulthood

With the advancement in age, emotional understanding and expression become increasingly sophisticated. Adolescents become more aware of their own emotional experiences and begin to develop a greater capacity for empathy and perspective-taking, which allows them to understand and respond to the emotions of others (Eisenberg & Morris, 2002). During this time, individuals also begin to develop more complex emotional regulation strategies, such as cognitive reappraisal (Gross, 2015).

As Indian children grow into adolescence, the cultural norms of emotional restraint become more pronounced. Adolescents are expected to exhibit emotional maturity and self-control, particularly in the context of social relationships (Chadda & Deb, 2013; Sondhi, 2017). In Indian culture, adolescents are expected to channel their emotions in a constructive manner, such as through community service or spiritual practices. Gender differences have also been observed in emotional expression. For instance, Kapadia (2017) reported that adolescent girls in India are expected to conform to gender norms, including modesty and compliance with authority figures. These expectations can limit their emotional expression and their ability to explore different aspects of their identity. Emotional expression by adults is often viewed as a sign of weakness, especially for men. Adults are expected to control their emotions, especially in public settings, and to express them in a manner that is consistent with cultural and social norms. Mostly, they express negative emotions such as anger and frustration through silence or indirect communication rather than through open displays of emotion.

In conclusion, it can be said that emotional development is a complex process that involves the interaction of genetic, neurological, environmental, and cultural factors. While some aspects of emotional expression may be innate, others are shaped by socialization, culture, and experience.

Variations in Expression of Emotions Across Time

The expression of emotions has changed over time, from oral to written to digital traditions. In oral traditions, emotions were expressed through tone of voice, facial expressions, gestures, and body language. In traditions like dance, theatre, and storytelling, emotions were conveyed through a combination of these different channels. Emotions were also expressed through dialogue and songs. The advent of written language made it possible to express emotions more accurately with the use of literary techniques such as metaphor, imagery, and symbolism. Emotions were communicated through language and dialogue. Poems are characterized by their simple, lyrical language and their deeply personal tone.

Digital technologies have enabled individuals to express their emotions in new ways through social media platforms, messaging apps, and other digital communication mediums. Emojis, stickers, memes, and GIFs have become popular ways to convey emotions. It is now easier for individuals to connect with others and share their emotions in real time, regardless of their physical location. Online support groups, digital therapy, and mental health apps are available. These platforms have enabled individuals to connect with others who share similar experiences and emotions, creating a sense of community and support. However, some studies (e.g., Coma & Hancock, 2010) have found that digital communication can lead to more negative emotions and misunderstandings due to the lack of non-verbal cues and context.

Aesthetic Development

Aesthetic development refers to the acquisition of the ability to understand, appreciate, and create art and beauty. It is a process that takes place throughout a person's life and is influenced by various factors, including personal experiences, cultural background, and exposure to different art forms. As humans, we have a natural attraction to beauty, reflected in how we decorate our homes, the clothes we wear, and the music we listen to. This attraction to beauty is not simply a matter of personal preference but is rooted in our biology too. Studies have shown that the human brain responds positively to art and beauty, releasing dopamine, the neurotransmitter associated with pleasure or reward (Zeki, 1999).

Aesthetics is reflected in various Indian art forms and cultural practices. Bharata Muni's *Natyashastra* and sage Vatsyayana's *Kama Sutra* are two important texts that provide insights into aesthetics in the Indian context. The concept of *rasa* is closely linked to the idea of divine beauty. The *shringara rasa*, for example, is associated with the beauty of the divine couple, Radha and Krishna. The poetry of *Bhakti* poets, such as Kabir, Surdas, Mirabai, and Tulsidas, expresses the devotee's love and devotion towards the divine through poetic language and imagery.

Aesthetics is also prevalent in other Indian art forms like paintings, dance, and temple architecture. They reflect the deep connection between art, spirituality, and human emotions. Paintings like Madhubani (found in the Mithila region of Bihar), Tanjore (from Tamil Nadu), Warli (in tribal regions of Maharashtra), and Pattachitra (in tribal areas of Odisha) are known for their intricate designs and use of natural materials. The classical dance forms including Bharatanatyam (Tamil Nadu), Kathak (North India), Odissi (Odisha), and so on are characterized each with its unique style, movements, and expressions. The breathtaking architecture of Indian temples – Khajuraho Temples in Madhya Pradesh, Konark Sun Temple in Odisha, Meenakshi Temple in Madurai (Tamil Nadu), Brihadeshwara Temple in Thanjavur (Tamil Nadu) and Kailasa Temple in Ellora (Maharashtra), to name a few – particularly their intricate carvings, sculptures, and paintings on walls and ceilings evoke a sense of divine beauty and awe in the devotees. These paintings, dances, and architecture demonstrate the richness and diversity of Indian cultural heritage and its enduring influence on contemporary art and aesthetics.

The development of aesthetic sense begins in childhood. Children who are exposed to music, dance, and visual arts from a young age tend to have better cognitive and emotional development, as well as improved social and emotional skills (Bone & Fancourt, 2022; Pesata et al., 2022). In a study (Muralidharan & Srivastava, 1995), children living in the vicinity of temples in south India were found to be more cognitively competent. Chatterjee and colleagues (2022) reported improvement in the cognitive functioning of Bengali females due to their involvement in classical dancing.

The role of education in aesthetic development is crucial. Art classes, music lessons, and drama programmes expose children to different styles and techniques, helping them to appreciate and understand the nuances of different art forms and fostering their critical-thinking skills (Efland, 2002). Aesthetic development is also related to emotional and social development. Aesthetic experiences often evoke emotional responses that individuals learn to identify and articulate. For instance, the beauty of a sunset may evoke feelings of awe, wonder, and tranquillity. Through aesthetic experiences, individuals learn to express their emotions healthily and constructively.

Stress and Coping: A Developmental View

Stress refers to a physiological and psychological response to a perceived threat or challenge, which can be both positive and negative. According to Lazarus (1966), Lazarus and Folkman (1984), stress is the result of an individual's appraisal of a situation as threatening or challenging and their ability to cope with it. Stress is a natural part of life, and we all experience stress at some point in our lives. While moderate levels of stress can be beneficial and help us perform better, chronic stress can negatively affect our physical and mental health.

Stress can manifest in various physical, psychological, and behavioural symptoms. These symptoms vary widely from person to person and also differ depending on the duration and intensity of the stressor. The physical symptoms of stress include headaches, muscle tension, chest pain, rapid heartbeat, fatigue, and insomnia. These symptoms are thought to be a result of the body's natural fight-or-flight response to stress. Stress can affect our mental health, leading to symptoms such as anxiety, depression, irritability, and mood swings. Chronic stress can also impair cognitive functions, such as memory, attention, and decision-making. Some people may also experience panic attacks, phobias, and obsessive-compulsive disorder (OCD) as a result of stress (APA, 2019). The behavioural symptoms of stress include increased substance use, social withdrawal, overeating, and difficulty with work or school performance.

The causes of stress and its effect may vary across life stages. For example, factors like parental separation, exposure to violence, poverty, or neglect can cause stress during childhood (Shonkoff et al., 2012). During adolescence, stress is often associated with the developmental tasks of identity formation, peer relationships, and academic performance. In adulthood, work-related stress is common, which can lead to burnout and physical and mental health problems. In later adulthood, stress is often associated with the challenges of ageing, such as chronic health conditions, social isolation, and retirement. The ability to cope with stress in later life is influenced by individual factors, such as resilience and social support (Folkman, 2008).

The *National Mental Health Survey of India* (2016) estimated the prevalence of neurotic and stress-related disorders at 3.70% among adults aged 18+ years and above. The survey was conducted in 12 states across six regions of India. However, the estimates concerning the prevalence of stress among Indian people vary greatly, and it is difficult to draw any conclusion. The studies do agree about the prevalence of a higher degree of stress (20% to 70%) among adolescents and adults with gender and rural–urban variations (e.g., Bhaskar et al., 2015; Kumar & Akoijam, 2017). Adolescents use coping strategies such as positive reframing, planning, active coping, and instrumental support (Mathew et al., 2015).

In Indian tradition, stress is often viewed as a result of a disturbance in the balance of the three *doshas* (energies) – *vata*, *pitta*, and *kapha*. Ayurvedic treatment for stress involves balancing the *doshas* through diet, lifestyle modifications, and herbal remedies. Yoga and meditation also help in managing stress. Additionally, people adopt various strategies to manage stress, including seeking support from friends, family, or other sources; reinterpreting a stressful situation in a more positive or manageable way; and adopting meditational practices. In recent years, excessive stress is experienced by school children (see Box 9.5).

Box 9.5 Stress of Schooling Among Indian Children

The stress of schooling among Indian children has been a long-standing issue and has drawn the attention of various education commissions and policies. The stress among school children arises from three interrelated factors: academic performance, peer victimization, and discriminatory behaviours of the teachers. The pressure to perform well in studies is a major cause of stress (Verma et al., 2002). Peer victimization, both physical and relational or bullying, is also observed (Malhi et al., 2015). The discriminatory behaviour of teachers on account of students' caste, gender, religion, socio-economic status, disability, etc. also is a source of stress among school students (Kumar, 1983; NCERT, 2005). Addressing the stress of schooling among Indian children requires holistic, child-centred approaches, inclusive environments, and heightened teacher sensitivity.

Overview

The exploration of affective development has provided a rich understanding of emotions, delving into diverse perspectives and theories that contribute to the complexity of this psychological domain. From foundational concepts to cultural nuances, the chapter offered learners insights into the multifaceted nature of human emotions. The chapter began by unravelling the conceptions of affect and emotions, paving the way for a deeper analysis of different theoretical frameworks. The inclusion of an Indian perspective added a unique cultural dimension, elucidating the roles of *doshas*, *rasa*, *bhava*, and *bhakti* in shaping emotional experiences. This cultural lens not only broadened the scope of understanding but also underscored the importance of recognizing diverse influences on emotional development.

The exploration of *jitendriya* introduced learners to a concept that transcends individual emotions, emphasizing the significance of emotional self-regulation. This understanding forms a crucial foundation for the subsequent discussions on positive and negative emotions, culminating in the concept of *Sthitapragya*. *Sthitapragya* serves as a beacon, guiding individuals towards emotional stability and maturity, encapsulating the developmental journey of emotions.

Moreover, the chapter delved into the practical aspects of emotional development, aesthetic development, stress, coping, and resilience. By examining the stress of schooling among Indian children, the learners gained valuable insights into the real-world applications of the discussed concepts. In essence, this chapter has equipped learners with a comprehensive toolkit for navigating the intricate landscape of affective development. The knowledge gained will undoubtedly foster a nuanced understanding of emotions and their role in human development. As we conclude this exploration, we hope that learners emerge with not only a deeper appreciation for the intricacies of affective development but also with practical insights that can be applied in various contexts, contributing to personal growth and the well-being of others.

Key Terms

Aesthetic Development
Bhakti
Concept of Affect
Concept of Emotion
Cognitive View of Emotion
Development of Understanding and Expressing Emotions
Doshas – Vata, Pitta, and Kapha
Indian Perspective on Emotions
Jitendriya
Multi-Componential Perspective
Positive and Negative Emotions
Physiological Theory of Emotion
Rasa and Bhava
Social Constructivist View
Sthitapragya
Stress and Coping
School Stress

Questions for Reflection

1) How do diverse theories of emotions contribute to our understanding of the intricate nature of emotions, and in what ways do they intersect or differ?
2) How does the Indian conception of emotions (such as *doshas, rasa, bhava,* and the *bhakti*) shape the understanding and expression of emotions in this cultural context?
3) How does the concept of mastering one's senses contribute to emotional regulation and well-being, and how might this perspective differ from Western views on emotional control?
4) How do individuals acquire and enhance their emotional competencies over time, and what role does this competence play in shaping social interactions and relationships?
5) How does the notion of a balanced and composed individual (i.e., *Sthitapragya*), irrespective of external circumstances, align with or challenge contemporary views on emotional well-being?

Suggested Further Readings

Books

Barrett, L. F. (2017). *How emotions are made: The secret life of the brain*. Houghton Mifflin Harcourt.
Schore, A. N. (2003). *Affect regulation and the repair of the self*. W. W. Norton & Company.
Siegel, D. J., & Bryson, T. P. (2011). *The whole-brain child: 12 revolutionary strategies to nurture your child's developing mind*. Bantom.

Websites/Online Resources

American Psychological Association (APA) – Emotion (*www.apa.org/topics/emotion*)
Child Mind Institute (*https://childmind.org/*)
Developmental Science (*https://onlinelibrary.wiley.com/journal/14677687*)
Greater Good Science Center (*https://greatergood.berkeley.edu/*)
ZERO TO THREE (*www.zerotothree.org/*)

10 Moral Development

Contents

Introduction	204
Conceptions of Morality and Values	204
Theoretical Perspectives on Morality	205
Cross-National Studies on Values	209
Indian Perspective on Morality and Values	211
Box 10.1: The Concept of *Purushartha*	212
Box 10.2: The Concept of *Nishkama Karma*	212
Development of Values	213
Changing Patterns of Values Across Time	215
Education, Values, and National Development	216
Development of Social Notions	217
Overview	219
Key Terms	220
Questions for Reflection	220

Learning Objectives

After studying this chapter, the learner will be able to:

Explain theoretical perspectives on moral development;
Analyse the role of culture in the formation of values and morality;
Explore the role of family, peer group, education, religion, mass media, and culture in shaping value systems;
Analyse Indian perspectives on morality and values; and
Understand the significance of values in national development, democracy, human rights, and citizenship.

Introduction

Moral development is a multifaceted and intricate process that shapes an individual's understanding of right and wrong, influencing their ethical decision-making throughout life. Rooted in cultural, societal, and individual beliefs, morality and values play a crucial role in shaping human behaviour and societal norms. This chapter delves into various dimensions of moral development, examining conceptions of morality and values, theoretical perspectives, and some important cross-national studies. Additionally, it explores the unique Indian perspective on morality and values, shedding light on concepts like *purushartha* and *nishkama karma*. Furthermore, the discussion extends to the development of values across the lifespan, including adulthood and ageing, as well as the evolving patterns of values over time. The interplay of education, values, and national development is explored, along with the development of social notions (such as justice, human rights and duties, citizenship, and democracy) that contribute to the dynamic landscape of moral development. Through these lenses, the chapter aims to unravel the complexities of moral development and its profound impact on individuals and societies.

Conceptions of Morality and Values

Morality

Morality refers to the principles that guide individuals and societies in distinguishing right from wrong behaviour. Morality has been studied extensively by philosophers, theologians, and social scientists. One of the earliest moral philosophers, Aristotle (384–322 BCE), believed that morality was a product of rational thinking and the pursuit of excellence. Immanuel Kant (1724–1804) argued that morality was based on the concept of duty. In contemporary moral philosophy, there exists a wide range of theories and perspectives on morality. Each of them offers a different perspective on the nature of moral decision-making and related criteria.

Morality is also a deep-rooted concern in Indian culture and traditions, which emphasizes the importance of living a virtuous life, performing one's duties with sincerity, and avoiding harm to others. The ancient texts like the Vedas, the Upanishads, and *the Bhagavad Gita* lay down the foundations of *dharma*, which is the moral law and code of conduct for individuals and society. *Dharma* is based on the principles of righteousness, justice, and ethical behaviour. Another related concept is *karma*, which is the belief that every action has consequences. Therefore, it is essential to act morally and virtuously to ensure a positive outcome in the future. The concept of ahimsa or non-violence is also integral to many religious and philosophical traditions, including Hinduism, Buddhism, and Jainism. Ahimsa refers to the principle of avoiding harm to all living beings.

Buddhism emphasizes the concept of *karma* and the pursuit of enlightenment. The teachings of Jainism emphasize the importance of non-violence, truthfulness, and non-attachment while the teachings of Sikhism emphasize the importance of selfless service and moral responsibility. Mahatma Gandhi advocated the philosophy of *Satyagraha*, which means the pursuit of truth and non-violence. In contemporary India, the concerns of morality involve many dimensions. It is connected to various challenges and debates. For example, there is an ongoing discussion about the issues of capital punishment, euthanasia, and abortion. These issues raise questions about the values and principles that guide our moral decision-making and draw attention to the ethical implications of our actions.

Values

Values signify beliefs or principles that individuals or societies consider important or desirable. They shape the attitudes and behaviours of people and guide their decision-making. They can be cultural, social, or personal, and they often provide a framework for ethically sound decision-making. Cultural values are shared beliefs and practices that are socially shared by a community. These values often reflect the history, traditions, and norms of the culture and may include respect for authority, hospitality, and social harmony. Social values may include things like individualism, democracy, and equality. Personal values are individual beliefs about what is important or desirable in life. These values are shaped by a person's upbringing, experiences, and personality and may include principles like honesty, integrity, and compassion.

India is a land of diverse cultures, religions, and beliefs. This diversity is reflected in its value system and is deeply embedded in spirituality and the well-being of everybody. For long, the core values of respect, family, spirituality, education, hospitality, and non-violence continue to shape the Indian psyche. These values have been integrated into the Indian constitution as well. It may, however, be noted that the development of values is not merely a reproductive process; it is a creative process as well. The traditional and contemporary elements in society make demands for adjustment and adaptation on the part of individuals that get formulated as new patterns of values. In other words, values are not fixed but rather evolve in response to changing social and economic conditions.

Distinguishing Morality and Values

While morality and values are often intertwined, they are not the same. Morality is a broader concept that encompasses a range of ethical principles, whereas values are more personal and subjective beliefs about what is important, desirable, or worthwhile. Examples of morality include beliefs like honesty is good, lying and stealing are wrong, respect for human life is essential, compassion and empathy for others should be practised, fairness and justice in dealings should be upheld, and so on. Examples of values include freedom and autonomy, hard work and diligence, concern for family, personal growth and self-improvement, creativity and innovation, and so on. It may be noted that there may be some overlap between morality and values, as what one person considers a moral principle, another might consider the same a personal value. For example, some people may view honesty as a moral imperative while others may see it as a personal value they aspire to uphold.

Theoretical Perspectives on Morality

The concepts of morality and values have been dealt with by several thinkers and researchers. Prominent among them are Jean Piaget, Lawrence Kohlberg, Elliot Turiel, Carol Gilligan, and Richard Shweder. In the context of India, Mahatma Gandhi immensely contributed towards our understanding of morality. This section briefly describes their theoretical formulations.

Jean Piaget's Theory of Moral Development

Piaget's (1932) theory of moral development believed that children's moral reasoning develops in a predictable sequence through a series of three main stages: the heteronomous stage, the transitional stage, and the autonomous stage. The heteronomous stage (4–7 years) is characterized by rigid adherence to rules and the belief that rules are unchangeable and absolute.

During this period, children judge the morality of an action based solely on its consequences rather than on the intentions of the actor. The transitional stage (8–10 years) is characterized by a flexible understanding of rules and a growing recognition that rules can be modified through negotiation. During this stage, children begin to consider the intentions of the actor while making moral judgements. The autonomous stage (beginning around 11 years) is characterized by a fully developed understanding of rules and a recognition that rules are created and agreed upon by individuals within a society. In this stage, individuals make moral judgements based on both the intentions of the actor and the consequences of the action. However, many researchers (e.g., Turiel, 2006) believe that these stages are not as universal and cultural and individual differences affect the rate and nature of moral development. It is also argued that Piaget underestimated the role of social interactions in understanding moral development (Eisenberg et al., 2007).

Lawrence Kohlberg's Theory of Moral Development

Kohlberg (1981, 1984) developed a stage theory of moral reasoning. He proposed six stages of moral reasoning, which are grouped into three levels.

1) *Pre-Conventional Level*

At this level, children make moral decisions based on self-interest and external consequences, such as punishment or reward. The two substages in this level are:

Stage 1: Obedience and punishment orientation – This is reflected in the tendency to avoid punishment.
Stage 2: Individualism and exchange – It is focused on obtaining rewards.

2) *Conventional Level*

At this level, moral reasoning is based on societal norms and expectations. The two substages in this level are:

Stage 3: Interpersonal relationships and conformity – It emphasizes maintaining social order and authority.
Stage 4: Social order and maintaining the law – It is focused on maintaining social order by following laws and regulations.

3) *Post-Conventional Level*

At this level, individuals develop abstract reasoning abilities and begin to question societal values and norms. The two substages in this level are:

Stage 5: Social contract and individual rights – During this stage, the focus is on individual rights and the democratic process.
Stage 6: Universal Principles and Ethics – The stage reflects universal ethical principles.

Though Kohlberg's theory has been very influential and has been applied to different fields, including education, psychology, and law, the theory suffers from cultural bias and gender bias and has limited scope. The theory is primarily based on research conducted with male participants from Western industrialized countries (Helwig, 2006). It does not take into account women's moral reasoning, which is often based on care and concern for others (Miller, 1984). Miller et al. (2019) further opined that Kohlberg's method of moral dilemma interviews contain hypothetical scenarios. Moreover, it is limited in scope as it does not address the influence of emotions, social context, and cultural variability on moral decision-making (Lapsley & Narvaez, 2004).

Elliot Turiel's Distinct Domain Theory

Turiel (1983) proposed that moral development occurs in three distinct domains: moral, social-conventional, and personal. The moral domain is concerned with issues of harm, fairness, and justice while the social-conventional domain is concerned with social norms and rules, and the personal domain is concerned with the issues of personal autonomy and individual rights. It has been argued that individuals can differentiate between three domains from a young age (Turiel, 2006). The theory has been used to explain cultural differences in moral reasoning, as different cultures may prioritize the different domains of morality (Smetana, 2017).

Carol Gilligan's Theory of Moral Development

Gilligan (1982) studied the development of moral reasoning in women, particularly the ethics of care. Based on her interviews Gilligan found that women tend to emphasize the importance of caring for others and maintaining relationships. This approach to moral reasoning was distinct from the more abstract, principled approach to moral reasoning that Kohlberg had noted. Gilligan identified three stages of moral development. The first stage, the pre-conventional stage, is characterized by a focus on the self and individual survival. The second stage, the conventional stage, focuses on social relationships and conformity to social norms. During the third stage, the post-conventional stage, the focus is on individual rights and principles of justice. Gilligan argued that women tended to operate within the second stage of moral development, the conventional stage, which is based on an ethics of care. She (Gilligan, 1996) further proposed a contextual and relational approach to moral development, in which individuals are understood as embedded within specific social and cultural contexts and shaped by their relationships with others. The ethics of care suggests that moral decision-making should be based on the needs and experiences of others rather than on abstract principles of justice.

Gilligan's theory has been criticized for the reasons that it (a) has limited developmental scope as it does not adequately account for moral development beyond adolescence, (b) has limited applicability to men and other groups, (c) lacks strong empirical support, and (d) reinforces the notion that women are naturally more nurturing and empathetic than men, which may not be accurate.

Richard Shweder's Theory of Moral Relativism

Shweder (1991, 1996, 2000) argued that moral reasoning is not a universal, context-free process but is deeply influenced by the cultural beliefs and practices of the society in which it occurs. His work has highlighted the importance of cultural context in shaping moral beliefs and values. His research focused on a range of moral domains, including autonomy, community, divinity, and purity. He has studied how these domains are prioritized in different cultural contexts and how they shape individuals' moral beliefs and judgements.

In his work in India, Shweder focused particularly on Hindu culture and the concept of *dharma* in guiding moral decision-making. He argued that in Hindu culture, moral values are grounded in a sense of obligation to fulfil one's duties and responsibilities rather than individual desires or preferences. Shweder (Shweder et al., 1990) conducted in-depth interviews with women from a range of social classes and castes in the city of Bhubaneswar and asked them to discuss their moral beliefs and values. He found that the women emphasized the importance of fulfilling their duties and responsibilities to their families and communities. They expressed a strong sense of obligation to their husbands, children, and extended family members and felt that it was their duty to sacrifice their desires and preferences for the sake of others. Moreover, Shweder found that the women prioritized the well-being of the group over individual autonomy and upheld traditional practices and beliefs. The women considered "stealing" as morally wrong and against the "dharma" (Shweder & Much, 1987).

Jensen (2011) discusses the developmental patterns concerning the three ethics of autonomy, community, and divinity. The Ethic of Autonomy refers to the interests, well-being, and rights of individuals (self or other) as well as fairness between individuals. Taking responsibility for oneself and autonomy-oriented virtues such as self-esteem, self-expression, and independence are covered under this ethic. The Ethic of Community includes moral concepts about persons' duties to others and concern with the customs, interests, and welfare of groups. This ethic also comprises community-oriented virtues such as self-moderation and loyalty towards social groups and their members. The Ethic of Divinity is concerned with the spiritual or religious entities of the individuals. Here the moral goal is for the self to become increasingly connected to that which is pure or divine. This ethic taps divinity-oriented virtues such as awe, faithfulness, and humility.

According to Jensen (2011), the Ethic of Autonomy emerges early and stays relatively stable across adolescence and into adulthood. The Ethic of Community emerges early and rises throughout childhood and into adolescence and adulthood. The emergence of the Ethic of Divinity remains restricted, which emerges only in cultures that emphasize scriptural authority or supernatural entities (such as God). In the context of India, Pandya et al. (2021) found age and SES differences: older children employing the Ethics of Community and younger children the Ethics of Divinity. Further, high-SES children employed the Ethics of Autonomy more than low-SES children, who were more afraid of the fear of punishment. Another study (Bhangaokar & Kapadia, 2019) reported the maximum use of the Ethic of Community, closely followed by autonomy by Indian women.

Critiques of Shweder's theory argue that it overemphasizes cultural variability and neglects the role of individual differences in moral development. It has also been argued that Shweder's theory is too descriptive and does not provide clear guidance for understanding moral conflicts or making moral decisions. Despite these critiques, Shweder's work has had a significant impact on the study of moral development and has highlighted the importance of cultural context in shaping individuals' moral beliefs and values.

Mahatma Gandhi's Concept of Satyagraha

Gandhi (Mohandas Karamchand Gandhi) (1869–1948), regarded as the Father of the Indian Nation, dedicated his life to promoting the principles of non-violence, truth, and self-discipline. Gandhi's perspective on morality was rooted in the concept of *Satyagraha*, which means the pursuit of truth and non-violent resistance. He believed truth was the highest moral principle and sought it in every domain of life. According to Gandhi, truth was not merely a matter of intellectual understanding but a way of life that required self-discipline, self-control, and a commitment to serving others. Gandhi believed in the importance of non-violence as a moral principle, which was essential to creating a just and equitable society, and he practised it throughout his life as a means of bringing about social and political change. In addition, Gandhi emphasized the importance of self-discipline and self-control as key components of morality. Gandhi's views on morality continue to inspire people around the world. His philosophy has also been influential in the development of modern theories of non-violence and civil disobedience for promoting social justice and human rights.

Cross-National Studies on Values

Based on the premise that values vary across cultures and, therefore, different cultures tend to have different value systems, reflecting their unique historical, social, and economic contexts, several studies have been conducted to chart national/cultural differences. Some prominent studies are described here.

Milton Rokeach Value Survey

In his seminal work, Rokeach (1973) provided a framework for understanding how values influence human behaviour. Rokeach defined values as enduring beliefs that a specific mode of conduct or end-state of existence is personally or socially preferable. He distinguished between two types of values: instrumental (means-oriented) and terminal values (end-oriented). Instrumental values are concerned with how we achieve our goals, and terminal values refer to the goals or desired end-states. Values such as responsibility, hard work, honesty, punctuality, respect for others, self-discipline, and so on are instrumental values, and terminal values include happiness, inner peace, wisdom, freedom, equality, security, family harmony, self-fulfilment, a comfortable life, world peace, and so on.

Rokeach proposed that values can be organized into a hierarchy, with some values being more fundamental or abstract than others. The hierarchy of values varies across individuals and cultures. He further suggested that values can be classified as either personal (individual goals and aspirations) or social (well-being of society as a whole). Rokeach's theory provides a systematic framework for understanding values and their implications for human behaviour.

Geert Hofstede's Study of Cultural Dimension

Geert Hofstede (1984, 2001) introduced a framework for understanding cultural differences based on four dimensions: power distance, individualism–collectivism, masculinity–femininity, and uncertainty avoidance. This was based on a survey of IBM employees in 40 countries. A brief description of these dimensions is given here.

1) *Power distance* or the extent to which people in a society accept and expect power to be distributed unequally. In high power-distance societies, there is a greater acceptance of hierarchy and authority, whereas in low power-distance societies, there is more of an emphasis on equality and autonomy.
2) *Individualism–collectivism* or the extent to which people in a society prioritize individual interests versus group interests (for details, see Chapter 11).
3) *Masculinity–femininity* or the extent to which societies prioritize traditionally masculine values, such as competition, achievement, and assertiveness, versus traditionally feminine values such as cooperation, nurturing, and quality of life.

4) *Uncertainty avoidance* or the extent to which people in a society feel threatened by ambiguity and uncertainty. In high-uncertainty avoidance societies, there is a greater emphasis on rules, structure, and conformity, whereas, in low-uncertainty avoidance societies, there is more of an emphasis on creativity, flexibility, and risk-taking.

These dimensions are not absolute and do not apply to every individual within a society, but they provide a useful framework for understanding cultural differences and their implications for work-related values and practices.

Shalom Schwartz's Study of Basic Values

Schwartz (1992, 2012) examined the structure and content of human values across 20 countries. He identified ten basic human values that were present across all cultures. These are power (or the desire for social status and control over others), achievement (or the desire for personal success and competency), hedonism (or the desire for pleasure and enjoyment), stimulation (or the desire for excitement and novelty), self-direction (or the desire for independence and creativity), universalism (or the desire for social justice, equality, and tolerance), benevolence (the desire to help others and promote their welfare), tradition (or the desire to preserve cultural and religious traditions), conformity (or the desire to follow social norms and expectations), and security (or the desire for stability, safety, and protection).

The study found that the ten values could be grouped into four higher-order values: (a) openness to change, including self-direction, stimulation, and hedonism, (b) conservation, including conformity, tradition, and security, (c) self-transcendence, including benevolence and universalism, and (d) self-enhancement, including power and achievement. Cultural differences were also reported, with some values being more valued in certain cultures than others. For example, self-direction was more valued in Western cultures while conformity was highly valued in Asian cultures. Overall, the study provided evidence for the existence of universal human values and identified the underlying structure of human values across different cultures.

Harry Triandis's Individualism/Collectivism

Triandis (1995) has extensively examined the role of the cultural syndrome of individualism and collectivism in shaping human behaviour, attitudes, and values. According to Triandis, individualism and collectivism form a continuum. That is, these two dimensions exist in all cultures, some being high on one dimension and some on the other. Cultures high on individualism promote the development of traits like independence, autonomy, and self-reliance among their members. In contrast, traits like interdependence, harmony, and social relationships are promoted in collectivist cultures. In individualistic cultures, individuals are expected to be self-reliant, make their own decisions, and prioritize their own goals and interests over group goals. In contrast, collectivistic cultures emphasize social harmony, cooperation, and interdependence. Individuals are expected to prioritize the goals and interests of their respective groups (also see Chapter 8).

The World Values Survey

The World Values Survey (WVS) is a global research project covering 100 countries that seeks to understand how people's values and beliefs are changing over time and across different societies. The most recent wave 7 of data collection occurred between 2017 and 2020. Some of the key findings of the WVS include a decline in traditional religious beliefs and an increase in the importance of individualism and self-expression in developed countries, the persistence of strong family values in countries in Asia and the Middle East, an increasing acceptance of gender equality, and wide variation in attitudes towards democracy and political participation across different regions of the world.

Indian Perspective on Morality and Values

The Indian tradition considers the whole world as one family. The concept of *Vasudhaiva kutumbakam* (the world is one family) teaches us universal brotherhood and that all people of the world are interconnected and belong to one family, regardless of their race, religion, nationality, or any other differences. It promotes the values of tolerance, acceptance, and respect for diversity. The following verse from *Brihadaranyaka Upanishad* (1.4.14), one of the oldest texts, is often recited as a prayer for the peace and well-being of all beings:

ॐ सर्वे भवन्तु सुखिनः सर्वे सन्तु निरामयाः ।
सर्वे भद्राणि पश्यन्तु मा कश्चिद्दुःखभाग्भवेत् ।
ॐ शान्ति ॥

> (May all beings be happy, May all beings be healthy, May all beings experience prosperity, May no one suffer, Om Peace, Peace, Peace.)

The oral tradition prevalent in the Indian culture emphasizes the development of values such as *Priyamvada* (felicitous speech), *Satya* (truthfulness), *Dama* (restraint), *Dana* (charity), and *Daya* (compassion); all these are subsumed under the golden rubric of *dharma* (Mahadevan, 1978). The concept of *Priyamvada* promotes the idea that our words have the power to create harmony, build relationships, and heal wounds. It encourages us to speak with kindness, empathy, and compassion, even in challenging situations. The concept of *Satya* stresses the fact that truth is the foundation of all human relationships and that we must speak the truth ("Satyam vad, dharmam chara" or Speak the truth, follow righteousness). The virtue of *Dama* encourages us to cultivate the quality of *Vinaya* or politeness and self-control, *titiksha* or endurance, and discipline in our thoughts, words, and actions. The virtue of *Dana* (charity) emphasizes the importance of generosity and charity in our lives. It promotes the values of compassion, empathy, and gratitude and encourages us to cultivate a more altruistic and compassionate world view. The virtues of *Daya* and *Karuna* involve various forms of compassion, such as showing kindness and empathy towards others, practising forgiveness, and volunteering to help those in need.

Several saint poets in India have discussed the qualities of human beings. For example, Sant Kabir, a 15th-century poet, taught us the significance of values that promote peace, love, and compassion. The founder of Sikhism, Shri Guru Nanak Dev, in the 15th century, emphasized the importance of devotion, equality, and service to others. His message "Vaand Chhako" teaches us to share whatever God has given us with others and help those who are in need. The 16th-century poet, Sant Tulsidas advocated that human beings' only duty is to do good to others, and the only dereliction is the oppression of others. Tukaram, one of the greatest 17th-century Marathi poets, emphasized the importance of devotion, humility, morality, compassion, equality, inner peace, and service to others.

The Indian tradition, thus, emphasizes the development of a set of core values, including hard work, kindness, empathy, compassion, gratitude, honesty, forgiveness, self-control, contentment, tolerance, acceptance, helping the needy, non-violence, equality, wisdom, building relationships, respect for diversity, respect for living beings, sensitivity to the environment,

212 *Perspectives on Self and Affective Development*

inner peace, detachment from material beings, spirituality, and so forth, among human beings. The Constitution of India, in its Preamble, also asserts the values of secularism, democracy, justice, liberty, equality, and fraternity. The concepts of *purushartha* (Box 10.1) and *nishkama karma* (Box 10.2) have guided the value system in India.

Box 10.1   The Concept of *Purushartha*

Purushartha refers to the four goals of human life: *dharma, artha, kama,* and *moksha*. These goals together form the foundation of a well-rounded and fulfilling life. *Dharma*, the foundation of all other goals, refers to an individual's duty or moral obligation. This includes following religious or social norms, treating others with kindness and compassion, and acting in a way that is aligned with one's personal beliefs and values. *Artha* refers to material well-being or prosperity. *Artha* is often associated with finding a sense of purpose and meaning in one's work or occupation. *Kama* refers to enjoyment or sensual pleasure. It is about finding joy and satisfaction in one's relationships, work, and other aspects of life. *Moksha* refers to spiritual liberation/salvation or enlightenment. This includes achieving a state of higher consciousness, breaking free from the cycle of birth and rebirth, and attaining a state of ultimate peace and bliss.

The concept of *purushartha* has been an important part of Indian philosophy for thousands of years and continues to shape the way individuals think about their lives and goals. By emphasizing the importance of balancing material well-being with spiritual growth, and pleasure with duty and responsibility, *purushartha* provides a holistic framework for living a fulfilling and meaningful life.

Box 10.2   The Concept of *Nishkama Karma*

Nishkama karma is a concept that refers to the idea of performing actions without any attachment to their outcome. The term "nishkama" comes from the Sanskrit words "nish", which means without, "kama" means desire, and "karma" means action. Thus, *nishkama karma* can be translated as "action without desire" or "action without attachment". Performing actions without any attachment to the outcome is a key principle for achieving spiritual liberation or *moksha*. Lord Krishna tells Arjuna in the *Bhagavad Gita*:

कर्मण्येवाधिकारस्ते मा फलेषु कदाचन |
मा कर्मफलहेतुर्भूर्मा ते सङ्गोऽस्त्वकर्मणि || 2. 47 ||

("You have the right to perform your prescribed duty, but you are not entitled to the fruits of your actions".)

Since attachment to the outcome of actions can lead to negative emotions, such as greed, jealousy, and frustration, this situation often acts as a distraction in the pursuit of goals. The concept of *nishkama karma* is not only relevant to spiritual pursuits but also has practical applications in everyday life. By performing actions without attachment to the outcome, individuals can reduce stress and anxiety, increase focus and productivity, and cultivate a sense of inner peace and contentment.

The critics of *nishkama karma* argue that it can be a difficult concept to put into practice, as it requires individuals to let go of their attachment to personal desires and goals. However, as Miller (1986) argues, *nishkama karma* is not about inaction or detachment from the world, but rather it is about performing actions with the right attitude and intention. He suggests that the ultimate goal of *nishkama karma* is to cultivate a sense of detachment from the material world while also remaining engaged in the world and performing actions for the greater good.

Development of Values

The development of values is a gradual process that begins in childhood and continues throughout one's life. The process of value development involves a complex interplay of individual, societal, and cultural factors. This section discusses the role of some of these factors in value development.

Role of Family

Children learn values from their parents, peers, and the surrounding environment through the process of socialization. In a study (Kagitcibasi, 2005), it was found that parents who emphasized moral values, such as honesty, respect, and responsibility, were more likely to have children who internalized these values and displayed them in their behaviour. In the context of India, studies (e.g., Hazra & Mittal, 2018) have reported the constructive role of parents in the development of values in children. Indian parents mostly adopt the storytelling method and persuasion; storytelling was more often adopted by rural parents and storytelling and persuasion by urban parents (Srivastava, 1996). Karmakar (2015) reported an association between parenting style and the adoption of value regulation by children and adolescents. For adolescents, the authoritarian parenting style was positively linked to external and introjected regulation and the authoritative parenting style with integrated regulation.

Peer Groups

It has been established that, as children grow, they are more influenced by the values and attitudes of peers through observation and imitation. Children are more likely to adopt the values of their peers if they perceive them as credible, attractive, and powerful. Peer relationships were positively associated with the development of prosocial values (i.e., values related to helping others) in adolescents (Anand & Kaura, 2020; Padilla-Walker et al., 2018). Studies also report the association of peer group influence with decision-making and aggressive behaviour (Verma & Bansal, 2019).

Education and Religion

Schools and religious institutions often emphasize values such as compassion, empathy, and social responsibility (Turiel, 2005). The school culture and climate influence the development of values such as social responsibility, honesty, integrity, and concern for others. A variety of methods, including storytelling, role-playing, and group discussions, are used in schools in India (Dash, 2015). Studies (e.g., Singh, 2011; Thapliyal et al., 2015) have found a positive effect of value education programmes on the development of values among students. NCERT (2012) has developed a framework for value education in schools which, instead of teaching values as a separate subject, advocates for adopting a whole-school approach to value education in which values should be integrated into all activities of the school. The studies, thus, suggest that value-based education, if implemented properly, can be an effective tool for promoting positive values in Indian children.

Religion is also found to impact the development of values, such as humility, moral reasoning, and psychological well-being (Tongeren et al., 2018). As Narvaez and Lapsley (2005) have argued, religion provides a framework for understanding the world, and our place in it, and it can shape our beliefs and behaviours. In a study (Ahmed & Hammarstedt, 2011), it was found that in many countries people believe that morality is impossible without having faith in God (about 66% supported this notion in India). White et al. (2010) found that, in India, religion plays a primary role in the grounding of the moral order on which society is based and individuals behave, in addition to its being essential for well-being.

Mass Media

In recent years, a significant effect of mass media, which includes television, radio, newspapers, magazines, and the internet, on people's beliefs, attitudes, and behaviours has been reported. In a review of studies, Anderson et al. (2003) concluded that exposure to media violence is a significant risk factor for aggressive behaviour and desensitization to violence in children and adolescents. Exposure to television programming has a significant impact on the value development of young people. Adolescents exposed to television content with strong messages about gender equality displayed more positive attitudes towards gender roles and relationships (Ward & Grower, 2020).

Influence of Culture

The cultural syndrome of individualism–collectivism has been discussed in earlier chapters. In short, individualists display values such as independence, autonomy, and self-reliance. Interdependence, harmony, and social relationships are promoted in collectivist cultures. It has been reported that Indians regard responsiveness to the needs of others as an objective moral obligation to a far greater extent than do Americans (Miller & Bersoff, 1998). Another study (Miller et al., 2011) found that whereas US participants considered self-sacrifice for family and friends to be unsatisfying, Indians considered it a moral requirement to give priority to the needs of family and friends in the face of hardship and associated satisfaction with fulfilling such responsibilities. The responsibility of Hindu Indians towards the needs of their family or friends remains unaffected irrespective of their liking or disliking of the family members and friends. In contrast, European Americans felt less responsive to the needs of friends and family if they did not have a few common tastes and interests (Miller & Bersoff, 1998).

Indian culture, in general, places a strong emphasis on collectivism and family values, which influence the values of Indian children. Studies (e.g., Sinha & Verma, 1987; Triandis & Bhawuk, 1997; Verma, 1999; Verma & Triandis, 1999a) show that Indian children value social relationships and the well-being of the community over individual achievement studies. In a comparative study of Indian and US students, Verma and Triandis (1999a) found that Indian students opted for a higher percentage of collectivist (53%) and a lower percentage of individualist alternatives (47%) than American students who opted for 39% collectivist and 61% individualist alternatives. In another study, Sinha and Tripathi (1994a) compared achievement motivation and values in Indian and American college students. They found that while both groups place a high value on achievement and success, Indian students were more likely to prioritize social and spiritual values while American students prioritized individualism and material success. Because Indian society is context-sensitive and individuals behave according to *desh* (place), *kala* (time), and *patra* (person), Sinha et al. (2001) found that concerns for family or family members evoked a purely collectivist behaviour among Indian youth.

Verma and Triandis (1999b) explored how cultural values shape an individual's response to sociopolitical change. The study found that in India, individuals tended to respond to sociopolitical change with increased reliance on social support and a greater focus on the needs of the group. Chaudhary's (2004) work also highlighted that Indian adolescents stress social and relational concerns in their moral reasoning than their Western counterparts.

As regards the process of socialization of values among Indian children, Misra et al. (1999) found that the process is bidirectional, flexible, and co-constructional. Also, they observed that Indian mothers wanted their children to be sincere, that is, they should do their best in whatever way it may be. Misra (1991) found that older children display a higher level of moral judgement than younger children. Boys had a more mature judgement of moral values than girls. The high SES children showed more mature moral judgement at the young and middle-age levels than their low SES counterparts. The studies thus demand the importance of understanding the cultural context and historical experience in shaping values and attitudes in Indian society.

Value Development During Adulthood and Old Age

As value development is a continuous process, one might observe changes in values during adulthood and old age. With advancing age, values related to social connectedness, such as family, friendships, and community involvement, become increasingly important (Summer et al., 2018). Life experiences, such as personal crises or major life events, can also shape values during old age.

Value development during adulthood and ageing among the Indian population is a topic of growing interest. Research (Bhangaokar & Kapadia, 2009; Bhawuk, 2011) reports that taking care of the family's needs is the foremost *dharma* (duty, responsibility) during adulthood. With respect to performing gender roles and responsibilities during adulthood, Pandya and Bhangaokar (2022) found that, though both adult males and females accepted equal responsibilities for themselves within and outside the family, women's involvement was much on the higher side than that of men. Under the influence of modernization and urbanization, a shift in values among older adults, particularly in urban areas, towards independence, self-care, and self-expression rather than reliance on family and community is observed. While family and community continue to be highly valued, there may be shifts towards individualism and a focus on personal growth and spirituality.

Changing Patterns of Values Across Time

Throughout history, human societies have passed down their values and beliefs through various modes of communication, including oral, written, and now digital traditions. The shift from one mode of communication to another has often resulted in changes in the way values are transmitted and interpreted.

Oral traditions were the primary means of communication for most of human history. Stories, myths, and songs were passed down from generation to generation, providing a shared understanding of the world and its values. According to anthropologist Ruth Finnegan (1992), oral traditions emphasized community and the collective memory of a society, with the storyteller serving as a conduit for cultural transmission. However, oral traditions are also susceptible to alteration and loss over time, as memories fade and stories are adapted to fit the changing circumstances. Therefore, they emphasized values which focused on maintaining order in the community, social harmony, and the preservation of tradition.

The written traditions allowed societies to record and transmit their values with greater accuracy, wider circulation, and preservation of information. However, as historian Ong (1982) argued, written language creates a more individualistic and detached relationship between the writer and reader. In contrast to oral traditions, where the storyteller and audience are actively engaged in a shared experience, written texts can be consumed in isolation and with less direct emotional impact. The values associated with written cultures often included individualism, objectivity, and the pursuit of rational knowledge (Einstein, 1983).

In the contemporary digital era, values are increasingly transmitted through online platforms, social media, and other forms of digital communication. Digital technologies offer opportunities for values to be shared across vast distances and among diverse populations. However, as media scholar Turkle (2011) noted, digital communication can also lead to a superficial and fragmented understanding of values, as people consume information in short bursts and often without context or critical reflection. This makes value transmission a superficial or surface-level activity. Now, there is an increasing emphasis on instant gratification, individual expression, and the democratization of knowledge. The uninterrupted flow of information of all kinds is becoming a crucial challenge. Cybercrimes are increasing threats to the healthy growth of children and peace in society.

It is, however, important to note that the shift in value patterns from oral to written to digital tradition is not necessarily linear or exclusive. Some cultures and communities blend elements of all three traditions, and the values emphasized may differ depending on the context and medium of communication.

Education, Values, and National Development

Value education has been a part of the educational system in India for centuries. The ancient Indian scriptures and texts such as the Vedas, the Upanishads, *Ramayana*, *Mahabharata*, *Dharma Shastra* and *the Bhagavad Gita* constituted the primary sources of value education. Also, the teachings of social reformers and thinkers such as Mahatma Gandhi, Rabindranath Tagore, Swami Vivekananda, and Jyotiba Phule have guided value education.

Value education has been an important component of the recommendations of the various education commissions and policies. The Education Commission (also known as the Kothari Commission, 1964–66) recommended that education should aim at the development of the whole person, including moral and ethical values. It recommended that education should aim at character building, scientific temper, respect for manual labour, hard work, national consciousness, sense of social responsibility, social and national integration, the dignity of the individual, freedom, equality, justice, tolerance, peace, etc.

The National Policy on Education (NPE, 1986) recommended that value education should be included as an integral part of the curriculum. The policy stressed the need to promote Indian culture, traditions, and values, such as respect for elders, non-violence, tolerance, and social justice. The Policy recognized the importance of environmental education and the need to inculcate values such as conservation, sustainable development, and eco-friendliness among students. The National Curriculum Framework for School Education (NCFSE, 2000) recognized the importance of imparting social, moral, and spiritual values as well as about different religions in schools. The National Curriculum Framework (NCF, 2005) recommended the education of peace as a value, which includes tolerance, justice, intercultural understanding, and civic responsibility. The recent National Education Policy (2020) recommends fostering the holistic development of children (including cognitive, affective, and behavioural competencies), and a range of ethical, human and constitutional values, promoting life skills such as communication, cooperation, teamwork, resilience, and respect for diversity and respect for the local context, equity, and inclusion, scientific temper and creativity among children. Based on the policy, National Curriculum Framework for School Education (2023) has been brought out.

Apart from the school curriculum, many non-governmental organizations (NGOs) in India are also actively involved in promoting value education. For example, the Ramakrishna Mission, the Art of Living Foundation, the Chinmaya Mission, the Satya Sai Education Foundation, the Brahma Kumari Organization, etc. have launched several initiatives to promote human values among the Indian youth.

In recent years, the Government of India has launched several initiatives having implications for value development. The *Swachh Bharat Abhiyan* and the National Action Plan on Climate Change promote values such as environmental responsibility and sustainability. The National Voter's Day and the National Service Scheme promote values of civic responsibility and democracy among the citizens. The government has also been promoting innovation through various initiatives such as the Start-Up India programme, which aims to encourage entrepreneurship and innovation among the youth. These efforts are likely to have a far-reaching cumulative impact on national development.

Development of Social Notions

Social notions, such as justice, human rights and duties, democracy, and citizenship, form the backbone of societal structures, influencing how individuals interact with one another and contribute to the collective welfare. This section contains a brief description of the development of these notions.

Notion of Justice

The concept of justice is concerned with ideas of fairness, equity, and the distribution of resources and opportunities. According to Rawls (1971), justice involves ensuring that the basic rights and liberties of individuals are protected and also promoting social and economic equality. According to Amartya Sen (2009), a just society should provide its citizens with the capability to lead fulfilling lives. The Indian concepts of *dharma* and *karma* are linked to the importance of individual responsibility and accountability in the pursuit of justice. Mahatma Gandhi's philosophy of *Satyagraha* has inspired movements for justice and social change all around the world.

Earlier studies in India show that there was a preference for the conceptualization of justice in terms of the needs of the recipients rather than merit or equality (Aruna et al., 1994; Berman, Murphy-Berman, & Singh, 1985). This may be due to several reasons, including the allocator–recipient relationship, resource scarcity, and the like. In a recent survey, however, Krishnan (2011) reported that justice to the Indian people meant equality of various kinds (such as equal resources, equal opportunities, impartiality, and lack of discrimination) and giving people their due as well as rewarding people according to their contributions. Sensitivity to a potential recipient's need, fulfilling one's promises, and following reciprocity were among the least commonly mentioned meanings of justice to the Indian people (Krishnan, 2001; Krishnan & Carment, 2006; Krishnan et al., 2009; Pandey & Singh, 1997; Singh, 1994).

The concept of justice in Indian children begins to develop as early as the age of two or three. At this age, children are capable of recognizing and reacting to unequal distribution of resources or rewards (Sinha, 1985). Laddu and Kapadia (2007) examined the development of judgements of parental fairness among two groups (6–8 years and 10–12 years) of children. Young children agreed with parental judgements as they focused on the outcome of an act. Older children, on the other hand, had developed the ability to understand the intention behind the act and therefore did not agree with parental judgements on some occasions. Gender differences were also evident with older girls focusing more on the intention of the parents than boys.

It may be noted that children's understanding of justice is shaped by their experiences of socialization and interaction with others. Children who are exposed to fair and just social environments are more likely to develop a strong sense of justice and fairness. The organizations of activities such as Children's Parliament and Bal Panchayats encourage children to participate in decision-making processes and advocate for their rights. These initiatives provide children with the opportunity to develop leadership skills, critical thinking, and a sense of social responsibility.

Concepts of Human Rights and Duties

Human rights and duties are two sides of the same coin, and they are essential for the establishment of a just and democratic society. The Constitution of India enshrines a set of fundamental rights that are essential for the protection and promotion of human dignity and freedom. These rights include the right to equality, freedom of speech and expression, freedom of religion, right to life and personal liberty, and the right to education, among others. The Constitution also guarantees certain fundamental duties that citizens must fulfil to contribute to the welfare of society. These duties include respecting the Constitution and national symbols, promoting harmony and the spirit of common brotherhood, and protecting and preserving the natural environment. *Kartavya* (duty) is an important cultural concept in India that governs social relationships (Pande, 2013).

In addition to the Constitution, India has several legal frameworks and institutions that protect and promote human rights. The National Human Rights Commission (NHRC) is an independent body that investigates and addresses complaints related to human rights violations. The Protection of Human Rights Act of 1993 is an important legislation. The Scheduled Castes and Scheduled Tribes (Prevention of Atrocities) Act, 1989, and the Protection of Women from Domestic Violence Act, 2005, are some of the other legal frameworks that protect the rights of marginalized and vulnerable sections of society.

Human rights are closely linked to the concept of social justice in India. The principles of equality, non-discrimination, and inclusivity are integral to human rights, and they form the basis for addressing social inequalities, discrimination, and marginalization in Indian society. Human rights provide a framework for promoting social cohesion, tolerance, and understanding among diverse communities in India.

Concept of Democracy

The concept of democracy refers to a form of government in which the power is vested in the people, who rule either directly or through elected representatives. It is a system of governance based on the principles of equality, freedom, participation, and accountability. India has a long history of diverse and decentralized governance systems, including village councils or panchayats, which have practised democratic principles of decision-making and collective participation.

Children need to develop the concept of democracy from a young age as it helps them understand the importance of civic engagement, democratic values, and responsible citizenship. It can be done in different ways. First, the concept needs to be introduced in an age-appropriate manner. Younger children can be introduced to basic concepts such as fairness, equality, and sharing, through interactive activities, stories, and games. As children grow older, they can be taught about the principles of democracy, such as the right to vote, freedom of speech, and the importance of participation in decision-making processes. Age-appropriate resources, such as books, videos, and interactive websites, can be used to explain the concept of democracy. Second, children may be encouraged to participate in school and community activities, such as student council elections, debates, and discussions, which help them understand the value of participation in democratic processes. Third, adults, including parents, teachers, and other members of the community, can be positive role models by demonstrating democratic values in their actions and behaviours, such as respecting diversity, valuing different opinions, and promoting fairness and equality. Adults can also engage in discussions with children about current events, social issues, and democratic processes and encourage them to express their opinions and ask questions.

Notion of Citizenship

Citizenship refers to the status of being a member of a particular country or state and having the rights, privileges, and duties associated with that membership. It is a legal concept that defines a person's relationship with the state, their obligations to the state, and the state's obligations to them. Citizenship carries with it certain rights and privileges, such as the right to vote and the right to work and live in the country. Also, it comes with certain duties and obligations, such as paying taxes and obeying the laws of the country.

Education plays a vital role in shaping children's understanding of citizenship. A recent study by the Centre for Policy Research (2019) found that children who had access to quality citizenship education were more likely to demonstrate positive attitudes towards democracy and human rights and to engage in civic activities such as volunteering and community service. Furthermore, family, community, and mass media also play a significant role in shaping the concept in children.

It may, however, be noted that the concept of citizenship is not static and can change over time in response to societal, technological, and political developments. For example, debates on global citizenship have emerged in recent years, focusing on the responsibilities of individuals towards global issues, such as climate change, migration, and human rights, beyond national boundaries (for details, refer to Chapter 14). Furthermore, the concept of digital citizenship has gained prominence in the age of the internet and social media, highlighting the rights and responsibilities of individuals in the digital realm, including online privacy, freedom of expression, and digital literacy (Ribble, 2015).

Overview

The journey through the chapter has provided a comprehensive exploration of the multifaceted landscape of human values and ethical growth. By delving into the rich tapestry of theoretical perspectives and empirical studies, this chapter has illuminated the intricate process by which individuals navigate the path of moral understanding and conduct. The contributions of prominent theorists like Piaget, Kohlberg, Turiel, Gilligan, Shweder, and even Gandhi, underscore the significance of diverse vantage points in comprehending the nuances of morality. Cross-national studies have magnified the universal and culturally nuanced dimensions of values, enriching our understanding of their variations across societies. The studies, like those by Rokeach, Hofstede, Schwartz, and the World Values Survey, emphasize the importance of cultural context and historical legacies in shaping individuals' value systems. Furthermore, the Indian perspective has been interwoven throughout the chapter, emphasizing the fusion of ancient wisdom and contemporary ethical dilemmas. Concepts like *purushartha* and *nishkama karma* serve as poignant reminders of the profound resonance between cultural ethos and moral constructs.

As we journeyed through the chapter, we recognized the dynamic interplay of family, peer groups, education, religion, mass media, and culture in moulding individuals' values. The transformative potential of education catalyses nurturing holistic development and inculcating values that resonate with societal progress and harmony. The exploration did not stop at individual development; it extended to the societal realm, examining notions of justice, human rights, democracy, and citizenship. As societies evolve, so do their value systems, highlighting the need for continuous reflection and adaptability in the face of changing times.

In essence, this chapter has illuminated the intricate tapestry of moral development, underscored the importance of diverse perspectives, and emphasized the dynamic interplay of cultural, societal, and personal factors. It reminds us that the journey of understanding and practising morality is a shared endeavour that transcends boundaries and epochs, ultimately shaping the core of our collective human experience.

Key Terms

Approaches to Values
Changing Value Patterns
Cross-National Studies on Values
Cultural Factors
Developmental
Democracy and Citizenship
Development of Social Notions
Development of Values
Education, Values, and National Development
Ethics of Autonomy, Community, and Divinity
Human Rights and Duties
Instrumental Values
Indian Perspective on Morality and Values
Justice
Morality
Nishkama Karma
Pre-Conventional, Conventional, and Post-Conventional Morality
Purushartha
Role of Family, Peer Groups, Education, Religion, Mass Media, and Culture
Satyagraha
Social Learning
Theoretical Perspectives on Morality
Values During Adulthood and Ageing
Terminal Values

Questions for Reflection

1) How do conceptions of morality and values vary across cultures, and what factors contribute to these variations?
2) Reflect on the role of family, peer groups, education, religion, mass media, and culture in the development of moral values. How do these factors interact and influence an individual's moral development?

3) Explore the perspectives on morality presented by various theorists. How do these perspectives contribute to our understanding of moral development, and in what ways do they differ?
4) How do cultural differences impact moral development, and what insights can be gained from comparing moral values across different societies?
5) How have societal shifts and historical events influenced the evolution of moral values, and what implications does this have for the development of social notions such as justice, human rights, democracy, and citizenship?

Suggested Further Readings

Books

Brooks, D. (2015). *The road to character*. Random House.
Cohen, D., & Kitayama, S. (2019). *Handbook of cultural psychology* (2nd ed.). The Guilford Publications.
Haidt, J. (2012). *The righteous mind: Why good people are divided by politics and religion*. Allen Lane.

Websites/Online Resources

Character Education Partnership (*https://character.org/*)
Character Lab (*www.characterlab.org/*)
Greater Good Science Center – Ethics (*https://greatergood.berkeley.edu/ethics*)
Values and Ethics: From Living Room to Boardroom (*www.valuesandethics.org/*)

Part V
Social Understanding and Prosocial Development

11 Development of Social Understanding

Contents

Introduction	226
Theories of Social Understanding	226
Box 11.1: Understanding the Notions of Family, Group, and Nation	228
Cultural Syndrome of Individualism Versus Collectivism: Developmental Implications	230
Development of Social Understanding	232
Development Changes in Alternative Social Conceptions (or False Beliefs)	232
Box 11.2: Theory of Cognitive Dissonance	233
Understanding Other People	234
Box 11.3: The Concept of Money	235
Box 11.4: The Problem of Greed	235
Understanding of Social Dynamics	236
Development of Relationships	237
Development of Religious Identity	239
Development of Prejudice and Discrimination	240
Overview	241
Key Terms	242
Questions for Reflection	242

Learning Objectives

After studying this chapter, the learner will be able to:

Define social understanding, exploring its relevance in interpersonal contexts;
Analyse theoretical perspectives related to social understanding;
Evaluate developmental implications of individualistic and collectivistic perspectives;
Examine the cognitive processes involved in the development of false beliefs; and
Understand the development of interpersonal relationships.

DOI: 10.4324/9781003441168-16

Introduction

The Greek philosopher Aristotle said, "Man is by nature a social animal". A human infant comes into the world alone but opens his/her eyes amidst people surrounding her, be it parents, elder siblings, other family members, close relatives, and so on. All these people play a significant role in the development of the infant in diverse ways. The child slowly learns to behave like family members. She learns to communicate in the language spoken by her family or community, dresses as others in the community do, develops a taste for food eaten by the family or society, and adopts the customs, rituals, and norms of the family or community. That is, the lonely human infant first becomes a part of the family, and with advancing age acquires the characteristics of the peer group, community, village, school, and workplace, and ultimately becomes a proud citizen of a nation. In the present age of globalization, an individual is not limited to being a citizen of the country of birth but also becomes an active member of several international organizations. The process of transformation of the lonely human infant into a social being is, of course, a fascinating one.

Social development, thus, refers to the process through which individuals acquire and refine social skills, behaviours, and relationships through interaction with others. It encompasses the social, emotional, and cognitive changes that occur in the course of development. Social development is influenced by various biological, psychological, cultural, and environmental factors. This chapter begins with an exploration of foundational theories and examines the dynamic interplay between individuals and their social environments. It dissects the dichotomy of individualism versus collectivism, the nuanced realm of alternative social conceptions, and the understanding of other people. The chapter further unfolds the developmental intricacies of relationships, religious identity, the perplexing phenomena of prejudice and discrimination, and the evolving perceptions of status, roles, and responsibilities within organizations.

Theories of Social Development

Several theories have been proposed to explain social development across life stages. The salient features of the prominent theories of Piaget, Erikson, Bowlby, and Vygotsky are given here.

Jean Piaget's Cognitive Development Theory

Piaget (1954, 1965) emphasizes the role of cognitive processes in social development. It suggests that children's understanding of social concepts and norms develops as they actively construct knowledge through their interactions with the environment. Piaget argued that through social interactions, children gradually overcome egocentrism and develop the ability to take the perspective of others, known as decentration. Children's interactions with peers provide opportunities to learn from others, challenge their ideas, and develop a more sophisticated understanding of the social world.

Erik Erikson's Theory of Psychosocial Development

Erikson's (1950, 1968) theory proposes that individuals go through a series of psychosocial stages, each characterized by a unique developmental task or crisis. Successful resolution of these tasks contributes to healthy social development and the formation of a coherent identity. The stages are described as follows.

1) *Trust Versus Mistrust*

During infancy (0–1 year), the primary task is to develop a sense of trust in the world. Infants rely on their caregivers for the satisfaction of their basic needs, and if their needs are consistently met with love and care, they develop a sense of trust. However, if caregivers are inconsistent or neglectful, infants may develop mistrust and a sense of insecurity.

2) *Autonomy Versus Shame and Doubt*

Children (Early Childhood, 1–3 years) start asserting their independence and autonomy. They begin exploring the environment and making choices. If caregivers allow and support their independence while providing guidance, children develop a sense of autonomy. However, if caregivers are overly controlling or critical, children may develop feelings of shame and doubt.

3) *Initiative Versus Guilt*

In this stage (Preschool Age, 3–6 years), children become more curious and initiate activities. They start taking on responsibilities and asserting themselves. When caregivers encourage their initiatives and allow them to explore and express themselves, children develop a sense of purpose and confidence. If they face excessive criticism or restrictions, they may develop guilt and feel inadequate.

4) *Industry Versus Inferiority*

Children (School Age, 6–11 years) enter school and engage in tasks and activities that require them to develop competencies and skills. Success in these areas leads to a sense of industry and accomplishment. However, if they experience consistent failure or receive excessive criticism, they may develop a sense of inferiority and incompetence.

5) *Identity Versus Role Confusion*

Adolescence (12–18 years) is a crucial stage where individuals explore their sense of identity, seeking to answer the question, "Who am I?" They develop a sense of self and personal values, exploring different roles and possibilities. Successful resolution leads to a coherent identity while unresolved conflicts may result in role confusion and identity crises.

6) *Intimacy Versus Isolation*

Young adults (18–40 years) seek to establish close, meaningful relationships and intimate connections with others. They strive for emotional and physical intimacy. If they form successful relationships, they develop intimacy and a sense of connection. However, if they experience repeated failures or isolation, they may feel lonely and disconnected.

7) *Generativity Versus Stagnation*

Adults (40–65 years) in this stage focus on contributing to society and leaving a lasting impact through their work, relationships, and parenting. They aim to nurture and guide the next generation. Successful resolution leads to a sense of generativity and fulfilment, whereas unresolved conflicts can result in feelings of stagnation and a lack of purpose.

8) Integrity Versus Despair

In the final stage (65+ years), individuals reflect on their lives and contemplate their accomplishments and regrets. They strive for a sense of integrity, accepting the ups and downs of life and finding meaning in their experiences. Successfully resolving this stage leads to a sense of wisdom and acceptance while unresolved conflicts can lead to despair and a sense of regret.

It is important to note that Erikson's theory is based on the assumption that each stage builds upon the successful resolution of the conflict at previous stages. Additionally, cultural and environmental factors can influence the outcome of each stage. Studies conducted in Asian cultures have highlighted the importance of collectivism, interdependence, and filial piety as influential factors in psychosocial development (Keller & Lam, 2013). In the Indian context, factors such as caste, religion, socio-economic status, and family dynamics importantly influence psychosocial development (Syed & Fish, 2018).

John Bowlby's Attachment Theory

Attachment theory (Bowlby, 1969) emphasizes the importance of early social and emotional bonds between infants and their primary caregivers in shaping social development. The central premise of this view is that infants are biologically predisposed to seek proximity and contact with a caregiver as a means of survival and protection. Early attachment behaviour is characterized by a set of instinctual behaviours such as crying, smiling, and clinging, which are aimed at eliciting a caregiving response. The caregiver's responsiveness and sensitivity to the infant's signals play a crucial role in the formation of attachment bonds (see also Chapter 2). Adequate and secure attachment is a prerequisite for healthy social behaviour.

Albert Bandura's Social Learning Theory

The social learning theory of Bandura (1977) proposes that individuals acquire social behaviours and skills through observation, imitation, and reinforcement. Chapter 8 contains details of the theory.

Lev Vygotsky's Sociocultural Theory

This theory (Vygotsky, 1978) emphasizes the role of cultural and social interactions in shaping cognitive and social development. It highlights the importance of social scaffolding and the zone of proximal development (ZPD) in facilitating learning and development. Related to it is Barbara Rogoff's (1990) concept of apprenticeship in thinking (see also Chapter 6).

These theories provide valuable frameworks for understanding social development. It may be pertinent to note that multiple theories often complement each other in explaining the complexity of social development across different life stages. At this point, it is important to understand the concepts of family, group, and nation (Box 11.1).

Box 11.1 Understanding the Notions of Family, Group, and Nation

The family is an integral part of human society, which provides emotional support, nurturing, and a sense of belonging. Traditionally, family refers to a group of individuals connected by blood ties, such as parents, siblings, and extended relatives. However, contemporary understanding acknowledges a broader range of relationships, including non-blood relatives, such as adopted children, stepfamilies, single-parent families, same-sex partnerships, and chosen families (formed within LGBTQ+ or Lesbian, Gay, Bisexual, Transgender, and Queer + communities). This expanded understanding of family emphasizes the importance of emotional bonds, commitment, and mutual care rather than solely relying on biological connections.

Traditionally, the Indian family structure was characterized by a joint family system, where multiple generations, including parents, children, grandparents, and sometimes even uncles, aunts, and cousins, lived together under one roof. This set-up fostered close-knit relationships, shared responsibilities, and a sense of collective identity. Filial piety, respect for elders, and the honouring of familial obligations were deeply ingrained values in Indian society. However, the family structure in contemporary India is evolving, reflecting societal changes influenced by urbanization, globalization, and individual aspirations.

Sinha (1988) noted the following changes in the Indian family: (1) nucleation or the transition from extended kin to a primary kin system, (2) the segregation of children from adults and individuation, (3) a change from indulgent to strict child-rearing, (4) inconsistencies in child-rearing, (5) the absence of clear-cut role models, (6) changes in the status, role, and employment of women, and (7) the impact of migration. In recent years, legislative measures have been taken which give equal status to women in matters of inheritance, participation in politics, and employment and to prevent discrimination on the grounds of sex. Also, with increasing education, economic opportunities, and migration, there has been a gradual shift from joint families to nuclear families, particularly in urban areas. This shift is accompanied by changes in gender roles, with women increasingly participating in the workforce and having greater agency in decision-making processes within the family.

The recent move towards the arrangement of "live-in relationships" is posing new challenges.

Thus, the concept of family continues to evolve, reflecting the changing dynamics of society and the recognition of diverse relationships. While biological relationships remain significant, the emphasis has shifted towards emotional connections, support, and care.

The Concept of Group: Exploring Human Collaboration

A group is defined as a collection of individuals who interact with one another, share common goals, and perceive themselves as a distinct entity. Within a group (or in-groups), members typically enjoy some level of interdependence and communicate and work together towards shared goals. The members of a group engage in regular communication, share common objectives, develop a shared identity, and perceive themselves as part of a cohesive unit. Groups often have an established structure with defined roles and hierarchies (such as leaders, coordinators, mediators, and followers) and develop their own norms, values, and rules that govern behaviour within the group.

There are several types of groups, such as formal, informal, primary, and secondary. The formal groups are intentionally created within an organizational or institutional setting to achieve specific objectives, such as work teams, project groups, and committees. The informal groups emerge spontaneously based on personal interests, social connections, or common affiliations. They are often seen in social circles, hobby clubs, and online communities. Primary groups are characterized by close, intimate, and long-lasting relationships. Families, close friends, and small social circles are examples of primary groups. Secondary groups are larger and more task-oriented. They are formed to accomplish specific goals or functions but may lack the strong emotional bonds found in primary groups. Academic classes, professional associations, and political parties are examples of secondary groups.

The groups play several roles such as helping in the socialization of individuals; providing emotional support, a sense of belonging, and companionship; and fostering collaboration among the members. Groups also serve as catalysts for social change, organizing collective action, advocating for rights, and challenging societal norms and injustices. Thus, groups are integral to human existence, shaping social, educational, and professional spheres. The concept of a group encompasses collective identity, interdependence, and shared goals.

The Concept of Nation

A nation can be defined as a group of people who share common bonds, such as a common language, culture, history, and territory. Anderson (2006) argues that nations are not naturally occurring entities but are socially constructed communities, imagined by their members who perceive themselves as part of a larger cohesive group. It is characterized by national identity, cultural identity (such as language, literature, art, music, cuisine, and religious practices), defined territory, history, and shared memory. Nationhood is often linked to a defined political structure and international relations.

India, the seventh-largest country in the world by geographical area and first in terms of population, is a land of rich cultural heritage, diversity, and history. It is a land of contrasts, where ancient traditions meet modern advances and where the past coexists with the present. The Constitution of India provides for a representative and participatory democracy, where citizens elect their leaders through regular elections. It has been the birthplace of several major religions, including Hinduism, Buddhism, Jainism, and Sikhism. It is known for its ancient practices of meditation, yoga, and Ayurveda, which have gained global popularity for their holistic approach to well-being. It is home to diverse ecosystems, including lush forests, deserts, beaches, and wildlife sanctuaries. In recent decades, India has emerged as a global player in technology and innovation.

Cultural Syndrome of Individualism versus Collectivism: Developmental Implications

Introduced by Hofstede (1980), individualism–collectivism is a cultural syndrome or a dimension referring to the extent to which individuals prioritize their own goals and self-interest (individualism) versus prioritizing group goals and interdependence (collectivism) within a given society. It describes the degree to which individuals consider themselves as distinct entities or as part of a collective identity. Individualism emphasizes personal freedom, autonomy, and self-expression. Individualists focus on personal achievement, goals, and rights. Fulfilment of individual needs and desires takes precedence over group obligations. Collectivism, on the other hand, emphasizes group harmony, cooperation, and interdependence. Collectivists focus on the needs and goals of the group or community. They value loyalty, conformity, and cooperation. To collectivists, group obligations and relationships take precedence over individual desires. Individualism, thus, refers to the separation from ingroups and independence from others, and collectivism can be characterized by the subordination of personal goals for collective goals and extended family relationships (Triandis, 1995). Based on their study in 37 countries, Owe et al. (2013) concluded that contextualism is an important part of cultural collectivism. In simple terms, as Levine et al. (2019) put it, individualists tend to operate according to self-interest, whereas collectivists operate according to group interests.

Individualism–collectivism varies on horizontal–vertical dimensions resulting in four distinct culture types (Shavitt et al., 2019; Triandis, 2001). These culture types are (1) horizontal individualism, in which people want to be unique; (2) vertical individualism, in which people want to do their own thing and also to be the best; (3) horizontal collectivism, in which people merge their selves with their ingroups; and (4) vertical collectivism, in which people are willing to sacrifice themselves for their ingroup and submit to the authority of the ingroup.

Attempts have been made to find out which regions of the world, and specific groups of individuals, are more individualistic or collectivistic than others. Results from a meta-analysis of studies (Oyserman et al., 2002) indicate that Europeans and Americans are both more individualistic and less collectivistic than members of other cultures. Asian and African countries are observed to be higher on collectivism. Many African cultures tend to emphasize communal values, extended family relationships, and collective decision-making. Ubuntu, a concept prevalent in many African societies, promotes the idea of interconnectedness, compassion, and community cooperation.

In India, collectivism is exemplified by the strong emphasis on family ties, intergenerational obligations, and communal celebrations. The joint family system, where several generations live together, highlights the importance of family cohesion, tolerance, and mutual support. While the joint family system in India supported the value of familism (Singh, 2013), the modern nuclear family is perpetually promoting the principle of individualism (Gopalakrishan, 2021). Concepts such as "dharma" (duty) and "seva" (selfless service) underscore the collective responsibility and obligation towards society. In a study (Sinha et al., 1999), it was found that Indian participants were more likely to prioritize collective well-being over individual well-being, whereas American participants were more likely to prioritize individual well-being. Verma and Triandis (1999a) also found that Indian students were more collectivistic than students in the United States.

Studies (e.g., Jha & Singh, 2011) show that India's rapid urbanization and exposure to global influences have led to the emergence of individualistic values. The younger generation, especially in urban areas, is more likely to prioritize personal goals, career aspirations, and individual rights and are increasingly challenging traditional norms and expectations. In another study (Sinha & Tripathi, 1994b), individualistic and collectivistic values were found to exist together. It is interesting to note that the Indians behave in a context-sensitive manner according to the context, that is, *desh* (place), *kala* (time), and *patra* (person). They remain collectivists in family and community settings. However, if compelling personal needs and goals are juxtaposed with the interests of family or friends, there is a shift towards, but not too extreme, individualist behaviour and intention (Sinha et al., 2001). In a recent study (Kathuria et al., 2022), it was found that Indian mothers endorse both relational and individualistic goals to a certain extent. After analysing some popular folk narratives from the Jatakas, Panchatantra, *Mahabharata*, and the *Ramayana*, Panda (2013) noted that Indians take the middle path.

Implications of Individualism–Collectivism for Development

The individualism–collectivism has implications for various aspects of human development. First, social relationships in individualistic cultures are more loosely knit, and relationships are often formed based on personal choice. In collectivist cultures, social relationships are more tightly knit, and individuals prioritize maintaining harmony within their social groups. Collectivists are more likely to prefer working in teams (House et al., 2004). Second, communication in individualistic cultures is more direct and assertive, whereas collectivist cultures prioritize indirect communication and avoiding conflict to maintain group harmony (Holtgraves, 1997). Third, individualistic cultures value personal decision-making and autonomy, whereas collectivist cultures emphasize group consensus and shared decision-making (Markus & Kitayama, 1991). Fourth, children are socialized to be self-reliant and assertive in individualistic cultures. In contrast, socialization in the collectivistic cultures emphasizes conformity, obedience, and respect for authority (Oyserman et al., 2002). Fifth, individualistic cultures foster independent self-concept, while the self-concept is more relational, and individuals define themselves about their social roles and relationships (Mascolo et al., 2004). Lastly, individualistic cultures often foster analytic thinking while collectivistic cultures tend to emphasize holistic thinking (Nisbett & Miyamoto, 2005). Thus, the concept of individualism–collectivism provides valuable insights into understanding cultural differences in societal values, behaviours, and interpersonal relationships.

Development of Social Understanding

The development of social understanding is a lifelong process. During infancy and early childhood, social development primarily revolves around forming attachments and developing trust with caregivers (Feldman, 2015). During middle childhood, the scope of social understanding expands as children start to interact with peers and form friendships. They learn skills such as sharing, taking turns, and cooperating. During adolescence, children seek peer acceptance and belonging. They strive for independence; develop an understanding of emotions, empathy, social norms, and self-identity; and establish relationships outside their families (Brown et al., 2002; Steinberg, 2008). Adulthood is characterized by forming intimate relationships, establishing careers, and contributing to their communities. In old age, the focus shifts to maintaining existing relationships and adapting to changing social roles. Older adults may face challenges such as retirement, loss of loved ones, and changes in health.

In the Indian context, social skills among urban children are more developed than their rural counterparts (Kapur et al., 1994). Middle childhood witnesses the acquisition of social norms and cultural practices (Goyal et al., 2019). Mothers' non-supportive behaviours result in the development of behavioural problems during middle childhood (Raval et al., 2014). It is during adolescence that a deeper understanding of emotions, moral reasoning, and social hierarchies develops. Behavioural problems of children in their social adjustment and social interaction skills are caused by the insufficiency of social competence, such as cooperation, empathy, and conflict resolution skills (Choudhery & Kaur, 2018).

Developmental Changes in Alternative Social Conceptions (or False Beliefs)

The concept of false beliefs refers to situations where individuals hold beliefs or ideas that are inconsistent with objective reality or factual evidence. False beliefs can arise due to cognitive biases, misinformation, subjective interpretations, or flawed reasoning processes. They can have a significant impact on an individual's perception, decision-making, and behaviour. Cognitive biases are of several types. A few examples are discussed here.

Confirmation Bias

This refers to the tendency to search for, interpret, favour, and recall information in a way that confirms one's pre-existing beliefs or hypotheses while disregarding contradictory evidence. For example, a person who strongly supports a particular political candidate may consume news only from sources that are known to be biased in favour of that candidate. They may ignore or dismiss information from opposing viewpoints. In a classical study, Festinger and Carlsmith (1959) examined the effects of cognitive dissonance (see Box 11.2) on individuals when they were forced to engage in behaviour that contradicted their beliefs or attitudes. The researchers recruited participants and asked them to perform a monotonous and boring task, which involved turning pegs on a pegboard for an hour. Afterwards, the participants were assigned to one of two conditions: control and experimental. The control group participants were simply paid $1 for their participation in the study. In contrast, the experimental group participants were paid $20 to tell a confederate (an actor in the experiment) that the task was enjoyable and exciting, despite knowing it was not.

After the experiment, the researchers measured the participant's attitudes towards the task. They found that participants in the experimental condition reported lower levels of enjoyment compared to the control group. Thus, the participants in the experimental condition experienced cognitive dissonance because their behaviour (lying about the task) conflicted with their internal belief that the task was boring. To reduce cognitive dissonance, participants in the experimental condition underwent a cognitive process known as "attitude justification". They convinced themselves that the task was indeed more enjoyable than they initially believed, aligning their attitudes with their behaviour. This cognitive process helped reduce the discomfort of dissonance.

Box 11.2 Theory of Cognitive Dissonance

Cognitive dissonance refers to the psychological discomfort or tension that arises when a person holds conflicting beliefs, attitudes, or values or when their behaviour contradicts their beliefs or values. The theory of cognitive dissonance, developed by Leon Festinger (1957), suggested that individuals have an inherent drive to maintain consistency and avoid conflicts or contradictions in their thoughts, beliefs, and actions. The experience of cognitive dissonance creates psychological discomfort, which motivates them to reduce the dissonance and restore cognitive harmony.

Cognitive dissonance can arise in various situations. For example, if someone believes that smoking is harmful to health but continues to smoke, it creates a conflict between his or her beliefs and behaviour. This inconsistency can lead to discomfort and internal tension in resolving the conflict. To reduce cognitive dissonance, individuals may change their beliefs or attitudes to align with their behaviour. Alternatively, they may change their behaviour to be in line with their existing beliefs or values. In some cases, individuals may also ignore or deny information that contradicts their beliefs to maintain consistency. Thus, cognitive dissonance plays a significant role in decision-making, attitude formation, and behaviour change.

Developmental Trajectories

There are variations in the onset of false belief understanding. A large body of evidence indicates that false belief understanding develops between three and five years across cultures (Ahn & Miller, 2012). Callaghan and colleagues (2005) reported that there was a synchrony in the onset of false belief reasoning that occurs between three and five years of age. Naito and Koyama (2006) reported that Japanese children developed false belief understanding between six and seven years of age. Liu et al. (2008) reported that Hong Kong children started performing false belief tasks around the age of 64 months, whereas Canadian children pass such tasks around 38 months. A study in India (Joshi et al., 2019) revealed that Indian children start performing false belief tasks between six and seven years of age.

In conclusion, false beliefs are cognitive states where individuals hold or accept beliefs despite evidence to the contrary. They can emerge from various sources such as susceptibility to misinformation, cognitive biases, and cultural or religious beliefs. The developmental trajectory of false beliefs varies across cultures.

Understanding Other People

Understanding other people refers to the ability of an individual to grasp and comprehend the perspectives, emotions, motivations, and experiences of others apart from oneself. It involves going beyond surface-level observations and actively seeking to comprehend the inner workings of another person's thoughts, feelings, and actions. Understanding other people implies developing empathy, compassion, and insight into their unique context, background, and world view. Rogers's (1961) work underscores the importance of creating a supportive and empathetic environment for understanding others. By practising unconditional positive regard, empathy, active listening, and authenticity, we can foster deeper connections, improve communication, and gain a more profound understanding of those around us.

Understanding other people involves actively listening, asking questions, and being open-minded to gain a deeper understanding of their thoughts, needs, and desires. It may, however, be noted that understanding other people is not about merely tolerating or accepting differences but embracing diversity and appreciating the richness that different perspectives bring. By embracing diversity and recognizing the influence of cultural backgrounds, we can enhance our understanding of others and foster inclusive relationships.

Covey (2013) has advocated for cultivating the following seven habits to effectively understand other people. Included among these habits are (1) being proactive by taking control of your actions and responses, (2) visualizing goals and desired outcomes before starting any task or project, (3) prioritizing and focusing on the most important tasks, (4) seeking mutually beneficial solutions through interactions with others, (5) listening empathetically and trying to understand others before sharing your thoughts and ideas, (6) valuing and embracing the differences and strengths of others to create innovative solutions, and (7) continuously improving and renewing yourself physically, mentally, emotionally, and spiritually. Brown (2018) has also echoed similar concerns. The concept of emotional intelligence also highlights the importance of understanding others' emotions and perspectives for building strong relationships, effective communication, and successful collaboration (Goleman, 2006). Thus, the development of understanding other people lies in fostering empathy, compassion, and meaningful connections, leading to improved communication, relationships, and a more inclusive and harmonious society. Related to it are the concepts of money and greed (Boxes 11.3 and 11.4).

Box 11.3 Understanding the Concept of Money

Money can be defined as any widely accepted medium of exchange that is used to facilitate transactions and represent value. It exists in various forms, including cash, bank deposits, and electronic currencies. Historically, various forms of money have been used, such as gold or silver, physical assets, fiat money, or government-issued currency, and now digital currencies like Bitcoin and decentralized cryptocurrencies have emerged.

Money serves three primary functions: (a) it facilitates the exchange of goods and services, (b) it provides a common measure for determining the value of goods, services, and assets, and (c) it retains its purchasing power over time, allowing individuals to save and accumulate wealth. For money to function as a medium of exchange effectively, it needs to fulfil certain conditions. First, it must be acceptable in exchange for goods and services. Second, it should be easily divisible into smaller units to accommodate various transaction sizes. Third, it should be able to withstand wear and tear to preserve its value over time. Fourth, it should be easy to carry and transport. Fifth, each unit of money should be the same as every other unit to ensure consistency and fungibility. Lastly, the availability of money should be controlled to prevent excessive inflation and maintain its value.

Cultural factors influence the spending pattern of money. For example, in collectivistic societies, interdependence demands establishing one's status in the community through large expenses on festivals, weddings, funerals, and so on (Cohen et al., 2019). The poor households spend a large sum on festivals. A study in Udaipur (Banerjee & Duflo, 2007) reported that about 10% of the median household spending is on festivals. In another study (Collins et al., 2009), it was found that in rural Indian households, about 56% of spending in the year a child is married is on the marriage. Poor families spend so lavishly on funerals that they skimp on food for months afterwards (Banerjee & Duflo, 2011). Rich people spend on death rituals to show their social position, the poor struggle hard to save face (Kaushik, 2018). In South Africa, funeral expenses account for almost seven months of income. The reason for the huge spending is that they do not want to lose face and also for improving the social standing of the family. In contrast, the spending on weddings, funerals, and ceremonies is about 1% of the amount in developed or individualistic countries (Akerlof & Shiller, 2015).

Box 11.4 The Problem of Greed

Greed is defined as an insatiable desire for excessive wealth, power, or possessions, beyond what is necessary or reasonable. It is characterized by a relentless pursuit of self-interest, often at the expense of others or ethical considerations. Greed often stems from deep-seated psychological factors, such as insecurity or a fear of scarcity. It is driven by a mindset of accumulation and the belief that acquiring more will lead to personal fulfilment and happiness. Frank (2012) argues that people tend to care more about their relative than their absolute position. No matter how well people do in absolute terms, they will not be happy if their peers do better.

> According to Keltner (2017), enduring power does not come from greed but from empathy and giving. This is what we all too often forget. We abuse and lose our power, at work, in our family life, and with our friends, because we have never understood it correctly. Power is not the capacity to act in cruel and uncaring ways; it is the ability to do good for others, expressed in daily life, and in and of itself a good thing.
>
> The consequences of greed are many. At the personal level, it leads to constant dissatisfaction, creating a perpetual cycle of desire and disappointment, undermining personal well-being and happiness. Greed can strain interpersonal relationships, as individuals prioritize their interests over the well-being of others. Excessive greed can lead individuals to engage in unethical or illegal practices to fulfil their desires. This can result in compromised integrity, loss of moral values, and harm to oneself and others. Greed also has social consequences, such as economic inequality, exploitative practices, corruption, and power imbalances.

Understanding Social Dynamics

Social dynamics refers to the study of how individuals and groups interact, influence each other, and form relationships within a social context. It focuses on the study of the way an individual's thoughts, emotions, and behaviours are influenced by the social environment. It examines the psychological processes that occur within groups, such as conformity, communication, group polarization, social influence, and interpersonal dynamics. Thus, social dynamics encompasses a wide range of areas, including group dynamics, social influence, conformity, leadership, social networks, and interpersonal relationships.

The study of social dynamics draws from various theoretical perspectives and research traditions. Kurt Lewin's (1951) field theory proposed that behaviour is a product of the interaction between an individual and their social environment [$B=f(P \times E)$, where 'B' refers to behaviour, 'P' the person, and 'E' the environment]. He focused on the interdependence between individuals and their social context. Lewin's work laid the foundation for studying social dynamics and highlighted the significance of group processes and interpersonal relations.

Compliance to Authority

Compliance is a form of interdependence, which is shaped by requests or demands from others. For example, if a particular behaviour is widely accepted or expected in a given context, individuals may comply with requests to engage in that behaviour to avoid social disapproval or gain social approval. In this context, Milgram (1974) aimed to understand the extent to which individuals would obey commands from an authority figure, even if it involved harming others. Milgram designed a controlled laboratory setting that simulated an authority figure instructing participants to administer electric shocks to a "learner" (a confederate) when the learner answered questions incorrectly. Milgram's research revealed shocking results: a significant proportion of participants complied with the experimenter's orders to administer increasingly dangerous levels of electric shocks, despite the apparent harm caused to the learner. Milgram's work highlights the potential for ordinary individuals to engage in harmful actions under the influence of authority figures.

In another classic study, Muzafer Sherif and colleagues (1961) conducted the Robbers Cave Experiment which aimed to investigate intergroup conflict and cooperation among a group of boys at a summer camp. The experiment took place in two stages. In the first stage, the researchers formed two groups of boys who had no prior knowledge of each other. The boys participated in various competitive activities, such as sports and contests. This resulted in the emergence of intergroup conflict, with each group developing negative stereotypes and hostility towards the other. In the second stage, the researchers introduced situations that required both groups to work together towards common goals. Results showed that intergroup conflict could be significantly reduced and intergroup cooperation enhanced by creating goals that necessitated the collaboration of both groups. The study, thus, highlighted the importance of shared goals and cooperative efforts in reducing prejudice and intergroup conflict and fostering positive intergroup relations.

Philip Zimbardo (2007) proposed the concept of the "Lucifer Effect" to illustrate how normal individuals can be influenced by social forces and engage in acts of evil or cruelty. He conducted the Stanford Prison Experiment in 1971 in which 24 male college students were randomly assigned to play the roles of prisoners or guards. The study was intended to run for two weeks. However, it was terminated after only six days due to the extreme and abusive behaviour exhibited by the participants playing the role of guards. They began to display authoritarian tendencies, dehumanizing and mistreating the prisoners. The prisoners, on the other hand, showed signs of distress, helplessness, and even some psychological trauma. In his book, Zimbardo (2007, p. 22) cited a poem from *Stray Birds 22* authored by Nobel Laureate Rabindranath Tagore which beautifully depicts the relationship between power and love.

Power said to the world, "You are mine".
The world kept it prisoner on her throne.
Love said to the world, "I am thine".
The world gave it the freedom of her house.

The first part of the poem suggests that power asserts dominance and control over the world, and the world is held captive and confined by the grip of power. In contrast, when love approaches the world with a sense of belonging and connection, the world grants it freedom and openness within its realm. It suggests that love brings liberation, acceptance, and a sense of belonging, allowing for the exploration and expression of one's true self. The quote beautifully reflects the dichotomy between power's tendency to dominate and restrict, whereas love fosters freedom, acceptance, and a sense of belonging. It conveys a deeper message about the contrasting nature of these two forces and their impact on the world and individuals.

Understanding social dynamics is a complex process that evolves throughout childhood and adolescence. Research by Wellman and Liu (2004) suggests that such understanding emerges around the age of 2–3 years and by age 4–5, they develop a more advanced understanding. According to Selman (1980), children progress through different levels: egocentric, social–informational, self-reflective, third-party, and societal. This development occurs gradually during middle childhood and early adolescence. By recognizing these developmental differences, educators, parents, and caregivers can provide appropriate support and foster healthy social interactions in children and adolescents.

Development of Relationships

Relationships refer to the connections or associations between two or more individuals, groups, or entities. Relationships are an integral part of the human experience, shaping our social interactions and emotional well-being. From friendships and familial ties to romantic partnerships, relationships provide us with a sense of belonging, support, and personal growth. However, the development of relationships is a dynamic process influenced by various factors such as communication, trust, shared experiences, and cultural norms.

Stages of Relationship Development

Knapp and Vangelisti (2000) have proposed a model of relationship development, which consists of five stages of coming together and five stages of coming apart. Included among the five stages of coming together are (a) Initiation Stage (or the first encounter and the formation of a basic connection, often marked by small talk and polite gestures, such as "hello", "How are you" etc.), (b) Experimenting Stage (e.g., small talks on a wide variety of topics in a superficial manner to identify mutual interests and compatibility), (c) Intensifying Stage (or sharing of more information about each other informally and affectionately), (d) Integration Stage (or assigning a label to their relationship such as a best friend), and (e) Bonding Stage (or forming an emotional or legal bond to continue their relationship). Coming apart includes the following five stages: (a) Differentiating Stage (or beginning to realize differences and being unhappy about the same, (b) Constricted Communication Stage (or restricted communication and avoidance of controversial topics and in-depth discussions), (c) Stagnation Stage (or the emergence of expectations of unpleasant communications), (d) Avoiding Stage (or minimal interactions and avoidance of each other), and Termination Stage (or physically and psychologically leaving the relationship).

The development and growth of relationships evolve. It requires open, honest, and effective communication between individuals and respecting their values, boundaries, and autonomy. Adaptability is also crucial for the growth and survival of relationships. Being open to change, accepting differences, and adjusting to new circumstances foster resilience and longevity in relationships.

Changes in Relationships: The Indian Experience

Social relationships in Indian society have undergone significant transformations over time, influenced by historical, social, and cultural factors. In the Vedic period, the relationship was rooted in the notion of indebtedness (*rina*), which invites playing roles as obligations to significant others including Guru, mother, father, guests and living beings such as animals. There was provision of five *Yajnas* (performances) to repay the debts (Misra & Kapur, 2014). Indian society has been predominantly an agrarian one, organized around kinship ties and caste-based social systems. Arranged marriage and patriarchy were of paramount importance. The *Manusmriti*, an ancient legal text, laid down guidelines for marital relationships and family structure. The medieval period witnessed the continuance of arranged marriage with variations across different regions and religious communities. The practice of polygamy was more prevalent among the ruling classes while monogamy remained the norm for the majority. The influence of Sufi saints and Bhakti movements played a significant role in shaping the spiritual and emotional aspects of relationships.

During the colonial era, while arranged marriages remained prevalent, the concept of love and companionate marriages began to gain traction, particularly among urban-educated elites. India's independence in 1947 brought forth a wave of social and political reforms aimed at modernization and equal rights. The Indian Constitution enshrined principles of gender equality, individual freedom, and social justice. The women's movement gained momentum, leading to changes in traditional gender roles and expectations. Inter-caste and inter-religious marriages became more acceptable, challenging old social taboos. With urbanization and globalization, there has been an increase in nuclear families, migration, and greater individual autonomy in relationship choices.

Development of Religious Identity

Religious identity refers to an individual's affiliation, beliefs, and identification with a particular religious tradition or faith. It encompasses a person's sense of belonging to a religious community, their religious practices, rituals, values, and the way they perceive and understand the world based on their religious framework. Religious identity can be deeply personal and may evolve as individuals engage in religious exploration, questioning, or experiences that impact their beliefs and practices.

Hardy et al. (2019) have identified seven interconnected but distinct dimensions of religious development. These are:

1) *Cognitive Dimension*: It refers to an individual's beliefs, knowledge, and understanding of religious concepts, doctrines, and teachings.
2) *Behavioural Dimension*: This dimension focuses on religious practices, rituals, and behaviours, such as prayer, worship, participating in religious ceremonies, and adhering to religious guidelines or moral codes.
3) *Affective Dimension*: The affective dimension includes feelings of awe, reverence, devotion, gratitude, joy, peace, and other emotional responses related to religious and spiritual experiences.
4) *Identification Dimension*: The identification dimension refers to an individual's sense of belonging and identification with a particular religious group or community.
5) *Well-Being Dimension*: The well-being dimension focuses on the relationship between religious engagement and individuals' subjective well-being and mental health.
6) *Spiritual Dimension*: The spiritual dimension encompasses individuals' subjective experiences of transcendence, meaning-making, and connection to something greater than themselves.
7) *Ecological Dimension*: The ecological dimension explores how religious beliefs and values influence individuals' attitudes and behaviours towards nature, environmental sustainability, social justice, and the well-being of others.

These dimensions are considered interconnected and overlapping, reflecting the multidimensional nature of religious development. They provide a comprehensive framework for understanding and studying the various aspects of religious development across different domains.

Religious Pluralism

Modernization and globalization have contributed to the rise of secular views and religious pluralism in many societies. As a result, individuals are exposed to diverse religious beliefs and practices, leading to a more fluid and pluralistic religious identity. In such contexts, individuals may adopt a syncretic approach, blending elements from multiple religions or adopting a non-exclusive religious identity (Ammerman, 2013).

Development of Religious Identity

Though a significant portion of children, adolescents, and emerging adults remain religious (Marks & Dollahite, 2017), a decline in religious beliefs in recent years among young people as compared to their parents and grandparents has been noted. Gale et al. (2023) argue that religious development among adolescents and young adults is influenced by four factors: (a) process (i.e., person–religion mismatch and family processes), (b) person (i.e., age, gender, mental health, personal agency, and experience), (c) context (e.g., home environment, culture, and community), and (d) time (i.e., historical events and the duration of proximal processes). Adolescents' religiosity is positively related to the parent–child relationship (Regnerus & Burdette, 2006).

The development of religious identity begins in childhood in interaction with parents and other family members. Children listen to religious stories and participate in religious ceremonies, which shape their initial understanding and connection to their religious identity (Smith, 2003). During adolescence, individuals begin to explore, question, and develop their identity. In the Indian culture certain rituals, called *samskaras*, are performed which help adolescents develop their religious identity (refer to Chapter 1 for details). Adolescents may also seek connections with peers who share similar religious beliefs and engage in religious activities independently of their families. In adulthood, individuals' religious identity is often influenced by personal experiences, education, and exposure to diverse perspectives. Some individuals may deepen their religious commitment and become actively involved in religious communities or participate in religious practices and rituals. Others may experience a shift in their religious identity, adopting new beliefs. The elderly people confront existential questions and also face the prospect of mortality. In many religious cultures, such as Hinduism and Buddhism, a greater emphasis is placed on religious practices and spirituality in the later stages of life, turning to religion for comfort and guidance.

Development of Prejudice and Discrimination

Prejudice is a social phenomenon that involves holding negative attitudes and beliefs about individuals or groups based on preconceived notions or stereotypes. This refers to the tendency to evaluate members of one's group (or in-group) favourably more than members of the other groups (or out-groups) (Hewstone et al., 2002). The bias may take the form of in-group favouritism and out-group derogation. Trust, positive regard, cooperation, and empathy are extended to in-group members, and outgroup members are treated with fear, hatred, or disgust. One can observe the inter-group difference (i.e., between in-groups and out-groups) in our day-to-day behaviour. Identification with in-groups creates relatively high status, provides a positive social identity, and enhances self-esteem among in-group members (Tajfel & Turner, 1979), helps derive satisfaction (Leonardelli & Brewer, 2001), reduces uncertainty (Hogg, 2000), satisfies the need for self-preservation (Solomon et al., 1991) and desire to promote intergroup hierarchies and for their in-groups to dominate their out-groups (Sidanius & Pratto, 1999).

Prejudice arises from multiple sources. The first source is the socialization process, transmitting stereotypes and biases across generations and reinforcing prejudiced attitudes. The second source is limited or negative contact with members of different social groups. The third source of the formation of prejudice is the tendency of human beings to simplify the complex world around them. This cognitive tendency leads to the formation of stereotypes and biased judgements. For example, in a study (Tripathi & Srivastava, 1981), it was found that relatively deprived Muslims would sort out their negative social identity problems by devaluing or downgrading the comparison out-group. There is also a tendency to distinguish members of the in-group from others based on social positioning and identity construction (Sen et al., 2016). The fourth source of prejudice is socio-economic disparities and political ideologies. In societies with inequality and limited resources, groups may compete for access to these resources, leading to prejudice and intergroup conflict.

The expression and manifestation of prejudice vary across different life stages. Studies have shown that children as young as three years old demonstrate preferences based on race, gender, and other social categories (Dunham et al., 2008). Adolescents tend to identify strongly with their peer groups and may engage in stereotyping and discriminatory behaviours to establish their own identity and maintain group cohesion. Peers, media influences, and societal norms play crucial roles in shaping adolescents' attitudes and behaviours. Gender bias tends to increase during adolescence, with girls becoming more aware of and conforming to traditional gender stereotypes (Bigler & Liben, 2007).

As individuals transition into adulthood, their experiences and interactions with diverse individuals and groups may impact their attitudes towards prejudice and bias. While some individuals may become more open-minded and inclusive, others may hold onto deeply ingrained prejudices. Factors such as education, exposure to diverse perspectives, and intergroup contact are associated with reduced prejudice. In contrast, individuals who face threats to their own social identity, economic insecurity, or a lack of exposure to diversity may be more prone to maintaining or even reinforcing prejudiced beliefs (Schmitt & Branscombe, 2002). As individuals age, they may become more resistant to change, less likely to challenge their existing beliefs, and more susceptible to cognitive biases. Socialization processes, cohort effects, and historical experiences can also shape the attitudes of older adults.

Overview

In conclusion, it becomes evident that developing an understanding of the social world is a multifaceted journey with profound implications for individual growth and societal cohesion. Throughout this chapter, we discussed the intricate tapestry of concepts, theories, and developmental milestones that contribute to our comprehension of the social world. From understanding the nuanced dynamics of individualism and collectivism to grappling with the complexities of false beliefs, our journey took us through the cognitive landscapes that shape our social interactions. The exploration of relationships, from their inception to maturity, provided insights into the intricate threads that bind individuals together. Also, we navigated through the terrain of diverse social phenomena, including the development of prejudice and discrimination.

The accompanying boxes served as windows into specific topics such as family, group, and nation, as well as delving into the intriguing realms of cognitive dissonance, the concept of money, and the problem of greed. These supplementary discussions aimed to deepen our understanding of the intricate web of social concepts and behaviours. It is crucial to recognize that the journey towards enhanced social understanding is perpetual. The insights gained here are not merely static knowledge but tools for ongoing reflection and refinement. Armed with a nuanced comprehension of social dynamics, relationships, prejudice, and identity development, we are better equipped to navigate the complex social landscapes that characterize our interconnected world.

May this chapter serve as a stepping stone, inspiring continued curiosity and critical examination of the rich and ever-evolving field of social understanding. The journey towards becoming socially adept individuals is a continuous one, and with each step, we contribute to the collective tapestry of human interaction and understanding.

Key Terms

Attachment	Group
Cognitive Dissonance	Individualism and Collectivism
Development of Social Understanding	Money
Developmental Crisis	Nation
Development of Alternative Social Conceptions (False Beliefs)	Prejudice and Discrimination
	Religious Identity
Family	Roles and Responsibilities
Greed	

Questions for Reflection

1) How do cultural factors, particularly the cultural syndrome of individualism versus collectivism, impact the development of social understanding in individuals?
2) In what ways do alternative social conceptions or false beliefs undergo developmental changes, and how does this evolution contribute to an individual's overall social understanding?
3) How does the theory of cognitive dissonance play a role in shaping and influencing social understanding?
4) How does the understanding of concepts like money and the problem of greed influence an individual's social perceptions and interactions?
5) How does the development of relationships contribute to the overall growth and maturation of an individual's social understanding?

Suggested Further Readings

Books

Bond, M., & Bond, M. S. (2015). *The power of others: Peer pressure, groupthink, and how the people around us shape everything we do*. One World.

Brooks, D. (2011). *The social animal: The hidden sources of love, character, and achievement*. Random House.

Gopnik, A., (2016). *The gardener and the carpenter: What the new science of child development tells us about the relationship between parents and children*. Farrar, Straus and Giroux.

Pinker, S. (2014). *The village effect: How face-to-face contact can make us healthier, happier, and smarter*. Spiegel & Grau.

Websites/Online Resources

Center on the Developing Child at Harvard University (*https://developingchild.harvard.edu/*)
Social Development Research Group (SDRG) at the University of Washington (*www.sdrg.org/*)

12 Human Strengths and Their Development

Contents

Introduction	244
Defining Human Strengths and Virtues	244
Positive Emotional States and Processes	244
Happiness and Well-Being	245
Positive Cognitive States and Processes	247
Understanding the States of Consciousness	250
Life Skills: Building Blocks for Success	252
Teamwork: An Essential Skill for Success	253
Prosocial Behaviour: Building a Caring Society	255
Overview	258
Key Terms	259
Questions for Reflection	259

Learning Objectives

After studying this chapter, the learner will be able to:

Understand the concept of human strengths and virtues;
Describe how different positive emotional states and processes contribute to overall well-being;
Analyse positive cognitive states and illustrate their importance in personal development and resilience;
Explain the mystery of consciousness including their potential impact on personal growth and well-being;
Recognize essential life skills for personal and professional success; and
Explain how prosocial behaviour contributes to the development of a caring and supportive society.

DOI: 10.4324/9781003441168-17

Introduction

This chapter focuses on the positive dimensions that shape our individual and collective well-being. It begins with a contemplation of human strengths and virtues, laying the foundation for a nuanced exploration of the positive aspects of the human experience. Among the positive emotional states and processes, the concepts of happiness and well-being are explored. It further examines the positive cognitive states and processes, such as wisdom, optimism, hope, courage, and self-efficacy, which take centre stage as essential elements in the tapestry of personal development. The realm of consciousness is explored through the lenses of mindfulness, flow, and spirituality, offering insights into the mysteries that shape our inner worlds. Life skills such as communication, cooperation, teamwork, resilience, and digital literacy emerge as indispensable building blocks for success. The narrative further unfolds with a focus on prosocial behaviour, examining the intricacies of building a caring society through altruism, gratitude, love, and forgiveness. The discourse thus explores the facets that empower individuals to lead fulfilling lives and contribute to the creation of a compassionate and harmonious world.

Defining Human Strengths and Virtues

Human strengths and virtues refer to the positive qualities, characteristics, and attributes of individuals that contribute to well-being, personal growth, and the flourishing of societies. They comprise the inherent capacities and values that enable individuals to lead fulfilling lives, build positive relationships, and make meaningful contributions to their communities. These strengths and virtues have been explored in various fields, including psychology, philosophy, sociology, religious studies, and political science. The emerging field of positive psychology, in particular, has focused on identifying and cultivating strengths and virtues to enhance well-being and positive functioning. This chapter takes a look at the development of some of these human strengths and virtues. The deployment of strengths and virtues appropriately across the different stages of life is critical to navigate in life.

While concern for human strengths and virtues did receive attention in some quarters of psychology, for a major part of the 20th century the discipline primarily followed a disease model of human functioning and focused on studying defects, illness, and the like and developing ways to compensate for that. Seligman (2002) argued that "Psychology is not just the study of disease, weakness, and damage; it also is the study of strength and virtue" (p. 4). Seligman and Csikszentmihalyi (2000) declared that there is a need to move from examining the worst things in life to the study of the positive qualities of humans that enable them to thrive and excel in various areas of life. Examples of human strengths include creativity, resilience, empathy, optimism, integrity, perseverance, and adaptability. These strengths can be innate or developed over time through experiences, education, and personal growth.

Likewise, humans have certain virtues, such as moral and ethical qualities, that guide individuals' thoughts, actions, and behaviours. Virtues are regarded as universal and timeless principles that promote human well-being and social harmony. Seligman and his colleagues have identified six core virtues that are found across cultures and periods. These virtues are wisdom and knowledge, courage, humanity, justice, temperance, and transcendence (see Aneesh Kumar et al., 2018; Peterson & Seligman, 2004; Singh et al., 2016).

Positive Emotional States and Processes

Positive emotional states refer to a range of pleasant feelings and experiences. These emotions, such as joy, gratitude, love, contentment, amusement, serenity, hope, inspiration, and so on, are perceived as enjoyable and uplifting feelings. Negative emotional states, such as sadness, anger, fear, anxiety, guilt, shame, or frustration, lead to unpleasant feelings and are typically associated with discomfort, unhappiness, and overall negative affect.

The emotional processes refer to the subjective, physiological, and behavioural mechanisms underlying the experience, regulation, and expression of positive or negative emotions. These processes influence how individuals perceive and interpret the world around them, how they respond to events and situations, and how they maintain or enhance positive emotional states. Positive emotional processes help in evaluating events or situations in a positive and favourable light; adopt emotional strategies like reappraisal, emotional resilience; and emotional contagion; or the spread of positive emotions from one person to another in social interactions or groups, which creates a ripple effect, leading to enhanced well-being and positivity in social environments. Happiness is one such positive emotion. Negative emotional states, on the other hand, often trigger physiological responses associated with stress, such as increased heart rate, elevated blood pressure, heightened muscle tension, and release of stress hormones like cortisol. They create a cognitive bias which results in negative interpretations, overgeneralization, magnification of negative events, or rumination on negative thoughts.

Happiness and Well-Being

The quest for happiness is a universally cherished goal in life. Happiness refers to the feelings of pleasure, contentment, and satisfaction. It has multiple components, such as positive emotions including feelings of joy, gratitude, and love; life satisfaction; and a sense of purpose and meaning in life (Diener et al., 2018).

The conceptualization of happiness varies across cultures. In individualistic cultures, happiness is seen as a subjective and personal achievement as people in these cultures see themselves as autonomous and independent entities. In contrast, people in collectivistic cultures view themselves as intertwined and interrelated with other people. To them, happiness is more relational, intersubjective, and collective in scope (Kitayama & Markus, 1994). It is also to be noted that being happy or unhappy also takes the form of a personality trait where social comparison information plays a significant role (Lyubomirsky & Ross, 1997). Happy people perceive, evaluate, and think about the same events in more positive ways than unhappy ones. Happy people are relatively better equipped to manage ups and downs, as well as stresses in life. Happiness can be increased by practising gratitude and mindfulness, engaging in hobbies, and setting achievable goals (Fredrickson, 2009).

The question that arises is what is the role of money in happiness. Research has shown that though money cannot buy happiness, a certain amount of money is needed to keep life's narratives moving. Once comfortable, more money provides diminishing returns on happiness (Diener, 2000). In a study conducted by the World Bank (cited in Wilfensohn, 2004), it was found that though money is important to the poor, they desire to have a voice in matters related to them, an ability to contribute to their future, and a yearning to be heard, which makes them happier.

Happiness is associated with a range of positive outcomes, such as improved physical and mental health, enhanced social relationships, and increased resilience in the face of adversity. Seligman (2002) noted that happier people tend to be more sociable, better looking, or even healthier, on average, than less happy people.

Culture and Happiness: The Indian Perspective

The Indian view recognizes the natural desire of all human beings to be happy at every stage and every aspect of life. For example, in daily life, the youngsters' greetings are responded to by the elders with the blessing "Khush Raho" (be happy). *Sarve bhawantu sukhina* (let all people be happy) has been the highest ideal of human life. According to *Bhagavad Gita*, a happy state indicates a larger accommodative mental space within the individual (Menon, 1998). Hasya (comic) has been identified as one of the *rasas* by Bharata Muni in *Natyashastra*. The Vaiśeṣika school of Indian thought recognizes *sukha* (pleasure) as one of the 24 *gunas* (qualities) of human beings. It generates such symptoms as gratification, affection, and the brightness of the eyes.

Of the four goals of human beings (i.e., *dharma, artha, kama*, and *moksha*), *kama* seems to correspond most directly to *sukha* (or pleasure, happiness). However, the acquisition of power and wealth (i.e., *artha*) and religious merit (i.e., *dharma*) are also equally important as these have the potential to let people enjoy pleasure at a later time. Further, the Hindu view of *prarabdha karma* (accumulated deeds) assumes that happiness and sorrow are the results of actions performed in present and past lives. It is, therefore, possible that the right actions in the present life may be accompanied by sorrow, and wrong actions by happiness, as a result of the consequences of one's deeds in the past lives (Chaturvedi, 2001). The *Swastika* is the most auspicious symbol in the Hindu tradition. It is drawn, carved, or sculpted at the place of worship on every auspicious occasion. *Swastika* stands for universal well-being ("swasti" means the well-being of one and all, and "ka" means symbol). Thus, *Swastika* indicates happiness, safety, fertility, and prosperity (Kamat, 2023).

In a study, Srivastava and Misra (2013) analysed Sanskrit *suktis* (or good words). *Suktis* are usually small with one or two sentences but are seeped in timeless wisdom which has served as a guide to people for ages. They collected 529 *suktis* having reference to happiness. The majority of the *suktis* (about 82%) were related to happiness and a small number (18%) discussed unhappiness. The researchers also examined the construal of happiness among school students and teachers by administering self-report measures. A large majority of students (62%) and teachers (about 75%) reported that they were very happy. In a recent NCERT survey (Sibia et al., 2022) on school students across the country, happiness was found to be the most common emotion, followed by frequent mood swings and feeling anxious about studies, examinations, and results.

The Analysis of Sanskrit *suktis* and responses of students and teachers showed some salient features of happiness in the Indian context.

1) Happy people show characteristics such as contentment, control over desires and non-attachment, equanimity in opposites, freedom, perseverance and hard work, and the ability to relate with others.
2) Happiness is not simply concerned with the gratification of material senses; rather, it is concerned with finding true peace and fulfilment.
3) Happiness and unhappiness are cyclic where one inevitably follows the other. If there is happiness there is bound to be unhappiness too. The noted poet Kalidas compared it with a rotating wheel where sometimes happiness and sometimes unhappiness takes the front side.
4) Happiness and unhappiness are considered complementary to each other. Indian tradition believes that the search for knowledge begins with the realization of suffering (*dukkha*), and *moksha* is treated as liberation from suffering (Srivastava & Misra, 2012). It is believed that the end of one marks the beginning of the other. Indeed, the Indian view believes that unhappiness is not always to be avoided, it gives meaning to life in certain ways. Misery evokes good qualities of the self or *sadgunas*, such as *jnana* (knowledge), *aisvarya* (prosperity), *sri* (welfare and prosperity), *virya* (prowess), *yasas* (reputation), and so on. It pushes a person to explore new avenues in life that were unsought earlier. It makes one humble and strong at the same time. Hence, misery is viewed as growth-oriented and a developmental process.

5) Personal and social circumstances are considered to cause happiness or unhappiness. Existentially, the foremost source of unhappiness is ignorance. Verma (1994) noted that the reasons for sorrow are (a) the conception of a limited self; (b) the emergence of the quality of restless mobility; (c) dependence on external objects as sources of *sukha* (pleasure); and (d) the fear of separation from the source of *sukha*.

Research in India has shown a positive association of happiness with traits like conscientiousness, extraversion, and emotional stability (Hafen et al., 2011). Social circumstances, such as strong social and familial ties and religiosity and spirituality (Singh et al., 2022) are positively related to happiness. Suar and colleagues (2020) identified several factors of happiness including interpersonal relationships, leisure activities, positive self-evaluation, achievements, comfort, prosocial behaviours, food, recognition, adventure, and material possessions. Factors such as loneliness, poverty, and family conflict inhibit the experience of happiness (Biswas-Diener & Diener, 2006; Srivastava & Shukla, 2018). The students see happiness in terms of social relationships and accomplishments. The concept of a happy life among Indian farmers relates to immediate economic values, self-development, family welfare, and social goods to a great extent. In short, strong social connections, spirituality, job satisfaction, cultural activities, and economic stability are some of the factors that contribute to happiness in India.

Positive Cognitive States and Processes

Positive cognitive states and processes consist of human qualities that are essential for personal growth and well-being. Included among these qualities are wisdom, optimism, hope, and courage. By nurturing these facets of our cognitive framework, we can lead a more fulfilling and meaningful life.

Wisdom: Illuminating Paths to Personal and Collective Well-Being

Since the beginning of civilization, wisdom has been considered a rare and superhuman quality, a gift of God. Wisdom refers to a deep understanding of human nature, and life experiences, and the ability to apply this knowledge thoughtfully and compassionately. The development of wisdom is a lifelong process, which involves learning from both positive and negative life events. In a study involving 26 cultures, including India, from six continents, Lockenhoff et al. (2009) reported that there was a widespread consensus about an increase in wisdom and a decrease in the ability to perform everyday tasks during old age.

According to Baltes and Smith (2008), wisdom consists of a combination of cognitive, reflective, and affective qualities. It encompasses factual knowledge, procedural knowledge, and metacognitive knowledge. It integrates knowledge with values, enabling people to make judgements that align with ethical and moral principles. Wisdom involves the capacity for critical and reflective thinking. Due to this, wise people can consider multiple perspectives, weigh evidence, and make informed judgements. They can balance short-term and long-term goals, personal and collective interests, and immediate gratification and delayed rewards. Wise people are pragmatic in the sense that they possess problem-solving skills and the ability to adapt their knowledge to changing circumstances. Wisdom encompasses a social dimension too, considering the impact of actions and decisions on others and the common good. Wise individuals have a concern for social justice, equity, and the well-being of others, and they use their wisdom to promote positive change in society. Cross-cultural variations in the conceptualization of wisdom have been noted. For example, in a study (Takahashi & Bordia, 2000), it was found that the term "wise" in the West (American and Australian respondents) is characterized as similar to "experienced" and "knowledgeable", whereas the Asian respondents (Indian and Japanese) associated "wise" most closely with "discreet", "aged", and "experienced".

Wisdom has been associated with numerous positive outcomes, including greater life satisfaction, emotional well-being, successful ageing, and improved decision-making. Research has shown that individuals with higher levels of wisdom tend to exhibit better interpersonal relationships, empathy, and prosocial behaviours (Staudinger & Glück, 2011). Researchers are realizing that wisdom can be taught. For example, Sternberg (2004b) proposed to foster wisdom by teaching certain skills and ways of thinking in schools as part of educational curricula.

Indian mythology is rich with stories of wise individuals who imparted profound wisdom and guidance to others, including Lord Krishna, Rishi Valmiki, Rishi Vyasa, Rishi Vishwamitra, and Rishi Narada, to cite a few. Suvasini et al. (2000) analysed the discourse between Lord Krishna and warrior Arjuna in *Bhagavad Gita* to understand the characteristics of wise people. Some of the key characteristics that emerged from this analysis are self-knowledge, detachment, equanimity, compassion, humility, and devotion to the divine.

Optimism: Embracing the Bright Horizon

Optimism denotes a positive mindset, characterized by an inclination to expect positive results, even in difficult situations, and focus on opportunities and possibilities. According to Seligman (1991), optimism is not simply an innate trait but can be cultivated through cognitive and behavioural strategies. Seligman suggests that by identifying and challenging negative, pessimistic thoughts, individuals can reframe their thinking patterns and develop a more optimistic outlook. He introduces the ABCDE model, which stands for Adversity, Beliefs, Consequences, Disputation, and Energization. It involves identifying the Adversity (the negative event), exploring the Beliefs (the thoughts and interpretations surrounding the event), examining the Consequences (emotional and behavioural outcomes), engaging in Disputation (challenging negative beliefs and finding alternative explanations), and generating positive Energization (motivating oneself with new, optimistic perspectives).

Carver and Scheier (2014) discuss dispositional optimism, which refers to a person's inherent tendency to be optimistic or pessimistic. According to them, optimistic people exert effort, whereas pessimistic people disengage from effort. A distinction has been made by Dweck (2006) between a fixed mindset and a growth mindset. Individuals with a fixed mindset believe that their abilities, intelligence, and talents are fixed traits that cannot be significantly developed or changed. On the other hand, individuals with a growth mindset believe that abilities and intelligence can be developed through effort, learning, and persistence. They see failures and setbacks as opportunities for growth and view challenges as a means to improve their skills. Research has shown positive associations between optimism and markers of better psychological and physical health, such as lower risk of cardiovascular disease, improved immune function, better physical and mental health, and experience enhanced overall well-being. Also, optimists have better social connections (Carver & Scheier, 2014).

In India, the concept of optimism has its roots in early Vedic thought. People believed that everything was possible through prayer, magic, natural forces, and cooperation with the gods (Bharti & Rangnekar, 2019). Consider the following Vedic statement:

तमसो मा ज्योतिर्गमय । मृत्योर्मा अमृतं गमय ॥

(Tamaso mā jyotirgamaya, mṛtyormā amṛtaṃ gamaya)

Lead me from darkness to light is the essence of the first part of this prayer. It is a plea to move from a state of spiritual ignorance or darkness to a state of enlightenment and wisdom. The second part is a request to transcend the cycle of life and death and attain the state of eternal existence. In essence, this mantra is a spiritual aspiration for guidance towards enlightenment, knowledge, and liberation from the cycle of birth and death and from mortality to immortality. Research shows that Indian people are more optimistic than the British (Joshi & Carter, 2013) and Japanese (Nishaat, 2022). Optimism is associated with psychological well-being (Soni & DeSousa, 2016).

Hope: Welcoming Possibilities

Hope is a powerful positive cognitive state that plays a significant role in human motivation, resilience, and well-being. The following statement from the *Rigveda* is a prayer asking for the arrival of noble and auspicious thoughts from all directions.

आ नो भद्राः क्रतवो यन्तु विश्वतः । (Ā no bhadraḥ kratavo yantu viśvataḥ)
(May noble thoughts come to us from all directions)

Hope refers to the optimistic outlook that one's goals are attainable, and one should pursue and achieve those goals, even in the face of challenges and obstacles. In his seminal work *The Psychology of Hope*, Snyder (1994) conceptualized hope as comprising two main components: agency and pathways. Agency refers to the individual's belief in their capacity to initiate actions and influence outcomes while pathways involve identifying multiple routes to achieve goals. Research shows that hopeful students are more likely to set challenging goals, put in the effort, and persist in the face of setbacks, leading to better academic performance (Snyder et al., 2002). Employees with higher levels of hope tend to be more motivated and adaptable and demonstrate higher job satisfaction and performance (Cheavens et al., 2006). Hopeful individuals are more resilient in the face of adversities and better equipped to cope with stressful situations (Feldman & Snyder, 2005).

Hope is an essential element of the Indian world view and is expressed in many ways. The embarking of Lord Ram on a journey to rescue Sita from demon king Ravana and the pleading of Savitri with Yama not to take her husband Satyavan's life, to cite a few, are such stories. The philosophy of non-violence and *Satyagraha* (truth force), propagated by Mahatma Gandhi, inspired millions and gave hope for a peaceful and just society. Likewise, Sri Aurobindo regarded hope as a powerful force that inspires personal growth, spiritual evolution, and the realization of divine potential. Swami Vivekananda's teachings inspire people to have hope in their ability to transform their lives and contribute positively to society. Hope is positively related to spirituality, faith, personal growth, well-being, life satisfaction, meaning in life, mindfulness and happiness, self-esteem, and so on (Kraft & Choubisa, 2018).

Courage: Unleashing the Brave Heart Within

The concept of courage encompasses the ability to confront fear, uncertainty, danger, or adversity and take action despite its potential negative consequences. It involves facing challenges, standing up for one's beliefs, and persevering in the face of obstacles. Courageous behaviour always involves a certain degree of risk and ambiguity. Courage can be of different types, such as physical (e.g., bravery), moral (e.g., speaking out against injustice), emotional (e.g., expressing love or forgiveness), intellectual (e.g., engaging in critical thinking), and social (e.g., maintain relationship with others in case of adversities) (Ryan, 2014).

Courage can be cultivated and developed through various processes, including facing fear, developing self-efficacy, managing emotions, building resilience, and demonstrating bravery in various contexts. Research suggests that individuals who experience fear but can regulate their emotional responses and maintain goal-directed behaviour are more likely to demonstrate courageous actions (Blascovich & Mendes, 2010). The self-efficacy theory (Bandura, 1997) highlights that by building a belief in one's ability to overcome challenges, individuals are more likely to exhibit courageous behaviours. Exposure to positive role models, mastery experiences, and supportive environments also contribute to the development of courage. Courage is closely linked to resilience. Research suggests that individuals who possess higher levels of courage are more likely to exhibit resilience in the face of challenges and adversity (Fletcher & Sarkar, 2013).

In Indian tradition, courage is celebrated and exemplified through various historical and mythological narratives. Arjuna's brave fighting against formidable opponents in the Mahabharata war at Kurukshetra, Shivaji Maharaj's courage in leading a resistance against the Mughal rule, Raja Ram Mohan Roy's fight for the abolition of practices such as Sati (widow burning), Guru Nanak Dev's journeys to spread the message of love, equality, and spiritual unity, to cite a few, are examples of courage displayed by the Indian legends.

Thus, courage encompasses facing fear, adversity, or danger and taking positive action despite potential negative consequences. It manifests in various forms, including physical, moral, emotional, intellectual, and social courage. Courageous acts involve confronting and managing fear rather than the absence of fear itself.

Understanding the States of Consciousness

States of consciousness contain a diverse spectrum of human experiences, which open doors to self-awareness, connection, and transcendence. Mindfulness, flow, and spirituality emerge as dynamic and transformative states.

Mindfulness: A State of Heightened Awareness

Mindfulness is a practice that involves bringing one's attention to the present moment in a non-judgemental and accepting way, including thoughts, sensations, and emotions. It is often cultivated through meditation techniques and can be applied to various aspects of life, such as daily activities, relationships, and work. It encourages a state of curiosity and acceptance, allowing individuals to observe their experiences.

Mindfulness has deep roots in Indian traditions and practices like yoga and meditation. One of the well-known mindfulness practices is Vipassana, which means "insight" or "clear-seeing". In Vipassana meditation, the practitioner cultivates mindfulness by observing the breath and bodily sensations, as well as thoughts and emotions, in a non-judgemental and accepting manner. The aim is to develop a deep awareness and understanding of the nature of reality and the impermanent and interconnected nature of all experiences. Kabat-Zinn (1994) has developed a "Mindfulness-Based Stress Reduction (MBSR) Programme", which has been widely implemented and studied in the United States.

Studies have found that mindfulness meditation training leads to improvements in attention, self-regulation, and stress reduction (Tang et al., 2007). Another study by Holzel et al. (2011) used functional magnetic resonance imaging (fMRI) to show that mindfulness training can lead to changes in brain structures associated with attention, compassion, and self-awareness. Moderate effects of mindfulness-based interventions have been reported in the treatment of various psychological conditions, including anxiety, depression, and chronic pain (Goyal et al., 2014).

In the Indian context, attempts have been made to find out the correlates and effectiveness of mindfulness practice on the personality and health of people. For example, a study conducted at Kaivalyadham Yoga Institute (Menon et al., 2014) found that mindfulness was positively correlated with conscientiousness and negatively with neuroticism. Another study (Chandna et al., 2022) reported positive correlations between five levels of mindfulness (i.e., *observing, describing, acting with awareness, non-judging of inner experiences, and non-reactivity to inner experience*) and self-efficacy and self-esteem. Mindfulness reduces anxiety and depression and improves the quality of life (Pal et al., 2022). Thus, the practice of mindfulness improves mental health, reduces stress, and enhances overall well-being.

Flow: The Power of Optimal Experience

Coined by Hungarian psychologist Csikszentmihalyi (1990, 1997, 2008), flow represents a state of deep concentration and enjoyment that leads to enhanced performance and a sense of fulfilment. Flow is a psychological state of optimal experience where individuals feel fully immersed and focused in an activity. The term "optimal experience" describes those occasions where we feel a sense of exhilaration or a deep sense of enjoyment, which we cherish for long and that becomes a landmark in our lives. It may be noted that enjoyment is different from pleasure. We derive pleasure when our biological or social needs are met, such as eating food when hungry. Enjoyment is a feeling that occurs not only after the fulfilment of biological and social needs but also when we achieve something beyond expectations, characterized by a sense of novelty and accomplishments. Thus, while pleasure is dependent on external stimuli, enjoyment comes from within and helps in self-improvement.

The experience of flow is characterized by several distinct qualities. The individuals in a state of flow experience a complete absorption in their activity, losing track of time and their surroundings. Flow is often associated with a sense of effortless control, where the individual feels capable of meeting the challenges presented by the task at hand. When the task is too easy, individuals may become bored, whereas if it is too difficult, they may become anxious or overwhelmed. Flow occurs when there is a perfect match between the individual's skills and the level of challenge, leading to a state of optimal engagement and enjoyment. The individual becomes absorbed (*talliin* or *tanmay*) in performing the task. Some common examples of activities that can induce flow include playing a musical instrument, engaging in a challenging game or sport, solving complex problems, painting, writing, or even performing routine tasks with a mindful and focused approach.

Flow experiences have been linked to enhanced performance and creativity, increased well-being, satisfaction, and intrinsic motivation, as individuals derive a sense of joy and fulfilment from the activity itself. Researchers have developed several measures to assess the experience of flow, such as the Flow State Scale and the Flow Channel Scale, which capture different aspects of the flow experience (for details, Nakamura & Csikszentmihalyi, 2009).

Spirituality: Awakening the Connection to the Infinite

Spirituality refers to the search for meaning, purpose, and connection with something greater than oneself. Spirituality encompasses various dimensions, including the quest for ego-transcendence, inner growth, self-reflection, and a sense of interconnectedness with others, nature, or a higher power. It involves exploring existential questions, contemplating one's values and beliefs, and seeking a sense of harmony, peace, and purpose in life. Pargament (1997, p. 32) defined spirituality as a "search for the sacred".

Research on spirituality has shown numerous positive effects on individuals' well-being and mental health such as greater resilience, better coping skills, and enhanced subjective well-being (Koenig, 2012). A study (Wagani & Colucci, 2018) conducted with students who were part of a spiritual community in India and actively involved in spiritual practices indicated that spirituality gave them a sense of meaning in their lives, even when they were in difficult situations, including when they felt psychologically unwell. Spirituality, however, has negative aspects as well which need to be avoided. For example, the belief that difficulties are caused by God in the form of punishment needs to be avoided. Spirituality is a phenomenon of adulthood which increases during middle and late adulthood. Wink and Dillon (2002) reported that women became more spiritual than men in the second half of adulthood.

The search for spirituality varies across cultures. Indigenous cultures often have deeply rooted spiritual practices and beliefs, emphasizing a holistic world view, with a strong focus on maintaining harmony with nature and honouring ancestors. In Western cultures, individuals may seek spirituality through prayer, worship, religious rituals, and adherence to sacred texts. In New Age spirituality, individuals explore spirituality outside of organized religion. This can include a variety of practices such as mindfulness, yoga, energy healing, and the adoption of eclectic spiritual beliefs and practices.

Spirituality has been valued in Indian culture from time immemorial, and there are several examples of personalities who have excelled in the field of spirituality (Bhawuk, 2011). At its core, Indian spirituality emphasizes the unity of all beings and the interconnectedness of the universe. Through practices such as meditation, self-discipline, and devotion, individuals strive to transcend the limitations of the ego and experience a sense of oneness with the divine. The Vedanta system has proposed that the goal to be realized is to identify with higher consciousness and become the *Brahman*. This leads to the realization that *I am Brahman (Aham Brahmasmi)*, and everything is *Brahman (Sarvam khalvidam Brahman)*. This requires rigorous enquiry into the self, which involves listening, reflecting, and contemplating (*Shravan, Manan, and Nidhidhyasan*). In addition, the seeker has to follow rules of conduct in everyday life. The normal conceptualization of consciousness involving sleep, dream, and deep sleep (*Nidra, Swapn, and Sushupti*) is complemented by a fourth state called *Turiya*, which treats the waking state *as an* illusion.

Thus, efforts to refine the experience of consciousness offer profound opportunities for personal growth, self-discovery, and the exploration of the boundless potentials of the human mind. Modern psychologists have found mindfulness as an intervention to foster mental clarity and emotional balance; flow helps to unlock the potential for peak experiences and creative breakthroughs; and spirituality brings in a sense of purpose, interconnectedness, and a deeper understanding of the human experience.

Life Skills: Building Blocks for Success

Life skills are the essential building blocks that empower individuals to navigate the complexities of modern life with confidence and success. Among these skills, communication, cooperation, teamwork, resilience, and digital literacy shine as pillars of personal and professional growth.

Communication: The Skill of Connecting and Understanding

Communication skills are fundamental abilities that enable individuals to express their thoughts, ideas, and feelings effectively. Also, it involves the ability to listen actively and comprehend others. Strong communication skills are essential in both personal and professional contexts, as they facilitate the building of relationships, resolving conflicts, and conveying information.

There are certain distinguishable features of effective communication. First, effective communication involves not only the words we use but also our tone of voice, body language, and facial expressions (refer to Chapter 7). Second, active listening and the use of precise language are crucial. Third, effective communicators are adaptable to different situations and audiences, such as adjusting style, tone, and language to suit the specific context. Lastly, developing empathy and emotional intelligence allows us to understand others' perspectives, emotions, and needs.

Cooperation: The Skill of Working Together

In the present fast-paced and interconnected world, cooperation has emerged as a crucial life skill for personal, professional, and societal success. Cooperation is defined as the act of working together towards a common goal. The Yajurveda (32/8) verse "यत्र विश्वं भवत्येकनीडम्" (Where the world becomes one home) reflects the Indian ideal of a harmonious society where cooperation transcends boundaries, leading to unity, peace, and collective well-being.

Many of the challenges that we face in today's world require collaborative problem-solving. Cooperation enables individuals to pool their knowledge, skills, and perspectives, leading to more innovative and effective solutions. Organizations fostering a cooperative culture experience improved productivity, higher employee satisfaction, and increased innovation. It promotes social cohesion, reduces conflict, and cultivates a harmonious society (Batson et al., 2002).

As an instructional approach, cooperative learning is widely practised in the educational context. It involves structured activities where students work together in small groups to achieve common goals, fostering academic and social growth. In a meta-analysis of over 800 studies, Johnson et al. (2014) found that cooperative learning strategies consistently led to higher achievement scores across various subjects and grade levels. Cooperative learning also fosters social and emotional development (Kagan & Kagan, 2009) and helps in cultivating higher-order thinking skills among learners. Research in India also shows similar benefits of cooperative learning.

Teamwork: An Essential Skill for Success

Like cooperation, teamwork is also an essential skill to achieve a common goal. It involves the coordination, cooperation, and mutual support of team members, each contributing their unique skills, knowledge, and perspectives to achieve shared outcomes. The essential conditions for teamwork are effective communication, active listening, and the ability to work harmoniously and synergistically with others. In teamwork, each person shares his/her unique perspective, skills, and experiences, which are collectively utilized to tackle complex challenges. Collaboration within a team encourages brainstorming, open dialogue, and the exchange of ideas. This increases the chances of identifying creative problem-solving strategies.

In an insightful analysis, Gupta (2002) observed that culture plays an important role in the effective functioning of teamwork. It has been found successful in the Japanese context, which has a strong but benevolent and mutually satisfying hierarchical orientation. Its success in the Indian context would require special effort. As Indian society is hierarchically organized, the leader of the team needs to care, show affection, and take an interest in the personal well-being of team members.

Resilience: Skill for Thriving Amidst Challenges

Resilience is a life skill that enables individuals to adapt, persevere, and bounce back from challenges, setbacks, and adversity (Masten & Cicchetti, 2016). It is a quality that enables individuals to face adversity, overcome challenges, and maintain equilibrium in the face of life's ups and downs. It is similar to the concept of plasticity in human behaviour, where individuals change their habits, acquire new skills, and adjust their perspectives according to the requirements of the context. Resilience helps individuals cope with uncertainty, embrace change, and adapt to new situations. Also, it helps individuals manage stress, overcome challenges, and prevent the development of mental health disorders (Southwick & Charney, 2012). It fosters effective communication, empathy, and conflict-resolution skills, contributing to stronger connections and social support networks (Fredrickson, 2009).

The famous shloka from the *Bhagavad Gita* "कर्मण्येवाधिकारस्ते मा फलेषु कदाचन ।" (i.e., you have the right to perform your prescribed duty only, but never bother about the fruits of your actions) emphasizes the significance of resilience in the face of outcomes. It teaches us to focus on our efforts and actions rather than getting attached to the results. Several methods have been put forward for developing resilience. Included among these methods are building a supportive network of family, friends, mentors, and support groups; practising self-care; developing problem-solving skills; and cultivating optimism and positive thinking. In the context of India, intervention measures have been developed to improve resilience (Mehrotra et al., 2018). Thus, by cultivating resilience, individuals can enhance their overall well-being, professional success, and interpersonal relationships. With the right methods and support, anyone can develop resilience and face life's challenges with confidence.

Digital Literacy: An Empowering Skill for the Digital Age

Digital literacy involves acquiring a host of technical as well as cognitive and social skills necessary to engage with digital tools, networks, and content. First, there are some basic skills required to operate digital devices (e.g., typing, use of search engines, managing files), use software applications (such as Microsoft applications, Facebook, WhatsApp, and so on), and the internet. Second, it requires information literacy, such as the ability to critically evaluate the credibility, accuracy, and reliability of online sources, identify fake news, understand search strategies, citation and copyright, and privacy and security awareness. Third, digital literacy demands understanding netiquette (online etiquette) necessary to communicate clearly and respectfully through digital channels and collaborate with others using digital tools and platforms. Lastly, digital literacy includes an understanding of responsible and ethical behaviour in the digital world. This involves respecting intellectual property rights, protecting personal information and privacy, and engaging in safe and responsible online behaviour.

Digital literacy has increasingly become essential for individuals to participate fully in education, employment, civic engagement, and everyday life. However, one would observe a digital divide in society; individuals or communities having access to and effectively using digital technologies and those who do not have access to the device (Vassilakopoulou & Hustad, 2023). In developed countries, the digital divide in terms of access is almost closing, but there are inequalities in people's ability to make use of the resources. In developing countries like India, even access is limited. As per the National Family Health Survey 2019–21 (NFHS-5), only 57.2% of males and 33.3% of females had ever used the internet. The gap also exists in the usage of the internet and mobile phones based on area of residence (rural/urban), caste, and age. The digital divide needs to be reduced to utilize its advantages by all sections of society.

Digital Technology: Some Emerging Concerns

In the last few decades, digital technology has changed the way human beings interact with their world. The use of the Internet of Things (IoT) and Artificial Intelligence (AI) is found to have some positive and several negative effects. They are interfering with the development of human strengths and virtues such as empathy, attachment, compassion, trust, and morality. Digital technology is replacing engagement in play and physical activities in real time. In this way, digital technology interrupts with promotion of qualities like creativity, communication, imagination, self-control, and social harmony. It is estimated that the time young children spend on mobile and tablets has increased tenfold in the last five years. Excessive screen time is closely related to autism/language development/attachment, and behaviour issues. Platforms like YouTube, Snapchat, Facebook, and so on are proving harmful. Digital manipulation and exploitation have become a crucial challenge for parents. During adolescence sensation-seeking behaviour increases, and it needs to be supported by impulsivity regulation. It may increase delinquency, antisocial behaviour, and drug/alcohol addiction.

Indeed, the proliferation of digital technology is becoming a serious threat to the well-being of children and adolescents. Exposure to harmful content and advertising is becoming more powerful with the introduction of interactive technology. AI and tools like ChatGPT are complicating learning styles and other academic activities. As noted by Kapur (2024), digital devices have very limited scope for education. A heavy dose of entertainment detracts from academics, displaces reading, creates aversion to homework, and replaces the time spent with parents and siblings. She suggests that parents need to set limits to tackle gadget addiction. The very young should not be exposed to it. During 10–12 years' age, limited access should be given. Limits should be set for adolescents too. Attempts should be made to replace the use of digital gadgets with real-time activities and bonding. Unfortunately, the new technology spreads very quickly and the information about its impact lags. Therefore, awareness about advertisements of IoT and AI is needed. As Kapur (2024) has remarked "we need to plan how to prevent children from falling prey to the virtual world and promote their well-being by providing multipronged intervention strategies incorporating tradition preferred practices and contemporary evidence-based practices" (pp. 182–183).

This discussion illustrates the importance of life skills. By honing these life skills, we equip ourselves with the tools necessary to thrive in an ever-evolving world, unlock our potential, and contribute meaningfully to society's progress.

Prosocial Behaviour: Building a Caring Society

Prosocial behaviours encompass actions and attitudes that contribute to the development of harmonious relationships, social cohesion, and the well-being of individuals and communities. These behaviours are characterized by empathy, compassion, and the willingness to help, support, or cooperate with others. Included in some of the core prosocial behaviours are altruism, gratitude, love, and forgiveness.

Altruism: Helping Others

Kar Bhala, Hoga Bhala

—(Do good, and good will come to you.)

Altruism refers to selfless acts of kindness, compassion, and empathy towards individuals or groups to improve their well-being. It is a voluntary action of helping or benefitting others at one's own expense. It goes beyond simple acts of generosity and manifests in various forms, such as donating to charity, volunteering, or providing emotional support.

Altruistic acts are driven by intrinsic motivations, a genuine desire to alleviate the suffering of others, or promote their well-being. Social norms, cultural values, and personal experiences also shape altruistic tendencies. Related to altruism are concepts such as altruistic punishment, reciprocity, and cooperation. The concept of altruistic punishment, first introduced by Fehr and Gachter (2002), refers to a form of behaviour where individuals punish others for violating social norms, even when there is no direct personal gain or benefit to the punisher. Reciprocity involves the expectation that the other person will act similarly in a subsequent interaction. Cooperation has been discussed separately in this chapter.

The development of altruistic behaviour begins at a young age. Young infants (14–18 months of age) help other infants in finding objects beyond their reach, and they do it without reward or encouragement from adults. Chadha and Misra (2006) observed an increase in prosocial reasoning among Indian children with age. Altruism is positively associated with happiness, health, and well-being, reduced rates of depression and anxiety, longevity, and psychological well-being (see Filkowski et al., 2016). It fosters social cohesion by creating networks of support, enhancing interpersonal relationships, and building trust within communities.

Indian culture is rich with examples of altruistic behaviour, such as *seva* (selfless service) and *dana* (charity). Rishi Dadhich is revered as the epitome of altruism and sacrifice in Indian mythology. Baba Amte and Mother Teresa are among the other renowned altruistic figures in the current times. In India, what Gupta (2013) called "biosphere altruism", altruistic treatment is given to plants, animals, and even entire ecosystems and landscapes such as rivers, forests, and mountains. They are considered sacred and worshipped regularly.

Gratitude: Cultivating Connections

Gratitude involves acknowledging and expressing appreciation for the kindness, help, or benefits received from others, whether tangible or intangible. By expressing gratitude, individuals express their indebtedness towards others' positive actions and contributions. This strengthens interpersonal relationships, promotes positive communication, and enhances social connectedness (Algoe, 2012). Grateful individuals often exhibit higher levels of happiness, life satisfaction, and overall psychological well-being. Also, gratitude triggers a desire in others to reciprocate and contribute to the happiness and welfare of others (Watkins, 2014).

Gratitude is not just a static trait but evolves and deepens as individuals grow and experience life's challenges and joys. During childhood, children may begin to say "thank you" in response to receiving gifts or favours, but they don't fully grasp the emotional depth of gratitude. It is during adolescence that gratitude fosters empathy and prosocial behaviour from them. Young adults begin to reflect on the support they have received and start expressing gratitude by reciprocating acts of kindness and offering emotional support to others (Wood et al., 2008). As individuals enter midlife and beyond, they realize the importance of meaningful relationships, reflect on life accomplishments, and develop a sense of contentment and acceptance. Gratitude can serve as a buffer against stress and promote overall well-being in later adulthood.

In individualistic cultures, gratitude is often expressed more directly and explicitly. People may openly express thanks through verbal communication or written messages. In contrast, gratitude may be more subtly expressed to maintain harmony and avoid direct attention to oneself in collectivistic cultures (Chen et al., 2006). In India, people express gratitude in various ways including, saying "Thank You" (*Dhanyavaad* or *Shukriya*), touching feet (*pranam*), giving gifts, offering prayers and donations, feeding others (particularly the less fortunate ones), providing assistance in various ways, touching the forehead in *Anjali Mudra* (placing the palms together in a prayer-like manner at the forehead, accompanied by a slight bow), and so forth.

Love: The Power of Compassion and Connection

Love is an intense feeling of deep affection, care, and emotional attachment towards someone or something. It involves a profound sense of warmth, compassion, and a desire for the well-being and happiness of the loved one. The feeling of love induces in the individual emotions such as joy, happiness, feeling energized, warm, passionate, and so on (Mayer, 2021). Love knows no boundaries of age, gender, race, or cultural background. It is a universal emotion that can bridge differences and bring people together. It requires forming deep connections, bonding, making sacrifices for the well-being and happiness of others and providing care and support. However, variations in the meaning of love are observed across time, place, and culture (Mayer & Vanderheiden, 2021).

Robert Sternberg (1986) has advanced the "Triangular Theory of Love", which has three primary components: intimacy, passion, and commitment. Intimacy refers to the emotional closeness, connectedness, and bond shared between individuals. Passion represents the intense physical and emotional attraction or arousal that individuals feel for each other. Commitment refers to the cognitive aspect of love, where individuals are devoted to each other, maintain a long-term relationship, and are willing to work through challenges and conflicts. Based on this, Sternberg proposed seven different types of love, which are liking, infatuation, empty love (without intimacy or passion), romantic love, companionate love (characterized by intimacy and commitment but lacks strong passion), fatuous love (involving passion and commitment without deep emotional intimacy), and consummate love (an ideal form of love, encompassing all three components of intimacy, passion, and commitment). Mayer (2021) noted three aspects of love: human (or interpersonal qualities including trust and intimacy), transhuman (deep connection with spiritual powers), and individual (such as self-sacrifice).

The development of love is influenced by biological, psychological, and sociocultural factors. During early childhood, it is expressed through attachment to caregivers. During adolescence, romantic love and attraction become prominent. Young adulthood is marked by the development of more mature and committed romantic relationships. In late adulthood, love may shift towards more platonic relationships and companionships.

Love has a rich and diverse history in the Indian context. Its portrayal has been depicted through various literary works, art forms, and religious texts. For example, during the ancient Vedic period, love was often portrayed as a sacred and divine connection. The love between deities and their devotees symbolized the spiritual union between the individual soul (*Atman*) and the supreme cosmic soul (*Brahman*). *Bhagavata Purana* portrays the intense love and devotion of the devotee towards Lord Krishna. In an exemplary work, Bhawuk (2021) analysed the notion of *prema* (love) as used and expressed by the 15th-century Indian saint-poet Kabir in his *sakhis* or couplets. The analysis revealed eight themes of love: (a) it is non-transient, (b) cannot be hidden, (c) is difficult, (d) is a drink, (e) love for God is superior to material love, (f) without understanding, love is useless, (g) compassion is the root cause of love, and (h) love, detachment, and sadguru are interrelated.

Love finds expression in various Indian art forms like painting, sculpture, and dance. The depiction of love in temple sculptures, particularly in Khajuraho and Konark, showcased sensuality, eroticism, and the celebration of physical love as an integral aspect of human existence. Thus, love has been celebrated in various forms, from divine and spiritual love to romantic and emotional connections. It continues to be a powerful force that shapes relationships and influences the way people express their emotions in the Indian context.

Forgiveness: Healing Wounds

Forgiveness refers to the voluntary decision of the individual to release feelings of resentment, anger, or vengeance towards someone who has committed a perceived wrongdoing. It involves replacing negative emotions with positive feelings like empathy, understanding, and compassion. When individuals forgive, it can lead to increased trust and cooperation between them and the offending party (Van Vianen et al., 2018). This improved relationship quality can foster greater social cohesion within groups and communities. Forgiveness also helps in conflict resolution by de-escalating conflicts and reducing aggressive responses (Fehr et al., 2010). Research shows that older people are more willing to forgive others than younger people. Females are found to be more forgiving than males in the Indian context (Marigoudar & Kamble, 2014).

Cultural and religious factors significantly influence the practice of forgiveness. Some cultures and belief systems emphasize the value of forgiveness as a virtue and encourage individuals to display forgiveness as prosocial behaviour. In the Indian context, the one who forgives is considered to be the embodiment of bravery and equivalent to God. In Valmiki Ramayan, forgiveness has been accorded the highest value:

क्षमा दानं क्षमा यज्ञः क्षमा सत्यं हि पुत्रिकाः ॥ क्षमा यशः क्षमा धर्मः क्षमया निष्ठितं जगत् ।

(Forbearance is charity, forbearance is sacrifice, forbearance is truth, forbearance is glory and forbearance is virtue. O daughters, the universe is supported by forbearance.)

Prosocial behaviours, thus, serve as the cornerstone for fostering a compassionate and interconnected society. Acts of altruism create a network of support and cooperation, nurturing a community built on empathy and shared well-being. The practice of gratitude, love, and forgiveness further solidifies social bonds, promoting understanding, resilience, and a collective sense of compassion that is vital for building a caring and harmonious society.

Overview

The exploration of the development of human strengths in this chapter has provided a comprehensive overview of the multifaceted aspects that contribute to our well-being and flourishing. The chapter began by delving into the definition of human strengths and virtues, establishing a foundation for understanding the positive attributes that shape our lives. The examination of positive emotional states and processes highlighted the importance of cultivating emotions such as joy, gratitude, and resilience, emphasizing their role in fostering a positive and fulfilling existence. Similarly, positive cognitive states and processes, encompassing wisdom, optimism, hope, and courage, underscored the significance of nurturing our mental faculties for personal growth and achievement.

The chapter further explored the mystery of consciousness, exploring mindfulness, flow, and spirituality as transformative elements that contribute to a deeper understanding of ourselves and our connection to the world. Life skills were identified as essential building blocks for success, including effective communication, cooperation, teamwork, resilience, and digital literacy, which collectively empower individuals to navigate the complexities of contemporary life. Moreover, the discussion on prosocial behaviour shed light on the crucial role of altruism, gratitude, love, and forgiveness in building a caring and compassionate society. These virtues were presented as catalysts for creating meaningful connections and fostering a sense of community, contributing to the overall well-being of individuals and society at large.

In synthesizing these diverse elements, it becomes evident that the development of human strengths is a dynamic and interconnected process. As individuals cultivate positive emotions, nurture cognitive resilience, and acquire essential life skills, they contribute not only to their personal growth but also to the collective flourishing of society. This chapter serves as a road map for understanding and harnessing the inherent strengths within each individual, providing insights that can inspire positive change and contribute to the creation of a more compassionate and resilient world.

Key Terms

Altruism	Life Skills
Communication	Love
Cooperation	Mindfulness
Consciousness	Optimism
Courage	Positive Emotional States
Digital Literacy	Positive Cognitive States
Flow	Prosocial Behaviour
Forgiveness	Resilience
Gratitude	Self-Efficacy
Happiness and Well-being	Spirituality
Hope	Teamwork
Human Strengths	Wisdom

Questions for Reflection

1) How do you personally define and conceptualize human strengths and virtues based on your experiences and observations?
2) Give your opinion about how fostering happiness and well-being positively impacts an individual's overall life satisfaction and personal growth.
3) In what ways do positive cognitive states and processes contribute to an individual's resilience and ability to navigate life challenges?
4) Considering the exploration of consciousness in terms of mindfulness, flow, and spirituality, how might incorporating these aspects into daily life enhance one's overall sense of purpose and fulfilment?
5) How can the development of life skills positively influence personal and professional achievements?

Suggested Further Readings

Books

Claude-Hélène Mayer, C. H., & Vanderheiden, E. (Eds.). (2021). *International handbook of love: Transcultural and transdisciplinary perspectives*. Springer Nature.
Duckworth, A. (2016). *Grit: The power of passion and perseverance*. Scribner/Simon & Schuster.
Rath, T. (2007). *StrengthsFinder 2.0*. Simon & Schuster.

Websites/Online Resources

Greater Good Magazine (*https://greatergood.berkeley.edu/*)
Mindful.org (*www.mindful.org/*)
Positive Psychology Center (University of Pennsylvania) (*https://ppc.sas.upenn.edu/*)
TED Talks on Positive Psychology (*https://positivepsychology.com/positive-psychology-ted-talks/*)

Part VI
Towards Inclusive Development
Emerging Issues

13 Development under Vulnerable Circumstances

Contents

Introduction	264
Developmental Challenges in Adverse Circumstances	264
Family and Community Violence	266
Terrorism: Sources and Influences	268
Natural Disasters: Cyclones, Earthquakes, Tsunamis	269
Box 13.1: COVID-19 and Its Impact on Human Development	272
The Occurrence of War: Dark Aspects of Humanity	272
Understanding Conflict and Its Resolution	273
Street Children: A Vulnerable and Neglected Population	276
Box 13.2: Vulnerability and Resilience Among Orphaned Adolescents in Institutional Care	277
Overview	279
Key Terms	279
Questions for Reflection	280

Learning Objectives

After studying this chapter, the learner will be able to:

Understand various adverse conditions that hinder development;
Analyse sources and influences of violence and terrorism;
Learn how resilient communities can better cope with and recover from the aftermath of natural disasters;
Gain insights into conflict resolution methods; and
Understand the challenges faced by street children as a vulnerable population.

DOI: 10.4324/9781003441168-19

Introduction

In the realm of development under vulnerable circumstances, resilience and adversity take centre stage influencing human development. The chapter commences by delving into the developmental challenges that individuals face, affecting their personal growth. Family and community violence emerge as stark realities, presenting an ongoing struggle for safety and well-being. The complex web of terrorism is dissected, unravelling its sources and influences, with a spotlight on initiatives such as safe school declaration that aim to protect educational environments in conflict zones. Natural disasters, ranging from cyclones and earthquakes to tsunamis and the COVID-19 pandemic, punctuate the narrative, highlighting the resilience required to rebuild lives in the aftermath of such cataclysmic events. The occurrence of war exposes the dark aspects of humanity, prompting a contemplation on understanding conflict and its resolution. Within this challenging landscape, the plight of street children surfaces as a vulnerable and neglected population, inviting reflection on societal responsibilities. The chapter also sheds light on the nuanced interplay of vulnerability and resilience among orphaned adolescents in institutional care. This discourse thus explores the complexities of development under vulnerable circumstances, acknowledging the strength of the human spirit in the face of adversity and the collective responsibility to create a more compassionate world.

Developmental Challenges in Adverse Circumstances

What are Adverse Circumstances?

Adverse circumstances refer to challenging and unfavourable conditions that individuals or communities face, often hindering their well-being, development, and ability to lead fulfilling lives. Various factors, including natural disasters, armed conflicts, economic hardships, social inequalities, and health crises, can cause these circumstances. Some common examples of adverse circumstances are described here.

Natural Disasters

This includes events like earthquakes, hurricanes, floods, tsunamis, wildfires, and droughts. It can cause extensive damage to infrastructure, disrupt livelihoods, and displace communities, leading to significant hardships for those affected. It is estimated that an average of 134 million people are affected by natural disasters annually. Globally, between 1990 and 2019, flooding was the most common natural disaster (42%), followed by storms (30%) (Institute for Economics & Peace, Ecological Threat Register, 2020). The National Disaster Management Authority in India undertakes the responsibility of rescuing people affected by natural disasters.

Armed Conflicts

War and armed conflicts result in loss of lives, destruction of infrastructure, and widespread displacement. Civilians caught in conflict zones often endure trauma, limited access to basic needs, and human rights violations. The United Nations (n.d.) estimates that over 235 million people require humanitarian assistance due to conflict and violence.

Poverty and Economic Hardship

Living in poverty means inadequate access to food, clean water, healthcare, education, and other essential services, perpetuating a cycle of disadvantage. The World Bank estimates that over 700 million people live in extreme poverty, surviving on less than $1.90 per day (World Bank, 2021).

Infectious Disease Outbreaks

Global pandemics, such as the COVID-19 pandemic, can overwhelm healthcare systems, disrupt economies, and lead to loss of lives and livelihoods, particularly in vulnerable populations.

Forced Displacement

People forced to flee their homes due to conflict, persecution, or environmental disasters often face challenges in finding safety, shelter, and access to basic services in their host communities. The United Nations High Commissioner for Refugees (UNHCR, 2023) reports that at the end of 2022, there were 108.4 million forcibly displaced people globally.

Social Inequalities

Discrimination based on race, ethnicity, gender, religion, or other factors can lead to systemic disadvantages, limiting opportunities and perpetuating social divides.

Environmental Degradation

Pollution, deforestation, and climate change contribute to adverse circumstances by affecting ecosystems, biodiversity, and the well-being of communities that rely on natural resources. The Intergovernmental Panel on Climate Change (IPCC, 2018) warns of the significant adverse impacts of climate change on human well-being.

Lack of Access to Education

Limited access to education (particularly quality education) and educational resources hinder individual and community development and economic opportunities. Of those in school, a large number of children do not attain minimum proficiency levels in reading and mathematics.

Personal Crises

Family breakdowns, personal trauma, or unexpected life events such as the loss of a loved one can lead to adverse circumstances, impacting emotional and psychological stability.

Mental Health Issues

Exposure to adverse circumstances can lead to increased levels of stress, anxiety, depression, and other mental health problems.

Political Instability

Uncertain political situations, corruption, and lack of governance can create adverse circumstances, impacting citizens' rights and access to public services.

Developmental Scenario in Adverse Circumstances

Adverse circumstances present various challenges for human development. Meeting the basic needs of food, clean water, shelter, and healthcare is limited in areas affected by armed conflicts or natural disasters (UNICEF, 2023). Experiencing adverse events can lead to psychological trauma, including post-traumatic stress disorder (PTSD), anxiety, and depression. For example, refugees who have fled war-torn regions suffer from severe mental health issues before and during their displacement. Disruption in the education of displaced children hampers their cognitive and overall development (Save the Children, 2021). Living in adverse circumstances often means limited access to economic opportunities and resources, leading to persistent poverty (World Bank, 2021). Adverse circumstances can have a long-lasting impact on future generations. Children who grow up in such environments carry physical, emotional, and psychological scars into adulthood, perpetuating cycles of poverty and disadvantage (UNICEF, 2021).

Family and Community Violence

Violence refers to the intentional use of physical force or power against oneself, others, or property, leading to harm, injury, or damage. It can manifest in various forms, such as physical, psychological/emotional, or verbal aggression. Physical violence refers to the use of bodily force to inflict harm or injury, ranging from simple assaults to severe acts like murder. Psychological violence is characterized by actions that manipulate, control, or demean individuals without necessarily resorting to physical harm. Violence can take the shape of interpersonal violence (e.g., spouse abuse and homicide), intergroup violence (e.g., violence between members of two or more groups), and mass violence (e.g., terrorist acts and genocide). *Psychology of Violence*, a multidisciplinary research journal brought out by the American Psychological Association (APA), recognizes all forms of violence to be interconnected. A proper understanding of violence requires inputs across disciplines, such as psychology, public health, neuroscience, sociology, medicine, and other related behavioural and social sciences.

Family/Domestic Violence

Family or domestic or intimate partner violence involves abusive behaviours within the families, including physical violence, emotional abuse, sexual violence, and economic control. Cultural norms around gender roles influence the types and levels of violence within a society. For example, cultures that promote strict gender roles and traditional masculinity experience higher rates of domestic violence (Heise, 1998).

Sustainable Development Goal 5 (refer to Chapter 14) is concerned with eliminating all forms of violence against women and girls. Globally, about one-third of women suffer from domestic violence. The World Health Organization (WHO, 2021c) estimated a 26% prevalence of intimate partner violence in ever-married/partnered women aged 15 years or more globally in 2018. According to the National Family Health Survey (NFHS, 2019–21), about 29% of married women in India (rural=31.6%; urban 24.2%) in the age group 18–49 years have experienced domestic/sexual violence. Also, about 3% of pregnant women in the ages of 18–49 years have experienced physical violence during pregnancy. It occurs in multiple forms, such as physical, sexual, and emotional violence (Chaudhary et al., 2009; Sinha et al., 2012). Research reveals that abused women show increasing health problems such as injury, chronic pain, gastrointestinal and gynaecological signs including sexually transmitted diseases, depression, and post-traumatic stress disorder (Campbell, 2002). To safeguard women from domestic violence, the Government of India has enacted a law "The Protection of Women from Domestic Violence Act, 2005".

In the Indian tradition, domestic violence against women has been condemned and is considered contrary to the principles of *dharma* (righteousness), compassion, and respect for others. For example, the following shloka from *Manusmriti* (3.56) highlights the significance of respecting and honouring women.

यत्र नार्यस्तु पूज्यन्ते रमन्ते तत्र देवताः । यत्रैतास्तु न पूज्यन्ते सर्वास्तत्राफलाः क्रियाः ॥

(Where women are honoured, divinity blossoms there. Where they are not, all actions remain unfruitful.)

However, research in India shows the prevalence of negative attitudes and practices against women. In their study, Dhawan et al. (1999) found mild to severe forms of verbal abuse targeted towards women, particularly in families in urban and low education levels. The prevalence of inadequate sexual and reproductive healthcare among women and low levels of nutrition and care among their children due to incidences of domestic violence has been reported in the Indian context (Suri et al., 2022). In another study conducted on women in Kolkata and nearby areas (Chakraborty & De, 2019), it was noted that women suffer lifelong struggles with restricted space for themselves and several authority figures to control them. Thakur and Rangaswamy (2019) reported that women suffering from domestic violence experience physiological (such as aches and pains, nutritional deficiencies, reproductive), psychological (such as depression, low self-confidence, change in aspirations and ambitions, mistrust, rumination) and behavioural (such as crying, withdrawal, irritability, disturbed sleep) distress. Thus, much against the traditional wisdom, domestic violence against women is quite prevalent in India causing physical and psychological distress to them.

Community Violence

Community violence occurs within a community, often involving strangers or acquaintances. This form of violence can include physical assaults, shootings, gang-related violence, and other criminal acts. Community and family violence are linked, as individuals experiencing community violence may show aggression within their families. Similarly, family violence can spill over into the community through incidents such as domestic disputes turning violent in public spaces (Fitzpatrick et al., 2018).

In India, socio-economic disparities, particularly between different caste groups such as scheduled castes and scheduled tribes, have been a recurring cause of violence due to conflicts over resources and opportunities. Community violence is also sometimes orchestrated for political gains. Violent incidents deepen existing divides, leading to distrust, fear, and hatred among different communities. This polarization weakens the social fabric and hinders cooperation. The persistence of violence erodes the country's long-standing tradition of religious and cultural pluralism, threatening the social harmony that India is known for.

Efforts to address community violence have been undertaken at local, national, and international levels. For example, India has various laws and provisions in place to prevent violence and maintain law and order. These include the Indian Penal Code (IPC); the Protection of Children from Sexual Offenses (POCSO) Act, 2012; the Scheduled Castes and the Scheduled Tribes (Prevention of Atrocities) Act, 1989; the Dowry Prohibition Act, 1961; the Protection of Civil Rights Act, 1955; and the Criminal Law Amendment Act, 2013. It may, however, be noted that the implementation of these laws can sometimes be challenging due to various factors such as social attitudes, infrastructure, and the efficiency of the legal system.

Violence, however, cannot be controlled simply by making laws. Addressing violence requires a holistic approach that includes education, prevention programmes, conflict resolution training, mental health support, and measures to tackle systemic issues that contribute to violence (Pinker, 2011). In the context of India, it has been suggested that improving literacy, creating awareness regarding legal aid, and screening the victims of violence at primary health centres can minimize its effects. Similarly, in the case of family violence crisis helplines, shelters, counselling, and legal assistance for victims, as well as offender intervention and rehabilitation programmes may be useful (George et al.,2016; Nadda et al., 2018).

In conclusion, community and family violence are complex issues that require a comprehensive understanding of their underlying causes and far-reaching impacts. By addressing these forms of violence through evidence-based interventions and support systems, societies can work towards creating safer and healthier communities for all.

Terrorism: Sources and Influences

Terrorism is a devastating phenomenon that has been a matter of significant concern worldwide. It involves the use of violence, intimidation, and fear to achieve political, religious, or ideological objectives. In many cases, terrorism arises from political grievances, where certain groups feel marginalized or excluded from the political process. When people believe that their voices are not being heard through peaceful means, they resort to terrorism as a way to draw attention to their concerns. Poverty, unemployment, and lack of economic opportunities are other sources. Individuals don't become terrorists suddenly, but it is a gradual process and depends on the available opportunities. There is a general progression from social alienation to boredom, then occasional dissidence and protest before eventually turning to terrorism.

Randy Borum (2004), in his book *Psychology of Terrorism*, analysed the causes of terrorism and violence. According to him, three motivational factors contribute to becoming a terrorist: perceived injustice, identity, and belonging. Perceived injustice gives rise to a desire for revenge or vengeance. Because of perceived injustice, many terrorists need belonging, connectedness, and affiliation. Extremist ideologies and terrorist organizations offer them a sense of belonging and purpose. Institute for Economics & Peace (2015) reported that terrorist activity is correlated with the prevalence of political violence and violent conflicts in the country. Lack of respect for human rights, the existence of policies targeting religious freedoms, group grievances, and political instability also correlate with terrorism. In wealthier countries, a correlation between socio-economic factors, such as youth unemployment, drug crime, and terrorism was found in the study.

Some of the important terrorist activities in the world in the recent past include the 9/11 Attacks in the United States of America in 2001, the Beslan School Siege in the Soviet Russia in 2004, the London Underground Bombings in 2005, and the Boko Haram Insurgency (Nigeria). India has also been the victim of terrorism for long. In the recent past, several terrorist activities took place, such as bomb explosions in Mumbai in 1993, an attack on the Parliament building in New Delhi in 2001, bomb explosions on Mumbai's local trains in 2006, and a suicide bomber targeted a convoy of Indian paramilitary forces in Pulwama, Jammu and Kashmir in 2019. Studies (Kar, 2000; Shetty & Chhabria, 1997) following the Mumbai riots in 1992–93 found victims in a state of shock, fear, and helplessness; 33% expressed anger; 2% of these had attempted suicide; 21% of those interviewed had severe anxiety, 41% had paranoid thinking and obsessional symptoms; and the majority reported a loss of libido. PTSD features scored very high, a few were emotionally numb, and 36% had suicidal thoughts.

Development under Vulnerable Circumstances 269

At a young age, exposure to terrorism and violence can lead to significant psychological trauma. Children may experience anxiety, depression, nightmares, and post-traumatic stress disorder (PTSD), which can hinder their emotional and cognitive development. Terrorism often disrupts educational systems, causing children to miss out on formal schooling (UNICEF, 2018). Terrorist organizations actively target children and adolescents for recruitment, exploiting their vulnerability and impressionability. Terrorism disrupts the career aspirations and educational pursuits of young adults. As terrorism disrupts economic activities, adults face financial insecurity and psychological distress, affecting their overall mental well-being and ability to cope with challenges. Terrorism also deepens societal divisions, leading to mistrust and prejudice among adults, which hampers community cooperation and collective development (Neria et al., 2007). Thus, terrorism, fuelled by various sources such as political disenfranchisement, socio-economic factors, and ideological extremism, has profound effects on human development across different age groups.

Natural Disasters: Cyclones, Earthquakes, and Tsunamis

Natural disasters, such as cyclones, earthquakes, and tsunamis, have profound and long-lasting effects on the development of individuals across various stages of life. These disasters often result in significant physical, emotional, and socio-economic impacts, particularly on vulnerable populations, including children, adolescents, and older adults. The recent COVID-19 pandemic has also adversely affected human development to a great extent (Box 13.1).

Cyclones: The Large-Scale Tropical Storms

Cyclones, also known as hurricanes or typhoons, are large-scale tropical storms characterized by strong winds rotating around a low-pressure centre called the eye. Cyclones develop in tropical and subtropical regions when warm ocean waters evaporate, rise, and condense, releasing latent heat. At the centre of a cyclone is the eye, which is a relatively calm and clear area typically ranging from a few kilometres to tens of kilometres in diameter. The eye is surrounded by the eyewall, where the most intense winds and heaviest rainfall occur. The intensity of cyclones is measured on the Saffir-Simpson Hurricane Wind Scale (for hurricanes) or the Typhoon Intensity Scale (for typhoons). These scales range from Category 1 (weakest) to Category 5 (strongest). The Category 5 hurricanes/typhoons have wind speeds over 157 mph (252 km/hour). Cyclones bring heavy rainfall and storm surges. As the cyclone approaches land, its strong winds push ocean waters towards the coast, resulting in a surge of water that can inundate low-lying coastal areas. Some of the major cyclones that India faced recently are Cyclone Hudhud (2014), Cyclone Gaja (2018), Cyclone Fani (2019), Cyclone Amphan (2020), Cyclone Asani (2022), and Cyclone Biparjoy (2023).

Cyclones have catastrophic effects on communities, causing loss of life, damaging infrastructure, destroying homes, disrupting essential services, and disrupting economies. It also negatively influences the psychological make-up of people leading to diverse types of disorders (Norris et al., 2001). In a survey of 130 people exposed to the 1999 super cyclone (Suar & Khuntia, 2004), it was found that 50% of the survivors were suffering from PTSD, such as anxiety, externality, and depression, three months after the disaster. A higher incidence of PTSD was observed in victims belonging to a lower caste and low educational status and having obligations towards more members in large families. Mohanty (2002) found that the victims of the 1999 super cyclone had developed a "weaning syndrome", characterized by acquired dependence, the tendency to seek external support, and to continue under the safety of such support (Mohanty, 2002).

Earthquakes: A Natural Phenomenon Shaping the Earth's Surface

Throughout history, earthquakes have played a significant role in shaping landscapes and influencing the development of civilizations. Earthquakes are geological phenomena that occur due to the sudden release of energy in the earth's crust. This results in the generation of seismic waves that propagate through the earth, causing ground shaking and, in severe cases, leading to significant destruction and loss of life. The primary cause of earthquakes is the movement of tectonic plates, the large segments of the earth's crust that float on the semi-fluid asthenosphere. When these plates interact with each other, they can either collide (convergent boundary), or move apart (divergent boundary), or slide past one another (transform boundary). The stress and strain build-up at these plate boundaries leads to the sudden release of energy, resulting in an earthquake. The effects of earthquakes can range from minor tremors with no damage to catastrophic events that cause widespread destruction and loss of life. The severity of an earthquake is usually measured on the Richter scale or the moment magnitude scale (Mw). The damage caused by an earthquake depends on factors such as magnitude, depth, distance from the epicentre, local geology, and the level of preparedness of the affected community.

A few devastating earthquakes that occurred around the globe in the recent past are 2011 Tohoku Earthquake and Tsunami (Japan, Magnitude: 9.0), 2015 Nepal Earthquake (Nepal, Magnitude: 7.8), 2016 Kaikoura Earthquake (New Zealand, Magnitude: 7.8), 2017 Puebla Earthquake (Mexico, Magnitude: 7.1), 2018 Sulawesi Earthquake and Tsunami (Indonesia, Magnitude: 7.5), and 2019 Ridgecrest Earthquakes (California, United States; Magnitude: 6.4 and 7.1). India suffered the following earthquakes: the 1993 Latur Earthquake (Magnitude: 6.6), the 1997 Jabalpur Earthquake (Magnitude: 6.0), 2001 Kachchh (Gujarat) Earthquake (Magnitude: 7.7), 2004 Sumatra-Andaman Earthquake and Tsunami (Magnitude: 9.1), 2005 Kashmir Earthquake (Magnitude: 7.6), and 2011 Sikkim Earthquake (Magnitude: 6.9).

After an earthquake, the population often experiences hypervigilance, anxiety and depression, mental roadblocks, earthquake phobia, sleeping problems, and PTSD (Neria et al., 2008). PTSD is very common among young people. A study (Shrestha & Gopal, 2021) observed higher sensitivity to threats among children as a result of exposure to earthquakes in Nepal even after three years. Pistoia and colleagues (2018) studied the after-effects of the 2009 L'Aquila, Italy earthquake and found that students living in earthquake-affected areas had a general increase in anxiety and anticipation of threats. An interesting positive result was that earthquake victims developed expertise in recognizing facial expressions. It was probably because they started systematically paying attention to potential signs of approaching threats, such as emotional facial expressions.

In India, Kumar Ravi Priya (2004) studied the sufferings and healings of the 2001 Kachchh (Gujarat) earthquake after two years. The results showed that the earthquake brought socio-economic changes, such as the diffusion of caste and class boundaries, values, and mismanagement in the distribution of relief materials. Participants developed a belief in "moving on" (p. 49) in consonance with nature. In another study, Kumar (2007) trapped the children and their caretakers' versions of the 2001 Gujarat earthquake in a pilot research conducted in 2001. Children's narratives were full of themes of death, dismemberment of body parts, and procrastination of demonic hands in the disaster.

Tsunamis: The Unpredictable Oceanic Giants

The word "Tsunami" is derived from two Japanese words – "Tsu" means harbour and "nami" means wave. It is a series of extremely strong tidal waves that occur due to various ocean events, such as volcanic eruptions, earthquakes, or landslides. It is caused by underwater disturbances in the ocean, typically resulting from seismic events such as earthquakes, volcanic eruptions, or underwater landslides. Tsunamis are triggered by sudden vertical movements of the seafloor, which displace a large volume of water. Tsunamis can travel at speeds of up to 500 to 800 kilometres per hour in deep water, allowing them to cross entire ocean basins within a day. It can have wavelengths of hundreds of kilometres, making them much longer than typical wind-generated waves. In the open ocean, tsunamis may have a wave height of only a metre or less, but as they approach shallower coastal regions, they can grow to tens of metres (sometimes even over 30 metres) in height. When tsunamis reach coastal areas, their immense energy can cause widespread devastation.

Some of the recent important tsunamis worldwide are the 2004 Indian Ocean Tsunami, the 2010 Chile Earthquake and Tsunami, and the 2011 Tohoku Earthquake and Tsunami. Studies have examined the psychological and environmental effects of tsunamis. Doocy et al. (2013) reviewed the literature concerning the 2004 Indian Ocean tsunami which resulted in more than 225,000 deaths across 12 nations and the 2011 Japan tsunami which caused an estimated 28,000 deaths. Drowning was found a major cause of death and wounds, and lacerations and fractures were the major causes of injuries. Females, very young and old aged persons, were relatively more subject to death. Interestingly, it has been reported (Nobles et al., 2015) that the 2004 Indian Ocean tsunami led to an increase in the fertility rate. Mothers who lost one or more children in the disaster were significantly more likely to bear additional children after the tsunami. Also, women without children before the tsunami initiated family building earlier to rebuild the population in the affected community.

Over half the population affected by the 2004 Tsunami and surveyed indicated the need for some kind of psychosocial support (Vijaykumar et al., 2006). However, satisfactory psychosocial interventions were available only at a limited scale due to the lack of governmental facilities and coordinated care (Thara et al., 2008). It was only five years after the tsunami that the National Disaster Management Authority (NDMA) of India included psychosocial goals in its disaster plan, specifying the implementation of psychosocial support and mental health services (Padmavati et al., 2020). Srinivas (2015) studied the 2004 Indian Ocean Tsunami and its environmental impact. It was noted that the disposal of solid waste and disaster debris, contamination of soil and water, and extensive damage to environmental infrastructure, buildings and industrial sites were some of the major issues. The study highlighted the need for comprehensive capacity-building in areas such as strategic environmental assessment, integrated environmental management, coastal zone planning, and so on.

In conclusion, natural disasters such as cyclones, earthquakes, and tsunamis continue to pose significant challenges to human development and well-being. While these events are unavoidable and inherent to the earth's dynamic processes, their impacts can be mitigated through comprehensive disaster preparedness, early warning systems, and sustainable development practices. Investments in education, awareness, and capacity-building are essential to empower communities to respond effectively to the threats posed by these natural calamities. Only through a holistic approach, driven by cooperation between governments, organizations, and societies, can we minimize the human and economic toll of these disasters and foster a more resilient and sustainable future for all.

> **Box 13.1 COVID-19 and Its Impact on Human Development**
>
> The COVID-19 pandemic during the years 2020–22, caused by the novel coronavirus SARS-CoV-2, has had far-reaching consequences on various aspects of human life. Beyond its immediate health implications, the pandemic has significantly impacted human development across all stages, from prenatal to late adulthood.
>
> The pandemic introduced stressors affecting pregnant women, potentially influencing foetal development. Millions of children faced reductions in healthcare and school closures resulting in learning loss. Remote learning led to educational inequalities, exacerbating existing disparities in access to resources and support. The pandemic heightened stress and anxiety levels among adolescents, with potential long-term implications for mental health. A large number of young people lost their jobs and livelihoods. Older adults have been disproportionately affected by the virus. The isolation measures and fear of infection have contributed to declines in mental health and exacerbated existing social isolation among this population. The understanding of the effect of the pandemic is still emerging.

The Occurrence of War: Dark Aspects of Humanity

War is a state of organized and often prolonged conflict between different groups or nations, characterized by the use of armed forces and violence. Throughout human history, wars have been waged for various reasons, including territorial expansion, resource acquisition, political ideologies, religious beliefs, and economic interests. References to war can be found in numerous historical records and literary works. In the 20th century, two devastating global wars were witnessed: World War I (1914–18) and World War II (1939–45). These wars involved the majority of the world's nations, caused immense loss of life, and reshaped the geopolitical landscape. The Vietnam War (1955–75) was a prolonged conflict between North Vietnam, supported by communist allies, and South Vietnam, backed by the United States and its anti-communist allies. It left a lasting impact on both nations. The Gulf War (1990–91) was a conflict between Iraq and a coalition of nations led by the United States after Iraq invaded Kuwait. The Afghanistan and Iraq Wars, held in the post-9/11 era, saw the United States and its allies engage in conflicts in Afghanistan (2001–present) and Iraq (2003–11). In recent years, the Russo-Ukrainian war commenced in February 2022 and the Israel–Palestinian war in October 2023.

The causes of war are multifaceted and vary significantly across different contexts and historical periods. Some common factors include resource scarcity in terms of land, water, and minerals, ideological and religious differences, political and socio-economic factors (e.g., struggles for power, political control, and socio-economic disparities), and ethnic and cultural tensions driven by historical grievances or feelings of identity and superiority.

Research shows differences in the prevalence, nature, and acceptance of violent behaviour across different societies and cultures. These variations can be influenced by historical, social, economic, and political factors and a particular community's values, norms, and beliefs. For example, Triandis (1995) noted lower levels of aggression in certain situations in individualistic societies as people are encouraged to solve conflicts through peaceful means and compromise. In contrast, collectivistic societies place a higher value on group harmony and loyalty, which may lead to increased incidents of aggression when defending the group's interests or honour. In some societies (e.g., agrarian and herding), the perceived threat to one's honour leads to retaliatory violence (Nisbett & Cohen, 1996).

The consequences of aggression and war are devastating, affecting all aspects of society. Loss of countless human lives is the major consequence of war, which leaves behind grieving families and shattered communities. Violence and war force millions of people to flee their homes, leading to a global refugee crisis and humanitarian challenges. The conflict zones experience the destruction of critical infrastructure, such as schools, hospitals, and utilities, disrupting essential services for civilians. Survivors of violence and war often suffer from severe psychological trauma, leading to post-traumatic stress disorders and long-term mental health issues. Wars also impose significant economic costs on nations, leaving little room for investment in critical sectors like education, healthcare, and infrastructure. This phenomenon, often referred to as the "guns vs. butter" dilemma, inhibits the growth of human capital and the overall well-being of societies.

In conclusion, violence and war have been persistent aspects of human history, causing immense suffering and hindering societal progress. Understanding the root causes and consequences of violence and war is crucial for developing strategies to build a more peaceful and compassionate world. Efforts towards conflict resolution, empathy, and peaceful coexistence are vital for creating a future free from the devastating impact of violence and war.

Understanding Conflict and Its Resolution

Conflict can be broadly defined as a disagreement, clash, or opposition between two or more individuals or groups or ideas over differing interests, values, opinions, or goals. It is a natural part of human interactions and can occur in various contexts, such as personal relationships, workplaces, politics, or international affairs. Conflicts can arise due to a variety of factors, including misunderstandings, competition for resources, ideological differences, historical grievances, or power struggles. Deutsch (1973) differentiated between constructive and destructive conflict. Constructive conflict can lead to positive outcomes, such as problem-solving, better decision-making, and improved relationships. In contrast, destructive conflict can escalate tensions, lead to hostility, and impede resolution.

Conflict can be of different types, such as:

1) Approach–approach conflict: This type of conflict occurs when you have to choose between two desirable outcomes (i.e., you would like to have both of them, but you have to choose one of them.
2) Avoidance–avoidance conflict: This type of conflict occurs when you have to choose between two unattractive outcomes (i.e., you want to have neither of them but have to choose one).
3) Approach–avoidance conflict: This type of conflict occurs when ONE event or goal has attractive and unattractive features (i.e., you like some aspects of it but don't like other aspects.
4) Multiple approach–avoidance conflict: This type of conflict occurs when you have to choose between two or more things, each with desirable and undesirable features.

Conflict can occur at various levels. It can take the form of interpersonal (or between two or more individuals), intrapersonal (or internal struggle within an individual's thoughts, emotions, or desires), organizational (within an organization or workplace setting), intergroup (between different groups within a society, organization, or community), ideological (or opposing beliefs, values, or ideologies between individuals, groups, or nations), cultural (differences in cultural norms, customs, and practices of individuals from different cultural backgrounds or in multicultural societies), socio-economic (arising due to disparities in wealth, income, or access to resources), political (opposing political ideologies, policies, or leadership preferences), environmental (disagreements over natural resources, land use, pollution, or conservation efforts), and armed conflict/war (which necessitates the use of force and violence between organized groups). It may be noted that conflicts can sometimes overlap or evolve from one type to another. Moreover, conflicts can have both positive and negative consequences, as they may lead to growth, change, and resolution or, in extreme cases, to violence and destruction. Resolving conflicts effectively requires understanding the underlying causes, effective communication, empathy, and a willingness to find mutually agreeable solutions.

Conflict Resolution Strategies

To address conflicts effectively, various strategies and approaches can be employed (Folger et al., 2013; Pruitt & Kim, 2004). These approaches are mentioned here.

Collaboration

Collaborative conflict resolution emphasizes open communication, active listening, and joint problem-solving. Deutsch et al. (2011) highlight the significance of active listening, empathy, and mutual understanding as essential tools for effective conflict resolution. They also emphasize the value of open and honest communication in fostering collaboration and finding mutually acceptable solutions.

Compromise

Compromising involves seeking a middle ground by making concessions and reaching a mutually acceptable agreement. It requires a willingness to give up certain preferences to achieve a balanced outcome.

Accommodation

This entails yielding to the demands or wishes of others to maintain relationships or promote harmony. It may involve acts of generosity, empathy, or selflessness.

Competition

Competition involves pursuing one's interests or goals without considering the interests of others. While it can lead to quick resolutions, it may strain relationships and create winners and losers.

Avoidance

Avoidance strategies involve minimizing or ignoring conflicts altogether, often by sidestepping the issues or withdrawing from the situation. However, avoidance can lead to unresolved tensions and underlying resentments.

Developmental Changes

The use of conflict resolution strategies varies across life stages and is influenced by cognitive and emotional development. For example, Dhillon and Babu (2015) found that older children

(10-year-olds) had a larger number of conflicts over facts and opinions than their younger counterparts (6-year-olds). Physical aggression as an issue for conflict as well as a strategy to deal with conflict was more common among younger children. Peer interactions and guidance from parents and teachers play crucial roles in shaping these strategies (Hughes, 2015). In another study (Srivastava & Lalnunmawii, 1989), students from grades 4, 6, and 8 were asked to describe "What would you do if a boy of your class abuses you or if a girl of your class threatens to beat you". The responses were categorized into no conflict (e.g., do nothing or I would cry), mediated conflict (e.g., report to the teachers or parents), and direct conflict (e.g., I will hit back). More number of younger children preferred the use of direct conflict than the older children.

Adolescents are more assertive and attempt to exert control. They start experimenting with avoidance or withdrawal as a means of conflict resolution (Laursen & Collins, 2009). In adulthood, conflict resolution strategies tend to become more nuanced and varied. Adults typically have developed greater communication skills, emotional intelligence, and problem-solving abilities. They are more likely to engage in negotiation, compromise, and collaboration to resolve conflicts. In the Indian context, Gupta and her colleagues (2016) conducted a study in which 14% sample were baby boomers (born between 1946 and 1964), 17% were Generation Xers (born between 1963 and 1983), and 69% belonged to Generation Y ("millennials", born after 1983). Sixty-nine per cent of those surveyed were male. They identified two conflict resolution styles: avoidance (consisting of resignation and withdrawal) and approach-oriented (consisting of confrontation, compromise, and negotiation). Participants from three generations and genders preferred approach-based strategy over avoidance, with negotiation being the most preferred style across generations and genders. Baby boomers were found to have a significantly higher preference for confrontation than those in Generation Y. Generation Y chose withdrawal significantly more than baby boomers as their conflict resolution style. In addition, male baby boomers were more likely than female boomers to use resignation as a conflict resolution style. It is important to note that individuals within each stage may exhibit variations based on personal characteristics, experiences, and cultural influences. Additionally, conflicts themselves can differ in nature, intensity, and significance, which can further impact the choice of resolution strategies.

Cultural Variations

Different cultures approach conflicts in diverse ways, depending on their cultural norms, values, communication styles, and social structures. For example, people in individualistic cultures, emphasize assertiveness and direct communication to express one's needs and preferences in conflict resolution. In contrast, conflict resolution in collectivist cultures involves indirect communication, mediation by respected elders, and a focus on preserving group cohesion. In high-context cultures, like those in Japan, China, Korea, India, Arab countries, and many African cultures, communication is more implicit, and meaning is often embedded in the context of the situation. Conflict resolution may involve reading between the lines and understanding non-verbal cues to grasp the full meaning of a message. Low-context cultures, common in North America and Western Europe, emphasize explicit communication. Conflict resolution may be more straightforward, with individuals explicitly stating their grievances and seeking direct solutions (Hall & Hall, 1990).

Likewise, in cultures with high power distance (e.g., many Asian and African countries), there is a significant power gap between individuals or groups. Conflict resolution may involve deference to authority figures or hierarchical decision-making. In contrast, low power distance cultures (e.g., Scandinavia) may adopt more egalitarian approaches to conflict resolution (Hofstede, 1984). Also, cultures vary in their time orientation, with some emphasizing the past and tradition (e.g., Middle Eastern cultures) and others focusing on the present or future (e.g., Western cultures). This can impact the perception of time urgency (e.g., quick or delayed solutions) in conflict resolution (Hall & Hall, 1990). It is, however, essential to note that cultures are not monolithic, and individuals within a culture may still exhibit diverse conflict-resolution approaches. When dealing with cross-cultural conflicts, sensitivity to cultural differences and effective communication strategies are crucial for successful resolution.

In the Indian tradition, conflict resolution strategies are deeply rooted in cultural and philosophical principles that have evolved over centuries. These strategies aim to promote harmony, mutual understanding, and peaceful resolution of conflicts. Ahimsa (non-violence) is a fundamental principle in Indian philosophy. Indian tradition places great emphasis on dialogue and negotiation as means of resolving conflicts. The concept of "Samvad" (dialogue) encourages individuals to engage in meaningful conversations to resolve conflicts peacefully. Another widely practised strategy has been mediation and conciliation. The traditional practice of panchayats (village councils) serves as a forum for resolving disputes through mediation. The mediators, known as *Panchas*, facilitate discussions between conflicting parties and help them reach a mutually acceptable resolution. Mediation and conciliation emphasize compromise, consensus-building, and finding win-win solutions. Following *dharma* (the path of righteousness) and adopting practices such as mindfulness, self-reflection, and cultivating wisdom have been followed since ancient times for conflict resolution.

Conflict is, thus, an inevitable part of human interaction, encompassing a wide range of types and contexts. By understanding the nature and typologies of conflict, individuals and societies can develop effective strategies for conflict resolution, fostering healthier relationships and promoting constructive dialogue.

Street Children: A Vulnerable and Neglected Population

Street children are one of the most vulnerable and marginalized groups in society. The term "street children" refers to children who live and work on the streets, often without any adult supervision or protection. Described as "invisible children", they are found in urban centres and even some rural areas worldwide. The exact number of street children in India is difficult to determine due to the transient nature of their lives. However, various estimates suggest that there are about 18 million street children in India (Juris Centre, 2022). As regards the profile of street children, Mathur (2009) found that the majority of them were boys (71%); belonging to the age group 8–12 years (44%), followed by 12–16 (40%) and 5–8 (16%) of age groups. The reasons for migration to the city were (i) the search for better employment opportunities; (ii) the lure of city life; and (iii) family problems in the villages. The majority of the children lived with their families. Children worked on jobs that did not require skill training. Some of them were also involved in begging.

Street children typically come from poor families or difficult home situations, and they often leave their homes due to factors like abuse, poverty, neglect, or family breakdown. Based upon other studies, Mathur (2009) listed significant causes of working and street children in India. These are economic marginality, mass migration of rural families to urban centres, inappropriate education system, chronic poverty, unemployment, overcrowded homes, parental abuse, drug abuse, alcoholism, parents abandoning children because of economic pressures, and children running away from stressful situations at home. Another study (Dutta, 2018) found factors such as extreme poverty and a lack of awareness among illiterate parents regarding educational opportunities and healthcare to be responsible for driving children on the streets.

The consequences of life on the streets are dire. Street children face physical and emotional abuse, sexual exploitation, drug addiction, and exposure to violence. Child abuse, particularly sexual assault, is common among street children (Kacker et al., 2007). A lack of proper nutrition and healthcare leads to health issues, including high rates of malnutrition, respiratory illnesses, and infections. Their exclusion from formal education results in limited cognitive development, reducing their potential for upward mobility and socio-economic advancement. The cycle of poverty is perpetuated as street children grow up with limited access to education and job opportunities. This further marginalizes them, restricting their integration into mainstream society and reinforcing the cycle of poverty for future generations.

Nanda (2008) studied the health conditions of street children in Delhi and found that the health conditions of working street children are miserable. The majority of the available health services are out of reach of street children, and there are multiple obstacles faced by street children in accessing healthcare services. Another study (Sharma & Verma, 2013) examined the lives of girls on streets in the cities of New Delhi (India), Jakarta (Indonesia), Manila (Philippines), and Pretoria (South Africa). Results indicated that these girls were at maximum risk of being involved in antisocial activities with peers, being low on problem-solving, and high on depression and mental health-related problems.

Several governmental and non-governmental organizations in India, for example, Consortium for Street Children, SOS Children's Villages of India, Salaam Balak Trust, Butterflies, Pratham, Railway Children India, and Save the Children India, are actively working to address the needs of street children. They provide food, shelter, education, healthcare, and vocational training to help these children reintegrate into society. However, exposure to harsh reality at an early age results in a premature loss of innocence. Integrated Child Protection Scheme (ICPS) is a government-run initiative that aims to provide a safety net for vulnerable children, including street children, by establishing and strengthening child protection mechanisms at the state and district levels. It supports various programmes and services to ensure street children's safety, care, and rehabilitation. Box 13.2 provides the details of challenges faced by orphan children.

Box 13.2 Vulnerability and Resilience Among Orphaned Adolescents in Institutional Care

The vulnerable group of children includes orphans, abandoned children, victims of abuse, child trafficking survivors, those affected by HIV/AIDS, and more. With a lack of robust foster care alternatives, child-care institutions (CCIs) serve as the primary means for providing alternative care to these children. Mishra and Sondhi (2019) found that, before entering the institution, most orphaned participants had faced challenging circumstances, marked by a lack of necessities like food and clothing, an unfavourable social environment with delinquent peers, abusive and addicted adults, and an unsafe neighbourhood. A high prevalence of alcohol abuse among fathers and domestic violence within families is very common. Nearly half of the participants reported experiencing physical abuse from a parent. Abandonment, homelessness, and begging for food are also prevalent in this group of vulnerable children. From an early age, male and female children assume economic and domestic responsibilities, respectively, in the family. Parents or caregivers place these children in CCI to alleviate the financial strain of raising them.

Entering an institutional facility elicits a mix of emotions among children. While it offers a sense of security, it also requires adapting to the new environment. This phase is marked by intense crying, thoughts of running away, requests to staff to contact relatives, and repeated pleas to return home. However, the thought of previous deprived and abusive living conditions forces them to adapt to the new situation. Studies indicate that the psychological aftermath of maltreatment encompasses conduct disturbances, disruptive behavioural issues, attention disorders, and mood disorders (Sroufe et al., 2000). These challenges further impede the development of bonds with new family members, including staff and fellow residents. The most detrimental consequence of these behavioural difficulties is an unsettled state caught between a yearning to return to parents or relatives and an inability to connect with those in the institution. If left unaddressed, this internal conflict may evolve into a severe attachment disorder, affecting all aspects of a child's development and potentially leading to significant psychopathology in adulthood.

Theory of Resilience for Orphaned Adolescents in Institutional Care

Mishra and Sondhi (2021) developed a grounded theory of resilience for orphaned adolescents in institutional care that found that the pathway towards resilience has significant roots in pre-admission living circumstances. The child's immediate environment before admission is laden with numerous risk factors threatening safety and survival. In this challenging context, the child yearns to break free from suffering but faces helplessness without supportive forces. The subsequent theory delves into processes and factors reigniting the desire to overcome adversity. This renewed desire becomes a driving force, enhancing the protective value of resources post-institutional admission. Once rekindled, it serves as a motivating goal, aiding adjustment to the new residence. Additionally, aligned with certain personal and environmental factors, this desire influences two crucial periods during the institutional stay: (a) initial maintenance and (b) long-term adjustment, with the former significantly impacting the latter.

Social Reintegration: From Institution to Independence

Children in institutional care typically remain until the age of 18. Upon reaching this age, they are required to transition out to integrate into the community. Pursuing the objectives of adulthood imposes emotional and physical strains, especially for adolescents in institutions who lack the safety and support typically provided by traditional families, amplifying the challenges they face. While studies on the transition outcomes of Indian youth in care have been scarce, existing data consistently reveals various challenges experienced by care leavers (CLs). These challenges encompass difficulties in securing housing and employment, ongoing education, addressing physical and mental health issues, inadequacies in life skills and challenges in mobilizing psychosocial support (Ahuja et al., 2017, Modi et al., 2016). Recognizing these challenges, which remain mostly unaddressed by the system, Mishra et al. (2024) have proposed a mentorship curriculum to enable readiness for a successful transition of institutionalized adolescents. The curriculum covers seven core areas – creating a sense of belonging and community, preparing the adolescents for life after transition, enabling clarity on future vision and goals, building psychosocial competency, enhancing employability, promoting rational decision-making, and problem-solving.

One way to instil this readiness for transition is through ensuring ongoing adult support and guidance. Mentoring programmes, therefore, can be a potentially effective intervention strategy to improve outcomes for CLs. Mentors can offer residents the chance to acquire vital social and practical skills crucial for successful reintegration. They can also facilitate supportive social connections and the practice of essential social skills for initiating and maintaining relationships. Additionally, the mentor–resident bond acts as a protective buffer, mitigating risk factors and fostering resilience (Werner, 2005).

Rachna Mishra
University of Delhi

Overview

In conclusion, the exploration of development under vulnerable circumstances has illuminated the myriad challenges that individuals and communities face in adverse conditions. From the pervasive impact of family and community violence to the profound disruptions caused by terrorism and natural disasters, the chapters have delved into the complexities of navigating development amidst adversity. The dark aspects of humanity are unveiled in the occurrences of war, with its devastating consequences on both individuals and societies. Understanding conflict and its resolution emerges as a crucial aspect of fostering sustainable development and rebuilding shattered communities. The section on street children shed light on a particularly vulnerable and neglected population, emphasizing the need for targeted interventions and compassionate policies to address their unique challenges. Recognizing and addressing the root causes of their vulnerability is essential for promoting inclusive development.

In essence, this chapter underscores the resilience of individuals and communities in the face of adversity, highlighting the importance of comprehensive strategies that address the multifaceted nature of developmental challenges in vulnerable circumstances. Moving forward, a holistic approach that integrates social, economic, and educational interventions will be paramount for fostering sustainable development and creating a more equitable and resilient global society.

Key Terms

Accommodation	Earthquakes
Avoidance	Family Violence
Adverse Developmental Circumstances	Influences of Terrorism
Children in Orphanage	Natural Disasters
Conflict	Street Children
Conflict Resolution	Tsunamis
Cyclones	War
Developmental Changes	

Questions for Reflection

1) How do individuals in adverse circumstances experience and navigate developmental challenges, and what factors contribute to their resilience in the face of adversity?
2) Reflecting on the impact of family and community violence, what supportive interventions can be implemented to mitigate long-term effects on the safety and well-being of individuals?
3) How can societies work towards preventing radicalization and fostering resilience against the negative impacts of terrorism on individuals and communities?
4) How do traumatic events such as natural disasters and war influence the development of individuals?
5) Reflect on the plight of street children as a vulnerable and neglected population. What developmental interventions can be implemented to improve their well-being and prospects?

Suggested Further Readings

Book

UNICEF. (2020). *Mental health and psychosocial support for children in humanitarian settings: An updated review of evidence and practice.* www.corecommitments.unicef.org/kp/unicef-updated-mhpss-2020- evidence- and-practice-review.pdf

Journal Article

Peek, L. (2008). Children and disasters: Understanding vulnerability, developing capacities, and promoting resilience – An introduction. *Children and Disasters, 18*, 1–29.

Website/Online Resource

UNICEF – Children in Emergencies and Crisis Situations *(www.unicef.org/emergencies)*

14 Sustainable Development and Lifelong Learning

Contents	
Introduction	282
Nature of Sustainable Development	282
Box 14.1: Sustainable Development Goals	283
National Schemes Related to Human Development in India	284
Sustainable Development and Lifelong Learning	286
Development of Attitudes and Skills for Sustainable Development	287
Box 14.2: Development of 21st-Century Skills	288
Box 14.3: Development of Vocational Skills	289
Box 14.4: Global Citizenship Education	290
Role of Culture in Sustainable Development	291
Examples of Good Practices Across the World	292
Overview	293
Key Terms	294
Questions for Reflection	294

Learning Objectives

After studying this chapter, the learner will be able to:

Appreciate the multidimensional nature of sustainable development;
Recognize how lifelong learning empowers individuals to adapt to changing circumstances and contribute to sustainable progress;
Evaluate real-world examples of sustainable development initiatives;
Understand the symbiotic relationship between cultural diversity and sustainable development; and
Appreciate the significance of global citizenship education in fostering a sense of global interconnectedness and shared responsibility.

DOI: 10.4324/9781003441168-20

Introduction

This chapter explores the nexus of sustainable development and lifelong learning, where the imperative of nurturing an enduring, inclusive, and ecologically balanced future takes centre stage. The chapter begins by unravelling the multifaceted nature of sustainable development and sustainable development goals. It then takes you to the panorama of national schemes related to human development in India, offering a glimpse into the country's commitment to fostering sustainable growth. The role of education in shaping a responsible global citizenry is highlighted. The chapter then explores the development of attitudes and skills for sustainable development, with a focus on 21st-century skills, vocational skills, and global citizenship education. The cultural dimension takes centre stage while examining the role of culture in sustainable development, recognizing its influential role in shaping attitudes and practices. The narrative expands to showcase examples of good practices across the world, illustrating how communities and nations are steering towards sustainability. This intellectual odyssey uncovers the critical intersections that pave the way for a resilient and harmonious global future.

Nature of Sustainable Development

Sustainable development is a concept that seeks to balance economic, social, and environmental goals to meet the needs of the present generation without compromising the ability of future generations to meet their own needs. It involves using resources wisely, minimizing waste and pollution, and ensuring that development activities do not lead to the depletion of natural resources or the degradation of ecosystems.

The origins of sustainable development can be traced back to the Brundtland Report, officially known as "Our Common Future", published in 1987 by the World Commission on Environment and Development (WCED). The report defines sustainable development as "development that meets the needs of the present without compromising the ability of future generations to meet their own needs". The report emphasized the importance of intergenerational equity and highlighted the critical role of environmental conservation in achieving long-term prosperity.

Sustainable development has three main pillars: economic sustainability, social sustainability, and environmental sustainability. Economic sustainability focuses on fostering economic growth, improving the quality of life, and reducing poverty while ensuring that resources are used efficiently and do not lead to overexploitation. Social sustainability seeks to promote social inclusion, equity, and justice. It involves ensuring access to education, healthcare, and basic services for all members of society and reducing disparities between different social groups. Environmental sustainability centres on safeguarding the natural environment and conserving resources. It involves minimizing pollution, promoting renewable energy sources, protecting biodiversity, and mitigating climate change.

Various international agreements and initiatives support the implementation of sustainable development goals. One of the most notable initiatives is the United Nations' 2030 Agenda for Sustainable Development, adopted in September 2015 at the United Nations Headquarters in New York (United Nations, 2015b). This agenda consists of 17 Sustainable Development Goals (SDGs) (Box 14.1) and 169 targets aimed at addressing various global challenges, including poverty, hunger, health, education, gender equality, clean water, clean energy, climate action, and biodiversity conservation (for details, https://sdgs.un.org/goals). The Paris Agreement, adopted in 2015, is another significant global effort that aims to combat climate change and limit global warming to well below 2 degrees Celsius above pre-industrial levels. Overall, sustainable development is an ongoing process that requires cooperation and collaboration among governments, businesses, civil society, and individuals to create a more sustainable and equitable world for current and future generations.

Box 14.1 Sustainable Development Goals

Goals	Description
1	End poverty in all its forms everywhere
2	End hunger, achieve food security and improved nutrition, and promote sustainable agriculture
3	Ensure healthy lives and promote well-being for all at all ages
4	Ensure inclusive and equitable quality education and promote lifelong learning opportunities for all
5	Achieve gender equality and empower all women and girls
6	Ensure availability and sustainable management of water and sanitation for all
7	Ensure access to affordable, reliable, sustainable, and modern energy for all
8	Promote sustained, inclusive and sustainable economic growth, full and productive employment, and decent work for all
9	Build resilient infrastructure, promote inclusive and sustainable industrialization, and foster innovation
10	Reduce inequality within and among countries
11	Make cities and human settlements inclusive, safe, resilient, and sustainable
12	Ensure sustainable consumption and production patterns
13	Take urgent action to combat climate change and its impacts
14	Conserve and sustainably use the oceans, seas, and marine resources for sustainable development
15	Protect, restore, and promote sustainable use of terrestrial ecosystems, sustainably manage forests, combat desertification, and halt and reverse land degradation and halt biodiversity loss
16	Promote peaceful and inclusive societies for sustainable development, provide access to justice for all, and build effective, accountable, and inclusive institutions at all levels
17	Strengthen the means of implementation and revitalize the global partnership for sustainable development

(*Source*: https://sdgs.un.org/goals)

Psychosocial Aspects of Sustainable Development

The journal *Psychology and Developing Societies* carried out a thematic issue in 2017 (vol. 29, issue 2) on the psychosocial basis of sustainable development. In its editorial, the journal opined that psychology has entered into the discussion on sustainable development quite late. It argued that

> When sustainable development is defined as addressing the needs of the future generations without compromising on the needs of the present generation, it is left unsaid "who" defines these needs and "whose" needs are in focus. All "needs" have a social and cultural context.
>
> (Editor's Introduction, 2017, p. vii)

Therefore, there is a need to factor in local cultures and voices of people. It was further argued that there is a need to identify psychological and social pathways to develop sustainable societies.

Commenting on the role of psychology, Jaipal (2017) underscored the necessity of adopting a more holistic and culturally aware approach to effectively address the challenges of sustainable development. He called for adopting a holistic model integrating all levels of functioning (e.g., biological, psychological, environmental etc.). Indigenous theories are particularly important, which can guide in the creation of environments that promote both physical health and mental well-being and also foster societal sustainability. The research literature is replete with studies that show that socio-economic inequality negatively influences societal development (for details, see Leviaton, 2017). Based on the study of kibbutz communities, Leviaton (2017) found that physical social capital (such as socio-economic inequality) and psychosocial capital (such as social interaction and support, participatory decision-making, availability of information, involvement in the civic, social, and political activities, quality of working life, and so on) influence the levels of peoples' health and well-being.

To show how psychosocial pathways can help in building a sustainable environment, Tripathi and Singh (2017) reported a long-term social intervention effort spanning around 15 years which aimed at liberating a group of individuals trapped in debt bondage in rural India. The social capital emerged as a significant predictor of sustainability perceptions in the study. Social capital is of two types: bonding and bridging. Bonding social capital represents close ties among the members of the group and positively affects sustainability perceptions. In contrast, bridging social capital refers to connections beyond the immediate group, which negatively influences sustainability perceptions. In another study (Mishra, 2017), the quality of relationships between people, in addition to economic and health conditions, emerged as an important component of the notion of a happy life in a rural tribal community in India. These studies underscore the importance of local context that needs to be additionally factored into the larger framework of sustainable development.

National Schemes Related to Human Development in India

With a focus on human development, the Government of India has launched several schemes for the benefit of its people. Some of the important schemes are described here.

Mahatma Gandhi National Rural Employment Guarantee Act (MGNREGA)

This scheme guarantees 100 days of wage employment to every rural household whose adult members volunteer to do unskilled manual work. MGNREGA is considered a landmark legislation in India, aiming to address issues of rural unemployment and poverty by providing employment opportunities to those in need. Third-party studies show that MGNREGA has benefitted several rural households and provided social protection, livelihood security, and democratic empowerment (Government of India, 2022).

National Health Mission (NHM)

The NHM aims to provide accessible, affordable, and quality healthcare to all citizens, particularly in rural areas, with a special focus on maternal and child health services. It has, however, been observed that the mission places limited emphasis on preventive healthcare, such as health education, awareness campaigns, and immunization programmes.

Samagra Shiksha

Samagra Shiksha is a comprehensive scheme to improve the quality of school education. It is an integrated and holistic approach to address the various needs of school education in India. It aims to enhance the quality of education, bridge gender and social category gaps, provide access and infrastructure, promote vocational education and skills development, and strengthen and support the entire educational ecosystem from preschool to higher secondary levels. Samagra Shiksha has resulted in increased enrolment, improved infrastructure, increased gender parity, and enhanced teacher training (Mehta, 2023).

Pradhan Mantri Jan Dhan Yojana (PMJDY)

This financial inclusion scheme provides a range of financial services like the availability of a basic savings bank account, access to need-based credit, remittances facility, insurance, and pension to all households in the country. The scheme faces the challenge of keeping the accounts live and creating awareness among people about financial inclusion (Ravikumar, 2018).

Pradhan Mantri Awas Yojana (PMAY)

This scheme aims to provide "Housing for ALL" which includes affordable housing to all urban and rural poor by 2022. Identification of beneficiaries, quality of construction, and delays in disbursal of funds are some of the challenges of the scheme (Sharma, 2020).

National Food Security Act, 2013

Under the NFSA, subsidized food grains are provided to approximately two-thirds of the population to ensure food security. It marks a paradigm shift in the approach to food security from welfare to the rights-based approach. It covers about 75% of the rural and 50% of the urban population.

Beti Bachao Beti Padhao (BBBP)

The BBBP addresses the declining child sex ratio and promotes the education of girls. A study (Jaiswal et al., 2020) found that the campaign for BBBP has successfully created awareness in general. The study also pointed out some deficiencies, such as functional and clean toilets in schools, as a hindrance to the scheme. There has also been a gap in terms of budgetary planning and monitoring (Arora, 2022).

Swachh Bharat Abhiyan

Also known as the Clean India Mission, it is a nationwide cleanliness and sanitation campaign initiated by the Indian government. Launched on October 2, 2014, the campaign aims to make India clean and open-defaecation-free by promoting hygiene, sanitation, and waste management practices (Government of India, 2014). VerKuilen and colleagues (2023) reviewed the studies related to the success of the Swachh Bharat Mission and found that while 60% of the population in India practised open defaecation in 2016, 19% practised the same in 2021. Also, studies (e.g., Biswas et al., 2020; Caruso et al., 2022; Namdev & Narkhede, 2020) have reported that having a latrine at home does not necessarily indicate its use. Reasons for continuing with open defaecation include financial constraints, lack of water supply, governmental mistrust, cultural beliefs, and personal preference (VerKuilen et al., 2023).

Digital India

This initiative aims to transform India into a digitally empowered society and knowledge economy by expanding digital infrastructure and services. Launched in July 2015, the programme aims to leverage technology and digital infrastructure to improve governance, service delivery, and digital literacy across the nation. It has shown a positive impact in different fields (Beriya, 2021).

Skill India

The Skill India initiative aims to empower the country's workforce with employable skills. The primary goal of the Skill India movement is to bridge the gap between the demand for skilled labour and the availability of a skilled workforce.

The Fit India Movement

This movement aims to promote physical fitness and encourage people to lead an active and healthy lifestyle. The campaign aims to make fitness a part of every Indian's daily routine, regardless of age or background.

These are just a few examples of national schemes in India related to human development. These schemes are designed to foster inclusive growth. As India continues to advance on its path of human development, the successful implementation and continuous evaluation of these schemes will remain imperative for achieving sustainable and equitable growth for all its citizens.

Sustainable Development and Lifelong Learning

Sustainable development and lifelong learning are two interrelated concepts. Sustainable development is concerned with meeting the present requirements without affecting meeting the requirements of future generations. Lifelong learning emphasizes the continuous acquisition of knowledge, skills, and competencies throughout one's life. It empowers individuals to adapt to the evolving challenges of a rapidly changing world. This has been prominently included in SDG 4 (ensure inclusive and equitable quality education and promote lifelong learning opportunities for all). English and Carlsen (2019) pointed out that lifelong learning is also viewed as critical for the attainment of many other SDGs, such as gender equality (SDG 5), decent work and economic growth (SDG 8), health and well-being (SDG 3), responsible consumption and production (SDG 12), and climate change mitigation (SDG 13). Learning literacy and numeracy is a continuous aspect of lifelong learning (English & Carlsen, 2019). It fosters critical thinking, problem-solving abilities, creativity, and resilience, enabling individuals to navigate uncertainties and thrive in diverse environments.

In today's digital age, technology serves as a powerful enabler of lifelong learning. Online platforms, Massive Open Online Courses (MOOCs), and other digital resources democratize access to education, reaching individuals worldwide. Technology is required for addressing new socio-economic developments that involve automation, artificial intelligence, and big data. Supporting transversal skills development and social cohesion demands lifelong learning. This is also required in case of migration of people, both within the country and between countries, the working population, and asylum seekers. Lifelong learning encourages curiosity, a thirst for knowledge, and a commitment to ongoing self-improvement. It enables individuals to embrace change positively and seek growth opportunities.

In India, the government attempts to foster lifelong learning through schemes like the National Skill Development Mission, the Digital India initiative, and adult learning. These programmes promote skill development and digital literacy among the youth and adults. Adult education is an ongoing programme which aims to promote learning, including literacy and numeracy, vocational skills, and so on, among individuals who have crossed the age of formal schooling (15 years and above). Also, a centrally sponsored scheme of Padhna Likhna Abhiyan was launched in 2020. The Government of India has recently introduced The New India Literacy Programme (Press Information Bureau, 2022), which covers all aspects of the adult education programme. The National Education Policy 2020 has suggested adopting innovative strategies for adult education.

Thus, sustainable development and lifelong learning are inseparable pillars of societal progress, propelling humanity towards a more equitable and prosperous future. By promoting sustainable practices and empowering individuals with the capacity for continuous learning, we can tackle global challenges, such as poverty, inequality, and environmental degradation.

Development of Attitudes and Skills for Sustainable Development

Achieving sustainable development necessitates the cultivation of specific attitudes and skills among people. It is essential to equip individuals and communities with the mindset and abilities to make informed and responsible choices. It further requires cultivating a collective consciousness dedicated to preserving our planet and securing a better future for all.

Attitudinal Change

Achieving sustainability requires a fundamental shift in attitudes and behaviours across individuals, communities, governments, and businesses. Embracing responsible consumption is the first step in the direction of attitude change. Discarding "throwaway culture" and using goods and services that possess social, economic, and environment-friendly attributes (De Pelsmacker et al., 2005) is required. Individuals need to change from passive buyers into conscious agents who consider the environmental and social impacts of their choices. Threats to climate change can be minimized by adopting low-carbon lifestyles and supporting renewable energy initiatives. Research suggests that personal values and attitudes play a significant role in determining individual commitment to climate change mitigation actions (Stern, 2000). Environmental identity or the extent to which individuals perceive themselves as part of the natural environment is positively correlated with pro-environmental behaviour ((Whitmarsh, 2008). Research also suggests that future time perspectives and personality traits like agreeableness and openness are positively associated with sustainable behaviour (Eastman et al., 2019).

Biodiversity conservation is another aspect of attitudinal change. Biodiversity loss disrupts ecosystems and jeopardizes food security, clean water availability, and climate regulation. Developing a positive attitude towards nature and recognizing the intrinsic value of biodiversity is essential. Education and exposure to natural environments have been found to positively influence pro-environmental attitudes and behaviours (Chawla, 2007).

As pointed out earlier, social development is an important aspect of sustainable development. Addressing poverty, inequality, and social injustices is imperative. Empathy and a willingness to understand the perspectives of marginalized communities are key factors in promoting inclusivity (Agyeman et al., 2002). In the business sector, corporate attitudes need to shift from profit maximization to triple-bottom-line accounting (economic, social, and environmental) for long-term success. A report by UN Global Compact and Accenture (2013) emphasizes that companies' attitudes towards sustainability strongly influence their ability to adapt to a changing business landscape.

Empowering local initiatives is crucial for sustainability. Individuals and communities should take ownership of their development which fosters a sense of responsibility and ensures that solutions align with specific needs and circumstances. In this context, two mass movements in India are worth noting. The Chipko Andolan (or Embrace the Trees) during the 1970s in India aimed to protest against deforestation and promote ecological conservation. Similarly, the Narmada Bachao Andolan aimed to protest against the construction of large dams on the Narmada River. The movement advocated for the rights of displaced communities, emphasizing sustainable and equitable development.

Formal and informal education should include sustainability-related topics to raise awareness about the urgent challenges facing our planet. References like the UNESCO Education for Sustainable Development (ESD) emphasize the need for transformative learning experiences that empower individuals to become change agents for sustainable development.

Skills Required for Sustainable Development

A diverse range of skills needs to be adopted by the stakeholders to achieve sustainable development. In this context, systems thinking is a crucial skill that enables individuals to understand and analyse complex problems by considering the interactions and interdependencies among the various components of a system. It involves viewing a situation or issue as a whole and recognizing that the parts of a system are interconnected and influence each other. This approach, according to Sterman (2002), helps identify potential leverage points for positive change and minimizes unintended consequences of development initiatives. There is a need to foster skills required for success in the 21st century (Box 14.2). By fostering these skills, we can make significant strides towards creating a sustainable future for generations to come (Stafford-Smith et al., 2017).

In conclusion, the development of attitudes and skills for sustainable development is a multifaceted and dynamic process that requires the collective efforts of individuals, communities, organizations, and governments. By fostering a deep sense of responsibility and empathy towards the environment, and promoting a culture of innovation and critical thinking, we can contribute to the preservation of our planet's resources. Education plays a pivotal role in shaping attitudes and skills for sustainability. Boxes 14.3 and 14.4 contain the development of vocational skills through sustainable development and global citizenship education, respectively.

Box 14.2 Development of 21st-Century Skills

The 21st century is characterized by rapid technological advancements, globalization, and a changing economic landscape. As a result, individuals need to possess a unique set of skills to succeed in this environment. These skills enable individuals to adapt to change, collaborate with others, and solve complex problems. UNESCO (2015) has identified a set of skills that it considers essential for individuals to thrive in the modern world. It emphasizes that these skills are important for individuals to not only succeed in the modern economy but also contribute to a more peaceful, just, and sustainable world. These skills include the following.

Learning to Learn or the ability to engage in self-directed learning and adapt to new situations).

Creativity and Innovation or the ability to think creatively, generate new ideas, and develop innovative solutions to complex problems.

Critical Thinking or the ability to analyse information, evaluate evidence, and make well-reasoned judgements.

Communication and Collaboration or the ability to communicate effectively and work collaboratively with others.

Information and Media Literacy or the ability to find, evaluate, and use information from a range of sources, including digital media.

ICT (Information and Communication Technology) Literacy or the ability to use digital technologies to access, analyse, and communicate information.

Social and Emotional Skills or the ability to understand and manage emotions, develop empathy and respect for others, and work effectively in diverse teams.

Global Citizenship or the ability to understand and respect different cultures, appreciate global interdependence, and act ethically and responsibly towards the environment and society.

Box 14.3   Development of Vocational Skills

In the modern world, the development of vocational skills is essential to secure sustainable livelihoods for individuals and also to contribute to the overall socio-economic progress of a nation. For this, it is essential that people develop vocational skills that align with sustainable practices.

There are several opportunities for vocational skill development in sectors like green energy, sustainable agriculture and farming, waste management, ecotourism, and so on. For example, in the green energy sector, there are opportunities to acquire skills in solar panel installation, wind turbine maintenance, and energy-efficient construction. In India, the "Suryamitra" programme, launched by the National Institute of Solar Energy, Gurugram, has trained thousands of people in solar energy technologies, enabling them to become entrepreneurs or contribute to the country's ambitious renewable energy goals.

Likewise, vocational skills in agriculture are essential for promoting food security and reducing the ecological impact of farming practices. Initiatives like the Sustainable Agriculture Education (SAgE) Project in the United States provide hands-on training in organic farming, water conservation, and soil health. Sikkim (an Indian state) follows 100% organic farming. The state has phased out chemical fertilizers and pesticides and achieved a total ban on the sale and use of chemical pesticides in the state (Heindorf, 2019). The transition has benefitted more than 66,000 farming families. By promoting regenerative agricultural practices, these programmes contribute to preserving biodiversity and mitigating climate change.

With the escalating problem of waste management, vocational skills in recycling and waste treatment are crucial for sustainable development. In Brazil, the "Reciclar pelo Brasil" programme educates waste pickers on efficient recycling techniques, enhancing their livelihoods while reducing the environmental burden. Similarly, vocational training in ecotourism and sustainable hospitality is needed. Countries like Costa Rica have integrated sustainable tourism practices into their vocational training programmes to preserve biodiversity-rich areas and promote responsible tourism.

In India, various skill development programmes have been launched. For example, Pradhan Mantri Kaushal Vikas Yojana (PMKVY) provides skill training to youth across the country and enhances their employability. National Skill Development Corporation (NSDC) is a public-private partnership that collaborates with various training partners and organizations to promote skill development in different sectors. Focused on rural youth, Deen Dayal Upadhyaya Grameen Kaushalya Yojana (DDU-GKY) provides skill training and employment opportunities to help them secure better livelihoods. The National Council of Vocational Education and Training (NCVET) has developed National Skills Qualifications Framework and has proposed to start skill development courses in sectors like agriculture, automotive, electronics, green jobs, IT-ITes, life sciences, and telecom. Udaan is a special initiative by the Ministry of Home Affairs that provides skill development training to the youth of Jammu & Kashmir to enhance their employability. National Apprenticeship Promotion Scheme (NAPS) promotes apprenticeship training and bridge the gap between industry demands and the skills of the workforce. Several private companies, industry bodies, and NGOs run skill-training programmes to cater to the specific requirements of different sectors. These efforts have long-term implications for sustainable development.

Box 14.4 Global Citizenship Education

Global citizenship refers to the individuals' responsibilities and rights that go beyond national boundaries and act as members of a larger community worldwide. It stresses the importance of the interconnectedness of the world and working together to address global challenges such as poverty, climate change, access to healthcare measures during pandemics, migration and refugee crises due to political instability, and social injustice. According to UNESCO (2015), global citizenship involves four key competencies: (a) understanding and respecting diversity, (b) valuing human rights, (c) understanding and addressing global challenges, and (d) taking action to promote a more just and sustainable world.

Global Citizenship Education (GCE) is an educational approach that aims to develop individuals who are aware of global issues, culturally sensitive, and actively engaged in promoting a more just, equitable, and sustainable world. GCE equips individuals with the knowledge, skills, and attitudes necessary to address global challenges, embrace cultural diversity, and work collaboratively towards positive change on both local and global scales (UNESCO, 2014).

The concept of GCE has been recognized and promoted by various organizations and institutions, including the United Nations Educational, Scientific and Cultural Organization (UNESCO) and other international bodies. UNESCO, in particular, has been actively advocating for GCE to be integrated into national education policies and curricula around the world.

Different countries promote global citizenship education in their unique ways. For example, global citizenship education in Japan has been integrated into the school curriculum as part of "kokoro" (heart education). The programme encourages students to develop values such as compassion, respect, and cooperation, promoting a sense of global awareness and understanding beyond national boundaries. In South Africa, the curriculum includes elements that encourage respect for cultural differences and address historical injustices. By fostering empathy and understanding, South Africa strives to build a nation of global citizens committed to promoting peace, reconciliation, and human rights. In Canada, there is an appreciation of diverse cultures, social justice, and environmental sustainability. Initiatives like "Me to We" encourage young Canadians to take action on global issues and make a positive impact on the world. The curriculum in the United Arab Emirates incorporates lessons on tolerance, peaceful coexistence, and appreciation for diverse perspectives. By fostering a spirit of global citizenship, the UAE aims to contribute to a more interconnected and harmonious world.

The value system in India emphasizes several key principles that are relevant to fostering global citizenship. Some key elements of the Indian value system related to global citizenship education include respect for diversity, Ahimsa (non-violence), *vasudhaiva kutumbakam* (the world is one family), inclusiveness and social justice, tolerance and acceptance, *seva* (service to others), living in harmony with nature, and so forth. These values provide a foundation for individuals to develop a sense of global responsibility and contribute positively to the world community. The National Curriculum Framework (NCF) 2005 and the National Education Policy 2020 recognize the importance of holistic education and have emphasized the need to foster values of global citizenship, environmental consciousness, and ethical behaviour among students. Furthermore, various non-governmental organizations and educational institutions have taken initiatives to promote global citizenship education. However, challenges remain, including the need for a comprehensive and systematic integration of global citizenship education across all levels of education.

Role of Culture in Sustainable Development

Culture is a reservoir of wisdom, offering insights into sustainable living practices that have evolved over centuries. One can observe diverse practices across cultures that have been followed by generations having implications for sustainable development. For instance, India's agricultural practices have been heavily influenced by cultural traditions and knowledge. Over generations, many farmers follow agroecological methods, such as intercropping and mixed cropping, which promote biodiversity, reduce the need for chemical inputs, and enhance soil fertility. Agroecology is beneficial for production of both a huge quantity as well as good quality food, medicinal crops, etc. (Tripathi et al., 2015). Terrace farming is widely practised in the hilly regions of India to prevent soil erosion and conserve water.

India is home to numerous sacred groves and areas of forests protected by local communities due to their religious and cultural significance. These groves are considered sacred spaces dedicated to deities and spirits. As a result, they remain untouched and serve as crucial biodiversity hotspots. The preservation of sacred groves reflects the cultural reverence for nature and contributes to the conservation of rare and endangered plant and animal species. Several regions in India, particularly in arid and semi-arid areas, have developed traditional water harvesting systems. For instance, the "baoli" (stepwell) in Rajasthan is an ancient structure that collects and stores rainwater during the monsoon season for use throughout the year. The handicraft traditions in India use eco-friendly and locally sourced materials. Artisans employ sustainable techniques in their crafts, such as natural dyeing, handloom weaving, and upcycling materials. Supporting traditional handicrafts not only preserves cultural heritage but also fosters sustainable livelihoods for local communities. These examples and several other practices highlight the significance of India's cultural traditions in promoting sustainable development.

Like India, terrace farming is also practised in China and Peru, which prevents soil erosion and conserving water resources (Deng et al., 2021). The Maasai people in Kenya have practised pastoralism for centuries, adopting rotational grazing methods to prevent overgrazing and maintain the health of grasslands. Their traditional practices exemplify a sustainable approach to livestock management that preserves natural ecosystems.

Ecotourism is another way of fostering sustainable development. Ecotourism is defined as "responsible travel to natural areas that conserves the environment, sustains the well-being of the local people, and involves interpretation and education" (The International Ecotourism Society, 2015). Tourists are involved in the observation and appreciation of nature as well as traditional culture. The Government of Karnataka has developed ecotourism treks in districts including Bengaluru, Bellagavi, and Bellari. The Guna Yala (San Blas) indigenous community in Panama manages its tourism activities sustainably, preserving its cultural traditions, pristine environment, and unique way of life. By sharing their culture with visitors, they encourage cultural appreciation and environmental awareness.

Bhutan presents a unique approach to development. It focuses on Gross National Happiness, which emphasizes maintaining the balance between material well-being, environmental conservation, and cultural preservation. This philosophy guides policymaking in the country, resulting in initiatives such as the preservation of forests and biodiversity, the promotion of organic agriculture, and the prioritization of happiness and well-being over pure economic growth (The Centre for Bhutan & GNH Studies, 2023).

India's rich cultural heritage has influenced various sustainable development practices over the centuries. For example, Indian farmers possess a wealth of traditional knowledge related to agricultural practices, seed saving, and pest management. This knowledge has been honed over generations and is often region-specific.

Examples of Good Practices Across the World

Good practices for sustainable development related to energy generation, waste management, reforestation, subjective well-being, etc., are being followed throughout the world. Some of these practices are mentioned in this section.

In the field of renewable energy, Costa Rica has made significant progress primarily through hydropower, wind, geothermal, and solar resources (*France 24*, 2023). In 2017, the country ran on 100% renewable energy for 300 consecutive days. Sweden has successfully implemented a waste-to-energy programme, where more than 99% of household waste is converted into energy. The country imports waste from neighbouring countries to maintain a constant supply for its energy plants. Germany has embarked on an ambitious energy transition to phase out nuclear and coal power in favour of renewable energy sources. This transition has resulted in significant growth in renewable energy capacity and a move towards a more sustainable energy system. Masdar City is a planned sustainable urban development project in Abu Dhabi, UAE. It aims to be a carbon-neutral city, powered entirely by renewable energy sources.

San Francisco has implemented innovative waste management strategies, achieving high recycling and composting rates. The city has also banned plastic bags and Styrofoam containers to reduce plastic pollution. The successful implementation of these initiatives has made San Francisco one of the leading cities in the United States in terms of sustainable waste management practices (United States Environmental Protection Agency, 2023). The Netherlands has embraced the concept of a circular economy, aiming to reduce waste and maximize resource efficiency. Initiatives include sustainable product design, recycling, and remanufacturing processes. The Dutch government collaborates with businesses and citizens to promote circularity, reducing the environmental impact of goods and services.

In 2019, Ethiopia launched the Green Legacy Initiative, a massive reforestation campaign to plant four billion trees in four years. This initiative aims to combat deforestation, enhance biodiversity, and mitigate climate change impacts. The country achieved significant milestones, including planting more than 350 million trees in a single day.

Rather than solely focusing on economic growth, Bhutan measures its progress using the Gross National Happiness (GNH) index, which considers factors like environmental conservation, cultural preservation, and social well-being. This holistic approach to development has led to policies prioritizing sustainable practices and promoting citizen well-being.

India has also been actively engaged in various sustainable development practices. The Jawaharlal Nehru National Solar Mission is one of the world's largest renewable energy expansion plans. Its goal is to increase the capacity of solar power in India to 100 GW. The state of Gujarat has a solar power policy that encourages the development of solar projects, both utility-scale and rooftop installations. The Rewa Solar Park in the state of Madhya Pradesh is one of the world's largest single-site solar power projects exemplifying India's commitment to renewable energy expansion.

The Pradhan Mantri Ujjwala Yojana (PMUY), launched in 2016, aims to provide clean cooking fuel to poor households, especially in rural areas. The scheme offers free LPG (liquefied petroleum gas) connections to eligible women from below-poverty-line families. The Swachh Bharat Abhiyan is another example. India has been actively involved in reforestation efforts to combat deforestation and biodiversity loss. Several states have undertaken tree-planting drives to increase forest cover. For example, in the state of Maharashtra, the government launched the "Miyawaki" method of afforestation, which involves planting a diverse mix of native tree species to restore ecosystems and improve environmental conditions. These examples demonstrate India's commitment to sustainable development and environmental conservation.

Thus, sustainable development and lifelong learning are interconnected pillars essential for fostering resilient societies. By promoting ongoing education and skill acquisition throughout individuals' lives, we empower them to contribute to sustainable development, addressing environmental, economic, and social challenges for a harmonious and equitable future.

Overview

The concept of sustainable development embodies the synergy between societal progress, economic growth, and environmental responsibility. It is an ongoing journey that demands a comprehensive understanding of the intricate interplay between these elements. The concept of sustainable development also needs to incorporate the psychosocial characteristics of people. In India, various national schemes have been devised to bolster human development, emphasizing the significance of education, healthcare, and skill enhancement. The amalgamation of sustainable development principles with lifelong learning cultivates a potent tool for individual empowerment, enabling people to chart a course towards a more promising future.

Sustainable development nurtures a holistic set of attitudes and skills essential for its realization. Through initiatives like vocational skill development, individuals are equipped with practical expertise that aligns with sustainable practices, amplifying their potential contribution to society. Global citizenship education further fosters a sense of interconnectedness, underlining the shared responsibility to safeguard the planet's health and prosperity.

The linkage between cultures and sustainable development emphasizes the importance of preserving diverse traditions while embracing modernity. This harmonious coexistence is vital for ensuring that development is not only ecologically sound but also culturally enriching. Encouragingly, numerous instances of commendable sustainable development practices can be observed worldwide. These range from innovative renewable energy projects to community-driven conservation efforts, showcasing the feasibility and effectiveness of sustainable approaches.

In a world striving for equilibrium between advancement and preservation, sustainable development, coupled with lifelong learning, emerges as a beacon of hope. As we navigate the complexities of our era, we must continue to cultivate a shared commitment to fostering a balanced, inclusive, and prosperous future for all. Through synergizing education, development, and environmental stewardship, we can collectively embark on a transformative journey that transcends boundaries and paves the way for a more harmonious world.

Key Terms

Attitudes and Skills for Sustainable Development
Cultures and Sustainable Development
Development of 21st-Century Skills
Development of Vocational Skills
Economic Competencies and Sustainability
Fostering a Connected World
Good Practices Related to Sustainability
Global Citizenship Education
Human Development in India
National Schemes
Skills
Sustainable Development
Sustainable Development Goals
Sustainable Development and Lifelong Learning

Questions for Reflection

1) How does the nature of sustainable development align with your values and understanding of societal progress?
2) Reflecting on the Sustainable Development Goals, which goal resonates with you the most, and how do you perceive your role in contributing to its achievement?
3) In the context of lifelong learning, how can the development of attitudes and skills for sustainable development enhance an individual's adaptability and resilience in the face of evolving challenges?
4) What is needed to foster a mindset of responsible and informed citizenship for sustainable development?
5) How can cultural diversity be leveraged as a strength to promote sustainability, and what challenges might arise in incorporating cultural perspectives into sustainable development initiatives?

Suggested Further Readings

Books

Brundtland, G. H. (1987). *Brundtland report: Our common future*. United Nations.
Kolbert, E. (2014). *The sixth extinction: An unnatural history*. Henry Holt and Company.
Sachs, J., Kroll, C., Lafortune, G., Fuller, G., & Woelm, F. (2021). *The decade of action for the sustainable development goals: Sustainable development report 2021*. Cambridge University Press.
Wals, A. E. J., & Corcoran, P. B. (2012). *Learning for sustainability in times of accelerating change*. Wageningen Academic Publishers.

Websites/Online Resources

Coursera – Sustainable Development Courses
MIT OpenCourseWare – offers free access to course materials on sustainability
United Nations Sustainable Development Goals (SDGs) Platform
World Economic Forum – Sustainable Development Impact

Glossary of Sanskrit Terms

Abhidhā (अभिधा): Verbal power to convey the literal meaning of words. It is the potency of words to convey their conventional dictionary meaning.
Abhyudaya (अभ्युदय): Prosperity; progress; development.
Adhyavasāya (अध्यवसाय): Study; reflection.
Ahaṃkāra (अहंकार): Ego sense. Conception of one's individuality. The making of self; egotism; Awareness of the existence of I.
Ahiṃsā (अहिंसा): Non-violence; harmlessness. It is one of the Yamas in Yoga which requires abstention of injury to any life. The practice of mental, verbal, and behavioural Ahimsa develops friendship with all beings and forms a universal principle (Maha Vrata). The term has not merely the restrictive meaning of non-killing, but the positive and comprehensive meaning of "love embracing all creation". Mahatma Gandhi used it in this sense.
Ānandamaya (आनन्दमय): Blissful sheath; Beatitude.
Anitya (अनित्य): Non-eternal; Temporary.
Annaprāśana (अन्नप्राशन): A saṃskāra in which a baby is given food. It is held when the child is between five and eight months old and is fed with solid food for the first time.
Antaḥkaraṇa (अन्तःकरण): Conscience, internal or inner instrument, often used to refer to mind.
Antyeṣṭi (अन्त्येष्टि): Last saṃskāra; cremation performed after death and includes shrāddha rites. It involves paying homage to departed ancestors. Prayers are offered to gods.
Anubhāva (अनुभाव): Overt expressions accompanying the durable (Sthayi) and transitory (Vyabhicari) emotions (bhavās). They are of verbal, physical, and physiological types.
Anumāna (अनुमान): Inference or deduction. It is a method of knowing (pramāna).
Apar ā vidyā (अपरा विद्या): Lower level of knowledge as held in Adavita Vedanta. It deals with the phenomenal world through sensory experience and reason. The higher level of knowledge (parā vidyā) is attained in altered states of consciousness such as the fourth state (turiyavastha).
Artha (अर्थ): Meaning; purpose; wealth; One of the puruṣārthas (life goals).
Āsana (आसन): Posture; It is a state of perfect firmness of body and provides delight.
Asmitā (अस्मिता): Ego-consciousness; I-ness; The sense of "I" am. It is the identification of the seer with the instrumental power of seeing. The difference between the seer Ātmā and the instrument that sees buddhi is necessary.
Āśrama (आश्रम): A hermitage; There are four Āśramas or stations in life: brahmacharya (studentship), gṛhastha (the household), vanaprastha (living in the jungle), and sannyasa (ascetic).
Ātmā (आत्मा): The Self; The principle of life.
Avidyā (अविद्या): Generally lack of knowledge; ignorance, partial knowledge; It is reflected in mistaking the transient for permanent, the impure for the pure, pain for pleasure, and not self for self. It is the source of all the other obstacles. Patanjali designates avidyā as the breeding ground of all affliction.
Bhakti (भक्ति): Devotion or love; channelling of the intellect, emotions and self towards a higher purpose, devotion to god or a deity.
Bhavā (भाव): Emotion.
Bhoga (भोग): Enjoyment or suffering; Experiencing the fruits of one's actions; Feelings of pleasure and pain.
Brahmā (ब्रह्म): Expanding one. All embracing divine spirit, cosmic principle of reality, supreme reality. Indivisible, ubiquitous, formless, infinite, eternal, indescribable three aspects being, consciousness

and bliss sat-chit-anand. The supreme being, the cause of the universe, the all-pervading spirit of the universe.

Buddhi (बुद्धि): Intellect; discrimination; aspect of mind closest to pure consciousness; one of three aspects of the inner instrument antaḥkaraṇa.

Buniyādī Tālīma (बुनियादी तालीम): A scheme of education initiated by Mahatma Gandhi at Wardha. It emphasized on holistic education involving use of mind, hand, and heart.

Ćitta (चित्त): The stuff of consciousness realized as memory, cognitive processes, ego, instinctual tendencies from earlier lives' vāsanās and saṃskāras.

Ćūḍākaraṇa (चूड़ाकरण): Tonsure; it is held during a male child's first and seventh year of life. This involves shaving (mundana) of the boy's head.

Dāna (दान): Charity, helping, giving, doing good to others, it should be selfless and has religious moral feeling.

Daya (दया): Mercy, sympathy for the suffering of others, compassion. Benevolence, kindness, favour.

Dharma (धर्म): Duty; the righteous way of living, characteristics; duties appropriate for one's station in life; one of the four puruṣārthas.

Dhyāna (ध्यान): Meditation, absorption in the object of meditation.

Duḥkha (दुख): Suffering, sorrow, pain.

Gṛhastha (गृहस्थ): House holder, second station (Āsramas) of human life.

Guṇa (गुण): A single thread, a quality, property, an attribute; three major strands or components of prakṛti, the primordial materiality of the universe i.e., sattva, rajas, and tamas referring to tranquillity, activity, and inertia, respectively.

Guru Śiṣya (गुरु शिष्य): Teacher-disciple; they constitute one unit called sandhi and teaching was exploration (Sandhan); in traditional Gurukul, the Guru promoted holistic development of the student.

Indriya (इन्द्रिय): Sense; hearing, touch, sight, taste, and smell known as jnanendriyas.

Itihāsa (इतिहास): It means this is how it was; thus indeed it was; it tells about what happened in the past; Ramayana and Mahabharata, Valmiki and Vyasa.

Jitendriya (जितेन्द्रिय): One who has full control over the senses/passions.

Jñāna (ज्ञान): Cognition, wisdom, knowledge of reality.

Kāma (काम): Wish, desire, longing; desire for love; god of love and passion; one of the puruṣārthas.

Kāma Sūtra (काम सूत्र): A text attributed to Vatsyayana related to sexuality, eroticism, and emotional fulfilment; considering this as part of puruṣārthas philosophy and theory of love, nature of love, finding a partner, maintaining one's love life. It was composed in third century BC. It's a popular reference to erotic ancient literature.

Kāraṇa Śarīra (कारण शरीर): There are three bodies: gross body Sthula Śarīra, subtle body Sukshma Śarīra, and causal body Kāraṇa Śarīra. It is causal body merely the cause or seed of the subtle body and the gross body.

Karma (कर्म): Action; work; deeds; It includes any type of action including thought and feeling. There are three kinds of karma: sanchita accumulated actions, prayārabdha a portion of karma allowed for being worked out, and agami actions of the future.

Karṇa Vedha (कर्ण वेध): Ear-piercing occurs between the ninth and the twelfth months. It was performed on boys and girls both. Now it is restricted to girls.

Karuṇā (करुणा): Compassion, pity, tenderness. Action to alleviate the suffering of the afflicted ones.

Kleśa (क्लेश): Affliction, pain or suffering, obstacles disturbing the equilibrium of the mind.

Koṣa (कोष): Sheath; Tatttiriya Upanishad states Jiva as a multi-layered entity consisting of five nested sheaths, with the body on the outside (annamaya), followed by bodily functions (pranamaya), sensory capacities (monomaya), cognitive functions (vijnanamaya), and blissfulness (ananandamaya).

Lakṣaṇa (लक्षणा): Indication; a kind of power of words.

Lakṣmī (लक्ष्मी): The goddess of beauty and fortune, consort of Vishnu.

Madhyamā (मध्यमा): Vak as goddess of speech and divine entity. The conceptualization of speech is in terms of four stages. Parā, Paśyantī, Madhyamā, and Vaikhari. Human beings speak only the fourth level. Para represents the transcendental consciousness. Madhyama (middle) represents the mental consciousness. It is intermediate unexpressed state of sound. The language we speak is vaikhari. It represents the physical consciousness. It is the manifest and grossest level of speech form of speech. Pashyanti is the first visible manifestation of speech and less subtle than para vak.

Manana (मनन): Mind-generated understanding. Its rational understanding.

Mānasa (मानस): The mind. It has capabilities for differentiation and integration and for doubting and deciding. Also, used for the aggregate of Ćitta, buddhi, mānasa, and ahaṃkāra.

Mokṣa (मोक्ष): Release or emancipation; freedom from transmigration from the perpetual chain of actions and their consequences and the consequent cycle of birth, death, and rebirth. The state of embodied liberation is called jivanmukta.

Nididhyāsana (निदिध्यासन): Continuous or persistent contemplation; last stage of self-realization.

Nidrā (निद्रा): The state of sleep is when there is an absence of awareness thus cessation of bodily experience can be termed as sleep. In waking state, one gets drawn out into the external world. It is a state of forgetfulness of the world.

Nirvāṇa (निर्वाण): Eternal bliss; liberated from existence.

Niṣkāma Karma (निष्काम कर्म): Performing actions over which people have control but there is no desire for their fruits. Action is always superior to inaction. By not bothering about fruits, the individual remains in peace. The fruits of actions are bound to come to the doer of actions performing actions.

Nitya (नित्य): Eternal, everlasting, constant.

Nivṛtti (निवृत्ति): Non attachment; life path of renunciation; no false ego or sense of lordship; attention is directed inward, it allows peace and fulfilment; inward contemplation leads to desire lessness. Turning inward and being uninfluenced by worldly desires.

Niyama (नियम): Principle, The second limb of Patanjali yoga. It has four components i.e. sauch (cleanliness), santosha (contentment), svadhyaya (self-study/reflection), and ishvar pranidhana (surrender to a higher power/god); if these qualities develop, then a good society is built. Kriya yoga talks about tapah (austerity), svadhyaya, and ishvar pranidhana.

Nyāya (न्याय): It literally means justice, rules, or judgment. It is one of the six orthodox schools of Indian philosophy. It emphasizes logic and epistemology. Nyaya sutra is ascribed to Gautam. This system accepts perception, inference, comparison, and testimony of reliable (Apta) people.

Oṃ (ॐ): The sacred syllable om is composed of a, u, and m; Universal mantra considered to be origin of all mantras; cosmic vibration of universe; same as sacred syllable Aum, called pranava.

Pañca Karma (पञ्च कर्म): A method to cleanse the body of the unwanted waste after lubricating it. It includes preventive, curative, and promotive interventions for various diseases. These include vaman, virechana, basti, nasya, and raktamokshana. Thus, they involve laxative measures, herbal enemas, vomiting therapies, nasal rinsing, and phlebotomy.

Prajñā (प्रज्ञा): Faculty of insight; wisdom; awareness.

Prāṇamaya (प्राणमय): The sheath consisting of vital air. It involves vital forces and the psychic nervous system.

Prāṇāyāma (प्राणायाम): Control of the subtle life forces breath/prana, often by means of special breathing practices. Breath control.

Prārabdha Karma (प्रारब्ध कर्म): Actions, deeds in the past life; sanchita karma which is seen through the present body.

Pratyāhāra (प्रत्याहार): It denotes conquest of senses and mind. Drawing back, restraining and withdrawal of senses, mind and consciousness from contact with external objects and then drawing them inwards towards the seer. This is the foundation of renunciation. Pratyahara is the outcome of the practice of yama, niyama, asana, and prāṇāyāma.

Pravṛtti (प्रवृत्ति): Rolling forward; moving onward, advance, manifestation, approach. Path of action.

Puruṣārtha (पुरुषार्थ): Life goals; these include Dharma, Artha, Kāma, and Mokṣa; It provides an inclusive approach to life. Dharma is central and other goals need to be pursued in consonance with dharma.

Rāga (राग): Desire, passion, pleasure; Pleasure leads to desire and emotional attachment. It is an affliction. Attending to pleasurable experiences ignites desire and a sense.

Rajas (रजस्): One of the three gunas/strands of prakṛti. It is the active principle, roughly equivalent to energy.

Rāmāyaṇa (रामायण): Epic attributed to sage Valmiki. It provides narrative account of the life of Lord Rama, the 7th incarnation of Lord Vishnu. It has been adapted and rewritten in many Indian and foreign languages. Ram Rajya is famous model of administration devoted to social welfare and well-being of the people.

Ṛṇa (ऋण): The Indian view of life maintains that an individual is born in society and has obligations to those people (e.g. parents, teachers, other living beings) who nurture and provide support. An individual is indebted to them and tries to respect them and extend support to them. This forms the basis of intergenerational communication, cultural continuity, and maintenance of values in society.

Śabda (शब्द): Word. The words of trustworthy persons who have attained knowledge aptā are sources of knowledge. Bhartrihari has observed that all knowledge is illumined through the word.

Sadguṇa (सद्गुण): Positive qualities, virtues.

Samādhi (समाधि): It is the last stage of yoga sadhana. At the peak of meditation, the sādhaka moves to this state. His body and senses are at rest and his faculties of mind and reason are alert as if he is awake, yet he has gone beyond consciousness. There is no duality between the knower and the known.

Saṃnyāsa (संन्यास): Renunciation. The fourth stage in the Āśrama scheme. The person renounces worldly and materialistic pursuits and dedicates life to spiritual pursuits. A form of asceticism.

Saṃskāra (संस्कार): Impressions left behind by experiences and actions that are considered as shapers of future experiences and behaviours.

Saṃtati (संतति): Offspring; a person's child.

Saṃvāda (संवाद): Discussion between two individuals.

Sāṅkhya (साङ्ख्य): A school of Indian philosophy founded by sage Kapil. It enumerates 25 tattvas which constitute the whole universe. These include puruṣa (cosmic spirit), prakṛti (cosmic substance), mahat (cosmic intelligence), ahaṃkāra (individuating principle), mānasa (cosmic mind), indriyas (ten abstract sense powers of cognition and action), tanmatras (five subtle elements – sound, touch, form, flavour, and odour), and mahabhutas (five sense particulars – the great elements of ether (space), air, fire, water, and earth).

Śarīra (शरीर): The body enveloping the soul. Vedanta advances three frames of body. 1. Sthula, the gross frame, consisting of the anatomical sheath of nourishment (annamaya kośa), it is material and perishable body which is destroyed at death, 2. Sukshma, the subtle frame, consisting of the physiological sheath (pranamaya kośa) including the respiratory, circulatory, digestive, nervous, endocrine, execratory, and genital systems, the psychological sheath (manomaya kośa), functions of awareness, feeling and motivation, and the intellectual sheath (vijnanamay kośa) affecting the intellectual processes of reasoning and judgment derived through subjective experience, and 3. Karana the causal frame, consisting of the spiritual sheath of joy (anandamaya kośa).

Sarvidaya (सर्वोदय): Universal uplift. Desire for progress of all. Mahatma Gandhi used it as the ideal for his philosophy and work. Saint Vinoba Bhave used it to ensure equality in society.

Sattva (सत्व): One of the three components of guṇas of prakṛti in Samkhya school. It is characterized by illumination, subtlety, and lightness. It is considered as the finest quality of mind.

Satya (सत्य): Truth, real, genuine, honest, virtuous. It is one of the Yamas in Yoga thought.

Śiṣya (शिष्य): See Guru Śiṣya.

Smṛti (स्मृति): Memory; recollection; refers to scriptures/code of law (e.g. Yajnavalkya Smṛti).

Śravaṇa (श्रवण): Listening; knowing from sensory data; study.

Sthitaprajña (स्थितप्रज्ञ): State of transcendence through control of sensory input by mind control practices. Establishment in divine consciousness, one established in wisdom, whose intellect is stable. Firm in judgment or wisdom, free from any hallucination.

Sukha (सुख): Happiness.

Suṣupti (सुषुप्ति): A stage of consciousness, the state of the mind in dreamless sleep.

Svapna (स्वप्न): Dream.

Svarāja (स्वराज): Self-rule.

Svasti (स्वस्ति): Well-being.

Tamas (तमस्): One of three gunas of prakriti; darkness or ignorance, one of the three qualities or constituents of everything in nature.

Tāṇḍava (ताण्डव): A special dance performed by Lord Siva.

Tri Doṣa (त्रिदोष): Three body humours. Body is made up of tissues dhatus, waste products malas and doshas energetic forces. Tri Doṣa – vata, pitta, and kapha assist in the creation of various tissues of the body and to remove any unnecessary waste product from the body. They influences all the activities of body and mind. They are dynamic energies balancing doṣa in the body are necessary. Vata is characterized by the mobile nature of wind, air energy, pitta embodies the transformative nature of fire energy, and kapha reflects the binding nature of water energy.

Tṛpti (तृप्ति): Complete satisfaction.

Turīyavsstha (तुरीय): Fourth state.

Tyāga (त्याग): Renunciation.

Upanayana (उपनयन): Thread ceremony. It takes place during the child's eighth year. It symbolizes the child's readiness for receiving sacred knowledge. The boy wars a sacred thread of three strands.

Vaikharī (वैखरी): A state of vak or speech. See Madhyama.

Vāta (वात): One of the doṣas. See Tri Doṣa.

Veda (वेद): Knowledge; The sacred texts considered as revealed literature sruti, consisting of four collections samhitas called Rgveda – hymns to gods, Samveda -priest's chants, Yajurveda – sacrificial formulae in prose, and Atharvaveda – magical chants. They are called Apaurusheya. Each Veda has broadly two divisions i.e. mantra and brahmana; the latter includes Aranyaka (theology) and Upanishads (philosophy).

Vibhāva (विभाव): Causal factors related to rasa. Some are primary on which the emotions rest (alamban) and other are exciting (uddipan) causes. They reinforce the basic emotional tone.

Vidyā (विद्या): Knowledge. It has two types parā and aparā. Knowledge purifies and leads to emancipation.

Vidyārambha (विद्यारम्भ): Beginning of studies; performed when the child commences education. Usually takes place in the fifth year at the child's home. The gods are invoked and worshiped. The child pays homage to the teacher. The teacher writes some characters and recites them one by one. As the child repeats them consecutively.

Vijñānamaya Koṣa (विज्ञानमय कोष): See Koṣa.

Vīrya (वीर्य): Vigour, strength, virility, enthusiasm.

Vivāha (विवाह): Marriage is one of the saṃskāras. It is the beginning of grihastha asrama.

Vyabhicārī (व्यभिचारी): Transitory emotions. These minor emotions are diverse. Sage Bharat has identified 33 such emotions including repose or withdrawal (nirveda), debility or weakness (glāni), jealousy (asuyā), pride (mada), indolence (ālasya), depression (dainya), anxiety (cintā), shame (vridaā), agitation (āvega), and joy (harṣa).

Vyañjanā (व्यञ्जना): Suggested meaning. It indicates suggestion of the emotion through the primary meaning. Thus, it shows expansion of meaning far beyond the literal sense. It adds beauty and glory to the poem by suppression in expression.

Yajña (यज्ञ): Derived from Sanskrit root yaj, it means to worship and offering. It is a ritual involving sacrifice, devotion, offering, oblations, and libations. It involves acts to do good without expecting anything in return. It is a ceremony with an actual or symbolic offering. The five great yajña include bhuta yajña (offered to living beings), manushya yajña (sacrifice to fellow human beings), pitr- yajña (sacrifice to ancestors), deva yajña (sacrifice to gods), and brahma yajña (sacrifice to Brahmanas). In essence, these are sacred duties to be performed as a way of life for living in harmony. To this end, we need to recognize our right place within the larger scheme of things. We should be sensitive to ourselves, to others, and to the environment.

Yama (यम): The first limb of yoga consisting of satya (truthfulness), ahimsā (abstention of injury to any life), asteya (non-stealing), aparigrah (not being acquisitive), and brhamacarya (celibacy).

Yoga (योग): Joining, union, yoking; a system of spiritual development; a school of Indian philosophy; systematized by sage Patanjali, it has eight limbs: *yama, niyama, āsana, prāṇāyama, pratyāhara, dharanā, dhyāna,* and *samādhi.*

References

Acharya, A., Vankar, G. K., & De Sousa, A. (2018). An exploratory study of fears among adolescent students from an urban cohort in India. *International Journal of Adolescent Medicine and Health*, *30*, 20160003. https://doi.org/10.1515/ijamh-2016-0003.

Adlakha, D., Krishna, M., Woolrych, R., & Ellis, G. (2020). Neighbourhood supports for active ageing in urban India. *Psychology and Developing Societies*, *32*, 254–277.

Adolph, K. E. (2008). The growing body in action: What infant locomotion tells us about perceptually guided action. In R. Klatzy, M. Behrmann, & B. MacWhinney (Eds.), *Embodiment, ego-space, and action* (pp. 275–321). Erlbaum.

Afridi, F., Barooah, B., & Somanathan, R. (2014). *School meals and classroom attention: Evidence from India*. Mimeo and Indian Statistical Institute.

Agrawal, S. (2023, July 21). The silent home: Exploring the impact of 'empty nest syndrome' on parents. *Indian Express*. https://indianexpress.com/article/lifestyle/life-style/empty-nest-syndrome-parents-children-relationship-mental-health-challenges-loneliness-8737188/

Agyeman, J., Bullard, R. D., & Evans, B. (2002). Exploring the nexus: Bringing together sustainability, environmental justice and equity. *Space and Polity*, *6*, 77–90.

Ahmed, A., & Hammarstedt, M. (2011). The effect of subtle religious representations on cooperation. *International Journal of Social Economics*, *38*, 900–910.

Ahn, S., & Miller, S. A. (2012). ToM and self-concept: A comparison of Korean and American children. *Journal of Cross-Cultural Psychology*, *43*, 671–686.

Ahuja, C., Bensley, A., Huh, J., Levy, J., Nayar-Akhtar, M., & Gupta-Ariely, S. (2017). Transitioning OSC mental health profiles: A two-year longitudinal study of aftercare and alumni from Udayan Care. *Institutionalised Children Explorations and Beyond*, *4*, 40–51.

Ahuja, K. K., Banerjee, D., Chaudhary, K., & Gidwani, C. (2021). Fear, xenophobia and collectivism as predictors of well-being during Coronavirus disease 2019: An empirical study from India. *International Journal of Social Psychiatry*, *67*, 46–53.

Ainsworth, M. D. S., Blehar, M. C., Waters, E., & Wall, S. (1978). *Patterns of attachment: A psychological study of the strange situation*. Lawrence Erlbaum.

Akerlof, G. A., & Shiller, R. J. (2015). *Phishing for phools: The economics of manipulation and deception*. Princeton University Press.

Algoe, S. B. (2012). Find, remind, and bind: The functions of gratitude in everyday relationships. *Social and Personality Psychology Compass*, *6*, 455–469.

Allik, J., & McCrae, R. R. (2004). Toward a geography of personality traits: Patterns of profiles across 36 cultures. *Journal of Cross-Cultural Psychology*, *35*, 13–28.

Allport, G. W. (1937). *Personality: A psychological interpretation*. Holt, Rinehart, and Winston.

American Psychological Association. (2019). *Stress effects on the body*. APA. www.apa.org/topics/stress/body.

Ammerman, N. T. (2013). *Sacred stories, spiritual tribes: Finding religion in everyday life*. Oxford University Press.

Anand, K., & Kaura, N. (2020). The effect of peer pressure on value orientation of adolescents and young adults. *International Journal of Indian Psychology*, *8*, 774–782.

Anand, P., Bakhshi, A., Gupta, R., & Bali, M. (2021). Gratitude and quality of life among adolescents: The mediating role of mindfulness. *Trends in Psychology*. https://doi.org/10.1007/s43076-021-00077-z

Anandalakshmy, S. (1994). *The girl child and the family. A study in 22 Centres in India*. Development of Women and Child Development, Ministry of HRD, Government of India.

Anandalakshmy, S. (2013). Through the lens of culture: Studies on childhood and education in India. In D. P. Chattopadhyaya (Gen Ed.), *History of science, philosophy and culture in Indian civilization (vol XIII, part 3, G. Misra, Ed.), Psychology and psychoanalysis* (pp. 191–218). Centre for Studies in Civilizations.

Anandalakshmy, S., & Bajaj, M. (1982). Childhood in the weaver's community in Varanasi: Socialisation for adult roles. In D. Sinha (Ed.), *Socialization of the Indian child* (pp. 31–38). Concept.

Anandalakshmy, S., Chaudhary, N., & Sharma, N. (2008). *Researching families and children: Culturally appropriate methods*. SAGE.

Anderson, B. (2006). *Imagined communities: Reflections on the origin and spread of nationalism*. Verso Books.

Anderson, C. A., Berkowitz, L., Donnerstein, E., Huesmann, L. R., Johnson, J. D., Linz, D., & Wartella, E. (2003). The influence of media violence on youth. *Psychological Science in the Public Interest, 4*, 81–110.

Aneesh Kumar, P., Toney, S. G., & Sudesh, N. T. (Eds.). (2018). *Character strength development: Perspectives from positive psychology*. SAGE.

Angom, S. (2008). *Good practices of mid-day meal scheme in Manipur*. NUEPA.

Annett, M. (2002). *Handedness and brain asymmetry: The right shift theory*. Psychology Press.

Appadurai, A. (1996). *Modernity at large: Cultural dimensions of globalization*. University of Minnesota Press.

Arnett, J. J. (1999). Adolescent storm and stress, reconsidered. *American Psychologist, 54*, 317–326.

Arnett, J. J. (2000). Emerging adulthood: A theory of development from the late teens through the twenties. *American Psychologist, 55*, 469–480.

Arnett, J. J. (2004). *Emerging adulthood: The winding road from the late teens through the twenties*. Oxford University Press.

Arnett, J. J. (2007). Emerging adulthood: What is it, and what is it good for? *Child Development Perspectives, 1*, 68–73.

Arnett, J. J. (2015). *Emerging adulthood: The winding road from late teens through the twenties* (2nd ed.). Oxford University Press.

Arora, A. (2022). *'Beti Bachao, Beti Padhao' scheme: A critical analysis*. Observer Research Foundation.

Aruna, A., Jain, S., Choudhary, A. K., Ranjan, R., & Krishnan, L. (1994). Justice rule preference in India: Cultural or situational effect? *Psychological Studies, 39*, 8–17.

ASER. (2024). *ASER 2023 beyond basics- rural*. ASER.

Atkinson, R. C., & Shiffrin, R. M. (1968). Human memory: A proposed system and its control processes. In K. W. Spence & J. T. Spence (Eds.), *The psychology of learning and motivation* (Vol. 2, pp. 89–195). Academic Press.

Awasthi, P., Mishra, R. C., & Singh, S. K. (2018). Health-promoting lifestyle, illness control beliefs and well-being of the obese diabetic women. *Psychology and Developing Societies, 30*, 175–198.

Aydlett, L. (2011). Neonatal behavioral assessment scale (NBAS). In S. Goldstein & J. A. Naglieri (Eds.), *Encyclopedia of child behavior and development* (pp. 1004–1005). Springer.

Azuma, H., & Kashiwagi, K. (1987). Descriptions for an intelligent person: A Japanese study. *Japanese Psychological Research, 29*, 17–26.

Babu, N. (2009). *Development of theory of mind and mental state language in children*. Concept Publications.

Baddeley, A. D., & Hitch, G. J. (1974). Working memory. In G. H. Bower (Ed.), *The psychology of learning and motivation* (Vol. 8, pp. 47–89). Academic Press.

Balasundaram, P., & Avulakunta, I. D. (2022). *Bayley scales of infant and toddler development*. StatPearls Publishing.

Baldwin, J. M. (1895). *Mental development in the child and the race: Methods and processes*. Macmillan.

Baltes, P. B. (1987). On the incomplete architecture of human ontogeny: Selection, optimization, and compensation as foundation of developmental theory. *American Psychologist, 52*, 366–380.

Baltes, P. B., & Baltes, M. M. (1990). Psychological perspectives on successful aging: The model of selective optimization with compensation. In P. B. Baltes & M. M. Baltes (Eds.), *Successful aging: Perspectives from the behavioral sciences* (pp. 1–34). Cambridge University Press.

Baltes, P. B., & Reese, H. W. (1984). *Life-span developmental psychology: Introduction to research methods*. Lawrence Erlbaum Associates.

Baltes, P. B., & Smith, J. (2008). The fascination of wisdom: Its nature, ontogeny, and function. *Perspectives on Psychological Science, 3*, 56–64.

Baltes, P. B., Staudinger, U. M., Maercker, A., & Smith, J. (1999). People nominated as wise: A comparative study of wisdom-related knowledge. *Psychology and Aging, 14*, 411–426.

Bandura, A. (1977). *Social learning theory*. General Learning Press.

Bandura, A. (1986). *Social foundations of thought and action: A social cognitive theory*. Prentice-Hall.

Bandura, A. (1997). *Self-efficacy: The exercise of control*. W.H. Freeman.

Bandura, A., Ross, D., & Ross, S. A. (1961). Transmission of aggression through imitation of aggressive models. *Journal of Abnormal and Social Psychology, 63*, 575–582.

Banerjee, A. V., & Duflo, E. (2007). The economic lives of the poor. *Journal of Economic Perspectives, 21*, 141–167.

Banerjee, A. V., & Duflo, E. (2011). More than 1 billion people are hungry in the world. *Foreign Policy, 186*, 66–72.

Bar-On, R. (1997). *The emotional quotient inventory (EQ-I): Technical manual*. Multi-Health Systems.

Barac, R., Bialystok, E., Castro, D. C., & Sanchez, M. (2014). The cognitive development of young dual language learners: A critical review. *Early Childhood Research Quarterly, 29*, 699–714.

Bard, P. (1928). A diencephalic mechanism for the expression of rage with special reference to its inhibitory control. *Archives of Neurology and Psychiatry, 20*, 254–272.

Barry, H., & Paxson, L. M. (1971). Infancy and early childhood: Cross-cultural codes 3. *Ethnology, 10*, 466–508.

Basu, S., Zuo, X., Lou, C., Acharya, R., & Lundgren, R. (2017). Learning to be gendered: Gender socialization in early adolescence among urban poor in Delhi, India, and Shanghai, China. *Journal of Adolescent Health, 61*, S24–S29.

Batson, C. D., Ahmad, N., Lishner, D. A., & Tsang, J.-A. (2002). Empathy and altruism. In C. R. Snyder & S. J. Lopez (Eds.), *Handbook of positive psychology* (pp. 485–498). Oxford University Press.

Baumeister, R. F., Campbell, J. D., Krueger, J. I., & Vohs, K. D. (2003). Does high self-esteem cause better performance, interpersonal success, happiness, or healthier lifestyles? *Psychological Science in the Public Interest, 4*, 1–44.

Baumrind, D. (1991). The influence of parenting style on adolescent competence and substance use. *Journal of Early Adolescence, 11*, 56–95.

Baveja, B. (2019). Culture, cognition, and pedagogy. In G. Misra (Ed.), *Psychology: Vol 1: Cognitive and affective processes* (pp. 61–110). Oxford Academic.

Bayley, N. (2006). *Bayley scales of infant and toddler development* (3rd ed.). Harcourt Assessment.

Behera, J., & Acharya, S. S. (2020). Assessing the impact of ICDS on child undernutrition status in India. *Man & Development, XLII*. http//www.crrid.res.in/journal.

Bem, D. J. (1967). Self-perception: An alternative interpretation of cognitive dissonance phenomena. *Psychological Review, 74*, 183–200.

Benet-Martínez, V., & Karakitapoğlu-Aygün, Z. (2003). The interplay of cultural syndromes and personality in predicting life satisfaction: Comparing Asian Americans and European Americans. *Journal of Cross-Cultural Psychology, 34*, 38–60.

Berger, K. S. (2011). *The developing person through the life span*. Worth Publishers.

Beriya, A. (2021). *Digital India programme: Going full circle* (ICT India Working Paper #56. Center for Sustainable Development). Earth Institute, Columbia University.

Berk, L. E. (2017). *Child development*. Pearson.

Berman, J. J., Murphy-Berman, V., & Singh, P. (1985). Cross-cultural similarities and differences in perceptions of fairness. *Journal of Cross-Cultural Psychology, 16*, 55–67.

Bevli, U., Ghuman, P. A. S., & Dasen, P. R. (Eds.). (1989). *Cognitive development of the Indian child*. NCERT.

Bhangaokar, R., Gokhale, A., Pasta, S., & Roy, G. (2023). *Triguna (Sattva, Rajasa and Tamasa)* personality traits and *Karma Yoga*: Developmental trends among Indian adults. *Psychological Studies, 68*, 502–511.

Bhangaokar, R., & Kapadia, S. (2009). At the interface of 'dharma' and 'karma': Interpreting moral discourse in India. *Psychological Studies, 54*, 96–108.

Bhangaokar, R., & Kapadia, S. (2019). Gendered boundaries, cultured lives: The underexplored dimensions of duty (Kartavya) in the Indian family context. *Psychology and Developing Societies, 31*, 252–282.

Bhangaokar, R., & Kapadia, S. (2021). Human development research in India: A historical overview. In G. Misra, N. Sanyal, & S. De (Eds.), *Psychology in modern India: Historical, methodological, and future perspectives* (pp. 281–297). Springer.

Bharti, T., & Rangnekar, S. (2019). Employee optimism in India: Validation of the POSO-E. *Benchmarking: An International Journal, 26*, 1020–1032.

Bhaskar, K., Watode, K. J., Kishore, J., & Kohli, C. (2015). Prevalence of stress among school adolescents in Delhi. *Indian Journal of Youth and Adolescent Health, 2*, 4–9.

Bhatia, K. V., & Pathak-Shelat, M. (2019). *Challenging discriminatory practices of religious socialization among adolescents: Critical media literacy and pedagogies in practice.* Palgrave Macmillan.

Bhatia, S., & Ram, A. (2001). Rethinking 'acculturation' in relation to diasporic cultures and postcolonial identities. *Human Development, 44*, 1–18.

Bhatia, T. K. (2017, June 28). *Bilingualism and multilingualism from a socio-psychological perspective.* Published online. https://doi.org/10.1093/acrefore/9780199384655.013.82.

Bhatia, T. K., & Ritchie, W. C. (2004). *Bilingualism in South Asia: Pedagogical perspectives.* Multilingual Matters.

Bhattacharyya, P., & Pradhan, R. K. (2015). Perceived paternal parenting style and proactive coping strategies of Indian adolescents. *International Journal of Psychological Studies, 7*, 180. https://doi.org/10.5539/ijps.v7n2p180

Bhattacharyya, R. (2016). Street violence against women in India: Mapping prevention strategies. *Asian Social Work and Policy Review, 10*, 311–325.

Bhawuk, D. P. S. (2011). *Spirituality and Indian psychology: Lessons from the Bhagavad Gita.* Springer Science & Business Media. https://doi.org/10.1007/978-1-4419-8110-3

Bhawuk, D. P. S. (2021). Prema in Kabir's Sakhi: Indigenous perspective on love. In C.-H. Mayer & E. Vanderheiden (Eds.), *International handbook of love: Transcultural and transdisciplinary perspectives* (pp. 223–242). Springer Nature.

Bhogle, S. (1981). Socialization among different cultures. In D. Sinha (Ed.), *Socialization of the Indian child* (pp. 3–10). Concept.

Bhogle, S. (1983). Antecedents of dependency behaviour in children of low social class. *Psychological Studies, 28*, 92–95.

Bhogle, S. (1991). Child rearing practices and behaviour development of a girl child. *Indian Journal of Social Work, 52*, 61–69.

Bialystok, E. (2017). The bilingual adaptation: How minds accommodate experience. *Psychological Bulletin, 143*, 233–262.

Bigler, R. S., & Liben, L. S. (2007). Developmental intergroup theory: Explaining and reducing children's social stereotyping and prejudice. *Current Directions in Psychological Science, 16*, 162–166.

Biswas, R., Arya, K., and Deshpande, S. (2020). More toilet infrastructures do not nullify open defecation: A perspective from squatter settlements in megacity Mumbai. *Applied Water Science, 10*, 96–99. https://doi.org/10.1007/s13201-020-1169-4

Biswas-Diener, R., & Diener, E. (2006). The subjective well-being of the homeless, and lessons for happiness. *Social Indicators Research, 76*, 185–205.

Bjorklund, D. F. (2023). *Children's thinking: Cognitive development and individual differences* (7th ed.). SAGE.

Blakemore, S. J., & Choudhury, S. (2006). Development of the adolescent brain: Implications for executive function and social cognition. *Journal of Child Psychology and Psychiatry, 47*, 296–312.

Blascovich, J., & Mendes, W. B. (2010). Social psychophysiology and embodiment. In S. T. Fiske, D. T. Gilbert & G. Lindzey (Eds.), *Handbook of social psychology* (Vol. 1, pp. 194–227). John Wiley & Sons.

Bonds, S. (2012). *Food for thought: Evaluating the impact of India's mid day meal program on educational attainment* [Undergraduate Honors Thesis]. University of California.

Bone, J. K., & Fancourt, D. (2022). *Arts, Culture & the brain: A literature review and new epidemiological analyses.* Arts Council England.

Boroditsky, L. (2001). Does language shape thought? Mandarin and English speakers' conceptions of time. *Cognitive Psychology, 43*, 1–22.

Borum, R. (2004). *Psychology of terrorism.* University of South Florida.

Bowlby, J. (1969). *Attachment and loss, Vol. 1: Attachment.* Basic Books.

Brazelton, T. B. (1992). *Touchpoints: Your child's emotional and behavioral development.* Addison-Wesley.

Bronfenbrenner, U. (1979). *The ecology of human development.* Harvard University Press.

Brown, B. (2018). *Dare to lead: Brave work. Tough conversations. Whole hearts.* Random House.

Brown, B. B., & Larson, J. (2009). Peer relationships in adolescence. *Handbook of Adolescent Psychology, 2*, 74–103.

Brown, B. B., Larson, J., & Saraswathi, T. S. (Eds.). (2002). *The world's youth: Adolescence in eight regions of the globe*. Cambridge University Press.
Bruneau, E. G., Pluta, A., & Saxe, R. (2012). Distinct roles of the "shared pain" and "theory of mind" networks in processing others' emotional suffering. *Neuropsychologia, 50*, 219–31.
Bruner, J. S. (1961). The act of discovery. *Harvard Educational Review, 31*, 21–32.
Bruner, J. S. (1983). *Child's talk: Learning to use language*. Norton.
Bruner, J. S. (1990). *Acts of meaning*. Harvard University Press.
Bruner, J. S. (1996). *The culture of education*. Harvard University Press.
Buchanan, C. M., Romer, D., Wray-Lake, L., & Butler-Barnes, S. T. (2023). Editorial: Adolescent storm and stress: A 21st century evaluation. *Frontiers in Psychology, 14*, https://doi.org/10.3389/fpsyg.2023.1257641.
Budhia, M., Neogi, R., & Rathi, M. (2022). Empty nest syndrome: Its prevalence and predictors in middle aged adults in Eastern India. *Indian Journal of Psychiatry, 64*. https://doi.org/10.4103/0019-5545.341672.
Bulletin of Registrar General of India. (2022). *Bulletin on maternal mortality*. https://censusindia.gov.in/census.website/data/SRSMMB
Burns, W. E. (2001). *The scientific revolution: An encyclopedia*. ABC-CLIO.
Cabeza, R., Albert, M., Belleville, S., Craik, F. I. M., Duarte, A., Grady, C. L., Lindenberger, U., Nyberg, L., Park, D. C., Reuter-Lorenz, P. A., Rugg, M. D., Steffener, J., & Rajah, M. N. (2018). Maintenance, reserve and compensation: The cognitive neuroscience of healthy ageing. *Nature Reviews Neuroscience, 19*, 701–710.
Callaghan, T., Rochat, P., Lillard, A., Claux, M. L., Odden, H., & Itakura, S. (2005). Synchrony in the onset of mental-state reasoning: Evidence from five cultures. *Psychological Science, 16*, 378–384.
Campbell, J. C. (2002). Health consequences of intimate partner violence. *The Lancet, 359*, 1331–1336.
Cannon, W. B. (1927). The James-Lange theory of emotions: A critical examination and an alternative theory. *The American Journal of Psychology, 39*, 106–124.
Carlson, B. M. (2019). *Human embryology and developmental biology* (6th ed.). Elsevier.
Carr, L. (2022). *12 inspiring quotes from B.K.S. Iyengar*. www.doyou.com/12- inspiring-quotes-from-b-k-s-iyengar-guru/.
Carraher, T. N., Carraher, D., & Schliemann, A. D. (1985). Mathematics in the streets and in schools. *British Journal of Developmental Psychology, 3*, 21–29.
Caruso, B. A., Sclar, G. D., Routray, P., Nagel, C., Majorin, F., & Sola, S., Koehne, W. J., & Clasen, T. (2022). Effect of a low-cost, behaviour-change intervention on latrine use and safe disposal of child faeces in rural Odisha, India: A cluster-randomised controlled trial. *Lancet Public Health, 6*, e110–e121. https://doi.org/10.1016/s2542-5196(21)00324-7
Carver, C. S., & Scheier, M. F. (2014). Dispositional optimism. *Trends in Cognitive Sciences, 18*, 293–299.
Case, R. (1992). The role of central conceptual structures in the development of children's thought. *Monographs of the Society for Research in Child Development, 57*, 1–138.
Caspi, A., Harrington, H. L., Milne, B., Amell, J. W., Theodore, R. F., & Moffitt, T. E. (2003). Children's behavioral styles at age 3 are linked to their adult personality traits at age 26. *Journal of Personality, 71*, 495–513.
Cattell, R. B. (1946). *Description and measurement of personality*. World Book.
Cattell, R. B., Cattell, A. K., & Cattell, H. E. P. (1993). *16PF Fifth Edition Questionnaire*. Institute for Personality and Ability Testing.
Cattell, R. B., Eber, H. W., & Tatsuoka, M. M. (1970). *Handbook for the Sixteen Personality Factor Questionnaire (16PF)*. Institute for Personality and Ability Testing.
Cattell, R. B., & Schuerger, J. M. (2003). *Essentials of 16PF assessment*. John Wiley & Sons.
Centre for Policy Research. (2019). *Towards an understanding of citizenship education in India: A multi-city study*. Centre for Policy Research.
Chadda, R. K., & Deb, K. S. (2013). Indian family systems, collectivistic society and psychotherapy. *Indian Journal of Psychiatry, 55*, S299–309. https://doi.org/10.4103/0019-5545.105555.
Chadha, N., & Misra, G. (2006). Prosocial reasoning and behaviour among Indian children: A naturalistic study. *Psychology and Developing Societies, 18*, 167–199.
Chakkarath, P. (2013). Indian thoughts on human psychological development. In D. P. Chattopadhyaya (Gen Ed.), *History of science, philosophy and culture in Indian civilization (vol XIII, part 3, G. Misra, Ed.), Psychology and psychoanalysis* (pp. 167–190). Centre for Studies in Civilizations.
Chakraborty, C., Afreen, A., & Pal, D. (2021). Crime against women in India: A state level analysis. *Journal of International Women's Studies, 22*, 1–18.

Chakraborty, R., & De, S. (2019). Be(com)ing a woman: Body, authority and society. *Psychology and Developing Societies, 31*, 283–314.

Chakraborty, T., & Jayaraman, R. (2019). School feeding and learning achievement: Evidence from India's midday meal program. *Journal of Development Economics, 139*, 249–265.

Chandna, S., Sharma, P., & Moosath, H. (2022).The mindful self: Exploring mindfulness in relation with self-esteem and self-efficacy in Indian population. *Psychological Studies, 67*, 261–272.

Chao, R. K., & Tseng, V. (2002). Parenting of Asians. In M. H. Bornstein (Ed.), *Handbook of parenting* (Vol. 4, pp. 59–93). Lawrence Erlbaum.

Chaplin, T. M., & Aldao, A. (2013). Gender differences in emotion expression in children: A meta-analytic review. *Psychological Bulletin, 139*, 735–765.

Chatterjee, S., Banerjee, N., Chatterjee, S., Bardhan, S., Saha, S., & Mukherjee, S. (2022). Cognitive ability improvement in Indian classical dancing: A study in Bengalee females. In D. Chakrabarti, S. Karmakar, & U. R. Salve (Eds.), *Ergonomics for design and innovation* (pp. 727–737). Springer.

Chaturvedi, V. (2001). Causality of Karmic justice. *Journal of Indian Council of Philosophical Research, 18*, 129–156.

Chaudhary, A., Girdhar, S., & Soni, R. K. (2009). Epidemiological correlates of domestic violence in married women in the urban area of Ludhiana, Punjab, India. *International Journal of Health, 9*, 1–5.

Chaudhary, N. (2004). Moral reasoning of Indian adolescents. *Journal of Moral Education, 33*, 179–193.

Chaudhary, N. (2013). *Parent beliefs, socialisation practices and children's development in Indian families: A report*. University Grants Commission (Major research project).

Chaudhary, N., Gupta, D., & Kapoor, S. (2021). Social conventions and moral obligations in young children's care: Illustrations from rural families of northern India. *Psychology and Developing Societies, 33*, 258–287.

Chaudhary, N., & Shukla, S. (2019). Family, identity and the individual in India. In G. Misra (Ed.), *Psychology, Vol. 2: Individual and social, processes and issues* (pp. 143–189). Oxford University Press.

Chauhan, S. D. (2011). *A study of mid-day meal programme in the government primary schools of Gwalior city of Madhya Pradesh*. http://shodhganga.inflibnet.ac.in/handle/10603/32848

Chawla, L. (2007). Childhood experiences associated with care for the natural world: A theoretical framework for empirical results. *Children, Youth and Environments, 17*, 144–170.

Cheavens, J. S., Feldman, D. B., Woodward, J. T., & Snyder, C. R. (2006). Hope in cognitive psychotherapies: On working with client strengths. *Journal of Cognitive Psychotherapy, 20*, 135–145.

Chen, C. S., & Farruggia, S. (2002). Culture and adolescent development. *Online Readings in Psychology and Culture, 6*. https://doi.org/10.9707/2307-0919.1113

Chen, F. S., Boucher, H. C., & Tapias, M. P. (2006). The relational self-revealed: Integrative conceptualization and implications for interpersonal life. *Psychological Bulletin, 132*, 151–179.

Chen, M. J. (1994). Chinese and Australian concepts of intelligence. *Psychology and Developing Societies, 6*, 101–117.

Chen, X., & Padilla, A. M. (2019). Role of bilingualism and biculturalism as assets in positive psychology: Conceptual dynamic GEAR model. *Frontiers in Psychology, 10*. www.frontiersin.org/articles/10.3389/fpsyg.2019.02122.

Cheng, F. K. (2020). From an aging person to an elegant senior: A humanistic approach to viewing older adults. *Frontiers of Nursing, 3*, 191–202.

Choi, I., & Nisbett, R. E. (2000). Cultural psychology of surprise: Holistic theories and recognition of contradiction. *Journal of Personality and Social Psychology, 79*, 890–905.

Chomsky, N. (1957). *Syntactic structures*. Mouton de Gruyter.

Chomsky, N. (1965). *Aspects of the theory of syntax*. MIT Press.

Choudhery, A., & Kaur, G. (2018). Social competence: Imperative for adolescents. *IMPACT: International Journal of Research in Humanities, Arts and Literature, 6*. 25–40.

Cobb, N. J. (1995). *Adolescence: Continuity, change, and diversity*. Mayfield Publishing Company.

Cocodia, E. A. (2014). Cultural perceptions of human intelligence. *Journal of Intelligence, 2*, 180–196.

Cohen, D., Shin, F., & Liu, X. (2019). Cultural psychology of money. In D. Cohen & S. Kitayama (Eds.), *Handbook of cultural psychology* (2nd ed., pp. 599–629). The Guilford Press.

Cole, M. (1996). *Cultural psychology: A once and future discipline*. Harvard University Press.

Collins, D., Morduch, J., Rutherford, S., & Ruthven, O. (2009). *Portfolios of the poor: How the world's poor live on $2 a day*. Princeton University Press.

Coma, C. L., & Hancock, J. T. (2010). Reading between the lines: Linguistic cues to deception in online dating profiles. *Journal of Communication, 60*, 413–433.

Commons, M. L., & Richards, F. A. (2003). Four postformal stages. In J. Demick & C. Andreoletti (Eds.), *Handbook of adult development* (pp. 199–219). Kluwer Academic/Plenum Publishers.

Cooley, C. H. (1902). *Human nature and the social order*. Scribner.

Coren, S. (1993). *The left-hander syndrome: The causes and consequences of left-handedness*. Vintage.

Coren, S., & Halpern, D. F. (1991). Left handedness: A marker for decreased survival fitness. *Psychological Bulletin, 109*, 90–103.

Cornelius, D. J. K., & Balakrishana. (2012). Inclusive education for students with intellectual disability. *Disability, CBR and Inclusive Development, 23*, 81–83.

Costa, P. T., Jr., & McCrae, R. R. (2008). The revised NEO Personality Inventory (NEO-PI- R). In G. J. Boyle, G. Matthews, & D. H. Saklofske (Eds.), *The SAGE handbook of personality theory and assessment, Vol. 2. Personality measurement and testing* (pp. 179–198). SAGE.

Covey, S. R. (2013). *The 7 habits of highly effective people: Powerful lessons in personal change*. Simon & Schuster.

Cramer, H., Anheyer, D., Lauche, R., & Dobos, G. (2018). A systematic review of yoga for major depressive disorder. *Journal of Affective Disorders, 241*, 632–647.

Crittenden, P. M. (1990). Internal representations of attachment relationships in mothers and their toddlers in India. *Child Development, 61*, 857–870.

Cruz-Jentoft, A. J., Bahat, G., Bauer, J., Boirie, Y., Bruyère, O., Cederholm, T., Cooper, C., Landi, F., Rolland, Y., Sayer, A. A., Schneider, S. M., Sieber, C. C., Topinkova, E., Vandewoude, M., Visser, M., Zamboni, M., Writing Group for the European Working Group on Sarcopenia in Older People 2 (EWGSOP2), and the Extended Group for EWGSOP2. (2019). Sarcopenia: Revised European consensus on definition and diagnosis. *Age and Ageing, 48*, 16–31.

Crystal, D. (2003). *English as a global language* (2nd ed.). Cambridge University Press.

Crystal, D. (2006). *How language works*. The Overlook Press.

Csikszentmihalyi, M. (1990). *Flow: The psychology of optimal experience*. Harper & Row.

Csikszentmihalyi, M. (1996). *Creativity: The psychology of discovery and invention*. Harper Perennial.

Csikszentmihalyi, M. (1997). *Finding flow: The psychology of engagement with everyday life*. Basic Books.

Csikszentmihalyi, M. (2008). *Flow: The psychology of optimal experience* (2nd ed.). Harper Perennial Modern Classics.

Cummins, J. (1979). Cognitive/academic language proficiency, linguistic interdependence, the optimum age question, and some other matters. *Working Papers on Bilingualism, 19*, 121–129.

Dalal, A. K. (2006). Social interventions to moderate discriminatory attitudes: The case of the physically challenged in India. *Psychology, Health & Medicine, 11*, 374–382.

Darling, N., & Steinberg, L. (1993). Parenting style as context: An integrative model. *Psychological Bulletin, 113*, 487–496.

Darwin, C. (1859). *On the origin of species by means of natural selection, or the preservation of favoured races in the struggle for life*. John Murray.

Das, J. P. (1994). Eastern views of intelligence. In R. J. Sternberg (Ed.), *Encyclopedia of human intelligence* (pp. 387–391). Macmillan.

Das, J. P. (2013). Indian perspectives on intelligence and consciousness: From antiquity to modernity. In D. P. Chattopadhyaya (Gen Ed.), *History of science, philosophy and culture in Indian civilization (vol XIII, part 3, G. Misra, Ed., Psychology and psychoanalysis* (pp. 479–513). Centre for Studies in Civilizations.

Das, J. P., & Dash, U. N. (1989). Schooling, literacy and cognitive development: A study in rural India. In C. K. Leong & B. S. Randhawa (Eds.), *Understanding literacy and cognition* (pp. 217–244). Plenum.

Das, J. P., & Naglieri, J. A. (1997). *Cognitive assessment system*. John Wiley & Sons.

Das, J. P., Naglieri, J. A., & Kirby, J. R. (1994). *Assessment of cognitive processes: The PASS theory of intelligence*. Allyn & Bacon.

Das, S. (2022). *The Hindu concept of three bodies: Body, mind, and existence*. www.sanskritimagazine.com/hindu-concept-three-bodies-body-mind-existence/

Das Gupta, M. (1996). Life course perspectives on women's autonomy and health outcomes. *Health Transition Review, 6*, 213–231.

Dasen, P. R. (2022). Culture and cognitive development. *Journal of Cross-Cultural Psychology, 53*, 789–816.

Dasen, P. R., & Mishra, R. C. (2011). Introduction: The cultural context of schooling. In P. R. Dasen & R. C. Mishra (Eds.), *Handbook of cultural psychology* (pp. 1–20). The Guilford Press.

References

Dasgupta, U., Mani, S., Sharma, S., & Singhal, S. (2023) Social identity, behavior, and personality: Evidence from India. *The Journal of Development Studies*, *59*, 472–489.

Dash, D. (2015). Effectiveness of storytelling approach in inculcating values identified by NCERT among the 6th grade learners of Odisha state. *Scholarly Research Journal for Interdisciplinary Studies*, *3*, 2583–2590.

Dash, M. (1991). *Analysis of cognitive and speech related processes in relation to reading efficiency and IQ* [Unpublished M.Phil. Dissertation]. Utkal University.

Dash, U. N., & Mahapatra, S. (1989). Development and differentiation of simultaneous and successive planning processes. *Psychological Studies*, *34*, 75–83.

Davidson, R. J., & Scherer, K. R. (2019). *Handbook of affective sciences*. Oxford University Press.

Dawson, J. L. M. B. (1977). Alaskan Eskimo hand, eye, auditory dominance and cognitive style. *Psychologia*, *20*, 121–35.

De Pelsmacker, P., Driesen, L., & Rayp, G. (2005). Do consumers care about ethics? Willingness to pay for fair-trade coffee. *Journal of Consumer Affairs*, *39*, 363–385.

DeCasper, A. J., & Fifer, W. P. (1980). Of human bonding: Newborns prefer their mothers' voices. *Science*, *208*, 1174–1176.

Deci, E. L., & Ryan, R. M. (1985). *Intrinsic motivation and self-determination in human behavior*. Springer Science & Business Media.

Deci, E. L., & Ryan, R. M. (2000). The "what" and "why" of goal pursuits: Human needs and the self-determination of behaviour. *Psychological Inquiry*, *11*, 227–268.

Deng, C., Zhang, G., Liu, Y., Nie, X., Li, Z., Liu, J., & Zhu, D. (2021). Advantages and disadvantages of terracing: A comprehensive review. *International Soil and Water Conservation Research*, *9*, 344–359.

Denham, S. A. (1998). *Emotional development in young children*. The Guilford Press.

Denham, S. A., Blair, K. A., DeMulder, E., Levitas, J., Sawyer, K., Auerbach-Major, S., & Queenan, P. (2003). Preschool emotional competence: Pathway to social competence? *Child Development*, *74*, 238–256.

Deutsch, M. (1973). *The resolution of conflict: Constructive and destructive processes*. Yale University Press.

Deutsch, M., Coleman, P. T., & Marcus, E. C. (2011). *The handbook of conflict resolution: Theory and practice*. John Wiley & Sons.

Dhankar, N. (2020). Educational importance of Indian home and street games and toys. *Online International Interdisciplinary Research Journal*, *8*, 226. www.oiirj.org.

Dhasmana, P., Singh, G. M., Srinivasan, M., & Kuma, S. (2018). Anger and psychological well- being: A correlational study among working adults in Uttarakhand, India. *International Journal of Medical Sciences and Public Health*, *7*, 296–300.

Dhawan, N., Punetha, D., Sinha, Y., Gaur, S. P., Tyler, S. L., & Tyler, F. B. (1999). Family conflict/violence patterns in India. *Psychology and Developing Societies*, *11*, 195–216.

Dhillon, M., & Babu, N. (2015). Peer conflict among Indian children in school settings. *Psychological Studies*, *60*, 154–159.

Diamond, A. (2002). Normal development of prefrontal cortex from birth to young adulthood: Cognitive functions, anatomy, and biochemistry. In D. T. Stuss & R. T. Knight (Eds.), *Principles of frontal lobe function* (pp. 466–503). Oxford University Press.

Diamond, A. (2013). Executive functions. *Annual Review of Psychology*, *64*, 135–168.

Diener, E. (2000). Subjective well-being: The science of happiness and a proposal for a national index. *American Psychologist*, *55*, 33–43.

Diener, E., Oishi, S., & Tay, L. (2018). Advances in subjective well-being research. *Nature Human Behaviour*, *2*, 253–260.

Dixit, P., Gupta, A., Dwivedi, L. K., & Coomar, D. (2018). Impact evaluation of integrated child development services in rural India: Propensity score matching analysis. *SAGE Open*, *8*(2). https://doi.org/10.1177/2158244018785713

Dolan, R. J. (2002). Emotion, cognition, and behavior. *Science*, *298*, 1191–1194.

Doocy, S., Daniels, A., Dick, A., & Kirsch, T. D. (2013). The human impact of tsunamis: A historical review of events 1900–2009 and systematic literature review. *PLoS Currents*, *5*. ecurrents.dis.40f3c5cf61110a0fef2f9a25908cd795.

Drèze, J., & Goyal, A. (2003). Future of mid-day meals. *Economics and Political Weekly*, *38*, 4673–4683.

Dreze, J., & Sen, A. (2013). *An uncertain glory: India and its contradictions*. Princeton University Press.

Due, R. (2000). Self-knowledge and moral properties in Sartre's "being and nothingness." *Sartre Studies International, 6*, 61–94.

Dunham, Y., Baron, A. S., & Banaji, M. R. (2008). From American city to Japanese village: A cross-cultural investigation of implicit race attitudes. *Child Development, 79*, 572–586.

Durkheim, E. (1897). *Suicide: A study in sociology*. Routledge.

Dutta, K., Singh, V. K., Chakraborty, P., Sidhardhan, S. K., Krishna, B. S., & Dash, C. (2017). Analyzing big-five personality traits of Indian celebrities using online social media. *Psychological Studies, 62*, 113–124.

Dutta, N. (2018). Street children in India: A study on their access to health and education. *International Journal of Child, Youth and Family Studies, 9*, 69–82.

Dutta, R. (1983). *Socialisation in an impoverished agricultural community: An ecological perspective* [Unpublished Masters' Dissertation]. University of Baroda.

Dweck, C. S. (2006). *Mindset: The new psychology of success*. Ballantine Books.

Dweck, C. S. (2017). *Mindset: The new psychology of success*. Random House.

Dwivedi, C. B. (2019).The mundane and incorporeal aspects of yoga psychology. In G. Misra (Ed.), *Explorations into psyche and psychology: Some emerging perspectives* (pp. 92–189). Oxford University Press.

Eagly, A. H., & Wood, W. (2013). The origins of sex differences in human behavior: Evolved dispositions versus social roles. *American Psychologist, 68*, 408–423.

Eastman, J. K., Modi, P., & Gordon-Wilson, S. (2019). The impact of future time perspective and personality on the sustainable behaviours of seniors. *Journal of Consumer Policy, 43*. https://doi.org/10.1007/s10603-019-09440-1.

Editor's Introduction. (2017). Psycho-social bases of sustainable development. *Psychology and Developing Societies, 29*, vii–ix.

Efland, A. (2002). *Art and cognition: Integrating the visual arts in the curriculum*. Teachers College Press.

Eisenberg, N., Cumberland, A., Spinrad, T. L., Fabes, R. A., Shepard, S. A., Reiser, M., Murphy, B. C., Losoya, S. H., & Guthrie, I. K. (1998). The relations of regulation and emotionality to children's externalizing and internalizing problem behavior. *Child Development, 69*, 499–512.

Eisenberg, N., Fabes, R. A., & Spinard, T. L. (2007). Prosocial development. In W. Damon & R. M. Lerner (Eds.), *Handbook of child psychology: Vol. 3. Social, emotional, and personality development* (pp. 646–718). Wiley.

Eisenberg, N., & Morris, A. S. (2002). Children's emotion-related regulation. In R. V. Kail (Ed.), *Advances in child development and behavior* (Vol. 30, pp. 189–229). Academic Press.

Eisenberg, N., Spinrad, T. L., & Eggum, N. D. (2010). Emotion-related self-regulation and its relation to children's maladjustment. *Annual Review of Clinical Psychology, 6*, 495–525.

Eisenstein, E. (1983). *The printing press as an agent of change: Communications and cultural transformations in early-modern Europe*. Cambridge University Press.

Ekman, P. (1973). Cross-cultural studies of facial expression. In P. Ekman (Ed.), *Darwin and facial expression: A century of research in review* (pp. 169–222). Academic Press.

Ekman, P. (1992). An argument for basic emotions. *Cognition & Emotion, 6*, 169–200.

Ellsworth, P. C., & Smith, C. A. (1988). Shades of joy: Patterns of appraisal differentiating pleasant emotions. *Cognition and Emotion, 2*, 301–331.

Emmons, R. A. (2000). Is spirituality an intelligence? Motivation, cognition, and the psychology of ultimate concern. *International Journal for the Psychology of Religion, 10*, 3–26.

Emmons, R. A., & McCullough, M. E. (2003). Counting blessings versus burdens: An experimental investigation of gratitude and subjective well-being in daily life. *Journal of Personality and Social Psychology, 84*, 377–389.

English, L. M., & Carleson, A. (2019). Lifelong learning and the Sustainable Development Goals (SDGs): Probing the implications and the effects. *International Review of Education, 65*, 205–211.

Ericsson, K. A., & Lehmann, A. C. (1996). Expert and exceptional performance: Evidence of maximal adaptation to task constraints. *Annual Review of Psychology, 47*, 273–305.

Erikson, E. H. (1950). *Childhood and society*. W. W. Norton & Company.

Erikson, E. H. (1968). *Identity: Youth and crisis*. W. W. Norton & Company.

Evans, G. W., & Kim, P. (2013). Childhood poverty and health: Cumulative risk exposure and stress dysregulation. *Psychological Science, 24*, 1544–1554.

Eysenck, H. J. (1967). *The biological basis of personality*. Thomas.

Eysenck, H. J. (1990). Biological dimensions of personality. In L. A. Pervin (Ed.), *Handbook of personality: Theory and research* (pp. 244–276). The Guilford Press.

Eysenck, H. J., & Eysenck, S. B. G. (1964). *Manual of the Eysenck personality inventory*. University of London Press.

Eysenck, H. J., & Eysenck, S. B. G. (1975). *Manual of the Eysenck personality questionnaire (junior and adult)*. Hodder and Stoughton.

Fehr, E., & Gachter, S. (2002). Altruistic punishment in humans. *Nature, 415*, 137–140.

Fehr, R., Gelfand, M. J., & Nag, M. (2010). The road to forgiveness: A meta-analytic synthesis of its situational and dispositional correlates. *Psychological Bulletin, 136*, 894–914.

Feist, J., Feist, G. F., & Roberts, T. (2018). *Theories of personality* (9th ed.). McGraw-Hill.

Feldman, D. B., & Snyder, C. R. (2005). Hope and the meaningful life: Theoretical and empirical associations between goal-directed thinking and life meaning. *Journal of Social and Clinical Psychology, 24*, 401–421.

Feldman, R. (2015). *Social development in infancy: A contemporary introduction*. Psychology Press.

Ferguson, C. A., & Menn, L. (1996). *Phonological development: A cross-linguistic perspective*. Blackwell Publishing.

Ferjan, N. R., Ramírez, R. R., Clarke, M., Taulu, S., & Kuhl, P. K. (2017). Speech discrimination in 11-month-old bilingual and monolingual infants: A magnetoencephalography study. *Developmental Science, 20*, e12427. http://dx.doi.org/10.1111/desc.12427

Festinger, L. (1957). *A theory of cognitive dissonance*. Stanford University Press.

Festinger, L., & Carlsmith, J. M. (1959). The cognitive consequences of forced compliance. *Journal of Abnormal Psychology, 58*, 203–210.

Feuerstein, G. (1998). *The yoga tradition: Its history, literature, philosophy and practice*. Hohm Press.

Field, T. (2016). Yoga research review. *Complementary Therapies in Clinical Practice, 24*, 145–161.

Filkowski, M. M., Cochran, R. N., & Haas, B. W. (2016). Altruistic behavior: Mapping responses in the brain. *Neuroscience and Neuroeconomics, 5*, 65–75.

Finkelstein, M. A. (2009). Civic engagement and the transition to adulthood. *The Future of Children, 19*, 159–179.

Finnegan, R. (1992). *Oral traditions and the verbal arts*. Routledge.

Fishman, J. L., Raval, V. V., Daga, S. S., & Raj, S. P. (2014). Metaemotion philosophy among Asian Indian immigrant mothers in the United States. *Qualitative Health Research, 24*, 875–889.

Fitzpatrick, K. M., Bold, K. W., & Eckenrode, J. (2018). Community violence and child maltreatment: A test of the spillover hypothesis. *Development and Psychopathology, 30*, 321–336.

Fjell, A. M., Walhovd, K. B., Fennema-Notestine, C., McEvoy, L. K., Hagler, D. J., Holland, D., Brewer, J. B., & Dale A. M. (2014). One-year brain atrophy evident in healthy aging. *Journal of Neuroscience, 34*, 16374–16381.

Flanagan, D. P., & Ortiz, S. O. (2011). The psychoeducational assessment of culturally and linguistically diverse students: A model from the PASS theory of intelligence. *School Psychology Review, 40*, 576–591.

Flavell, J. H., & Miller, P. H. (1998). Social cognition. In D. Kuhn & R. Siegler (Eds.), *Handbook of child psychology: Vol. 2: Cognition, perception, and language* (pp. 851–898). Wiley.

Fletcher, D., & Sarkar, M. (2013). Psychological resilience: A review and critique of definitions, concepts, and theory. *European Psychologist, 18*, 12–23.

Folger, J. P., Poole, M. S., & Stutman, R. K. (2013). *Working through conflict: Strategies for relationships, groups, and organizations*. Routledge.

Folio, M. R., & Fewell, R. R. (2000). *PDMS-2 Peabody developmental motor scales* (2nd ed.). PRO-ED Inc.

Folkman, S. (2008). The case for positive emotions in the stress process. *Anxiety, Stress & Coping, 21*, 3–14.

France 24. (2023). *Costa Rica, a renewable energy paradise*. www.france24.com/en/tv-shows/focus/20230303-costa-rica-a-renewable-energy-paradise

Frank, R. H. (2012). *The Darwin economy: Liberty, competition, and the common good*. Princeton University Press.

Frankenburg, W. A., & Dodds, J. B. (1967). The Denver developmental screening test. *The Journal of Pediatrics, 71*, 181–191.

Fredrickson, B. L. (2009). *Positivity: Groundbreaking research reveals how to embrace the hidden strength of positive emotions, overcome negativity, and thrive*. Crown Archetype.

Freud, S. (1900). *The interpretation of dreams*. Basic Books.

Freud, S. (1905). Three essays on the theory of sexuality. In *The standard edition of the complete psychological works of Sigmund Freud, Volume VII (1901–1905): A case of hysteria, three essays on sexuality and other works* (pp. 123–246). The Hogarth Press.

Freud, S. (1920). *Beyond the pleasure principle* (Standard ed.). The Hogarth Press.

Freud, S. (1923). The ego and the id. In *The standard edition of the complete psychological works of Sigmund Freud, Volume XIX (1923–1925): The ego and the Id and other works* (pp. 1–66). Norton & Company.

Fromm, E. (1941). *Escape from freedom*. Farrar & Rinehart.

Gale, M., Justin J. Hendricks, J. J., Dollahite, D. C., & and Marks, L. D. (2023). Perspectives on lifespan religious and spiritual development from scholars across the lifespan. *Religions, 14*, 362. https://doi.org/10.3390/rel14030362.

Galton, F. (1869). *Hereditary genius: An inquiry into its laws and consequences*. Macmillan.

Ganguli, H. C. (2008). *Fear of death and Bhagawat Gita: A psycho-philosophic analysis*. Global Vision.

Gard, T., Noggle, J. J., Park, C. L., Vago, D. R., & Wilson, A. (2014). Potential self-regulatory mechanisms of yoga for psychological health. *Frontiers in Human Neuroscience, 8*, 770. https://doi.org/10.3389/fnhum.2014.00770.

Gardner, H. (1983). *Frames of mind: The theory of multiple intelligences*. Basic Books.

Gardner, H. (1991). *The unschooled mind: How children think and how schools should teach*. Basic Books.

Gardner, H. (1993). *Multiple intelligences: The theory in practice*. Basic Books.

Gardner, H. (1999). *Intelligence reframed: Multiple intelligences for the 21st Century*. Basic Books.

Garg, N. (2022). Gratitude and work-family enrichment among Indian female workforce: Exploring the mediating role of psychological capital. *International Journal of Work Organisation and Emotion, 13*, 1–17.

Gates, G. A., & Mills, J. H. (2005). Presbycusis. *The Lancet, 366*, 1111–1120.

Gathercole, S. E., Pickering, S. J., Ambridge, B., & Wearing, H. (2004). The structure of working memory from 4 to 15 years of age. *Developmental Psychology, 40*, 177–190.

Genesee, F. (2015). Myths about early childhood bilingualism. *Canadian Psychology/Psychologie Canadienne, 56*, 6–15.

George, J., Nair, D., Premkumar, N. R., Saravanan, N., Chinnakali, P., & Roy, G. (2016). The prevalence of domestic violence and its associated factors among married women in a rural area of Puducherry, South India. *Journal of Family Medicine and Primary Care, 5*, 672–676.

Gesell, A. (1928). *Infant and child in the culture of today: The guidance of development in home and nursery school*. Harper & Brothers Publishers.

Gesell, A. (1933). Maturation and the patterning of behavior. In C. Murchison (Ed.), *A handbook of child psychology* (pp. 209–235). Russell & Russell/Atheneum Publishers.

Gesell, A. (1940/1993). *The first five years of life*. Buccaneer Books.

Ghai, A. (2019). Disability, exclusions, and resistance: An Indian context. In Z. Hasan, A. Z. Huq, M. C. Nussbaum, & V. Verma (Eds.), *The empire of disgust: Prejudice, discrimination, and policy in India and the US* (pp. 243–262). Oxford Academic.

Gibbs, R. W. (2006). *Embodiment and cognitive science*. Cambridge University Press.

Gilligan, C. (1982). *In a different voice: Psychological theory and women's development*. Harvard University Press.

Gilligan, C. (1996). Moral orientation and moral development. In M. M. Baltes & T. D. Nesselroade (Eds.), *Life-span developmental psychology: Personality and socialization* (pp. 223–243). Lawrence Erlbaum Associates.

Gire, J. (2014). How death imitates life: Cultural influences on conceptions of death and dying. *Online Readings in Psychology and Culture, 6(2)*. https://doi.org/10.9707/2307-0919.1120

Gold, D. (1987). *The lord as guru*. Oxford University Press.

Goldberg, L. R. (1992). The development of markers for the Big-Five factor structure. *Psychological Assessment, 4*, 26–42.

Goleman, D. (1995). *Emotional intelligence: Why it can matter more than IQ*. Bantam Books.

Goleman, D. (2006). *Emotional intelligence: Why it can matter more than IQ*. Bantam Books.

Goodnow, J. J. (1976). The nature of intelligent behaviour: Questions raised by cross-cultural studies. In L. Resnick (Ed.), *New approaches to intelligence*. Erlbaum.

Gopalakrishan, K. (2021). Changing scenario of family system in India: An analysis against the backdrop of changing social values. *International Journal of Social Sciences, 10*, 1–12.

References

Government of India. (2014). *Swachh Bharat Mission*. Ministry of Housing and Urban Affairs. [Website]. https://swachhbharatmission.gov.in/

Government of India. (2015). *Pradhan Mantri Jan Dhan Yojana (PMJDY), launched by the Prime Minister Shri Narendra Modi on 28th August 2014, celebrates its first anniversary*. Ministry of Finance (Press Information Bureau).

Government of India. (2022). Study to assess the impact of MGNREGS. *Ministry of Rural Development*. https://rural.nic.in/en/press-release/study-assess-impact-mgnregs.

Govinda, R. (Ed.). (2011). *Who goes to school? Exploring exclusion in Indian education*. Oxford University Press.

Govinda, R., & Sedwal, M. (2017). *India education report: Progress of basic education*. New Oxford University Press.

Gowramma, I. P., Gangmei, E., & Behera, L. (2018). Research in education of children with disabilities. *Indian Educational Review, 56(2)*, 7–93.

Goyal, M., Singh, S., Sibinga, E. M., Gould, N. F., Rowland-Seymour, A., Sharma, R., Berger, Z., Sleicher, D., Maron, D. D., Shihab, H. M., Ranasinghe, P. D., Linn, S., Saha, S., Bass, E. B., & Haythornthwaite, J. A. (2014). Meditation programs for psychological stress and well-being: A systematic review and meta-analysis. *JAMA Internal Medicine, 174*, 357–68.

Goyal, N., Wice, M., Aladro, A., Kallberg-Shroff, M., & Miller, J. G. (2019). Culture and the development of views of agency: Perspectives from storybooks, parents, and children. *Developmental Psychology, 55*, 1096–1110.

Greenfield, P. M. (1998). The cultural evolution of IQ. In U. Neisser (Ed.), *The rising curve: Long term gains in IQ and related measures* (pp. 81–123). American Psychological Association.

Grigorenko, E. L., Geissler, P. W., Prince, R., Okatcha, F., Nokes, C., Kenny, D. A., Bundy, D. A., & Sternberg, R. J. (2001). The organisation of Luo conceptions of intelligence: A study of implicit theories in a Kenyan village. *International Journal of Behavioral Development, 25*, 367–378.

Grolnick, W. S., Deci, E. L., & Ryan, R. M. (1997). Internalization within the family: The self-determination theory perspective. In J. E. Grusec & L. Kuczynski (Eds.), *Parenting and children's internalization of values: A handbook of contemporary theory* (pp. 135–161). John Wiley & Sons.

Grosjean, F. (2010). *Bilingual: Life and reality*. Harvard University Press.

Gross, J. J. (1998). The emerging field of emotion regulation: An integrative review. *Review of General Psychology, 2*, 271–299.

Gross, J. J. (2001). Emotion regulation in adulthood: Timing is everything. *Current Directions in Psychological Science, 10*, 214–219.

Gross, J. J. (2015). Emotion regulation: Current status and future prospects. *Psychological Inquiry, 26*, 1–26.

Grossman, B., Wirt, R., & Davids, A. (1985). Self-esteem, ethnic identity, and behavioural adjustment among Anglo and Chicano adolescents in West Texas. *Journal of Adolescence, 8*, 57–68.

Grusec, J. E., & Hastings, P. D. (2015). *Handbook of socialization: Theory and research* (2nd ed.). Guilford Press.

Guha, S., & Murthy, K. (2017). Understanding the role of toys in child development: Special focus on traditional Channapatna toys. *Indian Journal of Applied Research, 7*. https://doi.org/10.36106/ijar.

Gupta, A. (2013). Altruism in Indian religions: Embracing the biosphere. In D. Vakoch (Ed.), *Altruism in cross-cultural perspective* (pp. 101–112). Springer.

Gupta, A., Gupta, S. K., & Nongkynrih, B. (2013). Integrated child development services (ICDS): A journey of 37 years. *Indian Journal of Community Health, 25*, 77–81.

Gupta, P., Bhattacharya, S. Neelam, N., & Kunte, M. (2016). Boomers like to confront, generation Y is okay with withdrawal, but they all love to negotiate in India. *Conflict Resolution Quarterly, 33*, 403–435.

Gupta, R. K. (2002). Prospects of effective teamwork in India: Some cautionary conjectures from a cross-cultural perspective. *Indian Journal of Industrial Relations, 38*, 211–229.

Hafen, C. A., Singh, K., and Laursen, B. (2011). The happy personality in India: The role of emotional intelligence. *Journal of Happiness Studies, 12*, 807–817. https://doi.org/10.1007/s10902-010-9228-4.

Hall, E. T., & Hall, M. R. (1990). *Understanding cultural differences: Germans, French and Americans*. Intercultural Press.

Hall, G. S. (1904). *Adolescence: Its psychology and its relations to physiology, anthropology, sociology, sex, crime, religion and education* (Vol. 2). D. Appleton and Company.

Hardy, S. A., Nelson, J. M., Moore, J. P., & King, P. E. (2019). Processes of religious and spiritual influence in adolescence: A systematic review of 30 years of research. *Journal of Research on Adolescence, 29*, 254–275.

Harkness, S., Super, C., & Keefer, C. (1992). Culture and ethnicity. In M. D. Levine, W. B. Carey, & A. C. Crocker (Eds.), *Developmental behavioural paediatrics* (pp. 103–108). Sounders.

Harkness, S., & Super, C. M. (2020). Culture and human development: Where did it go? And where is it going? *New Directions for Child and Adolescent Development*, 101–119. https://doi.org/10.1002/cad.20378

Hart, B., & Risley, T. R. (1995). *Meaningful differences in the everyday experience of young American children*. Paul H Brookes Publishing.

Harter, S. (2012). Emerging self-processes during childhood and adolescence. In M. R. Leary & J. P. Tangney (Eds.), *Handbook of self and personality* (2nd ed., pp. 680–716). The Guilford Press.

Havighurst, S. S., Wilson, K. R., Harley, A. E., & Prior, M. R. (2011). Tuning in to Kids: An effectiveness trial of a parenting program targeting the emotional development of preschoolers. *Journal of Family Psychology*, *26*, 56–65.

Haynes, C. J. (2009). Holistic human development. *Journal of Adult Development*, *16*(1), 53–60.

Hazra, S., & Mittal, S. (2018). Role of parenting in moral development: An overview. *The International Journal of Indian Psychology*, *6*, 168–174.

Heckman, J., Pinto, R., & Savelyev, P. (2013). Understanding the mechanisms through which an influential early childhood program boosted adult outcomes. *American Economic Review*, *103*, 2052–2086.

Heindorf, I. (2019). *Sikkim's state policy on organic farming and Sikkim organic mission, India*. https://panorama.solutions/en/solution/sikkims-state-policy-organic-farming- and-Sikkim-organic-mission-India.

Heine, S. J., Lehman, D. R., Markus, H. R., & Kitayama, S. (1999). Is there a universal need for positive self-regard? *Psychological Review*, *106*, 766–794.

Heise, L. L. (1998). Violence against women: An integrated, ecological framework. *Violence Against Women*, *4*, 262–290.

Helwig, C. C. (2006). What is good reasoning? Examining Kohlberg's theory. In M. Killen & J. G. Smetana (Eds.), *Handbook of moral development* (pp. 391–416). Psychology Press.

Herba, C. M., Landau, S., Russell, T., Ecker, C., & Phillips, M. L. (2006). The development of emotion-processing in children: Effects of age, emotion, and intensity. *Journal of Child Psychology and Psychiatry*, *47*, 1098–1106.

Hewstone, M., Rubin, M., & Willis, H. (2002). Intergroup bias. *Annual Review of Psychology*, *53*, 575–604.

Hill, P. L., & Edmonds, G. W. (2017). Personality development in adolescence. In P. L. Hill (Eds.), *Personality development across the lifespan* (pp. 25–38). Elsevier Academic Press.

Hochschild, A. R. (1983). *The managed heart: Commercialization of human feeling*. University of California Press.

Hoff, E. (2013). *Language development* (5th ed.). Wadsworth Cengage Learning.

Hofstede, G. (1980). *Culture's consequences: International differences in work-related values*. SAGE.

Hofstede, G. (1984). *Culture's consequences: International differences in work-related values*. SAGE.

Hofstede, G. (2001). *Culture's consequences: Comparing values, behaviors, institutions, and organizations across nations*. SAGE.

Hogg, M. A. (2000). Subjective uncertainty reduction through self-categorization: A motivational theory of social identity processes and group phenomena. In W. Stroebe & M. Hewstone (Eds.), *European review of social psychology* (pp. 223–255). Wiley.

Holloway, D. S. (2006). Review: Toward a nuanced understanding of child development in Japan. *Human Development*, *49*(6). https://doi.org/10.2307/26763912

Holtgraves, T. (1997). Styles of language use: Individual and cultural variability in conversational indirectness. *Journal of Personality and Social Psychology*, *73*, 624–637.

Holzel, B. K., Carmody, J., Vangel, M., Congleton, C., Yerramsetti, S. M., Gard, T., & Lazar, S. W. (2011). Mindfulness practice leads to increases in regional brain grey matter density. *Psychiatry Research: Neuroimaging*, *191*, 36–43.

Horn, J. L., & Cattell, R. B. (1967). Age differences in fluid and crystallized intelligence. *Acta Psychologia*, *26*, 107–129.

House, R. J., Hanges, P. J., Javidan, M., Dorfman, P. W., Gupta, V., & GLOBE Associates (2004). *Leadership, culture and organizations: The GLOBE study of 62 nations*. SAGE.

Hughes, J. N. (2015). Conflict resolution strategies among preschool children: Links to persistent behavior problems. *Early Childhood Research Quarterly*, *32*, 133–141.

Indian Academy of Pediatrics. (2021). *Guidelines for parents: Normal development and when to suspect abnormal development?* Indian Academy of Pediatrics.

Inhelder, B., & Piaget, J. (1958). *The growth of logical thinking from childhood to adolescence*. Basic Books.

Institute for Economics & Peace. (2015). *Global terrorism index: Measuring and understanding the impact of terrorism*. Institute for Economics & Peace.

Institute for Economics & Peace. Ecological Threat Register. (2020). *Understanding ecological threats, resilience and peace*. http://visionofhumanity.org/reports

IPCC. (2018). *Summary for policymakers. In global warming of 1.5°C*. www.ipcc.ch/sr15/chapter/spm/

Iqbal, N., & Dar, K. A. (2022). Gratitude intervention and subjective well-being in Indian adolescents: Examining the moderating effects of self-esteem. *Child Indicators Research, Springer; The International Society of Child Indicators, 15*, 263–278.

Iverson, J. M., & Goldin-Meadow, S. (2005). Gesture paves the way for language development. *Psychological Science, 16*, 367–371.

Jaipal, R. (2017). Psychology at the crossroads: Sustainable development or status quo? *Psychology and Developing Societies, 29*, 125–159.

Jaiswal, R. K., Sinha, A., Dhawan, P., Sundar, R., Alawadhi, A., & Rangarajan, R. (2020). *An evaluation of India's Beti Bachao Beti Padhao scheme*. National Council of Applied Economic Research.

James, W. (1884). What is an emotion? *Mind, 9*, 188–205.

James, W. (1890). *The principles of psychology*. Henry Holt and Company.

Jayaraman, R., & Simroth, D. (2015). The impact of school lunches on primary school enrollment: Evidence from India's midday meal scheme. *The Scandinavian Journal of Economics, 117*, 1176–1203.

Jeffery, P., & Jeffery, R. (1996). *Don't marry me to a plowman! Women's everyday lives in rural north India*. Westview Press.

Jensen, L. A. (2011). The cultural-developmental theory of moral psychology: A new synthesis. In L. A. Jensen (Ed.), *Bridging cultural and developmental approaches to psychology: New syntheses in theory, research and policy* (pp. 3–25). Oxford University Press.

Jha, S. D., & Singh, K. (2011). An analysis of individualism-collectivism across Northern India. *Journal of the Indian Academy of Applied Psychology, 37*, 149–156.

Jhangiani, T., Dutta, M., Arundhati, Banerjee, T., & Jochan, G. M. (2022). Empty Nest Syndrome Scale-Indian Form (ENS-IF). *International Journal of Indian Psychology, 10*(4), 612–627. https://doi.org/10.25215/1004.059.

Ji, L. J., Zhang, Z., & Nisbett, R. E. (2004). Is it culture or is it language? Examination of language effects in cross-cultural research on categorization. *Journal of Personality and Social Psychology, 87*, 57–65.

Jin, H., Crimmins, E., Langa, K. M., Dey, A. B., & Lee, J. (2023). Estimating the prevalence of dementia in India using a semi-supervised machine learning approach. *Neuroepidemiology, 57*, 43–50.

John, A., & Montgomery, D. (2012). Socialization goals of first-generation immigrant Indian parents: A Q-methodological study. *Asian American Journal of Psychology, 3*, 299–312.

John, O. P., Donahue, E. M., & Kentle, R. L. (1991). *Big five inventory* (BFI) [Database record]. APA PsycTests.

Johnson, D. W., Johnson, R. T., & Smith, K. A. (2014). Cooperative learning: Improving university instruction by basing practice on validated theory. *Journal on Excellence in College Teaching, 25*, 85–118.

Joshi, M. S., & Carter, W. (2013). Unrealistic optimism: East and West? *Frontiers in Psychology, 4*, 1–15.

Joshi, P., Singh, K., Marimuthu, P., & Tripathi, R. (2019). The development of false belief understanding in Indian Children: A preliminary report. *Journal of Indian Association of Child and Adolescent Mental Health, 15*, 72–85.

Julka, A. (2003). *Inclusive education in practice: Awareness package at upper primary level*. NCERT.

Julka, A. (2007). *Meeting special needs in schools: A manual*. NCERT.

Juris Centre (2022). *Academics, analysis and everything in between*. https://juriscentre.com/2022/03/16/street-kids-of-india-a-grave-perspective/#_ftn11

Kabat-Zinn, J. (1994). *Wherever you go, there you are: Mindfulness meditation in everyday life*. Hyperion.

Kacker, L., Kumar, P., & Varadan, S. (2007). *Child protection, protection of children from harmful work*. Ministry of Women and Child Development.

Kagan, S., & Kagan, M. (2009). *Kagan cooperative learning*. Kagan Publishing.

Kagitcibasi, C. (2005). Autonomy and relatedness in cultural context: Implications for self and family. *Journal of Cross-Cultural Psychology, 36*(4), 403–422.

Kakar, S. (1978). *The inner world: A psychoanalytic study of childhood and society in India* (2nd ed.). Oxford University Press.

Kakar, S. (1979). *Indian childhood: Cultural ideas and social reality*. Oxford University Press.

Kamat, J. (2023). *Indian culture: Swastik in Indian culture*. www.kamat.com/indica/culture/sub-cultures/swastika.htm.

Kane, P. V. (1968). *History of dharmasastra* (Vol. I). Bhandarkar Oriental Research Institute.
Kapadia, S. (2008). Adolescent-parent relationships in Indian and Indian immigrant families in the US. *Psychology and Developing Societies, 20*, 257–275.
Kapadia, S. (2017). *Adolescence in urban India: Cultural construction in a society in transition.* Springer.
Kapadia, S. (2019). Socialization and parenting: Mapping the Indian landscape. In G. Misra (Ed.), *Psychology, Vol. 2: Individual and social, processes and issues* (pp. 53–124). Oxford University Press.
Kapadia, S., & Bhangaokar, R. (2013). Imageries of youth as a life stage in India. In D. P. Chattopadhyaya (Gen Ed.), *History of science, philosophy and culture in Indian civilization (vol XIII, part 3, G. Misra, Ed.), Psychology and psychoanalysis* (pp. 219–253). Centre for Studies in Civilizations.
Kapadia, S., Karnik, R., & Ali, R. (2005). *Parenting adolescents: A view from western India.* Paper presented at the Asian-African Region Seminar on Parenting Across Lifespan: Challenges and Opportunities, Vadodara.
Kapadia, S., & Sayajirao, M. (2009). Cultural perspectives on parenting in the context of globalization and acculturation: Viewpoints from India and Canada. *The International Journal of Interdisciplinary Social Sciences, 3*, 171–178
Kapur, M. (1995). *Mental health of Indian children.* SAGE.
Kapur, M. (2016). *Psychological perspective on childcare in the Indian indigenous health systems.* Springer.
Kapur, M. (2021). *Parents: Beware of the digital demon.* Vitasta Publishing.
Kapur, M. (2024). *From Freud to Zuckerberg and back.* Storywell Books.
Kapur, M., Girimaji, S. R., Prabhu, G. G., Reddy, G. N. N., & Kaliaperumal, V. G. (1994). Home environment and psychosocial development of pre-school children in south India. *NIMHANS Journal, 12*, 41–51.
Kapur, P., & Misra, G. (2003). Image of self in the Sikh community: Continuity of the core and global presence. *Psychology and Developing Societies, 15*, 103–116.
Kar, G. C. (2000). Disaster and mental health. *Indian Journal of Psychiatry, 42*, 3–13.
Karmakar, R. (2015). Does parenting style influence the internalization of moral values in children and adolescents?. *Psychological Studies, 60*, 438–446.
Kastenbaum, R., & Costa, P. T., Jr. (1977). Perspectives on death. *Annual Review of Psychology, 28*, 225–249.
Kathuria, T., Kapadia, S., & Friedlmeier, W. (2022). Links between maternal emotion socialization goals and practices in an urban Indian context. In M. Klicperova-Baker & W. Friedlmeier (Eds.), *Xenophobia vs.patriotism: Where is my home? Proceedings from the 25th Congress of the International Association for Cross-Cultural Psychology* (p. 297). https://scholarworks.gvsu.edu/iaccp_papers/297
Kathuria, T., Kapadia, S., & Friedlmeier, W. (2023). Emotion socialization in the Indian cultural context. *Online Readings in Psychology and Culture, 6*(1). https://doi.org/10.9707/2307-0919.1178
Kaul, V., Bhattacharjee, S., Chaudhary, A. B., Ramanujan, P., Banerji, M., & Nanda, M. (2017). *The India early childhood education impact study.* UNICEF.
Kaul, V., & Sankar, D. (2009). *Early childhood care and education in India.* National University of Educational Planning and Administration.
Kaur, R. (2021). Estimating the impact of school feeding programs: Evidence from mid-day meal scheme of India. *Economics of Education Review, Elsevier, 84*(C). https://doi.org/10.1016/j.econedurev.2021.102171.
Kaushik, A. (2018). Can you afford to die? Estimates of expenditure on rituals and impact on ecology. *Economic and Political Weekly (Engage), 53*.
Keller, H. (2007). *Cultures of infancy.* Erlbaum.
Keller, H., & Lamm, B. (Eds.). (2013). *Identity and development: From cultural to individual perspectives.* Psychology Press.
Keltner, D. (2017). *The power paradox: How we gain and lose influence.* Penguin Books.
Khera, R. (2006). Mid-Day meals in primary schools: Achievements and challenges. *Economics and Political Weekly, 41*, 4742–4750.
Khubchandani, L. M. (1978). Language policy and education in the Indian subcontinent. In R. Wodak & D. Corson (Eds.), *Encyclopedia of language and education* (Vol. 1). Springer.
Kim, U., & Rohner, R. P. (2002). Parental warmth, control, and involvement in schooling: Predicting academic achievement among Korean American adolescents. *Journal of Cross-Cultural Psychology, 33*, 127–140.

References

Kitayama, S., & Markus, H. R. (1994). The cultural construction of self and emotion: Implications for social behavior. In S. Kitayama & H. R. Markus (Eds.), *Emotion and culture: Empirical studies of mutual influence* (pp. 89–130). American Psychological Association.

Kitayama, S., & Markus, H. R. (1999). Culture and the self: Implications for cognition, emotion, and motivation. In R. F. Baumeister (Ed.), *The self in social psychology* (pp. 339–371). Psychology Press.

Knafo, A., & Plomin, R. (2006). Prosocial behavior from early to middle childhood: Genetic and environmental influences on stability and change. *Developmental Psychology, 42*, 771–786.

Knapp, M. L., Hall, J. A., & Horgan, T. G. (2013). *Nonverbal communication in human interaction* (8th ed.). Cengage Learning.

Knapp, M. L., & Vangelisti, A. L. (2000). *Interpersonal communication and human relationships* (4th ed.). Allyn & Bacon.

Koenig, H. G. (Ed.). (2012). *Handbook of religion and health* (2nd ed.). Oxford University Press.

Kohlberg, L. (1981). *Essays on moral development: Vol. 1. The philosophy of moral development*. Harper & Row.

Kohlberg, L. (1984). *The psychology of moral development: The nature and validity of moral stages*. Harper & Row.

Kolb, B. (2019). Brain development during early childhood. In S. Hupp & J. Jewell (Eds.), *The encyclopedia of child and adolescent development* (pp. 1–14). John Wiley & Sons.

Konantambigi, R. M., Meghani, S., & Modi, A. (2008). Non-formal education in a tribal setting: Strategies for qualitative changes in children. *Psychology and Developing Societies, 20*, 65–98.

Kraft, A. M., & Choubisa, R. (2018). Hope in the Indian psychology context: Philosophical foundations and empirical findings. In A. M. Krafft, P. Perrig-Chiello, & A. Walker (Eds.), *Hope for a good life – Results of the Hope-Barometer international research program* (pp. 131–163). Springer.

Krishnan, L. (1998). Child rearing: The Indian perspective. In A. K. Srivastava (Ed.), *Child development: The Indian perspective* (pp. 25–55). NCERT.

Krishnan, L. (2001). Justice perception and allocation rule preferences: Does social disadvantage matter? *Psychology and Developing Societies, 13*, 193–219.

Krishnan, L. (2011). Culture and distributive justice: General comments and some insights from the Indian context. In G. Misra (Ed.), *Handbook of psychology in India* (pp. 205–225). Oxford University Press.

Krishnan, L., & Carment, D. W. (2006). Senior/Junior recipient status and reward allocation in India and Canada. *Psychology and Developing Societies, 18*, 15–35.

Krishnan, L., Varma, P., & Pandey, V. (2009). Reward and punishment allocation in the Indian culture. *Psychology and Developing Societies, 21*, 79–131.

Kroll, J. F., & Dussias, P. E. (2017). The benefits of multilingualism to the personal and professional development of residents of the US. *Foreign Language Annals, 50*, 248–259.

Kubler-Ross, E. (1969). *On death and dying*. Macmillan.

Kuhl, P. K. (2007). Is speech learning "gated" by the social brain? *Developmental Science, 10*, 110–120.

Kuhl, P. K., Tsao, F. M., & Liu, H. M. (2003). Foreign-language experience in infancy: Effects of short-term exposure and social interaction on phonetic learning. *Proceedings of the National Academy of Sciences, 100*, 9096–9101.

Kumar, A., & Dixit, V. (2014). Forgiveness, gratitude and resilience among Indian youth. *Indian Journal of Health and Wellbeing, 5*, 1414–1419.

Kumar, A., Mehra, A., & Avasthi, A. (2021). Euthanasia: A debate – For and against. *Journal of Postgraduate Medicine, Education and Research, 55*, 91–96.

Kumar, K. (1983). Educational experience of scheduled castes and tribes. *Economic and Political Weekly, 18*, 1566–1572.

Kumar, K. (1991). *Political agenda of education: A study of colonialist and national ideas*. SAGE.

Kumar, K. (1996). *Learning from conflicts*. Orient BlackSwan.

Kumar, K. (2007). *Education and society in India*. Routledge.

Kumar, K. S., & Akoijam, B. S. (2017). Depression, anxiety and stress among higher secondary school students of Imphal, Manipur. *Indian Journal of Community Medicine, 42*, 94–96.

Kumar, K. S., & Oesterheld, J. (Eds.). (2007). *Education and social change in South Asia*. Orient Longman.

Kumar, M. (2007). A journey into the bleeding city: Following the footprints of the rubble of riot and violence of earthquake in Gujarat, India. *Psychology and Developing Societies, 19*, 1–36.

Kumar, R. P. (2004). Survivors' suffering and healing amidst changing socioeconomic forces in two years of post-earthquake Kachchh. *Psychology and Developing Societies, 16*, 41–60.

Kurtz, L. F. (1992). Group environments in self-help groups for families. *Small Group Research, 23*, 199–215.

Labouvie-Vief, G. (2015). *Integrating emotions and cognition throughout the life-span*. Springer.
Laddu, N., & Kapadia, S. (2007). Children's judgments of parental fairness: An Indian perspective. *International Education Journal, 8*, 244–253.
Lakatta, E. G., & Levy, D. (2003). Arterial and cardiac aging: Major shareholders in cardiovascular disease enterprises: Part I: Aging arteries: A "set up" for vascular disease. *Circulation, 107*, 139–146.
Lamarck, J. B. (1809). *Philosophie Zoologique, ou Exposition des Considérations Relatives à l'Histoire Naturelle des Animaux* [Zoological Philosophy, or an Exposition of Considerations Relative to the Natural History of Animals.]. Dentu.
Lange, C. G. (1885). *Om Sindsbevægelser (On mental processes)*. Danmarks og Norges Litteratur.
Lapsley, D. K., & Narvaez, D. (2004). A social-cognitive approach to the moral personality. In D. K. Lapsley & D. Narvaez (Eds.), *Moral development, self, and identity* (pp. 189–212). Lawrence Erlbaum Associates.
Lashkar, S. (2021). Domestic violence on adolescent girl child: A case study in a selected urban area of Assam, India. *Academia Letters*, Article 895. https://doi.org/10.20935/AL895.
Laursen, B., & Collins, W. A. (2009). Parent-child conflict during adolescence. In R. M. Lerner & L. Steinberg (Eds.), *Handbook of adolescent psychology* (pp. 356–388). John Wiley & Sons.
Lazarus, R. S. (1966). *Psychological stress and the coping process*. McGraw-Hill.
Lazarus, R. S. (1991). *Emotion and adaptation*. Oxford University Press.
Lazarus, R. S., & Folkman, S. (1984). *Stress, appraisal, and coping*. Springer.
Leary, M. R. (1999). Making sense of self-esteem. *Current Directions in Psychological Science, 8*, 32–35.
Lenneberg, E. H. (1967). *Biological foundations of language*. Wiley.
Leonardelli, G. J., & Brewer, M. B. (2001). Minority and majority discrimination: When and why. *Journal of Experimental Social Psychology, 37*, 468–485.
Lerner, R. M. (2008). The contributions of Paul B. Baltes to the transformation of the field of child development: From developmental psychology to developmental science. *Research in Human Development, 5*, 69–79.
Leung, A. S. M. (2005). Emotional intelligence or emotional blackmail: A study of Chinese professional service firm. *International Journal of Cross-Cultural Management, 5*, 181–196.
Leviatan, U. (2017). Physical social capital and psychosocial social capital as mediators between socio-economic inequality and expressions of well-being and health in Israeli Kibbutz populations. *Psychology and Developing Societies, 29*, 160–199.
Levine, B. R., Harrington, J. R., & Uhlmann, E. L. (2019). Culture and work. In D. Cohen & S. Kitayama (Eds.), *Handbook of cultural psychology* (2nd ed., pp. 630–649). The Guilford Press.
Levine, S. C., Ratliff, K. R., Huttenlocher, J., & Cannon, J. (2012). Early puzzle play: A predictor of preschoolers' spatial transformation skill. *Developmental Psychology, 48*, 530–542.
Lewin, K. (1951). *Field theory in social science: Selected theoretical papers*. Harper & Brothers.
Lewin, R., & Foley, R. A. (2004). *Principles of human evolution*. John Wiley & Sons.
Lewis, M., & Brooks-Gunn, J. (1979). *Social cognition and the acquisition of self*. Plenum Press.
Liu, D., Wellman, H. M., Tardif, T., & Sabbagh, M. A. (2008). Theory of mind development in Chinese children: A meta-analysis of false belief understanding across cultures and languages. *Developmental Psychology, 44*, 523–531.
Lockenhoff, C. E., De Fruyt, F., Terracciano, A., McCrae, R. R., De Bolle, M., Costa, P. T. Jr, Aguilar-Vafaie, M. E., Ahn, C. K., Ahn, H. N., Alcalay, L., Allik, J., Avdeyeva, T. V., Barbaranelli, C., Benet-Martinez, V., Blatný, M., Bratko, D., Cain, T. R., Crawford, J. T., Lima, M. P., Ficková, E., Gheorghiu, M., Halberstadt, J., Hrebícková, M., Jussim, L., Klinkosz, W., Knezević, G., de Figueroa, N. L., Martin, T. A., Marusić, I., Mastor, K. A., Miramontez, D. R., Nakazato, K., Nansubuga, F., Pramila, V. S., Realo, A., Rolland, J. P., Rossier, J., Schmidt, V., Sekowski, A., Shakespeare-Finch, J., Shimonaka, Y., Simonetti, F., Siuta, J., Smith, P. B., Szmigielska, B., Wang, L., Yamaguchi, M., & Yik, M. (2009). Perceptions of aging across 26 cultures and their culture-level associates. *Psychological Aging, 24*, 941–954.
Lodefoged, P., & Johnson, K. (2011). *A course in phonetics*. Wadsworth.
Lodhi, P. H., Deo, S., & Belhekar, V. M. (2002). The Five-Factor model of personality: Measurement and correlates in the Indian context. In R. R. McCrae & J. Allik (Eds.), *The five-factor model of personality across cultures* (pp. 227–248). Kluwer Academic/Plenum Publishers.
Logan, S. W., Barnett, L. M., Goodway, J. D., & Stodden, D. F. (2017). Comparison of performance on process-and product-oriented assessments of fundamental motor skills across childhood. *Journal of Sports Sciences, 35*, 634–641.
Lutz, C., & White, G. M. (1986). The anthropology of emotions. *Annual Review of Anthropology, 15*, 405–436.

Lyubomirsky, S., & Ross, L. (1997). Hedonic consequences of social comparison: A contrast of happy and unhappy people. *Journal of Personality and Social Psychology, 73*, 1141–1157.

Madaan, P., Saini, L., & Sondhi, V. (2021). Development assessment scale for Indian infants: A systematic review and perspective on dwindling cutoffs. *Indian Journal of Pediatrics, 88*, 918–920.

Magan, D., Mehta, M., Sarvottam, K., Yadav, R. K., & Pandey, R. M. (2014). Age and gender might influence big five factors of personality: A preliminary report in Indian population. *Indian Journal of Physiology and Pharmacology, 58*, 381–3888.

Mahadevan, T. K. (1978). Priyamvada: The Hindu perception of excellence. *The Illustrated Weekly of India, 37*, 20–26.

Main, M., & Solomon, J. (1986). Discovery of an insecure-disorganized/disoriented attachment pattern: Procedures, findings and implications for the classification of behavior. In T. B. Brazelton & M. W. Yogman (Eds.), *Affective development in infancy* (pp. 95–124). Ablex Publishing.

Malhi, P., Bharti, B., & Sidhu, M. (2015). Peer victimization among adolescents: Relational and physical aggression in Indian schools. *Psychological Studies, 60*, 77–83.

Malhotra, S., & Dutta, A. (2019). The role of maternal expressiveness and emotion regulation in the emotional development of Indian infants. *Early Child Development and Care, 189*, 1823–1833.

Malina, R. M. (2001). Physical activity and fitness: Pathways from childhood to adulthood. *American Journal of Human Biology, 13*, 162–172.

Mandal, M. K., & Dutta, T. (2001). Left handedness: Facts and figures across cultures. *Psychology & Developing Societies, 13*, 173–191.

Mandal, M. K., Pandey, G., Singh, S. K., Asthana, H. S. (1992). Hand preference in India. *International Journal of Psychology, 27*, 433–442.

Marigoudar, S. B., & Kamble, S. V. (2014). A study of forgiveness and empathy: A gender difference. *Indian Journal of Positive Psychology, 5*, 173–177.

Marks, L. D., & Dollahite, D. C. (2017). *Religion and families*. Routledge.

Markus, H. R., & Kitayama, S. (1991). Culture and the self: Implications for cognition, emotion, and motivation. *Psychological Review, 98*, 224–253.

Martin, C. D., Dering, B., Thomas, E., & Thierry, G. (2009). Brain potentials reveal semantic priming in both the "active" and the "non-attended" language of early bilinguals. *Neuroimage, 471*, 326–333.

Mascolo, M., Misra, G., & Rapisardi, C. (2004). Individual and relational conceptions of self in India and the United States. *New Directions for Child and Adolescent Development, 104*, 9–26.

Maslow, A. H. (1943). A theory of human motivation. *Psychological Review, 50*, 370–396.

Maslow, A. H. (1954). *Motivation and personality*. Harper & Row.

Maslow, A. H. (1968). *Toward a psychology of being*. Van Nostrand Reinhold.

Masten, A. S., & Cicchetti, D. (2016). Resilience in development: Progress and transformation. In D. Cicchetti (Ed.), *Developmental psychopathology* (3rd ed., vol. 4, pp. 271–333). John Wiley & Sons.

Masten, A. S., & Narayan, A. J. (2012). Child development in the context of disaster, war, and terrorism: Pathways of risk and resilience. *Annual Review of Psychology, 63*, 227–257.

Masuda, T., Rissell, M. J., Li, M. L. W., & Lee, H. (2019). Cognition and perception. In D. Cohen & S. Kitayama (Eds.), *The Handbook of cultural psychology* (pp. 222–245). The Guilford Press.

Mathew, N., Khakha, D. C., Qureshi, A., Sagar, R., & Khakha, C. C. (2015). Stress and coping among adolescents in selected schools in the Capital City of India. *Indian Journal of Pediatrics, 82*, 809–816.

Mathur, M. (2009). Socialisation of street children in India: A socio-economic profile. *Psychology and Developing Societies, 21*, 299–325.

Matsumoto, D. (2006). Culture and nonverbal behavior. In V. Manusov & M. L. Patterson (Eds.), *The SAGE handbook of nonverbal communication* (pp. 219–235). Sage.

Matsumoto, D., & Hwang, H. C. (2012). Culture and emotion. *Journal of Cross-Cultural Psychology, 43*, 91–118.

Matsumoto, D., Yoo, S. H., & Nakagawa, S. (2008). Culture, emotion regulation, and adjustment. *Journal of Personality and Social Psychology, 94*, 925–937.

May, R. (1958). *Existence*. Basic Books.

Mayer, C. H. (2021). Meaning-making through love stories in cultural perspectives: Expressions, rituals and symbols. In C. H. Mayer & E. Vanderheiden (Eds.), *International handbook of love: Transcultural and transdisciplinary perspectives* (pp. 895–922). Springer Nature.

Mayer, C. H., & Vanderheiden, E. (2021). Voicing the stories of love across cultures: An introduction. In M. C.-H. Mayer & E. Vanderheiden (Eds.), *International handbook of love: Transcultural and transdisciplinary perspectives* (pp. 3–22). Springer Nature.

Mayer, J. D., & Salovey, P. (1997). What is emotional intelligence? In P. Salovey & D. Sluyter (Eds.), *Emotional development and emotional intelligence: Educational implications* (pp. 3–31). Basic Books.

Mayer, J. D., Salovey, P., & Caruso, D. (2000). Models of emotional intelligence. In R. J. Sternberg (Ed.), *Handbook of intelligence* (pp. 396–420). Cambridge University Press.

McAdams, D. P. (1996). Personality, modernity, and the storied self: A contemporary framework for studying persons. *Psychological Inquiry, 7*, 295–321.

McAdams, D. P. (2011). Narrative identity. In S. J. Schwartz, K. Luyckx, & V. L. Vignoles (Eds.), *Handbook of identity theory and research* (pp. 99–115). Springer.

McAdams, D. P. (2018). The five-factor model in personality: A critical appraisal. *Journal of Research in Personality, 73*, 137–151.

McAdams, D. P., & Olson, B. D. (2010). Personality development: Continuity and change over the life course. *Annual Review of Psychology, 61*, 517–542.

McCord, B. L., & Raval, V. V. (2016). Asian Indian immigrant and white American maternal emotion socialization and child socio-emotional functioning. *Journal of Child and Family Studies, 25*, 464–474.

McCrae, R. R., & Costa, P. T., Jr. (1987). Validation of the five-factor model of personality across instruments and observers. *Journal of Personality and Social Psychology, 52*, 81–90.

McCrae, R. R., & Costa, P. T., Jr. (2013). Introduction to the empirical and theoretical status of the five-factor model of personality traits. In T. A. Widiger & P. T. Costa, Jr. (Eds.), *Personality disorders and the five-factor model of personality* (pp. 15–27). American Psychological Association.

McCrae, R. R., & Terracciano, A. (2005). Universal features of personality traits from the observer's perspective: Data from 50 cultures. *Journal of Personality and Social Psychology, 88*, 547–561.

McDougall, W. (1908). *An introduction to social psychology*. Methuen & Co. Ltd.

McManus, C. (2009). *Right hand, left hand: The origins of asymmetry in brains, bodies, atoms and cultures*. Harvard University Press.

Mead, G. H. (1934). *Mind, self, and society: From the standpoint of a social behaviorist*. University of Chicago Press.

Mead, G. H. (1967). *Mind, self, and society: From the standpoint of a social behaviorist*. University of Chicago Press.

Medland, S. E., Duffy, D. L., Wright, M. J., Geffen, G. M., & Martin, N. G. (2006). Handedness in twins: Joint analysis of data from 35 samples. *Twin Research Human Genetics, 9*, 46–53.

Mehrotra, S., Narayanan, A., & Tripathi, R. (2018). Understanding resilience: Global trends and Indian research. In G. Misra (Ed.), *Psychosocial interventions for health and well-being* (pp. 59–81). Springer.

Mehta, A. C. (2023). *Status & challenges of Samagra Shiksha*. https://educationforallinindia.com/status-challenges-of-samagra-shiksha-2023/.

Menon, P., Doddoli, S., Singh, S., & Bhogal, R. (2014). Personality correlates of mindfulness: A study in an Indian setting. *Yoga Mimansa: A Journal of Scientific and Philosophico- Literary Research in Yoga, 46*, 29–36.

Menon, S. (1998). The ontological pragmaticity of Karma in Bhagavad Gita. *Journal of Indian Philosophy, 16*, 44–52.

Menon, U. (2013). The Hindu concept of self-refinement: Implicit yet meaningful. *Psychology and Developing Societies, 25*, 195–222.

Menon, U., & Shweder, R. A. (1994). Kali's tongue: Cultural psychology and the power of "shame" in Orissa, India." In S. Kitayama & H. Markus (Eds.). *Emotions and culture* (pp. 241–284). American Psychological Association.

Menon, U., & Shweder, R. A. (1998). The return of the "white man's burden": The encounter between the moral discourse of anthropology and the domestic life of Hindu women. In R. A. Shweder (Ed.). *Welcome to middle age! (and other cultural fictions)* (pp. 139–188). University of Chicago Press.

Mery, F., & Burns, J. G. (2010). Behavioural plasticity: An interaction between evolution and experience. *Evolutionary Ecology, 24*, 571–583.

Mesquita, B., Vissers, N., & Leersnyder, J. D. (2015). Culture and emotion. In J. D. Wright (Ed.), *International encyclopedia of the social and behavioral sciences* (2nd ed., vol 5, pp. 542–549). Elsevier.

Messinger, D., & Fogel, A. (2007). The interactive development of social smiling. In R. V. Kail (Ed.), *Advances in child development and behavior* (pp. 327–366). Elsevier.

Milgram, S. (1974). *Obedience to authority: An experimental view*. Harper & Row.

Miller, B. S. (1986). Nishkama karma: The right action of non-attachment. *Journal of Indian Philosophy, 14*, 357–375.

Miller, D. T. (1984). Women's moral reasoning: A critique of Kohlberg's theory. *Psychological Bulletin, 95*, 448–463.

Miller, G. A. (1956). The magical number seven, plus or minus two: Some limits on our capacity for processing information. *Psychological Review, 63*, 81–97.

Miller, J. G., & Bersoff, D. M. (1998). The role of liking in perceptions of the moral responsibility to help: A cultural perspective. *Journal of Experimental Social Psychology, 34*, 443–469.

Miller, J. G., Das, R., & Chakravarthy, S. (2011). Culture and the role of choice in agency. *Journal of Personality and Social Psychology, 101*, 46–61.

Miller, J. G., Wice, M., & Goyal, N. (2019). Cultural psychology of moral development. In D. Cohen & S. Kitayama (Eds.), *Handbook of cultural psychology* (pp. 424–446). The Guilford Press.

Minturn, L. (1966). *The rajputs of Khalapur India*. John Wiley.

Mishra, R. C. (2014). Piagetian studies of cognitive development in India. *Psychological Studies, 59*, 207–222.

Mishra, R. C. (2017). Meaning of happy life for the Kharwars in India in their journey towards development. *Psychology and Developing Societies, 29*, 221–245.

Mishra, R., & Datta, S. (2024). *Designing a mentorship curriculum for assisting social reintegration among youth in institutional care in India*. [Manuscript under review].

Mishra, R., & Sondhi, V. (2019). Fostering resilience among orphaned adolescents through institutional care in India. *Residential Treatment for Children & Youth, 36*, 314–337.

Mishra, R., & Sondhi, V. (2021). Theorizing pathways to resilience among orphaned adolescents in institutional care in India. *Children and Youth Services Review, 124*, 105972. https://doi.org/10.1016/j.childyouth.2021.105972.

Mishra, R. K., & Baveja, B. (2014). Understanding the cultural situatedness of learning: Implications for pedagogy. *The International Journal of Pedagogy and Curriculum, 20*, 19–32.

Misra, G. (1991). Socio-cultural influences on moral behaviour. *Indian Journal of Social Work, 52*, 1404–1436.

Misra, G. (1995). Introduction. *Psychology and Developing Societies, 7*, 111–114.

Misra, G. (2004). Emotion in modern psychology and Indian thought. In K. Joshi & M. Cornelissen (Eds), *Consciousness, science, society and yoga*. Centre for Studies in Civilizations.

Misra, G. (2005). The science of affect. In K. Ramakrishna Rao & S. B. Marwaha (Eds), *Towards a spiritual psychology: Essays in Indian psychology*. Samvad.

Misra, G., & Gergen, K. J. (1993). On the place of culture in psychological science. *International Journal of Psychology, 28*, 225–243.

Misra, G., Kapur, M., & Srivastava, A. K. (1998). Emerging trends and future perspectives: A reprisal. In A. K. Srivastava (Ed.), *Child development: The Indian perspective* (pp. 266–283). NCERT.

Misra, G., & Kapur, P. (2014). Recovering the potentials of non-western psychological perspectives: Combining Chinese and Indian perspectives. *Culture & Psychology, 20*, 440–450.

Misra, G., & Kashyap, R. (2016). Self-construal and coping strategies among American and Indian college students. *Journal of Social Psychology, 156*, 633–647.

Misra, G., Sanyal, N., & De, S. (Eds.). (2021). *Psychology in modern India: Historical, methodological, and future perspectives*. Springer.

Misra, G., & Srivastava, A. K. (2002). Towards integral intelligence. In P. Boski, F. J. R. van de Vijver, & A. M. Chodynicka (Eds.), *New directions in cross-cultural psychology* (pp. 193–208). Polish Psychological Association.

Misra, G., Srivastava, A. K., & Gupta, S. (1999). The cultural construction of childhood in India: Some observations. *Indian Psychological Abstracts and Reviews, 6*, 191–218.

Misra, G., Srivastava, A. K., & Misra, I. (2006). Culture and facets of Creativity: The Indian experience. In J. C. Kaufman & R. J. Sternberg (Eds.), *The international handbook of creativity* (pp. 421–455). Cambridge University Press.

Misra, G., & Tripathi, K. N. (1998). Cognitive development. In A. K. Srivastava (Ed.), *Child development: The Indian perspective* (pp. 75–111). NCERT.

Misra, I., Suar, D., & Mandal, M. K. (2008). How good people are at estimating their own performance? A study of the relationship between hand preference and motor performance. *Psychology and Developing Societies, 20*, 111–125.

Misri, S. (1986). Child and childhood: A conceptual construction. In V. Das (Ed.), *The word and the world*. SAGE.

Mitchell, S. A., & Black, M. J. (1995). *Freud and beyond: A history of modern psychoanalytic thought*. Basic Books.

Mlacic, B., & Milas, G. (2015). Personality changes during adolescence across cultures. In J. D. Wright (Ed.), *International encyclopedia of the social & behavioral sciences* (2nd ed., pp. 863–869). Elsevier.

Modi, K., Nayar-Akhtar, M., Ariely, S., & Gupta, D. (2016). Addressing challenges of transition from children's home to independence: Udayan Care's Udayan Ghars (Sunshine Children's Homes) & aftercare programme. *Scottish Journal of Residential Child Care, 15*, 87–101.

Mohanty, A. K. (1982). Cognitive and linguistic development of tribal children from unilingual and bilingual environments. In R. Rath, H. S. Asthana, D. Sinha, & J. B. P. Sinha (Eds.), *Diversity and unity in cross-cultural psychology* (pp. 78–86). Swets Zeitlinger, B.V.

Mohanty, A. K. (1990). Psychological consequences of mother tongue maintenance and multilingualism in India. In D. P. Pattanayak (Ed.), *Multilingualism in India* (pp. 54–66). Multilingual Matters.

Mohanty, A. K. (2002). The weaning syndrome: Acquired dependence among super cyclone victims in Orissa. *Psychology and Developing Societies, 14*, 261–276.

Mohanty, A. K. (2006). The multilingualism of the unequal and predicaments of education in India: Mother tongue or another tongue? In O. Garcia, T. Skutnabb-Kangas, & M. Torres Guzman (Eds.), *Imagining multilingual schools: Language in education and glocalization* (pp. 262–283). Multilingual Matters.

Mohanty, A. K. (Ed.). (2019). *The multilingual reality: Living with languages*. Multilingual Matters.

Mohanty, A. K., & Babu, N. (1983). Bilingualism and Metalinguistic Ability among Kond Tribals in Orissa (India). *The Journal of Social Psychology, 121*, 15–22.

Mohanty, A. K., & Das, S. P. (1987). Cognitive and metalinguistic activity of unschooled bilingual and unilingual tribal children. *Psychological Studies, 32*, 5–8.

Mohanty, A. K., Dash, U. N., & Sahoo, R. N. (1994). *Cognitive development of unilingual and bilingual tribal children: Effects of schooling and age*. ICSSR Project Report. Utkal University.

Mohanty, A. K., Panda, M., Phillipson, R., & Skutnabb-Kangas, T. (Eds.). (2009). *Multilingual education for social justice: Globalising the local*. Orient BlackSwan.

Mohanty, A. K., & Perregaux, C. (1997). Language acquisition and bilingualism. In J. W. Berry, P. R. Dasen, & T. S. Saraswathi (Eds.), *Handbook of cross-cultural psychology, Vol. 2: Basic processes and human development* (2nd ed., pp. 217–253). Allyn & Bacon.

Mohanty, A. K., & Saikia, J. (2004, August 2–6). *Bilingualism and intergroup relationships in tribal and non-tribal contact situations*. Paper presented in the XVII Congress of the International Association of Cross-Cultural Psychology, Xian.

Mohanty, S. (2017). *Effect of yoga on physical and psychological health of children with visual impairment* [Unpublished Doctoral Dissertation]. Swami Vivekananda Yoga Anusandhana Sansthana.

Monroe, S. M., & Simons, A. D. (1991). Diathesis-stress theories in the context of life stress research: Implications for the depressive disorders. *Psychological Bulletin, 110*, 406–425.

Moore, K. L., Persaud, T. V. N., & Torchia, M. G. (2019). *The developing human: Clinically oriented embryology* (10th ed.). Elsevier.

Mundy-Castle, A. C. (1974). Social and technological intelligence in western and non-western cultures. *Universitas, 4*, 46–52.

Muralidharan, R. (1971). *Motor development of Indian children* (mimeographed). NCERT.

Muralidharan, R. (1986). *A comparison of the developmental norms of Indian children as obtained by the cross-sectional and longitudinal studies, 2 to 5 years*. NCERT.

Muralidharan, R., & Srivastava, A. K. (1995). Temple ecology and cognitive development: A report from south India. *Psychology and Developing Societies, 7*, 47–64.

Murman, D. L. (2015). The impact of age on cognition. *Seminars in Hearing, 36*, 111–121.

Murthy, S. R., & Dharmayat, S. (2020). Relationship between home environment and psychomotor development in Urban and Rural children: A cross-sectional study. *Indian Journal of Physical Therapy and Research, 2*, 41–46.

Nadda, A., Malik, J. S., Rohilla, R., Chahal, S., Chayal, V., & Arora, V. (2018). Study of domestic violence among currently married females of Haryana, India. *Indian Journal of Psychological Medicine, 40*, 534–539.

Nagar, A., Chowdhury, A., Bhandari, A., Sengar, G., & Kumari, J. (2021). Effect of self-esteem and gratitude on personal growth in Indian students. *International Journal of Social Sciences and Humanities Invention, 8*, 6497–6503.

Naito, M., & Koyama, K. (2006). The development of false-belief understanding in Japanese children: Delay and difference? *International Journal of Behavioral Development, 30*, 290–304.

Nakamura, J., & Csikszentmihalyi, M. (2009). Flow theory and research. In C. R. Snyder & S. J. Lopez (Eds.), *Oxford handbook of positive psychology* (2nd ed., pp. 195–206). Oxford University Press.

Nambi, G., Inbasekaran, V., Khuman, R., & Devi, S. (2011). Role of Sthitipragya in chronic pain management. *Indian Journal of Traditional Knowledge, 10*, 670–674.

Nambissan, G. B. (2020). Caste and the politics of the early 'public' in schooling: Dalit struggle for an equitable education. *Contemporary Education Dialogue, 17*, 126–154.

Namdev, G., & Narkhede, V. (2020). Reasons of open defecation behavior in rural households of Bhopal, Madhya Pradesh, India. *National Journal of Community Medicine, 11*, 103–106.

Nanda, S. (2008). *Working street children's perceptions of their health, illness and health- seeking behaviour- A qualitative study in New Delhi, India* [Unpublished Master's thesis submitted to the Department of International Health]. Royal Tropical Institute, KIT.

Nanthakumar, C. (2018). The benefits of yoga in children. *Journal of Integrative Medicine, 16*, 14–19.

Naragatti, S. (2020). The study of yoga effects on health. *International Journal of Innovative Medicine and Health Science, 12*, 98–110.

Narvaez, D., & Lapsley, D. K. (2005). The psychological foundations of everyday morality and moral expertise. In D. K. Lapsley & F. C. Power (Eds.), *Character psychology and character education* (pp. 140–165). University of Notre Dame Press.

National Curriculum Framework. (2005). *National Curriculum Framework*. NCERT.

National Curriculum Framework for Foundation Stage. (2022). *National Curriculum Framework for Foundation Stage*. Government of India (Ministry of Education).

National Curriculum Framework for School Education. (2000). *National Curriculum Framework for School Education*. NCERT.

National Curriculum Framework for School Education. (2023). *National Curriculum Framework for School Education*. National Steering Committee for National Curriculum Frameworks and NCERT.

National Education Policy. (2020). *National Education Policy*. Government of India (Department of Education).

National Family Health Survey. (2019). *National Family Health Survey (NFHS-5) 2019-21-Compendium of fact sheets-India and 14 states/UTs (Phase II)*. Government of India (Ministry of Health & Family Welfare).

National Human Rights Commission. (2014). *Rights of transgender persons in India*. https://nhrc.nic.in/sites/default/files/transgenderpersons.pdf

National Institute of Nutrition. (2011). *Dietary guidelines for Indians: A manual*. National Institute of Nutrition.

National Mental Health Survey of India. (2016). *National Mental Health Survey of India, 2015–16: Mental Health Systems*. NIMHANS.

National Policy on Education. (1986). *National Policy on Education*. Government of India (Ministry of Human Resource Development).

Nayak, I., Siddhanta, A., & Panda, B. K. (2022). Does empty nest elderly experience more depressive symptoms than non-empty nest elderly? Evidence from longitudinal aging study in India. *Hospital Topics, 11*, 1–12.

NCERT. (2005). *National focus group on problems of scheduled caste and scheduled tribe children*. NCERT.

NCERT. (2012). *Education for values in schools: A framework*. NCERT.

NCERT. (2015). *Including children with special needs: Upper primary stage*. NCERT.

NCERT. (2018). *NCERT Barkha series level 1 to 4*. NCERT.

NCERT. (2021). *National achievement survey: National report – classes III, V, VIII, and X*. NCERT.

NCERT. (2022a). *Toy-based pedagogy: A handbook-Learning for fun, joy, and holistic development* (Part I). NCERT.

NCERT. (2022b). *Pre-Assessment Holistic Screening Checklist for Schools (PRASHAST)*. NCERT.

NCERT. (2023). *Integrating transgender concerns in schooling process: A module for school staff*. NCERT.

Neisser, U., Boodoo, G., Bouchard, T. J., Jr., Boykin, A. W., Brody, N., Ceci, S. J., Halpern, D. F., Loehlin, J. C., Perloff, R., Sternberg, R. J., & Urbina, S. (1996). Intelligence: Knowns and unknowns. *American Psychologist, 51*, 77–101.

Neria, Y., Gross, R., Litz, B., Maguen, S., Insel, B., Seirmarco, G., Rosenfeld, H., Suh, E. J., Kishon, R., Cook, J., & Marshall, R. D. (2007). Prevalence and psychological correlates of complicated grief among bereaved adults 2.5–3.5 years after September 11th attacks. *Journal of Traumatic Stress, 20*, 251–262.

Neria, Y., Nandi, A., & Galea, S. (2008). Post-traumatic stress disorder following disasters: A systematic review. *Psychological Medicine, 38*, 467–480.

NIPCCD. (2009). *Research on ICDS: An overview* (Vol. 3). NIPCCD.

Nisbett, R. E. (2003). *The geography of thought: How Asians and Westerners think differently . . . and why*. Free Press.

Nisbett, R. E. (2019). Culture and intelligence. In D. Cohen & S. Kitayama (Eds.), *The Handbook of cultural psychology* (2nd ed., pp. 207–221). The Guilford Press.

Nisbett, R. E., & Cohen, D. (1996). *Culture of honor: The psychology of violence in the South*. Routledge.

Nisbett, R. E., & Miyamoto, Y. (2005). The influence of culture: Holistic versus analytic perception. *Trends in Cognitive Sciences, 9*, 467–473.

Nisbett, R. E., Peng, K., Choi, I., & Norenzayan, A. (2001). Culture and systems of thought: Holistic versus analytic cognition. *Psychological Review, 108*, 291–310.

Nishaat, A. (2022). Comparative study of realistic optimism between India and Japan university students. *IAFOR Journal of Psychology & the Behavioral Sciences, 8*, 55–67.

Nobles, J., Frankenberg, E., & Thomas, D. (2015). The effects of mortality on fertility: Population dynamics after a natural disaster. *Demography, 52*, 15–38.

Norris, F. H., Byrne, C. M., & Diaz, E. (2001). *50,000 disaster victims speak: An empirical review of the empirical literature, 1981–2001* (Best Practices Project prepared for the National Center for PTSD and the Center for Mental Health Services). Department of Psychology, Georgia State University.

Nunez, R. E., & Sweetser, E. (2006). With the future behind them: Convergent evidence from Aymara language and gesture in the crosslinguistic comparison of spatial construals of time. *Cognitive Science, 30*, 401–450.

Nussbaum, M. C. (1994). *The therapy of desire: Theory and practice in Hellenistic ethics*. Princeton University Press.

Ochs, E., & Schieffelin, B. B. (2011). The theory of language socialization. In P. A. Duff & S. May (Eds.), *The handbook of language socialization* (pp. 1–21). Springer.

O'Connor, A., & Daly, A. (2016). *Understanding physical development in the early years: Linking bodies and minds*. Routledge.

Ong, A. D., Bergeman, C. S., Bisconti, T. L., & Wallace, K. A. (2006). Psychological resilience, positive emotions, and successful adaptation to stress in later life. *Journal of Personality and Social Psychology, 91*, 730–749.

Ong, W. J. (1982). *Orality and literacy: The technologizing of the word*. Methuen.

Orth, U., Erol, R. Y., & Luciano, E. C. (2018). Development of self-esteem from age 4 to 94 years: A meta-analysis of longitudinal studies. *Psychological Bulletin, 144*, 1045–1080.

Orth, U., & Robins, R. W. (2014). The development of self-esteem. *Current Directions in Psychological Science, 23*, 381–387.

Owe, E., Vignoles, V.L., Becker, M., Brown, R. Smith, P.B., Lee, S.W., Easterbrook, M., Gadre, T., Zhang, X., Gheorghiu, M., Baguma, P., Atarko, A., Aldhafri, S., Zinkeng, M., Schwartz, S.J., Shneyderman, Y., Villamar, J., Mekonnen, K.H., Regalia, C., Manzi C., Brambilla, M., Caglar, E., Gavriliuc, A., Martin, M., Jianxin, Z., Lv, S., Fischer, R., Milfont, T., Torres, A., Camino, L., Kreuzbauer, R., Gausel, N., Buitendach, J., Lemos, F., Fritsche, I., Moller, B., Harb, C., Valk, A., Espinosa, A., Jaafar, J.L., Yuki, M., Ferreira, M.C., Chobthamkit, P., Fulop, M., Chybicka, A., Wang, Q., Bond, M.H., Gonzalez, R., Didier, N., Carrasco, D., Cadena, M.P., Lay, S., Gardarsdottir, R., Nizharadze, G., Pyszczynski, T., Kesebir, P., Herman, G., Bourguignon, D., De Sauvage, I., Ozgen, E., Guner, U.E., Yamakoglu, N., Abuhamdeh, S., Macapagal, M., Koller, S.H., Amponsah, B., Misra, G., Kapur, P., Trujillo, E.V., Balanta, P., Ayala, B.C., Gallo, I.S., Gill, P.P., Clemares, R.L., Campara, G., & Jalal, B. (2013). Contextualism as an important facet of individualism-collectivism: Personhood beliefs across 37 national groups. *Journal of Cross-Cultural Psychology, 44*, 24–45.

Oystermen, D., Coon, H. M., & Kemmelmeier, M. (2002). Rethinking individualism and collectivism: Evaluation of theoretical assumptions and meta-analyses. *Psychological Bulletin, 128*, 3–72.

Padilla-Walker, L. M., Carlo, G., & Memmott-Elison, M. K. (2018). Longitudinal change in adolescents' prosocial behaviors toward strangers, friends, and family. *Journal of Research on Adolescence, 28*, 698–710.

Padmavati, R., Raghavan, V., Rera, H., Kearns, M., Rao, K., John, S., & Thara, R. (2020). Learnings from conducting mental health research during 2004 tsunami in Tamil Nadu, India. *BMC Public Health, 20*, 1627. https://doi.org/10.1186/s12889-020-09733-y

Pal, A., Mukhopadhyay, P., & Dawar Pal, N. (2022). Effects of a mindfulness based intervention on mental well-being and quality of life in Indian adults: An early attempt for integration into community clinical practice. *International Journal of Community Medicine and Public Health, 9*, 2183–2189.

Paltasingh, T., & Bhue, P. (2022). Efficacy of mid-day meal scheme in India: Challenges and policy concerns. *Indian Journal of Public Administration, 68*, 610–623.

Pan, Y., & Detterman, D. K. (2013). Predicting academic achievement using the PASS theory of intelligence. *Journal of Intelligence, 1*, 30–47.

Panda, M. (2013). Madhyam marg: How it constitutes Indian mind? *Psychology and Developing Societies, 25*, 77–107.

Pande, N. (2013). Kartavya: Understanding selfless acts. *Psychology and Developing Societies, 25*, 109–132.

Pandey, J., & Singh, P. (1997). Allocation criterion as a function of situational factors and caste. *Basic and Applied Social Psychology, 19*, 121–132.

Pandey, N. M., Misra, I., & Tiwari, S. C. (2018). Interventions for enhancing health and well- being among Indian elderly. In G. Misra (Ed.), *Psychosocial interventions for health and well-being* (pp. 157–174). Springer.

Pandit, S. A., & Satish, L. (2014). When does yoga work? Long term and short term effects of yoga intervention among pre-adolescent children. *Psychological Studies, 59*, 153–165.

Pandith, P., John, S., Bellon-Harn, M. L., Manchaiah, V. (2022). Parental Perspectives on storybook reading in Indian home contexts. *Early Childhood Education Journal, 50*, 315–325.

Pandya, N., & Bhangaokar, R. (2022). Equal but different: Views on gender roles and responsibilities among upper class Hindu Indians in established adulthood. *Journal of Adult Development*, 1–11. https://doi.org/10.1007/s10804-022-09417-4.

Pandya, N., Jensen, L. A., & Bhangaokar, R. (2021). Moral reasoning among children in India: The intersection of culture, development, and social class. *Applied Developmental Science, 27*, 1–20.

Papadatou-Pastou, M., Ntolka, E., Schmitz, J., Martin, M., Munafo, M. R., Ocklenburg, S., & Paracchini, S. (2020). Human handedness: A meta-analysis. *Psychological Bulletin, 14*, 481–524.

Paranjpe, A. C. (2009). In defence of an Indian approach to the psychology of emotion. *Psychological Studies, 54*, 1–22.

Paranjpe, A. C. (2013). The concept of dharma: Classical meaning, common misconceptions and implications for psychology. *Psychology and Developing Societies, 25*, 1–20.

Pargament, K. I. (1997). *The psychology of religion and coping: Theory, research, practice*. The Guilford Press.

Pascoe, M. C., & Bauer, I. E. (2015). A systematic review of randomised control trials on the effects of yoga on stress measures and mood. *Journal of Psychiatric Research, 68*, 270–282.

Pathak, P. (1990). *Developmental assessment scales for Indian infants*. M. S. University of Baroda.

Patnaik, B., & Babu, N. (2001). Relationship between children's acquisition of a theory of mind and their understanding of mental terms. *Psycho-Lingua, 31*, 3–8.

Pattanayak, D. P. (1988). Monolingual myopia and the petals of the Indian lotus: Do many languages divide or unite a nation? In T. Skutnabb-Kangas & J. Cummins (Eds.), *Minority education: From shame to struggle* (pp. 379–389). Multilingual Matters.

Pattanayak, D. P., & Illich, I. (1981). *Multilingualism and mother tongue education*. Oxford University Press.

Pearson, K., & Lee, A. (1903). On the laws of inheritance in man: I. Inheritance of physical characters. *Biometrika, 2*(4), 357–462.

Perry, B. D. (2002). Childhood experience and the expression of genetic potential: What childhood neglect tells us about nature and nurture. *Brain and Mind, 3*, 79–100.

Pesata, V., Colverson, A., Sonke, J., Morgan-Daniel, J., Schaefer, N., Sams, K., Carrion, F. M. E., & Hanson, S. (2022). Engaging the arts for wellbeing in the United States of America: A scoping review. *Frontiers in Psychology, 12*, 791773. https://doi.org/10.3389/fpsyg.2021.791773

Peshawaria, R., & Venkatesan, S. (1992). *Behavioral Assessment Scales for Indian Children with Mental Retardation (BASIC-MR)*. National Institute for the Mentally Handicapped.

Peterson, C., & Seligman, M. E. P. (2004). *Character strengths and virtues: A handbook and classification*. Oxford University Press.

Phatak, A. T., & Khurana, B. (1991). Baroda Developmental Screening Test for infants. *Indian Pediatrics, 28*, 29–35.

Piaget, J. (1932). *The moral judgment of the child*. Routledge & Kegan Paul.

Piaget, J. (1936). *Origins of intelligence in the child*. Routledge & Kegan Paul.

Piaget, J. (1952). *The origins of intelligence in children*. International Universities Press.
Piaget, J. (1954). *The construction of reality in the child* (M. Cook, Trans.). Basic Books.
Piaget, J. (1957). *Construction of reality in the child*. Routledge & Kegan Paul.
Piaget, J. (1964). Cognitive development in children: Development and learning. *Journal of Research in Science Teaching*, *2*, 176–186.
Piaget, J. (1965). *The moral judgment of the child*. Free Press.
Piaget, J. (1972). Intellectual evolution from adolescence to adulthood. *Human Development*, *15*, 1–12.
Piaget, J. (1977). *The development of thought: Equilibration of cognitive structures*. The Viking Press.
Pinker, S. (1994). *The language instinct: How the mind creates language*. Harper Collins.
Pinker, S. (2011). *The better angels of our nature: Why violence has declined*. The Viking Press.
Pistoia, F., Conson, M., Carolei, A., Dema, M. G., Splendiani, A., Curcio, G., & Sacco, S. (2018). Post-earthquake distress and development of emotional expertise in young adults. *Frontiers in Behavioral Neuroscience (Section. Emotion Regulation and Processing)*, *12*. https://doi.org/10.3389/fnbeh.2018.00091
Plomin, R., DeFries, J. C., & Loehlin, J. C. (1977). Genotype-environment interaction and correlation in the analysis of human behavior. *Psychological Bulletin*, *84*, 309–322.
Prabhu, G. S., Yen, J. T. M., Amalaraj, J. J. P., Jone, E. T. Y., & Kumar, N. (2016). Anger management among medical undergraduate students and its impact on their mental health and curricular activities. *Educational Research International*, Article ID 7461570. https://doi.org/10.1155/2016/7461570.
Prabhu, P. H. (1954). *Hindu social organisation*. Popular Book Depot.
Press Information Bureau (2022, February 16). *Government approves 'New India Literacy Programme, a new scheme of Adult Education for FYs 2022–27*. https://pib.gov.in/PressReleasePage.aspx?PRID=1798805
Procopio, M. (2001). Handedness and schizophrenia: Genetic and environmental factors. *British Journal of Psychiatry*, *179*, 75–76.
Pruitt, D. G., & Kim, S. H. (2004). *Social conflict: Escalation, stalemate, and settlement*. McGraw-Hill.
Radhakrishnan, S. (1923). *Indian philosophy* (Vol. 1). Oxford University Press.
Radhakrishnan, S., & Moore, C. A. (1957). *A source book in Indian philosophy*. Princeton University Press.
Raina, M. K. (2002). Guru-shishya relationship in Indian culture: The possibility of a creative resilient framework. *Psychology and Developing Societies*, *14*, 167–198.
Raina, M. K., Srivastava, A. K., & Misra, G. (2001). Explorations in literary creativity: Some preliminary observations. *Psychological Studies*, *46*, 148–160.
Raisa, Z. H., Karuppali, S., Bhat, J. S., & Bajaj, G. (2019). Thinking about what he thinks of what I think: Assessing higher theory of mind abilities in Indian bilingual children between 3.0 and 8.11 years of age. *Indian Journal of Psychiatry*, *61*, 167–176.
Raisz, L. G. (2005). Pathogenesis of osteoporosis: Concepts, conflicts, and prospects. *The Journal of Clinical Investigation*, *115*, 3318–3325.
Rajkumar, A. P., Yovan, S., Raveendran, A., & Russell, P. S. S. (2008). Can only intelligent children do mind reading: The relationship between intelligence and theory of mind in 8 to 11 years old. *Behavioural and Brain Functions*, *4*, 51. https://doi.org/10.1186/1744-9081-4-51
Ram, U., Strohschein, L., & Gaur, K. (2014). Gender socialization: Differences between male and female youth in India and associations with mental health. *International Journal of Population Research*, Article ID 357145. https://doi.org/10.1155/2014/357145.
Ramachandran, V. (2004). *Snake and ladders: Factors influencing successful primary school completion for children in poverty context: A qualitative study (South Asia Human Development Sector Series; No. 6)*. World Bank.
Ramamurti, P. V., & Jamuna, D. (2010). Geropsychology in India. In G. Misra (Ed.), *Psychology in India (Vol 3: Clinical and health psychology)*. Pearson.
Ranjani, H., Jagannathan, N., Rawal, T. Vinothkumar, R. Tandon, N., Vidyulatha, J., Mohan, V. Gupta, Y., & Anjana, R. M. (2023). The impact of yoga on stress, metabolic parameters, and cognition of Indian adolescents: A cluster randomized controlled trial. *Integrative Medicine Research*, *12*(3). https://doi.org/10.1016/j.imr.2023.100979.
Rao, N., Umayahara, M., Yang, Y., & Ranganathan, N. (2021). Ensuring access, equity and quality in early childhood education in Bangladesh, China, India and Myanmar: Challenges for nations in a populous economic corridor. *International Journal of Educational Development*, *82*, 102380. https://doi.org/10.1016/j.ijedudev.2021.102380.

Raval, V. V., & Martini, T. S. (2011). "Making the child understand:" Socialization of emotion in urban India. *Journal of Family Psychology, 25*, 847–856.

Raval, V. V., Raval, P. H., & Deo, N. (2014). Mothers' socialization goals, mothers' emotion socialization behaviors, child emotion regulation, and child socioemotional functioning in urban India. *Journal of Early Adolescence, 34*, 229–250.

Ravikumar, T. (2018). Pradhan Mantri Jan-Dhan Yojana: An evaluation. *Journal of Business Management, 17*, 9–13.

Rawls, J. (1971). *A theory of justice*. Harvard University Press.

Regnerus, M. D., & Burdette, A. (2006). Religious change and adolescent family dynamics. *The Sociological Quarterly, 47*, 175–194.

Rentfrow, P. J., & Jakola, M. (2019). Geographical variation in the big five personality domains. In D. Cohen & S. Kitayama (Eds.), *Handbook of cultural psychology* (2nd ed., pp. 768–792). The Guilford Press.

Ribble, M. (2015). *Digital citizenship in schools: Nine elements all students should know* (3rd ed.). International Society for Technology in Education.

Roberts, B. W., & Mroczek, D. (2008). Personality traits change in adulthood. *Current Directions in Psychological Science, 17*, 31–35.

Rogers, C. R. (1946). Significant aspects of client-centered therapy. *American Psychologist, 1*, 415–422.

Rogers, C. R. (1951). *Client-centered therapy: Its current practice, implications and theory*. Constable.

Rogers, C. R. (1961). *On becoming a person: A therapist's view of psychotherapy*. Houghton Mifflin Harcourt.

Rogoff, B. (1990). *Apprenticeship in thinking: Cognitive development in social context*. Oxford University Press.

Rogoff, B. (2003). *The cultural nature of human development*. Oxford University Press.

Rogoff, B., & Mejía-Arauz, E. G. (Eds.). (2014). *The cultural nature of human development*. Oxford University Press.

Rogoff, B., & Mejía-Arauz, R. (2022). The key role of community in learning by observing and pitching into family and community endeavours. *Journal for the Study of Education and Development, 45*, 494–548.

Rokeach, M. (1973). *The nature of human values*. Free Press.

Roland, A. (1988). *In search of self in India and Japan*. Princeton University.

Roopnarine, J. L., Krishnakumar, A., & Vadgama, D. (2013). Indian fathers: Family dynamics and investment patterns. *Psychology and Developing Societies, 25*, 223–247.

Rosenberg, M. (1965). *Society and the adolescent self-image*. Princeton University Press.

Rothbart, M. K., & Bates, J. E. (1998). Temperament. In W. Damon (Ed.), *Handbook of child psychology: Vol. 3. Social, emotional, and personality development* (5th ed., pp. 105–176). Wiley.

Rotter, J. B. (1966). Generalized expectancies for internal versus external control of reinforcement. *Psychological Monographs: General and Applied, 80*, 1–28.

Rowe, J. W. (2023). Successful aging: Evolution of a concept. *The Journal of Nutrition, Health & Aging, 27*, 194–195.

Ruble, D. N., & Martin, C. L. (2018). Gender development. In *Handbook of child psychology and developmental science* (pp. 1–60). John Wiley & Sons.

Rumelhart, D. E., & McClelland, J. L. (1986). *Parallel distributed processing: Explorations in the microstructure of cognition* (Vol. 1). MIT Press.

Ryan, R. M. (2014). The importance of psychological courage in leadership and organizations. *Consulting Psychology Journal: Practice and Research, 66*, 83–92.

Ryan, R. M., & Deci, E. L. (2000). Self-determination theory and the facilitation of intrinsic motivation, social development, and well-being. *American Psychologist, 55*, 68–78.

Saarni, C. (1997). Emotional competence and self-regulation in childhood. In P. Salovey & D. J. Sluyter (Eds.), *Emotional development and emotional intelligence: Educational implications* (pp. 35–69). Basic Books.

Sabbagh, M. A. (2017). Theory of mind across cultures. In *The Oxford handbook of developmental psychology, vol. 2: Self and other* (pp. 399–413). Oxford University Press.

Sahithya, B. R., Manohari, S. M., & Vijaya, R. (2019). Parenting styles and its impact on children – A cross cultural review with a focus on India. *Mental Health, Religion & Culture*. https://doi.org/10.1080/13674676.2019.1594178.

Saikia, H., Bhattacharyya, N., & Baruah, M. (2023). Review of educational toy design elements and their importance in child development from a cognitive perspective. *The Pharma Innovation Journal*, *12*, 1030–1033.

Salovey, P., & Mayer, J. D. (1990). Emotional intelligence. *Imagination, Cognition and Personality*, *9*, 185–211.

Salthouse, T. A. (1996). The processing-speed theory of adult age differences in cognition. *Psychological Review*, *103*, 403–428.

Salthouse, T. A. (2009). When does age-related cognitive decline begin? *Neurobiology of Aging*, *30*, 507–514.

Salthouse, T. A. (2010). Selective review of cognitive aging. *Journal of the International Neuropsychological Society*, *16*, 754–760.

Sapir, E. (1921). *Language: An introduction to the study of speech*. Harcourt, Brace, and Company.

Sarangi, S. (2021, July 22). *16 Sanskaras in Hinduism and their relevance from the past to the present*. www.prathaculturalschool.com/post/16-sanskaras-in-hinduism.

Sarangpani, P. M. (2003). *Constructing school knowledge: An ethnography of learning in an Indian village*. SAGE.

Saraswathi, T. S. (1976). Changes in immediate memory span: A longitudinal study of children from 3–5 years. *Indian Educational Review*, *11*, 65–69.

Saraswathi, T. S. (1999). Adult-child continuity in India: Is adolescence a myth or an emerging reality? In T. S. Saraswathi (Ed.), *Culture, socialization and human development* (pp. 214–232). SAGE.

Saraswathi, T. S. (2011). *Reconceptualizing lifespan development through a Hindu perspective*. Oxford University Press.

Saraswathi, T. S., & Dutta, R. (1988). *Invisible boundaries, grooming for adult roles: A descriptive study of socialization in a poor rural and urban slum setting in Gujarat*. Northern Book Centre.

Saraswathi, T. S., & Dutta, R. (1990). Poverty and human development: Socialisation of girls and the urban and rural poor. In G. Misra (Ed.), *Applied social psychology in India* (pp. 141–169). SAGE.

Saraswathi, T. S., Menon, S., & Madan, A. (2018). *Childhoods in India: Traditions, trends, and transformations*. Routledge.

Saraswathi, T. S., & Oke, M. (2013). Ecology of Adolescence in India Implications for Policy and Practice. *Psychological Studies*, *58*, 353–364.

Saraswathi, T. S., & Pai, S. (1997). Socialization in the Indian context. In H. S. R. Kao & D. Sinha (Eds.), *Asian perspectives on psychology* (pp. 74–92). SAGE.

Saraswathi, T. S., & Sundaresan, J. (1979). Perceived maternal disciplinary practices and their relation to development of moral judgment. *International Journal of Behavioral Development*, *3*, 91–109.

Sarma, A. (2014). *Parental pressure for academic success in India*. Arizona State University.

Saucier, G., & Simonds, J. (2006). The structure of personality and temperament. In D. K. Mroczek & T. D. Little (Eds.), *Handbook of personality development* (pp. 109–128). Erlbaum.

Save the Children. (2021). *Protecting children in conflict*. www.savethechildren.org/us/what-we-do/emergency-response/war-and- conflict.

Schachter, S., & Singer, J. (1962). Cognitive, social, and physiological determinants of emotional state. *Psychological Review*, *69*, 379–399.

Scheff, T. J. (1990). *Microsociology: Discourse, emotion, and social structure*. University of Chicago Press.

Scherer, K. R. (1997). The role of culture in emotion-antecedent appraisal. *Journal of Personality and Social Psychology*, *73*, 902–922.

Scherer, K. R., & Ekman, P. (1984). Arousal, stress, and emotion. In R. Plutchik & H. Kellerman (Eds.), *Emotion: Theory, research, and experience* (vol. 1, pp. 263–287). Academic Press.

Scherer, K. R., & Wallbott, H. G. (1994). Evidence for universality and cultural variation of differential emotion response patterning. *Journal of Personality and Social Psychology*, *66*, 310–328.

Schlegel, A., & Barry, H. (1991). *Adolescence: An anthropological inquiry*. Free Press.

Schmitt, M. T., & Branscombe, N. R. (2002). The meaning and consequences of perceived discrimination in disadvantaged and privileged social groups. *European Review of Social Psychology*, *12*, 167–199.

Schutte, S., Ruhe, C., & Sahoo, N. (2023). How fear of violence drives intergroup conflict: Evidence from a panel survey in India. *Terrorism and Political Violence*, *35*, 229–247.

Schwartz, S. H. (1992). Universals in the content and structure of values: Theoretical advances and empirical tests in 20 countries. In M. P. Zanna (Ed.), *Advances in experimental social psychology* (vol. 25, pp. 1–65). Academic Press.

References

Schwartz, S. H. (2012). An overview of the Schwartz theory of basic values. *Online Readings in Psychology and Culture, 2*(1), 11. https://doi.org/10.9707/2307-0919.1116.

Scott, S. A. (2013). Saraswathi, T.S. In K. D. Keith (Ed.), *The encyclopedia of cross-cultural psychology* (pp. 1124–1125). John Wiley & Sons.

Seiter, L. N. (2009). *Emerging adulthood in India* [M.Sc. Dissertations]. Brigham Young University. https://scholarsarchive.byu.edu/etd/1978.

Seligman, M. E. P. (1991). *Learned optimism*. Pocket Books.

Seligman, M. E. P. (2002). *Authentic happiness: Using the new positive psychology to realize your potential for lasting fulfilment*. Free Press.

Seligman, M. E. P., & Csikszentmihalyi, M. (2000). Positive psychology. An introduction. *American Psychologist, 55*, 5.

Selman, R. L. (1980). *The growth of interpersonal understanding: Developmental and clinical analyses*. Academic Press.

Sen, A. (2009). *The idea of justice*. Harvard University Press.

Sen, P., & Chakraborty, A. S. (Eds.). (2024). *Death and dying in northeast India: Indigeneity and afterlife*. Routledge.

Sen, R., Wagner, W., & Howarth, C. (2016). Transcending boundaries: Fundamentalism, secularism and social capital in multi-faith societies. In R. C. Tripathi & P. Singh (Eds.), *Perspectives on violence and othering in India* (pp. 215–234). Springer.

Serpell, R. (1979). How specific are perceptual skills? A cross-cultural study of pattern reproduction. *British Journal of Psychology, 70*, 365–380.

Serpell, R. (1982). Measures of perception, skills, and intelligence. In W. W. Hartup (Ed.), *Review of child development research* (Vol: 6, pp. 392–440). University of Chicago Press.

Seymour, S. (1974). Child rearing in India: A case study in change and modernization. In D. Mouton (Ed.), *Socialization and communication in primary groups* (pp. 177–192). Routledge.

Seymour, S. (1976). Caste/class and child-rearing in a changing Indian town. *American Ethnologist, 3*, 783–796.

Seymour, S. (1999). *Women, family, and child care in India: A world in transition*. Cambridge University Press.

Shanwal, V. K. (2004). *Emotional intelligence: The Indian scenario*. Indian Publishers and Distributors.

Sharma, D. (2003). *Childhood, family and sociocultural changes in India: Reinterpreting the inner world*. Oxford University Press.

Sharma, D., & Verma, S. (2013). Street girls and their fight for survival across four developing countries. *Psychological Studies, 58*, 365–373.

Sharma, M. K., & Marimuthu, P. (2014). Prevalence and psychosocial factors of aggression among youth. *Indian Journal of Psychological Medicine, 36*, 48–53.

Sharma, N. (1999). *Understanding adolescence*. National Book Trust.

Sharma, S., Deller, J., Biswal, R., & Mandal, M. K. (2009). Emotional intelligence: Factorial structure and construct validity across cultures. *International Journal of Cross-Cultural Management, 9*, 217–236.

Sharma, S. N. (2020). Evaluation of implementation of Pradhan Mantri Awas Yojana (Urban). *Think India Journal, 23*, 1–13.

Shavitt, S., Cho, H., & Barnes, A. J. (2019). Culture and consumer behavior. Culture and work. In D. Cohen & S. Kitayama (Eds.), *Handbook of cultural psychology* (2nd ed., pp. 678–698). The Guilford Press.

Sherif, M., Harvey, O. J., White, B. J., Hood, W. R., & Sherif, C. W. (1961). *Intergroup conflict and cooperation: The Robbers Cave experiment*. The University Book Exchange.

Shetty, H., & Chhabria, A. (1997). Bombay riots. In *Proceedings of national workshop on psychosocial consequences of disasters*. NIMHANS.

Shetty, L., Reddy, G. G., Krishnan, P., Toby, I., Shwetha, T., & Annapoorna, K. (2022). Effects of yoga on cognitive functions among adolescents. *Advances in Mind-Body Medicine, 36*, 4–7.

Shonkoff, J. P., Garner, A. S., Siegel, B. S., Dobbins, M. I., Earls, M. F., McGuinn, L., & Wood, D. L. (2012). The lifelong effects of early childhood adversity and toxic stress. *Pediatrics, 129*, e232–e246.

Shrestha, N., & Gopal, B. (2021). Psychological problems among children three years after the earthquake in Nepal. *Journal of Indian Association for Child and Adolescent Mental Health, 17*, 12–34.

Shweder, R. A. (1991). *Thinking through cultures: Expeditions in cultural psychology*. Harvard University Press.

Shweder, R. A. (1993). The cultural psychology of emotions. In M. Lewis & J. Haviland (Eds.), *Handbook of emotions*. Guilford Press.

Shweder, R. A. (1996). Moral maps, "first world" conceits, and the new evangelists. In D. K. Lapsley & F. C. Power (Eds.), *Character psychology and character education* (pp. 371–406). University of Notre Dame Press.

Shweder, R. A. (2000). What about "female genital mutilation?" And why understanding culture matters in the first place. *Daedalus, 129*, 209–232.

Shweder, R. A. (2004). Deconstructing the emotions for the sake of comparative research. In A. S. R. Manstead, N. Frijda, & A. Fischer (Eds.), *Feelings and emotions: The Amsterdam symposium* (pp. 81–97). Cambridge University Press.

Shweder, R. A., Balle-Jensen, L., & Goldstein, W. (1995). Who sleeps by whom revisited: A method for extracting the moral goods implicit in praxis. In J. J. Goodnow, P. J. Miller, & F. Kessell (Eds.), *Cultural practices as contexts for development: New directions for child development*. Jossey-Bass.

Shweder, R. A., Mahapatra, M., & Miller, J. G. (1990). Culture and moral development. In J. W. Stigler, R. A. Shweder, & G. Herdt (Eds.), *Cultural psychology: Essays on comparative human development* (pp. 130–204). Cambridge University Press.

Shweder, R. A., & Much, N. C. (1987). Determinants of meaning: Discourse and moral socialization. In W. Kurtines, M. Gewirtz, & L. Jacob (Eds.), *Moral development through social interaction* (pp. 197–244). Wiley.

Sibia, A. (2006). *Life at Mirambika: A free progress school*. NCERT.

Sibia, A., Shukla, R., & Chakraborty, S. (2022). *Mental health and well-being of school students – A survey*. NCERT.

Sibia, A., Srivastava, A. K., & Misra, G. (2005). *Identification and nurturance of emotional intelligence in primary school children: An exploration*. NCERT.

Sidanius, J., & Pratto, F. (1999). *Social dominance: An intergroup theory of social hierarchy and oppression*. Cambridge University Press.

Singh, A. (2011). Evaluating the impacts of value education: Some case studies. *International Journal of Educational Planning & Administration, 1*, 1–8.

Singh, A. P., & Misra, G. (2012). Adolescent lifestyle in India: Prevalence of risk and promotive factors of health. *Psychology and Developing Societies, 24*, 145–160.

Singh, A. P., Park, A., & Dercon, S. (2014). School meals as a safety net: An evaluation of the midday meal scheme in India. *Economic Development and Cultural Change, 62*, 275–306.

Singh, J. K., & Misra, G. (1997). The experience of anger and aggression in Indian youth: Some preliminary observations. *Trends in Social Science Research, 4*, 231–242.

Singh, J. K., Misra, G., & De Raad, B. (2013). Personality structure in the trait lexicon of Hindi, a major language spoken in India. *European Journal of Personality, 27*, 605–620.

Singh, K., Bandyopadhyay, S., & Saxena, G. (2022). An exploratory study on subjective perceptions of happiness from India. *Frontiers in Psychology, 13*, https://doi.org/10.3389/fpsyg.2022.823496

Singh, L., Hui, T. J., Chan, C., & Golinkoff, R. M. (2014). Influences of vowel and tone variation on emergent word knowledge: A cross-linguistic investigation. *Developmental Science, 17*, 94–109.

Singh, K., Junnarkar, M., & Kaur, J. (2016). *Measures of positive psychology: Development and validation*. Springer.

Singh, M., Khan, W., Osmany, M. (2014). Gratitude and health among young adults. *Indian Journal of Positive Psychology, 5*, 465–468.

Singh, P. (1994). Perception and reactions to inequity as a function of social comparison referents and hierarchical levels. *Journal of Applied Social Psychology, 24*, 557–565.

Singh, R. P. B. (2013). The Hindu family in Indian society: Perspectives and prospects. In M. Angellio (Ed.), *The family in the cultures and societies of Asia* (pp. 19–48). Asiatica Ambrosiana.

Singh, S., Awasthi, S. Kapoor, V., & Mishra, P. (2023). Childhood obesity in India: A two- decade meta-analysis of prevalence and socioeconomic correlates. *Clinical Epidemiology and Global Health, 23*, 101390, https://doi.org/10.1016/j.cegh.2023.101390.

Singh, V. (2019). Impact of social media on social life of teenagers in India: A case study. *Journal of Academic Perspective on Social Studies, 1*, 13–24.

Sinha, A., Mallik, S., Sanyal, D., Dasgupta, S., Pal, D., & Mukherjee, A. (2012). Domestic violence among ever-married women of reproductive age group in a slum area of Kolkata. *Indian Journal of Public Health, 56*, 31–36.

330 References

Sinha, C. (2014). Cognitive development in multilingual children. *Journal of Neurolinguistics, 29,* 43–56.
Sinha, D. (1974). *Mughal syndrome.* Tata McGraw-Hill.
Sinha, D. (1977). Some social disadvantages and development of certain perceptual skills. *Indian Journal of Psychology, 52,* 115–132.
Sinha, D. (1981). (Ed). *The socialisation of the Indian child.* Concept.
Sinha, D. (1982). Toward an ecological framework of deprivation. In D. Sinha, R. C. Tripathi, & G. Misra (Eds.), *Deprivation: Its social roots and psychological consequences* (pp. 25–35). Concept.
Sinha, D. (1988). The family scenario in a developing country and its implications for mental health: The case of India. In P. R. Dasen, J. W. Berry & N. Sartorius (Eds.), *Health and cross-cultural psychology: Towards applications* (pp. 48–70). SAGE.
Sinha, D., & Naidu, R. K. (1994). Multilayered hierarchical structure of self and not-self: The Indian perspective. In A. M. Bouvy, F. J. R. Vijver, P. Boski, & P. Schmitz (Eds.), *Journey into cross-cultural psychology* (pp. 41–49). Swets & Zeitlinger.
Sinha, D., & Tripathi, R. C. (1994a). Achievement motivation and values: Indian and American similarities and differences. *Journal of Cross-Cultural Psychology, 25,* 384–400.
Sinha, D., & Tripathi, R. C. (1994b). Individualism in a collectivist culture: A case of coexistence of opposites. In U. Kim, H. C. Triandis, Ç. Kagitçibaşi, S. C. Choi, & G. Yoon (Eds.), *Individualism and collectivism: Theory, method, and applications* (pp. 123–136). SAGE.
Sinha, D., Tripathi, R. C., & Misra, G. (1982). *Deprivation: Its social roots and psychological consequences.* Concept.
Sinha, J. B. P., Sinha, T. N., Verma, J., & Sinha, R. B. N. (2001). Collectivism coexisting with individualism: An Indian scenario. *Asian Journal of Social Psychology, 4,* 133–145.
Sinha, J. B. P., Tripathi, R. C., & Reddy, N. V. (1999). Values, attitudes, and interpersonal behavior in a collectivistic culture: A study of India. *Journal of Cross-Cultural Psychology, 30,* 233–245.
Sinha, J. B. P., & Verma, J. (1987). Structure of collectivism. In C. Kagitcibasi (Ed.), *Growth and progress in cross-cultural psychology* (pp. 123–129). Swets & Zetlinger.
Sinha, K. K. (1985). *Developmental trends in distributive justice: An information integration analysis* [Unpublished Doctoral Dissertation]. University of Bihar.
Sinha, M., & Chauhan, V. (2013). Deconstructing Lajja as a Marker of Indian Womanhood. *Psychology and Developing Societies, 25,* 133–163.
Sirois, F. M., & Wood, A. M. (2017). Gratitude uniquely predicts lower depression in chronic illness populations: A longitudinal study of inflammatory bowel disease and arthritis. *Health Psychology, 36,* 122–132.
Skinner, B. F. (1938). *The behavior of organisms: An experimental analysis.* Appleton-Century-Crofts.
Skinner, B. F. (1957). *Verbal behavior.* Appleton-Century-Crofts.
Slobin, D. I. (1996). From "thought and language" to "thinking for speaking." In J. J. Gumperz & S. C. Levinson (Eds.), *Rethinking linguistic relativity* (pp. 70–96). Cambridge University Press.
Smetana, J. G. (2013). Moral development: The social domain theory view. In P. D. Zelazo (Ed.), *The Oxford handbook of developmental psychology (vol. 1): Body and mind* (pp. 832–863). Oxford University Press.
Smetana, J. G. (2017). Current research on parenting styles, dimensions, and beliefs. In M. R. Sanders & A. Morawska (Eds.), *Handbook of parenting and child development across the lifespan* (pp. 175–205). Springer.
Smith, C. (2003). Theorizing religious effects among American adolescents. *Journal for the Scientific Study of Religion, 42,* 17–30.
Smith, L. B. (1995). From fragments to modules: A developmental perspective on cognitive science. *Artificial Intelligence, 72,* 25–46.
Snyder, C. R. (1994). *The psychology of hope: You can get there from here.* Free Press.
Snyder, C. R., Shorey, H. S., Cheavens, J., Pulvers, K. M., Adams, V. H., & Wiklund, C. (2002). Hope and academic success in college. *Journal of Educational Psychology, 94,* 820–826.
Solomon, S., Greenberg, J., & Pyszczynski, T. (1991). A terror management theory of social behaviour: The psychological functions of self-esteem and cultural worldviews. In M. P. Zanna (Ed.), *Advances in experimental social psychology* (pp. 91–159). Academic Press.
Sondhi, R. (2017). Parenting adolescents in India: A cultural perspective. *Child and Adolescent Mental Health,* 91–108. https://doi.org/10.5772/66451.
Soni, P. V., & DeSousa, A. (2016). A study of relationship between optimism and well-being in undergraduate students. *Global Journal for Research Analysis, 5*(2), 103–105.

Southwick, S. M., & Charney, D. S. (2012). *Resilience: The science of mastering life's Greatest challenges.* Cambridge University Press.

Sowislo, J. F., & Orth, U. (2013). Does low self-esteem predict depression and anxiety? A meta-analysis of longitudinal studies. *Psychological Bulletin, 139,* 213–240.

Squires, J., & Bricker, D. (2009). *Ages and Stages questionnaires: A parent-completed child monitoring system.* Paul H Brooks.

Srinivas, H. (2015). *The Indian Ocean tsunami and its environmental impacts. GDRC Reseaarch Output E-023.* Global Development Research Center.

Srinivas, M. N. (1966). *Social change in modern India.* University of California Press.

Srinivas, M. N. (1996). *Indian society through personal writings.* Oxford University Press.

Sriram, R. (2011). The role of fathers in children's lives: A view from urban India. *Journal of the Association for Childhood Education International, 87,* 185–190.

Sriram, R. (2023). The Indian father as children see. *Psychological Studies, 68,* 177–189.

Sriram, R., & Navalkar, P. G. (2012). Who is an 'Ideal' father? Father, mother and children's views. *Psychology and Developing Societies, 24,* 205–237.

Srivastava, A., & Shukla, A. (2018). Subjective happiness and differential loneliness among Indian adults. *Journal of Humanities, Arts and Social Science, 2,* 1–10.

Srivastava, A. K. (1987). Incidence of left-handedness in Mizo children: Examining ecology and urbanisation effects. *Personality Study and Group Behaviour, 7,* 87–93.

Srivastava, A. K. (1996). *Role of acculturation in development of values among children: Maternal views.* NCERT.

Srivastava, A. K. (1998). Child development: Conceptual, methodological and applied challenges. In A. K. Srivastava (Ed.), *Child development: The Indian perspective* (pp. 1–24). NCERT.

Srivastava, A. K. (2009). Dynamics of schooling. In G. Misra (Ed.), *Psychology in India (vol. 2: Social and organisational processes)* (pp. 357–406). Pearson.

Srivastava, A. K. (2013). Intelligence – general, emotional, multiple. In K. D. Keith (Ed.), *The encyclopedia of cross-cultural psychology* (pp. 733–741). John Wiley & Sons.

Srivastava, A. K., & Lalnunmawii (1989). Cooperative-competitive behaviour and conflict resolution style among Mizo children: A cultural perspective. *Psychology and Developing Societies, 1,* 191–205.

Srivastava, A. K., & Misra, G. (1999a). An Indian perspective on understanding intelligence. W. J. Lonner, D. L. Dinnel, D. K. Forgays, & S. A. Hayes (Eds.), *Merging past, present and future* (pp. 159–172). Swets & Zeitlinger.

Srivastava, A. K., & Misra, G. (1999b). Social representation of intelligence in the Indian folk tradition: An analysis of Hindi proverbs. *Journal of Indian Psychology, 17,* 23–38.

Srivastava, A. K., & Misra, G. (1999c). What it means to be an intelligent person? Views of the lay people. *Indian Psychological Review, 52,* 123–133.

Srivastava, A. K., & Misra, G. (2001). Lay people's understanding and use of intelligence: An Indian perspective. *Psychology and Developing Societies, 13,* 25–48.

Srivastava, A. K., & Misra, G. (2007). *Rethinking intelligence: Conceptualising human competence in cultural context.* Pearson.

Srivastava, A. K., & Misra, G. (2012). Cultural perspectives on nature and experience of happiness. In A. K. Dalal & G. Misra (Eds.), *New directions in health psychology* (pp. 109–131). Sage.

Srivastava, A. K., & Misra, G. (2013). *Experience and consequences of happiness: A study of happiness among school students and teachers.* NCERT (ERIC) (mimeographed).

Srivastava, A. K., Sibia, A., & Misra, G. (2008). Research on emotional intelligence: The Indian experience. In R. J. Emmerling, V. K. Shanwal, & M. K. Mandal (Eds.), *Emotional intelligence: Theoretical and cultural perspectives* (pp. 135–152). Nova Science Publishers.

Sroufe, L. A., Duggal, S., Weinfield, N., & Carlson, E. (2000). Relationships, development, and psychopathology. In A. J. Sameroff, M. Lewis, & S. M. Miller (Eds.), *Handbook of developmental psychopathology* (2nd ed., pp. 75–91). Kluwer Academic Publishers.

Stafford-Smith, M., Griggs, D., Gaffney, O., Ullah, F., Reyers, B., Kanie, N., Stigson, B., Shrivastava, P., Leach, M., & O'Connell, D. (2017). Integration: The key to implementing the sustainable development goals. *Sustainability Science, 12,* 911–919.

Staudinger, U. M., & Glück, J. (2011). Psychological wisdom research: Commonalities and differences in a growing field. *Annual Review of Psychology, 62,* 215–241.

Steinberg, L. (2008). *Adolescence* (8th ed.). McGraw-Hill.

Sterman, J. D. (2002). All models are wrong: Reflections on becoming a systems scientist. *System Dynamics Review, 18*, 501–531.

Stern, P. C. (2000). New environmental theories: Toward a coherent theory of environmentally significant behavior. *Journal of Social Issues, 56*, 407–424.

Sternberg, R. J. (1985). *Beyond IQ: A triarchic theory of human intelligence*. Cambridge University Press.

Sternberg, R. J. (1986). A triangular theory of love. *Psychological Review, 93*, 119–135.

Sternberg, R. J. (1997). *Successful intelligence*. Plume.

Sternberg, R. J. (2003). A broad view of intelligence: The theory of successful intelligence. *Consulting Psychology Journal: Practice and Research, 55*, 139–154.

Sternberg, R. J. (2004a). Culture and intelligence. *American Psychologist, 59*, 325–338.

Sternberg, R. J. (2004b). What is wisdom and how can we develop it? *The American Academy of Political and Social Science, 591*, 164–174.

Sternberg, R. J. (2020). *Culture and intelligence*. https://doi.org/10.1093/acrefore/9780190236557.013.585

Sternberg, R. J. (2021). Adaptive intelligence: Its nature and implications for education. *Education Sciences, 11*, 823. https://doi.org/10.3390/

Suar, D., Jha, A. K., Das, S. S., & Alat, P. (2020). What do millennials think of their past, present, and future happiness, and where does their happiness reside? *Journal of Constructivist Psychology, 34*, 1–17.

Suar, D., & Khuntia, R. (2004). Caste, education, family and stress disorders in Orissa supercyclone. *Psychology and Developing Societies, 16*, 77–91.

Suar, D., Mandal, M. K., Misra, I., & Suman, S. (2013). Patterns of hand preference and unintentional injuries among Indian attempted hand switchers and hand nonswitchers. *Laterality, 18*, 652–670.

Subhashini, P. (2017). *Design and development of computer assistive technology system for differently abled students*. Avinashilingam Institute for Home Science and Higher Education for Women.

Subramanyam, Y. S., & Chadha, R. (2002). Contemporary fatherhood: Perceptions of 11-13-year-old sons. In V. Veeraraghavan, S. Singh, & K. Khandelwal (Eds.), *The child in the new millennium* (pp. 225–232). Mosaic Books.

Suchday, S. (2015). Anger and globalization among young people in India. *New Directions in Child and Adolescent Development, 147*, 77–84.

Sumner, R., Burrow, A. L., & Hill, P. L. (2018). The development of purpose in life among adolescents who experience marginalization: Potential opportunities and obstacles. *American Psychologist, 73*, 740–752.

Sundararajan, L., Misra, G., & Marsella, A. J. (2013). Indigenous approaches to assessment, diagnosis, and treatment of mental disorders. In F. A. Paniagua & A. Yamada (Eds.), *Handbook of multicultural health: Assessment and treatment of diverse populations* (2nd ed., pp. 69–88). Elsevier.

Super, C. M., & Harkness, S. (1986). The developmental niche: A conceptualization at the interface of child and culture. *International Journal of Behavioral Development, 9*, 545–569.

Suri, S., Mona., & Sarkar, D. (2022). *Domestic violence and women's health in India: Insights from NFHS-4* (Occasional Paper No. 343). Observer Research Foundation.

Suvasini, C., Misra, G., & Srivastava, A. K. (2000). Psychology of wisdom: Western and Indian perspectives. *Journal of Indian Psychology, 18*, 1–32.

Syed, M., & Fish, J. (2018). Revisiting Erik Erikson's legacy on culture, race, and ethnicity. *Identity: An International Journal of Theory and Research, 18*, 274–283.

Tajfel, H., & Turner, J. C. (1979). An integrative theory of intergroup conflict. In W. G. Austin, & S. Worchel (Eds.), *The social psychology of intergroup relations* (pp. 33–37). Brooks/Cole.

Takahashi, M., & Bordia, P. (2000). The concept of wisdom: A cross-cultural comparison. *International Journal of Psychology, 35*, 1–9.

Tan, U., Tan, M., 2001. Testosterone and grasp-reflex differences in human neonates. *Laterality, 6*, 181–192.

Tang, Y. Y., Ma, Y., Wang, J., Fan, Y., Feng, S., Lu, Q., Yu, Q., Sui, D., Rothbart, M. K., Fan, M., & Posner, M. I. (2007). Short-term meditation training improves attention and self-regulation. *Proceedings of the National Academy of Sciences, 104*, 17152–17156.

Tarapore, F. Z. (1998). Play and development. In A. K. Srivastava (Ed.), *Child development: The Indian perspective* (pp. 228–249). NCERT.

Telles, S., Singh, N., Bhardwaj, A. K., Kumar, A., & Balkrishna, A. (2013). Effect of yoga or physical exercise on physical, cognitive and emotional measures in children: A randomized controlled trial. *Child and Adolescent Psychiatry and Mental Health, 7*(1), 37. https://doi.org/10.1186/1753-2000-7-37.

Teti, D. M., Shimizu, M., Crosby, B., & Kim, B. R. (2016). Sleep arrangements, parent-infant sleep during the first year, and family functioning. *Developmental Psychology, 52*, 1169–1181.

Thakur, A., & Rangaswamy, M. (2019). Expressions of women survivors of domestic violence: Idioms of distress. *Psychological Studies, 64*, 377–389.

Thakur, G. P., & Thakur, M. (1986). Hindi adaptation of Eysenck Personality Questionnaire (adult). *Indian Journal of Clinical Psychology, 13*, 81–86.

Thakur, S., Parihar, R., Kapila, S., Barwal, V. K., & Rattan, S. (2022). Spiritual intelligence in relation to mental health: A study among Indian adolescents. *International Journal of Research and Review, 9*, 614–622.

Thapan, M. (1991). *Life at school: An ethnographic study*. Oxford University Press.

Thapan, M. (2020). Perspectives in the sociology of education and NEP 2020: A conversation with Professor Meenakshi Thapan. *The JMC Review, 4*, 294–307.

Thapliyal, G., Bisht, D., & Dhatt, H. K. (2015). Impact of value education programme among school students: An experimental study. *American Research Thoughts, 1*, 1223–1232.

Thara, R., Rao, K., & John S. (2008). An assessment of post-tsunami psychosocial training programmes in Tamilnadu, India. *International Journal of Social Psychiatry, 54*, 197–205.

The Centre for Bhutan & GNH Studies. (2023). *Launch of the 2022 GNH index results*. www.bhutanstudies.org.bt/launch-of-the-2022-gnh-index-results/

The International Ecotourism Society. (2015). *What is ecotourism?* https://ecotourism.org/what-is-ecotourism/

Thomas, A., & Chess, S. (1977). *Temperament and development*. Brunner/Mazel.

Thomas, J. R., French, K. E., & Hayes, J. C. (1982). The role of knowledge of results on hand-eye coordination. *Journal of Motor Behavior, 14*, 20–27.

Thompson, R. A. (2014). Stress and child development. *The Future of Children, 24*, 41–59.

Thorat, S., & Attewell, P. (2007). The legacy of social exclusion: A correspondence study of job discrimination in India. *Economic and Political Weekly, 42*, 4141–4145.

Thorat, S., & Lee, J. (2005). Caste discrimination and food security programmes. *Economic and Political Weekly, 40*, 198–201.

Thorat, S., & Newman, K. (2010). Caste and economic discrimination: Causes, consequences and remedies. *Economic and Political Weekly, 45*, 45–58.

Tirtha, S. S. (1998). *The ayurvedic encyclopedia: Natural secrets to healing, prevention, & longevity*. Ayurveda Holistic Center Press

Tiwari, T., Singh, A. L., & Singh, I. L. (2009). The short-form revised Eysenck personality questionnaire: A Hindi edition (EPQRS-H). *Industrial Psychiatry Journal, 18*, 27–31.

Tom, P., & Gisli, T. (2017). Designing toys to support children's development. *Journal on Educational Psychology, 11*, 1–10.

Tomasello, M. (2003). *Constructing a language: A usage-based theory of language acquisition*. Harvard University Press.

Tomkins, S. S. (1962). *Affect, imagery, consciousness: The positive affects* (Vol. 1). Springer.

Tongeren, V., Daryl, R., Davis, D. E., Hook, J. N., Rowatt, W., Worthington, E. L. (2018). Religious differences in reporting and expressing humility. *Psychology of Religion and Spirituality, 10*, 174–184.

Tottenham, N., Hare, T. A., & Casey, B. J. (2011). Behavioral assessment of emotion discrimination, emotion regulation, and cognitive control in childhood, adolescence, and adulthood. *Frontiers in Psychology, 1*, 1–9.

Trawick, M. (1992). *Notes on love in a Tamil family*. University of California Press.

Triandis, H. C. (1989). Self and social behavior in differing cultural contexts. *Psychological Review, 96*, 506–520.

Triandis, H. C. (1995). *Individualism and collectivism*. Westview Press.

Triandis, H. C. (2001). Individualism – collectivism and personality. *Journal of Personality, 69*, 907–924.

Triandis, H. C., & Bhawuk, D. P. S. (1997). Culture theory and the meaning of relatedness. In P. C. Earley & M. Erez (Eds.), *New perspectives on international industrial/organizational psychology* (pp. 13–52). The New Lexington Press.

Triandis, H. C., & Suh, E. M. (2002). Cultural influences on personality. *Annual Review of Psychology, 53*, 133–160.

Tripathi, N., Singh, R. K., Pal, D., & Singh, R. S. (2015). Agroecology and sustainability of agriculture in India: An overview. *EC Agriculture, 2*, 241–248.

Tripathi, R. C., & Ghildyal, P. (2013). Selfhood in search of Godhood. *Psychology and Developing Societies, 25*, 43–76.

Tripathi, R. C., & Singh, S. (2017). Psychosocial pathways towards a sustainable society: The role of greed, altruism and social capital. *Psychology and Developing Societies, 29*, 200–220.

Tripathi, R. C., & Srivastava, R. (1981). Relative deprivation and intergroup attitudes. *European Journal of Social Psychology, 11*, 313–318.

Tsai, J. L., & Clobert, M. (2019). Cultural influences on emotion: Established patterns and emerging trends. In D. Cohen & S. Kitayama (Eds.), *Handbook of cultural psychology* (2nd ed., pp. 292–318). The Guilford Press.

Tucker-Drob, E. M. (2011). Neurocognitive functions and everyday functions change together in old age. *Neuropsychology, 25*, 368–377.

Tucker-Drob, E.M., de la Fuente, J., Köhncke, Y., Brandmaier, A.M., Nyberg, L., & Lindenberger, U. (2022). A strong dependency between changes in fluid and crystallized abilities in human cognitive aging. *Science Advances, 8*, 1–10.

Tulving, E., & Thomson, D. M. (1973). Encoding specificity and retrieval processes in episodic memory. *Psychological Review, 80*, 352–373.

Turiel, E. (1983). *The development of social knowledge: Morality and convention*. Cambridge University Press.

Turiel, E. (2005). *The development of social knowledge: Morality and convention*. Cambridge University Press.

Turiel, E. (2006). Thought, emotions, and social interactional processes in moral development. In M. Killen & J. G. Smetana (Eds.), *Handbook of moral development* (pp. 7–35). Psychology Press.

Turkle, S. (2011). *Alone together: Why we expect more from technology and less from each other*. Basic Books.

Tuske, J. (2021). The concept of emotion in classical Indian philosophy. In *Stanford encyclopedia of philosophy*. https://plato.stanford.edu/entries/concept-emotion-india/

Uberoi, P. (2003). The family in India: Beyond the nuclear versus joint debate. In V. Das (Ed.), *The Oxford India companion to sociology and social anthropology* (p. 1073). Oxford University Press.

UN Global Compact & Accenture. (2013). *A new era of sustainability: UN Global Compact-Accenture CEO Study*. https://unglobalcompact.org/library/451.

UNESCO. (2014). *Global citizenship education: Preparing learners for the challenges of the 21st century*. UNESCO.

UNESCO. (2015). *Rethinking education: Towards a global common good?* https://unesdoc.unesco.org/ark:/48223/pf0000232983

UNHCR. (2023). *Global trend reports*. www.unhcr.org/global-trends- report-2022.

UNICEF. (2018). *Education under attack 2018*. www.unicef.org/reports/education-under-attack-2018

UNICEF. (2021a). *Generation now: Our commitment to adolescents and young people*. www.unicef.org/reports/generation-now-our-commitment- adolescents-and-young-people

UNICEF. (2023b). *The state of the world's children 2023*. www.unicef.org/reports/state-worlds-children-2023

United Nations (2015a). *World population prospects: The 2015 revision: Key findings and advance tables*. Department of Economic and Social Affairs, Population Division, United Nations.

United Nations. (2015b). *Transforming our world: The 2030 agenda for sustainable development*. https://sdgs.un.org/2030agenda

United Nations. (2019). *World population prospects 2019: Highlights*. United Nations Department of Economic and Social Affairs, Population Division.

United Nations. (n.d.). *Sustainable development goals 16: Peace, justice and strong institutions*. www.un.org/sustainabledevelopment/peace- justice/

United States Environmental Protection Agency. (2023). *Zero waste case study: San Francisco*. www.epa.gov/transforming-waste-tool/zero-waste-case-study-san- Francisco

Universal Declaration of Human Rights. (1948). *Universal Declaration of Human Rights*. United Nations.

Uzgalis, W. (2022). John Locke. In E. N. Zalta & U. Nodelman (Eds.), *The stanford encyclopedia of philosophy*. https://plato.stanford.edu/archives/fall2022/entries/locke/.

Valsiner, J. (1987). *Culture and the development of children's action: A cultural-historical theory of developmental psychology*. John Wiley & Sons.

Van Gordon, W., Shonin, E., Sumich, A., Sundin, E., & Griffiths, M. D. (2013). The meditative basis of sthitipragya: A Buddhist approach to the acquisition of emotional intelligence. *Journal of Psychosomatic Research, 74*, 361–370.

Van Vianen, A. E., De Dreu, C. K., & Tyler, T. R. (2018). Investigating the social context of forgiveness: Affective valence, offender status, and forgiveness. *Frontiers in Psychology, 9*, 1186.

Vargha-Khadem, F., Gadian, D. G., Copp, A., & Mishkin, M. (2005). FOXP2 and the neuroanatomy of speech and language. *Nature Reviews Neuroscience, 6*, 131–138.

Vassilakopoulou, P., & Hustad, E. (2023). Bridging digital divides: A literature review and research agenda for information systems research. *Information Systems Frontiers, 25*, 955–969.

Vaughan, F. (2002). What is spiritual intelligence? *Journal of Humanistic Psychology, 42*, 16–33.

Verenikina, I. (2010). *Play and learning in early childhood settings*. Oxford University Press.

VerKuilen, A., Sprouse, L., Beardsley, R., Lebu, S., Salzberg, A., & Manga, M. (2023). Effectiveness of the Swachh Bharat Mission and barriers to ending open defecation in India: A systematic review. *Frontiers in Environmental Science, 11*, 1141825. https://doi.org/10.3389/fenvs.2023.1141825

Verma, A., & Poffenberger, T. (1970). *Social change and perception of change in child rearing practices in a suburban Indian village*. M.S. University of Baroda Press.

Verma, J. (1994). A note on an indigenous approach to understanding sorrow. *Psychology and Developing Societies, 6*, 187–192.

Verma, J. (1999). Collectivism in the cultural perspective: The Indian scene. In J. C. Lasry, J. Adair, & K. Dion (Eds.), *Latest contributions to cross-cultural psychology* (pp. 228–241). Swets & Zetlinger.

Verma, J., & Triandis, H. C. (1999a). The measurement of collectivism in India. In W. J. Lonner, D. L. Dinnel, D. K. Forgays & S. A. Hayes (Eds.), *Merging past, present, and future in cross-cultural psychology* (pp. 256–265). Swets & Zeitlinger.

Verma, J., & Triandis, H. C. (1999b). The psychological impact of socio-political change: A cross-cultural analysis. *Political Psychology, 20*, 37–61.

Verma, R., & Bansal, A. (2019). Decision making among adolescents in relation to peer pressure. *The International Journal of Indian Psychology, 7*.

Verma, S., & Saraswathi, T. S. (2002). Adolescents in India: Street urchins or Silicon Valley millionnaires? In R. Larson & T. S. Saraswathi (Eds.), *The world's youth: Adolescence in eight regions of the globe* (pp. 105–140). Cambridge University Press.

Verma, S., & Sharma, D. (2003). Cultural continuity amid social change: Adolescents' use of free time in India. *New Directions for Child and Adolescent Development, 99*, 37–51.

Verma, S., Sharma, D., & Larson, R. W. (2002). School stress in India: Effects on time and daily emotions. *International Journal of Behavioral Development, 26*, 500–508.

Vijaykumar, L., Thara, R., John, S., & Chellappa, S. (2006). Psychosocial interventions after tsunami in Tamil Nadu, India. *International Review Psychiatry, 18*, 225–231.

Vishwanath, R., Kamath, A. G., Thomas, N., Guddattu, V., & Praharaj, S. K. (2023). Pattern of acquisition of theory of mind in pre-schoolers: A cross-sectional study from South India. *Asian Journal of Psychiatry, 81*, 103443.

Vygotsky, L. S. (1978). *Mind in society: The development of higher psychological processes*. Harvard University Press.

Wadhwani, P. (2014). Changing Connotation of Intelligence – Embracing IQ, EQ, SQ. *Modern Research Studies: An International Journal of Humanities and Social Sciences, 1*, 406–426.

Wagani, R., & Colucci, E. (2018). Spirituality and wellbeing in the context of a study on suicide prevention in North India. *Religions, 9*, 183. https://doi.org/10.3390/rel9060183

Wahi, S., & Johri, R. (1994). Questioning a universal theory of mind: Mental-real distinctions made by Indian children. *The Journal of Genetic Psychology: Research and Theory on Human Development, 155*, 503–510.

Wang, Y., & Lobstein, T. (2006). Worldwide trends in childhood overweight and obesity. *International Journal of Pediatric Obesity, 1*, 11–25.

Ward, L. M., & Grower, P. (2020). Media and the development of gender role stereotypes. *Annual Review of Developmental Psychology, 2*, 177–199.

Watkins, P. C. (2014). *Gratitude and the good life: Toward a psychology of appreciation*. Springer.

Watson, J. B. (1913). Psychology as the behaviorist views it. *Psychological Review, 20*, 158–177.

Watson, J. B. (1919). *Psychology from the standpoint of a behaviorist*. J B Lippincott Company.

Wellman, H. M., & Liu, D. (2004). Scaling of theory-of-mind tasks. *Child Development, 75*, 523–541.

Wentzel, K. R., & Wigfield, A. (2018). *Handbook of motivation at school* (2nd ed.). Routledge.

Werner, E. E. (2005). Resilience research. In R. D. Peters, B. Leadbeater & R. J. McMahon (Eds.), *Resilience in children, families, and communities*. Springer.

Wertsch, J. V. (1985). *Vygostky and the social formation of mind*. Harvard University Press.

White, S. C., Devine, J., Jha, S., Gains, S. (2010). *Religion, development and well-being in India* (Working Paper 54). International Development Department, University of Birmingham.

Whiting, B. B. (Ed.). (1963). *Six cultures: Studies of child rearing*. John Wiley.

Whiting, B. B., & Whiting, J. W. M. (1975). *Children of six cultures*. Harvard University Press.

Whitmarsh, L. (2008). Are flood victims more concerned about climate change than other people? The role of direct experience in risk perception and behavioral response. *Journal of Risk Research, 11*, 351–374.

WHO-ICMR Study. (1991). *Development and field testing of simple indicators of growth and psychosocial development of children*. National Institute of Nutrition.

Whorf, B. L. (1956). *Language, thought, and reality: Selected writings of Benjamin Lee Whorf*. MIT Press.

Wink, P., & Dillon, M. (2002). Spiritual development across the adult life course: Findings from a longitudinal study. *Journal of Adult Development, 9*, 79–94.

Wizarat, K. (2009). *Study of best practices adopted in mid-day meal scheme in Uttar Pradesh*. NUEPA.

Wober, M. (1974). Towards an understanding of the Kinganda concept of intelligence. In J. W. Berry & P. R. Dasen (Eds.), *Culture and cognition* (pp. 261–280). Methuen.

Wolfensohn, J. D. (2004, November 8). Tryst with destiny: Globalisation can be India's hour of glory. *The Times of India*, p. 14.

Wood, A. M., Maltby, J., Gillett, R., Linley, P. A., & Joseph, S. (2008). The role of gratitude in the development of social support, stress, and depression: Two longitudinal studies. *Journal of Research in Personality, 42*, 854–871.

Woodyard, C. (2011). Exploring the therapeutic effects of yoga and its ability to increase quality of life. *International Journal of Yoga, 4*, 49–54.

World Bank. (2021). *Fragility, conflict, and violence*. www.worldbank.org/en/topic/fragilityconflictviolence.

World Health Organization (WHO). (2021a). *Adolescents' health*. www.who.int/news-room/fact-sheets/detail/adolescents-health.

World Health Organization (WHO). (2021b). *Obesity and overweight*. www.who.int/news-room/fact-sheets/detail/obesity-and-overweight.

World Health Organization. (2021c). *Violence against women prevalence estimates, 2018: Global, regional and national prevalence estimates for intimate partner violence against women and global and regional prevalence estimates for non-partner sexual violence against women*. WHO.

Yadav, C. S. (2020). Incredible "Handmade in India" toys on the brink of extinction. *International Journal of Disaster Recovery and Business Continuity, 11*, 561–571.

Yalom, I. D. (2008). *Staring at the sun: Overcoming the terror of death*. Jossey-Bass.

Zeki, S. (1999). Art and the brain. *Journal of Consciousness Studies, 6*, 76–96.

Zimbardo, P. G. (2007). *The Lucifer effect: Understanding how good people turn evil*. Random House.

Zimmerman, B. J., & Bandura, A. (1994). Impact of self-regulatory influences on writing course attainment. *American Educational Research Journal, 31*, 845–862.

Zohar, D., & Marshall, I. (2000). *SQ: Connecting with our spiritual intelligence*. Bloomsbury.

Index

Abhidha 143
Abhinivesha 189
abstract thinking 31, 113
accommodation 45, 111, 274
adaptation 45, 111, 123
adolescent development 30–32
Advaita Vedanta 119
adverse circumstances, developmental challenges in 264–265
aesthetic development 198–199
aesthetics in Indian art forms 198–199
affect 127, 185; negative 185; positive 185
affective: competencies 104; regulation model 127
afforestation, Miyawaki method of 293
agreeableness 176
ahamkara 120
ahimsa 16, 204, 208
Allport's trait theory 178
alterable-transformative model 92
alternative schooling 134
alternative social conceptions 232–234
altruism 255–256
Alzheimer's disease 35
anal stage 42, 172
anand 170
anganwadis 28
anger 39, 193, 244
animism 113
antahkarana 119
anthropometric measures 67
anumana 141
armed conflicts 264
artha 15, 154, 212
artificial intelligence 255
artificialism 113
asanas 122, 155
ashram dharma, stages of 14–15, 48, 168; *brahmacharyashrama* 14; *grahasthashrama* 14; *sannyasashrama* 15; *vanaprasthashrama* 15
Ashtadhyayi 141
asmita 189
assessment tools 26
assimilation 45, 111

atma jnana 14
atman 14, 38, 170
atmanam viddhi 168
attachment, styles of: disorganized 26; insecure-avoidant 26; insecure-resistant 26; secure 26
attachment, theory of 26, 44, 228
attending and receiving initial sounds 146–147
attention 125
autonomy *vs.* shame and doubt 43, 227
avidya 120, 189
avoidance-avoidance conflict 273–274
ayu 13
ayurveda 119, 189
ayushman bhava 13

baby's: crying 90; feeding 90; sleep patterns 90
balance between body, mind and spirit 119
balancing between languages 149
balwadis 28
Bandura's Social Learning Theory 175, 228
baoli 292
behaviourism 44
belief about celestial events 92
Beti Bachao Beti Padhao 285
bhakti 133, 188, 191
bhava 188, 189, 190; *bhaya* 190; *hasa* 190; *jugupsa* 190; *krodh* 190; *rati* 190; *sama* 190; *shoka* 190; *utsaha* 190; *vismaya* 190
bilingualism 27, 147–152
bilinguals, types of 148; balanced 148; compound 148; coordinated 148; early 148; late 148; limited 148; non-balanced 148; partial 148; productive 148; proficient 148; receptive 148; sequential 148; simultaneous 148; subordinated 148
biodiversity conservation 287
biological age 13
biological theory 172–173
birth rates 69
Blastocyst 24
body language 154
Body-Mass Index (BMI) 70
bonding social capital 284
Brahman 14, 120, 252

Brihadaranyaka Upanishad 211
Brundtland report 282
Bruner's socio-cognitive theory 45, 116–117
buddhi 119, 129; *dharam* buddhi 130; *pap* buddhi 130
buniyadi talim 18

California Q-sort 181
Cannon-Bard theory 186
case studies 58
Cattell's 16 personality factors 177
centration 112
cephalocaudal law 75
cereals and millets 70
child: development 7; growth standards 68
child development, role of toys 79–80
child-rearing 97–98; father's role in 98–99
children with disabilities 101–102
chipko andolan 288
chitta 120
chromosomes 24
chronological age 13
chronosystem 47
circular reactions, types of 112
citizenship 219
closed-ended questions 55
co-construction 115
code-mixing 149; -switching 149
cognition: dynamic nature of 110, 115; Indian perspective on 119; individual differences in 115
cognitive competence 103–104, 130
cognitive development: in old age 36–37; role of yoga 122; schooling and 133–136
cognitive dissonance theory 233
cognitive representation: enactive 45, 116; iconic 116; symbolic 113, 116
collaborative learning 117, 274
collectivism, characteristics of 231
collectivistic cultures 89–90, 196
communication skills 252–253, 289
community violence 266, 267–268
competencies, development of 103–105
competition 274
compliance to authority 236–237
compromise 274
concrete operational stage 29, 45, 113
confirmation bias 233
conflict 273–275; approach-approach 273; approach-avoidance 273
conflict and its resolution 273–276
conformity 210
conscientiousness 176
conservation 112
Constitution of India 218
constructivism 45, 116
contentment 244
context sensitivity 130
contextual factors 114

conventional level 206
cooperation 253
coordinated secondary schemes 112
courage 249–250
COVID-19 pandemic 264, 265, 272
creativity 132–133, 244, 289
creoles 152
Criminal Law Amendment Act 267
critical period 156
critical thinking skill 289
cross-sectional design 50
cross-sequential design 51
crude death rate 69
cultural: ethos 48; identity 230; sensitivity 60; tools and symbols 115, 117
cultural apprenticeship 115
cultural psychology 115
cultural syndrome: individualism and collectivism 230–232
cyclones 269–270

dama 211
dana 211, 256
Darwin's theory of evolution 43
daya 211
death: denying society 38; instinct 42; a life-stage 37–39
decenter 113
deductive reasoning 113
deeksha 48
Deen Dayal Upadhyaya Grameen Kaushalya Yojana 290
deep structure 145
defence mechanisms 42, 171; denial 39, 171; displacement 171; intellectualization 171; projection 171; rationalization 171; regression 171; repression 171; sublimation 171
dementia 35
democracy 218–219
depression 39
development 4, 5, 7; multi-contextual 7; multi-cultural 8; multi-directional 7; multidisciplinary 8; theories of 42–49
developmental milestones for Indian children 76
developmental niche 47
dharana 133, 191
dharma 15, 16, 97, 127, 180, 204, 212; *shastra* 97, 120, 121
dhyana 133, 180, 191
dietary considerations 74
digital: citizenship 219; India 285–286; literacy 254–255
discovery learning 117
disease model 244
Domestic Violence Act 266
domestic/ family violence 266–267
dominance 177

doshas 189
Dowry Prohibition Act 267
dualistic view 119
dukkha 246
dvesh 188, 189

early adulthood 33–34
early auditory experiences 147
early childhood 27–28
early language acquisition 149
earthquakes 270
ecological: approach 46–47; model 47
economic sustainability 282
ecotourism 292
ectoderm 24
education 10
effortful emotion processes 188
ego 42, 171
egocentrism 31, 112
ego integrity *vs.* despair 43
Ekman's theory 153
Ellsworth and Smith's component process model 188
embeddedness in Indian context 91–93
embryonic development 24
emergent design 52
emerging adulthood 32–33
emojis 154
emotional: competence 130; competence model 127; coping with negative states 194, 244–245; stability 177
emotional development 195–198; cultural factors 196–197; environmental factors 197; socialization and 196
emotional intelligence 126–127; Indian view of 127
emotions: cognitive theories of 186–187; concept of 185; ego-focused 196; Indian perspective on 188–192; multi-componential theories of 187–188; other focused 197; physiological theories of 185–186; positive and negative 192–194; theories of 185–188; understanding and expressing of 195–198
empathy 244
empty nest syndrome 12
encoding and input processes 118
endoderm 25
enlightenment 204
entrepreneurial competence 130
environment(al) 6; degradation 265; sustainability 11, 282
equality 217
equilibration 111
equitable participation and access 60
Erikson's psychosocial theory 42–43, 226–227
ethical considerations 59–60
ethics of autonomy 208; care 207; community 208; divinity 208

ethnography 58–59
Ethnologue 140
Euro-American context xvii
euthanasia 39
evolution 5
executive functions 35
existential psychology 46
exosystem 47, 48
experimental method 56
expertise 115
exploration and discovery, period of 31
extraversion 173, 176
eye-hand coordination 67
Eysenck Personality Inventory 173
Eysenck Personality Questionnaire 173

facial expressions 154
false beliefs, development of 234
families: blended 87; grandparents 87; joint 87, 229; non-blood relationships 229; notion of 228–229; nuclear 87, 229; same-sex 87, 229; single-parent 87, 229; step 229
fear 194, 245
fine motor: development 75–76; skills 67
Fit India Movement 286
flow: experience of 251; nature of 251; outcomes of 251
focus group design 58
foetus 25
forced displacement 265
forgiveness 258; gender differences in 258
formal groups 229
formal operational stage 30, 45, 113
FOXP2 gene 156
Freud's psychoanalytic theory 171
fruits and vegetables 71
frustration 245

gender equality 10, 93
gender socialization, cultural variations in 90
general amenities 47
general conceptual structures 115
general geographic environment 47
generations: alpha 9; baby boomers 9; millennials 9; silent 9; X 9; Z 9
generativity *vs.* stagnation 34, 43, 227
genital stage 42, 172
genocide 266
germinal stage 24
Gesell's theory of maturation 43
gestation 25
gestures 154
Gilligan's theory of moral development 207
global citizenship: education 290–291; skill 289
gratitude 192, 244, 256–257
greed 235–236
green legacy initiative 293

Gross's emotion regulation theory 188
gross motor: development 75; skills 67
Gross National Happiness 292, 293
group: concept of 229; goals 230; types 229–230, 240
growth 4, 5; chart 67–68; velocity 68
guided participation 115
guilt 245
gunas 180
gurukul system 28
guru-shishya parampara 155; relationship 135–136

handedness 78–79; cultural factors in 78; incidence of 78
handedness development, theories of 78
hand-eye coordination 79
happiness 192, 245; Indian perspective of 245–247; and money 245; outcomes of 245; and well-being 245–247
Head Start Program 28
health norms 70–71
healthy living 81–83
hedonism 210
hemisphere: left 78; right 78
heredity 6
hijra 102
Hochschild's social constructionist theory 187
Hofstede's cultural dimensions of values 209–210
holistic development 9, 16; and yoga 82–83
hope 244, 249
human development: role of culture 9, 10; scope of 20
Human Development Index xvi
human-divine axis 92
humanistic approach 46
humanistic theory 173–174
human rights and duties 218
human strengths and virtues, definitions of 244

ICT skill 289
id 42, 171
identity, concept of 113; identity formation 31
identity vs. role confusion 43, 227
imaginary audience 31
imitation 157
immunization schedules 71–72
Implicit Association Tests 181
Indian family, changes in 229
Indian Penal Code 267
indigenous: approach 48; theories 284
indigenous toys and play, diversity in 80
individualism-collectivism 92, 109, 210, 230, 231–232
individualistic cultures 90, 196
inductive reasoning 113
industry vs. inferiority 43, 227

infancy 25
infatuation 257
infectious disease outbreaks 265
informal groups 229
information and media literacy skill 289
Information Processing Theory 118–119
informed consents 59
in-groups 240
initiative vs. guilt 43, 227
Inner World, The 96
inspiration 244
institutional settings 47
integral philosophy 48
integral yoga 18
Integrated Child Development Services Scheme 28–29, 73
integrity 244
integrity vs. despair 228
intellective concepts, indigenous 119–121
intelligence:123; adaptive 123; analytical 125; changing conceptions of 123; creative 125; crystallized 34; cultural variations in 128–132; emotional 126–127; fluid 34; Indian conception of 129–130; multifaceted nature of 122–128; multiple 124–125; quotient 122; PASS model of 125–126; practical 125; spiritual 128; technological 129; tests 18; triarchic theory of 125
internalization 114
Internet of Things (IoT) 255
interview method 56–57; semi-structured 57; structured 57; unstructured 57
intimacy vs. isolation 43, 227
intrinsic motivation 256
intuition 120
invisible children 276
in-vitro fertilization 24
involuntary response 49
IQ tests 122–123
irreversibility 113
itihasas 121

James-Lange Theory 186
janampatri 92
Jawaharlal Nehru National Solar Mission 293
jitendriya 127, 191
jnana 120
jnanapith awardees 133
joy 244
justice 217

Kabir's *sakhis* 257
kama 15, 212
kapha 189
karma 16, 127, 180, 20; yoga 180
karuna 211
kindergarten 28

kinnar 102
kleshas 189
Kohlberg's Theory of Moral Development 206–207
kokoro 291

lajja 30, 192–193
lakshana 143
Lamarck's theory of inheritance 43
language: discourse 146; morphemes 145; phonemes 144; pragmatics 145; semantics 145; subsystems of 144–146; syntax 145
language acquisition device 143, 156
language and thought 114, 152–154
language development 140; cultural variations in 156–157; stages of 141–142; theories of 143–144
language development, stages of 141–142; babbling 142; holophrastic 142; multi-word 142; pre-linguistic 141; telegraphic 142; two-word 142
language families in India 140; Austroasiatic languages 140; Dravidian languages 140; Indo-Aryan languages 140; Sino Tibetan languages 140
language in Indian tradition, significance of 141
language manifestation, Indian view of 142–143
language proficiency development 149
late childhood 29–30
latency stage 42, 172
laterization 78
Lazarus's Appraisal Theory 186
learning, cultural variations in 116
learning to learn 288
Lewin's Field Theory 236
life instinct 42
life skills 252–255
life-span perspective 7
liking 257
lingua fracas 152
literacy rate in India 150
longitudinal design 50–51
long-term memory 35, 118
looking-glass self 88
LOPI 116
love: aspects of 257; human 257; individual 257; transhuman 257; triangular theory of 257
love, types of 244, 257; companionate 257; consummate 257; empty 257; fatuous 257; romantic 257
love and belonging 46
lucier effects 237
Lutz and White's Cultural Theory of Emotions 187

Mac Arthur Studies 36
Macro system 8, 47
madhyama 143
Mahabharata 97, 103

man a social animal 226
manan 252
manas 119, 154
Manusmriti 37, 97, 267
Masculinity-Femininity 209
Maslow's concept of self-actualization 173–174
maturity 5
me to we initiative 291
meditation (*dhyan*) 122
mental and emotional well-being 82
mental health issues 265
mesoderm 8, 24, 47
MGNREGA 16, 284
microsystem 8, 47
Mid-day meal Scheme 72–73
middle adulthood 34
Milgram Study 236
Million Words Study 156
mind, aspects of 42; consciousness 42, 119, 250–251; sub-consciousness 42; unconsciousness 42, 171
mind-body connection 74
mindfulness 120, 250–251; -based stress reduction program 250; correlates of 251
minimizing harm and risks 60
Mirror Test 165
mixed method research 53–54
moksha 15, 38, 168, 212
money: concept of 235; functions of 235; spending patterns of 235
monistic view 119
monogamy 238
moral development 30; contextual and relational approaches 207; levels of 206–207; types of 205–207
moral domain 207
morality 204; theoretical perspectives on 205–209
morality and values, conceptions of 204–205; Indian perspective on 211–213
Moro reflex 146
mortality rates 69
mothering, many by many 91
motivational competencies 104–105
motor development 67; factors affecting 77; pattern of 75–76
motor skills, assessment of 77
mudras 155
Mughal rule in India 103
multilingual education 20
multilingualism 27, 152
multiple approach-avoidance conflict 273
multiple intelligences: bodily-kinesthetic 124; existential 124; inter-personal 124; intrapersonal 124; linguistic-verbal 124; logical-mathematical 124; musical 124; naturalistic 124; visual-spatial 124; theory of 124
multiple mothering 91

342 *Index*

Nada Brahman 140
Narcissistic tendency 179
Narmada *bachao andolan* 288
nation, concept of 230
National Action Plan on Climate Change 217
National Apprenticeship Promotion Scheme 290
National Curriculum Framework (2005) 117
National Curriculum Framework for Foundational Stage 29
National Disaster Management Authority 271
National Early Childhood Care and Education (ECCE) Policy 29
National Education Policy (2020) 29, 81
National Family Health Survey 266
National Food Security Act 285
National Health Mission 284
national identity 230
National Policy on Education (1986) 29
National Program for Organic Production 82
National Service Scheme 217
national territory 230
National voter's day 217
natural disasters 264, 269–272
nature-nurture controversy 6, 156
Natyashastra 133, 190
NCERT's module for school staff 103
neeti 97
negative attitudes and practices against women 267
Neo-Personality Inventory 181
Neo-Piagetian theories 115
neonate 25
netiquette 255
neurological factors 196
neuroticism 173, 176
nidhidhyasan 252
nidra 252
nirvana 168
nishkama karma 204, 212–213
non-normative influences on development 9
normative age-graded influences on development 8
normative history-graded influences on development 8
nursery books 80–81
Nyaya Sutra 141, 154

obedience and responsibility 49
obesity 70
objectivity 51
object permanence 112
observation 57–58
observational learning 44
official languages 140
old age 35–36
Om 141
open-ended questions 55
openness and opportunity, period of 31
openness to change 177, 210

openness to experience 176
operant conditioning 44
optimal experience 251
optimism 248–249; ABCDE model of 248
oral stage 42, 172
organic living 81–82
organismic factors 8
orphaned adolescents 277–279
Ossification 66
Osteoporosis 35
otherness 49
Our Common Future 282
out-groups 240

Padhna Likhna abhiyan 287
panchayats 276
panch kosha 121; *anandamaya* 14, 121, 168; *annamaya* 14, 121, 168; *manomaya* 14, 121, 168; *pranamaya* 14, 121, 168; *vijnanamaya* 14, 121, 168
para 142
para speech communication 154–155; variations in 155
parallel distributed processing 118–119
parallel play 113
paraya dhan 93
parenting styles: authoritarian 94; authoritative 94, 196; neglectful 94; permissive 94; types of 93–94
pashyanti 142
pastoralism 292
peers and peer groups 88
peer victimization 200
PEN model 172
perfectionism 177
perseverance 244
personal: agency 174; crisis 265; domain 207
personality 164
personality, cultural variations in 179–180; Five-Factor model of 176; Indian view of 180; theories of 170–178; trait theories 175–178
personality development 178–179; measurement of 181
personality traits: *rajasika* 180; *sattvika* 180; *tamasika* 180
person-centered therapy 46
PF Questionnaire 181
phallic stage 42, 172
physical development 82; Indian approach to 74–75
physical growth 66; assessment of 67; milestones in 68
physical social capital 284
physiological arousal 186; needs 46
Piaget's theory of: cognitive development 45, 110–114, 226; moral development 205–206
pitta 189

planning 125
plasticity 4, 8
political instability 265
polygamy 238
population pyramid 11
positive emotional states and processes 244–245
positive psychology 244
post-conventional level 206
post-formal thought 33
Post-Traumatic Stress Disorder (PTSD) 266
posture 154
poverty alleviation 11
poverty and economic hardships 264
power 210
power distance 209
pragya 120–121
prakriti 154
pramana 141, 154
pranayama 155, 180
PRASHAST 102
pratyahara 191
pratyaksha 141
pre-conventional level 206
pre-operational stage 45, 112–113, -thinking 27, 112
prefrontal cortex 196
prejudice and discrimination, development of 240–241; expression of 241; sources of 240–241
prema 257
Prevention of Atrocities Act 267
primary appraisals 186
primary circular reactions 111
primary groups 230
primitive reflexes 25
priyamvada 130, 211
Projective Techniques 181
promise and possibilities, period of 31
prosocial behavior 127, 255–258
Protection of Children from Sexual Offences (POCSO) Act 29
Protection of Civil Rights Act 267
proximo-distal law 75
psychanalytic approach 42
psychological age 13
psychological trauma 265
psychology of violence 266
psychophysiological response 49
psychosexual development 42, 172
psychosocial capital 284
psychoticism 173
puberty 30
pulses and legumes 71
purushartha 48, 180, 204, 212

questionnaire 55–56

raga 188, 189
Ramayana 97, 10
randomization 56
rasa: *adbhuta* 190; *bhayanka* 190; *bibhitsa* 190; *hasya* 190; *karuna* 190; *raudra* 190; *shantha* 190; *shringara* 190; *veera* 190
rasa and bhava, concepts of 189–190; theory of 190
rashiphal 92
reasoning 177
Reciclar pelo Brasil programme 289
reciprocal determinism 44, 175
reciprocal relationships 48
reflexes 111
reinforcement 44
relationships, changes in 238–239; development of 237–239
reliability 55
religious identity, development of 239
research approach: qualitative 52–53; quantitative 51–52
resilience, development of 254
resources, distribution of 217
respect for diversity 60
response categories 49
Rights of Persons with Disabilities Act 101
rinas 15, 238
Robbers Cave Experiment 236–237
Rokeach Value Survey 209
Rotter's concept of locus of control 175
RTE Act 134
rule-consciousness 177

sacred: persons 92; places 92; times 92
sadness 244
samadhi 191
Samagra Shiksha 29, 134, 284–285
samaskaras 15, 48, 92; *annaprasana* 15; *antyesti* 15; *chudakarna* 15; *karnavedha* 15; *namakarna* 15; *upanayana* 15, 91; *vidyarambh* 15; *vivaha* 15
samkhya system 119
samvad 276
sanskrit *suktis* 130
santati 92
Sapir-Whorf Hypothesis 153
sarcopenia 35
sarvodaya 16, 17
satya 16, 211
satyagraha 204, 208–209
scaffolding 114
Scandinavian Smorgasbord xv
Schachter and Singer's Two-Factor Theory 186
Scheff's Interactionist Theory 187
schema 45, 110
Scherer and Ekman's Component Process Model 187

secondary appraisals 187
secondary circular reactions 111
secondary groups 230
secondary traits 178
security 210
self- 164; across life stages 168; actualisation 46; awareness 164, 168; biological foundation of 165; compassion 168; concept 165; cultural factors in development of 170; direction 210; discipline 208; during adolescence 169; during adulthood 169; during early childhood 168–169; during middle childhood 169; during old age 169–170; enhancement 210; esteem 46, 165, 167–168; identity 165; in Indian thought 170; regulation 114, 165; reliance 177; social and cultural aspects of 166; theories of 166–167; transcendence 210; worth 167
self, types of: authentic 164; ideal 164; independent 166; personal 164; relational 166; social 164
self-determination theory 167; self-efficacy theory; self-perception theory 167
self-report measures 54, 181
sensitivity 177
sensorimotor Stage 45, 111–112
sensory memory 118
serenity 244
seva 256
Seymour's study of child-rearing 95–96
shabda 141, 154
shame 245
shaping 123
shared memory 230
sharira: *karana* 14; *sthula* 13; *sukshma* 14
short-term memory 118
shramadana 16–17
shravan 252
shukshma sharira 14
Shweder's theory of moral relativism 207–208
silence and pauses 154
simultaneous processes 126
Six Cultures Study 95
skill India 286
skills, 21st century 288–289
smriti 121
social age 13
social and emotional skills 289
social and environmental factors 74
social boldness 177
social capital, types of 284
Social Identity Theory 166–167
social: competence 129, 130; development 226–228; dynamics 236–237; harmony 49, 83; self 164; sensitivity 127; sustainability 282
social-conventional 207
social inequalities 265
social interaction and collaboration 116, 146

socialization: agents of 87–91; continuity and change in 99–101; cultural variations 89–91; family and 87; nature of 86; pattern in India 94–101; peer groups 88; primary and secondary 86; religious institutions and 89; role of education in 88–89
socially mediated process 116
social understanding, development of 232
sound 141; cross-cultural variations 147; patterns of 147
speech 141
spiral curriculum 117
spiritual: growth 83; intelligence 128; spirituality 251–252
sruti 121
stage-wise differentiation 98
Start-up India program 217
stereotypes 240
Sternberg's Triangular Theory of Love 257
sthitipragya 194–195
stimulation 210
storage processes 118
storm and stress, period of 31
street children 276–277
stress: causes of 199; manifestation of 199
stress and coping 199–200
stress due to academic reasons 200
stress of schooling among Indian children 200
study of socialization practices in Gujarat 97
study on weaver's community 96
subjective experience 174
subjective meaning 52
successive processes 126
sukha 246
superego 42, 171
surface structure 145
surveys 54–55
Suryamitra Program 289
sushupti 252
sustainable agriculture education (SAgE) project 289
sustainable development: attitudinal change for 287; goals 283; holistic model of 283; lifelong learning 286–287; nature of 282; pillars of 282; psychological aspect of 283–28; role of culture 291–292; skills for 288; sustainable development goal 5, 266; targets 282
sustainable tourism 290
swabhaava 180
Swachh Bharat Abhiyan 217, 285
swapn 252
Swaraj 16
Swastika 246

tabula rasa 17
Tagore's *stray birds poem* 237
Taittiriya Upanishad 121
tandav 79

tantric 188
Tat Tvam Asi 170
teamwork 253
temperament 178–179; difficult 179; easy 178; slow-to-warm-up 179
temporary (a*nitya*) 120
tension 177
Teratogens 25
terrace farming 292
terrorism 268–269
tertiary circular reactions 112
thanatology 39
theory of apprenticeship 115–116
theory of mind 131–132, 165–166
thinking: analytical 130; cultural variations in 130–131; holistic 130
three language formula 151
throwaway culture 287
time orientation 127
titiksha 211
Tomkin's Affect Script Theory 186
toy-based pedagogy 80
traditional physical activities 74
transgender persons 102–103
triangulation: data 53; method 53; researcher 53; theory 53; time 53
triguna, components of 180; *rajas* 180, 188; *sattva* 180, 188; *tamas* 180
triple-bottom-line accounting 287
trust *vs.* mistrust 43, 227
truth 208
tsunamis 271
Turiel's Distinct Domain Theory 207
turiya 252

udaan 290
uncertainty avoidance 210
understanding other people 234–236
universal grammar 143
universalism 210

vaand chhako 211
vaikhari 143
vak 141

Vakyapadiya 142
validity 55
values: across time 215–216; basic human 210; conservation of 210; cross-national studies 209–211; cultural dimensions of 229; development of 213–215; in digital era 216; during oral traditions 216; during written traditions 216; family, gender equality, self-expression and 211; higher-order 210; influence of culture on 214–215; instrumental and terminal 209; value education 216–217
variables 56; dependent 56; independent 56
vatta 189
vedana 188
Vedas 121
vigilance 177
vinaya 211
vipassana meditation 250
vocational skills, development of 289
voice, tone of 154
voluntary response 49
vratas 127
vyanjana 143
Vygotsky's Sociocultural Theory 187, 228

war 272–273
warmth 177
waste management strategies 293
waste-to-energy programme 293
we-self relationship 91
wisdom 120, 128, 179, 247–248
working memory 29, 118
World Value Survey 210–211

yajns 15, 238
Yajurveda 121
Yama and Niyam 122
Yoga and Ayurveda 74
Yoga Sutras 120, 133, 188
yugas 123; dvapara 123; kali 123; satya 123; treta 123

zone of proximal development 18, 45, 114
zygote 24